DESTRUCTION AND CREATION:
PERSONAL AND CULTURAL TRANSFORMATIONS

Destruction and Creation:

Personal and Cultural Transformations

Proceedings of

The Fourteenth International Congress

For Analytical Psychology

Florence, 1998

Mary Ann Mattoon
Editor

DAIMON
VERLAG

Florence 1998 – Destruction and Creation: Personal and Cultural Transformations
edited by Mary Ann Mattoon.
The translators of individual papers are given on the final page of each translation.

Contents

Jungian Psychology in a Changing World

Body and Psyche

Culture Diversity

Psychology and Art

Alphabetical List of Authors

Editor's Preface

The Fourteenth Congress for Analytical Psychology was held August 23-28, 1998 in the ancient city of Florence, Italy. The setting, described by attendees as "elegant," was the Palazzo dei Congressi, Villa Vittoria. The 565 participants included 364 IAAP members (analysts), 161 training candidates, and 40 "auditors." In addition, 125 day cards were issued.

The International Association for Analytical Psychology (IAAP), the professional organization of Jungian analysts, held its first Congress in 1958, the second in 1962, both in Zurich. Since then, such meetings have been triennial and held in various cities, including London, Rome, San Francisco, Jerusalem, Berlin, Paris, and Chicago.

The IAAP was founded in 1955, with 40 members. At the time of the first Congress, the membership had increased to 150, in eight member societies. When the 1998 Congress convened, there were 38 groups. At the meeting three new groups were added: Georgia (USA); Salzburg (Austria) and Venezuela. The post-Congress membership is 2278: approximately 57 percent female, 43 percent male.

The theme, "Destruction and Creation: Personal and Cultural Transformations," is especially appropriate to the Italian setting, with that nation's history of destruction, both from nature and from human activity, and its tradition – especially in Florence – of creative individuals and institutions. The theme is fitting, also, to the context of Jungian psychology, with its emphasis on these and other pairs of opposites, with their integral role in psychic wholeness. Acknowledging, also, that destruction is indispensable to creation, some Jungians prefer the term "creative unconscious" to the traditional "collective unconscious."

Of the 145 proposals offered, 43 were accepted and presented. The papers of the morning plenary sessions are listed here in the order of their order of presentation. The afternoon presentations are grouped by general areas with varying relationships to the theme, and different lengths, in proportion to the time allotted for each presentation. Usually four offerings were available simultaneously in each of the two afternoon time periods. Many afternoon meetings featured single presenters, while seven panels, of two to nine members each, gave opportunity for many individuals to present their ideas and research. Presenters are identified by their place of practice and the society through which they are voting members of IAAP. The Table of Contents lists the presentations that were made, with a few exceptions.

Some presenters decided not to submit papers for publication. These omissions are: Luigi Aversa and others (Round Table *Psicologia Analytica: Ipotesi di Sviluppo*, Analytical Psychology: Hypothesis of Development); Louise Mahdi and Barry Williams (Nature, Spirit and the Rites of Passage); Seth Rubin (Research), and Patrick Tummon (Dancing between Heaven and Hell: Reflections on the Archetype of the Self, from a South African Perspective).

The program represented by the papers in this book was embedded in a number of "extracurricular" offerings, which provided relaxation and community-building. These included a welcome reception and dinner, and a gala closing dinner with Renaissance music. One evening featured dinner in private homes, another a concert by a vocal ensemble. Guided tours (one each day) were offered to selected sites in Florence and its surroundings.

A "Social Dreaming Matrix," led by Helen Morgan and Keith Reed, met before the morning plenary on four successive mornings. Other meetings were organized around the following topics and subgroups (leaders' names in parentheses): training candidates (Jaqueline Mendelsohn and Bernard Rozran); editors of Jungian publications (John Beebe); developing groups in new cultural settings (Murray Stein); Jungians in the university (Renos Papadopoulos/Andrew Samuels); dissemination of Jung's works (Christian Gaillard); Sandplay (Harriet Friedman/Ruth Ammann); graduates of the Zurich Institute (Joanne Wieland-Burston); the IAAP newsletter (Renos Papadopoulos).

A business meeting attended by delegates of the societies was held mid-week, to elect officers and make policy decisions. For the first time, several smaller societies were elected to the Executive Committee.

***

The official languages of the Congress were English, French, German and Italian. For the plenary sessions, simultaneous translation was provided in each of the three languages not being used by the speaker. For some of the afternoon sessions, simultaneous translation was provided in selected languages. If a paper was delivered in a language other than English, it has been translated and the original language indicated at the end of the paper, along with the translator's name. Each reference is cited in the language chosen by the presenter.

The goals of the editing have been to clarify and enhance each author's contribution, while retaining individuality of writing style but consistency in notation and usage: references, spelling, and type style such as italicization. Due to space limitations, many of the papers were reduced in length (by their authors) for publication here.

References to Jung's *Collected Works* are indicated in the text by CW volume number and paragraph number. Other Jung references include:

Let-1 and Let-2 = Jung's *Letters*, Vols. 1 & 2.

MDR = *Memories, Dreams, Reflections*

ZS = *Zarathustra Seminars*

FJ = *Freud-Jung Letters*

Freud's works are indicated, insofar as possible, as SE (*Standard Edition*) and their volume numbers.

Other citations in the text follow the format of the *Publication Manual* of the American Psychological Association. They indicate author and date, each keyed to a reference at the end of a paper or group of panel papers. "See" references indicate the source of an idea without a direct quotation. References in each list are in the language chosen by the author. Except for the "Supervision" panel, all the references for a given panel are collected at the end of that chapter.

Punctuation and spelling follow British or American practice, according to the choice of the author. The terms "patient," "client" and "analysand" are used as the individual author sees fit. The identity of each such individual to whom an author refers is disguised. Graphics are placed as much in keeping with the author's request as possible, taking into account optimal use of space.

Manuscripts were typed on computer diskette by Beverly Pothen Cicchese. Jennette Cook Jones assisted the editor with refining some translations from French and Italian. Final proof-reading was done by Bonnie L. Marsh.

Mary Ann Mattoon
Minneapolis, Minnesota, USA
June 1999

Introduction to the Congress

Luigi Zoja
IAAP Vice-President
Centro Italiano di Psicologia Analitica

The focus of the Congress, as envisioned by the Program Committee, was not rhetorical: not merely to hold a Congress on the subject of creation. Rather, the goal was to talk intentionally about destruction first, and then creation.

From the time that Jungian thought came to us, we have thought of something that is unified. We search for totality. When we consider something that is luminous, we search to complete it with a shadow. Thus, we can say that the psyche wishes not only to create, but also to destroy. The unity of creation and destruction during the height of the Renaissance impacts us greatly.

It was in Florence that the "infamous" Nicolo Macchiavelli claimed his place in the realm of political theory. (When mentioning his name, we think of a political assassin. In fact, the word "*malichiavelli*" defines the names of the nails used to nail Jesus Christ to the cross.) The existence of the destructive shadow is the price of action and of power.

But in Florence, the psychic truth whereby shadow corresponds to light, and destruction corresponds to creation, become both material and literal. Florence is home to the largest concentration of art in Italy. According to estimates authored by UNESCO, Italy has more than 40 percent of the art treasures of the world, including 100,000 churches, 40,000 castles and fortresses, and 3,500 museums.

Nature and humankind provide this immense wealth of creation with works of destruction. Italy is a land of volcanoes and landslides. Forty-five percent of its surface is at seismic risk. In the last few years, numerous works of art in Central Italy have been swallowed up by earthquakes.

Humans try to do their part. Even though enormous strides have been made in the area of art cataloguing and conservation, approximately 35,000 objects a year disappear from our collections and museums. That is almost 100 per day. Even the love of beauty kills beauty itself. Venice is sinking, not only under pressure from the sea; it is being crushed by only 69,000 inhabitants but more than 15 million tourists per year.

But are we sure that malicious nature (the tidal waves, earthquakes, volcanoes: the destructive shadow of Mother Earth) and human pillaging (the dark plundering shadow of bright, inventive impulse) are Creativity's enemies that have never helped to extend life? Actually, the volcanic eruptions at Thira (Santorini) and Vesuvius have assaulted but also saved large quantities of Minoan and Roman objects that would have been lost forever, erased from time and from humankind's selfishness. In fact, humankind has always tried to erase any signs of previous cultures if they were the least bit different. Only in recent years (recent in relation to the history of humanity), within the last two centuries, the boundless curiosity of Western people has allowed the systematic collection of these traces.

For example, colonial powers have snatched away huge treasures from Mediterranean Europe and non-European countries. But it is difficult to decipher where their actions were negative and where they were positive. The plunder may have given back its life to something that was about to be lost. It may have been a destructive gesture: the final humiliation of an invaded land. But it could have been creative: the beginning of an absolute respect for art, for creation itself. The creative intention cannot escape from the destructive shadow. But destructive intent involves the creative shadow. Nothing is deep without its opposite.

Now let us take a step backward and think of the birth of a work of art. Not only is the destructive gesture something that can follow creation in order to preserve it. It can be the initial condition, the original action that frees up the creative act.

Behind the Renaissance debate regarding the differences between painting and sculpture there is something much less specialized: a timeless and universal depth which is of great interest to Platonic thought and Jungian psychology. Benedetto Varchi raised with various artists the question of the nobility of art.

Michelangelo, master in all expressive forms of art, preferred sculpture. While writing to Varchi in Rome in 1549, Michelangelo did not just state his preference, but defined clearly the various forms of sculpture. The truest form of sculpture is not clay. Using clay is closer to painting: adding a substance to give form. Color, clay; it doesn't matter: something limited, not a complete living process. One does not put and then take away, create and destroy.

According to Michelangelo, true sculpture "is created by means of removing." To take away, unwrap, eliminate, destroy the unnecessary material that is in nature, in the marble block. To create is not to add, but rather to reduce. Humankind does not need to give or place a form in the world. Form already exists in things. Humans must produce an idea and liberate this idea from the excess stone.

In this regard, *"I Prigioni"* (The Prisoners) are Michelangelo's most representative works. These works portray prisoners as the subject. At the same time, they show that each of Michelangelo's sculptures was a "prisoner" with a block of marble. To create a sculpture meant to destroy its prison.

In looking at a block of marble, Michelangelo tried to see this ideal, solitary form. The artist is the person who assaults the block with a scalpel, unwraps the excess material, breaks the chains in which the form is held prisoner, and splits open the superfluous marble.

The sculptor is someone who destroys with a sovereign strength and having freed the idea, stops, exhausted by his own aggressiveness. This shows the striking "unfinished" style of *"I Prigioni"* and Michelangelo's other sculpture.

The work of art is not polished. There still remains much residue on the block of marble. Its power and its movement derive precisely from this. The work expresses not only the prisoner's wish to tear himself away from captivity, but also the idea's wish to come out from the material. This idea is grasped/caught in the moment in which it is done, when the sculptor struggles to shatter the marble's surface that suffocates it.

The sculpture is not a static and polished final product; it is a rough image of the struggle. In the language of psychology, it is not the product of the ego. It is the archetype that wants to take form and, to do so, asks the ego to free it from its wasted condition that is yet immobile and inorganic.

Thus, centuries before Jung, Michelangelo gave us proof of the existence of the archetype. He demonstrated that the work of the artist is not to create work from on high. Rather, the job of creating a work of art is to feel it, sense it, differentiate it, and free it from the primordial sleep that envelopes it inside the marble. Entrenched in a Platonism that for him was not academic philosophy but life's truth, the Renaissance artist's "unfinished" style was an internal need –

many centuries earlier than when modern expressive conventions with far less vitality followed a similar train of thought.

Michelangelo's chisel can be used as a metaphor for analytic commitment. From an individual and clinical point of view, the Jungian analyst is not so much trying to heal patients' illnesses as to help them uncover the waste that imprisons them. The analyst is trying to destroy the psychic calcification, the impersonal stone that covers the true and individual form of each one. The analytic process is an attempt to rediscover the harmony that the archetype keeps under the surface of everyday presumptions. It is a value that has been there forever, and yet requires destruction-creation in order to be liberated.

However, the Jungian analyst also has a cultural responsibility. Today when one sees that a group of young people have taken a hammer to a work of art, one cannot be satisfied just to call the police. One must ask oneself why Michelangelo's chisel – the unity of both destruction and creation – has been forgotten for centuries. One must ask why has it slipped away and only thugs have thought to wake it from its slumber.

Translated from the original Italian by Elizabeth Teefy

Welcome by the Presidents
of the Italian Societies

Marco Garzonio (Milan)
President, Central Italiano di Psicologia Analitica

We begin our Congress in a particular moment. We find ourselves contending with problems and difficulties that infest psychoanalysis and all schools of psychotherapy, including Analytical Psychology.

In a period of increasing globalization, we all know how much we are interconnected. In Italy, we are witnessing a proliferation of schools of psychotherapy, and training does not always involve a personal analysis. Growing numbers of therapists are being introduced into the system. They are therapists who have been educated in the conviction that one can learn psychotherapy from books, academic courses, and exams, and that psychotherapy learned this way is not very different from psychotherapy learned from the long and difficult process of working on oneself.

In Italy, the government and the universities have done their part in feeding illusions and equivocations. We are at the beginning of a struggle to inject a bit of clarity into the subject; we want to obtain public recognition of the specificity of psychoanalytic psychotherapy, of its "otherness."

There is no doubt that Analytical Psychology, too, is in a very delicate moment. Choices, clarifications, redefinitions have become necessary. The "original sin" – if we can call it that – begins with Jung. Or rather with the two Jungs, as they have been called: the empirical Jung, continual researcher, aware of the relativity of every point of view; and the Jung who is committed to the idea of the objective psyche – almost a "dogmatic" Jung.

Here is an example. Among analysts in training, we note something of a split between traditional Jungian theory and the clinical side of our work which is, after all, our response to the difficulties and the suffering of men and women, now at the end of the millennium. Our students work easily with our most familiar categories (e.g., archetype, anima, animus, shadow); they apply them with originality to myths, fairy tales, and literary works and characters. These same students, at the same time, use Freudian or neo-Freudian interpretive models (e.g., Bion, Klein, Kohut, Winnicott) when they discuss their clinical work. This approach is from an "ecumenical" point of view, if those "appropriations" – not always adequately assimilated – are not the fruit of the impasse caused by our insufficient elaboration of clinical theory.

As we begin our Congress, our wish for ourselves may be contained in a prospective interpretation of the title of our Congress. Probably none of us thinks that "creation and destruction" represent merely an evocative antinomy. And I imagine that a large number of colleagues are convinced that "transformation" can be viewed as a strictly psychological individuative process, with none of the consoling, pacifying overtones of a new religion. Let us begin this Congress by setting ourselves three tasks:

1. A renewed dialogue with other schools of psychoanalysis. Several years ago, Aryeh Maidenbaum and Stephen A. Martin called for a discussion of Jung, Freud, and anti-semitism. We could declare the 100th anniversary of *The Interpretation of Dreams* (1999) a common anniversary for all schools of psychoanalysis. And we might explore our debt to that work of Freud.

2. Further exploration of the theoretical and clinical aspects of our own school. Our next Congress might be dedicated to a search for a possible Jungian "clinical theory, with the various national institutes beginning their reflections on this subject now.

3. Initiatives directed at the "outside world" (from publishing to cultural debate), valorizing exchanges, social sensitivity, openness to collective needs. Opening the windows and letting in fresh air may be good for us. Our work here will be tiring, but full of hope. Nationally and internationally, welcoming and hospitable, the city of Florence, welcoming and hospitable, can be taken as a living metaphor: city of art and of antique wealth and beauty, but not just a museum. It is a living, breathing city, with its people, its shops, its streets, its surrounding industries.

We of CIPA are determined to continue our work to keep alive our collaboration with AIPA. This collaboration has been particularly successful of late in maintaining the survival of the patrimony of experience and progress of the two "historical" institutes, in guaranteeing the formation of our candidates, and in satisfying the expectations of our "public."

On the international level, we hope to find in IAAP a culture of rules that are certain and rigorous, which guarantees members of institutes of proven tradition working relationships based on reciprocity, on the value of everyone's contributions, on rules that are clear, transparent, shared.

Here at the Congress, we will elect new officers. We assure them our full collaboration as they seek to guarantee that the work of everyone will be anchored to precise ethical and political rules. Patients, other schools of psychotherapy and public opinion will judge us by our behavior, not by our good intentions. And Jungianism will be what we are: "creative" (as we all hope) or "destructive."

***

Concetto Gullotta (Rome)
President, Associazione Italiana per lo Studio della Psicologia Analitica

On behalf of the Italian Association of Analytical Psychology, I extend a warm welcome to the city of Florence. We are certain that this Congress, organized by the International Association with the invaluable collaboration of several of our Florentine colleagues, will be an occasion for cultural and personal enrichment for each of us. We intend to establish here in Florence that same atmosphere of friendship and community which we are accustomed to enjoying at our conferences, and which encourages colleagues from every part of the world to become acquainted.

Surely each of us has felt already, even before arriving in Florence, the special attraction that this city offers. Florence is, in the collective imagination, the Renaissance city *par excellence*. That process of cultural and anthropological transformation, which had begun in the preceding centuries and ushered Europe into the Modern Age, was completed here. And those artists who were the principal players in that transformation and who gave it shape and image lived and worked right here.

Human beings as individuals were becoming more and more the center and the measure of things, and the relationship with the world that surrounded them was characterised ideally by harmony and proportion. Perhaps the clearest symbol of this concept is Leonardo da Vinci's drawing of "The Man," in which the correct proportions of the human body correspond with those of the superimposed circle and square.

The logo for our conference partially reproduces Leonardo's symbol, making explicit reference to that Renaissance ideal. But today, precious little remains of that ideal; over the subsequent centuries that conception of the world has been transformed, has evolved, has borne positive and negative fruit, and seems finally to have reached its state of crisis in this twentieth century of ours. However, regardless of all the crises and transformations, we still recognize in that vision of the world some primary elements in our present way of being and of conceiving ourselves, primarily the notion of the individual.

This conference in part re-proposes these same themes: To what extent is our profession as analysts influenced by the profound social and cultural transformations that we are experiencing? In what ways are we to interact with the decline of that "concept of modernity" which originated at the time of the Renaissance? The drive to search out new cultural models could cause us to lose the memory of our roots. The tension in creating the new may lead us to the destruction of our awareness of the past. From this point of view Analytical Psychology, on the level of both collective and individual culture, has a specific role: keeping the value of memory and the sense of historical continuity alive, in terms of our professional activity with individual patients as well as the contribution that we can make to the larger contemporary cultural debate.

These are, of course, complex themes, which will echo through the discussions of the coming days. I hope everyone will have an enjoyable week here in Florence, alternating the intensity of the cultural debate with the pleasures of an encounter with our host city and with our colleagues who are also our friends.

Plenary Sessions

Duccio's Prayer

Mediating Destruction and Creation with Artists in Analysis

Mary Dougherty
Chicago, Illinois, USA
Chicago Society of Jungian Analysts

In 1311, Duccio completed the Maestà, the largest free-standing altarpiece ever to be painted in Italy: five and one-half meters high, five meters wide, with the image of the Passion of Christ on one side and that of the Virgin Enthroned on the other. Duccio inscribed this prayer around the base of the Virgin's throne: "Holy Mother of God, be thou the cause of peace for Siena and, because he painted thee thus, of life for Duccio." In the words of the fourteenth century chronicler,

> *On the day on which it was carried to the Duomo, the shops were locked up and ... all the populace and all the most worthy ... next to the said panel with lights lit in their hands; and then behind were the women and children with much devotion; and they accompanied it right to the Duomo making procession round the Campo ... sounding all the bells in glory, out of devotion for such a noble panel as was this (White 1979, pp. 96-97).*

When I first saw the Maestà, I was moved by the image of the Virgin and by the inscribed prayer. In the succeeding years, however, it has been Duccio's prayer that has captivated my imagination. As I have worked with artists in analysis, his prayer has come to represent for me the symbolic attitude of an artist in relation to creative work – a work that is not only an ego possession, but is also a mediatory product connecting to a source of meaning toward which both artist and community can turn.

When Duccio prayed, "Holy Mother of God, be thou the cause of peace for Siena," he addressed the Virgin as the acknowledged political and religious protectress of Siena. In doing so, the artist participates in a communal religious belief, namely, that it was She who could bring peace to the Sienese after years of war with the Florentines. When he prayed, "because he painted thee thus," Duccio acknowledged his unprecedented artistic achievement as and established the basis upon which he could then plead for his mortal life and for his eternal soul. In sum, Duccio's prayer not only acknowledged the Maestà as his ego achievement, but also embodied his symbolic attitude toward the work, both for himself and for the Sienese.

In contrast to my interpretations of his prayer as representing the artist's symbolic attitude in relation to his work, Duccio's inscription has been interpreted by art historians as a plea for eternal fame as an artist. Although this may be a modern gloss on medieval experience, Duccio's prayer does indeed stand as one of the earliest examples of an identifying signature on a work of Western art. It therefore marks the beginning of increased self-awareness of artists as artists and the growing valuation of their artistic creations apart from religious or communal functions.

This symbolic attitude toward artistic work, like the function of art itself, has shifted from Duccio's time to our own. Making art, which once served multiple functions – including the mediation of meaning – is now largely restricted to serving aesthetic ends. Twentieth century aesthetics has split artists from engaging a symbolic attitude in relation to their work.

When Duccio completed the Maestà, works of art functioned as channels for the numinous to flow into the community (see Neumann 1974). From Duccio's time on, the function of art and the role of artists increasingly shifted from glorifying the divine to representing human concerns. Rather than seeking eternal salvation, artists increasingly sought artistic fame and upward social mobility. These major shifts in the function of art reflected the growing emphasis on secularization, differentiation and specialization within the culture. In spite of these shifts, however, the artistic tradition of Realism continued to be flexible enough to contain and to incorporate spontaneous impulses from the unconscious within gradual innovations and refinements of artistic form (see Ehrenzweig 1967).

By the nineteenth century, the invention of photography had usurped the traditional role of artists to represent reality. The surface of art became increasingly fragmented by unconscious contents no longer contained within the artistic tradition of Realism and the focus of art increasingly became the exploration of the formal properties of art-making itself. With the withdrawal of libido from the solidly modeled outside world, the fragmentation of form and the resulting influx of the irrational carried artists inward into contact with the creative unconscious as the source of new vision. Although artists gave expression to this vision, they did so from ego stances which dissociated this vision from its source in the creative unconscious.

If medieval art was made for God's sake, and Renaissance art for humanity's sake, then twentieth century art has been made for Art's sake; with the exception of a few blips, the aesthetics of modernism have defined art as separate from life (see Gablik 1984). This separation has promoted the reification and the commodification of art objects and has privileged the aesthetic mode above other modes of experience, thereby restricting the former multiple functions of art (see Dewey 1987). Despite post-modernism's de-idealization of the art object and re-contextualization of art within social and political life, art's freedom from instrumental use continues to be championed in the formal education of artists and in the world of art.

For contemporary artists, therefore, the goal has become the production of unique objects which represent technical, formal or expressive innovations. In contrast to earlier times when innovations in form were gradually enfolded into the artistic tradition, the goal of innovative art is to surpass former works of art as progressive steps in the course of art history. Such demonstrations of uniqueness determine the commercial worth of a work of art. This focus on innovation and uniqueness encourages artists to identify with their ego intentions for their work and to see their artistic productions as ego possessions. Spontaneous eruptions of unconscious contents manifesting in the work tend to be valued by artists as formal or expressive elements and co-opted to fuel further art-making, rather than insight. Reparative strivings as well as compensatory dynamics expressed in the creative work, therefore, are repressed. Artists then come to see themselves as the source of the creation rather than as a medium for the creative source. This view promotes an inflated identification with the creative unconscious, splits off narcissistic deficits, and forges the artistic self in opposition to any infringements on their autonomous pursuit of art – including relational needs and physical limitations (see CW7, 235). Rather than serving a symbolic function, the art-making process often functions in collusion with an unconscious self-care system that holds the personality of the artist in an infantile, paranoid-schizoid stage of development (see Kalsched 1996).

In my clinical practice, which is informed by my training as an artist and as an art therapist, I understand that all aspects of a creative endeavor reveal unconscious contents. In the two examples that follow, my focus is not on the artistic productions, but the working process of my analysands, both to protect their privacy and to describe their experiences.

"Alice" is the embodiment of the "born artist." She recalled her four-year-old self ecstatically in love with drawing. She remembered her father assuring her that she would never run out of art supplies. In her mid-thirties, Alice came into analysis because she felt depressed about her relationship to a man who saw himself as her friend but not as an intimate partner. She did not want to disclose her intense longing for him as a lover for fear of losing him as a friend. Interwoven within the story of her current relationship were stories of herself as the youngest in a large family in which she felt "always left in the wake of a boat she had missed." She was the "moody one" in the family, the isolated outsider. Alice recited from memory a poem she wrote at age nine:

> *Silver slits cut the morning cloud cover*
> *inviting trees to glow*
> *A cool wind shakes the*
> *trees and wraps my bones*
> *setting the mood for another day*

Alice recalled that this poem had provided her with solace. I noted to myself, however, that despite the promise of light, it was a "cool wind" that wrapped her child-self and set her mood. My sense was that this poem expressed Alice's idealization of her isolation, which transformed her moodiness into a noble solitude. She would convey these child parts of herself to me by enacting various moods. Sometimes she entered a session with a listless, haughty reluctance, holding herself at a distance and only barely tolerating my comments; at other times she arrived desperately depressed, wanting me to fix her life magically so that she could "get on with it." What was remarkable was that in any given session, Alice's mood – whether distanced or depressed – would shift instantly to a sunny animation whenever she spoke about her creative work.

Alice is a prolific maker who engages her creative work with an enormous capacity to tolerate the chaos and frustration inherent in the creative process. When technical challenges forestalled the completion of a large work just weeks prior to a solo exhibition at a major museum, Alice came up with five alternatives within a week and a half. With each new idea, she carefully and steadily worked though its formal possibilities and technical limitations. Despite the anxiety that naturally accompanied the time pressure, Alice resisted the temptation to grasp at and run with a less than completely considered potential solution. Within her artistic life, she also demonstrated a genuine relatedness in working with others, including on a wide range of creative projects. Creative work comprises the functional part of Alice's life. This flexibility and relatedness in connection to her work were not present, unfortunately, in her non-artistic relationships, or in her ability to attend to the practical necessities of life.

As the analysis proceeded, I began to point out how she seemed to protect herself and her work from the encumbrances of intimate relationship by longing for the unavailable man while avoiding the present one. Both responses left her without the "wrapping" that a holding relationship provides. Later, I remarked that, although she appeared to make use of her therapy, I sensed that there were ways she was withholding herself from me. In the next session, Alice told me that my remark had the effect of making her pull back from me because it bothered her that I knew something she didn't. She added, "It's like expecting an orgasm and pulling back from it." I did not address directly the transference implications of the metaphor. Rather, I suggested that she pulled back from her discomfort at my having noticed her ambivalent feelings about me: that my knowing about her feelings made her feel too close and too vulnerable. Alice responded that, indeed, she did pull back from orgasm when she was with a man she loved because it too made her feel too vulnerable.

In this exchange, I believe we contacted a regressed, undeveloped aspect of Alice's child-self: a self left behind in the wake of her older siblings, an undeveloped relational self left behind in the development of her creative self. Alice can endure the chaos and frustration of "not knowing" in relation to her creative work, but when her core vulnerability is touched humanly, her logos function attacks and humiliates her undeveloped relational self, and she retreats into a noble isolation while longing for the unavailable other, or falls into an immobilizing depression.

My experience with patients like Alice has led me to question theories that promote the creative process as healing-in-itself (see Kohut 1978), and those theories that, even further, suggest that creative work can substitute for interpersonal relationship and human love. I question any stand that over-emphasizes the creative dynamics of the art-making process and avoids the destructive dynamics. The notion that an artist's sense of self can be repaired by using creative work, which represents the self, simply perpetuates the cultural stereotype of the separateness of the artist from relational needs and communal ties. In the case of Alice, whose relationship to the creative process is quite functional, working within such a theory would miss the critical lack of development that she suffers in the rest of her life and would solidify her creative work as her only object relation.

When artists make their work, they pursue – whether they know it or not – both aesthetic and psychological goals. However, their psychological goals often remain unconscious because artists lack both a cultural context as well as a conscious attitude that can observe and mediate the symbolic representations expressed in their work. Prior to the development of a symbolic attitude, creative work can be pursued as a manic defense against primitive affects never mediated by an adequate maternal presence (see Kavaler-Adler 1993). This defensive stance is reinforced by our culture's vision of the artist as one who transcends relational needs or physical limitations in favor of the autonomous pursuit of art. The perpetuation of this omnipotent fantasy promotes an over-identification with the creative archetype and isolates the artist's vulnerable self in an illusion of self-sufficiency (see Modell 1975).

In valuing the psychological aspects of the creative process, I am not de-valuing the aesthetic ones. As object relations theorists remind us, the aesthetic experience can hold the self in a state of reverie that viscerally reverberates with our infant experience of maternal reverie, thereby contributing to cohesion and continuity-of-self experience. Such a state of being holds us in an existential moment sufficient in itself, like a "good enough mother," without words or thought (see Winnicott 1971; Bollas 1993). As Jungians, we would add that such a moment brings us into contact with the "wordless occurrences" of the archetypal world as they arise into life from their source in the collective unconscious. However, as Jung himself reminds us, aesthetic formulation needs human understanding and language, for it is in linking the aesthetic and the psychological, the structural and the spontaneous, the formal and the pragmatic, that art regains the capacity to mediate personal and cultural transformation – as exemplified in Duccio's prayer. Otherwise, the individual artist can be overwhelmed by the archetypal dynamics of either creation or destruction when the crucial tension of opposites necessary for the creative process becomes ruptured. The damaging personal effects of such an imbalance are revealed in my next case example.

During our initial telephone conversation, "Thomas" said he was referred to me by a Jungian analyst who knew that many of my clients are artists. In a charming, non-offensive way, he asked if I would accept barter payment: art for therapy. Having once made that mistake with disastrous results, I said I had not found bartering to be useful since we both need to be paid for our endeavors; and further, that when I acquire art, I pay for it. I suggested we meet to determine if we could arrive at a fee we could both manage. We succeeded in doing so.

As our work began, Thomas revealed a life spent trying to appease others. As a child he failed miserably in school, but had a precocious ability to appease his worried teachers and parents by convincing them that his problems were just temporary. They were not. He moved into adulthood with a deeply-rooted anxiety. At 21, he decided to become an artist and to face problems on his own. Although he went to college, he had essentially taught himself the technical and formal elements of art as well as the history of artists and their working methods through intensive and rigorous study. His knowledge was impressive, but my sense was that his anxiety limited his connection to what he knew as an artist, in much the same way that his anxieties had interfered with his learning as a child. In spite of these limitations, Thomas had become a highly successful artist who supported himself through the sale of his work.

During sessions, Thomas would often "rev" himself up, uttering remarks such as, "My vision is strong enough to control my culture." Concurrently, whenever he compared himself to other artists, he would fall into paranoid states of inferiority. I acknowledged that the need for his world to be a point of reference with the culture was consistent with art world assumptions, but that putting such pressure on his work and on himself could prevent both him and the work from coming fully into being.

Unlike Alice, Thomas did not find his studio to be a place of solace. When he began a body of work, he immersed himself in an intuitive manipulation of visual motifs. Working relentlessly, he gathered intensity and focus – so much intensity and so much focus that he forgot to eat or to sit down. He even forgot to breathe. Thomas described his painful process: "I only know how to make something beautiful by throwing myself at the work." He trusted his intuitive ability to "pull off" a successful work of art. However, he longed to find a way of working that truly nurtured him, a way more balanced between the containment of conscious structure and the freedom of intuitive response – but the constant pressure to produce for the next exhibition, to earn money for the next year, seemed to preclude his ability to develop any other way to work. Meanwhile, his stomach ached and he felt isolated and unable to meet the practical demands of everyday life.

Thomas's relationship to his work was replicated in his other relationships. Whether he was producing the perfect dinner party, or producing himself as the all-giving lover, he remained caught in a cycle of his own relentless and enervating intensity – an intensity from which others eventually extricated themselves. Feeling abandoned, unseen and confused, Thomas attempted to repair his isolation by throwing himself back into work. In our sessions, I experienced myself as audience to these performances of himself. When I offered an interpretation, he either ignored it or incorporated it into his monologue as his own insight. He thus defended himself against having to engage my thoughts as separate from himself, in order to protect vulnerable internal structures incapable of shared experience. This destructive dynamic not only attacked my sense of competence, but also diminished his own experience of feeling held in the transference.

While the therapeutic endeavor seeks to help the patient make use of the analyst's insights, Thomas' unconscious usurping of them functioned to blind him to his dependency upon me. By maintaining authorship, he pushed away the very containment he longed for. So I pushed back, often using gentle humor, saying something like, "I don't mean to interrupt – but perhaps we could reflect together on what you just said." My job was not to let him push me off the analytic stage, but rather to maintain connection by insinuating myself into his solo performances, despite his great discomfort. In so doing, I allowed him to experience himself in the presence of me, having my own experience – an experience separate from, but not destructive of his experience. At the same time, I confronted his culturally-sanctioned, omnipotent isolation as an artist, which coincided with the omnipotence of his own internal self-care system.

As Thomas gradually came to tolerate my presence in the transference/countertransference relationship, several dreams imaged the destructive dynamics that severed his connection to both internal and external holding. Dream image #1: *Thomas came upon a large cavernous space. He had the feeling that he was looking down into an ancient temple. In a far corner of this temple he saw a small boy spinning.* Thomas associated the feeling of "spinning" to the anxiety he holds in his stomach; he associated the anxiety in his stomach to his desperate attempts as a child to get adult approval in the face of failing in school. In identifying the boy as only four or five, he realized how early he had learned to "rev" himself up to make things all right.

Dream image #2: *Thomas was holding himself off the ground by hanging onto a rope. Looking down, he could see that there was a goat trying to butt him. He then looked up and realized that the rope was not attached to anything.* This image of himself holding onto a rope attached to nothing reveals the omnipotent illusion and the underlying anxiety that has permeated his life. We traced his affective associations back to his feeling detached from his parents and teachers: that he holds himself now the way he learned to hold himself then, through the intensity of his self-performance detached from external support and vitiated by an underlying invasive fear. I suggested to him that this way of holding himself also inhibited his ability to trust his connection to me. I then asked about the goat. Thomas was familiar with the story of the scapegoat as the one who carries the rejected parts of the group and is sent away to wander alone in the wilderness. Through his associations, we came to see the goat as carrying the rejected parts of himself: his disembodied instinctuality and primal vulnerability. And now this goat was back, butting away at the system of his manic defense that held him above his own suffering and removed him from relationship to others.

These dreams allowed Thomas to name and to perceive consciously the destructive feeling states that dominated his psychological and creative life. "Spinning" and "self-holding" became the terms he used to describe the anxiety and tension that racked his body when he made his work. He came to see that his exclusive reliance on his intuitive intensity spun him into a relatively closed system that disconnected him from using consciously his full artistic intelligence to structure his working process. While the spin of his intensity funneled unconscious elements directly into his work, it also collapsed the potential symbolic space in which he could observe and experience these elements in a way that could ground his artistic process.

In continuing to track parallels between his work and his life, we saw that he performs his art-making in the same way he performed for teachers in school: to gain external approval in order to mitigate internal turmoil. We imagined his spinning as an internal psychic intensity that cocooned his terrified child-self against the fear of failing. I suggested, further, that his defensive spinning separated him from an embodied experience of himself and interfered with his ability to focus. It was also perhaps a cry for help and a refusal to function. I suggested further that his failing in school may have been his only way to stop the spin – to establish a sense of himself separate from his performance. His present physical symptoms could be viewed as an unconscious pressure to stop the spin of his manic production in order to experience himself outside his creative process.

By bridging this gap separating his artistic process from his psychological life, we created a space in which Thomas could stop spinning and begin to experience his split-off primitive feeling states. I could then speak to him of his experiences as a traumatized infant-self who had sought the holding of an internal or archetypal intensity because he lacked an adequately embodied maternal holding to humanize this intensity. Needless to say, our contacting these split-off affects intensified both his physical symptoms and his psychic rage within the transference. He became frustrated with me because the analytic work was not making him feel better. He was also devastated to discover that he could not leave analysis because, as he said, "I cannot find my way back by myself." For the next year and a half, Thomas fought to maintain his omnipotent self-holding to ward off feeling the full impact of his isolation and loneliness.

Just as Thomas resisted experiencing primitive feeling states, he also resisted his emerging awareness of the compensatory nature of the unconscious. He understood how he had used his working process to resist the rest of his life, but was perplexed by my suggestion that it could also inform his life. That is, when he operated on the "pliable stuff" of his artistic medium to retrieve a work from chaos, he was also retrieving a bit of himself from his internal chaos (see Milner 1993). In his eyes, seeing the reparative potential of his artistic process diminished the importance of his creative work. Similarly, acknowledging the prognostic movement of the psyche within the work challenged his artistic ego as the sole source of his artistic productions.

As Thomas' resistance gave way to the holding in our analytic relationship, the compensatory power of the psyche revealed itself in dreams and in spontaneous healing images. Significantly, he experienced a greater capacity to structure his working process in ways that both contained and channeled his intuitive intensity. By engaging his artistic process as a reflection of his psychological life, and by tracing how his psychological life played out in his artistic process, Thomas's working process began to function as a mediatory product which enabled him to develop a capacity to observe consciously and to come to terms with the unconscious.

In analysis, engaging the artistic production as a mediatory product facilitates a conscious understanding and appreciation of unconscious manifestations in the work. Integration of unconscious opposition makes fullest use of the healing factor of psychic compensation. Jung quoted Sabrina Spielrein in linking the complex to the origin of the symbol within artistic expression: "Thus a symbol seems to me to owe its origin to the striving of a complex for dissolution in the common totality of thought. ... The complex is thus robbed of its personal quality. ... This tendency towards dissolution or transformation of every individual complex is the mainspring of poetry, painting, and every form of art" (CW5, 201).

Jung's description of the symbolic process explains how a work of art can function as a mediatory product to further individuation. Psychic products arise equally from conscious and unconscious sources. Purely unconscious products are no more symbolic than purely conscious ones; it is the attitude of the observing ego that can discover the symbol emerging from the collaboration of both. For the artistic process to function symbolically, the artist must not be aligned one-sidedly with either conscious ego intentions for the work or unconscious impulses that arise in the work. Rather, the artist must endure the liminal space and negotiate between these opposites. When the artist ego holds the tension of this middle ground, psychic energy regresses into the unconscious, activating the wordless occurrences of primary process and infantile experience as well as core archetypal energies – all seeking conscious expression. The artistic process then functions as a common channel, allowing the opposites to flow into the mediatory product of the creative work. What then may be revealed in the work is an intelligence and a meaning beyond the artist's intentions; this, in turn, can relativize the artist's ego and initiate a symbolic attitude.

In my case examples, Alice tends to focus on a conscious intellectual exploration of her work while repressing emotional expression, whereas Thomas tends to merge with an intuitive expression of the unconscious that is unstructured by his artistic intelligence. When one side of these opposites subordinates the other, the artistic product is not a symbol but, rather, a symptom of the suppressed other part. A work of art gains symbolic significance when it appeals to thinking as well as to feeling and stimulates sensation as much as intuition. A symbolic attitude neither replaces technical and conceptual competence nor imposes a particular style or content. Rather, the symbolic function of a work of art is based in the attitude of the maker toward the artistic production both during and after the making process. A work of art has the potential to function symbolically for the community when the artist has tolerated the holding of the opposites in order to allow the making process to function as a channel for the "wordless occurrence" to incarnate into form.

With this in mind, let us return to Duccio and imagine his attitude as he stands before the Maestà, this work that took him two and three-quarters years to realize: this work that is an amalgamation of design constraints and technical innovation, of artistic tradition and expressive invention, of religious efficacy and political necessity. As he stands before his work and relates to it, the image begins to mediate between his human intention and the eternal source to which he now prays.

I believe that the symbolic attitude embodied in Duccio's prayer can inspire our analytic work with artists. Our task is to serve human artists so that their lives are no longer sacrificed for art, a condition that spins them into abstraction and suspends them above human connection. We can do this by neither pathologizing nor idealizing their creative work, but by differentiating and mediating the destructive and creative dynamics that underlie their work. We do this so that these artists may begin to experience their work as a vehicle through which both grace and ordinary understanding might infuse their lives.

References

Bollas, C. (1993). Aesthetic moment and search for transformation. In P. L. Rudnytsky (Ed.), *Transitional Objects and Potential Spaces: Literary Uses of D.W. Winnicott*. New York: Columbia University Press.

Dewey, J. (1987). *Art as Experience*. Republished in *Late Works of John Dewey*, (Vol. 10). Carbondale: Southern Illinois University Press.

Ehrenzweig, A. (1967). *The Hidden Order of Art: A Study in the Psychology of Artistic Imagination*. Berkeley: University of California Press.

Gablik, S. (1984). *Has Modernism Failed?* New York: Thames & Hudson.

Kalsched, D. (1996). *The Inner World of Trauma: Archetypal Defenses of the Personal Spirit.* London/New York: Routledge.

Kavaler-Adler, S. (1993). *The Compulsion to Create: A Psychoanalytic Study of Women Artists.* London/New York: Routledge.

Kohut, H. (1978). *Searches For the Self*, Vol. II. Madison, CT: International Universities Press.

Milner, M. (1993). The role of illusion in symbol formation. In P. Rudnytsky (Ed)., *Transitional Objects and Potential Spaces: Literary Uses of D.W. Winnicott.* New York: Columbia University Press.

Modell, A. (1975). A narcissistic defense against effects and the illusion of self-sufficiency. *International Journal of Psychoanalysis, 56*: 275-82.

Neumann, E. (1974). *Art and the Creative Unconscious.* Princeton, NJ: Princeton University Press.

White, J. (1979). *Duccio: Tuscan Art and the Medieval Workshop.* London: Thames & Hudson.

Manifestation of the Archetype in Children's Reality

Caterina Vezzoli
Milan, Italy
Association of Graduate Analytical Psychologists
Zürich Institute

Research done over a three-year period consisted of 1085 dreams and drawings of children in two elementary school classes in Northern Italy. The teachers of these classes informed the children's parents about the research and the parents gave their formal consent. The teachers also asked their pupils to write, if they wished, about a dream – in order to learn as much as possible about their dreams.

Thirty-nine pupils participated: 17 female, 22 male; ages 8 to 11 years. Fourteen pupils (six female, 8 male) were followed for three consecutive years, while thirteen (eight female, five male) were followed for two years. The remaining twelve (three female, nine male) were followed for one academic year.

The children responded with enthusiasm. They felt valued and, above all, they seemed to enjoy recounting and drawing their dreams. The teachers acted as important intermediaries in the research work. They did not intervene, nor did they comment on the content of the children's dreams. However, with the utmost respect and sensitivity, they collected the narratives. At the end of the project, the teachers reported significant improvements in the children's correct spelling and handwriting and in their expressive capacity (oral and written) including in the telling of their dreams.

The Approach to the Research

The researchers initiated the study because of an interest in unconscious productions of the latency stage of psychological development. Parting from the assumption that, through dreams and drawings, it would be possible to observe the psyche in action as a self-regulating system, a homogeneous sampling – with regard to age, environment and scholastic situation – was chosen. To limit the field of inquiry, attention was given to the following observations: 1) the development of the ego complex in "normal" children; 2) the mutual influence between the archetypal image and the ego complex; 3) the relation between the ego complex and the maternal and paternal complexes.

During the period of research, there was no contact between me and the children, whose everyday lives were unknown to me. The flow of dreams was irregular. To guarantee the maximum freedom to write or not write their dreams, initially there was no deadline for the descriptions of dreams. Eventually, it was decided that school compositions would be not more than once a month. Conducting research for three years was motivated by the need to continue observations for a long stretch of the latency period, and on the consideration that a symbolic process needs time to be born and developed.

The psychological "normalcy" of the sample was predicated on the hypothesis that the subjects had a base of ego development and were able to withstand and interact with unconscious stimulus. Thus, from the beginning of the research, it was clear that there were no pupils with a diagnosis of infantile psychosis or autism. The ability to symbolize presupposes an ability to tolerate and experience object separation, ambivalence, guilt and loss. There were no cases with a psychopathological diagnosis. The lack of diagnoses did not guarantee the absence of at-risk cases. Two of the children were handled by social workers because of their families' economic circumstances.

To draw dream images was a way to expand on the dream's content. In addition, drawing seemed to guarantee some distance from the content, if it became too heavy.

Research Results

It is clear that my background as an analytical psychologist influenced the interpretation of the material but, in the execution of my research, I tried to ensure that the material would be open to a variety of possibilities. More than once I was tempted to report the dreams and drawings without comment, letting all of them speak for themselves but I commented on some aspects of the dreams and drawings and disregarded others. I tried to stay consistent with my observation on which the research was based: that the creative process makes up a part of the process of destruction-construction-transformation of the ego complex.

The narration freely chosen by all the children follows the typical structure of a fairy tale or dream: situation, exposition, development, lysis. The drawings illustrate parts of the dreams and/or complement them. The dynamics expressed through color allowed me to understand where was the emotion described in the dream. Dream and drawings are complements to each other. Drawing is an integral part of the symbolization process, allowing the dreamers to expand upon the dream contents.

The research materials make it clear that, in the search for meaning, children of the latency stage are involved in a creative process where moments of destruction and regression alternate with moments of growth and progression. In this way, they transform and integrate the archetypal material.

In each dream, a problem is declared. In most dreams the problem is connected to emancipation from a dependent and ambivalent situation, to growth, to becoming an individual. This declaration is a path whose goal is individuation.

Numerous times in a year or more, each child presents an archetypal image, around which the ego complex is focused and developed. The material confirms that such a heroic and grandiose identification, projected by the psyche as a self-regulatory system, allows for a solution to be found and for the development of new identities and new possibilities.

The quantity and variety of collected material confirms that, in the latency period, the ego complex organizes itself by identifying, evolving and separating from the paternal and maternal complexes. The psychic energy in play creates great tension and sacred, archetypal images emerge. The ego complex structures itself and is stimulated by the independence supplied by the archetypal image.

In the report of results here, selected examples of dreams and drawings are presented in chronological order. Dreams and drawings are from pupils of the same age and the same class, at more or less the same time. For Silvia and Massimo, longer sequences show different phases of their journey: the various ways that the ego complex tries to assert itself.

Example: Identification with the parent

Three dreams of eight-year-old Tiziano show the idealized and compensatory identification with a parent of the same sex, as well as the spontaneous emergence of a grandiose identification with archetypal images.

Dream and Drawing 125 (September)

Figure 1

One night I dreamt that I was at sea in a boat with my Dad. My Dad was paddling while I was watching some fish and holding onto the sail. The sails were big and blue. I was watching the sea and the clouds in the sky. My Dad was rowing fast and we were getting farther from the seashore.

Tiziano says he was holding on to the sail, but in the drawing (Figure 1), he shows himself well planted in the boat and as big as his father. The father is at the helm and holds the oars. Under the boat there are many fish; some emerge from the water.

We may take the figures in the drawing and the dream as the manifestation of the paternal and ego complexes. The paternal complex rows, that is, he expends the energy to propel the boat forward. But if the sails that Tiziano is attached to are maneuvered adequately, they could move the boat without oars. Thus, he is identified with the father's strength. If the ego complex is represented by Tiziano in the dream, he is not yet capable of giving direction to his identity, but lets himself be led by the paternal complex. Even though he says he is holding onto the sails, he could possibly move the boat himself. The ego is not very active, but is in the safety of the boat and in visual contact with the fish, the unconscious contents. The idealization of the father's strength is probably a compensation to feel strong. The sails represent the possibility of Tiziano's becoming skipper, to be driver of his own boat, to be an autonomous human being.

Dream and Drawing 127 (October)

Figure 2

I dreamt that I was in a factory and I was fixing cars. I was screwing in a screw of a minibus and after a bit I went home for supper. The morning after, I went again to the factory and I fixed lots of cars and minibuses.

In the drawing (Figure 2), the factory is in the center of the page. The motor vehicles are red; a worker in a blue jumpsuit is holding onto the controls of a car. There are many blackbirds in the sky. The theme of work appears. The metalworks laborer fixes up the automobiles. But above all, the theme of separation appears: a separation that is justified by necessity. One leaves the house in the morning to go to work. The black birds signify sad thoughts connected to separation.

Dream and Drawing 128 (November)

Figure 3

I dreamt that I was a shepherd with five or six sheep and that I was living in a hut and in the morning I was going out to pasture. I was away from home for 10 or so days with my sheep and then I was going back toward home where I would stop and sleep. I sent my sheep into a pen. In this dream I had a king's crown and shepherd's clothing.

In the drawing (Figure 3), the shepherd figure is regal and imposing with a crown, a big cape, boots, feet firmly planted on the ground, arms that are still a bit small, but one can see the fingers. The small sheep graze at the feet of the shepherd. They aren't all the same; they have different expressions.

The shepherd king is an archetypal image that transcends the image of the regal father. The image could be connected to religious upbringing: God as the Good Shepherd. All the children live in a very religious environment; their lives are influenced by the Church. However, Tiziano is the only one to choose a shepherd king.

Separation, as an experience of autonomy initiated in the previous dream, is proposed again and then rendered definitive. To take care of the sheep, one must go far from home; one lives in a hut and is alone. The image is a numinous manifestation of Tiziano's Self and, therefore, grandiose. However, the shepherd king is conscientious in his care of the sheep. The ego is able to take care of his nascent interests: an ego complex that is sufficiently coherent and able to sustain its functions.

Even though it departs from an identification with the parent, the unconscious is stimulated to explore different possibilities. Eventually, the new archetype appears. The archetype's energy supports the organization and the coherence of the ego complex.

Example: Reiteration and expansion of the theme of destruction and reconstruction

In dreams, the children expand freely on themes and fantasies that help them develop and consolidate the ego complex. As an example of this process of destruction-reconstruction, I chose eight-year-old Demis, who dreamed of being a king.

Dream and Drawing 167 (September)

Figure 4

I dreamt that I was King of a castle with many guards. I like to ride horses and have many animals in the castle. I like to have horses, cows and many animals. I liked my dream because I have many animals.

Demis draws (Figure 4) himself on a horse's saddle with his head held high and his feet in the stirrups. The emphasized saddle brings to mind a large penis. The king is on a draw bridge, with proud stature. He enters the castle; sentinels watch him from the bastions. The drawing is colorful and Demis is shown with a red cape and clothing. A grandiose image, a fable atmosphere and an emphasis on the importance of animals and a listing of animals. The animals reduce the grandiose component. The sentinels stand guard. They are aspects of the ego at the service of the Self. The colors and the animals tell us that Demis is in contact with his feelings and his instincts.

Dream and Drawing 169 (October)

Figure 5

I am a hunter. I shoot my rifle at a bird and it drops dead. Later a pheasant comes near me and keeps yelling, "Gra, gra, gra." It scares me and I escape to the forest. I hear a lot of sounds but all of a sudden I slip into a big cave where there was a big bear and a gorilla. I walk. After a bit I see an uninhabited house and find a lot of precious items. I take them and put them in a bag. Returning outside, I find a dead rabbit. I thought that the gorilla killed it. I take a step and find a dead mouse. Unafraid, I go to the cave and catch whoever killed the two animals. I wait and a big mammoth comes out. While I'm watching to see if it falls into the trap, my rifle falls right on its head. In that moment my mother wakes me up. (Figure 5)

The subjects of death, destruction and fear are recurrent themes in the dream. There is no color inside the cave; my hypothesis is that the emotions are too strong and too indistinct to be expressed and, because of this, are not colored. The gorilla and the bear are not in the drawing, but the bat is. The cave is a symbol of inversion of energy and in the drawing the bat, another symbol of inversion of energy, hangs its head. The birds are also drawn with their legs in the air, having been hit by bullets from the hunter's rifle. Outside the cave, everything is very colorful and Demis colors himself red like the king in the first dream. The crown was replaced by a hunter's cap with a feather in it. The cap is yellow like the crown.

In the drawing and in the story the motifs of death, loss of consciousness and fear are reiterated and lead to slipping into the cave and losing contact with the outside world. The theme of slipping into the cave indicates the turning inward of psychic energy; it refers to the capacity to look at oneself on the inside. The ego, consistently needing to renew itself, must confront dangers and unfamiliar places that reside within.

When he slips into the cave and encounters large animals, how can he not think about parental complexes that keep the ego complex in check and cause feelings of inability and depression? Still, destructive aspects can promote growth and lead to resolution of problems. In fact, Demis, always more active, succeeds in leaving and finds precious items. Then the theme of death returns outside. The active figure in the dream, the ego complex, sets a trap to catch the culprit. But what he finds is too much, even for a combative ego. Surprisingly, a large prehistoric animal symbolizing uncontrollable force appears. This content is too loaded with energy to confront upon the first encounter.

His actual mother comes at the end of the dream as bearer of reassuring everyday life although the assonance between mother and mammoth can't be ignored. The ego needs reinforcement in order to face the many facets of the complexes.

Dream and Drawing 278 (November)

I dreamt that I was Saint Francis and I was in the woods. The animals of the forest were hungry and thirsty and they didn't have an owner. There were only animals. I gave them something to eat and drink. These animals were a fox, a lamb, two hares, two kangaroos, a duck, two chickens, a rooster, a goat, a wildcat, a deer, a lion, a black panther, four turtles and four little snails: two yellow ones and two brown ones. I wore a bearskin and to hold it in place I had a cord tied tight. Everyday I gave them something to eat and drink and at night I had a wooden bed and a blanket of leaves. The animals and I slept outside under the stars. One day the animals got sick and I cured them.

Figure 6

In the drawing (Figure 6) there are all the animals listed in the dream along with nests in the trees and blackbirds. All the animals are well detailed in their color and characteristics. Note the rooster in the center of the picture who is making his sounds.

Demis says he is St. Francis, but isn't the young cock at the center of the drawing? The sound "Chicchirichi" is the call to wake up. St. Francis is smiling with his arms opened wide in a welcoming and prayer-like stance. During the Mass, the "Our Father" is recited with one's arms opened up in the same manner that Demis draws them in his picture. An aspect of asceticism and of transcendence is present in the image of St. Francis.

The animals are the well-differentiated instincts and St. Francis/Demis is in harmony with them. In the picture, St. Francis seems to be wearing a robe, but in the dream he is wearing a bearskin. The bear in the cave from the previous dream had been sacrificed and now he protects the new hero, the spiritual force. St. Francis is the grandiose image that represents new order. Surely Demis knows the story about St. Francis' rebellion against his father and how he went into the woods to live with the animals.

The ego complex needs to be renewed. The new order asserts itself by going into the woods, disappearing into nature, being able to take care of itself, taking care of the instincts and then curing them. The loneliness that occurs because of the rebellion against the parental complexes does not frighten if it is guided inwardly by the spiritual knowledge that one can rebel against the father. An ego complex independent of the parental complex knows how to take care of itself and its own instincts. There is nothing better than to have the stars in the sky as one's roof and a heavenly father to go to.

Example: The complex of the besieged ego

There were some dreams where certain situations arose in which the ego complex was besieged and ran the risk of being split. This was the case in eight-year-old Silvia's dreams and drawings, which she entitled "The stone monsters."

Dream and Drawing 41 (September)

Figure 7

One evening during vacation, I saw a very beautiful film. But at night I dreamt that the stone men were following me. It began like this: I began to run and then I saw men everywhere. Finally I was able to escape. When these men are near me and about to grab me, I wake up and I find myself on the floor.

Silvia is against the left wall and is touching it with her hands. The ground is slightly sloped where she is. The expression on her face is one of complete terror and there is no way out. The stone monsters are gray and red – like Silvia's dress – and they are running toward her. The first monster has his arms stretched out to grab Silvia. Silvia's countenance is one of fear.

The beginning of her dream is reassuring with its reference to a very beautiful film, but in the unconscious the opposite occurs. Silvia's ego, which is still fragile, is threatened by the gigantic stone men. The risk of disintegration is present. It is not possible to make out reassuring elements except for the ability to flee; hence, to escape the threat.

To tell and draw a dream (Figure 7) so terrifying demonstrates that the ego complex, even while threatened, succeeds in maintaining control. Theoretically, fear could be the emotion that allows for the disintegration and reconstruction process. But it is necessary to see if such a large and destructive emotion can be used for the organization of the ego.

Dream and Drawing 45 (November 23)

Last night I dreamt that me, my cousin Marianna and my very little

Figure 8

cousin, her name is Sabrina, we are lost at sea. Then a big shark jumped out and my cousins and I were really afraid and the shark said to us: I'm going to eat all three of you. All of a sudden, the water started rising around us and then it turned into a cement wall, there was only one window. My cousin and I tried to get to the window and at this point I woke up.

Color has vanished. The shark looms over the three girls. In the colorless picture (Figure 8), the waves make it so that one cannot see the bottom of the boat that looks open. The protagonists talk and scream "protect the baby," who is shown in a sort of basket. We can recognize the desire to protect the rising feminine identity. In the dream the water turns into a cement wall which protects the fragile ego from its attacker, but it also reminds us of a prison. The bigger girls try to escape the prison by climbing up to the window above. The overwhelmed ego's only defense against destructive forces is a miraculous transformation that allows it to be freed.

Miraculous salvation images that appear in children's dreams, a subject of much research, are connected with the transcendent function. In situations where the hero – the ego – is about to be overtaken, something miraculous occurs, such as water turning into a wall in Silvia's dream.

Dream and Drawing 229 (March 23)

Figure 9

My friends and I were going around on our bicycles. At a certain point, we arrived at a shipyard where they were working. In front of me my friends were jumping a lot, and then I tried to. My male friends yelled at me to watch out, but I had already fallen in a hole. As soon as I hit the bottom, my bike ricocheted and I got hurt.

Silvia draws herself (Figure 9) differently from the first dream. She is no longer the terrorized child, but the bold heroine on her bike seat, who faces up to dangers. She is wearing knee pads, a hat and pants. She is equipped to go out and face the outside world, which,

Daimon Verlag
Hauptstr. 85
CH-8840 Einsiedeln
Switzerland

Stamp

*Bitte als Postkarte
frankieren*

we can see from the background, has remained black and hostile. In addition, even though the bicycle is too big she handles it well, holding onto it with her feet on the pedals. Both Silvia and the bike are very colorful. The bike has red spokes and a red seat. The child has blond hair with a blue cap and red visor, blue shirt, orange pants, red knee pads. The features are definite.

The explanation of a similar change, from the fragile and frightened ego to one that is more solid, brings us to the dream. She is no longer alone and abandoned. Her male friends are in agreement with her; they warn her about the danger. Contrary to the previous dreams, she and her cousins and her friends are no longer afraid. It is no longer the adults who come to Silvia's rescue; rather, her peers warn her about the dangers. They bring her to confront her limits.

In her dream she says there is a shipyard. It is probably a building under construction. The work and dangers of constructing a less fragile ego are not finished, but there are some allies.

Silvia's series of dreams reminds us of the fairy tale "The Robber Bridegroom." A beautiful miller's daughter is betrothed to a rich suitor. The daughter is afraid of him and repulsed by him. When he invites her to his house in the woods, the maiden plucks up her courage and goes. But on her path she leaves a trace of seeds (lentils and chickpeas). The house is dismal and a bird gives her a warning. Nonetheless, she enters. An old woman explains to her that this is a den of thieves and she will be eaten. In fact, while hiding, she is witness to the killing of another maiden. But she succeeds in fleeing with the old woman. On the day of her betrothal, the maiden recounts her terrible adventures and shows everyone the finger of the dead girl. The bridegroom, along with his friends, is brought to justice.

Silvia's and the maiden's paths are similar. Like the beautiful miller's daughter, Silvia is afraid. In her dreams she first finds support from her mother and aunt, but afterward her friends offer help and encouragement to confront danger. She escapes the projections and will of the parental complexes.

The ego structures itself by integrating masculine aspects through identification with her male friends. It reorganizes the unconscious omnipotence of the parental complexes which are obstacles to structuring – building – a more solid ego complex. Thus, Silvia discovers in her drawings, and we hope in her life, the color of her emotions, her body, her existence and recovery – after the fear – also her happiness in play and adventure.

Example: From archetypal symbols to personal symbols.

Dream and drawing of Massimo, age eight 110 (September)

Figure 10

A man accuses a king of murder.

The interpretations one can make of Massimo's dream and drawing (Figure 10) are many. The chosen drawing shows the Egyptian god Anubi, half dog: the psychopomp that escorts the hero to the land of the dead in his journey to regain his identity. In the picture, the man who accuses the king has a regal stature. The rigid drawings could be due to the inability to draw movement. Nevertheless, the drawing shows a sentiment of tragic feeling.

Massimo could have seen illustrations of the god in a history book or on television, but the use of it is exclusive; none of his friends chose a similar symbol. The symbol engaged his fantasy and was chosen unconsciously to illuminate a problem.

The renewal of the sun and the passage of the threshold are mythological references suggested by the dream and drawing. This refers not only to the formation of the ego, but also to the renewal of the Self. The ego is derived from the Self and a complete Ego has the ability to assimilate and integrate positive and negative factors in such a manner that the personality is not split into antagonistic parts. For Massimo this journey could be dangerous.

If the king is a murderer, regardless of his demonstrated royalty, he runs the risk of being destroyed. The ego complex requires protection; perhaps the dog Anubi can furnish it. To rebel against the superpower of the paternal complex in order to structure the ego.

Dream and Drawing 111 (October)

I'm in a big war space shuttle and I'm fighting.

In the drawing (Figure 11) of the space shuttle a human form can be recognized. The aggressors are not identifiable; they have no faces or bodies. They are points. In the drawing the command comes from the space ship, "Hurray," in response to the "We surrender" of the enemies.

In Massimo's and his friend's dreams, outer space is prevalent, probably due to television. To live in outer space is a new challenge. The ego that separates itself from the identification

Figure 11

with the parental ego must find a new identity also through grandiose challenges. Massimo moves the challenge outside the domestic walls to have the greatest possibility of exercising his fantasy.

Massimo says "I am on a space shuttle." A space shuttle depends on the mother ship. But Massimo adds "big," as if to say that he has a certain degree of autonomy. Then he adds "war." He must fight to find his place in the universe. The loneliness of the space shuttle with so many enemies could be a representation of emotional loneliness. We do not know whether, in Massimo's life, he has experienced loneliness and abandonment. However, separation is a necessary condition to be freed from the parental complex.

The fantastic transposition in the sky allows for the representation of a conflict and of feelings that would be too difficult to accept and confront if one were on earth. A bit of time is necessary before the conflict comes down to earth. We can assume that conflicting subjects must first be represented far away and gradually closer up so that the ego develops the strength and coherence capable of withstanding the confrontation.

The ego represents itself as a grandiose power. Grandiosity is necessary in the construction of the ego complex that finds itself surrounded by enemies and conflicts which bombard it from every side. The next step would be to give a face to those conflicts and to identify the enemies.

Dream and Drawing 113 (November)

Figure 12

Robi, Franci and I are playing ball. The ball goes into the City Hall garden. I climb the fence, then a man and the police arrive. Franci shoots a stone with his slingshot at the man.

The hero is with his peers (Figure 12). The ball game and the school courtyard are symbolically the places and modality to discover himself as masculine. His father is the other man, but similar. The police defend the order, those rules that Massimo would like to break; his friends help him. A generation fight? It seems more an exaggeration of the persecutory male power that wishes to impede play.

The fight is to gain autonomy: the individuality that began with the king and continued into outer space, now is on the earth. The scenario is everyday life. The fight reached the school yard, the authorities arrived, and Massimo experienced the comfort of being in a group. By being with his friends, there is support to continue with the rebellion and to solidify ego strength.

Dream and Drawing 120 (February)

Figure 13

I was a sailor in a beautiful field. I was dressed in white pants and a white sweater with blue stripes, some black shoes and a white hat with a black pompom. I was dancing happily when all of a sudden I fell into a hole and into a tunnel that went to a castle. I left the tunnel and I began to sing and dance, but at a certain point rabbits, squirrels, little birds and an owl came out. The little animals told me that the king prohibited dancing and singing. I ran to the castle and jumped up on the windowsill. The king was a big mouse like a cat. I asked him why he forbade dancing and singing. He responded that he prohibited singing and dancing because he didn't know how to do them. I taught him how to sing and dance. Then I returned to the ship and I went away.

Massimo draws himself (Figure 13) just as he is jumping into the window where the mouse is. He is dressed as he describes in his dream, with big black shoes. He says "Jump." The roof of the house/castle is dark red and the brown door to the entrance is closed. The rest of the drawing is not colored.

Massimo offers an immediate interpretation of the persecutory aspect of the father. The king is terrible because he is envious of the *joie de vivre*. Massimo shows an ability to enter a relation with the king's persecutory and depressive aspects. Now the ego complex is sufficiently coherent to be not frightened by the power of the paternal complex.

To enter into a relationship with the wicked king, who is sad, demonstrates a desire for reparation and understanding. An ego that is sufficiently coherent no longer runs the risk of being swallowed up by the paternal complex. Massimo enters into relationship with female aspects and with the hero who saves the maiden, but danger is still lurking.

Dream and Drawing 246 (After summer vacation)

Figure 14

I was a sailor and I had a fat friend. One day my friend took a baby that I had found. He sold him to an old man who had to leave on a ship. I found out about this and I followed him and killed him and I made sure the baby came back on the ship and then we returned home all happy.

In the drawing (Figure 14), there is a storm and the boat is swaying to and fro. There is a jetty with a lighthouse where the fat boy with a red jacket is putting something into his mouth. Massimo, dressed in a sailor outfit, turns to the little child who is in a small boat attached to the wharf and says, "Pisellino" (Sweet Pea). The baby says, "Papa pa-pa." In the sky, a face laughs sardonically, perhaps a clown. The competition continues, but the ego does not risk being inflated with the fat boy. It regains its size and he becomes Dad. The term pisellino referring to the penis, is one of endearment used for small boys. The ego can be taken care of by the new, male identity.

Conclusions:

I hope to have conveyed the richness and creativity of the material that I collected. I conclude with a sentence taken from *The City of Magic*, a fantasy novel by Marion Zimmer Bradley. "Was it the end of her searching? Or was it the beginning? Or is it that all searching ends like this, with one last step toward the top of a high mountain, but only to make out the existence of new and unknown horizons?"

Translated from the original Italian by Elizabeth Teefy

Medication in the Materia

Doctorly Destructiveness or Chemical Creativity?

Frederick Steele
San Francisco, California, USA
C.G. Jung Institute San Francisco

"Medication in the Materia" is my catchy way of introducing a somewhat onerous topic: the interaction of Analytical Psychology with the currently red-hot clinical practice of psychopharmacology. The second title, "Doctorly Destructiveness or Chemical Creativity," bends this subject to the needs of our conference. The use of medication in psychoanalytic situations can be either creative or destructive and sometimes, in measure, both.

Over roughly the last decade – propelled by mixed motives born of the evolving standard of psychiatric care in the United States, scientific curiosity, and guilt over the possibility of doing less than the best for my patients – I have been pursuing the prescribing of pharmacological agents in the course of psychotherapy and analysis. This evolution in my interests and identity has felt more or less forced upon me, largely by external cultural and administrative pressures and, as such, has stood in clear distinction from the manner in which I have more commonly experienced individuation: growth from inside outward. Could it be that this topic – prescribing in analysis – has been rooted in me more deeply than I have realized?

When I was a child, there was really no religion in my nuclear household. My parents' interests were decidedly secular, and my mother was imbedded in what proved to be a life-long feud with her own mother about religious matters. Grandmother was an ardent Christian Scientist with an annoyingly persistent inclination to proselytize, while my mom was a Camel cigarette-smoking, hard-drinking, sarcastic skeptic and sometime agnostic. One of the resolutions of this distaff standoff was that I was offered up to the experience of Christian Science Sunday School from ages four to fourteen.

One of the central dogmas of Christian Science, the religious opus of Mary Baker Eddy, is articulated in "The Scientific Statement of Being." This was recited aloud and in unison every week at Sunday School. Excerpts include:

> *There is no life, truth, intelligence or substance in matter. All is infinite mind and infinite manifestation, for God is all-in-all. ... Spirit is the real and eternal; matter is the unreal and temporal. ... Spirit is God, and Man is His image and likeness.*
> *Therefore Man is not material, he is Spiritual.*

When ill, the hard-core Christian Scientist experiences a primacy of prayer to penicillin and seeks the counsel of a Christian Science adept called a practitioner rather than the services of a physician. The commitment of the devout is abstinent and rather severe. That my grandmother lived a healthy life to age 103 does give, in retrospect, a certain empirical spin to her history of irksome homiletics.

For decades now I have looked at my early religious lessons as horribly one-sided. Here I quote Emo Phillips, a quirky and idiosyncratic comic whose work I have admired: "I used to think that the mind was the most marvelous part of the human being; then I realized what was giving me that thought." Phillips adroitly gets at the solipsistic shadow I see in Christian Science, in myself, and sometimes in other places in our Jungian world as well. Jung (MDR) said:

> *All comprehension and all that is comprehended is, in itself, psychic, and to that extent we are hopelessly cooped up in an exclusively psychic world. Nevertheless, we have good reason to suppose that behind this veil there exists the uncomprehended absolute object which affects and influences us. (p. 352)*

To my reading, this quotation leaves us aloft in an ether of psyche alone, pondering the nature of that "uncomprehended absolute object" which may contain or inhere in matter.

Prescribing in the psychological context opens the practitioner to errors of two fundamental types. The first type of error – one for which I have a proclivity owing in part to my early Christian Science exposure and its subsequent amplification on Jungian themes – is to overestimate what the psyche or spirit can do therapeutically and thus bring harm to the patient through a failure to treat when appropriate somatic treatment is available. A kind of spiritual ambition or analytic inflation in the therapist, along with ignorance of the medical approach, is a common source of such errors.

In a protracted period of analytic work a dozen years ago, a very depressed Jungian-oriented analysand bent on "doing it without medications," as a matter of integrity and honor, had me colluding with her powerful animus in demanding what neither of us realized was therapeutically impossible. Ultimately my patient required emergency hospital admission and another physician to provide effective antidepressant medications.

No apparent loss of "soul" or of "depth" resulted from this intervention. Quite the reverse; afterward the patient was better able to do the analytic work and, as we took note of this together, it brought a powerful deflation of a shared analytic hubris. Neither of us ever forgot it.

Jung gave an interesting amplification to my notion of this type of error.

Brigitta of Sweden (1303- 1373) ... helped me to gain insight. ... In a vision she saw the devil, who spoke with God and had the following to say about the psychology of devils:
"Their belly is so swollen because their greed was boundless. ... A like greed is mine. Could I but win all the souls in heaven and on earth and in purgatory, I would gladly snatch them." So the devil is the devourer. Understanding ... is likewise a devouring. ... In wanting to understand, ethical and human as it sounds, there lurks the devil's will, which ... is a fearfully binding power, at times a veritable murder of the soul" (Let-I, p. 31).

Jung went on to make the point that unknowing lies at the center of the symbol, that the reification of understanding wounds and scars, that we must know and be ignorant at once. Knowing where understanding in the domain of the psyche should cease and when attention to the domain of the body should begin (and vice versa) is the charge to the contemporary practitioner of conscious mental health care.

Today's separation of biology and psychology is oddly complete, holding the provinces of body and mind discrete and discontinuous. It is as though one could pursue truth in the domain of soma or that of psyche separately, cleanly; each half is devoid of the contaminants and confusions of the other. Mental health care has become very material and not spiritual. The psychiatrist in the United States, for years regarded as a keeper of psychological mysteries, has once again become a medical doctor. Psychopharmacology conferences rarely mention psychotherapy.

The first major wave of contemporary psychopharmacological innovation has definitely hit the beach. The ambient American *Zeitgeist* would claim this wave as a sea-change, but let us look at the facts, taking dysthymia and major depressive episodes as our examples.

These two diagnostic groups together have a lifetime incidence of six percent in the United States today. That is to say, over 15 million Americans now living will suffer one or both of these conditions at some point in their lives. Of depressed patients, 85 percent can be helped to some degree by a psychopharmacological intervention alone. (In evaluating this kind of statistic, we need to remember that the placebo effect for anti-depressants in adults is about 35 percent.) Of the group that receives benefit, only half are symptom-free and in full remission. The others are advanced into more and more complex pharmacologic regimens, despite spotty prognostic acuity.

Errors derive also from providing a concrete response (medication) when a symbolic or spiritual approach is needed. This error underestimates psyche and invites the patient to project psychic content, inappropriately, onto the medication or the doctor. This constitutes what I have come to call "alchemical incest." Psychic contents thus projected can become as inextricably bound to their object as those contents that are confounded in therapeutic incest of the sexual type.

One of my dramatic symptomatic successes with prescribing occurred more than a decade ago. The patient was a handsome, clean-shaven, middle-aged engineering executive with neatly cut white hair and equally neatly cut gray wool pin-striped suits. For several weeks he had been losing weight, energy, and sleep; he did not have much to give at work. Very real cutbacks at his company had become threatening monsters of penury and displacement to him, though his own position, when objectively considered, looked secure.

He insisted that I call him by his first name, "Fred," though his domineering and upwardly mobile wife called him Jack. I met with her once at her request so that I "could get a clear picture of what's happened to Jack." Her father, like me, had been "a medical man," so that she addressed me with familial and Asclepian warmth as she told me what Fred/Jack's problems were. Her account was as superficial and external as Fred/Jack's own. Each spoke about Fred/

Jack's life in an entirely "persona" sort of way; neither of them appeared to possess differentiated consciousness of any other type.

I prescribed maprotiline (Ludiomil), a tetracyclic then relatively new to the market and being touted (as so many new antidepressants were) for rapid onset of antidepressant effects. Week to week we inched the dose upward and reviewed his symptoms and side effects, filling the hours with history-taking that tried to look like an approach to depth work, until at five weeks he responded beautifully to the medication. Energy returned, his sleep assumed its former pattern, and his dread of events in the workplace evanesced. Over the next few weeks he spoke philosophically about how much he had suffered during his depression and was exceedingly grateful to me in a classical patient-doctor kind of way, now that with my help it was "all behind" him.

Fred/Jack reduced the frequency of his visits and drifted away from my care, trailing renewals for medications. I felt wistful about the psychotherapy that did not take place. But Fred/Jack declared that he felt great as he went away. Here the doctor had done his work and the symptoms were relieved. But even now, years after these events, my memory is of a life unlived and of Fred's commitment to go on unliving. Medication had succeeded but individuation appeared to have been forestalled.

Here "alchemy" and "chemistry" look as if they are in contention. Fred/Jack chose the option of chemistry in relative isolation, viewed his symptoms entirely in the light of the medical model, and at the end of the day declared himself cured. My sense of the defeat of what we might call his "alchemical opus" of self-realization was unmistakable. The ostensibly cordial refill requests, which eventually came from outside California, were recurrent reminders of Fred/Jack's fixed projections onto the medications and me.

The concept of incest includes elements of the alchemical equation that bear on the story of Fred/Jack as I have told it. When we prescribe a chemical that transforms the patient we have rendered concrete not only the *prima materia,* the imaginal "stuff" of the therapeutic transaction, but also concretized the goal: Ludiomil (Prozac) as *lapis.* However satisfied the removal of symptoms makes us, we may have committed an "alchemical incest" of a sort. The goal has been achieved in the body by altering its chemistry. This in turn was enabled by providing a real – as contrasted with imaginal – substance, the medication. Part of the image of the Self is thus bound to the medication and becomes dependent upon it for actualization. It is an incest with a symptomatically good outcome.

Fred/Jack was the victim of such an "alchemical incest." We could argue that violence was done to the possibility of wholeness in his life. It is an irony of Fred/Jack's example that the medication provided a tool that could be used either to seek wholeness or to flee it.

Thus prescribing medications, from the alchemical perspective, can be tantamount to incest. Isn't incest always bad? If the medication can enable the tools of individuation I need a way out of my own incest argument, for this enabling product of the incest is clearly an opening to good. Jung gives me some help:

> *The instincts and the specific fantasy-contents are partly concrete, partly symbolical (i.e., "unreal"), sometimes one, sometimes the other, and they have the same paradoxical character when they are projected ... It is often almost impossible to say what is "spirit" and what is "instinct." (CW16, 362)*

If I paraphrase Jung in order to bring his language closer to that of our present discussion, I can construct an argument by analogy. My paraphrase:

> *Matters of the body and the specific fantasy-contents are to be seen as partly concrete, partly symbolic; sometimes one, sometimes the other, and as possessing this same paradoxical character when they are projected. It is often almost impossible to say what is symbolic and what is actual.*

It begins to sound as if one could have a "real" exchange, where "concrete" things occur, and still be very much in keeping with the opus. If this is so, we have a place to stand and defend conscious psychopharmacologic intervention against my own "incest" argument. Real exchanges can take place and incest need not be occurring. There are no easy rules here, only more clinical distinctions to be made with keen demands upon the perception and judgment of the clinician.

Contemporary neuroscientists and skillful practitioners are exploring empirically the domain of this potential incest in its biophysiological aspects. Their discoveries have brought us to a point where material and spiritual no longer need be held separate; they have given us assistance with our discriminations regarding incest and individuation. They have brought us into an era where – for many individuals – the pursuit of wholeness, the impulse to self-actualization, the process of individuation, and the alchemical opus all suffer no compromise in purity or prospect of fulfillment when psychopharmacological agents form part of their pathway. The "conscious psychopharmacological intervention" thus becomes the *modus operandi* for prescribing in the context of psychotherapy or analysis.

This phenomenon is easiest to see when a psychopharmacological intervention goes well. A couple of years ago I was referred a brilliant and successful young professional woman, "Susan." She was married and the mother of two young children. Somehow she found time for both family and profession and had been doing very well in both spheres for several years.

Her husband was an interesting and complex man doing well in his own field but possessed of an irascible and unpredictable temperament. That his father had committed suicide after a long series of psychiatric hospitalizations for depression was a significant part of his story and the probable source of his mocking disdain for psychiatry and psychotherapy. My patient's own angry alcoholic father had behaved during her childhood much as her husband did now. Her mother had been retiring and self-abnegating, trying to stay out of harm's way.

My patient's profession served both self-expression and refuge, but for the past year or two she had become worried that other members of her department were noticing a decrease in the quality and quantity of her work and were in league to have her removed from the firm. Yet no one had said anything of the kind to her, and Susan could produce no concrete example that would satisfy even her own self-observation. She had begun to dread meetings at which differences of opinion were likely to be expressed, and arranged her schedule to avoid them when possible. (In the past she had been an ardent exponent of her own point of view and enjoyed articulating it.) Susan's level of energy had fallen precipitously and she was sleeping fitfully, awakening early in the morning feeling as tired as when she had gone to bed. She was overwhelmed by the children and suffered from the sharply critical attacks of her husband when this left more work for him.

Susan had read *Listening to Prozac* before coming to our first meeting, and was an informed potential consumer with many interesting questions. At the heart of her concern was her intuition that medication would be effective. Where would that leave her with regard to her own self-definition? For how long would she then take it? Could she tell her husband?

Susan engaged me immediately in a natural and promising psychotherapy process (this was her first therapy experience) and candidly hoped that, whatever changes might follow from our discussions as to whether or not she was to take medication, I could become a positive father-figure for her and provide a relationship that would be not only comforting but altogether new. After five visits and a thorough exploration of her thoughts on the matter of medication she asked what I would recommend.

I started her on paroxetine (Paxil) which I advised for its sedating side-effect, anticipating that it might help her immediately with her sleep disorder. It did, and as she came to rest in its effects over the next three weeks, all her other symptoms melted away as well. She was restored to her former confident self at work, had the energy to meet each busy day, and felt right with her children once more. But she could not tell her husband that she was taking medication for depression.

Seeing such an objective success was a thrill for us both. I wondered whether Susan would even continue with her psychotherapy now that she hardly appeared to need it. But her tie to me only deepened. Over the next year the positive father transference she had hoped for gradually appeared. She seemed to take it for granted in the warmest, most innocent way, and wanted it not interpreted or drawn into attention much; it was as though she was basking in my consistent good will and restoring herself with it.

After a period of concentrated work on the anamnesis of her father's rages and shouting intimidations she confided to me that during her vacation some weeks earlier she had, on her own and without consulting me, discontinued her medication for ten days. Her former depressive worries had begun to return very quickly, coming in like a morning fog after only five or six drug-free days. She had gone back to her usual regimen and had seen her mood stabilize again before telling me about the episode. Her anticipation of the confession of all this had been the stimulus for recapturing all those images of the paternal emotional abuse. I passed the transference test by not blowing my stack at her for acting autonomously. Susan decided on her own to stay on the medication open-ended unless it really began to bother her in some tangible way. And she decided to tell her husband that she was taking it.

Susan's husband blew his stack at the news of the Paxil. Between the fact of the medication and the deception of her having taken it a year and more without telling him, he found just cause for a new round of his familiar rages.

"But I knew you would blow up just like this if I told you" was Susan's answer, bringing onto the table the habitual double-bind in which she was caught. The conflict which began over the Paxil led Susan and her husband into conjoint work with another therapist. A hoped-for spinoff of Susan's Paxil has been the husband's getting into his own individual therapy and beginning to work on his history and his temper.

In Susan's case the medication plays many roles: stimulus to seek care, content for initial tests of the prospective therapist, effective psychopharmacologic intervention, contract of trust through which the therapist/father's temper could be tested, pharmacologic resource and psychological lever for challenging the tempestuous hegemony of her husband, and part of the motivation for her husband's entry into treatment of his own. Where does the psychopharmacology end and the psychotherapy begin? What is chemistry; what is alchemy? Each is part of the other. Where the two cannot be separated we can raise my question of alchemical incest. But, unlike the case of Fred/Jack, it is hard here to spot any depotentiating effects attributable to Susan's medication regimen. The Paxil almost serves as co-therapist for parts of this extended project. Our Jungian approach need suffer no discontinuity when helpful pharmacologic agents are introduced consciously and carefully into ongoing analytic psychotherapy.

I have presented one instance (Fred/Jack) where the "alchemical incest" seemed both present and damaging and another (Susan) where synergy and synthesis result. In a third case, the meaning of the outcome is less clear, but the case boldly presents a fundamental dilemma.

"Martha" is a single woman of 40 who has been in psychotherapy most of her adult life. The times of progress and encouragement have been few. She has been working with me for several years. Her complaints center on recurrent symptoms of anxiety, dissociation, depression, and insomnia. Martha's most torturous symptom is her sleeplessness. This is tyrannical and persistent.

Over the years we have experimented with a variety of medications, including benzodiazepine anti-anxiety agents and hypnotics, tricyclic antidepressants, fluoxetine (Prozac), clomipramine, trazodone, buspirone, and others that I am no doubt forgetting. None of these has had a notable antidepressant effect, and not one has offered Martha more than temporary respite from insomnia. But in recent months we have had more luck. Though Martha was too activated on Prozac, she was able to tolerate Paxil when we very gradually moved the dosage upward. At present she is alternating 15 and 20 milligrams on successive nights and getting the best result with the insomnia that we have seen. She sleeps well nearly every night. Disappointingly, the Paxil has had surprisingly little effect on her other symptoms.

But there is a major footnote here. While her newfound sleep is exceedingly welcome to Martha, she now reports a continuous inner state that she describes by saying, "I've lost a little piece of my soul." I guess this would have to be called a "side effect."

My questions are these: Is what has been lost something essential to her, or an absence of jitteriness that has been present so long as to have come to feel essential? If we conclude that a part of her "soul" has been taken from her by the medication, what do we do then? Report this to her? Discontinue the medication and "honor" the insomnia? Agree that some soul has been lost but that this is worth the result?

In Martha's case, we have an odd outcome. It is partly salutary, partly alarming, partly healing, partly wounding. It possibly defeats one tension that should not be defeated – the pull of individuation – while it enhances her ability to sleep.

I have left a fourth case to the end, in recognition of the fact that adding dreams to the already teeming number of variables may make decisions impossible. But I want at least to offer some preliminary material.

"Peter" is a professor of arts and letters at a major university. He was 49 years and 11 months of age at our first appointment and very recently had separated amicably from his wife of 23 years. Both of them felt that they were needing to develop as individuals and that the patterns of their marriage (he on a control-trip and she excessively compliant) were stifling to both of them. They have one daughter who is a brilliant and rather independent-minded senior in high school. Peter gets along well with his estranged wife and his daughter and sees them each several times a week. He was working effectively and was not clinically depressed at the time we first met.

But one year before I met him Peter had suffered a major depressive episode which his internist had treated with 30 milligrams of Paxil. (This paper is *not* being brought to you by a grant from SmithKline-Beecham.) On the medication Peter's mood had returned to its "normal" dysthymic state and his uncontrollable weeping and demonic insomnia had ended.

Yet, on the Paxil, Peter had felt anything but whole – medicated, sedated, and impotent – and after six months of treatment had tapered off the medication before calling me. In our initial telephone conversation he reported that he had "been living most of [his] life in a state of melancholy" and was prepared to go on doing so, though in calling me, he was "seeking a state of mindfulness about [his] depression." The intensity of the recent depressive episode had "objectified this lifelong suffering" for him in a way that he thought warranted some reflective attention. He was aware that the mood could return with its earlier intensity and was wanting "to resist without medications if at all possible."

At our first face-to-face meeting Peter told me the story of his upbringing as the eldest child and only son in a Philadelphia metropolitan blue-collar ethnic neighborhood family where his tyrannical and unfeeling mother, whose lifelong *leitmotif* was an angry and endlessly recurring, "Why me?" controlled the family with an iron fist. Mother, 79 and gravely ill with an inoperable aortic aneurysm, had watched with my patient and his younger sister the slow death by alcohol of her sensitive but passive husband. When his father died, my patient was 17; he had to assume material responsibility for the family. Military service and Vietnam were Peter's springboard out of his family and opened the door for an exodus that he had anticipated ever since his deeply imaginative boyhood.

At our second meeting my patient discussed, in a "Why me?" tone what he felt was terribly unfair treatment both by potential publishers and university politics. Between the second and third sessions he called to report a frightening return of his depression and volunteered over the phone that he wanted to consider a return to medications at our next appointment.

At the third visit I began a course of bupropion (Wellbutrin), by my experience less sedating than Paxil, and far less likely to disrupt sexual function. In our discussion that hour he continued to catalogue perceived career injustices in the now-familiar "Why me?" tone.

By our fourth weekly appointment we had increased the Wellbutrin to our target dose without Peter's experiencing either side effects or anti-depressive effects. With some sense of urgency, he reported a dream.

I am at a large party, dressed in a bathrobe while others are more formally dressed, wandering through a crowd of unfamiliar faces, wondering when I will come to a place where I can change my clothes. The scene shifts and I am in a quiet parlor opposite my wife; she is attractively dressed, sitting on a love seat. There is an immediate sexual excitement that we both feel; she wordlessly indicates I should sit next to her. I do, and we begin to kiss and touch one another. Then all at once she changes positions and sits facing me at a right-angle with her feet against the side of my leg. The sexual feeling of course stops and we are at an impasse. Next I see her getting ready to go out on a date. She is dressed like Dorothy in "The Wizard of Oz." My potential feelings of jealousy are eased when I take note of how innocent and naive she appears to be.

By the fifth meeting he could feel the Wellbutrin taking hold and "closing the aching maw in the middle of my chest that is this endless weeping," as the Paxil had done six months before, though with distinctly different subjective qualities. At that visit he reported a dream, which he described as being very similar in pattern to dreams that had recurred throughout his adulthood.

I am standing across the room from a woman who is familiar to me. She is smiling silently and there is a warmth between us. There is a sexual feeling but no lust. I move across the room to be enclosed in her warm, tender embrace, realizing as I do so that there are women on each side of her, seven or eight in all, and that they are all part of a collective encompassing warmth.

Contrasting the two dreams, it is easy to think that a significant internal realignment is depicted in the movement from the first dream to the second. Peter's conscious attitude and mood both reflect this movement. There is an inner feeling of being sustained, presumably owing quite directly to the Wellbutrin, which appears contemporaneously with the second dream. Can we attribute a causal relationship to these two events? And if so, is the relationship to the feminine which appears in the second dream, a longstanding recurrent dream theme, to be regarded as salutary? Is this a healthy maternal embrace or a seductive regressive movement? Has our "alchemical chemical" provided feminine sustenance to Peter or has it given rise to a uroboric wish-state? Does the medication conspire to preclude a deeper look into the unconscious or open the door to an enhanced reflective process? How do we approach and answer such questions?

Perhaps by including another dream. Peter used the sixth, seventh, and eighth sessions to explore his relationships with his wife, daughter, and mother – spending by far the most time on the mother, fleshing out the story of her unfeeling and controlling ways. Over this two-week period, his mother began to go downhill rapidly with the extension of her aneurysm and it became clear that she was going to die soon. In the three weeks that separated visits eight and nine Peter travelled to his childhood home, attended his mother during her last, agonizing days, was with her when she died, handled the memorial service and went through some of her belongings. He did not suffer depression during this period.

He reviewed this story in summary fashion for me as we resumed our meetings, but then quickly got to his alarm over two evenings of break-through depression which occurred during the first weekend back in California. He had fallen into deep pits of despond plagued with suicidal thoughts, and in these was centering all his anguish on the difficulties in publishing his work. He saw himself as "whining" and expressed disgust with himself over his inability to control this behavior.

Peter was stunned and illumined when I told him that the whining was his version of Mother's "Why me?" and that it was this "mother inside him" who was culpable for his current misery. This was near the end of the hour but, while collecting himself to go, he reported a dream. It had come three days after his mother's death, while he was still staying at her house.

> *I am in my mother's house, looking down into the cellar. Believe me, it's not a basement, it's a cellar, a real pit. There is a crowd of people down there in the dark, filling the place. Someone is calling out to me, "You haven't even begun to work on what is down here."*

Peter and I looked at one another in recognition of the truth, one that was all the more compelling for its having been formulated and articulated by his own unconscious. He was worrying aloud about perhaps needing to come to therapy more frequently as he opened the door and left.

I can always update my knowledge of "chemistry" at a weekend medical conference on psycho-pharmacology; my work with Peter's dreams is a reminder about the alchemy.

The Infant and the Depressed Mother

Véronique Lemaitre
Grenoble, France
Société Française de Psychologie Analytique

My life is the story of a self-realization of the unconscious.
Life is sense and nonsense, or it holds sense and nonsense. I
anxiously hope that sense will overcome and win the battle.

C. G. Jung

My inquiry lies between these two propositions from Jung,
regarding the opposite potentials engraved in the unconscious: to
become oneself or to become crazy. The archetypal program can
spin endlessly in a process of deadly repetition. Jung shows the way
toward a possible return to the source through a regression to the
archetypal reservoir of energy that he calls incest with the mother
(CW5). The question of meaning finds its answers in the dialogue
established with the unconscious. What warrants having such a
dialogue?

I look for an answer to this question by way of the observation of
babies with their parents. This period of life is recognized universally as central for the building of personality and, according to our
methods, for the establishment of an ego able to establish a dialogue
with the unconscious. I make use of the accumulated findings of the
cognitive psychologists as well as of psychoanalysts over the past 20
years, concerning babies' abilities and interactions between parents
and infants, in order to understand the first moments of this dialogue.
And I am presenting the ways that I have devised, beyond the forays
of Michael Fordham and Erich Neumann.

By observing babies we have identified a frequent pathology (in
at least 15% of the mothers) whose long term effects on the child's
development are serious: post-partum depression, which interferes
with the cognitive and relational development of the baby exposed
to it. Let us evaluate how the mother's depression influences the
child's ability to establish a dialogue with the unconscious, which
the infant needs for growth and creativity.

The work of Stern (1985) offers the most coherent ideas about the development of a baby's psychic life, associating the working method of the cognitive school and the clinical observations of psychoanalysts. According to Stern, being equipped to sense the constants in all areas of perception allows a baby to differentiate what is from itself and what is from the other. The repetition of experiences allows the infant to build "theories," for predicting events that follow, and mastering them. In this way, the infant identifies little by little the external and internal sources of excitement, as well as the sequences of events that bring comfort.

We can evaluate the information available to the baby about itself and the other, and about what links the two. Therefore, we can size up the immense power of the mother's care. Her regulation of the constants depends only minimally on her free will; the essential part eludes her, whether it relates to outside events or to the influence of her unconscious life. The mother transmits her own relationship to what escapes her: her degree of flexibility and confidence, her aptitude for maintaining a dialogue with the unconscious.

Jung defined depression as a beneficial illness. It forces the ego to reassess its perception of its own power. Then it can evaluate the power of unconscious complexes with which to establish a dialogue in order to recover from depression. These complexes are organized by archetypes whose interplay can enrich the ego if it recognizes its weakness in relation to them. The central organizer of this process, the Self, can be seen as the unconscious matrix of the ego which, by its dimension of uniqueness, entirety and eternity, can compensate the vulnerability and mortality of the ego. The Self appeared (CW13) late in Jung's work – 1929 – as a potential of energy and organization that comes to the aid of an ego threatened with dissociation because of excessive internal tensions between unconscious complexes. The Self appears as a natural anti-depressant insofar as the ego can start a dialogue with it. It counterbalances what appeared at the beginning of his work as the prime source of life and creativity: the archetypal mother. The Self, as the central organizer of the individuation process carries the creative potential of an individual.

The experience of the Self brings together unification, that is, a reinforcement of the feeling of identity ("I am myself"), along with a harmonization with the world: "I am also the world." This experience is similar to Winnicott's idea of the primal relationship: the mother allows her baby to find the breast outside and to create it inside. The experience of the Self allows the constitution of the Winnicottian self, and the enduring feeling of existing is a measure of the quality of the ego-Self dialogue.

In order to establish a fruitful dialogue between the ego and the Self, I find that the infant must live the experience of the Self in the relationship with the mother sufficiently to allow the baby to relate this experience with those it can make with its own body and in contact with the inanimate world. It is also necessary that the parents be able, in the care they deliver to their infant, to respect the taboo of incest: not to use the infant as an object of their own satisfaction. If the taboo is respected, the Self will be projected onto the infant's body and the dialogue between ego and Self can happen through the bodily engagement in the exploration of the world. The triangle ego-father-mother can constitute the interface of communication between ego and Self, the key to the baby's feeling of being alive, and the basis of psychic creativity.

According to Lebovici (1983), the newly-born child meets in its parents' minds two babies: "fantastic baby," which comes from the parents' psychic lives when they were children, and "imaginary baby," which they were building during pregnancy.

More concretely, issued from inside the parents' bodies after a transit in the mother's body, the baby gives shape and image representation to what is inside, secret, inaccessible, at the same time as at the origin: the unique meeting between two gametes, a crossing of two lines, but also the mystery of human origins. We reach here the archetypal dimension: a projection of the Self onto the baby as a point from which everything comes and everything converges.

Winnicott (1969) described the mother's psychology after the birth as a necessary stage of "madness" to make her able to adjust to the needs of her baby. This "primal motherly preoccupation," starts at the end of the pregnancy, reaches its apex at the moment of birth and during the first few weeks, then fades progressively during the first three months of the baby's life.

Close to the state of being in love, this preoccupation seems to correspond to the moment when, for the mother, the Self is projected onto the newborn and when it depends on her that the dialogue ego-Self, projected onto the dialogue mother-baby, be of a good quality. This projection comes to the aid of the mother-baby relationship, functions as an archetypal organizer of the first moments of the newborn's life and is crucial for the child's future. It gives consistency to the sense of void that sometimes seems intolerable but inherent to this non-verbal communication. It gives the newborn a certain sense of familiarity, along with a share of power that imposes respect and helps the mother find the right distance. In the response that the mother brings to its requests, the baby discovers the level of interest she feels for the body which is the messenger of the person the baby is. Through her care, the mother provides the baby with a mirror in which to discover the Self and manufacture an ego. The mother-baby relation becomes the mold in which the baby's dialogue ego-Self develops. As Beebe (1997) has done with videotaping, let us look at the mirror function of the mother. Within a few weeks, the mother-baby duo has established specific sequences of interplay in which imitation takes center stage.

A three-weeks-old girl is lying on the changing table, with mother above her. Baby looks at her intensely while she is looking back: "Ooh … oh yes! You're happy!" She repeats over again with the same tone of voice and with the same rhythm. The baby is looking steadily at her mother and moving her lips in a quiet sucking motion. The mother: "Ah?, you want to play, do you? She imitates the baby who accentuates the imitation and gesticulates. Mother repeats the sound and gesture. Baby smiles. Mother smiles: "Oh yes, you like to play" and she kisses the baby.

This interactive sequence, which we can imagine is repeated at each changing, gives the baby an occasion to relate pleasurable sensory experiences with a type of relationship in which it experiences the pleasure of being with mother and having an influence over her. Mother gives attention, free in its expression, and she gives the lead to the baby. They create together an experience of the Self as a reality which both inhabits them and links them together. Tronik (1996) calls a "feeling of dyadic expansion" this feeling of happiness when being together, a motive for the communication that seems to be so strong between mothers and babies.

In a second example, a five-week-old boy tries to locate his hand, which just passed through his visual field. His gesture is too quick and he hits his forehead with his fist. He cries. His mother has followed the sequence from a distance, busy changing his diaper. She speaks to him: "Oh my poor baby. Oh yes, it is difficult to put your hand in your mouth. You'll make it, don't worry!" She turns the baby around so that he lies on his belly, putting his hand close to his mouth. She bends over to look at him. He looks at her too and sucks his fist quietly. She says: "There it is! You found it."

Anticipating his motor skills and helping them along gently, this mother encourages the self-exploration of her baby by fantasizing the pleasure he will have sucking his thumb so that he can do without her. After the above scenario, she informs the baby that she understands his intention (which is to discover his body and the means at his disposal), and she agrees with the satisfaction he feels. She encourages the development of the ego; the message of this sequence refers back to the representation of a Self internal to the baby, already disengaged from the relation with his mother.

Third example: The same sequence of gesture signs will produce another type of reaction with another mother: "Oh no, you want to scratch yourself. Slow down, give me your hands." While talking, she removes the hand from the baby's face and covers him with kisses. After a brief movement to escape, the baby lets his mother kiss him without reacting. It is difficult to read his expression and see if he is satisfied or not.

We can see here how the mother's worried interpretation of the baby's gesture cancels her exploratory intention (probably the same as in the previous example): the Self is extremely precious and must be left untouched. "Let me do it for you!" The Self here seems to belong to the mother and is accessible to the baby only through her intervention.

If the mother is a good mirror for her baby, that is, helping the child to decipher feelings and to select and differentiate behaviors that bring satisfaction, the complexity of the mother's answers informs the baby in many other areas. These interactive sequences are fairly constant in their content and their functional objective, but they are infinitely varied in context (e.g., presence of other persons, mother's mood). These variations are rich in information about what escapes the baby, the part of the environment on which the baby's nascent ego has no influence.

In my first example, it can happen that the mother does not react as usual when the baby initiates the game with little "mouth movements." She does not seem to understand the baby's invitation. According to the degree of motivation, the baby will give up or will try to invent new gestures to get the mother interested. From her feedback the baby will gather information on what preoccupies her. Then he experiences the difference between himself and his mother, and also about the elusive nature of the Self. If all goes well, the mother gets bored with the repetitive side of constant care and tries to go back to her previous occupations; the projection of the Self does not happen exclusively through the baby and touches on other relationships and activities.

A clinical experience sheds more light on the way a baby comes to an understanding of mother's psychological life and can (or cannot) link this "primal Eros," in which the baby is bathed, to the enigma of the mother's sexual attachments.

> *A young woman, used to establishing a dialogue with the unconscious, describes what she feels for her six-week baby boy: "I spent a bad night because of milk overflow. It is strange; it was the first time it happened. The lactating process was well established; I had never had a problem ... (silence). Last night, my husband came home later than usual and I resented this ... (silence). During the last breast-feeding of the night, the baby hurt me, he sucked too hard. Usually I lie in bed and fall asleep while breast-feeding ... In fact it becomes painful when I have had enough of it. Otherwise, it is rather pleasurable; it makes me fall asleep. When I want to be with my husband, the breast-feeding does not last as long. In fact, I am split between the temptation to be with my baby or with my husband. When I know my husband is home, I fall asleep during breast-feeding while thinking of him ..."*

Breast-feeding is a time of communication when the participation of both partners is at its fullest, involving mutual intimacy. Such a closeness, linking body areas as sensitive to excitation as the breast and the mouth, evokes for the mother the intimacy of sexual relationship. These images are especially close to consciousness since the baby is the result of this type of relationship. This example reflects the intensity of the internal conflict that this vivid feeling activates. It is because of the pleasure she can enjoy with her husband that this young woman accepts being used by her baby. The sleepiness which comes during breast-feeding shelters consciousness from images too excitingly erotic. Breast-feeding becomes a quiet moment for her: to feed the baby in an atmosphere of serenity, which is "good for his growth and balance."

The sexual excitement is diverted toward another scene. But if her husband does not come home at the time she expects him, anxiety grows and makes the excitation painful, due to her feeling that she is left defenseless against the baby's avidity, own desire of incestuous pleasure, and the guilt associated with it. The mother is torn between the necessity she perceives in her baby to experience the Self in an encounter with her through the intermediary of her breast, and her need to dissociate her sexual fantasies when she breast-feeds. The calm and the sleepiness possible when the husband is around appear to be the other side of the "lover's censure," which allows the mother to forget her baby in order to find her husband. Offered to her baby and unconscious of the sexual nature of the exchange, she appears like a Virgin Mother, sheltered from any incestuous sexual satisfaction. It allows her to live, in her unconscious, the incestuous relationship that the baby needs in order to activate the ego-Self dialogue.

This example shows how the ability to desexualize the images of pleasure taken with the baby can be missing. The exchange informs the baby of mother's inner experience and what is at play: the behavior of this mother (stopping the breast-feeding before the breast is quite empty) aims at protecting her baby from what she confusedly perceives as a sexual "perversion." She certainly has suffered more from it than the baby, who has spent a very good night. This behavior shows the strength of her psychic organization and her ability to communicate with the unconscious.

Thus, the delicate dynamics of excitation, of the mother as well as of the baby, create a vivid tension for the mother, according to Bydlowski (1997). Maternity is the occasion of an important psychological restructuring. It is a physiological crisis whose most frequent consequence is a depression from which the mother usually recovers easily. The child, on the other hand, retains the after-effects of it. Play has an essential place in the child's development, but how can the mother play if she is depressed? A nightmare can be the result when communication does not function. Crying babies, or those who do not show clearly that they are satisfied, can become persecutors for their mothers, who feel obliged to satisfy them or reproach themselves for being unable to do so. All these conditions unite to form a vicious circle or, rather, an interactive spiral that turns backward. The repetition of unsatisfying experiences on both sides adds to the level of anxiety and guilt, which aggravates the inability to play.

In a parallel research, Murray (1992) confirmed that post-natal depression lowers the quality of the communication between a mother and a two-month-old baby. It affects not only the mother's ability to understand her baby, but also her capacity to engage in play with her baby, for the fun of both. This alteration is statistically correlated with:

1) A less confident sense of attachment, and therefore a separation anxiety between them more difficult to cure.

2) Inferior cognitive performances at 18 months and 5 years and also a reduced creativity. (Boys are described as hyperactive and girls as overly watchful.)

3) An alteration of the capacity to relate with other children: at five years of age, they initiate contact less often and their attempts are not as successful as those in the control group.

Moreover, the quality of the interaction with the father seems to protect them effectively from difficulties of adaptation in school.

If these studies do not shed light on the specific way of functioning of these children, they do help us understand that an important part of their energy is diverted from their personal use. For what gain? We get some indications from the interaction between Julie and her depressed mother. Both parents are 25 years old.

First observation: Julie at four weeks. Her mother is very distressed. The baby is sleeping in her crib, cries when the mother tries to speak. She can't, it went too fast, the baby was born too early, she was not ready. She is too agitated to communicate with me. She speaks out without allowing me to say a word. The only moment when she speaks in a normal way is when she talks about her interrupted schooling, her guilt toward her parents. She obviously tries to go back to the time when she was not pregnant.

Second observation: eight days later. The father is present. Julie is crying. Her mother holds her. Julie opens her eyes and turns her head to find her mother. The mother does not see the move and rocks her to quiet her down, without looking at her. Julie cries and is restless. The mother finds a position in which the baby quiets down, curled up on her chest, face turned toward her mother. She falls asleep. The parents tell me their story, the complexity of each family and the heroic nature of their marriage, a lifeboat for the love and the happiness that neither had found at home. I help them to structure their own little family so that they will not separate and the mother will not remain alone with her baby.

A meeting every other day, with the baby present, asleep on her chest, helps the mother to face all that is surging up from her own childhood. She still cannot look at her daughter but takes fairly good care of her: understanding when the baby is hungry or needs to sleep, knowing how to quiet her down in her arms – showing me the position. Julie is easy to deal with and develops well. However, I receive two emergency calls because her parents cannot stop her crying.

Third observation: Julie at 9 weeks: Father comes along. Julie calls from her crib. It is feeding time. Without discussing it with his wife, the father gets ready to bottle-feed the baby, helped silently and efficiently by his wife. When everything is ready, she sits nearby and looks at them. The father's gestures are tender and experienced. He offers the bottle to Julie while softly talking to her. She looks at him intensely and, instead of taking the nipple, smiles at him. The father, very moved, responds vocally while smiling. The exchange lasts at least a minute before Julie starts feeding. Her father keeps looking at her. His wife and I both watch him. Again, Julie stops feeding and smiles while trying to utter a sound that the father reinforces. The mother is crying while looking at them. The father has not noticed and, happy, looks at me. I intervene to emphasize the beauty of this interaction, underlining the father's ability to communicate with Julie, who prefers to play with her father than to eat. I mention that the sight of this scene must be moving for the mother and also maybe a little painful. The mother then bursts into tears.

Fourth observation: eight days later, without the father. Julie cries in her crib. The mother takes her on her lap, facing her. She puts her face close to Julie's face, and the baby quiets down instantly and looks intensely at her. Her face does not reflect any emotion, but rather an uneasy expectation. Her mother withstands the gaze but doesn't say anything. Her face is frozen. This impassive moment lasts a painfully – for me – long time. The mother cries in silence, without moving. Julie is looking with an unexpressive face. Her mother averts her gaze and doesn't ask for help. I talk to her, though: "It is difficult for you." She murmurs "I am not good for her; I can't." I offer a halfway out: "Your tears are not so bad for her, but tell her what you will do when you take her and move her. She must be anxious about not being able to guess what's next. You should help her to anticipate what's going on." The mother's eyes lose their vagueness and her gaze returns to the here and now. She now looks at Julie in a lively way and smiles at her.

This depression is much more intense than most cases of post-partum depression. We can see all the mechanisms at play, as if through a magnifying glass. The mother is ambivalent toward her motherhood and afraid of hurting her baby. We can perceive the destructive impulse, a tempting shortcut in an attempt to come back to the time "before the pregnancy." The way of carrying the baby which quiets both mother and daughter is the one in which they rediscover the feelings from before the birth. The mother's care is appropriate at the level of gesture but actively disconnected from any value of communication: no look, no word which could be contaminated by and therefore contaminate, this wish to kill. Communication can start when the desire to kill can relate to the infantile hatred of the mother toward her own mother and her fear of abandonment. It is replaced by a depression in the true Kleinian sense ("I am in fact as bad as my mother"), which allows an exchange of looks with the baby but not yet a verbal exchange.

This type of triangular relationship is very difficult, as if mother and baby were sucked into a merging with each other, in a meeting place that has a morbid tone, but is attractive by the fact of their being together. This attraction is similar to that of a whirlpool drawing one into a watery abyss. I took a clue from the discreetly questioning expression on the little girl's face, to conclude that she would be better off if she knew with what sauce she would be devoured. But the power of the abyss was such that the formulation, which comes as I am writing and is made more vivid by the image of an ogre (this little darling is adorable enough to eat!), could not leave my lips. Struck by an identification with the mother, I remembered her first complaint, "I had not been warned during my pregnancy about what could happen," used to reestablish the capacity of the mother to identify with her daughter in a living dynamic.

One fact deserves to be underlined: it is remarkable that a ten-weeks-old baby could have had two interactive styles so different: immobility, astonishment at the mother; activity, seduction and a clear expression of her pleasure with her father, who is not depressed: an open face, speech discreet but free, a frank look without fear. What can Julie construct out of her contact with both of them? Her father offers her the ability to build the basis for an ego-Self dialogue from the pleasure of being together in an experience that integrates that pleasure with the satisfaction of influencing each other.

What does she develop from the contact with her mother? The mirror that her mother offers since her birth reflects little about Julie's personal experience: hunger, satiety and perhaps tiredness. The emotions seen in her face are reflected neither by the mother's expression nor by words telling what she feels. On the contrary, she is surrounded by her mother's emotional world – transmitted by her body language, her breathing, her heartbeat and what Julie can get out of her facial expression. She suffers repeatedly the sense that she has no power over this situation, except by reproducing from the inside what she perceives from her mother's body in her immobility. She succeeds then in establishing the most primitive level of communication: perception through active sensation of the physical state of the other. It all happens as if she were forgetting about herself in order to understand her mother, so as not to lose her.

If we translate things in term of ego-Self dialogue the depressed mother has lost contact with the Self, which was projected on her pregnant belly. The birth ruptured this unity which was sheltering her from the anguish of loss and brutally confronted her with the conflicts with the two families who did not agree with the marriage and the birth which came too fast. Once the egg was broken, she could only identify with the abandoned and vulnerable baby separated from her mother. The Self she is searching for with her daughter is like an inaccessible two in one, in which the child is trying to fit as best as she can while sacrificing her ego. My hypothesis is that, in parallel with this sacrifice, she will develop a knowledge of her mother's abusive internal world, about which she will be more familiar than with her own.

The mode of body imitation, as if to integrate the other's body, seems to me to open a way to understand the workings of the often astonishing intuition of psychotics. Seen from the child's point of view, the Self remains projected inside her mother, with the major flaw that it is accessible to her while the child's ego is developed only on the side of being and very little on the side of doing. The active potentiality of the ego will come to realization within the relation with the father, a supportive projection for the inaccessible Self. The stage is set for confusions of sex and generation to disturb the psychological evolution of this little girl.

How to help the baby of a depressed mother? Logic would dictate: to cure the post-partum depression as quickly as possible. But the means to do so are not so simple. Very often, an intervention within the first few weeks and a few interviews can reestablish a loving relationship between mother and child. But a delay often leaves traces in the form of an anxious preoccupation on the mother's side and an excessive closeness between her and her baby. In the case of Julie, it is probable that she will need help for herself: the projection of her Self onto her own body probably will be difficult without a previous disengagement of a relation with the mother based on a confusion between the Self and the mother. Only her confrontation with the inaccessibility of her parents will allow Julie to project the Self onto the love that links them and retrieve, by appropriation, a solid basis for her own feeling of identity. This will occur through a confrontation with her own sexual emotions.

I purposely gave a central place to the notion of "experience of the Self" and its connection with sexual pleasure. Thus I reintroduce sexuality into the context of Jungian thought, without which clinical work with infants seems to me impossible. To look at the parenting of babies from this perspective allows us to approach the sources of our ability to symbolize, and also the channels through which the intergenerational transmission is established. This sheds some light also on certain foundations of the psychoanalyst's talent.

At the time of Jung's birth, his parents were mourning their first son, Paul, who died as a newborn. Carl must have been aware of his mother's depression when he was a baby. Freud's mother also went through a difficult time when her second son died at seven months when Sigmund was only two. Thus, part of one's talent as a psychoanalyst lies in the creative use that one can make of the qualities one developed as a baby in contact with a depressed mother.

Translated from the original French by Martine Nagy

References

Beebe, S. (1997). *Les Interactions Précoces et le Dialogue Psychanalytique (Precocious Interactions and Psychoanalytic Dialogue)*. Conference in Paris.
Bydlowski, M. (1997). *La Dette de Vie*. Paris: Puf.
Lebovici, S. (1983). *Le Nourrisson, la Mère et le Psychanalyste*. Paris: Centurion.
Murray, L. (1992). Impact and post-natal depression on infant development. *Journal of Child Psychology and Psychiatry, 33*, 543-561.
Stern, D. (1985). *The Interpersonal World of the Infant*. New York: Basic Books.
Tronick, E. (1996). *Les Etats de conscience "dyadiquement en expansion" et le processus normal et anormal de Développement (The state of mind "dyadically in expansion," and the normal and abnormal process of development)*. International Conference of Perinatal Psychiatry, Monaco.
Winnicott, D.W. (1971). *"Jeu et Réalité"* (C. Monod & J.B. Pontalis, Trans.). Paris: Gallimard.
Winnicott, D.W. (1969). *From Pediatrics to Psychoanalysis*. (J. Kalmanovitch, Trans.) Paris: Payot.

Destruction and Containment in the Analytic Relationship

Takao Oda
Tokyo, Japan
Association of Graduate Analytical Psychologists
(Zürich Institute)

The vas belle clausum (well-sealed vessel) is a precautionary measure very frequently mentioned in alchemy, and is the equivalent of the magic circle. In both cases the idea is to protect what is within from the intrusion and admixture of what is without, as well as to prevent it from escaping. – C.G. Jung

The analytic container is equivalent to the *vas* (vessel) in alchemy. The alchemical vessel is essential to the alchemist; the analytic container is equally indispensable to the analyst. Both vessels and containers are the sites of a process of transformation; both alchemical and analytic works are performed through the imagination. Alchemists work both imaginally and with concrete vessels containing substances; analysts use dialogue and imagination. This very concreteness means that alchemists are often unconscious of the projection of their psyches onto their vessels and alchemical material; analysts can only visualize the containers and their contents. Analytic vessels, and the transformation process that occurs within them, are created out of the joint imagination of analyst and patient. Thus, analysts must be much more conscious of the imaginal dimension of the process.

It goes without saying that we as analysts have a deep concern for our patients' psychic transformation. Such transformation occurs more or less spontaneously in the analytic vessel when that vessel is constellated in the analytic space. Therefore, the constellation of a secure and protected container is crucial for the process of analysis. The analytic vessel is a living symbol, and it must function dynamically.

Although it must be well-sealed, it must not be completely impenetrable, lest it put us at risk of committing incest. The constellation of a sealed vessel and the development of a relationship between what is inside and what is outside are a dialectical process.

Alchemical Process and the Dynamics of Healing

Alchemists, *adept* and *soror mystica*, cooperate with each other in facilitating *opus*, the work. As Jung observed, there are some illustrations from alchemical texts in which we can see a vessel in the intermediate realm between *adept* and *soror* (e.g., CW12, p.276). The *adept* and *soror* would be unable to accommodate an alchemical vessel were there no space between them. Nor would the vessel function well if the physical and psychological distance between *adept* and *soror* were too narrow or, conversely, too great. Narrowing the psychological distance between them is the function of Eros, while psychic destructiveness increases that distance. Thus both Eros and Thanatos – destruction – are required for analysts to maintain an intermediate realm and to facilitate the constellation of a vessel within which it is able to contain the transformation process.

In alchemy the *coniunctio* describes the Eros aspect of relationship between *adept* and *soror*. *Coniunctio* involves a great risk of incest unless the *adept* and *soror* are well differentiated Jung discussed how *adept* and *soror* avoid incest through the alchemical *quaternio*. Forming the quaternity facilitates the transformation of the *prima materia* within the alchemical vessel.

Adept and *soror* in alchemy correspond to analyst and patient in psychotherapy. Schwartz-Salant (1989) studied alchemical imagination, emphasizing the value of *coniunctio* and the analytic dyad of analyst and patient. Yet, while his discussion is highly evocative, it is not only *coniunctio* and the dyad that are necessary, but also the constellation of the alchemical vessel between the analytic partners. Here the formation of the alchemical quaternity is indispensable for creating distance within fused, incestuous relationships.

As I have indicated, the function of *vas* or container, both in alchemy and psychotherapy, is very important. Jung said (CW9-II, 377) that the *vas* is often synonymous with the *lapis*, so that the constellation of a vessel and the transformation process that occurs within it are one and the same. The *coniunctio*, which bridges the distance between analyst and patient, and the *quaternio*, which intrudes upon them and ends their fusion, together form necessary and sufficient conditions for the constellation of a secure therapeutic vessel in the intermediate realm and the ensuring transformation that takes place within it.

We must not identify with the archetype of the wounded healer. An analytic vessel will not be constellated and the transformation process will not be initiated if we accept every wound into ourselves. It is necessary for us to discriminate between what is acceptable and what is unacceptable in order to form a therapeutic container. Acceptability and discrimination are closely related to therapists' feelings and emotion. We have to use not only affirmative feelings but also destructive emotion as therapeutic tools. The archetypal wounded healer does not function well if analysts cannot experience anger and destructive feelings.

Alchemically, anger or destructiveness is related to the motif of the slaying, mutilation, or dismemberment of animals within the *vas*, the mortificatio of *Sol* or *Rex*. Jung quoted a passage from the seventeenth century *Theatrum Chemicum*, where Sol is speaking:

> *I announce therefore to all you sages, that unless ye slay me, ye cannot be called sages. But if ye slay me, your understanding will be perfect.*

Thus, *Sol* passes through various stages of transformation from the dragon, lion, and eagle to the hermaphrodite, and comments on the above passage as follows:

> *The idea that the dragon or Sol must die is an essential part of the mystery of transformation. The mortificatio, this time only in the form of a mutilation, is also performed on the lion, whose paws are cut off, and on the bird, whose wings are clipped. It signifies the overcoming of the old and obsolete as well as of the dangerous preliminary stages which are characterized by animal symbols. (CW14, 164)*

When analysts treat severely wounded patients, it is crucial to determine how to deal with the destructive emotion in both parties. When patients cannot experience anger or destructiveness, analysts must face voluntarily their own destructive emotion – in an imaginal way – for example, by slaying or mutilating animal symbols that, in their own minds, represent their patients and their own inner patient, in order to conquer the *nigredo*.

Analysts' Destructive Emotion

Lambert (1972) says that analysts' understanding and overcoming of the talion law – the principle of an eye for an eye – give them therapeutic potency (p. 325). Sedgwick (1994) adds: "It seems appropriate not to vent this [anger in the analyst] on the patient" (p. 141). Although they are quite right from the viewpoint of analysts' verbal communication with patients, they have not considered enough the meaning of analysts' experiencing anger or destructive emotion in their imagination. I call this sort of aggression "transformative aggression" (Oda 1997). Alchemical *mortificatio* is the archetypal basis of transformative aggression.

Searles (1976) intensively studied the analyst's emotions, including destructive ones, when he treats psychotic and borderline patients. He criticizes the therapist's emotional neutrality in classical psychoanalysis: "Far from finding myself immersed predominantly in an emotionally neutral apartness, I have to learn to be at home with various inner emotional reactions to the patients for which my … classically psychoanalytic training analysis ill equipped me" (p. 528).

In discussing the importance of hate in the countertransference when analysts treat psychotic patients, Winnicott (1949) said that analysts must not deny the hate that exists in themselves. Although he did not mention the transformative aspect of hate, he derived the psychotherapeutic value of analysts' destructive emotion from the parent-infant relationship:

> *Sentimentality is useless for parents, as it contains a denial of hate, and sentimentality in a mother is no good at all from the infant's point of view. It seems to me doubtful whether a human child as he develops is capable of tolerating the full extent of his own hate in a sentimental environment. He needs hate to hate. If this is true, a psychotic patient in analysis cannot be expected to tolerate his hate of the analyst unless the analyst can hate him. (p. 74)*

Two cases demonstrate the importance of an alchemical vessel in the intermediate realm, and the transformative aspect of analysts' woundedness and destructive emotion, when analysts are treating severely wounded patients. My work with "Yukiko" shows how important it is for us to face our own woundedness and that of our patients. Just after becoming an analyst, I met 36-year-old Yukiko. She was married and very much devoted to her job. Her lawyer had recommended that she see a psychiatrist at a university hospital because he suspected that she was mentally ill. As a psychiatrist, I met and examined her at the hospital.

When she began analysis with me, she was suffering from neurotic dissociation and medically untreatable sterility and hormonal problems. Despite the fact that she was depressed, with suicidal ideation, Yukiko always had a smile on her face during our sessions. At the same time, she demonstrated antisocial conduct in the form of repeated shoplifting. At the beginning of the analytic process, Yukiko told me that she felt another person had done the shoplifting. Later, however, she slowly began to admit that she herself had committed the antisocial acts.

Yukiko also had a history of psychosomatic disease. She was subject to eruptions of urticaria: hives accompanied by severe itching, during her menstrual periods. One night in winter, three months after beginning her analysis, Yukiko tried to commit suicide by throwing herself into the sea near a university town. I had never anticipated such an event. Fortunately, Yukiko was rescued from drowning by two male medical students who saw her as she walked into the sea. Just a few days after the incident, during our analytic hour, she spoke to me about her suicide attempt, again with a smile on her face.

As I review the process, I see that Yukiko had split her psyche into two parts. I was seeing the affirmative part. It was necessary for me to realize how she had split off her woundedness and destructive emotion when she was suffering from urticaria and committed shoplifting. Not being able to face fully my own inner patient, I could not facilitate the constellation of the wounded healer. I did not realize how deeply I had been wounded in my kindergarten days, without going through suffering similar to Yukiko's. Consequently, at this stage of Yukiko's analysis, it was difficult for me to realize how much she was wounded. Now I know that it was hard work for her to integrate safely the split shadow side of her personality.

The morning of the day that Yukiko tried to commit suicide she dreamt:

> *When I went to the lavatory there was vaginal bleeding. First I thought I was having my menstrual period. But, when I looked closely at the blood something white in it was pulsing with life. That something was a three-month-old fetus. It seemed that I had had a miscarriage. I felt ill.*

Jung emphasized that the *vas* is a kind of matrix or uterus from which the *filius philosophorum*, the miraculous stone, is to be born (CW12, 338). The therapeutic vessel is also the uterus in which the transformation of the psyche will occur. I believe now that the alchemical vessel did not function well; Yukiko had a symbolic miscarriage because 1 had not yet realized her split-off psychic wounds. Thus, the wounded healer had not been constellated.

When Yukiko tried to commit suicide, it seemed that the three-month-old-fetus as *filius philosophorum* had been aborted. However, the fetus was pulsing with life and Yukiko was rescued from her attempt to die. The therapeutic uterus or vessel would be reconstructed. She survived this crisis despite my inability to face fully my own woundedness.

The Reversal of the Usually Constellated Roles

By the time one year had passed since our beginning analysis, I had come to understand better Yukiko's woundedness – through her attempt to die – and had been able to facilitate the constellation of a container in the intermediate realm. In Yukiko's imagination, my body and the consulting room were functioning as a containing vessel, as we can see from the following dream:

> *I was being analyzed in an analytical hour with you. You were suffering from urticaria and itching. You left the consulting room and brought a syringe back with you. You asked me to give you an anti-urticaria injection to heal the itching of the disease. I gave you an injection in the session.*

In reality no anti-urticaria injection had ever been effective for Yukiko. But three days after the dream, she completely recovered from the chronic urticaria, and it never recurred. In the dream the therapist became a patient and the patient became a therapist. When the therapist was constellated in Yukiko's psyche and the patient was constellated in my psyche, a healing process was initiated. I call this healing phenomenon "the reversal of the usually constellated roles."

At that time, Yukiko had ceased her antisocial conduct. It may be that her shoplifting and destructiveness were contained within the vessel of my body and the consulting room when I was able to face my woundedness. Although Yukiko and I had not talked about her anger and destructive emotion, healing certainly took place.

It is even more difficult for analysts to face their patients' aggression and their own anger or destructiveness than it is to accept their woundedness. Meier (1949) quoted the oracle of Apollo, saying, "He who wounds also heals" (p. 5). One may say that the one who sends disease is also able to heal it. If we are to deal with patients' woundedness and destructiveness, we have to face our own woundedness and destructiveness. If we do not do so, the wounded healer will not be fully constellated.

A 38-year-old female borderline patient, "Hanako," was suffering from depression with suicidal ideation and bulimia. The patient was married and living with her husband and children. In childhood her mother used to ask Hanako to soothe her drunken father. Hanako had suffered from her father's abuse. The mother was unaware of the abuse, and did not protect her. Hanako had had episodes of wrist-cutting during her college days. A psychiatrist colleague of mine thought Hanako was suffering from depression and asked me to treat her psychotherapeutically. Hanako was more severely wounded and unstable than Yukiko.

Analysts must be differentiated from their patients and their inner patient if they are to facilitate the constellation of an analytic vessel with the dyad or quaternity as its content. In the second year of her analysis with me, Hanako complained about her depression, suicidal ideation, and family history. I felt wounded but did not blame her; I blamed myself that she was suffering. Hanako's and my fused relationship prevented us from forming a secure vessel in the intermediate realm. It seemed that her projective identification with me had been constellated against the background of her fused and abandoning relationship between her and her parents.

A dream of Hanako's shows that a protected vessel, and the dyad or quaternity which includes analyst and patient, had not yet been constellated.

I was living alone in a small, white, Western-style house. The house had two thin and transparent glass doors. One door opened onto a road and the other opened into my mother's house. The house was surrounded by grassland. While I was in the house, the door chimes rang. I could see no one when I went to the door that opened onto the road. Then I went to the other door that opened into my mother's house, but again I found no one. I could not get an unobstructed view of the gloomy rooms in the house. I asked who rang the doorbell. Nobody answered my question. I thought that someone might have

already intruded into my house. The cruel intruder might be a
murderer who would kill me. I was seized with fear.

Hanako told me that it was almost impossible for her to protect
herself from the murderer's intrusion because there were two doors.
She had feelings of dread. At that time I thought the patient was
projecting her inner bad object onto the destructive mother or
dreadful father. However, she may have projected her split-off cruel
inner figure onto her therapist. I had not yet realized that I myself
might have intruded into her house, because I had not experienced
anger or destructive emotion against her. I did not know how much
I had repressed or split off my anger and destructive emotion from
my childhood. The patient's house in the dream is a kind of
alchemical vessel, but this vessel is not a secure one that protects
what is within from the intrusion of what is without.

Slaying a Serpent

In the fourth year of her analysis with me, Hanako complained of
depression, empty feelings and binge eating with vomiting. She
became angry with me in our sessions because of her feelings of
abandonment. I felt that she was forcing me to split myself into two
opposites. One was a warm and kind analyst, the other a cruel one.
One moment Hanako would force a positive and idealized analyst
figure onto me. But immediately afterward she would make me a
cruel analyst figure. Hanako was manipulating me unconsciously
through her projective identification.

In one session I tried to combat both Hanako's projective identification with me and my projective counter-identification with her. I
asked her to pay for a telephone conversation with me. She verbally
expressed her aggression, telling me that she would not be able to
rely on me for help because I could not understand her depressed and
wounded psychic condition and because I asked her to keep a
distance when she was suffering. She also told me that she would
never come to see me again. I think that I was wounded by my own
abandonment feelings. Before this incident, when I was the object of
a patient's anger and rage, I had always felt wounded and depressed
and had partly identified with the archetypal wounded healer. This
time, when I was the object of Hanako's rage, I could face my own
woundedness and destructive emotion. I felt anger at her manipulative attitude.

In my imagination, in the intermediate realm between her and me, an unknown man with a knife was angrily cutting up a living serpent, which represented both Hanako and my inner patient. This image persisted throughout the analytic hour. As I continued to imagine that the man was cutting up the serpent in the intermediate realm and lived through the alchemical *imaginatio*, I began to feel slowly relieved and healed. This constellation of anger may have healed my woundedness and overcome both Hanako's projective identification and my projective counter-identification, and facilitated a psychic differentiation between us. A borderline patient's projective identification with the therapist comes from the patient's fused relationship with his or her archaic inner parents. If the analyst does not imaginally experience his or her own anger, such patients will deny and split off their own destructive emotion and, thus, continue to damage themselves and let intruders into the therapeutic vessel.

The motif of mutilation is significant both in alchemy and psychotherapy. In addition to emphasizing the importance of imaginally slaying or mutilating animals, Jung said (CW14, 155) that together with *Mercurius*, *Luna* sprinkles the dismembered dragon with her moisture and brings him to life again. The dew of *Luna* brings about the *albedo*. The *mortificatio*, in the form of a mutilation, signifies the passing of the old and obsolete, and the preliminary stages of alchemy. The serpent or dragon, as the *prima materia*, must undergo mutilation in order to be transformed. My image of a man mutilating a serpent was the *prima materia* in the intermediate realm. When I had accomplished this imaginal work, Hanako emerged from the *nigredo*.

Hanako did interrupt her therapy, but two weeks later asked to resume. Two weeks after the resumption, her depression with suicidal ideation and bulimia had improved considerably. She brought the following dream:

I was living in an apartment with my mother and my son, who was in elementary school. We three went to a department store to shop for a set of eight wooden sewing boxes that contained sewing needles and thread. My son interrupted a saleswoman with some questions while she was explaining the boxes to us. The saleswoman ordered my son to be silent and to hear her out. I protested against the saleswoman's conduct. I told her that she should not interfere with my son's talking, and that my son was allowed to say anything. It was not her job to teach my son how to behave. Her job was to explain the boxes to us. At that moment my mother, who was behind us,

*began to say something. It seemed to me that my mother did not stand
up for my son but for the saleswoman. I got angry with my mother
who interfered in my son's and my affair. I slapped my mother on the
mouth. Astonished at being slapped, my mother soon went home
alone. She was lying in bed wrapped in a futon mat.*
*The scene changed. Perhaps I had already moved to a new house
without my mother. Or perhaps I was going to move from the
apartment to a new place. There were lots of things to be moved, or
goods, already moved, were lying around.*

When we discussed this dream in our session, Hanako actually
got angry with her interfering mother. She associated her own eating
problems with slapping her mother on the mouth. I imagined
Hanako's apartment as a therapeutic vessel. In the second half of the
dream, the patient's rage against the interfering mother has facilitated her differentiation from the mother, overcoming the fused
relationship. My imagined aggression may have helped Hanako
overcome the projective identification with her manipulative mother,
dreadful father and me.

The analyst's transformative aggression facilitated the constellation of a secure therapeutic vessel in the intermediate realm. I had
allowed the patient's manipulative mother and dreadful father, or
myself, to intrude into the therapeutic vessel. When I imagined that
my inner therapist figure was angrily mutilating a living serpent
representing Hanako and my inner patient in the intermediate realm
between us, the *nigredo* was overcome and a secure and protected
alchemical vessel was constellated. Hanako then could drive the
mother out of the vessel. Imaginally experiencing anger or destructive emotion creates the intermediate space essential for the constellation of a therapeutic vessel between analyst and patient. From then
on, Hanako and I could discuss her destructive emotion in our
sessions.

Quaternity

The therapeutic vessel or the alchemical quaternity is important.
I have learned from my clinical experience that both the imaginal
coniunctio, which unites opposites, and the quaternity, which conquers the incestuous relationship with patients, are simultaneously
necessary for an analyst to assist in healing.

Exactly eight years after the beginning of her analysis, Hanako
had overcome most of her symptoms; she was no longer suffering

from depression or eating disorder. She had realized her own tendency to split and fuse and was able to work as a professional without much difficulty. She dreamed:

I went to an unknown clinic not far from my house because I felt ill and exhausted. The clinic was a simple old wood house, square, with two stories. I entered a consulting room through a corridor bringing my thick medical records with me. In the consulting room I saw an unknown gray-haired old doctor who was tall, slender and wore silver-rimmed spectacles. He was also a quiet and scholarly person. There were a table and two round stools on the wooden floor in the room. A strange machine was installed in the same room. I was sitting on one of the stools and the doctor was sitting on the other. I complained to the doctor of being exhausted. The platform of a train station was close to the clinic. I could see the platform through the open door of a wooden wall on the left-hand side. An unknown young man on the platform was looking at me while I was consulting the doctor. I asked the doctor to close the door so as not to be observed. He closed it for me. The doctor listened to me for some time and then left the room, without saying anything, to go to a forest to bring something back. After a while the doctor came back through the second door with an armful of branches. The branches had reddish berries. The doctor told me to watch what was going to happen. When he put only the branches, without berries, into the mouth of the machine, it started to work while making a noise. Then some powder, made from the branches, accumulated in a funnel-shaped container of the machine. I realized that he was making medicine. Afterward, the doctor put the reddish berries into another mouth. Some transparent troche-like medicines made from the berries accumulated in another container. He put one of the troche-like medicines into his mouth and then transferred it to my mouth using mouth-to-mouth feeding. I was astonished but I was able to endure the process of mouth-to-mouth feeding and could bear to hold the medicine in my own mouth. In a while, I began to feel well. A nurse looked into the consulting room through the third door and told the doctor, in an urging tone, that a patient was waiting to see him. The doctor suddenly became more practical. He told me that I was suffering from a cold and a sore throat. He added that I would recover from the illness before long. I went home from the clinic.

The doctor's mouth-to-mouth feeding represents a kind of *coniunctio*, although it is incestuous. Hanako associated the doctor's conduct to a similar situation with her husband during their engagement. She also associated the doctor with her analyst. The patient associated the nurse's urging attitude with her interfering mother.

The young man's intrusive behavior may be related to her father's abuse in her childhood. The man and nurse are intrusive. But it seems that, by looking into the consulting room, they prevented the doctor and patient from developing an incestuous relationship. There are two dyads: the doctor and the patient, and the young man and the nurse. The first dyad, representing Hanako and me, in the consulting room as a vessel, is facilitating *coniunctio* and protecting what is within from the intrusion of the other dyad. The second dyad is intrusive but it still functions constructively.

As we have seen, the *coniunctio* involves a great risk of incest. The two dyads form a quaternity that both facilitates the *coniunctio* and prevents the development of an incestuous relationship. The alchemical dyad of the therapist and patient has not been developed fully into a quaternity. In the future, the doctor might marry the nurse as his anima and the patient might marry the young man as her animus. However, as I have discussed, we can utilize the *nigredo* and the intermediate stages to the creation of the *lapis* as a tool in analysis. Hanako is much more differentiated and much less prone to splitting than she was because she has overcome both her antagonistic and her incestuous relationship with her analyst.

Conclusion

From my clinical experience I have learned how important it is that we, as analysts, be open to both our affirmative feelings and our own destructive emotion. In Yukiko's case, my woundedness and the inner wounded healer facilitated the constellation of a vessel in the intermediate realm. And the reversal of usually constellated roles occurred within the vessel. Although I fully faced neither her destructiveness nor my own destructive emotion, she did accomplish a sort of healing. In Hanako's case it was crucial for me to experience my own anger and destructive emotion in order to break through her projective identification and my projective counter-identification.

We must live through our patients' anger or destructiveness and our own destructive emotion in alchemical *imaginatio* when we treat severely wounded patients. The more we treat such patients, the more we have to face patients' and our own destructiveness. If we imagine, for example, that our inner therapists mutilate animals such as serpents or dragons as *prima materia*, which represent the patients and our inner patient, we will be healed and able to facilitate their transformation process. When we submit to the destructive emotion and mutilate the serpents, the *nigredo* will be overcome and an alchemical vessel will be constellated in the intermediate realm between the patients and us. Both the Eros and Thanatos aspects are necessary for the analyst to facilitate the constellation of a vessel, and to accomplish the *coniunctio* that heals psychic wounds and the *quaternio* that conquers the incestuous relationship.

Pursuing the goal of transformation is not most important. Rather, in the process, we can utilize the *nigredo* and the alchemical stages intermediate to the creation of the *lapis* as tools of analysis. In the process, two dyads form the quaternity; one dyad, within the vessel, develops the *coniunctio* and the other, outside the vessel, interrupts the incestuous therapeutic relationship. Both are essential for the dynamics of healing.

References

Lambert, K. (1974). Transference/counter-transference: Talion law and gratitude. In: M. Fordham, R. Gordon, J. Hubback & K. Lambert (Eds.), *Technique in Jungian Analysis* (Vol. 2). London: William Heinemann.

Meier, C.A. (1949). Ancient Incubation and Modern Psychotherapy (M.Curtis, Trans.). Evanston, IL: Northwestern University Press, 1967. New edition (1989) *Healing Dream and Ritual*, Einsiedeln: Daimon Verlag.

Oda, T. (1997). Rage and psychic transformation. In: M. Mattoon (Ed.), *Open Questions in Analytical Psychology*. Einsiedeln: Daimon Verlag.

Schwartz-Salant, N. (1989). *The Borderline Personality: Vision and healing.* Wilmette, IL: Chiron.

Searles, H.F. (1979). *Countertransference and Related Subjects: Selected papers.* New York: International Universities Press.

Sedgwick, D. (1994). *The Wounded Healer: Countertransference from a Jungian Perspective.* London/New York: Routledge.

Winnicott, D.W. (1949). Hate in the counter-transference. *The International Journal of Psycho-Analysis, 30,* 69-74.

Masochism: Sacred Suffering

Katherine Wattiker Olivetti
New York, New York, U.S.A.
New York Association for Analytical Psychology

Learn to suffer and you will understand how not to suffer.

Acts of John, The Apocryphal New Testament

The term "masochism" has evolved to describe a broad continuum of psychological and behavioral experiences in which pleasure mingled with pain is invited or endured willingly. It is inflicted and received, figuratively and literally, either at another's or at one's own hand. The pain-pleasure combination may be present in obvious and concrete forms, such as self-mutilation or ritualized sexual behavior, or it may appear in subtler characterological orientations and even in culturally sanctioned, albeit pathological, selflessness.

Where masochism organizes and informs one's psychology, regressive tides may sweep through the psyche, leaving wakes of fruitless destruction. Depression, despair, meaninglessness, fragmentation, and psychic pain are among its vestiges. Ego development flounders, sexuality is codified, the creative impulse aborts, the religious instinct goes astray, the transformational thrust miscarries, and a pathological process inhibits individuation. Thus, masochistic destruction is not creative, but pernicious and anti-transformational.

Traditionally, one thinks of masochism as a sexual pattern where one's pleasure climaxes when a partner imposes physical or psychological pain. Investigation reveals that the pain is not the *causa efficiens* (CW8, 530) of pleasure. Rather, anticipatory anxiety and submission – or in fantasy – to a partner experienced as more powerful, brings about and intensifies sexual arousal and pleasure.

In my analytic work, I have found other situations wherein the same unconscious dynamic – even without interpersonal sexual enactment – organized the person's behavior. Here the masochistic structure was cloaked in an attitudinal adaptation or a characterological orientation. Just as in the more overt sexual counterpart, two roles are narrowly scripted and habitually pre-determined. The drama is always the same: one small and helpless, seeing the other as grand and omnipotent. Pleasure comes when a regressive longing for merger and submission to the larger other is gratified. The longing that seeks expression in masochism is of archetypal intensity having, at its core, the religious instinct for a personal experience of the numinous.

My thesis emerges from work with a number of father-bound women, but I do not suggest that only one profile pre-disposes a woman to masochism, nor that masochism belongs only to the domain of female psychology. By exploring one manifestation of masochism, its essential features can be described sufficiently, making the patterns more easily identified in their several variations.

A case in point is a woman whose masochism was most blatant in her destructive relationships with men. Selected events from her psychic process expose themes embedded in the intricate reality of her life. While summation cannot do justice to the complex, idiosyncratic, and obscure ways her lived experience unfolded, I will describe what I have come to understand as the archetypal foundation of masochism.

Developmental Precursors

Acute anxiety, grief, and depression brought a single, 30-year-old office worker, "Linda," into treatment. Bright and attractive, her somewhat shabby appearance seemed not to fit her obviously educated manner. She spoke softly, and left long pauses, creating a seductive – although strangely synthetic – quality. As soon as she sat down, she began to weep, composing herself enough to say that she had just ended a painful two-year relationship. Linda had left her boyfriend several times. Even though consciously aware that she would be hurt again by his indifference, unavailability, and infidelity, she could not resist the urge to return to the relationship. When, as Linda put it, she "fell into his arms," intense gratification overshadowed the inevitable pain. This was not the first time she had been devastated by a relationship. Since adolescence, her life had been marked by one such relationship after another.

The oldest of four children and the only girl, Linda grew up in a small New England city where, by her description, the superficial aspects of white, middle-class family life appeared unremarkable. St. Mark's Episcopal Church, where the family worshipped, was also the setting of their social life. Her father was a deacon; her mother organized parish suppers. As a youngster, Linda attended Sunday school, sang in the choir, and belonged to the youth fellowship, but as an adult she no longer practiced her religion.

Linda's mother was an episodic alcoholic who maintained a sufficient level of functioning to fulfill the quotidian tasks of a homemaker. But at a deeper level, her drinking, depression, and narcissistic deficits created a maternal climate of psychological unavailability, unconscious aggression, and pronounced self-loathing.

The portrait Linda painted of her father, to whom she felt closer, was quite different. He was a charismatic, outgoing, self-made man. As a journalist, he rose through the ranks of the local daily newspaper, quickly becoming its senior editor. His narcissistic grandiosity, which required that he always be the center of attention, fueled the ambition which drove him to become elected to a high-profile public office.

Linda's early childhood was fraught with difficulties that hampered ego development. Parental narcissism made a particularly salient contribution to a masochistic tendency. Her mother's self-loathing, especially, interfered with her ability to receive and carry Linda's developmentally necessary and appropriate idealization. To Linda, her mother reflected unhappiness, depression, and a deficient sense of self. Personality traits, talents, abilities, and potentialities that could have been integrated via idealization and identification remained, for Linda, dormant and undeveloped in the unconscious. Instead of a healthy and resilient ego that was in keeping with the blueprint of the Self, the ego that developed was impoverished, vulnerable, riddled with lacunae and armored with defenses. In short, the failures in the developmental sequence of idealization-identification-integration produced an ego whose distorted growth did not foster its natural resemblance to her larger potential, the Self.

Instead of a kinship between the ego and the Self, dissonance between the two created a disturbed ego-Self axis (see Edinger, 1972). Consequently, the poor maternal experience evoked a field wherein the Self was projected onto the external.

If her mother could not tolerate receiving Linda's idealized projection, her father could not live without it. A partial differentiation between ego and unconscious occurred, and the importance of the father increased with the first stirrings of Linda's animus.

As Linda's father received – appropriately – both her libidinous attachment and animus projection, unfulfilled maternal needs persisted. This scenario over-determined Linda's relationship to the father. In Michael Fordham's language, the psychic effort included not only the integration of the deintegrates related to the father archetype but, because of the unmediated aspects of the mother archetype, the effort also included maternal repair and fulfillment.

That is, Linda's father complex attracted a "double dose" of psychic energy wherein the projection of the animus coincided with the projection of the Self. Two archetypal fields conflated so that a larger than life "father" was Linda's center of gravity: a huge, invisible magnet attracting and gripping her psychic energy, with doubled force. Early in treatment Linda dreamed:

The King of Hearts has corralled a small herd of horses. He bridles each of them and attaches a very long rein. He gets into a huge jeep, still hanging onto the bunch of reins, and drives off. The horses are dragged along, frantically galloping to keep up with him.

The images articulated poignantly the essence of Linda's father complex.

Feminine identity issues, stemming from the idealization problem of the maternal phase, further complicated the paternal phase. The projection of the Self was carried by the male parent. This burden of gender difference further strained the idealization-identification-integration sequence. Linda could not integrate ego traits, latent in the idealization, that she felt belonged exclusively to her father, and hence to the masculine. To retain distinct gender identity, she abdicated or repressed the father/masculine-associated qualities, even though they may have belonged rightfully to her authentic ego constitution and female identity. In the maternal phase, aspects of her ego had not been awakened fully and now, in the paternal phase, they were gender conflicted.

Linda proceeded in life, though psychic development was significantly compromised. The ego was impoverished, unevenly formed, diminished in feminine identity, unfulfilled in potential, and estranged in its kinship to the Self. The numinous idealization fell first to the father and, later in life, drew her to men who constellated her father *imago*, the grand and omnipotent other, her god.

Retreating from the Threshold

Linda's long string of painful relationships shared a common psychic motivation: her connections to the Self and to the animus were maintained through projection and merger.

As the story of her most recent relationship unfolded, she recalled previous ones. She remembered taking a painting course in college. Robert teased and demeaned her for thinking she had any artistic talent. Nonetheless, she continued to date him until he left her for another student. Jonathan never committed to making plans ahead of time. He always waited until the last minute to see if anything "better" became available. When he phoned, Linda dropped everything to be with him. Martin, a married man, came to town every once in a while. Linda always allowed him to stay in her home and he always convinced her to have sex with him. Even though she hated herself afterwards, she never refused his visits. And, in her most recent relationship, Linda discovered, soon after they met, that John dated and slept with other women. Each time she learned of an infidelity, she left him. When John promised to be faithful, she remained in denial of his pattern and returned to him.

The aftermath of this relationship re-awakened many traumatic experiences and brought earlier issues to the fore. In her analysis, as Linda reconstructed the loneliness, neglect and hurt of her childhood – through long periods of cathartic grief – a positive, idealizing transference predominated. We spent many sessions amidst intense reactions emanating from her ego's tenacious identification with the needy, dependent child. I was the omnipotent, idealized parent. Only with time, as we differentiated the child complex from her adult ego, did an observing ego emerge.

Linda gained insight into her masochism. In romantic relationships, she saw that she experienced the comfort of a blissful merger when she submitted to the partner who seemed like the omnipotent father/god. The same motif could be discerned in other situations and relationships which promised to gratify the neurotic desires of the wounded child. Ordinary daily events, as minor and seemingly insignificant as a conversation with a friend, were organized unconsciously by the small girl who reached for the omnipotent other, requiring always from that person responses that conformed to the powerful parental *imago*. Any of the friend's behaviors that might disrupt or evoke wrath were repressed, while those that assured the continued benevolence of the other were over-developed. Linda's submission, compliance, and repression of dangerous impulses had been necessary childhood adaptations to pathogenic parental narcissism. But the legacy in her adulthood was that, as she gravitated into a relationship, her adaptive behaviors pre-disposed her to the dependency, abuse, neglect, and abandonment of the masochistic role.

As treatment progressed, the negative transference emerged. I failed to gratify Linda, but reflected reality, set limits, maintained appropriate boundaries – and fell into inevitable analytic errors. Eventually aggression – which previously had been undifferentiated and unconscious – came forth. During this phase, I found that dream material reflected images of the aggression that had not yet taken anthropomorphic form. Evidently, until the analytic relationship provided a container for the dangerous impulses the unconscious aggression had remained embedded in the undifferentiated body/ psyche unity.

Over time, the aggression became accessible to the ego and she engaged it to restrict the habitual flow of energy into relationships. For example, when Linda tried to write, the constant ringing of the telephone interrupted her. She was the family "switchboard," for she could not limit her availability, even though it was at the expense of her writing. Gradually, she used her aggression to inhibit her automatic impulse to pick up the phone, thus detaching from her entanglements with family members. Progress consisted in allowing the answering machine to screen her calls. "Oh, I get it," she said one day. "If I consciously do the work, then my defenses don't have to do it in some other devious way!" Step by step, she learned to say no, she created boundaries, she kept to herself. Each time she engaged aggression on her own behalf, the defenses eased and the ego became stronger.

The process was not linear, neat, and tidy. Rather, the course of the analysis – progressing and regressing – was like creating a beach, accumulating sand little by little. Even though repetitive relationships and the regressive tides often washed away the gains, ever so slowly small ones would accrue.

Linda's acute moods and symptoms abated. She achieved an improved level of functioning and changed jobs: advancing from an unreliable, temporary position as an office clerk to a permanent and better compensated one as a legal assistant.

She then began to feel she wanted to write again. She had previously signed up for classes, but never completed them. She began stories and articles, but lost interest. Work piled up in a carton at the back of her closet. She continued to idealize her father, the journalist, and feared she would never write as he did. Nonetheless, with some nudging, she attended a writing class. With enthusiasm, she advanced toward her goal of one completed piece by the end of the semester. She was on the verge of greater autonomy. The healthier narcissism from such achievement would shift the balance of the masochistic scales, loaded so heavily toward the idealized father. By integrating and ascribing to herself those qualities heretofore the prerogative of the powerful father, his loss would be the ego's gain.

Linda's path was winding and spiraling as in any deep analysis; it was also confusing. In the midst of her seeming growth, a regressive pattern emerged, initially in faint suggestive strokes, but more clearly and distinctly, over time. At a critical point, something went wrong.

The week before the last class, Linda slipped the draft of her article into a large manila envelope and put it on her desk. She closed the flap, spreading open the small, metal clasp, and carefully turned the envelope over. She smoothed the creases on the face of the envelope, her hands moving over the paper, gently and tenderly, like a mother's hands smoothing the wrinkles of an infant's blanket. She was nearly there.

Early in the semester her teacher, Gary, had singled out Linda's work as potentially "publishable." Faithfully and patiently, after researching, editing, and re-writing, she passed in her revisions for feedback from him. A writer like her father, Gary was an attractive man, ten or so years older than Linda. Toward the end of the term, he suggested that they meet between classes to complete the final, finishing touches. Envelope in hand, Linda arrived at his office. After some discussion, Gary invited her for a drink. Flattered, Linda accepted his offer. One thing led to another, and Linda spent the night with him.

At the following session, Linda dragged into my office. She slouched into the chair, and cradled her head in both hands. Wisps of hair veiled her face and downcast blue eyes. Shaking her head, as if to say "No, no, no," and barely audible, she whispered, "I blew it – I really blew it – I've gone and done it again." slowly and heavily, she dug into the backpack at her feet and pulled out several sheets of rumpled paper. "Here," she said, as she handed me the pages. She forced out little truncated phrases of garbled words while stifling tides of rising and ebbing sobs. "This says it ... all ... read it ...

please ... hurts ... hurts too much ... can't tell it ... please ... just read ..."

The sheets were pages from her journal, written the day after she fell, suddenly and madly, in love with her teacher: "Thursday ... I had a terrible dream last night."

I was pregnant and it felt too good. Then suddenly I realize that I've had an abortion. There was blood, nothing but blood all over the place. ... How did this happen? We were working on the last few pages. I looked up, and it was as if for the first time I noticed how handsome he was. The streaks of gray at his temples made him look so distinguished ... Broad shoulders ... strong and steady. When our eyes met I was filled by His presence ... it fills me with life ... as if He lit the sun and my world came alive ... what I feel with him is the presence of the god, the father one who cares so and protects his most beloved daughter ... the sexual charge ... the intensity ... my life has meaning again ... it was like I was falling and sinking into this delicious wave of sweetness ... giving myself over to him ... I'll see him again tomorrow afternoon ...
Friday ... as I walked home I was still riding high on some inflated feeling cloud ... but I can feel it coming ... the guilt ... the dark bottomless pit ... again I pulled the plug ... again I shot a hole in the bucket ... all the water is running out ... it really hurts ... what have I done to myself?

The sequence of events that Linda reported illustrates the masochistic failure at a crucial moment in the transformational process. Her journal entry documents a significant dream theme. I found the theme of the failed birth (the loss, misplacement or death of infants; pregnancies that were aborted, miscarried or fizzled out; sick or tiny miniature babies) occurred often after the regressive masochistic episode.

From a reductive point of view, Linda's regression was a neurotic repetition of the painful events of early childhood. Libido flowed back along the familiar paths. But the regression also served a purpose. According to Jung's notion, the libido flows back to the imago "in order to find there the memory associations by means of which further development can take place" (CW8, 43). Linda's regressions brought the imago of the father to life but the repetitious cycling that looped back to this point was not fostering development. At this critical threshold the analysand fled the *angst* of autonomy and retreated to the familiar containment in a masochistic relationship; whose comfort was like a narcotic, obliterating anxiety, suppressing change, and easing the tensions of consciousness. While the regressive pattern may be the psyche's method of growth, it can also be a destructive, autonomous pattern, described by Ashcroft (1991) as masochism's "Syssiphean loop" (p. 140). Here was the crux of masochism's notorious intractability.

The gains of analysis – the insight, the understanding, the psychic differentiation, and the observing ego – were not enough bulwark for the powerful regressive tide. Linda's ego could not relinquish the gratification of the compulsive longings for a retrograde relationship. The capacity to integrate essential aspects of identity and to contain the tension, anxiety and discomfort that change generated were insufficient. The regressive merger with an idealized figure served to relieve the ego of the genuine and conscious suffering to be endured if transformation was to take place.

Masochism's Religious Core

The intense longing at the heart of the regression had another dimension. Clinical evidence, such as dreams presenting distinctly religious themes, or archetypal imagery as if "a great wind has swept through the house," and language like that of Linda's journal, characterized her experience. While the regressive merger ended in despair and depression, it began with a satisfying, if not ecstatic, experience of the numinous. This seemed to be the archetypal core of the complex. Gordon (1987) has suggested that masochism is the shadow side of the archetypal need to venerate. I see an additional dimension. Where a masochistic pattern prevails, not only does the archetypal need to venerate manifest, but also the religious instinct compulsively and relentlessly presses for a personal, viscerally felt experience of the numinous. As I reflected on this, it seemed that the intrapsychic dynamics of masochism had characteristics of a primitive religion. The ego of the masochist – consumed in merging with an omnipotent, idealized figure – dissolves in the way an innocent victim is sacrificed to secure the benevolent power of the god. Just as the propitiatory offering perpetuates rejuvenation of the godhead, so too the giving over of the masochist's ego preserves the power of an externally experienced "father god." The libido lost in dissolution of the ego is sucked into the vortex of the father complex, assuring its continued reign.

The masochist is fixated in this futile, "bipolar" cycling, from ecstasy to depression, from heaven to hell. When I considered the masochistic pattern through the lens of the religious instinct, Linda's masochism appeared as her own private religion, a phenomenon that Jung describes.

If the psychology of this dammed-up condition [the regressive flow of libido] is studied carefully and without prejudice, it is easy to discover in it the beginnings of a primitive form of religion, a religion of an individual kind altogether different from a dogmatic, collective religion.

Since the making of a religion or the formation of symbols is just as important an interest of the primitive mind as the satisfaction of instinct, the way to further development is logically given: escape from the state of reduction lies in evolving a religion of an individual character. (CW8,109)

Linda's masochism was the attempt to evolve an individual religion, but it was primitive and pre-symbolic. It had a god and a victim, but lacked a mediator or priest.

Profane Pain – Sacred Suffering

According to James (1955) the priest is "the official organ for maintaining a state of equilibrium between the sacred and the secular" (p. 13). Religious communities rely on the priest to fulfill specific religious functions in relation to the divine and, like a bridge, link the body of the faithful to their god: mediating, consecrating, reconciling, offering sacrifices, and bearing witness to the mystery of transformation. The priestly functions of consecration and sacrifice in traditional religious rituals seem to me to have analogues in the analytic process. The word "consecrate" comes from the Latin word *sacrare* – to render or make sacred. The priest takes ordinary substances, (e.g., bread and wine) and infuses them with new meaning. Linda would need to find the inner force to do the same by raising to consciousness the meaning of her regressive longings. By recognizing the symbolic essence of her longings, she sanctified them. In her experience, when she gave in to her longing she lost ground, became empty and depressed. Her pleasure devolved into pain. But when analytic insight exposed the symbolic meaning of her behavior, she could choose how she would relate to affect and desire. She could gratify the desire by a concretization, a profane re-enactment of the past. Of, if she held fast the meaning of desire and restrained herself from its gratification, a genuine sacrifice was offered.

Instead of the ego's being swallowed as the sacrificial victim, once meaning was made of the regressive urge, that urge itself was the potential sacrificial offering. Such a sacrifice brought torment and suffering, but a different pain. Paradoxically, by surrendering and choosing to suffer, the pleasure/pain pattern reversed. "By sacrificing ... the instinctive desire, or libido is given up in order that it may be gained in new form" (CW5, 671). When this sacrifice-making, priest-like function of the willing ego contained and bore the pressure created by blocking libido from its flow along the old, familiar route, there is an activation in the creative unconscious. The sacrificed libido, driven back into the psyche by not being dis-charged, is transformed. Instead of masochistic gratification leading to the meaningless pain of psychic destruction, sacrificial suffering leads to the meaningful – and bodily-felt – renewal and inner transformation. By enduring the anxiety when she behaved in a new, unfamiliar way, the transcendent function was activated.

In my work with Linda there were many aborted transformations. Eventually, adequate ego strength developed and adequate meaning was made of the regressive longings. During this time, she was tempted by the opportunity to regress anew into the familiarly configured relationship. When she chose to stand against this return, she dreamed:

> *Something special has happened. I can't remember the details, only the amazing, awesome feeling, and that someone has given me a gold fountain pen.*

The new third was born. It was a symbol that joined affect and image. The gold pen pointed the way toward what was needed for Linda to proceed on her individuation path. A key born of personal-ity, one whose integration had been troublesome because it was experienced as a numinous power of the father god, had to develop. The "gold pen," which previously belonged only to Linda's father, the journalist, was to become hers.

The Priestly Ego

In my practice with father-bound women who have masochistic features, healing requires that the ego transcend its defenses in order to achieve, in an individual psyche, functions that resemble those performed by the priest in a collective religion. Both the ego and the priest consecrate, sacrifice, reconcile, and mediate between the sacred and the profane. As the ego grows toward these functions, the birthing of an essential aspect of personality becomes possible. As long as an ego lancuna exists, individuation stalls and the masochistic pattern expresses the psyche's tenacious, though distorted, insistence on fulfillment.

To articulate what must be achieved, beyond the observing ego, I coined the term "priestly ego," to denote the ego function capable of bearing the tension of the opposites and facilitating the transcendent function. This priestly ego function replaces the old primitive religion of the masochist.

The term "priestly ego" seems appropriate also in that this specific aspect of the ego has a special relationship to the transpersonal. The masochist forever seeks an experience of the numinous, but is compelled by the ego lacuna into only the personal realm where concrete enactments fail to satisfy the religious instinct. The ego development, which turns the energy of masochism into new channels, also enables an inner experience of the numinous – an inner transformation that is individual, yet transpersonal. The ego then participates in giving birth to itself as a servant and as an incarnation of the Self in the outer world. The "priestly ego," and the process by which it comes into being, reconciles the conscious personality and the Self, and so carries forth the religious function of the psyche.

Conclusion

I have gathered my observations from several analysands with many similarities in background and in analytic process. Their masochism evolved from early wounding in the pre-oedipal, maternal phase of development and was then carried over to the oedipal, paternal phase. Difficulties in the idealization-identification-integration process in both phases fostered distorted, incomplete ego development, an over-determined father complex, and a powerful, unmetabolized idealization that drew its energy from two overlapping archetypal fields. The pathology is the pattern of recurrent regression, organized around the numinous idealization. While its purpose is to foster development, its results – without intervention – in condemning the masochist to an endless, futile cycle of despair.

There are many ways masochism can be described. For instance, it may be seen as a variation in the female child's oedipal drama. But reduction to the personal level and to sexual etiology does not provide sufficient insight into the intractability of the pathology, nor does it do justice to the religious imagery, language, affect, and process which is so evident.

Today I have tracked one manifestation of masochism and found it to be a pathology of religious instinct. When the masochism manifests more concretely, as in sexual practices of domination and submission, or self-inflicted mutilations, the flavor of religious ritual is even stronger. Could it be that the popular proliferation of masochistic patterns – in bedrooms, in internet chat rooms, in body-piercing studios, and in tattoo parlors – are current signs of the religious hunger for a bodily-felt, individual encounter with the divine? Where the myths and rituals of organized religion fail to mediate between the individual and the numinous, the religious ground goes dry and the religious instinct is unfulfilled. Eventually however, the way may be prepared for the emergence of new religious forms.

When I followed the thread of pathology that my analysands trailed through the labyrinth of psyche, I found that the potential healing of masochism lies in the ego's participation in certain "sacred" acts. By making meaning, the priestly ego consecrates. By choosing to relinquish desire, it sacrifices. By suffering the tensions of the opposites, it mediates. And by enduring the turmoil of transformation, the priestly ego participates in creation.

In my view, masochism – a fixation at a primitive phase of religious development – calls the physical body, affect, instinct, and image to reunion. Its transformation brings to life myth-making and symbol-making functions in a personal, yet transpersonal, way. When the archetypal foundation of masochism, the religious instinct for contact with the numinous, if fulfilled, the mystery of transformation is experienced, not at an altar of the collective, but within the *sanctum* of the individual.

References

Ashcroft, C. (1991). Some thoughts on masochism, blood and descent. *Harvest*, *37*, 40-50.
Edinger, E. (1972). *Ego and Archetype*. New York: Penguin Books.
Gordon, R. (1987). Masochism: The shadow side of the archetypal need to venerate and worship. *Journal of Analytical Psychology*, *32-3*, 227-240.
James, O.E. (1955). *The Nature and Function of Priesthood*. New York: Thames & Hudson.

Under the Volcano

Varieties of Anger and their Transformation

Jan Wiener
London, England
Society of Analytical Psychology

As analysts, we tend to use the word anger in an ambiguous and over-general way; it is actually a subtle, complex affect with many nuances of meaning. In the words of Aristotle (1976), "It is not easy to define how and with whom and for what reasons and how long one ought to be angry, or within what limits a person does this rightly or wrongly" (p. 162). I have become interested in why it is that for some patients in analysis, experiences of anger or "the darker passions" (Person 1993, p. 2) may be harnessed creatively into development that is life-enhancing and leads to growth while, for others, these experiences may remain suppressed, somatised, acted-out or in other ways rendered unusable in the service of the unfolding of the self.

The constellation of a major grievance rooted in a traumatic infancy is linked with hatred and can block, defensively, the harnessing of the healthy assertiveness necessary for separation, individuation and creativity. Aggression is the foundation stone of affects such as anger. To address the nature of grievance, we must differentiate anger from two other centrally-related affects, rage and hatred, in their manifestations in analysis and in terms of the dialectical relationship between ego and self. From my work with a male and a female patient in intensive analysis for some years, I found that, at critical times during both analyses, I was taxed severely in processing my own anger, in order to stay in touch with the hurt that was hidden by the psychic manifestations of the grievance.

Jung placed great emphasis on the psychology of affects: "The essential basis of our personality is affectivity. Thought and action are, as it were, only symptoms of affectivity" (CW3, 78). Affects are archetypal and emerge as patterns of experience, associated with unconscious fantasies and images in infancy. These are organized gradually as part of early object relationships, while the infant develops a sense of subjective identity.

A problem we have with understanding "anger" is that it overlaps with and is related to many other words. My own free associations to the word anger include: rage, aggression, assertiveness, self-affirmation, destructiveness, grievance, grudge, hatred, revenge, fury, indignation, power and evil. Definitions of anger are varied but most suggest, as does Jung (CW6, 681) that anger combines a psychic feeling state and a physiological innervation state.. Both body and mind are involved.

We have all experienced anger, which – as the seventeenth century poet Thomas Fuller wrote – "is one of the sinews of the soul." Some patients arrive consciously angry; others are unable to get in touch with their anger. The ego can become organized around anger. Thus, it is not just a free-standing affect but a property of all relationships. Models of the psychic functioning of anger in relationships are not yet well developed, but what we do know is that when anger is unconscious or suppressed in the patient, in the analyst, or within their relationship, it can be destructive. At its most dangerous, anger leads to cruelty, hatred, revenge and – collectively and culturally – to wars. William Blake wrote about the dangerous effects of suppressed, murderous anger in his poem, "A Poison Tree:"

> *I was angry with my friend,*
> *I told my wrath, my wrath did end;*
> *I was angry with my foe,*
> *I told it not, my wrath did grow.*

An illustration of two kinds of anger is found in Shakespeare's *King Lear*. The play is based on an old Celtic fairy tale in which an ageing King decides to relinquish his kingdom to his three daughters. In the play, Shakespeare explores the powerful emotions aroused between parents and children and immerses us chillingly in a study of the cruelest aspects of the human psyche. King Lear and Edmund – another character in the play – have both suffered what we would call today severe narcissistic wounds; they are angry.

Lear feels betrayed by his youngest daughter, Cordelia who, he feels, does not love him as much as he loves her. His grief and rage stir him to action in the famous quotation: "Touch me with noble anger." Lear becomes insane with rage. During the play, however, Lear's rage is transformed before he ultimately dies. When his rage is spent, his wound is transformed from a narcissistic grievance into a source of empathy with others.

Edmund is illegitimate, the younger son of the Earl of Gloucester; he will not inherit his father's wealth. As a consequence, Edmund is filled with intense envy and jealousy. He protests angrily against the assumption that he is low and vile because he is illegitimate and forges a letter in his brother's hand, threatening to kill their father for his wealth. Edmund coldly and ruthlessly sets out to turn his father against his brother. His career of crime is built on a narcissistic wound which becomes a life-long grievance and remains largely unmitigated and untransformed. He is relentless almost to his death.

In both cases, anger fuels a desire for revenge. Lear's rage is ultimately transformed and Edmund's hatred remains, as he puts it, "of mine own nature." In terms of psychic functioning, they illustrate contrasting forms of anger whose potential for transformation may be illuminated further by making a conceptual distinction between anger, rage and hatred.

Anger

I have borrowed part of the title of this paper, *Under the Volcano*, from Malcolm Lowry's powerful novel of the same name. Lowry's imaginative and original use of the hot, steamy visual imagery and symbolism of the volcano brings out the unpredictability of life in Mexico and the frightening, destructive eruptions of the main character, the alcoholic consul. The archetypal power of volcanic imagery also has considerable relevance in the consulting room and, in particular, as a metaphor to understand the vicissitudes of the affect of anger. The God of Israel began as a volcano God at Mount Sinai. Many patients talk of feeling as if there is a "volcano inside them" to convey the power of the anger they are experiencing and their fear of the possibility of dangerous eruptions with destructive consequences. For centuries, active volcanoes have been seen to represent the underworld of dangerous gods to whom sacrifices must be made. Sontag (1993) brings these fears to life when she writes about a volcano as a "monstrous living body, ... the slumbering giant that wakes, ... flushes the marrow out of your bones and topples your soul" (pp. 5-6). Redfearn (1992) discusses a volcano dream of one of his patients in terms of "uncontainable passions" (p. 101).

When we talk of volcanic eruptions, however, are we really talking about anger or the more intense, even violent emotion of rage? Here our terminology becomes confusing and it is necessary to pay careful attention to the conceptual differences between anger, rage and hatred.

Diamond (1966) compares anger with rage, using the metaphor of an electric switch: "Rage appears to operate via an 'on' or 'off' switching mechanism, with the 'on' position consisting of one constant voltage; anger ... can be controlled by way of a 'dimmer' switch, which modulates the relative intensity of the current" (p. 11). Diamond thinks that anger and rage spring from the same elemental source, although anger may be less intensely felt.

I believe that anger and rage are linked affects but, in terms of psychic functioning, they are different. Although anger is a complex emotion, in general it is aroused when desired goals are frustrated. As a way of overcoming obstacles, anger is usually conscious, ego-related, has a cognitive component and is, up to a point, controllable. Both ego and self are involved. In anger, the ego is acting as the executive of the self; in rage, it is overwhelmed by the self in its negative aspect. Anger is not necessarily destructive and is often part of normal, healthy narcissism or an attempt to regulate social interactions. It is part of the rhythmic deintegrative/reintegrative process wherein the self unpacks its archetypal potentialities by reaching out for real experiences. It is when angry feelings are unsatisfactorily mediated, leading to anxiety and splitting, that anger becomes disorganized or repressed and the capacity for rage may develop. Anger can be verbal, physical, direct, repressed, stifled, sublimated, hot or cold, a communication or a defence, but, as Person (1993) puts it, "anger represents a victory of assertion over intimidation, strength over fear" (p. 3).

Rage

Rage is hot, elemental and acute. It is a primitive affect arising from the unconscious. It is unpredictable, unbounded and danger-ous. We talk of "burning rage," of "boiling with rage" or of "blowing one's top." Rage captures the body and touches the self. The metaphor of a volcano is surely a more appropriate evocation of the archetypal experience of rage than of anger. Volcanoes erupt when the plates of the earth's crust collide. Melting minerals called magma become trapped in reservoirs and, ultimately, explode.

Rage is a result of a personal insult, a narcissistic wound often connected with shame. I like Lewis' (1993) idea of rage as a process:

"Shame leads to rage, which leads to more shame, which leads to more rage" (p. 159). It is a more primitive and diffuse experience than anger, and can be generated by an external or an internal assault on the self. Rage bypasses the ego. It comes straight from the self. The opposites of nature and culture come together but cannot make a new synthesis. Thus, like the plates of the earth's crust in a volcanic eruption, there is a violent internal clash. The pressure is too much and fears of annihilation are aroused. Rage comes from a collapsed or disintegrated sense of identity, when patients may feel as if they and their analysts are "exploding," like magma, or "falling to pieces." One patient needed to telephone me to make sure he had not "toppled my soul" after a particularly violent outburst of rage. The image of a blackened landscape following a volcanic eruption conveys expressively some patients' images of destruction, which may accompany an experience of rage. Rage threatens the very essence of our feelings about ourselves and, in its extreme, can lead to murder or the ultimate rage against the self, suicide.

Jung saw rage as a primitive, archetypal affect: "When we are beside ourselves with rage, we are obviously no longer identical with ourselves, but are possessed by a demon or spirit" (CW8, 627-628). Rage and madness are often intertwined and King Lear's words, "Touch me with noble anger," are really about rage. His temporary "madness" is surely different from the more coherent anger which seems to be more ego-related.

Hatred

Jung's preoccupation with the relationship between good and evil provides a relevant setting for a discussion of the nature of hatred. He rejected the Augustinian concept of *privatio boni*: to be evil means to be deprived of good. He believed that evil is much more than a turning away from good, and that good and evil are a logically equivalent pair of opposites. Hatred and love are also in a dialectical relationship. One is not an absence of the other, but rather they exist as a pair of opposites which struggle to coexist in an ambivalent relationship.

Hatred exists on a spectrum ranging from positive, benign hatred to a more malign, destructive form. Bollas (1987) talks of "loving hatred" where the aim is not destructive, but rather to act out an unconscious form of love in order to preserve a relationship. Blake's sentiment, "I was angry with my friend, I told my wrath, my wrath did end," seems to be more about benign hatred. We are also familiar with destructive and malignant hatred which is acted out in violent, sadistic acts towards others or the self. Here, hatred can be linked relevantly with Glasser's (1986) concept of sadism where the aim may be to inflict suffering on the other.

Hatred is much more focused than anger or rage and has usually become a stable part of the personality structure, as in Colman's (1988) idea of "the wound that will neither heal nor [contribute to] healing" (p. 77). Hatred involves several wishes: to destroy, to cause suffering and to control. It nearly always involves paranoid fears of retaliation. Whereas rage disrupts or fragments the ego, hatred sharpens it. Rage explodes; hatred smoulders and simmers. Lord Byron says in his poem "Don Juan":

> *Now hatred is by far the longest pleasure;*
> *Men love in haste but they detest at leisure.*

As Akhtar (1995) points out, "Rage is an immediate uncontrollable body response, hatred involves thoughts and can mean the suppression of muscular activity. ... Rage unshackles the self from the object, hatred traps the individual to the object" (p. 89). Hatred is paradoxical. It emerges from traumatic origins and involves primitive defence mechanisms of the self, such as splitting and projective identification, but it manifests itself at a sophisticated level of consciousness where ego fragments have coalesced, albeit in a distorted way, to form a fixed complex.

Grievance

The main theme of my paper is grievance, a central component of hatred. Some patients who suffer a severe early narcissistic wound develop a persistent grievance in a moral context involving blame. Patients with a grievance feel they have been wronged in some fundamental way and are the victims of gross psychic injury to which they cling determinedly (see Steiner, 1993). The clinging has three main functions. First, it is a means by which the integrity of the self may be preserved from further damage by the other. Second, it is a means by which patients may remain close to the object of their grievance in the hope of finding love. Third, it helps to prevent disintegration. Rage leads to hatred, which leads to grievance, then to hatred, more rage and so on. The grievance becomes self-destructive; its fixed quality stultifies creativity.

Clinical Illustrations

Two patients, "Robert" and "Barbara," have been in analysis with me three or four times a week for several years. Both have a central grievance; they hate their mothers. They have not had their aggression sufficiently well mediated, and they are left with a constant, conscious, simmering hatred for their mothers – which is projected unconsciously into me. I have been left sometimes with the feeling of being trapped; my own emotions are in danger of becoming uncontrollable.

Robert is a 50-year-old man who came into analysis after the break-up of an intense love affair. It had left him exceedingly depressed, with numerous somatic symptoms and a terror of dying. He is the second of four brothers and has a screen memory of being actively rejected by his mother. When he was two, she said to him, "I don't want you, go to your father." He feels that his mother actively disliked him while she loved his older and his youngest brothers. His mother had a serious phobia about germs and she seems to have selected Robert as the recipient of her projections to be the ill child. She repeatedly took him to hospital for chest X-rays, to which he attributes his recently-discovered sterility. He has a later, significant memory of being taken to visit his mother in hospital when he was three, after she had a miscarriage. He remembers seeing her through a glass screen and feeling extremely upset that he was not allowed to approach or touch her.

He frequently feels emasculated, particularly in his relationships with women and inevitably in his transference to me. Not only does he feel that his mother did not love him, but that she actually wished him dead. He seems to have erected an internal screen, or "concrete bunker" as he calls it, as a defence of the self to protect himself from her sadistic attacks, but this has left him impoverished, as the bunker splits him off from his emotions.

I like him and he takes his analysis very seriously, but he is compliant and very anxious about upsetting me, in case I erupt, as did his unpredictable mother. Any expression of irritation or anger feels to him dangerously destructive and must be suppressed. He wants me to remain the soothing mother at all times. All the affect appears in his dreams, which are often apocalyptic, violent and disturbing for us both. Dreams of natural disasters such as tidal waves and fires progressed to a series involving murder and mayhem, and then to dreams of damaged, distorted baby animals – a true archetypal hell. This raw energy rampages but cannot be lived, mediated and fully digested because it is blocked by his concrete bunker. If I am more challenging, I become his sadistic, retaliatory mother. Forced into this strait jacket, I have found myself overtaken with an overwhelming lassitude: a leaden, soporific feeling where I retreat into a passive, sleepy silence. My capacity to feel angry in a positive way that could help him is anaesthetized, and my imaginative capacities become deadened. I feel as if I am of no use to him.

Here is the deprivation and grievance. Robert's hatred towards his murderous mother could not be lived and mediated; it has become an enduring part of his personality. He is unconsciously identified with his aggressor mother. This has left him with no containing outlet for his aggression, which remains terrifying, encapsulated in an archaic form, and unavailable for expression and transformation within the analytic relationship. He needs this part of his personality to move forward in his masculine identity, but it remains unintegrated with his more passive, defensive persona, with which he is identified. Robert has experienced a violent assault on his core sense of himself, which leaves him impoverished – as the dream suggests. Coming alive in the analysis, which includes a space for anger and rage to find expression between us, also means grieving the absence of maternal love. To reach out for nourishing new seeds of life in our relationship, which might then be murdered for a second time, is a big risk and has taken many years to explore.

Barbara also came into analysis during a series of frightening somatic episodes, including a preoccupation with losing bowel control in public situations. This occurred at the juxtapositon of two difficult personal life experiences. Her marriage became less satisfying, leaving her with insecurities about the future and, at the same time, she needed to have surgery. Barbara has experienced a double narcissistic wound. She is illegitimate and feels she has no birthright. To be an unwanted child is the ultimate betrayal. She also experienced her adoptive mother, to whom she was sent at the age of 14 months, as critical and unloving. They fought bitterly until her mother died some years ago.

Barbara feels fundamentally unlovable. She frequently idealises men, but women – particularly authority figures – are often poisonous and not to be trusted. The basic wound is easily inflamed, making her angry and volatile but unable to reveal how hurt she feels. She becomes caught in a persecutory inner world and must remain alert at all times to keep her persecutors at bay. Any experience of rejection or conflict in her external world, and in the analysis with me, sets in motion a rapid, well-defined internal process like a toppling cascade of falling dominoes. Rejection leads to a feeling of deprivation, then to anger, contempt and outrage that she deserves better. Her aggression takes on a moral mode, which provokes a determined fight to make the rejecting others love her or change their minds about her. She remains fiercely attached to her attackers, omnipotently trying to change them. When she fails, she clings to the bad object, as this is better than nothing at all.

Barbara is a talented woman, intellectually gifted and very articulate, but she can use thoughts and words as weapons: to attack, defeat and distance. Quietness in sessions is rare, as if any potentially creative, more reflective, space between us will leave her open to dangerous attacks. She describes herself as a terrier working hard in her analysis. I sometimes experience this approach as her determination to remain self-sufficient: using a prickly, combative carapace persona to keep me at bay from her softer, immensely vulnerable core sense of self.

At the beginning of the analysis, I frequently felt as if whatever I offered was chewed up and spat out. When Barbara was distressed, I felt I could not soothe her. Moreover, my understanding was experienced as an attack, fuelling her anger and defensiveness. On one occasion, when we were having a particularly difficult time, she told me that she thought I planted things inside her which did not belong to her; they were alien. On another occasion, she told me that she could not say nice things to me in case I became complacent. Hatred seemed to be keeping our relationship alive. For a time, her aggression and contempt made me defensive, irritable and, on occasion, volatile. I was contributing to an enactment of her inner trauma. At these moments, I disliked her, and felt narcissistically wounded myself. It was only later, when she alerted me to her need for me to attend to the child in pain behind this hard carapace, that I found myself better able to process my countertransference affects. She was right. I was losing my analytic capacity, caught up unhelpfully with the process of her grievance. It was only after this realization that we both could attend more safely to her vulnerable child self, hiding in terror from danger.

Barbara's grievance takes the form of an unmediated archetypal dominant relationship between two extremes: hatred toward her mother and hatred toward herself. There is only a victim or a victimizer, a winner or a loser; either the other is all wrong or

Barbara is all wrong. As we gradually live out the pain and grievance within our relationship and understand it, both Barbara and I have had to face our capacity to hate and to accept it. She acknowledges that she has a "chip on her shoulder." I have had to face the full force of my uncomfortable, negative countertransference affects.

For Barbara, they explode into an excess of negative affect, causing difficulties in her relationships. This is an opposite pole of the same psychic constellation from Robert's. I experienced them first in the form of my own countertransference hatred: implosions into sleepiness with Robert and explosions of defensive anger with Barbara.

Primitive, archetypal hatred can be experienced and transformed into an ambivalent personal relationship encompassing both love and hate. This process is dependent on the analyst's ability to maintain a creative space in which fantasies can live, play and be contained. In my experience, this ideal is not always achievable. The strong psychic and bodily impact of hatred can become constellated in the relationship between ourselves and our patients. Our thinking capacities may be seriously impaired, constricting this creative space. Containing and processing the violent affects that may emerge during the work is, in turn, likely to depend upon our relationship to our own narcissistic needs and affects. As Winnicott (1947) has emphasized, our patients will be able to tolerate their own hate only if the analyst can hate them. But, paradoxically, our patients' evoking hatred in us can lead us to deny our hate. For a maternal grievance to be transformed, facilitating mourning, some essential work has to happen first within the analyst in order to process affects that result from the force of the inevitable projections and projective identifications from the patient.

Conclusions

The theme of this Congress is "Destruction and Creation." I have concentrated on personal transformations in my patients, in myself and within our analytic relationship. We use the term anger – like the term love – too generally, thereby masking subtly different emotions observable in clinical work. The primal self has the potential for both love and hate, for both creativity and destructiveness. Theoretical understanding of the manifestations of anger, rage and hatred in the consulting room can help to enhance our understanding of intrapsychic and interpersonal mental functioning, in particular the dialectical relationship between ego and self.

My searches have taken me, via a number of mazes, down one central path toward an understanding of grievance, a moral expression of hatred, which embodies a particular struggle between destructive and creative forces. As Kundera (1991) remarked, "hate traps us by binding us too tightly to our adversary" (p. 26). For such patients, clinging to their grievances helps to preserve the integrity of their defensive self structure. But when there is hatred and punishment embedded within the grievance, this can prevent or postpone the loss and mourning necessary for the ego to surrender some of its powers in the service of the self as a whole.

As analysts, we try to remain in touch with the hurt behind our patients' passions, often necessitating a parallel painful struggle to transform our own violent affects into knowledge. After a volcanic eruption, the soil recovers and becomes fertile. The best wine may be made from grapes that flourish from the ash on the slopes of a volcano.

References

Akhtar, S. (1995). Some reflections on the nature of hatred and its emergence in the treatment process. In S. Akhtar, S. Kramer & H. Parens (Eds.), *The Birth of Hatred*. Northvale, NJ/London: Jason Aronson.

Aristotle (1976). *The Ethics of Aristotle: The Nicomachean Ethis*. London: Penguin Classics.

Bollas, C. 1987). *Shadow of the Object: Psychoanalysis of the Unthought Known*. London: Free Association Books.

Colman, W. (1988). After the fall: Original loss and the limits of redemption. *Free Associations, 13*, 59-83.

Diamond, S.A. (1996). *Anger, Madness, and the Daimonic: The Psychological Genesis of Violence, Evil and Creativity*. Albany: State University of New York Press.

Glasser, M. (1986). Identification and its vicissitudes as observed in the perversions. *International Journal of Psycho-Analysis, 67-9*, 9-17.

Kundera, M. (1991). *Immortality*. London/Boston: Faber & Faber.

Lewis, M. (1993). The development of anger and rage. In R.A. Glick & S.P. Roose (Eds.), *Rage, Power and Aggression The Role of Affect in Motivation, Development, and Adaptation*. New Haven/London: Yale University Press.

Person, E.S. (1993). Introduction. In R.A. Glick, & S.P. Roose (Eds.), *Rage, Power and Aggression: The Role of Affect in Motivation, Development, and Adaptation*. New Haven/London: Yale University Press.

Redfearn, J. (1992). *The Exploding Self*. Wilmette, IL: Chiron.

Sontag, S. (1993). *The Volcano Lover: A Romance*. London: Vintage.

Steiner, J. (1993). *Psychic Retreats*. London: Routledge.

Winnicott, D.W. (1947). *Through Paediatrics to Psychoanalysis*. London: Hogarth Press.

Music and Melancholy

Marsilio Ficino's Archetypal Music Therapy

Peter Ammann
Zürich, Switzerland
Schweizerische Gesellschaft für Analytische Psychologie

I invite you on an imaginary journey, about 500 years back, to Florence in the second half of the fifteenth century, when that extraordinary cultural phenomenon in Italy we call the Renaissance took place. Not far from the town, in the surrounding hills, at a place called Careggi, we discover a villa which we are approaching slowly. The rising sun is just about to illuminate the typically reddish walls of the building. The singing birds announce a beautiful day.

Yet the closer we come to the house, the more our ears are enchanted by another kind of song. We are hearing a lovely male voice accompanied by the sounds of a lyre. Seduced by that magic music, we enter the house and follow the sounds that guide us through a long corridor to a small room. In the semi-darkness of the room we discover that the walls are decorated with astrological images. Most striking is the likeness of an old man. He is holding a sickle and is dressed in dark clothes. The sign above his head confirms our guess; the image depicts Saturn. On another wall, in a niche, we perceive the bust of Plato. In front of the impressive head stands a white candle.

In the soft light it casts, we distinguish a little hump-backed man. It is he who is singing so beautifully and accompanying his song by plucking a lyre. On the instrument, we see that it bears a picture of the divine Orpheus, surrounded by trees and animals. The dwarfish man wears a tunic and his head is crowned with a wreath of laurel. His eyes are fixed on a talisman lying on an altar in front of him. Incense is rising from little vases, filling the room with a dizzying smell of myrrh. The ground is richly strewn with heliotropes and other flowers (see Walker 1958, pp. 30-33).

The man who is singing, playing the lyre and celebrating this curious religious, magical ritual is Marsilio Ficino, who lived from

1433 to 1499. In 1459, Cosimo de' Medici, enthralled by Platonic and neo-Platonic philosophy, asked Ficino to translate Plato's work into Latin. He gave him a villa, which became the new home of Cosimo's dream, the Florentine Academy.

This is the house where, in our imagination, we were secretly watching Marsilio Ficino during one of his frequent magic rituals in which songs and music played the most important part. Let us recall the scenery once again. We are in a room whose walls are decorated with the images of the seven planetary gods: Saturn, Jupiter, Mars, the Sun, Venus, Mercury, and the Moon. In this room Marsilio Ficino is singing a hymn addressed to the Sun, such as the great Orpheus himself did once upon a time.

What was the purpose of this ritual? Marsilio Ficino suffered from melancholy, and the extraordinary ritual was a magic operation or, from our present point of view, a psychotherapeutic method. We might even call it an active imagination. Ficino intended to temper the melancholic influence of Saturn by conjuring up and attracting the benign influences of Jupiter, Venus and – above all – the Sun.

Ficino was a child of Saturn. In a letter to a friend, Ficino confessed:

> *Because of that excessive timidity, which you occasionally charge me with, I complain of my melancholy temperament, for to me it seems a very bitter thing, and one that I can only ease and sweeten a little by much lute-playing. ... Saturn me-thinks gave it me from the beginning, when in my horoscope he stood in the ascendant in the sign of the Aquarius. ... But where have I landed myself? ... I will try to find a way out, and either I will say that melancholy, if you must have it so, does not come from Saturn; or else, if it necessarily comes from him, then I will agree with Aristotle, who described it as a unique and divine gift. (Klibansky et al. 1964, p. 258)*

Ficino, in his letter, alludes to two ideas, both of which have their roots in Greek antiquity. During the beginning of the Renaissance they were reanimated, and culminated in Ficino's philosophy. The first is the neo-Platonic notion of Saturn, according to which the highest of the planets embodied, and also bestowed, the highest and noblest faculties of the soul, reason and speculation. The second idea is the Aristotelian doctrine of melancholy, according to which all great men were melancholics. Indeed, there seemed to be a correlation between the glorification of melancholy and Saturn in the circle of Ficino's Florentine Academy and the origin of the new concept of genius.

For a long time, even in the fifteenth century, melancholy was conceived as something only negative and evil. But then the idea forced its way, in that melancholy was not only a positive spiritual force, but actually a condition for creative work. Ficino's new doctrine of Saturn and melancholy grew out of the experience of an élite of humanists who discovered Saturn in a new and personal sense. They became aware of both the sublimity of Saturn's intellectual gifts and the dangers of its ambivalence. He conveyed weakness and susceptibility but also creative force. Yet, in contrast to the earlier view, these two states of mind were now conceived as a unity. Hence, creative men considered their melancholy a privilege. Ficino (1989) expressed this evolution in a magnificent formula which within a few decades became a proverb:

Saturn cannot easily signify the common quality and lot of the human race, but he signifies an individual set apart from others, divine or brutish, blessed or bowed down with the extreme of misery. (p. 251)

Saturn became the lodestar of the melancholic who, according to Ficino's formula, was distinguished as a person who breaks away from the collective and chooses to go the extraordinary, individual way. Thus the glorification of Saturn and melancholy in the Florentine circle of Ficino ultimately aimed at the *principium individuationis* (principle of individuation).

In 1489, when he was 56, Ficino (1980) published a book dealing with the symptoms and therapy of the Saturnine character. He wrote it for scholars like himself, students in letters who, in their intensive studies, suffer from melancholy. He made an astonishing statement:

Runners take care of their legs, athletes take care of their arms, musicians take care of their voices. ... Only the priests of Muses are so negligent ... that they seem to neglect totally that instrument with which they are able to measure and comprehend the whole world. This instrument is the spirit. (p. 4)

The spirit, we are told, is the instrument by which we are enabled to grasp the entire world. What is that spirit? In order to answer this question, we must recall briefly Ficino's view of humanity and the world.

According to the anthropological theory held during the Renaissance, the two basic components of human nature, the body and the soul, were connected by a third element described as the "medium." This bond was the *spiritus humanus*. As the microcosm corresponds to the macrocosm, the universe is similarly divided into matter, soul and the connecting bond, the spirit of the world. This *spiritus mundanus* flows through the whole universe and provides a channel of influence between the heavenly bodies and the sublunar world (see Klibansky 1964, 264-265).

Thus, the spirit of the world is a kind of mediator between the two extremes of soul and body. The planets, according to Ficino, send out rays which confer their astral qualities on that spirit, which passes them on to its counterpart, the *spiritus humanus.* Thanks to its intermediary position, it can pass the astral qualities on to body and soul. Melancholy, in this way, is a gift from Saturn to the souls and the bodies of humans. The scholar, or priest of the Muses, as Ficino likes to call him, has good reason to take care of his spirit: there is a direct connection between his intense mental activity, his spirit and his disposition for melancholy.

How do melancholy and the spirit, in Ficino's view, affect the human body concretely? Ficino thinks in the categories of antique medicine, according to which there are four humours in the human body. One of them is the black bile, in Greek *melaina chole.* Its predominance induces the mental state we call melancholy.

Astrologically, black bile is associated with the planet Saturn. Like Saturn, it favors contemplation and thinking. But intensive thinking, Ficino (1980) says, condenses the human soul and makes it similar to black bile. Thus,

> *of all scholars, those devoted to the study of philosophy are most bothered by black bile, because their minds get separated from their bodies and from bodily things. ... To the extent that they join the mind to bodiless truth, they are forced to separate it from the body. Body for these people never returns except as a half-soul and a melancholy one. (p. 7)*

But it is worth the suffering, because, as Ficino (1989) formulates,

> *Saturn, however, for the earthly life from which he himself is separate and finally separates you, repays you with a life celestial and everlasting. (p. 213)*

We modern psychotherapists can only agree with Ficino: that individuals who put mind above all other values get detached from concrete, sensual and instinctive life. They are raised into the realm of abstract ideas and remain cut off from "earthly life." They cannot enjoy life, and suffer from nostalgia to return to the collective stream of life, which they have left in their one-sided intellectual hubris.

Now what part does the spirit play with regard to melancholy? According to Ficino (1989), the medical doctors describe the *spiritus humanus*

> *as a vapor of the blood, pure, subtle, hot and clear. After being generated by the heat of the heart out of the more subtle blood, it flies to the brain, and there the soul uses it continually for the exercise of the interior as well as the exterior senses. This is why the blood subserves the spirit, the spirit the senses, and finally, the senses, reason. (p. 111)*

The scholar, through his continuous mental activity, uses his spirit with particular intensity. Therefore, he must replace it constantly from the more subtle part of the blood. This causes the remaining blood to become thick, dry and black. The flow to the brain is interrupted and thus the higher mental functions are cut off from the senses, the heart and finally the entire earthly body.

Let us translate Ficino's view into modern psychological language. The spirit, he says, is a very subtle body: not body and almost soul, not soul and almost body. It vivifies everything everywhere and is the immediate cause of all generation and motion. Thus it represents a kind of universal principle of life-energy. From a psychological point of view we could compare it to Jung's concept of libido in the sense of a general psychic energy. The soul, especially in its vital and emotional aspect, was projected into the blood since time immemorial. Thus, the spirit appears individually projected into the blood of the human body and collectively, as spirit of the world, into the spheres of the planets.

Melancholy, to him, is obviously a mental state in which the realm of deep, abstract thinking is cut off from the supply of spirit; that is, from the libido. From a Jungian perspective we could say: Melancholy is a depression of a conscious mind, on the one side dominated by excessive abstract thinking, on the other cut off from the personal (the microcosmic) as well as the collective (the macrocosmic) unconscious.

The libido has withdrawn into the unconscious. Today, we would observe carefully the manifestations of the unconscious, such as dreams, fantasies, and visions. What about our Renaissance doctor of the soul? What does he recommend to restore the supply of spirit?

Ficino, first of all, gives detailed advice on diet and regimen. He recommends wine, aromatic food, odors and pure, sunny air. All these remedies seem to have in common a quality of stimulation or slight intoxication that might cause a certain *abaissement du niveau mental* (lowering of attention): a relative approach of the conscious to the unconscious. Yet the most important remedy for the spirit, according to Ficino, is music. Why music? He (1989) explains: "If vapours exhaling from a merely vegetable life are greatly beneficial to your life, how much more beneficial do you think will be songs which are made of air to a spirit wholly aerial" (p. 213).

Ficino adopts Aristotle's theory, according to which the sense-organ is of the same substance as what is sensed. In this view the ear contains air – in reality it contains a liquid – and Ficino identifies this air with the spirit and calls it *spiritus aereus*. Whereas visual impressions have no direct contact with the *spiritus*, sounds – being moving air – communicate directly with the *spiritus aereus* (see Walker 1958, pp. 7-8).

Ficino emphasizes, again and again, that music has a stronger effect than anything transmitted through the other senses, because its medium – air – is of the same kind as the spirit. But there is another, more important, reason why sound affects the spirit more strongly than, for instance, sight; it transmits movement and is itself movement. Ficino, in his commentary on Plato's *Timaeus*, explains:

> *Although visual impressions are in a way pure, yet they lack the effectiveness of motion, and are usually perceived only as an image, without their real nature; normally therefore, they move the soul only slightly. ... But musical sound, by the movement of the air, moves the body; by purified air it excites the aerial spirit which is the bond of body and soul; by emotion it affects the senses and at the same time the soul; ... by its nature, both spiritual and material, it at once seizes, and claims as its own, man in its entirety. (Walker 1958, p. 9)*

Sound, thus, is moving air, animated and animating: a kind of living being. It moves, stimulates and animates the aerial human spirit, the linking bond between body and soul. Therefore, according to Ficino, music seizes humans not only partially, but in their physical and psychic wholeness.

Sounds do not render image as visual impressions do but, more important to Ficino, they render "the real nature of things." What is this real nature of things? It is the effectiveness of motion. Motion here, obviously, is not meant in a one-sided physical sense, but in the psychic sense of emotion. Thus music expresses the "real" nature of things: the emotions, affects and feelings that are linked to, or projected upon them.

The melancholic has lost the affective bond with things of this world. Therefore, the most effective means or remedy to re-establish the emotional relatedness with them is by directing music or songs to them.

Has the outstanding therapeutic role that Ficino assigns to music also an importance for our time? I believe so. A lecture by von Franz (1991) has the significant title "C.G. Jung's Rehabilitation of the Feeling Function in our Civilization." We must see Ficino's praise of music as a healing force on the background of the illness of our Western civilization. When Jung spoke in 1925 with Chief Ochwiay Biano, the Indian said that the whites were all mad. Jung asked why. Ochwiay Biano replied, "The whites say that they think with their heads. We think here," indicating his heart. "For the first time in my life," Jung commented, "someone had drawn for me a picture of the real white man" (MDR, p. 276). Our Renaissance therapist, Ficino (1989) exhorted his readers:

> *Remember that song is a most powerful imitator of all things. It imitates the intentions and passions of the soul as well as words; it represents also people's physical gestures, motions, and actions as well as their characters and imitates all these and acts them out so forcibly that it immediately provokes both the singer and the audience to imitate and act out the same things. (p. 359)*

How right is Ficino, though imitation is not always as obvious as, for instance, in Beethoven's Sixth Symphony, the famous *Pastorale*, dedicated to the peasants' country life. To the idea of imitation Ficino (1989) added a surprising additional dimension: "By the same power, when it (the song) imitates the celestials, it also wonderfully arouses our spirit upwards to the celestial influence and the celestial influence downwards to our spirit" (p. 359). Here Ficino again alluded to the doctrine, according to which the human spirit corresponds to the spirit of the world. Ficino, indeed, dedicates the third and last part of his *Book of Life* entirely to the question: how to bring your life in tune with the heavenly spheres of the planets.

The use of anything having the same qualities as a certain heavenly body will make our spirit similar to it and provoke the required influx of celestial spirit. This happens in the same way that a vibrating string by "sympathy" causes another, consonant, string to move and to make sounds. This attunement, according to Ficino, can be done in various ways. But it is music that again is recommended most strongly (see Walker 1958, pp. 13-14). Once again the

Figure 1

momentous reason is that music can influence the *spiritus humanus* more directly than anything else.

How can this magic operation of making the human spirit in tune with the spirit of the world be interpreted psychologically? Ficino's intention is, as we know, to temper the melancholic influence of Saturn. Consequently, his astrological songs are addressed to the compensating benign planets: the Sun, Jupiter, Venus and Mercury. The composition of these songs implies an intensive dealing with all things in this world ruled by those celestial bodies. Thus, we may say that the attunement of the human spirit to the spirit of the world is an attempt – consciously, by a kind of active imagination – to re-establish emotional relatedness with the archetypal realms of the planets from which Saturn has separated melancholics..

The realm from which melancholics are cut off, and which threatens them, is shown beautifully in paintings of "Melancholy" made by Lucas Cranach in the years between 1528 and 1533 (Figure 1). In the left corner above we see a dark, depressing cloud. The left side often represents the more unconscious side; it could correspond to repressed and therefore oppressing fantasies. In the black cloud a horde of witches under Satan's command is riding on pigs, goats, bulls, horses, dogs and cats – in a very menacing way – toward the woman representing Melancholy. It is the attack and cruel revenge of an offended goddess manifesting herself in her most negative aspect. The goddess, of course, is Venus. She was deposed from her throne and banished into hell by the Christian Church. Ficino, reviving neo-Platonism and amalgamating it with the Christian religion to a kind of new "Religion of the World," re-enthroned Venus, the neglected goddess, and gave her back the place she merits.

Ficino (1989) invited older people, especially, to avoid melancholic influences and to join Venus in her "gardens and green fields." He imagines the goddess herself reminding us: "I, my children, gave life to you (in case you didn't know) by pleasure and by motion. I therefore will preserve your life by a certain pleasure and a certain motion – although not the same kind" (pp. 203-205).

Venus is not the only grace Ficino implored in order to temper Saturn's obnoxious influence. "Venus is most friendly to Jupiter, just as Jupiter is to the Sun. … From these three Graces of the heavens … astrologers hope for and diligently seek our favors" (p. 263).

The three universal colors – green gold, and sapphire – are dedicated to these three Graces. Green is for Venus, gold for the Sun, and sapphire for Jupiter. If you want to capture the gifts of the heavenly Graces, Ficino advised "to look at these three powerful colours frequently." He, then, made a most astounding suggestion: "In the very depth of your house, you should construct a chamber, vaulted and marked with these figures and colors, and you should spend most of your waking hours there and also sleep" (p. 347).

These archetypal forms or figures of the whole world, as Ficino called them, painted on the walls of your most intimate room, are "not only to be looked at, but reflected upon in the mind." Ficino's intention is not so much to create an archetypal image outside but to evoke one inside. It is a matter of imagination, of active imagination. Consequently Ficino went on: "And when you have left your house, you will perceive, not so much the spectacle of individual things, but the figure and the colours of the universe (that is, the world in its wholeness!)" (p. 347).

Slowly closing the circle of our imaginary journey in the company of our archetypal therapist, I trust that you understand better his religious-magical rite. There we met Ficino in his most private room, playing the lyre and singing Orphic hymns, contemplating talismans and astrological images. A magical operation, an "active imagination" of a man haunted by melancholy, but determined to constellate the archetypal forces of the tempering, compensating planets.

A Jungian approach as a key for a better comprehension, in our time, of Ficino's philosophy and psychology seems natural and rewarding. It is not surprising that a Jungian such as James Hillman (1975) calls Ficino a "Renaissance Patron of Archetypal Psychology" and that he emphasizes the affinity between Neoplatonism and Jung. Indeed, while imagining Ficino in the most intimate chamber of his villa in Careggi, conjuring the spirit of the world by sounds and images, we cannot help recalling Jung himself withdrawing from the outer world into the secret world of his tower on Lake Zürich. He did not play an instrument, but he certainly painted and sculpted there, projecting his inner picture-book on the walls. We know something of what these paintings and active imaginations meant in re-establishing his relation with the healing forces of the archetypes. He was looking, not so much for perfection, but for equilibrium, wholeness. Ficino would call it "celestial temperateness."

Jung (CW12) analyzed a series of dreams by the famous physicist and Nobel-prize winner Wolfgang Pauli. In an unpublished seminar, Jung described Pauli as a man who lived exclusively in a world of thinking and had completely lost touch with the world of feelings and instincts. As Pauli confessed in one of his letters, his feeling problems had caused him such a deep personal crisis that he went to see Jung for help. His dreams dealt with the rehabilitation of the instinctive man and his feelings. Well known also is Pauli's impressive vision of the world clock which Jung (CW11) analysed in detail. The world clock rightly reminds Jung of "the antique idea of the musical harmony of the spheres." Less known are certain dreams of Pauli (Meier 1992) mentioned later in his letters to Jung in which music plays an important part. In 1953, five years before he died, Pauli completed a rather long active imagination, "The Piano Lesson," in which he had to have music lessons with a female piano teacher (Atmanspacher et al.1995, pp. 317-330). A subsequent dream deals with dancing (van Erkelens 1992, pp. 50-51).

Pauli is an outstanding representative of modern men and women who suffer from "the illness of the white man," turning one-sidedly to Saturnine thinking and, consequently, through their depressions and neuroses, compelled to re-establish contact with the world of Ficino's "Three Graces." On such a quest music played an essential role also for Wolfgang Pauli.

Let us return once again to Florence at the time of the Renaissance. Cosimo de' Medici's grandson, Lorenzo the Magnificent,

Figure 2

nurtured young artists such as Botticelli, Michelangelo, and Leonardo da Vinci, and transferred to their minds the ideas of Ficino. Yates (1964) discussed Botticelli's famous painting "Primavera" (The Spring), putting it into the context of Ficino's neo-Platonic Florentine Academy. She suggested that the picture can be seen as a practical application of Ficino's religious magic: a kind of talisman, an image of the world, arranged so as to transmit healthful, rejuvenating, anti-Saturnine influences to the beholder.

Here, in visual form, we can see Ficino's natural magic (Figure 2): on the left side Mercury, to his right the Three Graces. The central figure is Venus, with blinded Eros above her. On the far right side the wind of spring, Zephyr, blows and pursues the earth-nymph Chloris, who then is transformed into Flora, the herald of spring, which is the season of Venus.

Following Yates, let us look at the picture in the context of Ficino's philosophy. The wind blowing from the right down to Chloris and Flora corresponds to the *spiritus mundi*. In the flowery meadows of Venus we can take a walk, drinking in the scented air, laden with Venereal spirit from the planet. Inspired by the music of the spheres, we then join the Three Graces' joyful dance. In the middle, with her hair close-bound, Chastity looks at Mercury. The god is pointing to the sky, as if to say: "Don't pay too much attention to the spectacle of individual things; look at the image of the universe. Venus gives you pleasure, yes, but she lures you to the external things, while Saturn, through his pleasures, calls you back to the innermost things."

Here, our imaginary journey back into Ficino's view of the world comes to an end. It is the view of a world that is ensouled. Back, here and now, in our world full of problems of power games, racial conflicts, overpopulation, excessive growth, excess and – at the same time – lack of rationality, of destruction of our environment, both outside and inside, we wonder what message we can draw from our Renaissance philosopher and priest of the Muses.

You have felt, I am sure, the actuality of Ficino's message. He teaches us to re-enchant our world, to listen again to its cosmic music, and tune our soul to it in harmony in order to restore a corresponding vibration between the instrument of the macrocosm – our world – and of the microcosm – ourselves – the human beings.

References

Atmanspacher, H., Primas, H., & Wertenschlag-Birkhäuser, E. (Eds.). (1995). *Der Pauli-Jung-Dialog und seine Bedeutung für die moderne Wissenschaft.* Berlin: Springer.
Ficino, M. (1980). *The Book of Life.* (Charles Boer, Trans.). Dallas, TX: Spring Publications.
Ficino, M. (1989). *Three Books on Life.* Binghampton, NY: Center for Medieval and Early Renaissance Studies.
Hillman, J. (1975). *Re-Visioning Psychology.* New York: Harper & Row.
Klibansky, R.; Panofsky, E.; Saxl, F. (1964). *Saturn and Melancholy.* London: Nelson.
Meier, C.A. (Ed.) (1992). *Wolfgang Pauli und C.G. Jung, Ein Briefwechsel 1932-1958.* Berlin: Springer.
von Franz, M.-L. (1991). C.G. Jungs Rehabilitation der Gefühlsfunktion in unserer Zivilisation. In Stiftung für Jung'sche Psychologie, *Jungiana.* Küsnacht: Verlag für Jung'sche Psychologie.
van Erkelens, H. (1992). Wolfgang Pauli's Begegnung mit dem Geist der Materie. In Stiftung fur Jung'sche Psychologie, *Jungiana.* Kusnacht: Verlag fur Jung'sche Psychologie.
Walker, D. (1958). *Spiritual and Demonic Magic.* London: Warburg Institute.
Yates, F. (1964). *Giordano Bruno and the Hermetic Tradition.* London: Routledge & Kegan Paul.

Almost Two Thousand Years
and not a Single New God!

Nietzsche's Reception by Jung and Heidegger
in the Abyss of National Socialism

Günter Langwieler
Berlin, Germany
Deutsche Gesellschaft für Analytische Psychologie

In one of his last works the German Philosopher Friedrich Nietzsche took up an angry "critique of the Christian concept of God," through the stylistic medium of mocking contempt: "That the strong races of northern Europe did not reject the Christian God truly does their religious gift no honor." And somewhat later: "Since then they have created no other God! Almost two thousand years and not a single new God! Only still and as if justifiably, like an ultimate limit and extreme of God-creating power, of the creator spirit of men, this pitiful God of Christian monotonous-theism!" (KGW VI-3, p. 183).

Nietzsche could not publish *The Antichrist* because he was overtaken by serious psychological and physical illness (see Ross 1980). Does this amount to the outcry of a lunatic, a sick man who is no longer to be taken seriously? Or is Nietzsche speaking here in the person of the jester, the fool, the mad man? Is Nietzsche not also expressing, as if in a bequest – and precisely in the intensification of his feeling and thought with the approach of his illness and in the emotionalism of his words – an essential, although still hidden connection? Nietzsche addressed a fundamental dilemma of modern people, and succeeded thereby in a ground-breaking critique of our times. "God is dead" (KGW V-2, p. 159), another of Nietzsche's assertions: that is to say, the old God of Judeo-Christian monotheism is dead, because humans have declared him dead, but humans who delude themselves into thinking that they are creators, have not been able to create a new god. But what happens to humans when they proclaim "God is dead"? This was precisely the question that drove

Jung from the very beginning of his seminar on Nietzsche's *Zarathustra*.

Jung saw Nietzsche as someone who was so overwhelmed by the collective unconscious that he was involuntarily made conscious of the collective unconscious of his time: in a certain sense, a prophet (see ZS, p. 1300). Nietzsche asked himself the pressing questions of his time and ours. He was deeply convinced that "only the day after tomorrow belongs to me" (KGW VI-3, p. 165). He was concerned with a fundamental determinant of the crisis of European culture, which he saw as a crisis of Christianity. He wanted to overcome European nihilism, which was for him rooted in Platonic/Jewish/ Christian thought. He had an apocalyptic vision: "Our entire European culture has long been driven by an agony of tension that rose from decade to decade as if toward catastrophe: uneasy, violent, rushing like a stream that yearns for an end, that fears contemplation" (KGW VIII-2, p. 431).

One is reminded, by Nietzsche's mocking the "strong races of northern Europe," of the German National Socialists who dragged Europe into the abyss with their racial madness. Among the countless catastrophes of the twentieth century, German National Socialism, with its murder of millions of European Jews and the unchaining of the Second World War, represents a particularly shattering example of human destructiveness. Three thinkers fell into disrepute as intellectual pathbreakers of National Socialism: Nietzsche, Jung, and the German philosopher Martin Heidegger. My view is that the intellectual foundations of all three oppose those of National Socialism. Jung stands at the center of my considerations. In the early stages of National Socialism, he made use of his confrontation with Nietzsche in order to release himself from an initial fascination. In the course of his reception of Nietzsche, Jung – like Heidegger – became a messenger of bad tidings. Both warned of the impending dangers even though they remained passive and refrained from public statements when the need was greatest.

Let us consider first the "world of thinking" of Nietzsche, Jung and Heidegger with regard to a central section from *Zarathustra* called "The Vision and the Enigma" (KGW VI-1, pp. 193-198). Jung dealt with this part of *Zarathustra* in the fifth year of the seminars, 1938 (see ZS, pp.1256-1311). To Jung, Zarathustra was Nietzsche himself. The tales of Zarathustra gave Jung an extraordinary insight into the real processes of Nietzsche's unconscious. In this section, Nietzsche described a somber vision and an enigma. Zarathustra enters the darkness of the unconscious, which seems to him a storehouse of death. He remembers the ascent with a dwarf riding on his shoulders. For Jung, the dwarf personifies the unconscious. Insofar as Zarathustra turns the unconscious into a dwarf, he renders it small and unimportant and overlooks the fact that the dwarf is sly and crafty. The dwarf is a highly mythological figure. In alchemy he is like the spirit of gravity, eternal inertia, the spirit of lead. One should not provoke the dwarf; to do so symbolizes illness, which will destroy the mind.

For Jung, the dwarf on the shoulders is a typical demonstration of a possession. Everything that comes from behind comes out of the shadow, out of the darkness of the unconscious; and because we have no eyes there and – unlike primitive tribes – carry no amulet at the back of the neck, evil influences can take control of us. Through an alien possession, one is alienated from oneself. The right approach would be to turn around and look. Then one would receive an answer and could reconstruct the characters that are hidden within oneself.

Consciousness has a fundamental weakness so that it always can be overrun by unconscious material. Then what you assumed yourself to be disappears in the shadow and becomes an unconscious complex. To carry the other side, the shadow means to carry doubts about oneself. The one who is certain carries no cross, but thereby loses the human contact, the humanity that really carries the burden. For Jung, the tragic split in every kind of religious conviction is that the redeemed one is redeemed from his burden. Thus too with Zarathustra; he begins to preach, instead of asking the dwarf who he is.

In the second half of the section, the topic is the vision of the shepherd into whose mouth the snake crawled while the shepherd slept. Jung concluded that the snake represents the chthonic powers of the earth, the fertility of the earth and the fertility and power of a man. At the same time, the symbol is that of the hero who is devoured by a snake or dragon. Jung went further; speaking precisely, the image is one of interpenetration. The alchemical symbol for this is the *ouroboros*. Both interpenetrating parts destroy and are destroyed. Nature is unconscious, and humans are originally unconscious. Their great victory over nature is that they become conscious. Jung interprets the vision of the shepherd who bites through the head of the black snake as a victory of a human being and human consciousness over the darkness of nature. But even this interpretation was not enough for Jung; he questioned further. When does this symbol make its appearance? After the idea of the eternal, return of the same emerges. The moment without return means recognition of the singularity of the moment. This would be a moral accomplishment requiring heroic qualities. In Jung's view, Zarathustra does not accomplish this, and flees therefore into the idea of the eternal return. We will see later that Heidegger interprets this quite differently, in that he regards the concept of the eternal return directly in terms of the uniqueness of the moment, not like the dwarf, who regards it as a simple repetition in the sense of a circular movement.

Jung then looks at the symbol of the shepherd boy: the innocent, completely naive child of nature. Thus the contrast is particularly appalling; here the poisonous black snake, there the innocent sweet boy. As an example, Jung names the German Michel, a well-known figure in cartoons picturing the German mind. He never knows anything, is always misunderstood and has a wonderful sense of innocence. After all, he wanted only the best. His other side, his shadow, his second self, is the black snake.

Jung again broaches the interpretation of the snake. It is suggested by participants in Jung's seminars that it can be understood as the personification of all the least worthy aspects of the unconscious, as Satan. Jung takes the opposite approach: The snake also represents God. It is the *deus absconditus*, the God shrouded in darkness. When the Egyptian god Ra is not shining in Heaven, he is in the underworld hidden in a snake skin. He is both the Sun and the snake. He is the movement of alternation between day and night, the whole, a circle. For Jung, the black snake is thus the dark god, the God that Nietzsche declared dead.

This god now appears as a demonic power from below. When Zarathustra says: "No longer shepherd, no longer human being, – a metamorphosed one, an illuminated one who laughs!" (KGW VI-2, p. 198) this is in a certain sense the sunrise. As the metamorphosed one, the shepherd is also god, the rising sun, no longer human. In the uncanny laughter of the metamorphosed man, Zarathustra hears the superman. Jung calls it a mystery in the unconsciousness of humans that they cannot be free from the shadow. If we suppose that we can make a leap into the heavens and be the sun, then we can be sure that our other side is in hell. It is then only a question of time before the shadow has seized us. The savior is thus also always the great destroyer. God is also the black snake, and we fail to notice this only because of our shepherd-boy-like naivete.

The interpenetration of shepherd and snake is an image for a boundless subject. The human subject turns itself into God, like Nietzsche, who turns himself into Zarathustra and untimately transforms himself, in the form of the young shepherd, into the sun god of the illuminated superman. Thus, the process of the deification of the human subject is described as the inflation of the collective unconscious by means of archaic images of the divine.

In Heidegger's (1986a) view, Nietzsche's most fundamental concept is precisely that of the eternal return of the same. Nietzsche presents this concept in the form of an enigma. The concept comes to him in sight of the gateway that evidently should symbolize time – time and eternity. Heidegger holds that Nietzsche's essential thought is precisely this: to think of the eternal return of the same from the gateway, to conceive from the moment.

In order to understand this view, one must first comprehend the nature of nihilism from Nietzsche's point of view. "A nihilist," Heidegger quotes Nietzsche as saying, "is the man who judges that the world as it is should not be, and who judges that the world that should be does not exist. Therefore existence (acting, suffering, wanting, feeling) has no meaning." (KGW VIII-2, p. 30). For Heidegger, the meaninglessness of existence is bound tightly to Nietzsche's assertion that "God is dead." With this assertion, Nietzsche brings himself repeatedly back to the sense of emptiness. A complete isolation envelops humanity. The black snake, in Heidegger's interpretation, is the dreary eternal sameness and basic purposelessness and senselessness of nihilism. The snake cannot be torn out from without; that is, nihilism cannot be overcome from without, not "insofar as one merely puts in the place of the Christian god another ideal: reason, progress, social-scientific socialism, mere democracy." Heidegger continues: "All is in vain, if man does not bite into danger" (p. 200). In Heidegger's astonishing interpretation, the "bite" that should overcome nihilism from the ground up is the concept of the eternal recurrence of the same.

How can the concept be this "bite"? Insofar as this concept is rightly conceived, not as the dwarf conceives it. Humans overcome nihilism only when they consider the moment and put themselves in the place of someone facing the predicament of a rising nihilism. Heidegger (1986b) calls this "transposing oneself to the temporality of independent action and decision by looking forward to what is given as our task, and looking back at what is given as our endowment. ... This predicament itself is nothing other than what is opened up by transposing oneself into the moment. To think of eternity requires: to think the moment, which means transposing oneself to the moment of self-being" (p. 203).

The concept of the eternal return of the same does not mean that it has all happened once before; everything is inconsequential. Instead, the moment of self-being demands a decision; nothing is inconsequential, everything matters. Thus Heidegger in his interpretation arrives at a moral challenge of radical intensity.

Let us place ourselves at the moment of the beginning of Jung's Zarathustra seminar (May 2, 1934), to gain a historical-critical understanding of Jung's and Heidegger's reception of Nietzsche at the onset of National Socialism. Jung had gathered around himself a trusted group of 25 to 30 participants who had already taken part in his seminars. As he himself expressed it in a letter of April 1934, Jung had "collided with contemporary history" (von der Tann and Erlenmeyer 1993, p. 20). In December 1933, as editor of the *Zentralblattes für Psychotherapie*, which appeared in Germany, he had already formulated his commitments as follows: "Differences between German and Jewish psychology, evident and long recognized by thoughtful people, should no longer be obscured. This can only be advantageous for science." In February 1934 this was criticized by Bally in the *Neue Zürcher Zeitung* under the title "Germanic Psychotherapy." He wrote: "Jung does not reveal to us, … what particular value is promised by considering race in psychology." Bally reproached Jung on the grounds that, thanks to Jung's popularity, National Socialist scientific politics could register a success (cf. von der Tann & Erlenmeyer 1933, pp. 13-15).

In March 1934 Jung replied in the *Neue Zürcher Zeitung* in almost obstinately naive diction: "I concede I am careless, so careless that I do the most easily misunderstood thing that one can do in the present moment: I put the Jewish question on the table." He was not reluctant to declare that, according to his own personal equation, this involved the fundamental epistemological problem of psychology, namely, that the organ of knowledge is at the same time its object, and therefore every theory could be criticized as a subjective declaration. "Subjective idiosyncrasy is conditioned first by the individual, second by the family, third through nation, race, climate, locality and history" (von der Tann & Erlenmeyer, 1993, pp. 16-18). Jung wanted to use the "Jewish question" to intensify a scholarly confrontation about the question of the subjective. But, like the shepherd boy, did Jung not see then, the dark side of the preoccupation with race? Doesn't this obstinate persistence of Jung strike one as an alien obsession?

The label "Jew" meant something quite different to the National Socialists. It marked the inner and outer enemy, who in the beginning would be excluded and whose economic and social life would be destroyed, and who later would be consigned to an uninhibited annihilation free of every moral constraint.

Jung evidently was hard hit by the public criticism, imagined himself as the victim of a smear campaign, and felt that he was suspected of being a "bloodthirsty anti-Semite," which he was not. We can know this from the work of the historian Yerushalmi (1991), who discussed and considered Jung's remarks in the *Zentralblatt*, how they sounded in 1934 and how they may have affected Freud. In spite of all criticism, it is clear to Yerushalmi that Jung was neither Nazi nor anti-Semite in the usual sense.

These were the circumstances in which Jung decided to deal with *Zarathustra* in his next seminar. Now matter how self-assured Jung presented himself as being in public, he had fallen into a personal crisis with regard to his self-image and his scientific orientation. In this crisis he sought an orientation through *Zarathustra*. Why through Nietzsche? Nietzsche had had a powerful influence on scientists, artists and writers – not least on Freud, from 1890 on; Jung had read Nietzsche extensively since his studen t days and had been inspired by central Nietzschean concepts (see Bishop 1995). In his crisis after the split with Freud he had worked carefully through *Zarathustra* for the first time, as he noted in the *Zarathustra Seminar*. In an earlier paper Jung had pointed out the danger "that was hidden in the leap over Christianity" (CW7, 401) and in doing so referred to Nietzsche. For Jung, Nietzsche was much too important to be yielded up to appropriation and misinterpretation by the National Socialists, nor – ironically – from the other side, the warning against Nietzsche by National Socialist philosophers (see Safranski 1994).

In his Zarathustra seminar, Jung – carrying on his earlier engagement with Nietzsche – had attained his own critical position on National Socialism and thereby made a contribution to understanding it. The seminar itself took place in a closed circle and the stenographic transcription could not be circulated publicly, but Jung expressed himself publicly, in his Wotan article and in interviews (see von der Tann and Erlenmeyer 1993). He believed that he had warned repeatedly of the dangers of National Socialism. If he was not understood in this way, this was not only because he had not expressed himself clearly enough, but also because his critical references stemmed from an ambiguity that, in its political-moral explosiveness, was and is not taken truly seriously.

The problem is the question of God in our time. Jung raised exactly this question at the midpoint of the Zarathustra seminar: What happens to humans when they declare "God is dead"? National Socialism itself indirectly offers an answer to this question. The answers of Nietzsche, Jung and Heidegger, as different as their concepts and theoretical systems are, all answer the question in a way precisely opposed to the way National Socialism answers it. In the modern age, which has lasted for centuries, there is born out of doubt regarding God the human subject, a subject who brilliantly faces the world that is declared to be the object. Thus arises the person who says "I." The well-known assertion of Descartes, *"Ego cogito, ergo ego sum"* (I think, therefore I am) illustrates this development. But think also of the Renaissance, where the question of the relationship between creative humans and creator God was newly posed, as a few artists dared to say "I" and to paint the world as they saw it from their personal, individual perspectives. Thus, humans arrived at the reflection that they had created God in their own minds, in that God is not detectable in the empirical world of objects. God remains only as a psychological fact, an image of the divine.

Consequently, the human subject can have no foundation in anything more than itself. Belief in religiosity and the otherworldly "all-powerful creator, holy law-giver, and just judge" (Kant 1990, p. 165), lose their integrating, constraining and orienting power. The consequence is an all-embracing loss; humans stand on the brink of nothingness. The revolting subject pursues the mastery of nature in a systematic, scientific fashion as the goal of human activity and overlooks the "blond beast." The glorification of the beast was recognized by Heidegger in his 1940 lectures on Nietzsche, as the nihilistic consequence of the revolt of the subject. "For Nietzsche, subjectivity is absolutely the subjectivity of the body, i.e., of drive and affect. … In Hegel's metaphysics essentially understood *rationalitas* determines subjectivity; in Nietzsche's metaphysics *animalitas* (animality) is the theme. … The absolute essence of subjectivity necessarily manifests itself as the *bestialitas* of *brutalitas*. At the end of his metaphysics stands the proposition: *Homo est brutum bestiale*" (Heidegger 1986a, pp. 266-67).

Adorno and Horkheimer (1969) refer to the same connection, but from a completely different theoretical starting point. They stress the menace of the situation in which the human subject finds itself in our time. It is Jung's particular contribution to have emphasized the largely unconscious nature of these processes, the fundamental weakness of consciousness and rationality, and the pressure of archaic unconscious images of God, with the danger of the disintegration of the ego that is inflated by shadow images.

By contrast, National Socialism did not merely tolerate the dark side of the revolt of the subject but fully and completely embraced it. National Socialism based itself on the dark side, in that it proclaimed itself as the political movement of a "master race."

Because Nietzsche's assertion that "God is dead" coincides with the experience of many people, there existed and exists room for primitive images of the divine from the collective unconscious. Many Germans succumbed to megalomania through the impact of such archaic divine images. In an interview given to the American journalist H.R. Knickerbocker in October 1938, Jung described Hitler as a "mystical medicine man." The secret of his power was twofold; to an extraordinary degree, Hitler's unconscious had access to his consciousness and he let himself be driven by his unconscious: "Hitler … listens and follows. The true leader is always a follower" (von der Tann and Erlenmayer 1993, pp. 28-54). Attributing quasi-religious qualities to himself, Hitler said: "Providence has called me to be the greatest liberator of mankind. I am freeing mankind from the compulsion of a spirit grown too independent, from the dirty and humiliating self-torment of a chimerical conscience and morality" (Rauschning 1973, pp. 210-211).

Many Germans followed Hitler like the fanatic faithful of a religious sect and, like him, left conscience and morality behind. They were intoxicated by the archaic-religious ideas of power and redemption that he propagated, and imagined themselves as a chosen Aryan race. From the beginning, the National Socialists directed their complete hatred against the other chosen people, the Jewish people, and all those who would not or could not adhere to their megalomania. The inner opposition was physically annihilated, just like the sick and handicapped. Hitler's exercise of power was possible because he, as Goldhagen (1996) documents in a shocking fashion, had "willing executioners" among hundreds of thousands of "simple Germans," but that was not enough. He allied himself with science, industry, the military and an administrative machinery sworn to obedience and the fulfillment of duty. Arendt (1986) spoke of an "alliance between mob and elite" (p. 702).

In their intoxicating, seemingly invincible exercise of power, the National Socialists showed themselves restrained by nothing, until their destruction by the Allies, accompanied by somber stagings of self-destruction. The guiding image of the National Socialists was the German god of storm and war, Wotan. He was destructive through and through, an image of disintegration (see ZS, p. 870). According to this idea, National Socialism would be the murderous form, the dark side of the "revolt of the subject," that finally led to Auschwitz. In this regard, an essential connection should be noted. the monstrosity presented by National Socialism and the Holocaust is not thereby made any less an enigma. The shadow of the revolt of the subject defines anew the relationship between *animalitas* and *rationalitas* and shows the limits of a *moralitas* that grounds itself in the immanent without being able to secure a religious foundation. As early as 1937 Heidegger (1986c, p. 188) quoted Nietzsche's words: "One believes one can manage with a morality without a religious context, but this is necessarily the way to nihilism." *Animalitas* does not let itself be steered by *rationalitas*, but on the contrary makes the latter serve it.

An immanently grounded moral maxim, like the categorical imperative, is pushed *ad absurdum*, if the subject makes arbitrariness – one's own advantage – the common law. Thrown back on itself, the human subject can arbitrarily uphold or deny any maxim with the help of its *rationalitas*. Then the dams break – the dams against the pressure of archaic instinctive nature, the "*bestialitas* of *brutalitas*."

Nietzsche and Jung undoubtedly had sympathy for *animalitas*, but in designating *animalitas* as Dionysian they transfigured it into a gushingly admired ideal. Thus Jung (Let-I, p. 38) wrote in 1910 in a letter to Freud that psychoanalysis should gently turn Christ back into the wise-speaking god of the vine that he was, and by incorporating those archaic-infantile energies, reestablish the great beauty and purposefulness of ancient religion. What Jung found interesting in Nietzsche was the liberation of the Christian concept of God from the one-sidedness of the "God only of the good" (KGW VI-3, p. 180). Morality as determined by Christianity was considered to be cramped and hypocritical. But Nietzsche and Jung certainly had no morally unrestrained *animalitas* in mind.

The experience of Auschwitz is so central to the understanding of morality that Adorno (1966) reformulated Kant's categorical imperative: "One must think and act in such a way that Auschwitz is not repeated, that nothing similar happens" (p. 358). One must measure Jung and Heidegger by this standard and note a lack of engagement with and empathy toward the victims of the catastrophe they foresaw. Certainly it is a peculiarity of the conscience that it does not easily endure public displays and public acknowledgments of remorse and guilt, something that even Heidegger (1986c) has analyzed in detail (see p. 237). The voice of conscience is dumb; only one who is silent can hear it. In this respect Heidegger's silence was personally consistent. Jung too was silent, in order to show, "after the catastrophe," that he wanted to speak publicly again with his thesis of collective guilt. However psychologically correct this thesis was, little empathy for the frame of mind of the surviving victims of National Socialism was expressed in it, and Jung publicly took little of the collective guilt on himself.

Although Nietzsche, Jung and Heidegger had recognized the metaphysical, psychological and moral dilemma of our time, they were not immune to succumbing to it. In seeking to fill the yawning void, their intellectual models and concepts were ultimately not free of the grandiosity that Jung (ZS) had criticised as the "deification of mankind." This attitude is most clearly the case in Nietzsche, with his concept of the "superman." In Jung's case, the concept of the Self seems to be inflated into something godlike; when he speaks of the indestructible core of the Self, it is as if the Self is divine and not merely an image of the divine. Finally, in Heidegger's case, we find the advocacy of the *"Führer* principle": the accountability of inferior to superior and the commanding power of superior over inferior. As Jung expressed it, a political *"Führer* principle" of this sort derives from the father-son relationship, and ultimately in its absoluteness from the relationship of God the Father to his human son (see ZS, p.639).

Jung's and Heidegger's engagement with Nietzsche allowed them, in their characteristic indirect, introverted and cryptic way, to come to terms with their entanglement with National Socialism, without coming directly and openly into conflict with its intimidating claims to power. Jung and Heidegger were undoubtedly afraid. Nietzsche, the "uneasy eagle" (Ross 1980), had often secluded himself from his contemporaries, and called out great prophetic words from the distant heights. Jung and Heidegger followed him in this too; after initial extroversion, they quickly retreated from the political arena. But they called out very softly, to a small circle of hearers. Knickerbocker reported a notable episode from this time: Toward the end of their interview, Jung spoke with a patient on the telephone who complained that there was a hurricane in his bedroom that threatened to tear away his feet. "Lie flat on the floor, you're safe there," Jung had advised him. He evidently followed this advice himself.

We do not know whether either Jung or Heidegger suffered with the uncounted victims and the indescribable sufferings of contemporaries, because neither expressed himself publicly on this topic. However, both were guided by the example of Nietzsche's own distress: he had stamped the suffering subject with the image of the "madman." Heidegger (1977) referred to Nietzsche in 1943, at the deepest point of war, destruction and Holocaust. "Perhaps we recognize that neither the economic, nor the sociological, nor the scientific and technical perspectives suffice in thinking about what is happening in these times. What is given to our intellects to think is not any deeply hidden underlying meaning, but something nearer at hand, that we have constantly overlooked, precisely because it is so near at hand. To pay attention to this, and learn from it, it is enough for us to think for once of what the madman says about the death of God, and how he says it. Perhaps now we will not be so hasty that we fail to hear … that the madman "inaudibly cries: I'm searching for God! I'm searching for God!" (p. 266).

Jung's preoccupation with the image of the divine in our time was intended not only to leave open a place for God in the inner soul. The image of the divine is so tightly bound up with *moralitas* that it cannot even be decided whether *moralitas* depends on the existence of an image of the divine or whether the image of the divine depends on *moralitas* (see Kant 1990, Jonas 1987). In the field of tension between *rationalitas* and *animalaitas, moralitas* appears to be indispensible as a regulating agency. It alone can control the powerful libidinous and aggressive instinctive drives. *Rationalitas*, so proud of itself and so fond of itself, does not notice that it is ruled by *animalitas*. But *moralitas* is weakened because it can be sustained no longer by the *rationalitas* of the regulating agency of a monotheistic God who sets moral norms and enforces their observance. This agency proves to be a discriminating and above all precarious accomplishment of civilization, whose loss is associated with great dangers for our civilization.

The dilemma of the human subject in modern times appears insoluble: "God is dead!" and we cannot turn back to a naive faith. The full scope of the dilemma, however, is evident only when we bring to mind Jung's analysis: Spontaneously and unconsciously, archaic images of the divine step into the place of the "dead God" of the Judeo-Christian tradition. We find ourselves, as Max Weber put it, in an age of secularized polytheism (see Safranski 1997, p. 327). But this development is associated with a regression in *moralitas.* Internally, there comes a regression in collective ethics, a reduction of individual responsibility and guilt. Externally, the image of the "enemy" rules and, in relation to the enemy, other moral maxims are worth nothing.

Against these particularist tendencies, Jung set the representation of the *unus mundus.* He accepted Nietzsche's criticism of a "God only of the good," and sought to overcome this one-sidedness. A God who is also a God of evil; this is the answer to Job. Job kept his faith, and overcame the division between an exclusively good God and evil in the form of Satan. At the very end of one of the bloodiest centuries in human history, Jung's religio-psychological assessment, with its warning of the dangers of inflation from the archaic divine images of the collective unconscious, represents a not insignificant contribution to understanding and overcoming the destructive crises of our time.

Translated from the original German by Doug M. Jones

References

Adomo, T. (1966). *Negative Dialektik.* Frankfurt am Main: Surkamp Verlag.
Adorno, T. W. & Horkheimer, M. (1969). *Dialektik der Aufkärung.* Frankfurt am Main.: S. Fischer
Arendt, H. (1986). *Elemente und Ursprünge totaler Herrschaft.* München: R. Piper.
Bishop, P. (1995). *Jung's Annotations of Nietzsche's Works: An Analysis.* Nietzsche Studien, Vol. 24. Berlin/New York: W. de Gruyter.
Goldhagen, D. (1996). *Hitlers Willige Vollstrecker: Ganzgewöhnliche Deutsche und der Holocaust.* Berlin: Siedler.
Heidegger, M. (1977). *Holzwege.* Gesamtausgabe Band 5, Frankfurt am Main.: V. Klostermann.
Heidegger, M. (1986a). *Nietzsche: Der europäische Nihilismus.* Gesamtausgabe Band 48, Frankfurt am Main.: V. Klostermann.

Heidegger, M. (1986b). *Nietzsches Metaphysische Grundstellung im Abendländischen Denken.* Gesamtausgabe Band 44, Frankfurt am Main: V. Klostermann.

Heidegger, M. (1986c). *Sein und Zeit.* Tübingen: M. Niemeyer

Jonas, H. (1987). *Der Gottes Begriff nach Auschwitz.* Frankfurt am Main: Suhrkamp.

Kant, I. (1990, zuerst 1793). *Die Religion innerhalb der Grenzen der Bloßen Vernunft.* Hamburg: F. Meiner

Lesmeister, R. (1997). Veterbild und archetypische Strukturierung des Psychischen bei Jung. *Analytische Psychologie, 28-4,* 243-272.

Nietzsche, F., KGW: Kritische Gesamtausgabe Werke (Complete Critical Works). Berlin: de Gruyter.

Rauschning, H. (1973). *Gespräche mit Hitler.* Wien: Europa Verlag.

Ross, W. (1980). *Der ängstliche Adler.* Stuttgart: Deutsche Verlagsanstalt.

Safranski, R. (1994). *Ein Meister aus Deutschland: Heidegger und seine Zeit.* München/Wien: C. Hanser.

Safranski, R. (1997). *Das Böse oder Das Drama der Freiheit.* München/Wien: C. Hanser.

Tann, M. & Erlenmeyer, A. (Ed.). (1993). *Jung, C.G. und der Nationalsozialismus. Texte und Daten.* Deutsche Gesellschaft für Analytische Psychologie. Berlin.Yerushalmi, Y.H. (1992). *Freuds Moses. Endliches und unendliches Judentum.* Berlin: Wagenbach.

Theoretical Issues

The Return of the Prodigal

The Emergence of Jungian Themes
in Post-Freudian Thought*

Barbara D. Stephens

Los Angeles, California, USA
Society of Jungian Analysts of Southern California

Within the past few years the amount of interaction between the Freudian and Jungian communities has increased dramatically. Even though Jung pioneered professional dialogue among practicing therapists of different orientations, until recently Analytical Psychology in the United States has largely kept itself professionally ghettoized. The recent cross-fertilization demands a re-examination of established theory in order to establish a language sufficiently common to permit meaningful dialogue.

The respective psychologies of Jung and Freud are assumed to rest on different sets of assumptions, which are not washed away by apparent similarities in clinical approaches (see Nagy 1991). Thus, when we hear something Jung himself might say from the podium of a Psychoanalytic Congress, or a Freudian concept at this Congress, it may or may not indicate a shift in theoretical sub-structure. A number of Jungian concepts are emerging at the so-called "cutting edge" of psychoanalytic clinical theory; these concepts form an interrelated network. If one of them becomes a premise in a theoretical argument or a tenet in a belief system, the others will fall into a ready-made place around it.

Hegemony of Subjective Experience

After 1913, Jung's thoughts about reality moved steadily into a subjectivist stance. What began as a psychological value of an attitude that takes inner experience as objective, became an episte-

* An unabridged version of this paper has been published in *The Journal of Analytical Psychology*, 44-2.

mological assumption that the only certainty we have is our knowledge of the inner world. We are in effect imprisoned or – positively stated – enshrined in the symbolic realm of the psyche. Jung labeled this subjectivist view the "symbolic approach;" it is seeping into the Freudian community as an intersubjectivist "story" gets told.

Owen Renik (1993), a San Francisco psychoanalyst, holds that "it is *impossible* for an analyst to be in an objective position *even for an instant*" since "analytic technique, including listening, is *inescapably* subjective" (p. 560). Given that one of Jung's pioneering concepts is the existence and effect of the "objective" layer of the psyche, the archetypes – a subjectivist epistemology – seems a paradox. It is less paradoxical, but none the less problematic, if we consider that Jung was not as interested in the source of knowledge but in one's way of knowing the source. Since the archetypes cannot be known in themselves, but only in their manifestations, debate about their existence is considered as irrelevant for clinical practice as the existence of an unconscious was to the debates of the 1960s between behaviorists and depth psychologists. Their thesis went something like this: "We are not claiming that the unconscious doesn't exist; we're simply saying we don't need to posit its existence to account for etiology and treatment outcome."

This basic argument cannot be ignored as the Jungian and Freudian traditions move toward possible reconciliation. Recently the argument took an interesting form when Richard Noll (1994, 1997) attacked the validity of Jung's claims regarding the archetypes and issues of transcendence. His theses are still under heated discussion and careful analysis (see Stephens 1995, 1997; Shamdasani, 1998). Whether his evidence and method of argumentation will hold up to scrutiny does not detract from the importance of his earlier call for a "critical examination of Jung's professed 'evidence' for a 'collective' unconscious" (Noll, 1993).

Is any objectivity possible in a subjectivist universe? Structure-generating objectivity can exist in the context of the repeated performative language acts uttered in an "ethical discourse," where both analyst and patient submit their contributions to the judgment of the other. Throughout his life Jung was occupied with the function of symbols and their relation to an objective psychological reality. Psychoanalysts (e.g., Havens 1998) are now exploring this venue of objectivity through language symbols.

Centrality of the Subject and its Ineffable Nature

In a subjectivist universe the object of inquiry becomes the I-of-discourse, the Subject, with "experience-near" and "experience-distant" phenomena constituting the raw data of investigation rather than discrete drives and traits. It seems clear that the Subject has moved toward the center of psychological investigation, pushing ego-oriented investigations to the margins of psychoanalytic inquiry. Because of Strachey's de-spirited translation of Freud, among other cultural variants, I think it took non-German-speaking Americans much longer than Europeans to break through the limitations of ego psychology and begin conceptualizing in terms of the Freud's original *Das Ich*, the I. Lacan's (1977) decentering of the ego, Winnicott's (1960) "true self," Kohut's (1977) "bipolar self," Bion's (1965) "O" each move the concept of the self closer to an intensely relational process which is ultimately ineffable.

At a recent psychoanalytic conference in Los Angeles, one of the presenting analysts spoke of the "the God within" to describe his evolving concept of Subject/Self. The implications of such a conceptualization is exciting to ponder. "Vocatus atque non vocatus Deus aderit," Jung carved into the stone doorpost of his home, "Bidden or unbidden God will be present." His notion of the Self as *a priori* – a God-image – with an ability to unify and provide meaning are embedded in that carving. Jung had entered the room even if his theoretical presence went unnoticed and unacknowledged.

New language forms often emerge as theorists struggle to articulate an inner vision. This phenomenon seems to be simply the instinctual vestige of marking one's territory linguistically, but I see it more as a kind of intra-subjective dialogue. Language becomes more abstract and idiosyncratic in parallel with the deeper meanings that such theorists apprehend and attribute to the Self. They become, in effect, theoretical "poets," attempting to talk us into an experience of the hidden and ineffable nature of the Self. I see the current "poetry" as moving us toward an experience of our interdependent humanness which is not captured by our current use of such terms as self, selfobject, subject, object, other.

Philosophers, such as Francis Jacques (1991) are beginning to speak about the person, defining it as a "structural and dynamic integration of relations," whose reality is "irreducibly intersubjective" (p. 332). A person is not something that is, but something that is produced through dynamic relations on three levels of discourse:

the I, who has the capacity to receive the you of someone's address – who is me as a spoken you – and the he/she, a "third" as object of discourse. This "third" is an absent or distant Other, a relationship to which is essential for personal identity. "There is an unbreakable link between the three agencies of discourse – I, you and he/she. The result is a structural unit of enormous logical complexity, the person." (p. 30). Emmanuel Levinas, also a French philosopher, argues that the ground of our being as persons includes a fundamental ethical responsibility with alterity, otherness. By "having-the-other-in-one's-skin," I am inspired, and "this inspiration is the psyche" (1989, p. 104). The rich symbolism of a trinitarian concept of person whose identity is inseparable from its ethical responsibility to Otherness may offer analysts from both communities fertile territory for cooperative investigation of clinical material.

Role of Countertransference as Primary Data in Analysis

In a subjectivist universe, issues of countertransference move to center stage. A source of primary data about the patient is the analyst's overt and covert behaviors, once considered the psychic contagion of the patient's projected material. In 1946 Jung stated that by bringing activated unconscious content to bear upon the analyst, the patient "constellates the corresponding unconscious material [in the analyst]. ... Doctor and patient thus find themselves in a relationship founded on mutual unconsciousness" (CW16, 364). Still in his collaborative years with Freud, Jung initiated training analysis to help prepare analysts for the powerful reciprocal effects of this inter-penetrating psychic system.

When countertransference was addressed in the early Freudian community, it was considered a distortion in the analyst's clinical acuity and a personal psychological problem. More accurate clinical vision could be restored by a return to the analyst's own analytic work. Although some pioneering work on countertransference was done in the 1950s and 1960s, its significance as a source of valuable clinical material began to take hold only in the 1980s.

In 1991, Theodore Jacobs, a training analyst at the New York Psychoanalytic Institute, published a text on countertransference, *The Use of the Self.* It became a lightning rod for both the Freudian and Jungian communities. The title itself indicates a number of shifts that had already taken place in the Freudian community. A broader concept of the self has become more of an organizing principle than the ego, and countertransference is no longer a "problem;" it is a therapeutic resource. Jacobs wrote:

> *Although countertransference figures prominently in these pages, my concern is not with this phenomenon in a narrow sense. It is, rather, with the experiences of the analyst as they resonate with, comment on, and illuminate those of the patient. It is, in short, about the way two people communicate in the analytic situation and about how the analyst, by listening to himself, can better understand the communication (p. xxiii).*

The Jungian resonance in Jacobs' work was noticed. He and Renik were invited to present clinical material at an international conference sponsored by *The Journal of Analytical Psychology.* Jacobs' views on countertransference and its implications for redefining the "subject" of an analytic process also struck a chord in the Freudian community. An entire issue of the journal *Psychoanalytic Inquiry* (Vol. 17, 1997) was devoted to essays inspired by Jacobs' book. Referring to transactional phenomena, Jacobs indicated that a number of his colleagues were viewing it "in ways substantially different from those of their predecessors in both the classical and interpersonal school." He was quick, however, to add a caveat. It does not mean they are reformulating their traditional "view of human development [and] the role of the drives. ... Nor do they consider interpretive work at the interpersonal level to constitute the core of the analytic process" (p. 222). Jacobs says nothing directly about the archetypal dimension of the transference, nor is Jung quoted or referenced. But again, the surface dimensions of the landscape may indicate deeper theoretical shifts which have yet to emerge. It is one thing to give voice to new analytic experiences; it is another to find linguistic metaphors, appropriate to the Freudian tradition, to contain it.

The Nature and Transformational Aspects of Primitive Mental States

The shift in emphasis from the consideration of personality as a singularity to that of a cohesive multiplicity is captured partially in Goldberg's (1980) comment that "person" is a collective noun. As the world of theology was moving toward the concept of God as "verb" (Daly 1973), the analytic world of psychology was moving toward the concept of human as "nouns," subjects of psychological sentence-building revealing different layers of meaning and internal "grammatical" complexity. Jung referred to the manifestation of these nouns as "splinter psyches" (CW8, 202), collections of affect-images "which behaved like independent beings" within the personality (CW8, 253).

While psychoanalysts have not embraced the concept of a collective unconscious as explanatory of the formation of autonomous personality aspects, Jung's description of a complex is similar in tone to such clinical theorists as Bion (1957, 1958), Milner (1952, 1969, 1987) and the developmental research evidence of Stern (1985), each of whom describes aspects of the personality that are both autonomous and, at their core, unknowable. Just as there are Freudians who eschew any notion of a transcendent archetype as source material for complexes, there are Jungians who are repelled by the reductionism of some object-relations theorists. Despite some behaviors to the contrary in his practice, theoretically Jung embraced both dimensions, warning against the dangers of weighting them unequally. The fact that "history" has split them apart theoretically and clinically into various "schools" (Samuels 1985, 1996; Siegelman 1994) does not affect the integrity of Jung's original archetypal affect-imago object-relations psychology.

When a complex of the collective unconscious invades the ego, Jung described effects which sound similar to "unimaginable storms" (Jackson & Williams 1994) or the primitive states described by such analysts as Bion (1957), Meltzer (1968), Ogden (1989), and Rosenfeld (1971). For Jung, primitive states and defenses are not connotative – descriptions that point to realities beyond themselves – but denotative: explanations that hold an encapsulated meaning yet to be discovered. Steiner's (1993) descriptions of "psychic retreats," and the process of extricating oneself from those "perverse refuges" by "facing the reality of what belongs to the object and what belongs to the self" are established through the experience of loss" (p. 9) and the process of mourning, reminiscent of Jung's description of the pain and mortification incurred when portions of the ego are sacrificed for consciousness.

The Role of Desire and its Purposive Direction
Toward a Dual Experience of Self

That the intense relationship of Freud and Jung split over the concept of human desire is like an irony of black comedy. While the choice of the subdued Latin term "Libido" may have been necessary to the dialogue of a scientific community steeped in Victorian mores, in contemporary times the term "Desire" seems more popular and phenomenologically accurate. Libido/Desire is the energy that drives the psyche, the fuel that moves human thought and action. For Freud, Desire was fundamentally sexual in nature; for Jung it was psychic, a naturally occurring human purposive force, a will directed, not just toward specific objects, but toward the expansiveness of human consciousness and cultural development. In a Jungian universe an energic-finalistic perspective, rather than a causal-mechanistic one, fashions the story of relations between objects, the intensity of the energy flow, and the means by which the movement of desire is transformed into human drama. In my view this perspective is beginning to inform much of contemporary post-Freudian thought. The emphasis is not on discrete entities of analyst and analysand, but on the relationship, the dynamic linkage between them with their potential for "emergence." A term borrowed from recent explorations in the philosophy of science and neurobiology, emergence refers to a process whereby creative and novel forms erupt from within a system of multiple elements relating in multiple non-linear ways (see Tresan 1996). The process is subsequently self-generative, and moves toward more complex patterns of organization. The Jungian resonance is clear. In an ironic twist, Freud and Jung may be meeting once again at the place of Desire, ushered in by the scientists of biology and neuroscience.

Ultimately the purpose of Desire is to move a person toward consciousness through a dual experience of Self as immanent and transcendent. In Jungian psychology the transcendent Other is the archetypal order which is simultaneously immanent, embedded deeply within the human psyche and accessed through the symbolic. Some members of the psychoanalytic community seem particularly interested in exploring the clinical implications of myth and symbol (see Eigen 1998; Grotstein 1997). Only time will tell whether that exploration takes them all the way to Jung's perspective on the symbolic.

The Nature and Function of Symbols

The early dialogues between Freud and Jung about the nature and function of symbols illustrate a series of increasingly intense verbal misreadings, with each man pushing the other toward positions and consequences that neither fully gasped at the time. Jung wanted Freud to push beyond a semiotic vision of unconscious material which resorts to interpretations based only on phenomena previously known or made available through memory recall, free association or reconstruction toward a more fluid, ambiguous, yet purposeful vision, whose "chief importance lies in the fact that it has meaning for the actual present and for the future" (CW4, 674). Ironically that dialogue seems less intense between the two descendant groups today than within the Jungian "family" itself – which tends to reduce the symbolic value of the differing "schools" labeled classical, developmental, and archetypal to the categorization of specific theoretical ideas or modes of practice – a semiotic reading – rather than search for the deeper meaning of the theoretical eruptions and professional splits.

For Jung, true symbols had the power to connect the realms of conscious and unconscious, usher in meaning and potentially heal a damaged psyche, if they were embodied in human experience. Jung was critical of esoteric symbolic interpretations, which some consider the mark of a "Jungian," whose meanings were so equivocal that any correspondence between the symbol and real experience is lost. A symbol is not a representation as imaginal or artistic form, but something that "rises in the depths of the body" (CW16, 363). It is a representation of activity which has the capacity to give and promote life because it transforms unconscious energy into conscious experience. A word, an idea, a gesture, an image, an affect can function as a symbol capable of leading the analytic couple to a discovery of meaning and underlying developmental intention. A symbolic approach is evident in the work of such psychoanalysts as: Marion Milner, Wilfred Bion, Francis Tustin, Joyce MacDougal, Julia Kristeva, Thomas Ogden, Michael Eigen, Ted Jacobs and James Grotstein. Theoretical and personal differences aside, these clinicians approach analytic work as an exploration of unknown territory whose "maps" will be produced as the paths are traveled. Based on their published case material, I suspect they would all chorus Jung's refrain: "Each new case that requires thorough treatment is pioneer work, and every trace of routine then proves to be a blind alley. ... [It] is a most exacting business and sometimes it sets tasks which challenge not only our understanding or our sympathy, but the whole man" (CW16, 367). The symbolic approach is compatible with clinicians whose posture as analysts seems more person-driven than theory-driven.

On the surface it seems as if Freud and Jung have different ancestral lineages: Freud emerging from the physicalist group of Viennese neurobiologists and Jung from the more spiritualistic traditions of his psychiatric training in Switzerland. But beneath that surface, embedded in the clinical implications of their writings, may lie a fraternal professional twinship which, for a time, both recognized in the passion of their relationship (see Stephens 1998). They backed away from the potential implications of that first sighting and built separate kingdoms. In the final months of their relationship, Freud asked Jung a question: "The indestructible foundation of our personal relationship is our involvement with psychoanalysis ... Shouldn't we go on building?" (FJ, p. 304). Almost a century later, their clinical descendants may have begun to discover how we could.

The Prodigal Returns

Over the years, as I have heard Freudian language take on a more Jungian accent, I kept associating it to the image of the Biblical "prodigal," not the wasteful son of the Christian gospels but a more ancient meaning. The term prodigal is from the Latin *prodigere*, meaning to drive away.

The Jewish Bible describes the banishment of several sons: Cain, Ishmael, Esau, Joseph. My association was to Esau, the son of Isaac. The story is relevant to the emergence of Jungian themes in post-Freudian thought. Esau and Jacob were twin sons of Isaac and Rebekka. While sharing the same genetic inheritance, they were strikingly different on the surface. Esau was covered by a "hairy mantle" and enjoyed the "hunt." Jacob was smoothed-skinned and preferred the activities of the base camp. As the first born, Esau was in line for all the benefits of patrilineal descent. One day in his young adulthood Esau returned home from a hunt on the point of starvation. Jacob offered to trade him food for his privileged birthright. Esau accepted. Later, through trickery instigated by Rebekka, Jacob – disguised in goat-skins to resemble Esau's hairy body – fooled an aged, blind Isaac into passing to him the paternal blessing, another sign of privileged descent. Jacob now had it all, the birthright and the blessing. Esau wept with sadness and raged in fury. Rebekka sent Jacob away to protect him from Esau's suspected revenge. Years passed. Jacob, now a wealthy man, was returning to his ancestral home accompanied by his entourage. To do so, he passed through land controlled by Esau, who had similar wealth and power. Jacob sent a messenger laden with gifts, to seek Esau's permission to enter the land.

After the Freud-Jung split the two "brothers" went their separate ways. Each built his respective theoretical house, which flourished and produced – through multiple "wives"/disciples – a variety of lineages. There are Esau-Jacob dramas between our houses as well as in each among the lineage groups. They center around the creation of new ideas with accompanying problems of power. In any large family there is often fierce competition and envy about who gets to tell the "real" family story. The lineage group that gets to tell it is the one blessed by the father.

Jacob was the last of the patriarchs, the third generation after Abraham and Isaac. As Biblical scholar Aviva Zornberg (1995) points out, the "essential, dramatic directions have been plotted by his father and grandfather. ... What is left for Jacob to do? ... The role of the third generation is clearly the most complex, because in a sense everything has already been done" (p. 237).

Commenting on creativity across generations, literary scholar and critic Harold Bloom (1975) suggests that to be born later is a "crippling" experience. One cannot avoid what has already been said; one suffers from the dilemma of having been preceded. It is as if in speaking "one is not so much a man speaking to men as a man rebelling against being spoken to by a dead man (the precursor) outrageously more alive than himself." The creative thinker "dare not regard himself as being late, yet cannot accept a substitute for the first vision he reflectively judges to have been his precursor's also" (p. 19). The way out of this dilemma and to be free with one's creative thoughts is to "misread" the text. Original re-interpretations necessarily involve falsifications of the work of one's precursors. This "willful re-interpretation of all reality" must involve such misreading, because "every strong reading insists that the meaning it finds is exclusive and accurate" (pp. 69-70). In effect, one steals a birthright, or betrays through "misreading," which is paradoxically one's own vision. To "read strongly" the texts of our predecessors, Jung and Freud, we must find a way to be both faithful and "false," to submit to instruction and rebel, if we are to avoid being a mere replica (see Zornberg 1995, p. 239).

The Freudian community is just ending its third generation. We in the Jungian community are just beginning it. The impulse to misread is high in both camps, but perhaps even higher in ours. This is the generation that will push harder on its boundaries to find territory, within or outside the ancestral camp, to claim as its own. The creative misreadings may take both analytic communities to a more fully-developed theoretical base which combines the richness of both traditions in its clinical manifestations. Within our respective communities there are those who so fear a misreading that exclusionary lines are drawn around texts, which tend to give them a dangerous religious quality. Like Jacob, the communities fear the tribe will be decimated and the flocks scattered when the theoretical Esau arrives. Our attitude toward the approaching Esau depends upon our attitude toward the creativity of misreadings. Are they welcomed or feared? We return to our story.

Jacob looked up and saw Esau, accompanied by 400 men, coming to great him. He divided his camp in two, pushing those most beloved well to the rear. He moved out in front to greet his brother, respectfully bowing low to the ground until he reached him. What happened next is one of those dramatic scenes which has kept biblical sages pondering for centuries. "Esau ran to greet his brother. He embraced him, and falling on his neck, he kissed him, and they wept" (Genesis 33:4). In response to all the gift offerings and displays of obeisance, Esau responded: "I have enough, my brother; let what you have remain yours." The brothers are now equals, each with his own family and goods.

So who is the "prodigal" of depth psychology? That depends upon your family affiliation. Jung is the prodigal son of the Freudian community Since his break with Freud, Jung has been excluded from psychoanalytic discourse, banished as a clinically irrelevant "mystic" who has largely remained "unread lest the contagion of his thoughts be transmitted and his influence infect the orthodox" (Gallant 1996, p.3). But in some Jungian circles, things Freudian suffer the prodigal's fate and for the same reason, fear of contaminating the theoretical family or, worse, killing off its members on his return.

Every analogy limps compared to its original referent. To see the biblical twins, Esau and Jacob, as separate parts of ourselves is acceptable but to see them even remotely comparable to Freud and Jung is beyond the ken of some descendants of both tribes. They reason that, unlike Jacob and Esau, their striking outer differences confirm rather than mask separate progenitors. They may share a conceptual heritage but they are not seen as birthed from the same psychological or philosophical womb. Without an opportunity for an extended fraternal visit in which to explore the depth of our respective clinical work, it might be wiser to suspend final judgment about the commonality of genetic material, no matter how sound the philosophical arguments.

The emergence of Jungian themes in post-Freudian thought and Freudian themes in Jungian thought reminds me of a caesura. In music, a caesura is a pause or breathing at a point of rhythmic division in a melody. Until recently the Freud/Jung split has been treated as a caesura of birth, an irreparable cutting off of one body from another. However, I think a musical caesura is a more apt metaphor. As we take time conjointly to "breathe" and examine the nuances of our respective analytic work, rhythms of deeper, more common themes may be heard. Our "split" may represent two strong rhythmic elements in a long harmonic melody not yet played as a whole musical score. The separated Jung/Freud families may or may not decide to travel together, but in the meantime they have at least met again on the road. Perhaps if we consider our divergence the Otherness which demands a posture of ethical responsibility and courageous exposure, our meeting on the road will result in an embrace that significantly enriches our "songs and stories" as clinicians and persons.

References

Bion, W. (1957). Differentiation of the psychotic from the non-psychotic personalities. *International Journal of Psycho-Analysis, 38*, 266-77. Reprinted in *Second Thoughts*. London: Heinemann, 1967.

Bion, W. (1958). Attacks on linking. *Internationa Journal. of Psycho-analysis, 40*, 308-15. Reprinted in *Second Thoughts*. London: Heinemann, 1967.

Bion, W. (1965). *Transformations*. London: Heinemann.

Bloom, H. (1975). *A Map of Misreading*. New York: Oxford University Press.

Daly, M. (1973). *Beyond God the Father*. Boston: Beacon Press.

Eigen, M. (1998). *The Psychoanalytic Mystic*. Binghamton, NY: S. Freud Romanian Translation & Publication Fund.

Gallant, C. (1996). *Tabooed Jung: Marginality as Power*. New York: New York University Press.

Grotstein, J. (1997). Klein's archaic Oedipus complex and its possible relationship to the myth of the labyrinth: Notes on the origin of courage. *Journal of Analytical Psychology, 42*, 585-611.

Havens, L. (1998). Is psychoanalysis an experimental procedure? *Psychoanalytic Quarterly, 67-2*, 295-308.

Jackson, M. & Williams, P. (1994). *Unimaginable Storms: A Search for Meaning in Psychosis*. London: Karnac.

Jacobs, T. (1991). *The Use of the Self*. Madison, CT: International Universities Press.

Jacques, F. (1991). *Difference and Subjectivity: Dialogue and Personal Identity*. New Haven/London: Yale University Press.

Kohut, H. (1977). *Restoration of Self.* New York: International Universities Press.

Lacan, J. (1977). *Ecrits*. Alan Sheridan (Trans.). New York: Norton.

Levinas, E. (1989). *The Levinas Reader*. S. Hand (Ed.). Oxford/Cambridge: Blackwell.

Masson, J. (1984). *The Assault on Truth*. New York: Farrar, Straus & Giroux.

Meltzer, D. (1968). The relation of anal masturbation to projective identification. *International Journal of Psycho-Analysis, 49*, 396-401. Reprinted in *Sexual States of Mind*. Perthshire: Clunie Press (1973), 99-106.

Milner, M. (1952). Aspects of symbolism in comprehension of the not-Self. *International Journal of Psychoanalysis, 33*, 181-195.

Milner, M. (1969). *The Hands of the Living God*. New York: International Universities Press.

Milner, M. (1987). *The Suppressed Madness of Sane Men: Forty Years of Exploring Psychoanalysis*. London: Metheun.

Nagy, M. (1995). The truth of the matter. *The San Francisco Jung Institute Library Journal, 14*-2, 25-28.

Noll, R. (1994). *The Jung Cult: Origins of a Charismatic Movement*. Princeton, NJ: Princeton University Press.

Noll, R. (1997). *The Aryan Christ: The Secret Life of Carl Jung*. New York: Random House.

Ogden, T. (1989). *The Primitive Edge of Experience*. Northvale, NJ/London: Aronson.

Ogden, T. (1990). *The Matrix of the Mind: Object Relations and the Psychoanalytic Dialogue*. Northvale, NJ: Aronson.

Rosenfeld, H.A. (1971). A clinical approach to the psychoanalytic theory of the life and death instincts: An investigation into the aggressive aspects of narcissism. *International Journal of Psycho-Analysis, 52*, 169-78.

Samuels, A. (1985). *Jung and the Post-Jungians*. London/Boston: Routledge & Kegan Paul.

Samuels, A. (1996). Jung's return from banishment. *Psychoanalytic Review, 83*-4, 469-489.

Shamdasani, S. (1998). *Cult Fictions*. London/New York: Routledge.

Siegelman, E.Y. (1994). Reframing "reductive" analysis. *Journal of Analytical Psychology, 39*-4, 479-496.

Steiner, J. (1993). *Psychic Retreats*. London/New York: Routledge.

Stephens, B.D. (1995). Review of Richard Noll's "The Jung Cult." *Psychological Perspectives, 31*, 142-145.

Stern, D. (1985). *The Interpersonal World of the Infant*. New York: Basic Books.

Tresan, D.L. (1996). Jungian metapsychology and neurobiological theory. *Journal of Analytical Psychology, 41*-3, 399-436.

Winnicott, D. (1949). Hate in the countertransference. *International Journal of Psycho-Analysis, 30*:69-75.

Zornberg, A. (1995). *Genesis: The Beginning of Desire*. Philadelphia: Jewish Publication Society.

The Problem of Evil in Postmodern Reality

Roman Lesmeister
Hamburg, Germany
Deutsche Gesellschaft für Analytische Psychologie

How can one speak of evil in a psychologically meaningful way at the end of the twentieth century? I am not referring to the manifestation of evil but rather to some possible attitudes and their respective problems. My focus is on the question to what extent Jung's archetypal approach is suitable for establishing a psychologically meaningful discourse on evil.

"Evil" is not a genuinely psychological concept and especially not a depth-psychological/psychoanalytic one. The concept has its roots in the doctrine of morals, that is, ethics. Hence, it is based traditionally either in moral philosophy or moral theology. When we ask about evil, we cannot start with psychology. I consider it inevitable to consider first: what has become of evil since the era of enlightenment and what complicated status adheres to this venerable and demanding concept today. In this endeavor, I limit myself to some ground rules of philosophical discussion, largely because Jung has left this important tradition almost entirely out of consideration in his works, and therefore narrows his field of vision. I hope to demonstrate to which backgrounds of intellectual history Jung's archetypal theory of evil is to be related and onto which lines of thought development his ideas in this matter attach themselves, whether or not he was conscious of this.

The problem with which we are dealing consists in the fact that, approximately since the middle of the nineteenth century, a consistent theory of evil of spiritual-moral quality has not existed. Nietzsche's nihilistic critique put an end to the moral-philosophic and moral-theological convictions that had been common until then. Good and evil were unmasked either as symptoms of an atrophy of instincts driven by fear or as obsolete ideologic disguises for interests of power. At least it seemed that way. Schulte (1991), to whom we owe a superb overview of the career of evil within the time frame of the last two centuries, commented: "European nihilism – starting with the intellectual and artistic avant-garde and all the way into the broad public arena of the pluralistic mass societies – has caused a deep ideological and moral uncertainty as to which terms or moral concepts evil should still be talked about" (p. 324).

However the concept of evil may have been understood, the "nihilistic set-back" has not yet been reversed. The concept went hand in hand with changes in the societal worlds of existence and in the collective consciousness. These changes further drove the erosion of the understanding of evil. Part of the change is the final emancipation of the sciences, especially the natural sciences, from philosophic and theological handicaps, as well as the replacement of moral categories with pragmatic criteria of efficiency and functionality. The change allowed ethics to be interpreted only in the utilitarian manner of a capitalistic, techno-industrial reality.

Schulte (1991) described the results in their combined effect as "verbal neutralization of evil" (p. 323). The meaning of the concept was dispelled; the uncertainty that had been tied to its use was covered by conventions. The discourse on evil remained preserved, nominally, but what was meant by this discourse was less certain than ever and probably aroused less interest than ever. Into the place of a theory of evil stepped substitute formations, among which one can count the attempts, current until today, to reduce evil from an ethical category to biological or psychological factors that are empirically comprehensible: for example, the death drive, pathological types of aggression, and destructive narcissism. Postmodern pluralism and an intensified relativity of values have exaggerated further the difficulties of a concept of evil and have allowed a professional discussion that is marked by a helplessness in the face of evil and by a conspicuous intellectual tiring. "Evil has flagged," said H. Schuller, an expert of philosophic research, in a 1993 issue of *Der Spiegel*, and gains in the dimensions of experience and entertainment. Reflection on evil, however, has not advanced for a long time.

With this verbal neutralizing of evil, two great traditions of philosophy – which had determined the treatment of this topic since the enlightenment – have declined. One of these traditions had its starting point in Kant's (1793) view of radical evil in human nature. To the enlightened turning in the thoughts on morals and moral responsibility, Kant lent a decisive imprint by subjectifying evil without compromise, that is, by incorporating it into the human subject. For Kant, there can be only one origin of evil: the innermost areas of human nature. That is the price to be paid for the anti-metaphysical critique and for the enlightened abolition of other-worldly powers: the devil, and other demons. Kant pushed the replacement of evil into humans much further than is the case in Christian doctrine, where evil originates also in the human, who is stigmatized with original sin but where deliverance by the grace of God remains possible. This turning toward good is excluded by Kant. Consequently, his doctrine of evil falls into an inherent contradiction with the moral optimism regarding progress in the enlightenment. If Jung had taken this point of view, he would have had to take up Kant and not the church as an opponent, as he stubbornly fought to exonerate humankind from sole responsibility for evil.

Viewed from today's perspective, the history of the influence of radical evil in Kant unveils a double character. On the one hand, Kant's idea has set standards that have not lost validity up to the present. Insofar as evil was under serious discussion in the modern age, after the drastic break by the nihilistic critique of the nineteenth century, it was only this subjective evil for which the human being is responsible solely.

On the other hand, Kant's definition of subjective evil is exactly what was lost in the period that followed. Kant did not see a naturally predisposed defect in evil: no biological, anthropological or psychological deformation that governs the subject, more or less, in its motivations and actions. Rather, evil is that which is given, along with an option of freedom of the individual (see Safranski 1997). The human being is able to be evil by having a gift for reason and being free. Only the autonomy of the will, which is based on reason and with which Kant equips the human being, allows one to position oneself outside moral law and thereby to express an ethos which Kant names "radical evil."

In the tone-setting understanding of science of later times, no future was granted to the profound content of Kant's thought. Kant's idea of a capability for evil that is founded in the freedom of will proved to be incompatible with the notion of a universal determinism, be it of a biological or psychological nature, which had become binding in scientific thought since the mid-nineteenth century. The same holds true for the psychoanalytic theories that came from Freud or Jung and that emanate from a far-reaching determination by the unconscious. They do not have at their disposal a convincing concept of freedom of will – despite Jung's tentative approaches – and are little suitable to take up Kant's thought.

With the triumphal march of the nihilistic critique and the materialistic determinism in the natural sciences, a subjectively moral evil founded in the freedom of the subject was hardly imaginable anymore. Consequently, a different conception of evil that had formed as a reaction to Kant since romanticism was entirely discredited. An opposition soon formed against Kant's doctrine of a solely subjective evil that was rooted in human nature: an opposition that regarded Kant's solution to the problem highly unsatisfying. The representatives of the philosophical counterthought were: Franz von Baader, whose thought originated entirely in a Christian understanding of the world, and – above all – the philosophers of objective idealism, George Wilhelm Friedrich Hegel and Friedrich Wilhelm Joseph von Schelling. In Schelling (1809), especially, the old idea of an objective and transpersonal evil – an evil that comes from the outside or is mundane – experienced a philosophically magnificent resurrection and formulation.

One needs to understand why Kant's subjectification of evil and its ontological accommodation in human nature were so unacceptable to Schelling and his comrades-in-arms, whose thought was rooted deeply in a Christian understanding of the world. To conceive of evil as an integral part of the human essence, whose substance cannot be changed, tears open a deep and unbridgeable contradiction to the Christian concept of creation: God would have created something irreparably deficient, damaged, and incomplete in the human being who is supposed to be God's own image. This notion and the light it had to cast onto the nature of the God-creator was not acceptable to a Christian philosophy – as German idealism saw itself.

In the outlined problem lies the reason why the search for a theory of objective evil historically took place, inevitably, within a frame of theodicy: a justification of God in the face of suffering and evil in the world. If Kant was not correct or was not allowed to be correct, then a solution had to be found in which neither God nor the human being, his creation, came off too badly. Evil had to be given a place in the make-up of existence which could lie neither in God – whose perfection in good had to be protected – nor in the human being whose having been created in the image of God had to be preserved. One agreed that the human being could do evil only when the a *priori* conditions had been created on a higher level and a type of cosmic course-setting had taken place.

But this course-setting could not be blamed on the Creator. Then came into consideration a Fall of a higher order: the breaking-away of Lucifer before the break of the human being or the idea of a breaking-away of creation outside time, a creation that was driven away from the will of God by an awakened "self-will." In the majority of cases the different speculative constructions became viewed as failure due to intrinsic contradictions. Apart from that, they would not have had any substance in the face of the scientific, anti-metaphysical, and anti-religious critique of the late nineteenth century. With the large and speculative outlines of Schelling who, at the end of his long life stands like the monument of an extinct era in the rising modern age, the philosophical reflection on the possibility of a theory of objective evil breaks off for an undetermined time.

Jung was the one who took up the thread, broken by Schelling, against the background of the modern age based on a psychoanalysis that views itself as empirical. In a manner not atypical for him, Jung tackled the question of evil without concerning himself with the wounds that his concept had suffered during the intervening discussion. He treated the concept as if it had overcome the radical changes of the value and thought systems since the end of the nineteenth century. He made things easy for himself but kept the door open to say what was important to him.

Jung's contributions to the problem of evil can be found especially in several of his later works (CW11; CW9-II; Let-I & II), not least the exchange of ideas with Victor White. Rather than give an introduction to Jung's theory of evil, it is my intention to develop a certain understanding of what Jung is doing when he claims the existence of an objective (transpersonal) evil in the psyche – indeed, in the Self – and the representation of evil in the intrapsychic image of God. Toward the end of his life, Jung extended this assumption into an ever more encompassing doctrine of psychic and, finally, cosmic totality.

The theoretical apparatus that allowed Jung to assume a transpersonal evil in the Self – almost forces him to such an assumption – is based in the theory of archetypes. One could object that the archetypes describe a psychic reality and that, therefore, any statements on archetypal evil hold an entirely different epistomologic status from the metaphysical concepts of philosophy and theology that I have discussed and which match only by name the empirical-psychological facts of which Jung speaks. Jung often pointed out this essential difference. With all due respect to this conceptual differentiation, I am of the opinion that, when one extends a psychological concept such as the Self to the point where all transcendental matters and all traditional objects of metaphysics and theology find some room within, it does not matter whether one speaks of one or the other. The gnostics, as well, spoke of the Self and meant the world. The impreciseness in Jung's language of his later works, as well as the constant jumping back and forth between psychological and theological concept formations, shows that he could not maintain the differentiation upon which he insisted, or that he did not deem it necessary.

Thus the question is: What was Jung doing when he referred to archetypal evil, and thereby meant an evil that, in a psychic sense, is objective and transpersonal? On the one hand, he did something very antiquated. On the basis of an empirically interpreted psychology of the unconscious, he updated a notion of evil that up until then had been encountered only in metaphysical systems, that since the end of the last century had entirely changed direction, and that had practically lost all advocates outside the realm of theology. Jung's manner of thinking thus corresponds in formal respects entirely to that of his philosophical-theological predecessors, with one difference: that the empirically usable but transcendental concept of the archetype takes the place of the metaphysical instance. It was said earlier that human beings can do evil only because of the existence of a devil. Now it is said that persons are capable of doing evil because an archetypal structural precondition in the psyche predisposes them to do so.

Viewed epistemologically, Jung remains true to the objective-idealistic philosophy. And Jung, as a deeply religious spirit, inevitably had to fall into the tracks of the old debate of theodicy (see Lammers 1994). Here, as well, a far-reaching parallel between Jung and the philosophical tradition stands out in his basic intention as well as his logic of argumentation. With a knowledge of the historical standpoint, the conviction seems conclusive that Jung succeeded where his philosophical-theological predecessors failed on what to them seemed unthinkable anyway: To recognize evil as an autonomous power and to reconcile it with an image of God whose essence is Christian. That is the arch that reaches from the monster fantasy of the 12-year-old all the way to the Job work of the almost 80-year-old.

The significance of this achievement could not have escaped Jung himself. One could say, expressing it somewhat disrespectfully: He managed to save the Christian image of God – or that which he took as such – by means of a psychological back staircase. But the price he paid was high, and it did not bring him applause from those who considered themselves responsible professionally for such questions. In order to push forward to his solution, Jung had to undertake two elementary revisions for whose justification he strove passionately until the end of his life. First, he had to transfer evil into the innermost nature of God which, before him, nobody who still cared about this God had dared to do. That was, in a way, Jung's unintended answer to Kant: not the radically evil in the nature of the human being but rather the radically evil in the nature of God (psychologically stated: in the transpersonal God-image of the Self). But that was not enough, because nobody would have recognized this God as a Christian God. Therefore, Jung had to demonstrate, in his second step, that the Christian image of God in the doctrine of the church is not yet the complete or completely Christian image; that this image of God deals with a still-undeveloped God who remains in the process of development and who still has to integrate his dark side and his inherent evil. The entire dramaturgy of *Answer to Job* (CW11) serves as proof of this dynamic of conflict in the sphere of psychic objectivity that the human ego has not made, according to Jung, but into which it sees itself set.

But all of this constitutes only one side of the phenomenon discussed here. The second idea of Jung is a definition of archetypal (objective) evil with psychological content that is currently important and established in the conscious spiritual situation of the postmodern age. Jung treated good and evil as archetypal principles of the unconscious which, like everything in the Self, form a pair of opposites. But in the unity of the opposites is the fact that they lose their absolutes. They come to lose their rigid boundaries or even become identical with each other. Viewed from a perspective of the unconscious, we cannot be sure that something is not also the exact opposite of its first manifestation. This fundamental vagueness or ambiguity of the inner relationship, thanks to Jung, now holds true especially for the relationship between good and evil and consequently for questions of ethics and the conscience. "There is hardly another psychic phenomenon that brings the polarity of the soul out into the open more clearly than the conscience" (CW10, 844). "The highest and the lowest, the best and the vilest, the truest and the most deceptive things are often blended together in the inner voice in the most baffling way, thus opening up in us an abyss of confusion, falsehood, and despair" (CW17, 319).

Kant is behind the "inner voice" and the "moral law in me." But this voice is no longer unified or unambiguous. There are now two or more voices that no longer allow a reliable orientation. Jung determined that what analytic cognition has proved regarding phenomena of the soul is also true for moral impressions and judgments. When one penetrates the layers of conventional solidification and defensive mastery of anxiety, one arrives especially at ambivalence or ambiguity – characteristics that indicate the work of the unconscious. It now seems that Jung spoke of something that we know very well: a state in the proximity of which the awareness of the present tends more and more to adapt. Ambiguity – a lack of clarity that permeates all spheres of experience – and the irreducible uncertainty of values, boundaries, and areas of validity mark essentially that which sociologists call "postmodern consciousness." Baumann (1995) says:

> *Postmodern consciousness includes the fact that there are problems with insufficient solutions in our personal and social lives, tangled contradictions that cannot be untangled, ambivalences that are more than linguistic blunders crying out to be corrected, doubts that cannot be ruled out of the world through laws, and moral agonies that are not alleviated and especially cannot be healed by any remedies that dictate reason. Postmodern consciousness no longer expects to find the all-encompassing, total, and ultimate formula for a life without ambiguity, without risk, danger, or error, and it is deeply suspicious in the face of any voice that promises otherwise. Postmodern consciousness knows that every localized, specialized, and concentrated procedure, whether effective or not, spoils just as much as it cures if measured by its challenging goal. Postmodern consciousness has reconciled itself with the idea that the confusion of basic human nature will forever remain. This roughly constitutes what one can call postmodern insight. (p. 365)*

One may be surprised to encounter insights and conclusions that could have emanated just as well from Jung's pen but came from a contemporary author who did not count the psychology of the unconscious among his theoretical tools. Jung had a very sensitive and intuitive sensorium for the new experience of reality as outlined by Baumann, which places the subject into significant insecurity without any expectation of ever being released. Jung's relativistic psychology thus moves exactly at the peak of the times, and his contributions to the problem of ethics especially reflect that intellectual atmosphere in which the spiritual situation of the end of the twentieth century expresses itself – even if this atmosphere does not in general refer to archetypal conditions of the human psyche.

We have determined that Jung achieved a considerable balancing act in his thinking about the objective or archetypal evil; that he bridged a large gap across the modern age, because this thinking – and not only regarding the question of evil – has remained so curiously untouched by much of what constitutes the modern age. He bridged the gap by resting on one side on a metaphysical understanding of phenomena of the soul that can be traced back to gnostic roots. Clear and even absolute conditions seem to rule here. Evil is an objective and independent power that is equal to the one of good, is psychically substantiated and ontologized and is integrated into the order of existence, a part of the archetypal image of God in the Self. On the other side, this bridge has its supporting pillars in the spiritual-moral situation of radical change of the postmodern age, an era with an uncertain ending and, if looked at closely, an era whose certainties have all been lost and whose value concepts have gone into free-fall. Suddenly, everything becomes relative and blurred; evil is not necessarily what it seems. It is not a definable quality that can be held fast but rather an evasive fluid, the spirit out of the bottle, Mercury who can adopt thousands of different forms, no two of which need to be identical. As far as I know, Jung has never undertaken a serious attempt to identify the content of evil.

In the context of my observations so far, the question arises: What does the assumption of an objective or archetypal evil, as part of a theory of the collective unconscious, achieve and what status is to be attached to it? An attempt to answer that question must differentiate between empirical and nonempirical areas of validity. From the point of view of the nonempirical validity, the following possible interpretations would be conceivable:

1. Jung's conception of archetypal evil is an element of a normative theory or ethic. This interpretation suggests itself and was also drawn up by Jung himself (see CW10). Erich Neumann (1948) undertook the so far sole systematic continuation of this foundation of a "new ethic" with an archetypal foundation. In my work (Lesmeister 1995) I have shown, however, that Neumann has largely failed in the difficult attempt to derive a new ethical orientation – and

therefore one that takes into account the archetypal relativity of good and evil – from the normative ambiguity of the Self. In this connection, the suggestion of Lammers (1994) to distinguish between "Evil of Myth" and "Evil of History" and to separate thereby the structure of the intra-psychic image of God ("myth") and the question of concrete ethical decisions of behavior ("history") seems unconvincing. One can determine that the formulation of an ethic in the sense of Jung's representation of moral ambiguity is still to come.

2. Jung's conceptions of the archetypal evil and the conception of a Self or image of God that unites opposites are objective, hypostatized forms of representation of the conscious attitude of the occidental human being at the end of the twentieth century. That is, these conceptions are not elements of a scientific theory but of a myth. They constitute the myth of the postmodern frame of mind with the Self or image of God that unites opposites as the symbol or idol of this frame of mind. The ambiguity of the value concepts, the hopelessly entangled contradictions, and the growing impossibility of differentiating good from evil in the face of the gigantic complexity of the conditions of reality find their valid representation in a mythic image about which Feyerabend (1993) could express the dictum on that which has become a leitmotiv of postmodern times: "Anything goes!" In Jung's words, *complexio oppositorum*, anything is possible (CW18, 1640).

3. Jung's concept of archetypal evil is an expression of his effort to revive the dead God of Nietzsche and to reconcile this God with the conditions and requirements of the consciousness of the present – theodicy by psychological means. The representation of a simply good and perfect God is too childish and too simplistic to withstand an enlightened reflection and to be sufficient for the modern individual's demand for autonomy. A God who is not a loving father and onto whom one cannot attach oneself believingly and trustingly but who refers back to one's own responsibility as a being that is broken and full of contradictions, neither insults our intelligence nor our independence and finds more acceptance because, as a human being, one can recognize one's own image in such a God.

4. Jung's concept of archetypal evil serves as a defense in the psychodynamic understanding of the word. One has to consider that his conception could have emanated from the striving to navigate around the troubles and distress that arise from the solely human responsibility for evil. The idea, as Weisstub (1993) critically notes,

can be used to exonerate the subject of its responsibility for destructivity and the consequences thereof. Nevertheless, there is no reason why the phenomena of destruction and cruelty that are known to us should not be entirely attributable to the human ego. Jung's often-raised argument that the extent of the historical reality of evil surpasses all human capacity for responsibility does not represent a bullet-proof objection. The tragic situation of the human being of the modern age conceivably could consist exactly in that, like the magician apprentice of Goethe, the person is capable of creating conditions for being ethically overloaded. Jung refutes this possibility with stubbornness, and sometimes stereotypical argumentation, while allowing the assumption that, for him, factors that are unconscious were pushing for an exoneration of guilt. One can read *Answer to Job* in such a manner as if Jung had said: "It was not I, it was God, it was the Self, it was being," as it would read in Heidegger.

If the concept of archetypal evil is not only to describe an ethical category, if it is not to dissolve into a religious-ideological striving for legitimation, and if it is not merely to be the name for a new myth but is accorded the status of a theoretical concept, then its empirical content must be submitted to test. It would have to be shown that, with the aid of this concept, some phenomena can be understood that would not be understood or would be only partially understood without this concept or with the help of alternate concepts.

It looks as if we have hit the weakest point of construction here. Have we better understood the genesis and dynamics of human beings' committing murderous acts or such indescribable atrocities as in the Bosnian war, if we know that such impulses are based in the archetypal polarity of the psyche? Until now not much effort has been applied to the relationship between Jung's idea of archetypal evil and other concepts of inborn tendencies for destruction as, for instance, Freud's hypothesis of the death wish. One must assume that such suppositions – the archetypal disposition for evil or the death wish – are less suited to explain unique phenomena of destruction and atrocity but rather that their function consists in establishing a certain anthropology or a certain image of the human being. If the readiness for evil is anchored in biology and the archetype, then we cannot get free of it. We are testifying not only to the conditions of the here-and-now but also to the future of humankind. Freud and Jung stand close to each other as representatives of a not necessarily culturally pessimistic but yet decisively culturally sceptical view – a view that is still able to credit itself with just as much evidence at the end of the century as at its beginning. In contrast to Freud's biologically deterministic model, Jung's archetypal approach leaves more room for Kant's interpretation of evil as a capability or power of the subject. Briefly stated: Human beings do evil things not because a dark instinctive happening forces them to it but because they are capable of doing so and because conditions exist that make it seem justifiable to make use of this capability.

Translated from the original German by Yvonne Cherne

References

Baumann, Z. (1995). *Postmoderne Ethik*. Hamburg: Hamburger Edition.
Feyerabend, P. (1993). *Wieder den Methodenzwang*. Frankfurt: Suhrkamp.
Kant, I. (1793). Die Religion innerhalb der Grenzen der blossen Vernunft. In: *Werke in sechs Bänden*, hrsg. v. Wilhelm Weischedel, (Band IV). Darmstadt: Wissenschaftliche Buchgesellschaft, 1983.
Lammers, A.C. (1994). *In God's Shadow: The Collaboration of Victor White and C.G. Jung*. New York: Paulist Press.
Lesmeister, R. 1995). Über-Ich, Stimme des Selbst und depressive Position. *Analytische Psychologie, 26*-1, 1-18.
Neumann, E. 1948). *Tiefenpsychologie und neue Ethik*. Frankfurt: Fischer, 1984.
Safranski, R. (1997). *Das Böse oder das Drama der Freiheit*. Darmstadt: Wissenschaftliche Buchgesellschaft.
Schelling, F. (1809). *Philosophische Unterschungen über das Wesen der menschlichen Freiheit und damit zusammenhängende Gegenstände*. Frankfurt: Suhrkamp, 1988.
Schulte, C. (1991). *Radikal böse. Die Karierre des Bösen von Kant bis Nietzsche*. München: Fink.
Weisstub, E. (1993). Questions to Jung on "Answer to Job." *Journal of Analytical Psychology, 38*-4, 397-418.

Shame as a Teacher:
"Lowly Wisdom" at the Millennium

Ladson Hinton
Seattle, Washington, USA
Jungian Analysts, North Pacific

Can lust for knowledge sometimes be a moral transgression? Are there natural limits to experience? These are ancient questions which never should be ignored. In the contemporary world, the media constantly display an abundance of shadow and evil, with a steady résumé of crime, abuse, ethnic conflicts, and ecological disasters. Technology, with all its benefits, creates an alienating quality of speed and abstraction. The forces of globalization whip the process onward. Under this onslaught, the moral structure of individuals and communities steadily weakens. Is there a basic human wisdom that can provide moral orientation and tell us our limits?

Shame is the emotion of limits, and the price of wisdom. In Milton's *Paradise Lost*, the Archangel Rafael advises Adam to be "lowly wise." The Angel has been telling Adam a great deal about the meaning and purpose of things, and counsels patience. Knowledge will come in time. However, Adam's imagination and curiosity are too much. He eats the apple so that he will know what God knows – now. As a result, Adam and Eve are expelled from the Garden, and know shame for the first time. Shame came into the world to teach us about our relationship to the Self, and about our finitude. Usually, we think of shame as a symptom to be eliminated rather than its being useful or wise.

Shame can be an everyday guide to a humble knowing. Especially in hazardous times of personal and cultural liminality, such wisdom can be an anchor. When crossing new thresholds of awareness, we run the risk of becoming inflated and dangerous. Shame can provide a gradient, so that we do not undertake too much for our own good.

During the modern era the attitude toward shame, and toward emotions in general, has shifted radically. Certainty and perfection have become the ideal. After Descartes, embodied emotion was relegated to – and perhaps became – the unconscious of Western culture. One result of this disownment was the gradual loss of the natural moral bearings of individuals and communities. The Age of Reason has created its dark opposite. Our post-Enlightenment world is pervaded by violence, worship of power, and a shame-haunted narcissism.

In contrast, the Parzival Legend shows that shame functioned well as a guide within an intact, pre-Enlightenment world-view. From a very different perspective, recent scientific discoveries – that specific areas of the brain are specifically involved with shame – also help us to appreciate the innate primacy of shame. These neurobio-logical findings have begun to show the crucial role of shame in the formation of the emotional self.

My view is that the fundamental core of self is emotion and feeling, of which shame can be seen as the archetype, or generic modulator. It shapes our character, our ongoing sense of self. These varying perspectives have the common theme that shame can be, indeed, a guide to humble wisdom. As we create a pathway into the future at the millennium, we need – desperately – such a means of orientation.

Shame is the emotion that most frequently teaches humility and limits. When boundaries are overstepped, we feel shame. The parameters at issue may range from the person and society to the individual and the cosmos.

Practically speaking, we tend to see shame as a painful symptom, something to be done away with as soon as possible. The fact is that we are an unconsciously shame-ridden culture. Many theories of narcissistic and borderline disorders are based on it. Street talk is full of considerations of being "dissed" (disrespected). In the larger picture wars and revolutions, ethnic conflicts, and genocide seem substantially based in shame dynamics (see Hinton 1998; Wurmser 1981).

We tend to speak more of guilt than shame. Guilt is usually about some specific wrong: a hurtful thought or action, generally involving a certain person or situation (see Jacoby 1994; Williams 1993). In guilt, we usually fear some retribution. One can be guilty without doubting one's self-worth. It generally involves only a part of the self, of one's character. With guilt, there is a specific wrong, perhaps an illegal act, but often it can be remedied through some form of penance or penalty.

Shame can be social and somewhat superficial, or it can bring into doubt the very basis of one's own being. In shame, the self may be seen as flawed and inferior (see Morrison 1989). One may feel "mortified" and want to disappear. Its word origins refer to "keeping under cover" (Schneider 1997, pp. 29-30). This emotion is not readily resolved.

Due to "reasonable doubt," an individual might be acquitted formally of a crime. Often, however, the finding of "not guilty" would not resolve the issue for a morally sensitive person. Shame would continue, resulting in a period of self-examination. Such a person might ask, "How could I have been involved in such a thing? What does this say about my character?" For some people, spiritual questions would arise. A shame-provoked sense of finitude can have profound dimensions. Shame is therefore much more than merely social. Indeed, deep shame is often experienced completely alone.

Shame as an "Inferior" Emotion

In modern intellectual history, shame has generally been regarded as a "lesser" emotion. Shame-based cultures – generally non-Western – were seen as manifestations of a "primitive" or a "collective" ethos. Such cultures and communities were portrayed as dominated by a group-consciousness, an "irrational" preoccupation with "face," which constrained individual development. Guilt was propounded as a manifestation of a more advanced type of moral response. The "rational" individual of Western, supposedly guilt-oriented societies, was praised as being at the forefront of cultural evolution (see Shore 1996).

This view of the superiority of guilt was based on the European Enlightenment model of rational perfection as the ideal. From the guilt perspective, right and wrong behavior could be analyzed into neat models, which were followed by "civilized" Western people.

However, logical propositions about right and wrong look sensible only when seen in isolation in the textbooks of moral philosophers. In real human interactions, people do not behave like logical propositions. On the contrary, the French writer Alexis De Tocqueville commented on the prevalence of shame in the nineteenth century America he admired. In ancient Greece, the idealized land of our ancestral spirits, guilt was only a subdivision of shame (see Williams 1993). Anthropologists have shown the great complexity of "primitive" cultures. And the most refined Western cultures have shown themselves to be as capable of "barbarous" behavior as any others.

At this time in Western history, it is the lack of shame that we tend to bemoan as a sign of the decline in communal values. The O.J. Simpson trial was a dramatic, public instance of the difference between guilt and shame. Guilt is formal and legalistic. Shame is personal and cannot be excised by formal verdicts, or even specific penalties or their lack. When shame is missing, we feel that the wrong has not been set right, whatever the formal verdict of "guilty" or "not guilty." Clinically, focus on guilt often leads to superficial discussions with a rational bent. We often say "guilt" when we really mean "shame."

How did shame lose its conscious value in Western culture, and then reappear as a tormenting force in the contemporary psyche? We find important historical clues by examining the origins of the Enlightenment. Toulmin (1990) has researched those times, and brought new perspective to the subject.

The "Age of Reason" did not start with a group of brilliant intellects sitting in their armchairs and seeking a new model of truth. Like all thought, it originated amidst specific social and historical currents. The early seventeenth century, in general, was full of catastrophes. Cromwell wreaked havoc in England. There was a little Ice Age in Europe. Famine resulted in the countryside, and starving people thronged the cities. Apocalyptic pronouncements of the coming end of the world filled the air. Such was the atmosphere surrounding the birth of the "Enlightenment."

Toulmin's researches have brought out new facts about the life of René Descartes himself, who best symbolizes the birth of this world-view. Toulmin discovered that Descartes had close, emotional knowledge of the assassination of King Henry IV of France, and was directly present as an observer during the cruel Thirty Years' War. Descartes was immersed heavily in the most destructive events of his time, and these experiences surely influenced his reactive embracing of a geometric model of truth. *Cogito ergo sum* was a retreat from the bloody contingencies of body and emotion.

Descartes was similar in this to the older Plato, who had been disillusioned with the defeat of Athens and the death of Socrates. Such reactive idealism gave hope in difficult times. Descartes' life experience is conveyed by the epitaph he chose for his tombstone: "He who hid well, lived well" (Damasio 1994, p. 249).

Some Effects of the Enlightenment Model of Truth

Because of a general humility about the limitations of human knowledge, it was unusual to have severe penalties for theological deviations during the Middle Ages (see Toulmin 1990). Later, Francis Bacon and others warned of the dangers of "proud learning." The French philosopher Voltaire wrote on the idea of *portée,* or living within one's grasp or range.

As the Enlightenment ideal took hold, this cautious, humble approach to knowledge was forgotten. The absolute model of truth lent itself to severe forms of religious intolerance. The "parsimony" of science, as applied to religious dogma, translated into absolutism. When the model is geometric perfection there is not much room for messy compromises of theological differences.

The effect of the geometric model of knowledge finally resulted in the decline of religious belief. Myth was debunked as flawed and irrational, and the individual was left increasingly without moral anchors or guidelines. The Cartesian model, springing from a reactive horror against the events of the seventeenth century, took its revenge upon religion itself. Obsession with the rational perfecting of society replaced religion.

The French Revolution incarnated the Enlightenment ideal. All history was to be scrapped, including the months and days of the week. A new, scientific model was to predominate. It was said, for instance, that France would be better off if it lost a third of its population so that the resources could be more equitably distributed! It is not far from this idea to more recent models of revolution, progress, and perfection such as Stalinism, the so-called Cultural Revolution in China, and the genocides in Nazi Germany, Cambodia, and Rwanda.

In our post-Holocaust, post-modern times, we are again raising the questions of the limits of geometric models of truth. Awareness of these limits can lead us back to the tradition of a more tolerant, humble view of knowledge.

When the God-image is not mediated by religious and cultural forms, that energy does not disappear. It falls back into a psyche that already suffers from lack of structural coherence. As a consequence, the energy of the Self pervades the psyche in raw form. That is the present condition, both individually and collectively.

Narcissistic and "borderline" syndromes result when the psyche is overwhelmed with such unmediated energies of the Self. Buffeted by its raw energies, the narcissistic person fluctuates between extremes of grandiosity and inferiority. Inner structures and boundaries are overwhelmed. Since shame is the emotion of boundaries, the consequence is profound shame, along with chronic anxiety over the potential dissolution of the personality.

Borderline individuals represent the extremes of this modern condition. Such people are, for various reasons, susceptible to carrying our cultural projective identifications: the stuff we don't want. Borderline individuals are torn by shame and turmoil; the boiling, unassimilated energies of the Self; the shadows of the modern world. They carry too much for their own good, and, to our discomfort, mirror it back to us.

War, addiction, street crime, and the general decline of moral behavior are, to a substantial degree, desperate reactions to an overload of shame. If we can get "high" for a time, perhaps we can indeed be God, or at least have the illusion of an intact self. If we can humiliate other persons, other communities, or even entire nations, we can pass the shame onto them. A community haunted by shame is more susceptible to authoritarian manipulation; genocidal actions are the most extreme examples.

That we have despoiled our moral world is reflected in our despoliation of nature. As Zoja (1995) has pointed out, we unconsciously know our hubris in these things. We have offended Themis, the goddess of boundaries and limits. At the hidden core of our being we fear retribution through her counterpart, Nemesis. This is where we stand at the millennium.

Parzival: Shame as a Guide on the Path

Some old myths still have a numinous quality for the modern psyche, and make us aware of what we have lost. This seems particularly true for the Grail Legends. In these tales, we can see what it would be like to live in a coherent moral community, where shame is accepted as a teacher. In the poet Wolfram von Eschenbach's *Parzival*, shame repeatedly guides individuals toward the path of individuation and meaning. They welcome shame, because it helps them keep or regain their moral bearings.

One of the most unforgettable events of shaming in literature is Parzival's confrontation by Cundrie before the entire Arthurian court. Just as Parzival has been accepted in joy as a member of the Round Table, Cundrie publicly recounts to the court all Parzival's failures, most especially his failure to ask the questions which would have released the Grail King from his suffering. Parzival had failed in this deeper task because of the superficial shame of social propriety. When confronted by Cundrie, he suffers the deepest level of shame: a failure of one's integrity.

Eschenbach's description of Parzival's reaction to humiliation shows the perspective of those times. In the world of the high Middle Ages, shame was not seen as an inferior concern of conformists, but a guide to the knight who is serving the most sacred purposes. The author doubts whether merely a brave heart and manly breeding can help a person after such mortification. Answering his own questions about Parzival's character, Eschenbach (1980) says: "Nevertheless, he has a further resource, a sense of shame that reigns supreme over all his ways. ... A sense of shame is rewarded in the end by esteem and, when all is said and done, is the soul's crowning glory and a virtue to be practiced above all others" (p. 166).

In thinking of shame as a teacher, it is important to remember that Cundrie, who publicly mortified Parzival, is the first to inform him indirectly about his lost, speckled "shadow" brother, the "infidel" knight Feirefiz. At the marvelous conclusion of the story, it is Cundrie who is revealed as a messenger of the Grail, as well as a sorceress. It is she who proclaims Parzival's destiny as the new Lord of the Grail.

Parzival's assumption of the mantle of shame leads to his redemption and transformation. He is restored to accord with the heavens, with his true destiny as the Grail King. It is of interest to note that Emma Jung and Von Franz (1971) considered the Grail to represent the feeling function. Shame is a powerful teacher; it is clearly the vehicle that can lead to redemption and the deepest sense of integrity. Shame leads Parzival to the Grail of discriminated feeling, the truth of the heart.

The Psychobiological Immanence of Shame

There is a strong biological basis for seeing shame as a teacher. For the first few months of life, the infant is largely dependent on mother's soothing behavior to regulate the ebb and flow of its emotions. When that fails, and the infant is overwhelmed by emotions, one may see a "freezing-up" behavior. The object relations analyst Mel Knight (1998) has speculated that this is an early experience of finitude or shame. The neurobiologist and psychoanalyst Schore (1994), in his pioneering work, has found that an area of the brain specifically involved with shame, the orbito-frontal cortex, matures between 10 and 12 months of age. This shame cortex is connected with memory and inhibitory control, acting as a regulator for the cacophony of infantile affects. Such regulation – the basis of the emerging self – involves internalization of the interaction between self and other. These internal representations begin to act as modulators of affective states. The maturation of this cortex coincides with the growing motility of the child, as it moves toward becoming a more autonomous being. At this age, the child must learn to hear "no," and to inhibit its more dangerously exuberant impulses.

This function is largely right-brain. We know that the brain roughly doubles in size during the first two years of life, due to myelinization. However, there is a death of 15 to 85 per cent of neurons between infancy and childhood. There is a kind of "Darwinian" survival of areas and propensities in the brain. This survival is mediated by local hormonal influences in the brain itself, especially during "open periods" of development, such as Lorenz's imprinting mechanism. The mother, and especially her gaze, directly stimulates or fails to stimulate growth of inhibitory hormones in the evolving brain. This is a highly social, interactive process. The attuned mother is "inside" the infant, "metabolizing" the infant's emotions, literally shaping its brain.

A secure parent, confident of meaning and perspective, gives clear, attuned messages about behavioral and emotional management. Such a relationship is internalized as a stable, coherent structure of the self. Unfortunately, fragmentation of cultural myth seems to have created, over time, increasingly unsure and disconnected parents. Thus, they have become more narcissistic, with increasing problems in managing their own shame and self-esteem. This process has had its effects on the emotional configuration of their children. Over these last centuries, we have actualized increasingly what John Donne described in 1611 at the beginning of the modern age, *An Anatomy of the World*:

> *Tis all in peeces, all cohaerence gone;*
> *All just supply and all Relation:*
> *Prince, Subject, Father, Sonne, are things forgot,*
> *For every man alone thinkes he hath got*
> *To be a Phoenix, and that there can be*
> *None of that kind, of which he is but hee.*

Jung and the Emotional Self

Jung's own early research was on emotions. The Word Associa-tion Test, psychogalvanic skin responses, and his writings on com-plexes were substantially about emotions. He spoke of affectivity being the ground and basis of personality, and wrote that "Emotion is the chief source of consciousness" (CW9-I, 179). He described the highly differentiated subjective sense that human beings have of the interpersonal affective field. We possess this sense like an "instinct," similar to animals.

The nuclear element of a complex is its "feeling-tone," which Jung equated with its intensity of affect (CW5, 19). It is through emotion that the individual sorts out the relative value of inner, symbolic-emotional experiences, and shapes the structure of the personal self. Indeed, Jung said that it is through its feeling-value that the archetype exerts its influence on the "configurations" of our everyday, ongoing life (CW8, 411). Thus, affects have an innate "shaping" tendency, as well being the ground and source of con-sciousness. As Willeford (1987) has written, "The self has an evaluative aspect that has never been sufficiently stressed – and has never been made explicit enough – though Jung had it in mind when he regarded feeling and affectivity as essential qualities of the vital core" (pp. 149-50).

In fact, Jung said contradictory things about the affective spec-trum. Despite his ideas about the affective basis of personality, he made a great deal of the separation between emotion and feeling. He was very eager to preserve feeling as something conscious and rational, and quite different from emotion. In addition, he said that the dynamic, emotional pole of the archetype indeed provides the dynamism, but that the image provides the integrative element. That is, the archetypal image is the basic meaning-giving element, with a nobler role than affect. The wise animal sense of life, patterning through emotion and feeling, usually is not portrayed as the deciding factor in individuation.

In Jung's writings, the affectivity of complexes is frequently depicted as nuisance rather than guide. It is something that "gets in the way." Emphasis on the image as integrative guide for affects – the image originating from the "spiritual" or ultraviolet pole of the archetype – has fostered a tendency for Jungian psychology to "go upwards," away from the earth, away from emotion, body, and the psychobiological self. Thus the Cartesian split of mind and body has continued in Jungian psychology.

This split has manifested as a kind of polarity. On the one hand, the urge for transcendence through the image; on the other hand emotion, shadow, *nigredo*. In much of Jungian psychology, one gets a strong impression that transformation occurs through images of the transcendent, and that the meaningful patterning of life occurs through the "spiritual" or "ultraviolet" spectrum of experience. At its extreme, this leads to a romantic, seductive promise of being healed by the spiritualized archetype. This results in a kind of "symbolic excitement," rather than symbolic experience.

Idealized Image and Faustian Progress

Romancing the symbolic image can lead to a Faustian intoxication with the ideal. For the sake of his fantastic projects, Faust rejected *Sorge* (Care) for the earth. All Western individuals have this seductive myth of Progress somewhere in their psyches. It has expressed itself in the ideology of endless change and revolution. Actual revolution has subsided. Infatuation with the idealized image continues, creating a restless obsession with perfection at the expense of life. Technologies such as the Internet add to the endless possibility of knowing more, having more. We are alienated from Care: the immediate, emotional sense of earthy responsibility. The destruction of the environment continues. The search for a perfect happiness, to which we are entitled, and the pursuit of change race on.

For the sake of a progressive land development, Faust caused the murder of Baucis and Philemon, a gracious old couple who were close to the gods. He experienced no shame or guilt about his deeds.

Jung was plagued by his own Faustian heritage. Over the door at Bollingen, Jung carved: *Philemonis Sacrum – Fausti Poenitentia* (Shrine of Philemon – Repentance of Faust). He saw the Faustian moral problem as the key to the future of the modern world.

Mary Shelley wrote *Frankenstein* as a counter to Faustian romantic excesses (see Shattuck 1996). Can shame cool such collective and individual excess? Are we Faust, or are we Frankenstein? Can shame help teach us "lowly wisdom," so that we welcome Care once more?

Feelings are seen best on a continuum with affects, or as "cooled affects." Feeling presumes the internalized, functional memory of embodied emotional events (see Damasio 1994; Willeford 1987). That is, feelings are based on memories of emotions. The basic "drive" of the emotions is retained in feelings, which gives them their continuing "charge."

These embodied emotions have ways of deciding which are more efficient than thinking. Often rather automatic and out of conscious awareness, they are usually quite orderly. They are regular, functioning parts of our personal self-structures, shaping our ongoing internal and communal lives. This gives us a sense of cohesion, and is the basis of our continuing background awareness of self as process.

The emotional self is the original core of self. There is certainly not much syntactic communication in this early emergent self, when there seem to be only tones and vestiges of images. Shame becomes our teacher, with regard to primary shaping of character and acculturation. Autonomous self control and self-direction are not possible before the shame cortex develops. From the classic psychoanalytic view, renouncing of childhood omnipotence and the great leap away from primary narcissism take place during this early period when the shame cortex matures (see Schore 1996).

Without affects we would not be alive, since we would not connect with anything. We cannot think ourselves into having a self. Indeed, we would have no desire to do or think. Affects have direction and connection; they connect us to both self and others. In addition, the body-self's ongoing "background" feeling of aliveness is crucial to any vital sense of presence in the world. Thought and image are not independent entities, but are intertwined with emotion from the start.

Indeed, most of the ongoing, sorting and shaping processes of life are based in emotional feedback loops from the body. For the most part, embodied emotions and emotional memories sort things out for us in a very efficient way, before we even think about our choices. Intellectually intact individuals who have suffered neurological damage, which cuts them off from embodied emotion, have profoundly flawed judgment. These findings contribute a clear limit and humbling perspective to the inflated pretensions of "pure" thought.

Shame as the Archetype of Feeling

If "cooled affects" decide value, as feelings, and this shapes the structure of the personal self, what cools the affects? Shame, itself an emotion, would seem to be the "cooler," inhibitor, or dampener of the other emotions. Stewart (1996) suggested that shame is the archetype of feeling. He also viewed shame, and feeling in general, as crucial to a stable and viable culture. Indeed, he speculated that shame evolved directly as a function of the social needs of the mammalian species. As the generic modulator of emotion into feeling, shame enables us to be participating members of a moral community.

Shaping and maintaining a coherent self is an ongoing, valuing function. Its role is discrimination: the "regulation" or "taming" of affects into the function of "feeling." One could see this on a gradated scale of intensity, ranging from powerful – sometimes chaotic – affective states to refined feeling, or even "dead" feeling.

In the early years of infancy and childhood, the attuned – or non-attuned – mother modulates and mediates this process. Her strongest influence seems to be on right-brain development and function. Most of our ongoing, automatic evaluating of situations and behaviors, the emotional "tone" of our lives, there before thought, is regulated by the right brain structures (see Schore 1994), where the shame cortex resides. Later, language becomes more important, and the larger community takes on this "civilizing" function of cooling affects through shame.

Western culture has deified reason, and dismissed emotion and feeling. As a consequence, we have the modern, alienated individual, unable to maintain a sense of meaning and value. We have lost much of our capacity for evolved feeling, and we need to seek that Grail of lowly wisdom once more.

Conclusion: Shame and Humble Wisdom

We have journeyed through history, culture, neurobiology and psychology. All these perspectives show that shame is a universal teacher that can keep us close to the core of self. It is our psychobiological heritage, bringing culture and ethics deeply into our brains and minds.

Shame is frequently connected with the alchemical *nigredo*. If consciously suffered, shame can burn away artificialities of persona and, on another level, layers of the false self (see Jacoby 1994). Faithful embracing of shame will bring into awareness, in time, new patterns of deeper feeling. Such grounded feeling can reconnect us with the lineaments of order latent in the unconscious (see Van Eenwyk 1997).

Shame reduces us to that little clod of earth that we are. If shame is endured consciously, a kind of *kenosis*–emptying – results. This "emptying" is a deeper openness without the ego's preconditions. The fullness of Being may then manifest itself in new ways.

At the millennium, a time of deepest liminality and archetypal passage, powerful energies are constellated. The perspective of "lowly wisdom" is of great importance, as we confront important decisions about our personal lives, our moral communities, and the limits of science and material progress. We must sniff the air, taste the inner and outer currents, and allow our sense of shame to have its voice. Shame can be trusted to keep us modest and low until, like Parzival, we can glean answers with integrity.

To quote Wilamowitz, the German philologist, "To make the ancients speak, we must feed them with our own blood." Humbly accepting shame as our teacher, being "lowly wise," is the required sacrifice of our blood, so that we can hear those voices as new meaning – rather than new insanity – during our millennial passage.

References

Calasso, R. (1994). *The Ruin of Kasch.* Cambridge: Belknap Press.

Damasio, A.R. (1994). *Descartes' Error.* New York: Putnam's.

Eschenbach, W. von (1980). *Parzival* (A.T. Hatto, Trans.). London: Penguin.

Hinton, A.L. (1998). Why did you kill?: The Cambodian genocide and the dark side of face and honor. *The Journal of Asian Studies, 57*-1, 93-122.

Jacoby, M. (1994). *Shame and the Origins of Self Esteem.* New York: Routledge.

Jung, E. and von Franz, M.L. (1971). *The Grail Legend* (A. Dykes, Trans.). London: Hodder & Stoughton.

Knight, M. (1998). Personal communication.

Morrison, A.P. (1989). *Shame, the Underside of Narcissism.* Hillsdale, NJ: Analytic Press.

Schneider, C. (1997). *Shame, Exposure, and Privacy.* New York: Norton.

Schneiderman, S. (1995). *Saving Face.* New York: Knopf.

Schore, A. (1994). *Affect Regulation and the Origin of the Self.* Hillsdale, NJ: Erlbaum

Shore, B. (1996). *Culture in Mind.* New York: Oxford.

Shattuck, R. (1996). *Forbidden Knowledge.* New York: St. Martin's.

Stewart, L. (1996). The archetypal affects. In D. L. Nathanson (Ed.), *Knowing Feeling.* New York: Norton.

Toulmin, S. (1990). *Cosmopolis.* Chicago: University of Chicago.

Van Eenwyk, K.J. (1997). *Archetypes and Strange Attractors.* Toronto: Inner City.

Willeford, W. (1987). *Feeling, Imagination and the Self.* Evanston, IL: Northwestern University Press.

Williams, B. (1993). *Shame and Necessity.* Berkeley: University of California Press.
Wurmser, L. (1981). *The Mask of Shame.* Baltimore: Johns Hopkins University Press.
Zoja, L. (1995). *Growth and Guilt.* (H. Martin, Trans.). New York: Routledge.

The Reawakening of the Anima Mundi

Maria Luisa Spinoglio
Milan, Italy
Centro Italiano di Psicologia Analitica

One of Jung's most fruitful perceptions, which is tied to the dynamic of opposites, reminds us that the best is an enemy of the good and that every positive attitude, when pushed to the extreme, does not improve but tends to turn into its opposite. This is the law of *enantiodromia*. If I am climbing a mountain I step up to the peak but, if I think I will go higher – only one step higher – I fall into the void. In order to avoid a catastrophe I need simply to know the nature of the terrain and sacrifice the desire of the ego to climb further. I need to stop and begin the descent, thereby consciously and willingly inverting direction to avoid falling into the abyss.

Beyond the metaphor, matters become more complicated. Often, a necessary change is blocked by inertia and blindness or by the arrogance of the ego, which assumes itself to be limitlessly capable of continuing on the road that, until now, has shown itself to be advantageous – giving an unambiguous meaning to progress and growth. Just as knowledge is not equivalent to wisdom, unlimited growth is not synonymous with true progress. Life relies on change. The dynamic of opposites is the secret of perennial renewal and the possibility of a length that is not sclerosis and sterility. The *I Ching* (the Chinese book of wisdom) teaches us that the *yang*, after having reached its culmination, retreats in favor of the *yin* and vice versa.

The signs that our generation is passing through a crisis are obvious. Yet it is still difficult to be optimistic about humanity's capacity to benefit from these possibilities for a viable renewal. There are many indications that something is moving. But the process is still open and the danger is great. I hope for this work, and for the entire Congress whose topics converge on the value of transformation through crisis, that all of humanity might support natural change in the direction that the times require. Capra (1975) addressed the problem of freedom and competence in various fields, from physics to biology, medicine, psychology and economics. He pointed out the limits and the consequences of the "Newtonian-Cartesian" model that, for several centuries, has dominated in the Western world and is based on the presumed superiority of scientific, rational and linear thought. Linear thought is founded on mathematical, measurable and verifiable measurements that are held as "objective" criteria. The step from rationalism to mechanization brings us to a universe reduced to a machine with an enormous increase of scientific/technological baggage. From these applications we have enjoyed undeniable advantages and comforts. We are beginning to see, however reluctantly, the other side of the coin, with all its negative consequences on the ecological level as well as in the mental and psychic attitude. If we extend this reflection to other pertinent fields, such as great religious and philosophical systems, we realize that the dominant spirit of the times has conditioned even them. We find again the tendency toward control, toward rationalism and toward the undisputed faith in "Values" (capital V). This faith implies a generalization and acceptance that absolute good exists along with absolute truth, infallible science, and unbounded salvation. The spiritual has been set up against the material. Reduced to the experimental, nature has lost its very soul and the spirit has lost its roots.

How could this have happened, given the sincere desire for knowledge and the love of impassioned and disinterested research that we find in great scientists, philosophers and inventors? We need only think of Copernicus, Galileo, Bacon and Newton.

Instead of devaluing or demonizing the standards that have dictated guidelines and have also determined the development – both good and bad – of society, the crucial problem, according to Jungian thought, consists in the one-sidedness that always has informed the conscious and unconscious view of the world. This one-sidedness has existed since the time humans wearily came out of the clouds of undifferentiated oneness: an inevitable partiality in a system of rational thought based on Aristotelian principles of causality and non-contradiction. These universally-accepted principles force an unshakable dualism while splitting the internal and external worlds so that A cannot be B nor can white be black. Truth cannot be error nor can irrationality exist where there is reason. Where there is life there is no death and where there is consciousness there is no unconscious.

In the Middle Ages the spirit of the times was more inclined toward introversion and religious sentiment in a world view that was not based on external observation but rather divine Word of sacred scriptures. This required that both experience and life itself had meaning. No matter how much suffering there might be, one could never doubt the final judgment. Also darkness, ignorance, misery and above all injustice and unhappiness for a person who was unable to adhere to the dominant religious model because of nature or conviction.

Following the dualistic model in which one chooses A or B, excluding one or the other, it seems that we have jumped from the frying pan into the fire. From the obscurantism and fanaticism of the medieval religion that ended with witches at the stake and Galileo's imprisonment in chains, we have fallen into the arrogance of reason's reign in the modern era. It is sinking in heaps of garbage which technological wealth has produced. We have fallen also into moral aberrations which the two World Wars of the twentieth century have put forth, and into a cynical superficialism of mass culture.

In order to move out of dramatic and relentless narrowness, a broadening of consciousness is needed. This is the true objective of many groups, schools, religious or mystic centers which have continued to sprout up since the sixties in a somewhat serious and committed fashion. These groups undeniably converge in pointing out that something is moving away from the ashes of the old religions and systems of thinking. There is a tendency to move beyond the dualistic view of contrasting material-spiritual, body-mind, nature-culture, male-female, rational-irrational: to a reconciled and broader model in which one can resolve the duality in a complementary way without violence, conflicts or repression. It is the holistic vision of which, according to Capra, Jung was a precursor: complementarity as the key to the relationship between conscious and unconscious, and all opposites. Jung's introduction of Eastern and mystical thought, for which he was initially criticized, is now hailed – another sign of the change of times. This introduction is the most evident proof of the mastery of the limits of Western culture. The change is witness to the profound need for expansion, which does not deny the scientific patrimony and cultural achievements. Western culture is enriched by the wisdom and intuition of the East. Jung came to the unified view of the *Mysterium Coniunctionis* (CW14) after a profound experience which lasted more than

50 years. This experience consisted of psychological work on himself and on his patients where in he immersed himself continuously in the unconscious and looked for a way to cure the apparent absurdities of hallucinatory language and madness. He had to draw on images and symbols of alchemy – by then forgotten in current culture – in order to find the key to the individuation process. In addition, he re-read fairy tales, myths and other symbolic material that was considered marginal or appropriate only for children, to find the archetypal models which may be used for understanding the most important psychic processes.

The scientist Capra (1975) arrived with great amazement at a holistic view of the universe through the physical study of particles and recognized the great agreement with the intuitive vision of the mystics, especially in the East. In his second work (1982), he delved into and developed his research with the hope of clearing the path for researchers from other disciplines:

In the twentieth century, physics has gone through many conceptual revolutions which clearly reveal the limits of the mechanistic world view and which lead to an organic and ecological conception of the world which is not dissimilar, from certain aspects, to the conceptions of mystics from every time and tradition. The universe is no longer seen as a machine, composed of the multitude of separate parts, but rather it is a harmonious and indivisible whole. This whole is a net of dynamic relationships comprising in an essential way even the human observer, male or female, and his/her consciousness. The fact that modern physics, the manifestation of an extreme specialization of the rational mind, is making contact with mysticism, which is also the essence of religion and the manifestation of an extreme intuitive mind, shows very well the unity and complementarity of rational and intuitive modes of consciousness of yin and yang. Therefore, the physicists can furnish the scientific background for the behavioral and value changes of which our society has an urgent need. In a culture dominated by science, it will be much easier to convince our social institutions of the need for fundamental changes if we are able to give a scientific base to our discussions. This can be furnished today by the physicists. Modern physics can show other sciences that scientific thought does not necessarily have to be reductionist and mechanical and, that other holistic and ecological conceptions are scientifically correct. (pp. 42-43)

Jung also used scientific method in a coherent and serious fashion: the observation of symptoms and behavior of the patient. He also formulated hypotheses that are accepted only if they are useful to the understanding of the case and can be extended to analogous cases. With regard to proceeding, as a doctor, in an empirical and experimental fashion, Jung never had any doubt. Only through such a method could he decipher the most absurd paradoxes of the symbolic language. From 1911, the year of *The Psychology of the Unconscious* (later CW5, *Symbols of Transformation),* which goes beyond the mechanistic psychology of Freud, to 1956 (CW14), Jung sought to cure the split between the two forms of thinking that had been identified as the basis of human thinking: the intuitive and imagistic, symbolic on the one hand and the spoken, rational and scientific on the other. The right and left brain are no longer seen as contrasting nor do they surpass each other insofar as one is more archaic and primitive, but they are both valid support to the conscious and complementary forms to be integrated. In order to reach the objective of completeness, the person sees the Self as principal regulator and introduces, not by repression and one-sidedness, but by the recovery and integration of both aspects: conscious and unconscious, masculine and feminine, light and shadow.

The emergence of Capra's (1982) holistic view of the universe and the tendency toward the psychic totality by way of Jung's *coniunctio oppositorum* (union of opposites) highlight the recovery of a harmonious and revitalized vision of the earth. It is a single great living organism at the base of our very selves. It is the first material of alchemists and endowed with an intimate and innate sense, the tendency toward an order that is not only mechanistic but, as Teilhard de Chardin (1993) has said, a path toward a "guided evolution."

To feel the world in its vibrant unfolding and in the fullness of its beauty and vulnerability means to save it from within the soul. Because the difference between a robot, a machine, and a living being consists in this ineffable and inexplicable word "soul," which sets the beginning human as the seal of life. In arrogance and blindness, however, humans mistakenly have often attributed the soul as belonging only to ourselves. Thereby we break the harmony with other living beings – animals, plants and earth – the foundation and condition of our very existence. Thus, we fall into the trap of hubris: damaging the very source of life. It is not a matter of returning to the pantheism of the primitives and the original confusion of the *participation mystique,* but rather to broaden consciousness without sacrificing anything in the development and differentiation acquired in thousands of years of evolutive effort. One recognizes that which modern physics acknowledged at the subatomic level: the fundamental and unitary dynamism of matter in its perennial dance of life, a dynamism that Capra saw in the image of the dancing Shiva.

For Western humans it is difficult to revive harmony with the earth and acknowledge the *anima mundi*. For nearly 2000 years we have been accustomed, with the complicity of the church, to consider the material world to be the source of sin or something to exploit. Even though similar ideas are circulating increasingly, we are a long way from what the American Indian sages say, "We all have to learn to see ourselves as part of this earth, not as an enemy who comes from outside and seeks to impose his will. We, who know the secret of the Pipe, know also that, as a living part of this earth, we cannot do violence without hurting ourselves too" (Cervo Zoppo, quoted in Reicheis & Bydlinski 1994, p.15).

To understand the fundamental and urgent need, we must take responsibility consciously for recovering and integrating the world vision which is a living unity. I have chosen a case that seems emblematic because of the extreme good faith and innocence of the person. "Giovanni," a man who came to analysis at age 50, with obsessive symptoms and phobias about getting sick and fainting in public during official ceremonies. If the symptoms could have remained hidden, and primarily connected to private situations such as dressing and writing, the fear of a person who is often confined to public roles could have been contained without great conscious resistance. In fact, considering his age, he had a childish trust in analysis, a trust that was both moving and irritating. It was comprised of assumptions that had never been questioned and had caged him in a continuous fear of both failing and breaches of etiquette.

Giovanni was the first of three males, born at close intervals. He always sought the mother's favor and surpassed his brothers in unconditional and non-conflictual devotion to the values of the maternal world. From what his mother told him, only in his earliest years – during a precocious phase – did Giovanni allow himself to be vivacious, capricious and even aggressive. It was then that he was once discovered with a shoe in hand standing near his newborn brother's crib with the apparent intent of hitting him. From the time he was three years old he became a sweet and obedient child, an adolescent without any sexual curiosity – or any curiosity that would be considered even a minimal transgression within the cultural and sociological world of the mother who was an elementary teacher and held rigid Catholic principles. The level of his mother's expectations and their symbolic equivalent, Mother Church, constructed the supporting axle of Giovanni's entire development, determining the way he would face every situation and choice.

As the first, he was forced to remain the example, the straight, the just, the chaste – not because of personal pride but rather to placate that internal persecutor, an archaic super-ego inherited from the relentless maternal animus. The persecutor raised its finger, saying: "I do not transgress!" and pointed the way, moving it always further and higher. This was done with the complicity of his father, a state functionary and a very proper man in his irreproachable public life. He was ineffective and delegated Giovanni's entire education to his teacher-wife. Each evening, Giovanni's mother required from her children a recap of the entire day: a true confession that Giovanni never tried to avoid for he saw it not only as legitimate but also a precious opportunity to demonstrate his goodness.

Giovanni had a chair which was his only private space free from invasion and maternal judgment. The chair was where everything was under control and had to be in the utmost order and from which he received necessary reassurance. From that he went ahead, blindly believing in black and white, good and evil, correct and faulty, clean and dirty. All these were rigorously separated without possible confusion or doubts. The dirty, par excellence, was obviously sexuality which Giovanni held at bay in his greatest exercise of virtue. He conformed to his religious choice, which imposed on him formal chastity and was a refuge for Giovanni from possible transgression against the maternal world. The lack of a conscious conflict and the full adherence to the values of his mother and of the Church brought Giovanni to a brilliant and peaceful ecclesiastical career. The repression of his shadow was apparently possible and the ego believed to be at the service of higher Values in life: Goodness, Truth, Spirit, God. Only the symptoms that got progressively worse disturbed his serenity and forced him to come to analysis, opening the possibility to recover; above all, the strange vertigo that struck while he was in the presence of high prelates and in the great cathedrals from whose heights he could have had a catastrophic fall.

My intent is to go beyond the account of Giovanni's seven years of analysis. I want to show the key passage and the symbol of the turning point: how the unconscious guides the rediscovery and recovery of the immanent part of the archetype of Life in order to reestablish the psychic well-being that is founded on fullness and not on one-sidedness. In the first years of analysis, Giovanni's dreams were often about problems of the shadow: dirty cages, blockages, cynical characters, Nazis, slippery terrains and un-navigable seas. In other dreams, hungry and hostile animals recurred – often a black dog. Slowly, over five years, the atmosphere of the dreams changed. After having explored the most personal component of the neurosis, tied to the work on the shadow, we arrived at two dreams that can be used on a collective level as testimony of the need to widen the consciousness of the modern person, replanting roots in the earth. First dream:

> *I am on my knees (in prayer?) and I have on my right a type of bush or hedge beyond a metal grate. I hear a whistle. I think can there could be a snake and therefore I get up to look better. There is a big lizard. This becomes a rare bird, big as a sparrow yet more slight, a clear color (white-gray). Then in the bush a sign appears on which is written, more or less: Who sees the bird "so and so" very rare, communicates it. Emotion. Then I see the bird fly. I would like it to rest on my finger. I put out my finger and he lands there.*

After two days this dream:

> *I am biking with my mother. She is old but is riding. I am in front of her. We arrive at a narrowing of the road (between two strips) and some cows come to us. I am afraid that my mother will fall. Then I stop and pet one cow on the nose. Affectionate cow.*

The two dreams were brought up at the same session; they furnished guiding images for consolidating the most valuable work and provided encouragement in moments of stagnation. I see them as parallel, given that the unconscious produced them. Both of them deal with recovering, with love, the instinctual side which is represented by animals: the lizard-bird in the first dream and the cow in the second. These figures have two fundamental applications: the spiritual-paternal and the earth-mother. Jung often confirmed that the broadening of the conscious happens both on high and down low. Just as the extension of the bright spectrum expands toward the infra-red and ultraviolet area, an instinctual root of the spirit exists, as well as a spiritual valence of the instinct. To detach too much from the instinct, as happened to Giovanni, brings a breaking off from one's roots and an asphyxial and sterile wandering in both an abstract and pale pseudo-spirituality and on ephemeral and vertiginous heights. One is always on the brink of falling, not horizontally nor as a participant in the joy of sharing. The attainment of Values is illusionary as these are mere ideological strategies that substitute for true feelings. Where there is no incarnation there can be no passion. At best there can be exasperation and ideological tenacity.

Fanaticism and non-commitment are opposite expressions of the break between thought and feeling. These phenomena are common and thrive on the weakness of an ego that is indoctrinated precociously, detached from the wisdom of the instinct and left to risk everything in the maze of mass-media lures. Many tragedies of terrorism are understandable if we consider the narcissistic feature of the majority of ideological persons devoted to what they decide must be good for all. Strangely, however, they are not in touch with real needs, but are taken with the ideological certainty of their abstract Values; they are ready to sacrifice everything for incarnate ideals. The tension toward the spirit is not sustained nor guaranteed by the axis Ego-Other and, therefore, inflation which is the identification of the Ego with the Other impedes the pending catastrophe. Often the symptom of vertigo and the fear of falling from up high are present in narcissist personalities. It is the fear: the fascination of the puer regarding heights and the extreme attempt by the unconscious to warn of the danger of uprooting. Asthma, too – remembering Che Guevara's symptom – may indicate that one has pushed too high, in rarefied areas.

The appearance of the lizard in Giovanni's dream finally marks the reconfiguring of the missing element: the base animal from which he can set out again so that prayer is not a pure sterile exercise of pharasaical self-fulfillment but an efficacious and salvatory event for all. "Whoever sees the so and so bird, communicate it." The reptile, the most archaic animal in the evolutive chain, rapidly becomes a bird which is the animal symbol of the spirit because it belongs to the air and can fly high. One need only think of Zeus' hawk and the dove, the symbol of the Holy Spirit.

When the idealizations fall, the way opens to the recovery of immanence which is not an enemy of transcendence, just as the earth is not an enemy of heaven and *yin* is not an enemy of *yang,* but each pair is complementary. The pleasure of the here and now is rediscovered and a love is born for life and its small and great joys. There is also a love for each creature: the emotion in Giovanni's dream regarding the bird and his joy at feeling the small claws on his finger. The feeling of belonging to the whole earth and the pleasure of feeling at one with the entire universe as a single great organism is discovered. This signifies precisely to find again the *anima mundi* and to feel its presence: to vibrate on the same wavelength of life and to feel alive in the world. If the meaning of life is no longer "beyond," in the hereafter, in the eternal and transcendental Values which have transformed the most generous youth into martyrs and others into exploiters of the Earth, then the responsibility for this poor and precious world increases and with it the care not to let it further deteriorate.

To go beyond the idealization does not mean the loss of values and a fall into emptiness – a danger always present in the absence of psychological work – but rather it means a healing of the tearing and a recovering of that the material heart" (see Teilhard De Chardin 1976) and the *anima mundi*. Both of these guarantee meaning – toward evolution and life.

The other dream begins with the presence of the real mother, though transformed from the rigid guardian of historical reality. The dream ends with a caress on the cow's nose. The cow is the animal root of the archetype of the mother-nurturer; the sacred cow – as Isida, Era, Demetra – which is now found in the East as a sacred and untouchable animal. The personal mother complex is surpassed, opening to the archetypal component. At the same time the relationship is recovered, which can be loving only because the archetype of relationship is Eros with the earth and its creatures as in a new canticle of the creatures. The abstraction and dryness are surpassed, broadening consciousness, with further effort toward a circle rather than toward perfectionism. In this circle a holistic view is recovered in which microcosm and macrocosm mean the same thing. The dizziness too disappears because one no longer leans on emptiness; the ground is solid and is welcoming and nurturing.

A final note regarding the new meaning that the concept of development is assuming. It is no longer unlimited growth nor hypertrophic and monstrous: a concept already criticized by Hillman (1975). It is a recovery and integration which is also in accordance with recent neurophysiological and cerebral studies (see Liverio 1997). Some scholars have discovered a crucial relationship between nerve cells and vascularization by which it would no longer be possible to nourish the brain if it assigned its evolution to the increase in volume and to the progressive development of the cerebral cortex. In this latter process nerve functions are carried out by superior cerebral structures that are phylogenetically younger and dominate the functions of the structures and of the older centers. The only path of change could consist in a profound restructuring and internal reorganization and, therefore, a departure from the hierarchy, according to which newer is better: toward a synthesis and integration of old and new. It would be the scientific confirmation of the profound, mystical and religious perceptions. According to these perceptions, the future is entrusted to the wisdom of the past and to the importance of the psychological work of integrating and broadening the consciousness into an archetypal key. It is not a simple return to the past, which is an impossible operation as with all nostalgic utopias, but it is a renewal and revitalization in accordance with the evolution of life.

"Destroy the types of the past," the Indian philosopher Sri Aurobindo would say, "but keep their achievements and spirit intact, otherwise there will be no future."

Translated from the original Italian by Mara Teefy

References

Capra, F. (1975). *Il Tao della Fisica*. Milano: Adelphi.
Capra, F. (1982). *The Turning Point*. New York: Simon & Schuster.
Hillman, J. (1975). *Loose Ends*. Zurich: Spring Publications.
Liverio, A. (1997). Cervello ai limiti del possibile. *Corriere della Sera*, February 2.
Teilhard de Chardin, P. (1976). *Le Coeur de la Matiere*. Paris: Éditions du Seuil.

Jungian Psychology in a Changing World

Portraits of Suffering Trees

Destruction of Nature and Transformation of Consciousness

Roberto Gambini
São Paulo, Brazil
Schweizerische Gesellschaft für Analytische Psychologie

Psychology is not merely a science that one can use to observe deviant behavior, pathologies, lack of social adaptation or the many forms of human suffering. Understanding the workings of the mind and proposing some form of treatment to psychic pain is a noble cause carried on by psychology and always necessary, because human suffering has not decreased but, with progress, grown deeper. The challenge to understand why humans suffer is therefore ever greater.

But it is not enough to understand the mental working of the individual: the interplay between consciousness and the unconscious, the development of subjectivity. One needs to understand how individuals suffer the problems of the society they live in.

Society is a living body; community and culture can be sick. A good science is one that looks both to the whole and the part. As I come originally from the social sciences, I entered the field of reflection trying to understand great ensembles. Only later did I come to focus on the individual. Today I know they cannot be separated, or we will end up understanding neither one. In my analytic work I try from the start to locate the patient socially: life style, cultural traditions and family attitudes. Human beings do not live in a void, nor isolated inside an air bubble with their personal psychology, their complexes and personal characteristics. We live in and through human interchange. Isolation is a fiction; we are all connected, especially at the unconscious level, with one another and with nature. We need to examine to what degree all that is happening to nature is also happening in our psyches. To what degree are the problems that we inflict upon nature the outer manifestation of our inner conflicts? And the great drama underlying this question – well-known today, thanks especially to ecological activism – is human unconsciousness. That is, humans have not yet fully recognized that we keep doing something that is well described since Freud's early works: projection. We project upon nature an obscure inner area, which we believe to be exterior. A whole pattern of relationship between humans and their environment – trees, animals, water, air, cities – will change only if and when we become conscious of what we carry inside.

This relationship is, at present, the avant garde of psychological reflection: a realization of the old law of correspondences. Such a realization is the same as perceiving the human soul as spread out in the environment – a new version of Animism – with the significant difference that the new version implies a step forward, not an archaic trait as ethnocentric anthropologists saw it. This new standpoint enables us to perceive that it is not just the soul of the patient seeking help that is sick, but the *anima mundi* as well. Any therapist or thinker who wishes to have a social impact knows that treating individuals is not enough. The great sickness is that which affects the world's psyche. At that level a titanic problem is rooted and it can be dealt with only if this kind of thinking matures. This task cannot be ascribed solely to ecology, to environmental law, to politics, international treaties, state rules, public opinion, lobbying, or something else. All aspects of knowledge should come together for the task of treating the world's soul and avoiding the risk of the extinction of humankind.

We live in the sunset of a cycle that began with Christianity. The turn of the century is the right time to become conscious of this great danger of self-destruction. It is not easy to discuss this question because it is so close to sensationalism but, if one looks at relevant data, one can see how serious the situation is. Starting with overpopulation, all planetary problems are extremely grave. Pollution keeps growing and one-fourth of the earth's people live in extreme poverty. Not even the most advanced technology has brought any solution. Humanity keeps growing and its deepest problems grow too.

Our great challenge is therefore to find effective ways of expanding our consciousness. Working on what has deteriorated starts in each one's mind, and this is a march without leaders.

Trees are suffering in silence, but almost no one looks at them. We don't look at what is not interesting to us. If I lack a register in my mind I cannot perceive a corresponding outer object. Consciousness is selective; we capture reality not as a compact block, but as segments that are compatible with the present configuration of our consciousness. The task facing us is to alter and enlarge it, in order that a deeper layer of what we call "outer reality" can be processed psychologically.

I take as a starting point the way in which my consciousness unmistakably registered a question involving trees. When my wife and I returned from Zurich to Sao Paulo in 1981, after finishing our studies at the C.G. Jung Institute, we rented an apartment in a neighborhood full of trees. What we liked especially was the living room on the first floor, with glass windows from ceiling to floor that let us see a huge tree that almost came into our home. It was very good to live so close to that tree for a few years. My wife used to observe a bird building her nest on one of the branches and occupying it until the chicks flew away. One weekend we returned home and found that our beloved tree had been cut down by firemen, following orders of a retired police officer who lived across the street. In that day in 1984 – and only now can I see it more clearly – I promised myself that I would do something for the sake of trees. At that time I didn't know what, nor was I fully aware that I was making a serious vow.

In those days I still kept a correspondence with the late Dr. H.K. Fierz, who had been my analyst. Some days after the tree was felled I received from Küsnacht a black-trimmed envelope; I knew before opening what message it contained. His widow told me how and when he had died, at the same time the tree was cut. When I later shared this experience with her, Mrs. Antoinette Fierz answered: "When people have deep ties, distance makes no difference." His death was enacted right in front of me, a synchronicity both unforgettable and responsible in part for the track my reflection would follow.

There is a deep level in reality in which everything is connected with everything else. Once in a while this layer manifests itself. Once in a while our consciousness opens to perceive fragments of that level. By the same token, one can observe how one's mind works, how it remains tightly closed upon itself most of the time, while believing that it is seeing all there is "out there" to be seen.

Which invisible hand controls what we call reality and makes things happen in the way we are used to perceiving them? If an old Indian man from the Amazon were to give his opinion about desertification of a previously fertile area, or about an unquenchable fire destroying the rain forest, he would say that it has to do with people and their inner state. This is a pre-modern, pre-rational perception according to which outer unbalance can be corrected only if at least one person connects with the world's soul. Well, this has become now an outstanding post-modern approach! Perhaps it would be best to say that, in what we call reality, perceptible and imperceptible things do happen. Let us admit this fact, at least, and try to explore possible new accesses to the occult side. (I dare use this word, so loaded with old disparaging connotations.) For us working in psychotherapy this is fundamental, since we can observe only a small fragment of the processes our patients go through. The vital core, from which transformation originates, we cannot look at directly.

Field work began with my camera. In that same year of 1984 I was driving one day up a busy thoroughfare in Sao Paulo, formerly known for its beautiful garden houses, but now totally taken over by showrooms, noise, smoke, blasting sound and heavy traffic. Its threatened trees resist as well as they can. Suddenly I saw this scene, which I later photographed, while having a true insight: I realized in a second the drama lived by trees planted randomly by city workers under the electric web. In a particular case, seven palm trees were threatened with decapitation as soon as they started to interfere with transmission of energy. In that precise moment the plan was born to bring my camera along always, in order to register similar scenes. Once a certain number of photos portraying the suffering of trees had been reached I would try to convey, with my own words, what each one would say if only it could speak. But 11 years went by and I did nothing. The project lay dormant inside me like a capsule. Such things happen; sometimes a whole lifetime goes by and a person's beautiful encapsulated project is not realized. Something valuable and useful is not born. I use to call this an abortion (which by the way was the first subject I ever wrote about in psychology). Or it is a pregnancy that never comes to delivery. The fetus dries up, and so does the soul.

We must take care of our pregnancies. Mine took 11 years. I kept seeing that scene of the seven palm trees. I always registered it and felt it, but the work never began. Something must awaken what lies asleep. It can be an outer fact: an encounter with someone, a word, a request, a need, or an inner event, the pressure exercised by a dream, an activated symbol. For me, it awoke in this way: I was invited to meet – in his country house – the leader of an Afro-Brazilian religious cult. When we met, there was a bit of silence and we let it be, neither of us feeling that he should say intelligent words.

After a while we went out for a walk. He asked me if I was familiar with a spiritual entity called Oshossi, the lord of trees. I said I knew just a little bit and asked him to tell me more. He said Oshossi takes care of the spirit of trees; that excited me. I asked him what this entity might be feeling with all the forest devastation in Brazil. He didn't hesitate, but answered: "Oshossi must be very angry." We kept walking, looking silently at the trees. Then he said: "You have a spiritual guide aligned with Oshossi." That was our talk; it awoke my wish to act, doing the work that slept inside me. That was all. The next day I started. Today I have hundreds of photographs that speak for themselves.

This is the problem: a deep conflict between nature and technology, trees and electric wires. The comments I will make here refer all to the city of Sao Paulo: a great, fast and voracious megalopolis; a frightening socio-psychological phenomenon of disordered growth and unruled energy that characterizes the second largest city in the world. Regardless of what happens in other cities, what happens in this one is enough as a fact to be meaningful. Sao Paulo is the outpost of modern industrial development in Brazil and in Latin America; other cities may follow this model of unbalanced growth. In my home city, the conflict between nature and technology is acute and is shown completely naked, like a shadow crudely exposed.

Our trees are being attacked constantly and increasingly, as if their natural growth meant a dangerous threat. I didn't have to go out of my way; wherever I went I found what I was looking for. In order to give free passage to electric wires, a certain style of aggressive and random pruning is practiced so that some trees are penetrated and defoliated as if they were raped. Others are mutilated to the point of shapelessness, or crippled to such an extent that they can not survive. The rationale for this form of vandalism is that pruning is beneficial to the trees, since it is believed – falsely – they will grow again, perhaps even stronger than before. It is tragic that this type of occurrence becomes normal, imperceptible, undisputed and accepted. People grow more and more insensitive, and the process continues.

This false belief is my point. A tree has carried its future inside itself since it was a seed – as Aristotle said long ago. The idea of potentiality, also used by psychoanalysis, comes from Greek philosophy: What is going to develop is already present from the beginning, in a germinal state. With the unfolding of time, possibilities are actualized and become manifest realities. Thus, a little tree builds up an intelligent structure, a fully developed form. When a tree is pruned destructively, it loses its full form forever. It will make attempts to recompose that broken structure through intensified cell multiplication. Its life impulse, seeking preservation and progression, will give rise to sprouts and new branches, as if the tree wanted to live at all costs – and many do, albeit mutilated. But its original form never will reappear. A gothic cathedral can be rebuilt, as many were; even ruined frescoes can be restored. But the perfect majesty of an old, leafy tree, once lost, has no second chance. The question that I want to propose is: What has all this to do with us, with our soul? We are surrounded by mutilated and perverted forms; how are we affected by them?

Trees have come to represent something bad. What happens is a projection upon trees of negative contents that belong to us. So trees become negative objects in themselves and, when such actions are taken, there is a general feeling of relief, as if saying: "Good, we have cut out something evil." The next question is: What could this negative projection be? Which unconscious content has been projected? What kind of a problem could there be at the bottom of the modern urban human psyche that it cannot access in a conscious, direct way? The only answer I find is that it is the problem of spiritual growth.

Why do I say this? Because since time immemorial trees have been a symbol of human beings' inner growth. The Tree of Life appears in Genesis, in the Koran, in Aztec cosmogony, in that of Brazilian Indian mythology and in many other cultures. We are familiar with the Tree of Knowledge, the Tree of Truth, of Justice, of Good and Evil, of Happiness, of Bounty, of Genealogy. We contain inside our chests a respiratory tree, an inverted tree like the one conceived by the alchemists to represent the descent of the spirit into our flesh. Our heart arteries branch out like trees. We have trees all over our bodies: in the palms of our hands, in the nerve branching of our faces, in the circulatory vessels of our brains. Our physical health depends on the perfect shape of these trees. If they were pruned like the outer ones, our life would be endangered. And if the psychological or spiritual tree that represents the Self is distorted in our soul, our inner processes will be distorted.

Why is this antique symbol so apt for representing human life? Trees come from seeds. They must be planted in firm and fertile soil; they sprout and grow in an organized way. Roots correspond to our unconscious foundations in the invisible world, whence come the basic forces that maintain life. Roots are connecting channels through which vital energies are tapped and put into circulation. Root symbolism indicates that all life comes from Mother Earth in the form of sap. We are rooted in our unconscious, our bodies, our instincts and archetypal configurations; in our genealogy and the traditions transmitted from generation to generation, in our family psychology, in the place where we live or grew up. If one is uprooted abruptly from the tropics and transplanted to Alaska, one will have difficulty in tapping energy unless one's roots succeed quickly in perforating and penetrating this new soil. In tree symbolism every aspect is present: heaven and earth, matter and spirit, body and mind are connected by the trunk – formerly known as Axis Mundi – linking above and below, humans and gods. The tree trunk becomes – in temples – a Greek column. All architecture on pillars goes back to trees, our first abode since the dawn of humankind. The trunk is also the vertebral column structuring anatomical growth. The psychological equivalents of this rich symbolism can be detected in the "tree test," developed in the 1950s. Branches are the different aspects of the personality: its realizations, achievements, profession. An individuating person grows in all directions, like a leafy tree, like the lost Renaissance ideal of humanity.

All that happens to a human being is represented graphically in a tree; when we see a mutilated tree we face a symbolic image of an attack to life and to soul. Due to our lack of consciousness, we project upon trees our problem of not knowing how to grow. We cannot stand to see the full growth of trees because that reminds us of our shortcomings. The solution will not come with new laws forbidding people to attack trees, but can appear only if we overcome underdevelopment – which was my theme at the last Congress.

Mutilated trees are mirrors lining our boulevards. Wherever we go, we see our hidden psyche reflected in them. Not projection, but revelation.

Let us go back to the tree test. I have examined several of them that were lent to me by colleagues and found an astounding similarity between trees drawn by psychologically disturbed children and those we see around. This similarity led me to think that the suffering trees of Sao Paulo can be seen as a tree test done in a literal way by the population at large. That is, they are the mirror that reflects the deep unconscious conflicts of our soul.

A 12-year-old boy received the following school comments: "Problems of relationship. Parents had conflicts with each other and with him. Father spanked him and told him he was a good-for-nothing." His tree is completely brown, has no leaves and is cut at the root level. Some branches have the shape of saws or knives: a twisted tree with no sign of growth. One year before he drew this tree, his father had a violent jealousy attack; his mother left and when she returned home she found he had committed suicide in his car. The boy's growth stopped and he repressed his rage. When I see trees such as his in the city of Sao Paulo, I think of the death of an archetypal father whose absence breeds disorientation and freezes inner growth.

The increasing loss of organized form should be considered as the psychological undercurrent of chaotic urbanization. Sao Paulo, 17 million people in its metropolitan area, has lost its shape mainly in its peripheral belt: no planning, houses randomly clustered, destroyed nature, garbage all over. Promiscuity, poverty, hunger, ignorance, violence. An immense clandestine underground – the shadow – rules uncontested. In its origin, the antique city was the conquest of form and order over nature and chaos. The separation between inside and outside, the community and the others, was clearly delineated and marked by surrounding stone walls. In the 1950s, Brasilia was planned and built with the aim of becoming a symbolic center for the country and a model of ordered urban life. It failed, since its elegant design was eaten up by the barracks of the poor. The archetypal matrix of modern cities, as it is of Indian villages, is a mandala. But Third World cities have lost the mandala as a basis. Instead, what moves them forward is the chaotic strength of a shapeless but highly energized shadow.

When repeated attacks make survival impossible, trees slowly and silently start to die. Sometimes they look anorexic, or extremely sad. Some look suddenly very old; others remind us of hands with cut fingers. Some trees are chosen as the "right" site for garbage disposal. In some cultures, the base of a tree is considered as sacred ground, the spot where the divine manifests when it emerges from the earth along with the tree. In India, there are altars dedicated to Shiva at the feet of certain trees, displaying the iron trident that represents the God, flower garlands, saffron painted stones and votive lamps. Adepts of syncretistic Afro-Brazilian religions make offerings at the bases of trees; there one can see candles, bowls with food for the saints, and garbage. Probably the devout person is not aware of this mixture of pure and impure energies. The image reads: filth on the altar. Wouldn't this situation resonate somewhere in the adept's soul?

The suffering inflicted upon trees reflects an unrecognized pain in our own soul, due to loss of contact with spirit. Trees have always symbolized that connection. And so we can understand a little better one of the factors that keeps two thirds of humankind in a chronic state of psychological, political and economic underdevelopment.

208

"Raping the Soul"

An Experience of Active Imagination

Marta Tibaldi
Rome, Italy
Associazione Italiana per lo Studio della Psicologia Analitica

*Our fantasies always hover on the point of our insufficiency, where
a defect ought to be compensated.
A fantasy is more or less your own invention, and remains on the
surface of personal things and of conscious expectations. But active
imagination, as the term denotes, means that the images have a life
of their own and that the symbolical events develop according to
their own logic – that is, of course, if your conscious reason does not
interfere.*

C.G. Jung

In light of Jung's observations, I am using one of my experiences
of active imagination and its transforming effects on the psyche, to
illustrate how a destructive erotic image, such as rape, could be
integrated at the conscious and the creative level, activating the
transformation of destructive and creative images of Eros.

The experience to which I refer originates from a combination of
events – cultural, personal and imaginative. These events induced
me to reflect on a theme of great emotional impact such as erotic
destructiveness, and set off a process of internal transformation.

In January 1997, the press featured an open letter by Virginio
Merola, president of a district of Bologna afflicted by numerous
rapes. He wrote to answer the invitation, addressed to him by the
municipal council member who is responsible for the social politics
of the city, to initiate a discussion about the phenomenon of rape,
considered as a problem of male sexuality.

The letter was a plea to reflect on both the male and female roles
in our culture and the necessity of creating a language, common to
men and women, to recognize the reciprocal uneasiness with erotic
destructive modalities such as violence, rape, molestation or rude
comments. The magazine *Noi Donne* (January 1977) gave promi-

nence to the case, dedicating to Merola an entire cover with the title *Miracolo a Bologna* (Miracle at Bologna). As a woman, I appreciate the importance of the action. It was a fine letter, including from a psychological point of view. As an analytical psychologist, I did not want to reduce the initiative, as the press had done, only to the dimension of a "miracle," restricting the problem of the rape to a matter of greater consciousness, on the part of men, about the destructive aspects of their sexuality and avoiding the request for dialogue that Merola addressed to women.

The question of rape does not exhaust itself with men's acquisition of a greater consciousness of the destructive aspects of their sexuality; it bears instead on the awareness – for the man as well as for the woman – of the personal and cultural damage that the repression of more creative erotic modalities causes to both, interfering with reciprocal transformation.

For this reason I focused my reflection on the theme of the rape and, more generally, on the theme of Eros between men and women and its codification in our culture, going beyond the conscious and collective attitude, toward the experience of the imaginative consciousness. I went where the confrontation with deep masculine and feminine images leads to the integration of the destructive and creative erotic aspects of Eros and to the experience of the healing Eros, that transforms destruction into creation and death into life.

More personally, the occasion to deal with the theme of erotic destructiveness presented itself, thanks to the emotive and imaginative reaction that I experienced while working with a colleagues on deepening our understanding of certain themes of Jung. An active imagination was my imaginative response to a moment of sadness, induced by an intense emotive crisis of the group.

One of the participants had manifested his need of a greater involvement in a very destructive way, that led to his exclusion from the group. At that moment my perception was sorrow for his lack of respect toward our emotional reality. Immediately this image appeared to me: *It cannot enter the circle. It needs to move along the border; otherwise you destroy it.*

"Raping the Soul" is the title of the active imagination that, outside the group, I objectified in the form of writing. I am reporting and commenting only two images out of four: one of attempted rape and one of *coniunctio* (the other two concern respectively an image of death and one of rebirth). The two images I am reporting concern the reintegration of masculine aspects of erotic destructiveness and the possibility of their transformation through the comparison with the healing power of creative Eros. The text of this pair of images is as follows.

The soul says:
Thanks for saving me.
The union with the goddess is possible at the ritual culmination.
Propitious is the union of the goddess with the man.
Man, respect the goddess
...
Man, unite with the woman.
Woman, unite with the man.

A dream followed in which I discovered that *I was the daughter of a black father and had in my heritage both white and black genes.*

"Raping the Soul" and this dream were the imaginative impulses that led me to think about the theme of erotic destructiveness in a more complex way than my consciousness had suggested to me at the moment of the Merola letter and of the events in the group. Following "Raping the Soul," I considered a destructive erotic modality such as rape and, more generally, erotic modalities that cause suffering, as expressions of a distorted attempt at union with the female soul. I also thought about the divine aspects of Eros, about the ritual time they require and, finally, about the propitious nature of the union between man and woman, when it is realized under the benevolent view of the goddess. The dream makes me conscious that my genetic heritage had black genes, and it made me reflect on the possibility of my producing children of shadow.

Rape: Integration of Destructive and Creative Aspects of Eros.

One of the first effects the images of "Raping the Soul" had on my consciousness was, as I said before, that of contacting the phenomenon of rape in a more complex way. These images let me consider the theme of rape not only from the obvious viewpoint of destructiveness, but also as a deep expression of the necessity of masculine-feminine union, of human with divine Eros, of transformation and renewal beyond violent and destructive forms of Eros.

Following the directions of "Raping the Soul," I discovered – as, a few months later, had been clarified for me also by a figure of a "genius" in another active imagination – the path to the "treasure," to the richness of creative Eros, to the Eros that heals the wounds resulting from destructiveness:

Houses and roofs of a city and a black snake. A swallow looks down. The city is built on the snake. A white flower appears, a gardenia that changes into a lotus flower.
It is dark, I am in a cave. There is some light; I can move. I go deeper. There is a coffer with a treasure; it is full of golden coins. I look around. I am perplexed. I did not expect to find a treasure. I wonder what to do. I hear a voice telling me to get closer. I am afraid.
Come closer, says the voice; you can take the treasure. It belongs to everybody and to nobody. You do not take it away from anyone. Learn to take. The treasure is yours because you have found it. These treasures belong to those who reach them. After having reached them, you need to learn how to use them.
I answer: I need to come here, to watch the treasure, to get used to it. I did not ever think I could have such richness.
Again the voice: Learn. You need to be strong to have a treasure. Learn to be strong. To arrive at the treasure you need to go through the dark cave. This is the way. The dark cave leads us to the treasure.
Me: I shall go back to the surface and then back here, in the depth of the earth. I need to familiarize myself with this richness. Thanks.
The voice: I am here, at your disposal.

If we compare the proposal of the "Raping the Soul" with the treatment by the press of the phenomenon of rape, we can notice that it is much easier to alleviate the anxiety generated in us by shadow aspects of Eros, reducing a phenomenon such as rape to an exceptional and monstrous fact. That is, continuing to repress the destructive aspects of Eros that upset our conscience is easier than going through the darkness that frightens us but that represents the way to arrive at the treasure of creative Eros. Whether we like it or not, the phenomenon of rape forces us to come to terms with the unconscious need for union and transformation, although quite hidden in an obscure *prima materia*.

"As violent as rapes can be, the sexual component of the rape must not be underestimated in our hurry to accentuate the violent nature of the behavior. Whether distorted or violent, rape is always a matter of sex, and of sex that continues in love and in the wish for acceptance and union" (Te Paske 1987, p. 40).

With a better expression of Eisler (1996), we could call this sexual component "the human longing for connection" (p. 201): the unsuppressable need for a creative encounter of the masculine and the feminine, of the human and the divine aspects of Eros in the man as well in the woman, including through bodily experience.

It is the need of encounter that must not necessarily express itself – on the male side – in overwhelming or dominating behaviour or in the repression of the feminine soul and – on the female side – in passive submission, in defensive closing or in becoming masculine. Rather, the need for encounter is an opportunity for exchange and friendship: an experience of union with the deep feminine, an experience that is also a physical way toward spirituality – an act of love, an act of rebirth, a holy act connected to the goddess cult.

Dubose (nd) wrote that, in the patriarchal order, the removal of the transcendent feminine principle blocks a real *coniunctio* between male and female principles. Only the conscious reintegration of this transcendent feminine principle, as a "possible factor co-founding an order of a different nature" (p. 12), makes possible a propitious union between the masculine and the feminine.

To Hope Beyond Death.

But the experience developed by "Raping the Soul" did not relate only to the destructive and creative aspects in a collective phenomenon such as rape. It was also the chance for a journey through my feelings of despair and love.

To illustrate this journey, I would like to define the identity of the "goddess" and the nature of the ritual to which the images of "Raping the Soul" refer. The imaginal story, first offered as support to my feelings, was the mythological story of Isis and Osiris.

Thinking about a goddess of love, it would be easy to evoke the Greek Aphrodite. But following the directions that came from the deep images – a *prima materia* that changed into a green jelly until becoming a magnificent emerald – I have found myself in Egypt, before the "green god" Osiris and his bride Isis. As is well known, in Egypt at the same time the myth of Osiris is the myth of Isis; it is doubtless, the cult of feminine trust in the living power of love, feminine trust that goes beyond the physical experience of destruction.

The myth is a narration in which evil, put into action by a destructive male principle (Seth), even if lived and suffered in all its drama, is overcome creatively. Isis recomposes the dispersed limbs of the dead husband, re-forming the lost phallus. After the death, dismemberment and mutilation of Osiris, Isis can generate Horus, new and glorious progeny, the son who represents the renewed material world.

Osiris is the "tired god" and the god who, by a huge labor of Isis, comes back from the territories of death. He comes back to feminine love and perserverance, to the bride who responded to the destructive experience of evil with courage, sacrifice and devotion and who, with an indomitable trust in the power of love, can conceive a son after the killing, the dismemberment and the loss of the phallus. Plutarch tells us:

After his death Osiris begets a son, incredibly. That still could happen because of Isis, who suffered so much to have him back, with such a love force that overcomes the law of nature and is life itself. Her companion is a great god; her son Horus is too. Among the names of Isis there is "Mother of God," that identifies her as the archetype of a glorious posterity. But her feminine dimension includes something more. She is the only goddess to love her divine spouse with a human love, in devotion and sacrifice. The couple represents the essence of human beings, in the dramatic and unavoidable polarity of life and death.

After the victory of Horus over Seth – Plutarch calls him Typhon – the myth tells us that "the goddess not only did not condemned Tyfon to death but let him off completely." Isis, as "owner of earth" and "moist principle from which life has sustenance," did not want to nullify completely the opposite principle, represented by Typhon, who was identified in "everything arid and igneous." Plutarch explains: "This was because the goddess intended only to depotentiate him and then let him off, to keep intact the composition of the atmosphere. ... The cosmos cannot be perfect if the igneous element is missing." In this way Isis knew how to do justice to the madness and to the anger of Typhon, to "everything damaging and destructive, which nature has in itself." She showed human beings how the creative force of nature must not necessarily succumb to the destructive elements, but can overcome them in an infinite variety of solutions.

Plutarch explains the cosmic-natural everlasting dynamic in this way:

[Typhon] often is won by the force of generation and therefore imprisoned. Then he gets free and struggles against Horus, the earthly world, who can never escape the events of birth and death. Our life – he comments – is the fruit of a mixture, just as the cosmos is, but of a mixture that derives from being dragged by two opposite principles, which push us now right, now left, now forth, now back.

Isis represents – and here we are in my affective reading of the myth – a feminine modality that does not let herself destroy by negative erotic experiences or by bad advice of a destructive Animus. If, in spite of the killing, the physical dismemberment and the irremediable loss of the spouse's phallus – we could say the total loss of any vital masculine reference – she preserves intact the trust in the fecundity of a creative Animus, Isis represents a feminine aspect of the erotic creativity that generates children when everything speaks about death and destruction.

Thus the Isis attitude – this reflection could have a value both for the feminine and masculine intrapsychic dynamic and for the real relationship between men and women – is the fertile attitude, the "generatrix of children" attitude that activates erotic creativity in the apparent destruction of the positive masculine.

Isis is the feminine that is not annihilated in the "drying" action of destructiveness: the feminine that does not lose trust in every lively power of love and – thanks to her own faith, perseverance, courage and capacity to sacrifice herself – gives new vigor to the masculine fecundating power, that seemed to have been destroyed irrecoverably.

The myth tells us that, to find the spouse, Isis travels all over Egypt, building temples in each place in which the body parts of the spouse were scattered. She faces the impossibility of finding the phallus, the first part that Seth has thrown away and that the fish had devoured. For this reason she creates another one, vivifying it with her own love force.

Isis can represent therefore the feminine trust, the force, the courage and the perseverance that permit her to counteract the destructive experience, to rediscover the fecundating capacity of the masculine and to generate the son: the renewed masculine.

Removing the destructive aspects of the masculine Eros – as it has been done in the press and, in some way, in our group as an answer to the colleague – does not help to integrate the "dark" Eros. But it fosters the darker aspects, making them ever more dreadful and menacing. With the constructive and destructive elements of Eros in balance, recognizing one's own shadow relationship offers the feminine the opportunity to enforce the Isis qualities of the soul, receiving the healing power of love.

The Soul Companion and the Lava Stone

Everything said until now could describe my confrontation with a destructive erotic image such as the one of rape and the integration of a creative feminine aspect of Eros like the one represented by Isis. But I would wrong the totality of my experience of active imagination if I did not mention also the internal "soul companion," the positive Animus that has put me in touch with the masculine aspects of erotic creativity and who, accompanying me in this journey, supplied me with the energy to contact the healing power of Eros. Keeping in mind the directions contained in "Raping the Soul" is the man with whom the woman can unite, after following the directions of the goddess.

A dream marked the beginning of the work about my feeling:

After removing from my heart a metal plate, fixed with some bolts that had kept it blocked for a long time, my soul companion pours on the holes in my heart an unguent and massages it to soothe the pain and heal the wounds.

Unlike the figures of Seth and Osiris, whose function has been to stimulate the Isis qualities of my soul, the figure of the soul companion has been fundamental for recovering from the wounds of the destructiveness – wounds inflicted by a male wounded in his turn – and opening me to the experience of Eros that unites and renews creatively all aspects of existence. Leonard (1987) wrote in connection with the *coniunctio*:

Each soul marriage takes us before Being, before the ground that nourishes the soul. This soul marriage, interior marriage, royal or divine union, is for Jung a symbol of the culminating moment of the process of individuation. It is the symbol of the supreme union; in alchemy this symbol must "lead the work to its fulfillment, and to join, through love, everything its opposite, because love is stronger than death." In the last analysis, the divine marriage represents the union of the opposites through love and it is an archetype available in most cultures, religions, fairy tales, mythologies and also in dreams. (p. 198)

Taking the starting point from the archetypal plots that the author used to describe the stages leading to the soul marriage, I have found in Charles Perrault's story of *Beauty and the Beast* the narration that better fits what I was living in. Beauty is a feminine character who arrived at the experience of love when she decided to separate herself willingly from the paternal world. Without being deceived by the horrible forms of the Beast, or being confused by his enormous power, she chose to love him because her heart said so. The Beast is a masculine image who consciously renounces his own possessive and controlling will: letting Beauty go, he gives trust to the possibility that she will be back, out of love and not out of fear. He agrees to confront himself with his own vulnerability. Leonard explain:

The Beast is part of us we are afraid of, the terrible aspect of existence that menaces the control capacity of our Ego, the spontaneous and brute opening that marries us with the divine: without suspicion, without control, without conditions and manipulations of the Ego. When we are afraid of the Beast, when we fear the vigor of the vital force present inside us, when we fear the great union of life and death of which the Beast vibrates, often we try to put it behind bars, we avoid its danger, protecting ourselves and still always enchanted like spectators at the zoo. (p. 150)

In my experience with active imagination, a dream image took me before the same contradictory and paradoxical aspects of existence, indicating how the healing power of Eros exists beyond the scenes:

A pearl of incomparable beauty is encrusted with excrement. To appreciate and to enjoy its fine white light, it is necessary to insert my hands through the excrement, to pick up the pearl and clean it. One who stops on the surface can think that under the excrement there is nothing. One who knows how to look, instead, under the excrement finds the most precious pearl hidden. I pick it up, a white milky sphere that changes; it is the consecrated host shown to the faithful.

Back to the figure of the soul companion: his presence and the possibility of dialoguing imaginatively with him represented a constant source of creative energy with which I could face numerous destructive attacks from negative masculine images, such as the one of the raping man. His presence represented also a precious opportunity to give another shape to my feeling of love, taking to pieces and reassembling, in a more pleasant and creative way, the plans and the stories from which it had been made until then.

In this situation, a dream image gave me the measure of my internal situation:

I am at the sea with my soul companion, who keeps me close, staying behind me; together we look at the sea. On the left we see a city: two circular towers delimit the entrance. They are two big phalluses. The left one is down on the ground: the right one stands up. My soul companion tells me that the left one has been stricken in a battle, but it has been left there to remember, a testimony to struggle.

The presence of the soul companion has diluted many destructive experiences to which my erotic experience sent me back, making me separate from paternal and patriarchal patterns of suffering that – as Eisler (1996) writes – often concentrated more on death, punishment and pain than on sex, birth and pleasure.

We are used to experience, in our culture, the relationships between masculine and feminine mainly as hostile and violent relationships. Finding again internally the figure of the soul companion, who is very different from both the rapist and the idealized father, and marrying him in the soul marriage, means to unite the creative aspects of masculine Eros, healing the wounds that a culture like ours often inflicts on the souls of both men and women. As we know, the soul prefers the conciliatory and the private, enjoying the wholeness of existence and its paradoxes, and teaches the superior wisdom of love to human beings.

Back to my experience of active imagination and the images of the soul marriage, the dreams let me know – using the same symbol that is in the story of *Beauty and the Beast* – that the marriage will take place "when the leaves of the rose will fall." In the meanwhile, from the center of the earth arrives the wedding gift: a necklace of gold and lava stones.

This necklace is a symbol full of energy, that shows visually what I have tried to say in words. Jung wrote (MDR) that his dreams and his imagination have been "the incandescent magma from which springs the stone that must be sculpted." The lava stone necklace represents, in my experience, the crystallization of the incandescent magma of the destructive and creative aspects of Eros: the crystallized material, mounted in gold, that holds together the dark and the bright aspects of the erotic experience and decorates the bride for her soul marriage.

Comparing the first image of the attempted rape with the one of the necklace, it is possible to understand the way of transformation that my feeling has taken in this experience of active imagination. The bride and the spouse have exchanged their promise of love: words conquered at the end of a difficult and painful journey, expressing the full joy that springs from the erotic creativity:

I shall marry you with the moon ring, says the woman;
I shall marry you with the sun ring, says the man.

Conclusion

If destruction and creation belong to the dynamic of existence – and we know that it is so – destruction and creation mark the erotic experience of the human being. Destructive masculine aspects of Eros such as rape, the event in the group, the active imagination "Raping the Soul," the myth of Isis and Osiris, the image of the soul companion and the one of the necklace, make me think about some destructive and creative vicissitudes, both personal and cultural, of the erotic experience and about their possible transformation.

It is important to remember, once again, how this experience of active imagination started by a concomitance of facts that consciousness had considered in a too quick and unilateral way and that my feeling had proposed instead with images of a greater breadth. In retrospect, I consider the images of "Raping the Soul" a precious direction offered to me for my journey of individuation.

We know how much, in our culture, the relationships between men and women, between masculine and feminine are marked strongly by the dynamics of destructive power and by overwhelming ideals. In a culture such as ours, a great risk is that reciprocal suspicion enforces the vicious circle that makes the woman more sterile in her capacity to love and the man more impotent in his capacity to be fertile.

We can agree on recognizing how much our souls and our bodies suffer painfully the lack of a propitious union between male and female, between human and divine, between man and woman. It is a need of union that the phenomenon of rape shouts in a form highly dramatic and destructive, imposing on both masculine and feminine consciousness the weight of the reflection. At the same time, thinking in the direction of the soul companion and following the wisdom of the heart, we also know that only the alliance of the masculine with the feminine and the respect for reciprocal creativity, both physical and psychic, makes the human being the conscious author of reciprocal well-being.

At the entrance to the third millennium, we need gestures and words of soul that tell, with passion and enjoyment, stories of love and friendship of men and women and our common will to share creatively the pleasure of love.

Translated from the original Italian byDanielle Ruggiero,
revised by Robert Mercurio

References

Dubosc, F.O. (unpublished). *Il tesoro naascosto delle Mille e una Notte. Archeologia mitologica dei principi di genere.*

Eisler, R. (1996). *Il Piacere è Sacro. Il Mito del Sesso come Purificazione.* Milano: Frassinelli.

Leonard, L. (1987). *La Via al Matrimonio.* Roma: Astrolabio.

Te Paske, B. (1987). *Il Rito dello Stupro. Il Sacrificio delle Donne nella Violenza Sessuale.* Camo: R.e.d.

Destructiveness and Healing

Epistemological and Jungian Reflections

Renos K. Papadopoulos
London, England
Independent Group of Jungian Analysts

Destructiveness in its various forms has occupied a central place in both psychoanalysis and analytical psychology. In the main, psychoanalysis seems to have approached destructiveness through the notion of aggressive impulses, drives or instincts, whereas analytical psychology has placed its emphasis on the concept of shadow and the problem of evil in its treatment of the same subject. Both schools consider destructiveness one of the most fundamental issues in human nature. However, any such consideration is influenced (consciously or unconsciously) by a host of other factors: from philosophical views, cultural and theological positions as well as moral and ethical values, to the pragmatics of the socio-economic, political and historical realities. Consequently, destructiveness is a multifaceted and multidimensional phenomenon which cannot and should not be limited to the realm of any single discipline. Yet, because it is such an emotional issue, it is imperative that we focus our attention on the way we approach destructiveness before we embark on any further elaboration. It is essential that we reflect on the epistemology which we imperceptibly employ in approaching the subject of destructiveness.

Epistemological Concerns

Regardless of how one defines destructiveness, there are three over-arching factors that interweave: the position in which we locate ourselves in discussing destructiveness, the way we approach it (implicitly or explicitly) – either as a personal characteristic or a collective phenomenon – and our ideas about the aetiology of destructiveness.

As with any logical and philosophical pursuit, one must ask: Who is the person who is addressing the topic of destructiveness and under what circumstances? Within what context and for what purpose is this pursuit taking place? In answering these questions, our very position and identity as mental health professionals affect our approach to destructiveness.

At first glance, there seems to be nothing unusual in the idea that society recruits mental health professionals to assist with understanding and explaining destructiveness by providing psychological insights about it. Viewed from this perspective, mental health professionals are mere commentators who supply, mainly on demand, their particular expert opinion. This type of assistance is based on the formula that is used widely in society and which I have called "the Societal Discourse of the Expert" (Papadopoulos 1998a). This discourse governs the rules and regulations, the expectations and obligations, the positions, identities and relationships of everyone involved in the actions and interactions, belief systems and networks that are activated whenever we turn to experts for help in areas where specialist expertise is needed. The Societal Discourse of the Expert creates a certain type of interdependence among its actors which, at best, facilitates smooth and easier living conditions, and at worst, fosters exploitation and manipulation: authoritarianism on the side of the expert, and impotence on the side of the consumer. In the context of destructiveness, the Societal Discourse of the Expert has intricate ramifications which should make us re-examine the idea that what is happening is simply a recruitment of professionals to explain an area "where specialist expertise is needed."

On examining this further, it is important to observe that, as members of the mental health profession we are located on the side of health and, perforce, against non-health or pathology. Whatever phenomenon we address, we have this unavoidable predisposition, regardless of our awareness of it. When we see human pain and suffering, we cannot avoid formulating our observations and theories within this polarity. (Other professionals will view the same phenomena through their own lenses: for example, theologians in the language of good and evil and sociologists in terms of societal considerations.) Thus, insofar as destructiveness is humanly abhorrent, we will invariably pathologise it

We seem to be caught up in a debilitating conundrum: We cannot afford to "normalise" destructiveness, but we cannot delve more deeply into it in order to understand it more fully unless we adopt a less judgmental stance. This impossible situation has multifarious repercussions; one of them is exemplified by our attitudes towards the outbreak of new wars. After each eruption of violent hostilities or war we believe that we shall never forget it, that we shall learn from the horrible experience and thus avoid any repetitions. Yet, when the next outbreak occurs, we react as if we did not expect it to happen. Humanity seems to need to keep cleansing itself from the horrors of war by repeatedly "forgetting" them and thus renewing its innocence.

A simple explanation of this complex phenomenon is that, as human beings, we cannot afford to be neutral about destructiveness; inevitably, moral considerations influence our perception and judgement of destructiveness and violence. This means that there will always be an epistemological confusion (in mixing theoretical with moral dimensions) whenever we approach the subject of destructiveness.

Psychologising and Pathologising Destructiveness

Society faces a painful paradox because, on the one hand, the phenomenon of destructiveness itself, being widespread and affecting most of us, demands to be comprehended; on the other hand, what professionals offer provides no satisfactory explanation. It is not an understanding of the phenomenon of destructiveness but an anaesthetisation of the pain derived from the incomprehensibility of it, via ornate psychologisations and pathologisations. Unwittingly, we are used by society to explain away the disturbing complexity of destructiveness and replace it with sanitised theories. Under such pressure, we tend to employ causal-reductive approaches which isolate destructiveness and treat it as if we were investigating something that has nothing to do with us and our own nature.

By no means do I wish to suggest that destructiveness is "normal" or acceptable. But is placing it on the normal – abnormal polarity the only way to deal with it? Perhaps the first step towards a deeper understanding would be for us to appreciate the fact that we are trapped and imprisoned by and within these constraints, where the pathology narrative occupies a key position.

That is, a paradox exists that prevents us from developing a deeper understanding and appreciation of the multifaceted complexities of destructiveness and violence. If we could afford to avoid moralising, without ignoring the moral dimension, and equally avoid psychologising, without ignoring the psychological dimension, perhaps we could begin to contemplate that, after all, destructiveness may be a tragic facet of the human condition.

The Tragedy of Destructiveness

Returning to the three overarching factors, we now see that (a) our position as mental health professionals is coloured by the Societal Discourse of the Expert and we are thus entrapped within the dichotomous narrative of oppositionality (pathology-health); (b) as mental health professionals, we seem to be predisposed to approaching destructiveness as a personal (and indeed an intrapsychic) phenomenon, especially as a result of employing (mostly in an imperceptible way) the comforting but debilitating linear-causal epistemology; and (c) in terms of aetiology, we are divided according to the party lines of our analytical perspectives. This division is based on the debate that can be expressed roughly as follows: Is aggression an innate quality or drive or it is a reaction to external circumstances? We know that, as analysts, we do not have a good track record when it comes to addressing wider social issues; this may be the result of our internal over-involvement with this debate. By being preoccupied with our own internal theoretical arguments, we seem to have missed glaring external factors such as environmental pressures, socio-political realities, and historical legacies. Spasmodic expressions of concern about social issues appear not only to have little effect but they also exemplify the fact that we do not have, as yet, any approaches which could join together in a seamless way our theory, clinical practice and social concerns as citizens which may then provide us with coherent responses to societal expressions of destructiveness and violence.

As a consequence of the resulting epistemological confusion, narratives about destructiveness and war seem to occupy a paradoxical position in the western world; usually they are formulated as referring to either distant and irrelevant phenomena or to noble and heroic events. Stories of pain, terror, and atrocities are told as if they belonged to the past or as if they provide us with abstract moral lessons. Thus, when new conflicts erupt, we tend to react with some degree of confusion. In this manner, we seem destined not to learn from history but react with horror every time new armed conflict rears its head.

Destructiveness may be a tragic facet of our human condition: it is difficult to find any other word than "tragic" to describe it more appropriately, especially if we connect it with the original meaning of the word. "Tragedy" comes from *tragos* (goat); it was connected with the rituals performed by men dressed as goats in ancient Greek ceremonies. *Tragos* is also an onomatopoeic word which comes from *trogo* (to eat) and *traganizo* (to crunch). Thus, goats with their voracious appetites crunch anything in sight, regardless of whether it is good or bad for them. Indeed, there is something tragic in this potential self-destructiveness involved in the goat munching away at everything indiscriminately. Equally, impulsiveness and lack of discrimination are key characteristics of destructiveness. By emphasising the tragic aspect of destructiveness, we bypass the impossible questions as to whether it is inevitable or not, innate or reactive, personal or collective. By acknowledging the tragic element of destructiveness we accept that, as human beings, we are part of the tragedy of destructiveness. Our task then becomes the endeavour to locate ourselves as individuals, meaningfully within it, rather than explain it away.

Ordinariness and the Ecology of Violence

A consequence of understanding destructiveness as a tragic aspect of being human is that our position has the possibility of being shifted and, consequently, the arrogance of the "detached expert" can be replaced by compassion. From this new perspective, we may admit that destructiveness has always been part of our society. According to Heraclitus, "War is the father of all things." Conflict and strife, oppositionality and destructiveness are part of life and, in addition to their obvious negative effects, they may have a positive function. Therefore, we do not need to be fixed in a position from which we simply condemn destructiveness and distance ourselves from it. Usually, we tend to ascribe all kinds of bizarre and conspiratorial theories behind manifestations of destructiveness in order to distance ourselves from these allegedly inhuman phenomena. Yet, tragically, they may be much more "ordinary" than we would like to admit. This realisation makes us feel most uncomfortable. Accepting the ordinariness of destructiveness does not support its being innate or necessary; it merely acknowledges that, given the conditions in society and the vicissitudes of our existence, this phenomenon is fairly common.

This new perspective allows us to move away from the impossible dilemma that was posed above; how to avoid pathologising destructiveness without normalising it, which would imply condoning it. The way out is to create a new narrative within which the emphasis is on the ordinariness of destructiveness rather than its evaluation as either "normal" or "pathological." Hannah Arendt's famous expression "the banality of evil" aptly conveys this recognition; violent and destructive acts may be tragically more ordinary than we care to admit. It is threatening for us to accept the humanness of destructive acts: we are afraid to admit that they are committed by ordinary people; instead, we seem compelled to attribute inhuman and diabolical motivation to such acts.

In his novel *Captain Corelli's Mandolin*, Louis de Bernières – expresses in a most sensitive way – his thoughts about the ordinariness of destructiveness. He describes the situation when soldiers, after a period of anxious inactivity, experience action:

> *We found that there is a wild excitement when the tension of waiting is done with, and that sometimes it transforms itself into a kind of demented sadism once an action is commenced. You cannot always blame the soldiers for their atrocities, because I can tell you from experience that they are the natural consequences of the inferno of relief that comes from not having to think any more. Atrocities are sometimes nothing less than the vengeance of the tormented. (p. 61)*

The author does not judge or blindly condemn violence in an outright and dismissive fashion but, in a remarkably brave way, attempts to understand it. He characterises violence as a "natural consequence," not as good or bad, not as pathological or normal. Although he is not advancing a psychological theory and he is not using specialist language, "natural consequences" implies that atrocities, the actions themselves, are part of a bigger whole; one cannot focus exclusively on them, ignoring the rest. "Atrocities are sometimes nothing more than the vengeance of the tormented," means that the soldiers are brutalised and placed, unmercifully, within a cycle of violence which they did not instigate and which had begun before them. Violent acts are not committed, necessarily, by perverted individuals but by ordinary people who are caught up in tragic circumstances; most human beings are capable of violence. This narrative emphasises what could be called "the ecology of violence" rather than individual motivation. Moreover, this perspective locates us not as detached observers but makes us acknowledge that violence is also part of us, part of our lives. According to Jung, destructiveness is part of our shadow.

We cannot deny that our psychological and social worlds are full of shadow and violent elements. However, as human beings we have the capacity and resilience to be creative and constructive, especially when we are fully aware of these elements in ourselves. Jung accounts for these tragic circumstances by means of the archetypal shadow which, when it is activated in a particularly strong and gripping way, inevitably interconnects the wider collective with the personal (and indeed, intrapsychic) dimension; under these conditions, it is very unlikely that individuals will be able to resist this archetypal radiation and to maintain their own personal integrity. Thus, destructiveness reigns supreme and the archetype overwhelms all individualities. It is indeed frightening to acknowledge that this phenomenon is ordinary, despite its devastating effects.

Archetypal Fascination

The power of the archetype is manifested not only when it overwhelms individuals but also when it fascinates them. This phenomenon is equally common and ordinary. Destructiveness and violence are endemic in our society today. Violence sells and it strongly influences our art, literature, film, theatre and even fashion and design; so much so, that nowadays it is appropriate to refer to "designer violence." Destructiveness is chic, cool and hip. There is an ever-increasing ingenuity in how to present violence in artistic forms. At any given time, most films in any big city in the world are full of violent scenes. In a poem entitled "Reyerta" (The Fight), Lorca (1960) describes a fight with vivid descriptions of horrible and violent acts, all in a poetic way. Thus, he refers to the killing of the poem's hero: he "rolls down the slope dead, his body laden with lilies and a pomegranate on his brow. Now he rides a cross of fire on the highway to death." This lyric language is used to describe a ghastly piece of excruciating violence when a person was knifed to death by "clasp-knives, rendered beautiful with enemy's blood," which "glinted like fishes" (pp. 37-8).

The dilemma is that we cannot ignore the fascination and attraction destructiveness exerts on people and concentrate only on condemning it, because such an emphasis is not likely to produce many changes. On the other hand, it is not easy to acknowledge this fascination, and it is not comfortable to address these dark aspects of ourselves. Nevertheless, we know that violence can have an exhilarating and even liberating effect on the individual. This happens for at least four reasons:

1) In the act of violence, the individual does not need to think. As de Bernières said, there is a "relief that comes from not having to think any more." The "not thinking" here does not refer exclusively to cognitive thinking or the Jungian "thinking" function; instead, it relates to W.R. Bion's idea of the ability to create a space to reflect when one is overwhelmed by pressing impulses. Not having space to reflect provides a tragic kind of relief, as the person eradicates the pain caused by difficult considerations and by the awareness of inner contradictions and conflicts.

2) Gripped by a destructive archetype, people achieve a false "wholeness," insofar as they are dominated by "acting out" behaviour. Although acting out is frowned upon in psychoanalysis and analytical psychology, we fail to appreciate the attraction it may have, in mobilising the totality of the personality to act in unison. In acting out there is no division between thoughts, feelings and actions; all become one and action flows. This is tragically similar to the coveted aim of many spiritual practices which, after many years of hard and disciplined training, aspire to achieve moments or a state of being where action flows and inner divisions are abolished. By no means do I suggest that Zen meditation and impulsive acts of destructiveness are the same but it is imperative that we acknowledge the striking similarities.

3) Destructiveness can have a chilling purity that is extremely seductive. This observation is difficult to convey, but we can approximate it by connecting it with the process of archetypal possession where one polarity, devoid of personal content, dominates the individual. This possession has a numinous quality because, regardless of the content of the archetype, it is a distilled form of pure image and has an unmistakable and refreshing authenticity. Any purity exerts a powerful attraction and makes people wish to continue the connection with it. People offer themselves to protect this purity from any threat of contamination and commit atrocities in the name of defending and "cleansing" the perceived source of purity. This complex dynamic is close to the "Luciferian light" of evil.

4) Individual identity is subsumed by a wider collective identity. Within the context of personal identity, people are burdened by various conflicts and inner struggles; they feel refreshed when they shed this identity – even temporarily – by connecting with wider

forms of identity. Society has sanctioned times, places and conditions where this happens automatically, such as in sports competitions when a person becomes a fan, abandoning personal history and identity and feeling the exhilaration of joining with the crowd of supporters of a team. Numerous such sanctioned settings connect one with collective aspects of our identity in an innocuous and even growthful way: for example professional associations, community activities and family events. However, under certain conditions when destructive acts are played out on the societal plane, people become polarised and, as Jung (CW10) put it, "willy-nilly" a collective identity is imposed on them. The tragedy is that there are some paradoxical benefits of this imposition of a collective and a cancellation (however temporary) of the personal identity. Both victim and oppressor, or victim and saviour glow in the righteousness of their cause. A victim will feel self-righteous because, being an actual recipient of brutalisation, such a person does not need to get in touch with personal shadow material. After all, these people are not responsible for the calamity that has befallen them and therefore deserve our support, sympathy, love and eternal care. Although it may be less obvious why the oppressor may feel liberated, it becomes clearer when we remember that no perpetrators of violence see themselves as such; instead, they see themselves as selflessly serving the purity of their collective. The idea that the saviour feels liberated and infatuated by the role.

Towards an Ecology of Destructiveness

A serious appreciation of all these considerations leads to an emphasis on the "ecology of destructiveness," rather than isolated explanations and simplifications. The various roles that destructiveness imposes on people (victims, survivors, saviours, oppressors, observers, critics) are all interconnected within archetypal scenarios. In this way, destructiveness is seen not as an isolated and individual phenomenon but as part of a wider ecology. We can appreciate how we cannot be detached observers or commentators, how destructiveness is tragically more ordinary than we care to admit and that it has dark and shadow attractions. An ecological perspective can provide the safest possible framework to examine the psychological states which victims and survivors of destructiveness experience.

Jungian Reflections

In my own work with survivors of violence (Papadopoulos 1998b) I have endeavoured to apply the principles outlined above. Although this kind of work seems different from most analytic practices of one-to-one structure in private or hospital consulting rooms, the basic principles underlying them are remarkably similar. Moreover, Jungian insights can inform and enrich such approaches. These Jungian insights include the following:

1) Jung's alchemical metaphor of psychotherapy offers an apt illustration of the importance of a strong and clear vessel within which difficult and potentially disruptive material can be contained. A strong therapeutic vessel can enable the appropriate emotional proximity to the survivors and their experiences, in a way that would render any therapeutic work safe. Moreover, Jung's openness in employing creative ways of applying therapeutic processes is well known. He eschewed established therapeutic styles and was always looking for novel applications. More specifically, one of his particular sensitivities was the awareness of the limitations of our psychotherapeutic practices, due to their Eurocentric nature. Jung was one of the first European psychologists to draw our attention to this type of limitation and, as analytical psychologists, we are in a position to develop this awareness further.

2) The ordinary nature of human suffering is another central insight of Jung's approach, accompanied by his efforts to avoid pathologising psychological problems. Characteristically, he argued that "behind a neurosis there is so often concealed all the natural and necessary suffering the patient has been unwilling to bear" (CW16, 185). It could be said that Jung's efforts were directed towards making human suffering more accessible to people. He articulated this concern by emphasising the individual's developing a "personal myth": a narrative that accounts for the uniqueness of the individual within the context of collective narratives.

3) Instead of imposing on survivors techniques from traditional therapeutic frames (e.g. debriefing or emphasis on coping skills), my intent has been to empower them to develop their own new narratives within which their experiences would acquire different meaning. In this context, they need the presence of a helpful person who is well aware of the multiplicity of traps and possibilities inherent in therapeutic interactions (i.e., the varieties of transference/countertransference). In essence, what they need is the experience of what I

call "therapeutic witnessing." Thus, the "therapeutic presence" provides an actual human witness who can facilitate (with minimal intervention) the thawing and re-connection of the various parts of their personal and collective narratives which were frozen from the traumatic experiences.

4) The "witnessing" of their testimony (see Felman and Laub 1992) is not always verbal. Respecting that certain experiences must be shared in silence – due to their unspeakable horror and inhumanity – there were times when our shared silence honours the unutterable: We know what we are silent about and why. At other times, when referring to certain inhuman experiences, the very use of language attempts to re-establish the humanity of the person. For example, in narrating an episode where for days on end they had lived in filthy conditions, soiled by their own excrement, one of the ex-prisoners could not utter the words "human excrement" (or any other similar word); instead, he tortuously implied the word but without actually saying it. Thus, he was restoring his own human dignity even whilst narrating an inhuman experience).

Appreciating these phenomena as essentially archetypal experiences exerting powerful fascination, I am humbly aware that they may overwhelm my personality with their "archetypal radiation." The fascination is exerted at many different levels: meeting the people who have gone through such powerful experiences the content and the events they relate to, the overwhelmingly heroic feeling which imbues all the aid workers, and the variety of emotional reactions one has in these situations. However, this fascination extends to darker aspects of the human psyche in most complex ways. Shadow elements threaten to engulf the personality; destructive images acquire obsessive fascination. There is a real danger that therapeutic work in these situations becomes a vehicle for re-activation of these images. Polarisation of perceptions, ideas, personalities and situations threatens indiscriminate destructiveness. Under these distressing conditions, it is no wonder that "frozenness" emerges to save the individual from complete disintegration. We are dealing here with special types of defences of the self.

Analytical psychologists, led by Fordham (1974), have dealt in various ways with the particular types of defences that are aimed at protecting the very core of the self. However, most of them assume that predispositions developed in earlier stages of one's life are largely responsible for the emergence of these defences. Nevertheless, experiences in working with survivors of violence and disaster show that such defences can appear, tragically, in individuals without such early experiences. This phenomenon requires further investigation.

Finally, Jung did not shy away from acknowledging that some psychological phenomena are indeed connected with actual evil. Unless we respect the complexity of the multifaceted nature of destructiveness, in working with survivors of atrocities we are likely to fall into tragic positions from which we will psychologise evil and pathologise human suffering.

References

Felman, S. and Laub, D. (1992). *Testimony. Crises of Witnessing in Literature, Psychoanalysis and History*. London: Routledge.

Fordham, M. (1974). "Defences of the Self," *Journal of Analytical Psychology, 19*, 192-196.

Papadopoulos, R. K. (1998a). The tyranny of change. In *Proceedings of the Cumberland Lodge Conference,1996*. London: The Champernowne Trust.

Papadopoulos, R. K. (1998b). Destructiveness, atrocities and healing: Epistemological and clinical reflections. *The Journal of Analytical Psychology, 43*-4, 455-477.

The Millennium Rite of Passage

Ann Casement
London, England
Association of Jungian Analysts

The approaching millennium represents the most important rite of passage that any of us will ever experience. At such a time, the collective psyche is prone to portentous experiences, and events become imbued with sacred meaning. One recent event, in the shadow of the millennium, is the death of Diana, Princess of Wales, in September 1997. My main focus is the sacred/profane duality that surrounds major rites of passage, as linked to the paradoxes associated with royalty. The word "clinical" in my title points to my exploring all this in the alchemical container of Jungian analysis. My approach is married to that of social anthropology, interspersed with occasional visits to Frazer's (1971) *The Golden Bough*.

Jung differentiated collective consciousness from the collective unconscious: "Ego-consciousness seems to be dependent on two factors: firstly, on the conditions of the collective, i.e. the social, consciousness; and secondly, on the archetypes or dominants, of the collective unconscious" (CW8, 423). The first factor is the repository of the social, philosophical, ethical and religious problems of any one time. The second is timeless and in the realm of archetypal and instinctual contents. Royalty's secular and divine aspects transcend collective consciousness and unconscious while its two halves are rooted firmly in each of these realms.

Symbols emanate from the collective unconscious, whereas signs come from collective consciousness. Signs are symptoms of the subliminal process. A true symbol is an expression of an intuitive idea that cannot yet be formulated in any better way.

The death of Diana represented equally symbol and sign. For many, it was shrugged off as the product of media manipulation and mass hysteria; for others, the death had the effect of the symbol in mystifying and unifying large numbers of people. The impact of the symbol derives from its numinosity, which Jung defined as "A quality belonging to a visible object or the influence of an invisible presence that causes a peculiar alteration of consciousness" (CW12, 6).

A numinous experience has the full force of a confrontation with something that is as yet undisclosed but is experienced as fateful and meaningful. This kind of feeling often acts as a catalyst for unifying people on a collective level and leads to an experience of liminality and community. Turner (1995), that most Jungian of anthropologists, wrote of liminality as blending "lowliness and sacredness, homogeneity and comradeship." Community or *"communitas,"* the Latin version that he favors, Turner has described society as "an unstructured or rudimentarily structured and relatively undifferentiated ... community, or even communion of equal individuals who submit together to the general authority of the ritual elders" (p. 96).

Shortly after Diana's death, The London newspaper *The Economist* expressed its collective feeling of being mystified at the strength of its own reaction to the event. Here is an extract from a letter I sent in response:

> *[Re] your. ... overwhelming response to the extraordinary events of last week. What you describe is the mystifying, unifying, healing and changing power of the symbol. The feelings of community that have been engendered ... are another aspect of the symbol at work.*

Given the largely secular bias of *The Economist*, I was surprised to see my letter published at the top of the letters column. At the same time, it felt like another example of the huge role played by the media in Diana's outer life. Her more private side sought the solace of different forms of therapy. *Mercurius,* the alchemical name given to Hermes – that many-hued and wily deity – is the patron god of both communication and therapy. It is this Janus-like dual aspect always associated with that deity that we experience in the two sides of Diana.

The dual nature of what Jung called the Trickster is a reflection of Mercurius – half animal/half divine – a seemingly negative figure who yet manages to achieve through stupidity what others fail to achieve through wit or straightforward cleverness. The Trickster is compensatory to consciously-held views and goals and manifests through slips of the tongue, accidents and coincidences. Above all, in his power to bring transformation through new energy, he has the numinosity of all saviour-like figures.

Princess Diana embodied the duality associated with Mercurius. She presented to the media her outer carapace of glamour; the inner world of pain that was betrayed by those large, sad eyes she took to therapy. Both disciplines share the ruling deity of Mercurius but toward each he presents a different aspect. In his aspect of messenger, Mercurius is the god of the media, who infects journalists with an insatiable desire to find out secrets in order to be able to tell about them. In his aspect of psychopomp, he is the figure who guides the psyche at times of transition and liminality. It is this aspect of Mercurius/Hermes that is the god of therapy. In its course, this figure may be seen to be embodied by the therapist. Mercurius bestows on the therapist the privilege of being the repository of secrets, combined with the responsibility of being able to hold and contain them.

The Trickster plays an important part in my approach to Diana. This figure embodies compensatory energy both to the conscious attitude of the individual and also for the collective. That is, the Trickster points the way to what Jung calls "shadow": all that is denied and rejected because it is seen as inferior on a personal and collective level. Shadow, as an archetype, brings with it powerful affect when it is constellated, especially on a collective level. Once again, we are confronted with the duality of opposites: in this instance the duality of light equated with consciousness and ego, and dark equated with shadow. The opposites incorporated in Mercurius are each other's shadow; it is these opposites that are to be found in the media – and in therapy. This fact may go some way to explaining the uneasy relationship between the two: the media indulging in endless envious attacks on therapy and therapists while the latter, for their part, seem frozen into a state of paranoid projection onto the media.

Duality is a constant theme associated with Diana; another is the saint/whore projections she attracted to herself. This image of the sacred prostitute belongs to the pagan world before it was split by Christianity into the Virgin Mary and Mary Magdalene. It recurs in alchemical texts as the chaste bride and whore combined in the chaos of undifferentiated matter wherein lies the hidden deity (Mercurius) who contains the potential new life.

In life, Diana often was scapegoated as well as adulated and the sins of the many put on to her to carry. Thus, her death may be seen as a ritual sacrifice. The scapegoat performs for society that most cohesive function of all: providing a dustbin for the collective shadow. The redeemer is above all a scapegoat, by whose sacrifice a ritual act of catharsis or purging of all society's impurities takes place. After the rite of sacrifice comes the rite of incorporation, which was acted out collectively by the devouring of anything about Diana in the media. This act of incorporation both takes in and potentially integrates the energy of the savior; it also helps to salve the conscience of all concerned in the scapegoating and subsequent sacrifice. In this way, social glue is restored.

Panic of Sorrow

The awe with which the archetype of Death grips us all, and its place in the scheme of things, are well-understood by both Jung and the French sociologist Émile Durkheim. For Jung, death and rebirth are two sides of the same archetype or psychic reality at work in an individual – and in the collective – throughout life. When individual ego-consciousness and the social ego are confronted by a numinous event or image, the result may be a defeat for the ego, experienced as a death. In this death lies the potential new life which, incorporated, can lead to a further expansion of the ego.

The social order, for Durkheim (1965), was the focus of attention. He was always fascinated by anything that added to social glue; society was a numinosum. According to him, funeral or mourning rites were in a special category of their own. He named these "expiatory" rites, where sadness and sorrow are the dominant emotions. Rites of mourning produce a veritable "panic of sorrow," the social function of which is to draw the group together when its solidarity is threatened by the loss of an individual. In this way, the group reaffirms its permanence in the face of the transience of the individual.

For Durkheim, all ritual exists to shore up social cohesion. Religious ceremonial is the culmination, bringing together members of a society in an act of self-worship, the ultimate in social glue. Thus, in ritually sanctifying and worshipping Diana, people were taking part, ultimately, in their own sanctification. Durkheim's (1965) central thesis is that no religion is false.

Religious beliefs and practices undoubtedly seem disconcerting at times, and one is tempted to attribute them to some sort of a deepseated error. But one must know how to go underneath the symbol to the reality which it represents and which gives it its meaning. (p. 14)

Durkheim means "social" reality where Jung would substitute "psychic" reality. But apart from that the two probably would be in agreement with the rest of the statement. Ultimately, for Durkheim, the sacred referred to those things in society that are forbidden or set apart. Since this came about through an act of society, he concluded that the sacred force must be society itself.

Through a variety of acts sanctioned by British society in which they were embedded, Diana had royal/divine status conferred upon and later taken from her. Through marriage to a prince she was invested with the title "royal," but divested of it through divorce. However, this was a royal who had a deep intuitive understanding of the duality of the sacred and profane body of the monarchy; her life became increasingly one of privilege combined with an extraordinary empathy with the under-privileged. Her common touch, both literal and figurative, can also be seen as an antidote to the "King's Evil," an illness which only the monarch's touch can cure.

The term King's Evil was originally the rather fanciful name for scrofula, a tubercular swelling of the lymph glands that was popularly believed to be curable by the touch of royalty. Versions of this belief can be found at different times in other societies, but in England the custom was first adopted in the reign (1042-1066) of Edward the Confessor. It reached its zenith at the time of the Restoration when Charles II was said to have touched more than 90,000 people. The last royal healer in England was Queen Anne (1702-1707). The custom then dwindled out of existence until it was revived in recent years by Diana.

It is interesting to speculate why this phenomenon takes on new life at certain times. Charles II was restored to the throne with the monarchical powers claimed by his father somewhat modified, and had to demonstrate that he was fully aware of both the profane and the sacred aspects of the monarch. Being literally in touch with the common people would have been a way of demonstrating this duality. Diana seems to have been what Jung called a "feeling" type – someone who has a feel for the emotional needs of other individuals or of the collective. Out of her own suffering she was brought into touch with that of millions of others. In this way and in her own right she gradually assumed the mantle of divine and profane royalty. Diana's touch, in both its literal and metaphorical senses, contrasts with the actual monarch's seemingly being out of touch with the sentiments of the people. This was a point that was made, often forcibly, by the media at the time of Diana's death.

Sacred and Profane

In the symbolic form of Diana, the duality of the sacred and profane aspects of monarchy were seen to coalesce. Separated from the common (profane) world, the sacred appears in myths, sounds, ritual activity, people, and natural objects – all of which may come together to confer sacred status on an object, be it a person or an activity. Through the re-telling of a myth, the divine action that was done "in the beginning" is repeated. The repetition of the sacred action symbolically duplicates the power that originally established the world.

The sacred, which expresses the ultimate value and meaning of life, is the eternal reality. This reality is recognized to have been before it was known and to be known differently from the way in which common things are known, through myth or ritual activity. However, the duality of sacred/profane is complicated by the fact that the sacred itself can include the dichotomy pure/unpure. For instance, the Polynesian *tapu* designates something as not "free" for common use because of its extraordinary energy, which includes both generating and polluting forces.

Thus, anyone unprotected by special powers who comes into contact with the sacred can be polluted and destroyed by it. Incest, for example, is a prerogative of the gods and not allowed to ordinary mortals. Only a person who has entered the divine realm is pure; this transition was often marked by a ritual act of rebirth. The concept of the twice-born in India and in Christianity, along with Jung's alchemical model of death and rebirth, point to the actual material birth of an individual and to a subsequent symbolic rebirth.

There is a further ambiguity. What one person regards as sacred or profane is not necessarily so regarded by others. This ambiguity goes a long way in explaining the conflicting responses to what has come to be known as the "Diana phenomenon." The sacred sets the boundary of human capability but also represents the unlimited possibility that draws us beyond the limiting spatio-temporal structures of human existence. Only the sacred can fulfill humankind's deepest needs. Thus the reverence shown to the sacred is composed of both trust and terror.

Sacred Kingship

The concept of sacred kingship has been a human preoccupation since ancient times. This concept is related to what Jung calls the Self, which is for him the central and unifying principle of the whole psyche, both consciousness and the unconscious. The Self is no less than another image of the divine and often manifests in dreams or phantasies as a royal personage.

On the level of outer reality, the sacred ruler has been the possessor of supernatural powers, both beneficent and malevolent. In former times, power resided in one person who had the necessary physical and psychic strength over both people and objects. The king's power extended over everything in his community; only gradually was this power shared with others within the community. A residual belief from this era is that collective mores and national feelings of self-worth still are felt to derive from the transcendent position of the monarch. In Britain, for instance, the primacy of family life and values are felt to be encapsulated in the institution of the Royal Family.

Frazer (1971) concentrates on the study of divine kingship and power, and of how different societies deal with its loss in their ruler. In his chapter on the killing of the divine king – a widespread motif – Frazer devoted considerable space to Seligman's (1932) ethnological account of the Shilluk, a Nilotic people who inhabit the southern part of the Sudan and who numbered about 110,000 in the 1970s. In 1909 – when Seligman visited them – they were united in a single tribal state headed by a divine king to whom great reverence was paid; he was thought to derive his power from the spirit of the semi-divine hero who had founded the royal dynasty. Frazer gives a particularly colorful account of how the Shilluk went about their regular custom of putting the king to death whenever he showed signs of ill-health or failing strength.

For this tribal people, failing strength was directly equated with failing potency; when the king showed an incapacity to satisfy the sexual passions of his many wives, they would report this to the chiefs. The chiefs would signal the bad news of impending doom to the king by spreading a white cloth over his face and knees as he lay slumbering in the heat of the sultry afternoon. Execution soon followed, in a hut specially built for the occasion. The king was led into it; he lay down with his head resting on the lap of a nubile virgin. The hut was then walled up and the two were left to perish of starvation and suffocation. Later, this long, drawn-out process was ameliorated; the king was dispatched more quickly by being strangled, likewise in a hut built for the occasion.

The custom of putting the divine king to death at the first sign of his failing power is the Shilluk way of preserving the divine spirit by which he is animated "in the most perfect state of efficiency" (Frazer 1971, p. 353). Putting the king to death while he is still vigorous and physically attractive ensures that the divine spirit is transmitted to his successor whilst it is still unimpaired by weakness or old age.

Youth, vigor and sexual attraction are thus all necessary attributes of divine kingship. This necessity was evidenced after Diana's death by the debate about the monarchy and the succession. It may be that her death while still in full youth and vigor fulfilled the archetypal task of ensuring the continuing potency of the monarchy. Diana's death also served to draw attention to the aging Queen and Prince Charles, and to the populist idea that Charles should be passed over in favor of the young Prince William. Overnight it seemed that the great archetype of Death had conferred on Diana the divine status projected onto her by "the people." The monarch was seen to be out of favor because she was too remote and, in what appeared as a petty act of vengeance, she had removed Diana's royal status. Even the legitimacy of this act was questioned. Hence the monarch lost – at least temporarily – her status, which was now seen to reside instead in Diana and her heirs, her two sons.

Thus, the death of Diana has been a catalyst in focusing attention on reforming an institution which the British hold dear but which, at the same time, has become perceived as aloof and distant from ordinary people. The movement for reform of the monarchy is seen now to reside with Tony Blair, "the people's spokesman" and – one might say – high priest, who played such a significant role in enabling the transition of Diana to "the people's princess."

To elaborate further what this latter term may mean: Ritual sacrifice of Diana as scapegoat/savior leads to purification and to her coming to life in a different form; that is, to ritual rebirth. Death, both symbolic and actual, is the archetypal transformer of an individual's status from that of profane to that of sacred. (Again, reference to Jung's alchemical analogy is appropriate.) Death purified Diana of her mis-doings and sufferings and, in one great cathartic event, transformed her into a divine being. Identification with her as a savior figure dying for their sins holds out hope for millions of suffering, venal human beings that they too can experience this kind of salvation. In millions of people's panic of sorrow a new icon is born out of mass projection. Once again we see society worshipping itself by way of worshipping the icon. In this way, society itself can be seen to be divine and to confer divine status on the object of its reverence. As a result, social glue is reinforced, instilling sentiments of *communitas*. For a while, the feelings of degeneration that have been around as we approach the millennium are swept away in a great act of renewal and regeneration. In embodying divinity, royalty and humanity in one person, Diana has managed to fulfill all the criteria for a focal point of collective identification.

What we witnessed on a collective level in the extraordinary events of late 1997 was a panic of sorrow. This collective process links to individual process in the course of a long Jungian analysis.

A great part of the analytic process is taken up with mourning the loss of the past; leaving behind childhood and the whole of the first half of life in order to start on the path of individuating, that is, realizing one's own potential. Just as, for an individual in analysis, private emotions are connected to the greater realm of the collective unconscious, so for huge numbers of people after the death of Diana, private emotions – publicly expressed – connected personal experience to a feeling of being part of a group process: *communitas*. As Durkheim (1965) said of piacular rites: "Eventually one stops mourning, and one does so because of the mourning itself" (p. 448). This process represents the stage of rebirth into a new order, both for the individual and the collective.

Opus Contra Naturam

It was in his discovery of alchemy that Jung found the link between the past and his analytic approach. The most impressive example of this is his analysis of a series of alchemical pictures from the sixteenth-century *Rosarium Philosophorum* (CW16). Through analyzing the incestuous longings between the King and Queen depicted by the left-handed contact in the second picture, Jung extrapolated the experience of erotic and incestuous longings in any long-term analysis. The incestuous element evident in the *Rosarium* between the betrothed couple is symbolized in several pictures by the brother-sister relationship of Apollo and Diana or Sol and Luna. Also in the second picture, a dove descending between the incestuous pair with a rose in its beak unites their crossed roses and points to the spiritual or divine love awakening between them. The next two pictures show that the left-handed relationship is no more and their hands are connected by the uniting symbol of flowers.

If incestuous feelings can be contained (not acted out) in an analysis – the *opus contra naturam* – the incestuous libido may be transformed into spiritual libido; both analyst and analysand participate in a higher or royal marriage that leaves both personalities more fully integrated and evolved. Along the way, both are exposed to experiences of depression and death, but eventual rebirth may take place through the constellation of the symbol of new life, the divine child. Herein lies the true import of the analytic relationship.

The alchemical relationship depicted in the *Rosarium* relates to the psychologically incestuous union – not physical incest – of Diana and her brother, Charles Spencer. If incest, or "kinship libido," can be internalized and thus spiritualized rather than lived sexually, it has the possibility of activating the spirituality that is potential in everyone, and of bringing rebirth and new life.

The crowning moment of the funeral service was Spencer's eulogy, which contained some of the following words and phrases: symbol, compassion, transcended, joy, soul, God-given, goddess, anguish, love. How Jungian! Most moving of all was when he talked of his sister's "innermost feelings of suffering that made it possible for her to connect with her constituency of the rejected." One of the valuable things I learned from the pain engendered through the voyage of self-discovery that epitomizes Jungian analysis was exactly what Spencer had managed to convey in those poignant few words. What this means is a confrontation with the shadow, which affords the possibility of a rehabilitation of all the inferior, weak and despised parts of oneself. This experience leads to an ability to be open to the rejected parts of others.

There were two targets for Spencer's anger in the address. The first was the media; the second was a less direct attack on the royal family, when he pledged that Diana's "blood family" would make sure that her two sons would not be immersed in duty and tradition.

This is the voice of the brother/lover reclaiming the children of this psychological incestuous union with his sister/lover. Let us remind ourselves that incest is the prerogative of the divine and of royalty. This symbolic incestuous union, this *hierosgamos* as Jung terms it, touched and moved the world's soul.

Diana's death, like her life, has been a catalyst for the royal family and has already brought about change that appears likely to con-

Ann Casement

tinue. While she was alive, her affair with Dodi Fayed seemed to be a source of embarrassment to the establishment. She presumably had some inkling of this. Yet her death has put royalty back in the space it must inhabit between the sacred and profane, if it is to be a living symbol and also in touch with people's actual life experience. Once again we are brought face-to-face with the mercurial transformative quality that was so central to Diana's ways of being. She possessed, and was possessed by, a quality that must be extraordinarily uncomfortable for individuals on whom Mercurius bestows it. Like him, they have the quality of being all things to all people. I have talked with innumerable people since her death: family, friends, colleagues, patients, analysands, acquaintances. Each has a quite definitive view of Diana. She was, in the end, someone who attracted every kind of projection. And that, perhaps, is what is involved in the making of an icon – the very word being a derivative of the Greek *eikon*, meaning image.

Myths and alchemy provide maps for psychological development and insight. It is particularly at times when there is a collective panic of sorrow constellated around a major rite of passage such as the millennium that we turn to them for help and enlightenment. Alchemy was seen as heretical in medieval times because its lively imagery differed from an increasingly sexless Christianity – just as psychoanalysis later differed from Victorian rationalism and suppression. Jung alluded to alchemy as a grand projected image of unconscious processes, and was drawn to it because it represented a shift away from concretism to the capacity for symbolization and creative fantasy. Above all, it represented communion with a highly ambivalent god: base and impish on the one hand and divine on the other. My main thrust here is to point to this ambivalent deity as the ruler of the life and ultimate destiny of Diana, Princess of Wales, the icon of the millennium.

References

Durkheim E. (1965). *The Elementary Forms of the Religious Life: A Study in Religious Sociology* (J.Swain, Trans.). London: Allen & Unwin. New York: Macmillan.
Frazer J. (1971). *The Golden Bough: A Study in Magic and Religion.* London: Macmillan.
Seligman, C.G. (1932). *Pagan Tribes of the Nilotic Sudan.* London: G. Routledge & Sons.
Turner, V. (1995). *The Ritual Process.* New York: Walter de Gruyter.

Integration of the Self
in a New and Global Culture

Soren R. Ekstrom
Boston, Massachusetts, USA
New York Association for Analytical Psychology

The expanding role of the global marketplace has far-reaching consequences, some of which are only beginning to impact us. As the economy, communications, and mass culture move beyond national borders, permanent migration to affluent Western countries has increased. Adults, who spent their formative years in a different country, with different customs, often speaking a different language, are drawn to new educational and economic opportunities. But there is a price to pay and these new world citizens struggle with acculturation for a long time, perhaps a life-time, while its stresses force deep-seated personality problems to surface.

The effects of the global marketplace have been especially noticeable in the United States, a country founded on immigration. As an analyst living and practicing in an area which has long been desirable for immigrants, I have had the opportunity to work with many of these new members of what former President George Bush once called "the new world order."

I am one of these transplants, having moved to the United States after my training in Zurich, now some 25 years ago. My experience has made it easy for me to identify some of the typical reactions of a transplant into a new culture, a new language, and a new social circumstance – although I often have to remind myself that not all immigrants go through identical experiences nor with the resources I have had available.

Analytic work with those who have grown up in an entirely different culture has certainly been done before. My colleagues in Zurich, for example, taking their cues from Jung, have long been doing analysis with candidates and other "pilgrims" from all over the world. To dip into the process of individuation at the feet of the master's disciples, is, by now, a piece of the Jungian myth.

The patients I am going to discuss today are different in one important respect. They are not mere visitors, looking for a particular schooling and expansion of viewpoint. Instead they are people who entered treatment after they left their homelands and began making new homes. They experienced a fundamental change, a break with the past which had made them citizens, so to speak, of at least two countries, the old and the new. This fact makes quite a difference in their analytic work.

A Drive To Succeed

Naturalized citizens have been driven, traditionally, to succeed outwardly in their new circumstance. To prove that their decision to leave their home land was the right one, they often tend to measure their success or failure in concrete terms (see Sowell 1981). As patients, however, they often have difficulty verbalizing their developmental history. For fear that they will not be understood, they stop sharing past experiences – and they soon repress large portions of them. They live in what seems to be two psyches, one extravertedly oriented and concrete, the other tucked away in a language spoken no more, perhaps awakened only in dreams.

This split is reinforced by everyday experiences in the new homeland. People native to the area find it difficult to grasp the cultural milieu in which the immigrant's inner world was formed. It is too inconvenient, perhaps too disturbing, especially when the immigrant's history includes personal traumatic experiences such as abuse, neglect and blame for the political or economic system of the country of origin. At the same time, the immigrant's nostalgically romanticizing the homeland is often met with anger and defensiveness.

Because they are split off from their developmental and psychological history, immigrants are especially prone to periods of depression and self-doubt, conditions which easily trigger regressions. These periods may not be limited to the initial, more immediate acculturation. We would naturally expect depression and self-doubt to be strong features during the initial year in the new country, in line with the typical reactions to a difficult adaptation. Continuing depression often is a part of the immigrant's experience.

This fact was well articulated by a Swiss woman in her mid-thirties. She had studied in the United States for many years before she married an American and they settled in the Boston area. During their marital fights, she often would complain about how much she missed her homeland, making her husband feel guilty and responsible for her misery. In reflecting over her nostalgic ruminations, she recalled that she rarely felt the same sadness when she was a student expecting to return to Switzerland. Now, when this seemed out of the question, she had begun to forget all the personal reasons she had for wishing to live far away from her family, in particular needing to separate from her depressed mother whom the patient had taken care of since the patient's school days.

Typical Symptomatology

Initial problems of adaptation to a new culture may be summarized:

• Feelings of loss and separation, usually manifesting as a melancholic mood and an aversion to new forms of experience.

• Heightened images of childhood places and persons, such as the beauty of the home landscape and historical buildings.

These symptoms, although they may be quite severe, are understood easily as belonging to a difficult adaptation. They may include feelings of helplessness, dependency, and disorientation; but they are typically paired with a drive to become functional, useful, and adapted to the present. Often immigrants in this phase need to compare, to identify cultural peculiarities and to come to meaningful conclusions for their lives having brought them to this point.

When acculturation continues to be a problem, some additional changes occur, involving the core organization of the personality and revealing more long-standing and dysfunctional traits:

• Nostalgic reworking of personal history, repression of core memories of pain and hardship, and the infusion of a sense of special purpose and entitlements.

• Rageful complaints about the inadequacy of the political, economic and cultural system of the new country, along with negative comparisons with the idealized notion of the homeland.

Nostalgia, the first in this set of symptoms, involves some defensive features, such as cognitive distortions and displacement of affect. The analyst, who is unable to hear the narcissistic charge underlying these symptoms, may be tempted to present rational arguments against idealizing the old country. The patient is likely to respond to such a stance by feeling misunderstood and misjudged. The analyst may start to feel what others in the patient's life express as "So, if your home country is so wonderful, why don't you go back there!" The collective characterizations have now been given free reign and the unconsciousness of its sources has become shared. The treatment reaches an impasse from which it may never recover.

A more productive approach to the nostalgia is to view it as expressing a need for missing psychic resources, resources which perhaps never existed, but which the patient projects onto the old homeland. Thus, the nostalgic ruminations can be paradoxical carriers of new psychic life. By providing a safe environment for the patient to describe such longings, the stage is set for a later exploration of the personal traumas that made it necessary for the patient to risk leaving everything behind to seek a missing sense of inner unity.

The second symptom, rage against the customs of the new country, can be difficult to detect. A 50-year old divorced man, who grew up in Spain but had lived in the United States since he was a young adult, concealed his rage with such skillful jokes that it would be difficult for anyone not to be amused. However, it soon became apparent that his humorous descriptions of American tastes in food and clothing were only the tip of an iceberg. His daily life had become so marred by his efforts not to be contaminated by what he abhorred that he finally found himself living alone in the woods. Here he could pretend that he was not part of the market-driven world he had come to detest as American. As soon as he got in to his car, however, the rage would take over. Often with danger to himself and others, he would drive recklessly, cursing all the drivers of the cars he passed.

Such narcissistic rage is often what emerges as the cohesive glue to an otherwise fragile self, a self which, in spite of superficial adaptation, still remains organized around early wounding. These wounds originated in experiences of which the patient had some awareness but from which he was emotionally dissociated. He entered therapy after years of attending Alcoholics Anonymous AA meetings. He had now overcome his addiction, but was completely alienated from his ex-wife and two daughters and had hardly any friends.

Both his parents were alcoholics and had not been able to care for their two children. The mother felt that she had married beneath her class and remained closely attached to her own mother. When she was not drinking or in a rage, she would complain to her children about the life she could have lived if she had not had them.

When my patient was eight, his parents separated and the mother now openly favored her elder son, the patient's brother. Being sent away to a boys' school at age ten ended some of this misery, but the damage was done. When his mother later remarried an American, the patient was sent to an American boarding school. He was now a high school student and determined never to look back, instead finding family substitutes among his teachers and peers. Any mention of mother or brother would mobilize rage.

Theoretical Considerations

Jungian theory addresses many parts of the acculturation process. Depression, for instance, can be viewed as an activation of the unconscious, with an accompanying increase in charged and difficult fantasies which need to be made conscious. This understanding, instead of focusing on what causes the depression, finds particular values in the fantasies it produces.

In order to work with these fantasies, Jung developed the technique of "active imagination." The benefits of this approach for depression are described as follows:

> *Continual conscious realization of unconscious fantasies, together with active participation in the fantastic events, has, as I have witnessed in a very large number of cases, the effect firstly of extending the conscious horizon by the inclusion of numerous unconscious contents; secondly of gradually diminishing the dominant influence of the unconscious; and thirdly of bringing about change of personality. (CW7, 358)*

Immigrants' depressive fantasies typically have to do with the things left behind and which now seem unreachable; they express in images the feelings of loss of the secure connections to familiar circumstances. However, as Jung pointed out, the expressed content of an active imagination should not be taken to mean a wish to return to the old country.

In my working with immigrants suffering from recurring depressions, I have found Jung's view to be true. Their fantasies are usually quite vivid and easily accessible, but premature interpretation only leads to a surface understanding and confusion of inner and outer realities. Instead, it is in facing the passive and resigned nature of the patient's participation in the fantasies that progress can be made. When realizing the helpless and fatalistic approach reflected in the fantasies, there is often a sense that other choices are possible. A transcendent function has emerged to hold the tension of opposites, and consciousness is revitalized.

Contributions of Self Psychology

Regarding the rage against the new culture, additional approaches are necessary. In working with patients who easily go into rage, we are not talking about a usual anger or a fleeting expression of frustration from which the patient quickly recovers. This is rage of the narcissistic variety and can become a major obstacle, unless it is understood from the point of view of restoring, even temporarily, a sense of having an independent center of activity, a self capable of reflection and initiative.

Heinz Kohut, himself an immigrant, developed analytic approaches to such rage in his studies of narcissistic personality disorders (see Simpson 1994). His view of narcissism, as a necessary element in establishing and maintaining a meaningful connection to self, in many ways echoes Jung's understanding of the ego-self axis. Both understood the person's sense of self to be of primary importance, as a core structural element in the personality. While Jung focused on symbolic representations, Kohut understood the self developmentally within a narcissistic spectrum and described its various phases, from early archaic forms to fully mature ones.

> *My emphasis on the fact that narcissism need not be destroyed, but that it can be transformed is in tune with my support of a nonhypocritical attitude toward narcissism as a psychological force sui generis, which has its own line of development and which neither should – nor indeed could – be relinquished. In the psychoanalytic situation, too, the analyst's nonhypocritical attitude toward narcissism, his familiarity with the forms and transformations of this psychic constellation, and his uncensorious recognition of this biological and sociocultural value will diminish the analysand's narcissistic resistance and rage against the analytic procedure. (Kohut 1971, p. 647)*

In defining narcissistic rage Kohut focused on its being a response to actual or anticipated injury. He wrote:

> *Narcissistic rage occurs in many forms; they all share, however, a specific psychological flavor which gives them a distinct position within the wide realm of human aggression. The need for revenge, for righting a wrong, for undoing a hurt by whatever means, and a*

deeply anchored, unrelenting compulsion in the pursuit of all these aims, which gives no rest to those who have suffered a narcissistic injury – these are the characteristic features of narcissistic rage in all its forms and which set them apart from other kinds of aggression. (1971, p. 638)

From this perspective, experiences with rageful patients make it necessary for the analyst to set aside becoming allied with the patient's ego.

Although everybody tends to react to narcissistic injuries with embarrassment and anger, the most intense experiences of shame and the most violent forms of narcissistic rage arise in those individuals for whom a sense of absolute control over an archaic environment is indispensable because the maintenance of self-esteem – and indeed of the self – depends on the unconditional availability of the approving-mirroring selfobject or of the merger-permitting idealized one. (Kohut 1971, pp. 644-645)

Since unconditional availability seems beyond the scope of what any analytical relationship can offer, how could we, as analysts, realistically expect to work with these deeply disturbed patients? Not only are they defending against wounding which must have taken place very early in their lives, but their attacks are now directed at the analyst and the analytic situation itself.

As Jacoby (1991) pointed out, a first step is to extend our definition of the self. In Kohut's theoretical formulations, the emphasis is not on the self as an archetypal and intra-psychic content. Instead he stresses its function as a relational matrix, a bipolar entity, which he calls self and self-object. The latter being the internalized experience of an important – even a necessary – other, is initially the mother, in her empathic mirroring. She is thus the primary object in the infant's life and the experiences with her become a critical part of the self.

This relational view is very useful in its application to the treatment situation (see Mitchell 1988). Via the transference, the analyst may serve a similar function to the mother, especially when deficits in the area of early empathic self-object responses are being exposed. To serve such a function, however, the analyst must abandon, at least temporarily, the reliance on interpretations and other standard techniques. An empathic stance is required, based on the analyst's ability, via introspection, to attune to the patient's emotional state. Kohut (1957) viewed such a stance as an observational method, central to psychoanalysis, a mirroring based on the analyst's own introspection.

In working with the patient I described earlier, I soon learned that an empathic stance would lead to a great deal of progress, as long as I did not try to make generic interpretations by referring to memories he had mentioned of conditions in his childhood. The few dreams he reported contained little of what caused his rages and came mainly from awakenings and light sleep. We were left with the daytime material he presented and its underlying narcissistic charge. Carefully, and with a great deal of personal restraint, I reflected his affective states via my own similar experiences. As I did so, he began to claim his own understanding of his childhood and to relate with full emotion to his memories of utter deprivation and despair.

The Global Culture of Tomorrow

One of the particular consequences of living in a global culture is the creation of universal standards that are transferable from one country to another, especially in the skilled job market. As a result, we now can see a young generation of mobile adults for whom awareness of national culture is diminishing. The global culture, for these young adults, has much more significance. It is providing them with products marketed globally, as well as entertainment, information, and a sense of what is fashionable.

This was the case for a young German scientist in his thirties who entered the United States to do post-graduate work in his rather specialized field. Initially he was trying to overcome the wounds from the break-up with a French fiancçe before his departure. Further into the treatment, he also became involved, first with an English and then a Dutch colleague, but both relationships ended when the women left the country for professional jobs.

The uprootedness and loneliness this patient went through in these transient relationships echoed many of his childhood experiences. He seemed to have been a child with few friends and frail family relationships from the time he was a very small. He would occasionally talk to his mother over the phone about the mundane details of his life but felt his father had no interest in him beyond saying how nice it would be for the mother if he could find a position near home.

With the deepest despair, however, he would compare himself to his father, a successful industrialist, wondering if he ever would grow up and stop being so lonely. These self-incriminations were desperate attempts at restoring ideals that had crumbled under the pressure to deal with his sense of isolation and lack of self-affirmation. As his professor became available for comments and appreciation of his research, these attempts quickly disappeared. And the questions about his career choice also seemed to diminish, as our therapeutic relationship found a more solid ground.

The actual acculturation was relatively uncomplicated for this patient. He had few problems with the language, had plenty of opportunities to return home for visits and was generally at ease with most details in his everyday life. After some months of feeling isolated and in a foreign land, he began to look for opportunities to pursue his hobbies and interests, and the depression lifted.

From early on, the symptoms he manifested were mainly of the second, narcissistic kind. He would ambulate between nostalgic longing for those first months of being in love with his French fiancée, describing his daring pursuit of her, their courtship, and places he had a taken her. This would be followed by sharp self-incriminations, hopeless feelings of inadequacy and a sense that he would never find a suitable partner. Other times, with equal intensity, he would rage over her letters to him after the break-up, repeating particularly wounding phrases and denouncing what he saw as her cruel ultimatums to him.

I have described this case to illustrate how immigration, for certain patients, is less of an issue and how they have already incorporated into their lives the existence of a global marketplace. At the end of his post-graduate studies the patient applied for positions in several countries and it was the location of an available position that determined where he would live, not his country of origin, his national or cultural belonging.

What Constitutes Success?

As an analyst, I often ask myself how to judge the success of what I am doing. When working with immigrants, this question often takes on a somewhat different tone. I can no longer focus on obvious outer signs, since most of these patients have been determined to carve out an external identity which can be measured positively in financial and professional terms. They clearly entered analysis because something else was amiss, but often with symptoms worse than one would expect in view of their outer success.

In most cases, after the initial phase, a willingness to explore also developed. The best description is a search for inner resources, for self cohesion, and, from a Jungian perspective, a call to individuation. This in spite of devastating loss of meaningful family connections and growing up under family circumstances that provided only the barest affirmation of selfhood, resulting in early self deficits. Such deficits, overlaid with compensatory and defensive structures, typically took the form of daring adventurism and idealistic pursuits, but also a pseudo-vitality aimed at defending against depression and low self-esteem (see Morrison 1984).

In the cases I have described, there seemed to be little hope of repairing family connections. Career and outer achievement had become the main path to establishing self-worth.

On the other hand, less isolated patients are usually able to start their own families in the new culture, albeit with varying degrees of success. A radiologist, born in Asia, had been married for many years to an American, before he came into treatment on his wife's urging. He confessed to having been a workaholic, but a good provider. The marriage had seemed quite secure until their teenage daughter developed a problem with drugs. The shame and humiliation he experienced over the addiction led him to revert to an utterly patriarchal attitude. He refused to pay for her rehabilitation, scorned all mental health professionals, declared the American legal system to be bankrupt, and tried to force his wife to abandon their daughter. What to him had seemed like a good marriage now appeared headed for divorce; his wife was talking to lawyers and making her own financial decisions. As he saw his world crumble, he began to ask himself what he had become. He realized, that from the time he left home to go to school in Boston, his world had shrunk into his practice, his teaching colleagues, and the life of the medical school.

In working with the depressive episodes of patients such as this, Jung's technique of active imagination has proved to be very helpful in forming connections between the inner and outer world. Also common, however, is a cluster of symptoms, arising out of a nostalgic reworking of personal history and rage against the new culture and its institutions. This cluster can be classified as narcissistic injuries, rage, and personality structure. In my view, it would be a sign of failure if the analytic treatment did not address these deep-seated problems. A secure sense of self-worth and self-coherence also needs to be restored. It is fair to assume, in a social perspective, that one of the losses in globalizing the economy, with the associated alienation from community roots, family ties, and identifiable religious and cultural beliefs, is an increase rather than a decrease in these types of problems.

Being able to see choices and new opportunities was clearly very important to the immigrant patients with whom I have worked. In the end, however, this was possible only when a solid connection to inner resources and a sense of purposeful life progression was established.

General Reflections

Success in working with these patients is not always possible. Sudden withdrawal, unbearable shame, and festering rage may get the upper hand. However, if a therapeutic alliance is established before such departures, the immigrant is likely to resume the therapy.

I have been focusing on two areas which I have experienced as critical to such success: addressing depressive fantasies and responding to narcissistic rage. These are not particularly romantic tasks and they hardly permit the analyst to show how skillful he or she is in delivering brilliant interpretations based on perceived national or ethnic characteristics. In fact, I think it is critical for the Jungian community to understand that some elements in Jung's theories relate to a world of the past and an understanding that is ill-suited to the global culture in which we live today.

This is not to say that Analytical Psychology lacks appeal to those patients. On the contrary, it often has a particular resonance for them, in that it pays serious attention to questions of living in a modern world and the universality of our deepest beliefs and perceptions. But Jung's ideas – and those of psychoanalysis as a whole – emerged during a time when nationalistic and romantic ideas were the accepted norm and they formed an ideology that prevailed until recently, particularly in Europe (see Ellenberger 1970). To this way of thinking, national characteristics were imbedded deeply in the individual and consisted of genetic and ethnic differences. Many scholars (e.g., Lienhardt 1971) even believed this to imply some type of evolutionary hierarchy, from "primitive" to advanced European cultures. Later research has found no basis for these ideas. In fact, they are simplistic justifications for prejudicial thinking and were aimed at maintaining a political status quo for those who enjoyed great privileges (see Shweder 1991).

Nationalistic ideology also reflects a world far different from today's global marketplace. That world had more stable cultural patterns, very little migration and mobility, and different kinds of family structures. However, these benefits were paired with more authoritarian beliefs, few legal rights for women, rarity of divorces, and unavailability of reliable birth control. The existing mass communications, such as newspapers and books, typically did not cross language barriers and national borders.

As analysts, we need to embrace analytic approaches which reflect the world in which we live: a more global, more interdependent world. This challenge is perhaps most obvious when working with naturalized citizens. They are not merely representations of their land of origin. Their psychological make-up, as is every individual's, is complex and many-faceted and, often, more difficult for us to relate to than a person of our own national and cultural context. But we need to consider that they are probably rather atypical products of the culture they come from, whose otherness, in the first place, may have caused them to leave and seek a new belonging.

References

Ellenberger, H.F. (1970). *The Discovery of the Unconscious: The History and Evolution of Dynamic Psychiatry*. New York: Basic Books.

Jacoby, M. (1991). *Individuation and Narcissism: The Psychology of the Self in Jung and Kohut*. London/New York: Routledge.

Kohut, H. (1957). Introspection, empathy, and psychoanalysis. In P.H. Ornstein (Ed.), *The Search for the Self: Selected Writings of Heinz Kohut: 1950-1978*, (Vol. 1, pp. 205-232). New York: International Universities Press, 1978. (Originally presented at the Chicago Institute for Psychoanalysis, Nov., 1957).

Kohut, H. (1978). Thoughts of narcissistic rage. In P.H. Ornstein (Ed.), *The Search for the Self: Selected Writings of Heinz Kohut: 1950-1978* (Vol. 2), 615-658. New York: International Universities Press.

Lienhardt, R.G. (1971). Religion. In H.L. Shapiro (Ed.), *Man, Culture, and Society*, (rev. ed., pp. 382-401). London /New York: Oxford University Press.

Mitchell, S. (1988). *Relational Concepts in Psychoanalysis: An Integration*. Cambridge, MA: Harvard University Press.

Morrison, A.P. (1984). Shame and the psychology of the self. In P.A. Stepansky and A. Goldberg (Eds.), *Kohut's Legacy: Contributions to Self Psychology*. Hillsdale, NJ: Analytic Press.

Shweder, R.A. (1991). *Thinking through Cultures: Expeditions in Cultural Psychology*. Cambridge, MA: Harvard University Press.

Simpson, P. (1994). Heinz Kohut: His enduring influence today. *The Psychoanalytic Psychotherapy Review, 5-1*, 6-23.

Sowell, T. (1981). *Ethnic America: A History*. New York: Basic Books.

Archetypal Images
of Destruction and Creation

The Congress through the Feminine Looking Glass

International Women's Working Group
Ursula Wirtz, Switzerland, Coordinator
Maria Aparecida Freitas de Vilhena, Brazil
Lucia Azevedo, Brazil
Susan Bostrom-Wong, USA
Ursula Hohler, Switzerland
Ruth Ledergerber, Switzerland
Maria Meyer-Grass, Switzerland
Lisbet Myers Zacho, Denmark
Franziska Stüssi, Switzerland
*Laura Villares de Freitas, Brazil

How We Started

Comment from one of our members: "Congress 1995 in Zürich. I am disappointed and angry. I cannot identify with what was presented this first morning at our congress. My American friend who is sitting next to me shares my feelings. She refers to the presentations as a 'pissing contest.' We talk to our friends from different nations and soon discover they have similar feelings. We all long to have more experiential spaces and presentations in the IAAP Congresses, and also desire to work on feminine symbols."

A Dream as a Metaphor of a Two-year Process of Preparation

Our first meeting as a group took place in Zürich, August 1996. We hardly knew each other but we had a common goal: cooperation instead of competition; working together with pleasure and joy; using new methods, without hierarchical structures; exploring new ways of elaborating themes that are meaningful to us as women;

* With support from FAPESP (a São Paulo foundation for support of research)

experiencing, reflecting and giving creative form to these feminine symbols. This would not be a pissing contest. We decided to weave a web, uniting women from different countries, working in a feminine way, interlacing ideas and feelings. We agreed to pay attention to our dreams and to our responses to the powerful theme of the congress: Destruction and Creation. One week later a woman in the group had the following dream:

> *My dog is bleeding to death. She trots through the rooms, walks over books and manuals, everything is covered with blood. I am terrified and helpless. The dog collapses, is stiff and still bleeding, her backbone stretched out and her belly bulged out: typical hysterical "l'arc en cercle" I think and I run to the dog, pick up her head and gently hold her head in my hands to help her relax and soften. She is alive and sighs. I shout: Come! The people in the house arrive.*

The dream symbolized in many ways the experiences we as a group went through: our collective *abaissement du niveau mental*, the chaotic stages we passed through in terms of what we wanted and what was feasible. There was a loss of energy when we experienced facing the difficulties of finding dates to meet, meeting our own high expectations to achieve and the limitations that forced us down to earth again. The bloodlessnes that seemed to paralyze us was temporary. But the dog was not bleeding to death, only suffering as we were suffering, identified with the destructive archetypal energies constellated by the theme of the Congress.

Over Easter in 1998 our Danish colleague joined us for three intensive days of working together. Finally we were able to reflect on what was happening in our group. The dream helped us to find our way to understand what was happening to us and to shift our energy into taking action, working with pleasure, holding our own heads gently in our arms and sighing happily. Finally we had gotten rid of our numbness and reactivated our contact with the women from South and North America, shouting: Come! We are ready. How about you?

From April 1998 until the Congress started in August, ten women from four countries connected, to form our final working group. The Sunflowers, as we called ourselves, worked together via e-mail, fax, telephone and meetings. We created a web, wove a carpet that became manifest in the daily meeting "The Feminine Looking Glass" and the one-time workshop "Archetypal Images of Destruction and Creation." It was a moving synchronistic event, that the motif of the head was the major theme of the work the Brazilian women had prepared for our group, without knowing this dream.

We Experience, Reflect and Give Form
to Feminine Life Cycles

Myth Work

We (three women from Brazil) were stimulated by the desire to search for a genuine Brazilian theme which would express our cultural identity, and at the same time recover some of its origins. We started to read, study, discuss and research indigenous Brazilian myths, looking for one that would best express symbols of the feminine identity. One myth (Mindlin 1997, pp. 63-65, 159-161, 180-184) soon proved to be especially appealing: "The Voracious Head." It is a very old myth, found in many versions in the oral traditions of indigenous peoples. It touched us deeply and became a central symbol for the whole group.

According to the spirit of the working group, we took the myth as a starting point. Rather than looking for interpretations, we wanted it to be open to a multitude of associations and meanings. The versions we found had very different endings for the story. We created a collage of the first part of the myth, inspired by four indigenous versions.

Our intention was to promote an experience that would appeal strongly to sensations, emotions and feelings, thus facilitating a comprehensive involvement in the myth work. To accomplish this, we presented at the beginning a series of slide-images from Brazilian culture that emphasized feminine symbols. We also prepared a soundtrack of indigenous music which was played throughout the afternoon. After the slide presentation, we asked the participants to stand up and walk around the room, while we told in three voices the beginning of the myth. This is the text we read:

> *Once upon a time there was a beautiful young woman who had a young husband. He had loved her very much ever since they were children. He hunted for her and planted a large crop. So they lived well together and always slept in each other's arms, in the same hammock. They were very happy, in spite of a strange habit the woman had: Every night her head separated from her body and went in search of game meat and other food in other huts and villages.*

*Even though the husband hunted a great deal and managed to get
plenty of food, she always wanted to eat more in some other place.
Only the head went out to hunt. In other villages she took the meat
that was being smoke-cured and brought it home to eat. Was she too
greedy? Wasn't the meat, that her husband so lovingly brought her,
enough? It is also difficult to understand how the head could eat,
how the food she swallowed did not come out through the neck. The
truth is that at dawn the head fastened herself again to the body,
which had remained in the hammock, clinging to the husband.
Nothing could be noticed except for a little bit of blood on her neck
and a few drops on his chest.*

*[In one version the husband knew about his wife's habit but appar-
ently didn't mind.] It seems she had a lot of lice and didn't let anyone
pick them; it was the lice who wanted meat and so they cut off her
head. Another version says that she harboured the lice; she bit them
and ate only the heads. She used to say to her husband: "Wake up,
husband, the bat is sucking our blood, the lice are sucking us!" But
the husband was aware of nothing, he didn't hear anything, he didn't
know that every night his wife's head split from the body and flew
away. By morning she was always whole again. "Wake up, husband!
You sleep too much! There are too many lice and you don't wake
up!" This is how the young woman cried every night and, since the
husband remained quiet, the head went out alone.*

*There is yet another version which tells that, when she got meat in
other villages, she brought it to her hut to eat, but didn't let her
husband see it. He went out to work and she stayed at home eating
secretly. Every evening she tried to please her husband, calling him
to sleep in their hammock She coaxed him so that he would go to
sleep and she could get out. The only thing we are sure of is that no
one else in the village was aware of what was happening, until one
day ...*

At this point, where the narrative comes to a dilemma, we decided
to stop and open it to the participants. We asked them to create their
own versions of the ending, in small groups (see Figure 1). After 15
minutes of sub-group work, we asked everyone to form a big circle
to listen to the version of the Macurap indigenous people one, which
we again read in three voices:

*One night her mother decided to go gather yams for an important
party. If she didn't go before dawn she would not have time to
prepare enough beverage. She wanted to call her daughter to go with
her. She called and called but the daughter did not answer. She got
near the hammock and, horrified, saw the mutilated body, without
the head, in the arms of her son-in-law. She shrieked, waking the*

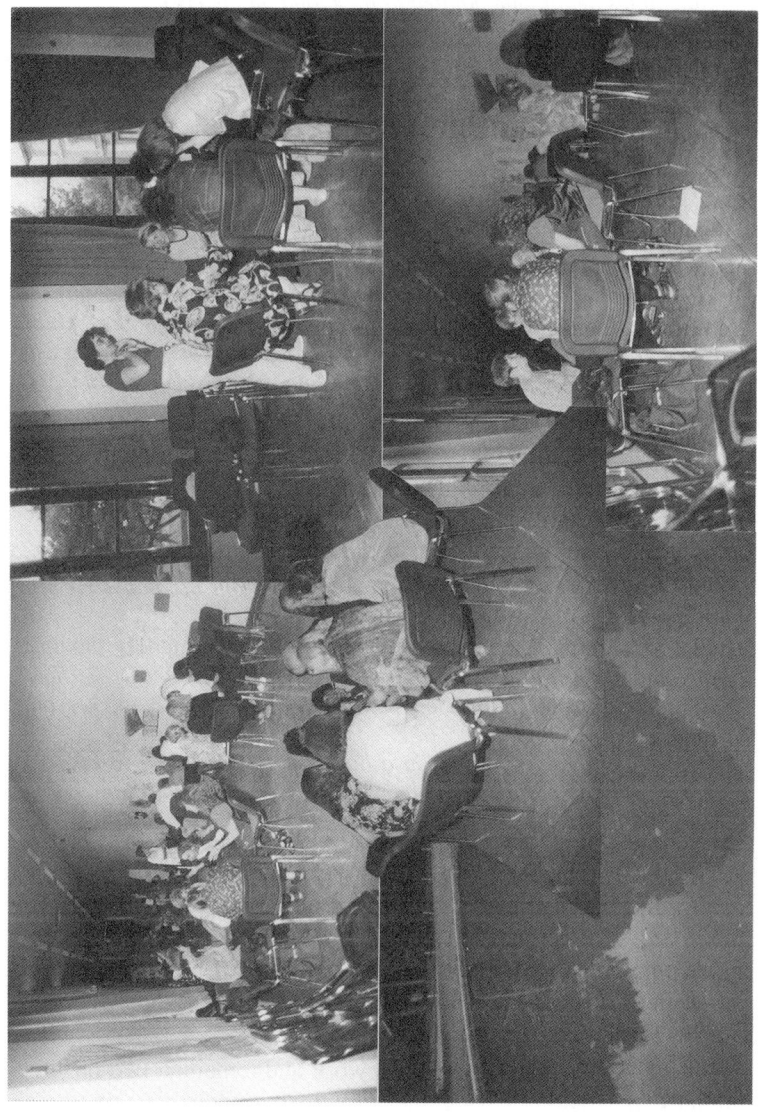

Figure 1

whole hut, crying for vengeance against the husband because of her daughter's death. She pointed at the blood on the neck.
"Of course I did not kill your daughter, I am crazy about her!" protested the innocent husband. "Wait only a little bit, until morning, and you will see how her head arrives and fastens herself again to this body." Nobody believed him; they took the body and buried it. The husband cried disconsolately.
At dawn there came the head flying quickly. She searched for her own body; she kept flying and going from one side to the other in the hut and couldn't find the rest of herself. Most distressed, she perched on her husband's shoulder. The woman's head never left him again. The husband became a man with two heads. Wherever he went, there was the other head, talking, watching, giving orders as a part of him. The worst was that the flesh of the head began to rot, because it was cut off from the rest. It had a vile smell, and became unbearable. And the beautiful body that always warmed him in the hammock every night when the voracious head went out, was no more!
The man began to go crazy. Nobody wanted to come near him, because of the stench. Even he was always nauseated. After much suffering, he decided to hunt for the woman-head. He left the meat a little far away, and ordered the head to go and eat. And so he managed to have the head detach herself from his body. He ran away.
The head, bewildered, since she couldn't find the friendly shoulder any more, made a nest on the way to the planted field. The head devoured anyone who passed. It was the shortest way, but everyone avoided it.
One day a young man was in a hurry and didn't want to take the longer way. The head went after him, wanting to devour him, but he was a very good runner, and managed to escape to the village and warn the others. The men took their swords and prepared themselves. She came rolling; since she had become only a head, she was a spirit. She didn't even let out blood any more, only the hellish stench. The men managed to split the head in small pieces. The stench persisted, they had to hold their noses. It was necessary for the shamans to treat ritually the foul smelling remains and throw them away.

After this we stopped the myth work and remained two or three minutes in silence, leaving the participants under the emotional impact of that indigenous ending, interwoven with their own endings. The energy and tension which were accumulated in this experience could be brought to the matrix work that followed, so that the participants had an opportunity to continue to experience and express the feelings, emotions, ideas and sensations.

This work was created in a group, for a group with subgroups. In this way we ensured the feminine aspect of the experience: containment, process, weaving, interaction and creation.

Matrix Work

With our matrix-work we wanted to leave behind rigid role-expectations, which are imposed upon women through various stages of their life. The work was meant to help us experience and become more conscious of our potential to embody many roles and archetypes. We have chosen three matrix-levels:

1. The biological life cycle: The female child, the girl and the young woman in puberty and adolescence, the young woman, the woman in middle age, the woman in the menopause, the woman between menopause and beginning old age, the old woman. A space was provided for what remained unsaid, unknown or forgotten.

2. Personal and archetypal experiences during certain stages of life: Which archetypes are dominant in this specific time of life? How did we, our clients, our mothers and daughters deal with them? How did they and how did we experience the archetype?

3. Destructiveness and creativity in these life stages: How do we experience destruction and creation in this period of life? What is our pain, shame and suffering during this time? In which form does lust, life energy and creativity show up in this period? What are we hungry and greedy for during this stage of life? When are we related to ourselves at this time of life? How do we experience time and space in this life stage? How do we experience transformation in this period? How do we experience the archetypal tension between the genders and within the restrictions of our society?

For each life stage we prepared a large bulletin board with pictures, paintings, poetry, texts and objects symbolizing each age level, to bring alive the archetypal energy. We invited all participants to work on these questions in groups or alone: reflecting, discussing, painting, doing collages or some other creative process (see Figures 2 and 3 on the following pages. We later met for sharing and feedback. We ended the workshop with a final ritual expressing our hopes and visions for the future.

Figure 2

Figure 3

The Congress through the Feminine Looking Glass

Our need to have a container for feminine views concerning the Congress and its deep stream of destructive and creative archetypal energies was like a seed falling into the earth at the beginning of our meetings and developing slowly but constantly from a tiny kernel to a beautiful, big sunflower in summer 1998. In this field of pulsating energy we had a room of our own for the daily meditations of the Congress through the feminine looking glass. This room of our own proved to be a very important and helpful element, a vessel for the alchemical process for many women during the congress.

Having the room and the opportunity to meet daily, to be able to drop in often, silently, was another important aspect of this process. This allowed many women to move through this process with its *nigredo* – the depression, anxiety and disorientation in the beginning – through *rubedo* – the full expression of our feelings of anger, lust, compassion, shame, wrath, joy – to the *albedo* of being alive again, connected to the mystery of life.

Amplifying our Feminine Looking Glass, it was:

A room of one's own.

A looking glass of images, impressions, moods, thoughts, visions.

A *temenos* for the feminine gaze, a sacred space to experience, paint, discuss and share.

A womb for the feminine matrix.

A safe place to speak out and become visible, to mourn and to regain strength.

An energetic field with Eros present, connecting and relating, binding together what was separate.

A melting pot of cultures, languages, gender; transcending boundaries of age, status, roles.

A feminine carpet, woven with love, solidarity and compassion.

A container for reflections and images, mirroring the archetypal dynamics of the Congress: Destruction and Creation.

Reference

Mindlin, B. (1997). *Moqueca de Maridos*. São Paulo: Editora Rosa dos Tempos.

Body and Psyche

Scarred Body, Scarred Psyche

Drawing the Jewel from the Wounds

Rose-Emily Rothenberg
Los Angeles, California, USA
Society of Jungian Analysts of Southern California

The experience of the mother's death reconfigures the newborn's psyche. Physical symptoms arising from the wound re-present this experience by reconfiguring the body. This reconfiguring takes the form of actual scars, of keloids that arise spontaneously, even in the absence of physical injury. Keloids are autonomous overgrowths of scar tissue that can occur when there has been trauma to the skin. Such growths are seen as a deformity in our culture, but for many indigenous people they are a window into another world.

Within this construct is my personal story. With the death of my mother shortly after my birth, the psyche went underground, like spirit descending into matter, and arose repeatedly in the form of spontaneous keloid scars. The orphan myth and the scars mirrored one another throughout my life. The emergence of the scars represented the unconscious in its raw, undifferentiated form, mediating the chaos and wisdom of the unconscious and offering protection and access to the inner world from which it arose.

Keloids consciously created by the art of scarification as practiced by indigenous people reflected my scars' opposite, and the psyche's opposite: a transformed, integrated state. Following the psyche's urge for initiation, I journeyed to Africa to interview shamans, to gain a deeper understanding of the symbolic nature of scarification rites, and to reconnect to the collective layer of the psyche that exists before the mother, the *prima materia* from which all things arise.

The Personal

I was six days old when my mother died and I came home alone to my father and two older sisters. A stepmother entered our lives just before my second birthday, and the door to spontaneous expression began to close. The door to the unconscious, however, remained open. My whole orphan experience was distilled into the first dream I remember from my childhood:

> *I am standing in the center of my childhood house in front of a barren tree that represents my mother. I am giving birth to black snakes from my arm.*

The tree in my dream stood in the center of my world. The snakes represented not only the psyche's reaction to the initial trauma of my mother's death and the coming of the stepmother, but also the solution to that trauma. The snake symbolized both the intrepid darkness and the healing spirit. It pointed to the potential inundation from the unconscious and necessitated the cohesiveness of the ego's attitude that could prevent it from happening. My libido, represented by the snakes born from my arm, had gone underground with the Self. Yet these snakes signaled the beginning of a new creation, the creation of consciousness.

The snakes born from my arm prophesied another event in my childhood. Before entering school, I had the required vaccination and, at the same time, had a mole removed from the other arm. The cuts reactivated the early trauma of my birth, and unsightly scars appeared on my arms as the healing tissue attempted to repair the wound. These wounds touched the unintegrated psychic material waiting for release. The large scars mirrored my psychological chaos in the physical world. My orphan psychology began to manifest physiologically.

The scars seemed to be speaking for me, conveying the suffering that I could not communicate in words. When the knife touched my skin and the nurturing mother was nowhere to be found, the wounds of my psyche were awakened. The doctors stood helplessly by as the scars grew into mountainous shapes on both my upper arms. Medical science had no cure.

The search for the psychological and metaphysical origins of my scar formation eventually merged with the search for my mother. Initially the scars carried the projection of despair about the dark side of life that brought death. Later they became a deformity that continued the suffering. It was as if the keloid wanted to give me something on which to project in order that it could carry some of the chaos, along with what needed to be redeemed and transformed. This dynamic announced itself to me first in a childhood book that had a lasting influence on me and may have prefigured the coming of the scars. The book was titled *Wee Fishie Wun* (Melissarato 1945). It is a story about a little black fish that turned into a beautiful goldfish. Tiny silver and gold beads were glued onto the fish. They were raised from the page as if from the skin and created a knobby effect that could be touched and felt. I especially loved touching those little beads. Although I was not conscious of it at the time, I was identifying with the longed-for transformation process they represented.

A second book had an equally profound effect on me and also may have contributed to the evolution of the scars. By contrast with *Wee Fishie Wun*, which reflects life and renewal, this book illustrates the pull toward death. Within a warm embrace, my father shared with me what was clearly his favorite book: *God's Man: A Novel in Woodcuts*, by Lynd Ward. He read and re-read this book to me, and it had a long-lasting influence. It is a story of an artist's Faustian pact and the painful life the artist leads following this ominous event.

The theme of danger accompanying new beginnings is recurrent in this book; it is what the orphan faces. The budding artist is launching into life anew and meets with darkness right away. He realizes the unbearable reality of betrayal when he sees a tattooed dollar sign on the body of a whore. He is held hostage by the shadows of his interior life and by his exterior life. The tale is a commentary on the dark unredeemed psyche. I was under its influence and under the influence of my father's anima. Together these influences created a fertile field for my receptivity to identifying with the prostitute and, more poignantly, to the tattoo which represented the dark side of the autonomous spirit.

I had to descend into the meaning of the keloids in order to discover this dynamic living spirit. Up to this point, I had scars only on my upper arms. When I went to college, I met someone I liked and admired, and we decided to be roommates. A large part of the Self was projected on to her. When she unexpectedly changed her mind and went off to room with someone else, my birth trauma repeated itself. My body reacted instantaneously. A rash of keloids appeared spontaneously across my chest. The scars had reappeared even though there had been no physical lesion to cause them. There had been a psychological one and, once again, they were a public expression of my anguish.

With the development of proliferating scars upon my chest, I was becoming aware that the scars were not going to go away and that new ones could be in the offing. An unknown force was living inside me and I experienced it as out of control. What I did not understand at the time was that the scars were containing the part of my psyche that was out of control, and the body was helping me to carry it.

Several years later I slipped and cut my knee. When I was recovering, I could see that a keloid was beginning to form on the wound. I was alarmed because this scar would be difficult to conceal. The medical profession couldn't help me, but I sought out a healing ritual. While it was in process, an image of God was invoked in me like the epiphanies that were experienced in Epidaurus. It was a deeply significant initiation for me, for it allowed me to make a conscious connection to the God image inside myself and to get a faint glimmer of God's reflection in the scars. The keloid on my knee did not materialize. That night I dreamed:

> *I am wearing a gown that has only one shoulder strap. My keloids have turned into flowers and have created the other strap.*

This was the first dream I had about the keloids and the first confirmation that the keloid could mean anything other than a physical deformity. That I had followed my inspiration to approach the scar in a meditation meant psychologically that I recognized a living connection to the Self as significant to healing. The keloids as flowers on my body represented my living connection with the spirit that would bring renewal. Furthermore, the keloid turning into a flower suggested that I could dispel the feeling that I was unworthy and defuse the ever-present temptation to fall into feeling inferior, the nemesis of orphan psychology.

The flower dream, reflecting the healing experience, suggested that I could transform my connection to the keloid, this ever-present obstacle to new life and, at the same time, transform the profound sense that I was damaged. It held the promise of my integrating the inferior side of myself and developing an authentic connection to the Self, the flower that blooms.

A dream I had as an adult illuminated the psychological dynamic that what is lower and experienced as inferior holds the promise of transformation. As I was preparing to give a talk on the keloid, I dreamed *I was giving a talk about frogs.* For many years I felt like a frog with keloids on my skin, and now the frog as a symbol of transformation was making its appearance. There was an unformed, embryonic aspect to my psychology, and the yet-to-be-revealed "superior" part of myself was buried inside. The scars represented the inferior frog-aspects and their repulsiveness. Yet, as a symbol of transformation, the frog exemplifies the promise of renewal. It represents the dark primordial aspect one carries deep within, and at the same time it is one's potential wholeness.

At crucial points my psyche underwent a significant change, despite the fear of moving into higher states of development. New birth signaled new life and with it came the memory of my mother's death and the darkness that attended it. My deep fear, although not conscious at the time, was that any new birth would be accompanied by another death. The pain of facing the unknown was an even larger component. These were the existential dynamics my body was expressing in the form of a scar. The scars arose at pivotal initiations in my life, such as entering elementary school and college. The scar on my knee also came at a time of transition: just before graduation. Further scars formed at my marriage and at the birth of my son.

Eventually, a dream suggested that I begin to paint. Without my conscious intention, two series of paintings of the keloid showed the dynamic of the transformation process. The first series revealed the light hidden within the darkness. In the first painting I wanted to create the birth umbilicus, and the containment it represented and that I had missed. Next I portrayed it as breaking up into little pieces resembling flowers: scattered pieces of the original container. The third painting contained these pieces, now enlarged and in their dark tumultuous aspects. In the fourth emerged the light.

In the second series I began with the red scar; in the second painting, water emerged out of the scar. The undervalued and despised – the flow of inner waters contained in the unconscious and in the keloid – burst forth and began to live. In the next painting, water fertilized the ground for the yet unborn parts of myself to come into being. Life sprang up.

The final painting was of a star made up of a multiplicity of small gold squares: my totality. This was an inner star and, like the keloid, a guiding light. Work on the keloid inevitably took me back to the birth trauma. I painted a picture of my mother, going off with death. I was the only "alive" image in the painting, witnessing the event. Bringing the image across the threshold from the unconscious, and putting it on the canvas, instilled it with life that had been long buried in my orphan and keloid wounds.

As I was painting I was immersed in a reverie about my mother. I wanted to bring her over to this side. I found a photograph of myself and one of her that I applied to the canvas as if we were holding hands. Bringing my mother across was bringing my identification with her into consciousness in order that a decided separation could take place. Coexistent with this, a more conscious relationship to the depths of the keloid was in the offing. The flower was coming into bloom.

The Cultural

In a book on Mesopotamian art (Strommenger & Hirmer 1964), I came upon some photographs of figurines found in a grave in Mesopotamia from the fourth millennium B.C.E. They were adorned with pellets of clay on their torsos, identical to the places my own scar formation had developed. I could scarcely believe what I saw.

According to anthropologists, the little figures were thought to have been placed in graves to provide comfort and dignity to the deceased in the next world. Because they were associated with the dead and presented features emblematic of the gods of the underworld, they were viewed as chthonic deities. They were thought, also, to symbolize fertility and life because the figurines were placed on the pelvis of the dead.

The keloid, as it evolved in me, seemed to authenticate this connection; I was being shown the archetypal roots through the figurines. I found more photographs, more amplifications and more discussion of the artifacts adorned with pellets, lines, grooves and body decorations that represented scarification. The keloid myth was unfolding before my eyes.

It was as if the scars reached into death to retrace my mother's steps back to the beginning of the first recorded images of woman. The practice of making figures showing scarification has gone on since prehistoric times. The art of body-marking is an age-old custom, now practiced most frequently by African tribes and by the aborigines of Australia and the South Seas.

These scarification rites are performed on specific occasions in the lives of the tribal members. Initiation ceremonies – the most commonly-known rituals associated with scarification – celebrate transformation, rebirth and the continuity of life. Scarification has been performed also for purposes of identification to prevent individuals' being taken into slavery, to mark achievements and times of mourning, and for psychological and physical healing. Body decoration is vital to many celebrations. In order to have a full and lasting effect on the initiate, the body must be involved ritually.

It was at times of my own outer world initiations – going to school, marriage and motherhood – that scars had appeared on my body. During these transitional events the keloid archetype appeared spontaneously; just as in traditional cultures the marks were deliberately carved into the initiate's body. The death and rebirth motif, personal and collective identification, and the need for protection and for a living relationship to the spirits in the hereafter were part of this ceremonial scarification. Those were the same potential meanings my own scars had for me.

Going to Africa

The transformational aspects that were carried first in the body and in the unconscious, and then later contemplated and studied, now could be experienced on the outside. The keloid research and my personal psychological development initiated my interest in interviewing shamans and meeting the scarified people in Africa. As well, I wanted to touch the mother and the archetype of the keloid in a more tangible form. I would go to West Africa, to Burkina Faso. My unconscious supported the journey via this dream:

> *I was taking a tour through Jung's house and looking at the "bare bones" of his furniture. His son gave me a key to the tower. I asked if it would open Jung's private room there and he said: "This key will open everything."*

Seeing the tower at Bollingen was something I had wanted to do ever since I read about it. This dream was saying my going to Africa would be the equivalent. Undertaking this journey was unique to me and was the key to building my own tower. The keloids were the centuries-old stones, the bare bones of my foundation. I had entered their world in art and active imagination and they had entered mine. I was about to leave my old containment and descend further into their world, and into a much larger piece of my totality. Jung clarified what was happening: "The unconscious itself initiates the process of renewal,..[a] process by which the self is "reborn" and enters into a state in which it can be experienced" (CW14, 548).

In Burkina Faso, my husband and I hired a guide who took us first to his village. There we were greeted by the women, as well as a few men that were there, many with beautiful scarified faces! The children came out from their hiding places and gathered around. They stood across from us in a group, staring and smiling; we stared and smiled back.

A wave of emotion flowed up in me, and I had an immediate sense that this is what I came for. This was where I finally could be myself. I was reunited with a source from which I had long been separated. The keloids had scarified me in a "natural way." In this "natural, indigenous world" of Africa, the image of my "natural" earth mother lived. Beyond this, the original family my Self had known long ago was now standing before me. They had come to welcome me home.

When we woke the next morning, the children gathered around us and the village chief came to see us, bearing a live chicken as a gift. We had given the elders some gifts we had brought and the chief was reciprocating. We asked if they would be willing to permit us to give the chicken as an offering to their ancestors by conducting a ritual sacrifice, in our honor. After a brief deliberation, they agreed. The sacrifice ceremony is a form of divination in which the entrails are examined to see if they are clean. If they are – and it is not always the case – it means that ancestors have accepted the sacrifice. The entrails of our chicken were clean.

The elders were especially pleased; they took a risk in offering to do a sacrifice for us and possibly offending their ancestors. We were told later by the son of the village chief that we were the first white people ever to make a sacrifice in that village. The elders told us that the ancestors would provide continuing protection while we were in Africa. During the subsequent three weeks, in third-world conditions with unbelievable heat (120ßF.), many diseases and unfamiliar food, the ancestors clearly protected us.

The chicken sacrifice prepared me to speak to the shamans about scarification. These interviews were like a living active imagination. Sitting with each shaman was like speaking with an ancient soul. I wrote in my journal: "Since the mother did not convey her wisdom directly, this is doubly important for me."

At the beginning of each interview, I said that I was interested in scarification; I explained that I had spontaneous scars and that I felt a bond with the healers because of it. Thus assured that I wasn't an anthroplogist there to study them, they were quite open and receptive to me.

The interviews centered around the three main reasons for scarification: healing, ethnic identification and initiation. Scarification for healing is currently well respected and still within the law in

West Africa, whereas other forms of scarification are officially forbidden. Scars made for initiation were mostly hidden, as were the ceremonies. Their marks are sacred to the initiates, and they fear that if the scars are seen by someone who does not have a respectful attitude, the meaning and intention of the scar can be taken away. The sacred must be veiled. That explanation affirmed the sacred side of the scar and my being so reluctant to show my own scars.

These shamans explained that the philosophy of healing and the ritual of body-marking is based on creating harmony between body and soul. When the psyche undergoes trauma, there is a need to match, quickly, a body scar to the psyche's scar. If one develops more psychological or physical illnesses, additional scars are applied. Scarification for identification is preventive; the highly visible scars are there mostly to produce a disconnection from a hurtful spirit source. During initiation ceremonies, a scar is applied to the body in order to align it to something the soul already has undergone. What is left over on the body becomes the seal that certifies the initiate's having gone through the process. A scar is applied as a seal that is permanent, affecting the initiate's long-term understanding. The scar makes a harmonious blend of spirit and matter.

In a colonial context, where the masses were put into inhuman conditions, the marks were created so that the body scar matched what the soul had gone through. The soul was scarred and the body scar mirrored it.

Unlike the Western view, with its focus on physical beauty, deformity in indigenous cultures is usually seen as a sign of great prosperity. Every time a scar develops, whether physically or symbolically, blood has been spilled. It is sacred. To be marked opens one to the spirit world and the door never closes.

Through these interviews I found confirmation that, whether purposefully made or spontaneous, the keloid elicits the spirit in the body that is naturally there. The keloid creates a link to the transpersonal world that for many modern people has disappeared. My own scars had connected me to the transpersonal, to the past, the present and the future simultaneously. My life circled around this central point; where the eternal touched the body, as it had at my birth, it manifested as scars.

One interview stood out, not so much because of its contents, but because of what it evoked in me. It was the only interview I had with a woman healer. I sat by her side. We didn't speak directly. Through a translator, my questions were addressed to a man sitting across from her who then translated to her and she spoke back to him. She and I did not look directly at one another but there was a feeling connection between us that was palpable.

The photograph of me shaking hands with the woman healer and my painting of bringing my mother into this realm as if we were holding hands had a striking similarity. At the deepest level, this is what the journey was about. I had to experience the mother, here in the "mother land" of the dark continent and in the context of what was "higher," my keloid research. That was the intended meaning of "bringing her across": bringing across the "higher" side of my psyche.

On our last day in Africa, our driver happened to ask a young woman along the road, whom he knew from his village, if she could direct us to get change for the road tax. When she came up to the car I noticed she had scars on her arm exactly like my scars. She also had a large keloid on her face. I could hardly contain myself and asked her if we could go off alone together. She showed me the scars on her back and her chest and I showed her mine.

Finding her was like "the jewel that is discovered in the most common place." She came out as if from nowhere at the end of our journey. After seeing many beautiful scarifications, and being protected in some precarious situations, I found her, a mirror image of myself, a stranger on the road, a soul sister who seemed to be waiting for me so that I could accomplish what I had come for. Scarred and scarified; the two merged as one.

Coming Home

The descent into Africa was going back into the wound to find the mother and, beyond that, it showed me the eternal element that surrounds birth and death. Going back to the ancestral land from which humankind emerged, I was searching for the experience of tradition that my mother could not give. It was as if, by giving the ancestral world a tangible reality, I could become fully born into this world of reality. A dream I had when I returned revealed that a healing had taken place in my identity as an orphan:

I am driving between the two main African cities we had actually visited on our trip. I camp out on a lawn by the road beside a big house. The woman of the house comes out and invites me in. She offers to have me join the family for dinner. My driver comes in and sings a song in my honor. It is a song of "love and courage." My blessing for the meal is: "My being here proves the existence of God."

My initiation went beyond the ego to include a conscious, experiential connection to the collective layer of the psyche, the archetypal layer, where one is not alone. My need to belong to my larger earth family was finally satisfied. My collective underpinnings, the expansive layer of the unconscious, had revealed itself to me. "Being here proves the existence of God" was saying: the autonomy of the psyche and the God image it represents exist and, when I participate in it through the work on my inner house, I feel its existence. Then I know I exist.

The keloid scar had become the alchemical stone for me. I equated scars with the "orphan stone" or the Philosopher's Stone, that was said to be both worthless and precious, the fateful set of opposites bestowed upon the orphan. The keloid scar had all the features of the stone; it was small and insignificant, and its symbolic meaning was sought by few. The scar reflected the suffering, held a great mystery and was unique in its persistence in spite of being rejected by those who wanted to be rid of it. It remained. The keloid represented the earthly substance of the body and the spiritual dynamic. It sought my attention throughout my childhood and into my adulthood, and the intense work I did with it guided my individuation process. The stone is seen in a new form each time it is created. It suggests change and when it is taken up and worked with, it can turn into something beautiful.

In a second dream *I am peeling off the scars on my arm. They look like a cluster of grapes.*

The keloids were the *prima materia* and the grapes were the *lapis*, the completion of the process. The keloids becoming grapes symbolized the transformation of something ordinary and, beyond that, something often despised, into something revered as divine. The divinity of the grape and its organic nature were a part of me. It meant I belonged to all of creation. I belonged to all of time. I had missed nothing. The body had offered me the initiation process I had missed at my birth, and this became the fruit of the vine.

The scars had been my constant companions, permanent fixtures that did not leave me. They belonged to early humans and thus to the historical part of my psyche. They were the part of the great continuum that I wore on my skin; pieces of the immortal were emblazoned there. Uniting the keloid with its collective beginnings connected me to mine. Learning about the metaphysical meaning of the scars, including their sacred and protective function, reaffirmed the spiritual meaning the scars had for me.

The scar that was worshipped in tribal custom is deemed in the modern individual "worthless" and "rejected." Although what comes up from the body and the unconscious begins in dark form, it is the jewel that has been lost; it carries the new potential. Arising as a spontaneous scar, it initiates rebirth and thus renews life.

At this time of great change, contemporary body-marking such as tattooing and body piercing may express the longing for a spiritual initiation to counterbalance the chaos created in the undifferentiated psyche as it moves toward a transformed, integrated state. Whether intentionally made or spontaneously arising, the keloid contains the indwelling spirit. It offers a link to the transpersonal world that for many modern people has disappeared. Yet what appears on the surface to be destructive, in fact carries a creative potential that can integrate matter and spirit, psyche and body. To carry these opposites and to shape them consciously is our challenge.

References

Melissarato, K. (1945). *Wee Fishie Wun*. New York: Cupples & Leon.
Ward, L. (1929). *God's Man: A Novel in Woodcuts*. New York: Jonathan Cape & Harrison Smith.
Strommenger, E. & Hirmer, M. (1964). *The Art of Mesopotamia*. London: Thames & Hudson.

Illness and Creativity

Paul Brutsche
Zurich, Switzerland
Schweizerische Gesellschaft für Analytische Psychologie

Jung introduces my topic, concisely and full of paradoxes: "A psychoneurosis must be understood, ultimately, as the suffering of a soul which has not discovered its meaning. But all creativeness in the realm of the spirit as well as every psychic advance of man arises from the suffering of the soul, and the cause of the suffering is spiritual stagnation, or psychic sterility" (CW11, 497).

This quote contains ideas that are remarkable but characteristic of Jung's way of thinking. Psychic illness ultimately results from a lack of meaning but also from a lack of psychic creativity. My reflection here aims at describing the various dimensions of the relationship between illness and creativity.

Jung's idea that people become neurotic or psychically ill because they do not experience their life as meaningful or their soul as fecund is an important one. We may experience ourselves and our everyday reality as being at a standstill because life appears to be made of seemingly mechanical repetitions, of an endless process. Our life may not give us a sense of meaning, although we derive satisfaction from numerous activities.

Leisure time becomes a problem. We do not know what to do when we are not working. It becomes difficult to find ourselves free to follow inner impulses, or to satisfy inner wishes in a playful spirit. We have trouble following creative impulses, out of sheer pleasure, instead of doing what is expected by something or someone in the outer world. We may find it difficult to formulate our own values or to have a personal opinion. We do not trust ourselves to refer to our own experience as a basis for our views.

Psychic creativity – as opposed to productivity – implies a desire and an ability to change, to fashion our own life. Such creativity may manifest as an experience of meaning that makes life worth living and gives it depth. A playful attitude allows the individual to reach beyond achievement, duties and obligations, and to fashion another form of experience. This attitude may translate into an ability to use personal experience in developing our own understanding and our own views.

Whenever these aspects of psychic creativity are missing, the individual experiences "the suffering of the soul" that does not feel genuine and that lacks meaning. The ultimate belief of living in harmony with oneself and with life is not there, and there is a subjective feeling of not being psychically healthy.

I have often observed a phenomenon in people who are in this situation; they feel vaguely ill, because – as we have seen – they are not able to fashion and to experience their life in a creative mode. And yet, curiously, they are not creative because they are not actually sick. They have avoided feeling ill or someone has spared them the experience of suffering, depriving them of an existential dimension. They avoid things that are unpleasant, disagreeable or disturbing. They were always and still are avoiding conflicts. They are caught in a paradisiacal "self-preservation" attitude. This unwillingness to bear pain then produces the neurotic suffering brought by a meaningless, boring life.

Or they may refuse to experience the helplessness connected to illness. This refusal to feel helpless causes the other type of suffering: the inability to let things happen in a creative manner, which would bring them the feeling of being alive. These people take on a heroic stance. Sheer willpower keeps them alive, but they do not realize that life itself is not involved – whereas it would be life that would fulfil their needs.

Some people may actively deny being ill. They were brought up in such a way that only positive aspects mattered and only normality was accepted. Being ill, which is not compatible with normality, cannot be seen as a reality. This attitude leads to suffering as a result of an obsession with normality. These people are doomed to lead an uncreative existence and may not be able to do anything without obeying collective norms.

Others avoid facing the precariousness of life. Because they don't want to accept that life is always perilous (or even "life-threatening"), they deny their own fears and pain every time they are faced with the abysmal doubts inherent in living. They then suffer from being dependent on the verdict of an authority outside themselves.

In many cases, the dimensions of suffering that belong to life have been suppressed. As Jung wrote, "Life demands for its completion and fulfillment a balance between joy and sorrow. Behind a neurosis there is so often concealed all the natural and necessary suffering the patient has been unwilling to bear" (CW16, 185).

There are consequences for therapy. We must accept that our patients may suffer from a lack of creativeness and that analysis should help them to discover and develop their own creativity. However, since this lack of genuine creativity – in the concrete context of one's life – is often paired with a refusal to accept the reality of natural suffering, the therapy must aim at enabling the patients to experience the suffering of the soul that will allow them to be creative.

We may ask ourselves whether the analytic relationship can enable people discover their psychic creativeness. I would say yes. An analytic relationship can serve to help the client to discover the creativeness that is buried in the soul, and elaborate a personal philosophy. For the process to take place, the therapist must have a specific attitude, the analytic vessel must fulfill specific conditions and the analysand must have certain experiences.

1. The therapist's attitude

a. We all know that the therapist must like people, be interested in their psychic realities, and value the other, within the field of tension joining spontaneous attraction and therapeutic Eros.

b. The therapist must be able, also, to have a genuine encounter with the patient: going toward the patient emphatically but reacting in a related mode, so that a lively confrontation may take place. The point is not to establish a comfortable, peaceful relationship; it is to find out about psychic truths. We may apply part of a motto Jung quotes (CW16, p. 167): "Bellica pax ... (A warring peace)." The quote is taken from John Gower's treatise on alchemy, but it may be used to express the fact that a therapeutic relationship is an intentional confrontation, never quite the same as a normal friendship.

c. The therapist must trust in the guidance provided by the psyche and in the client's ability to be receptive to its messages.

d. The therapist must be able to accept being put in question, being disapproved of and criticized, but also being appreciated and loved. Able to give up the role of the "healer" who knows more and directs the process, the therapist will be an interlocutor whose reactions are guided by the psyche and who helps constellate "soul aspects."

The attitude I have just described corresponds to Eros in its purest form. This type of Eros is found not only in therapy, but of course as a part of other relationships, or it can be missing in any interaction.

Many people have been wounded in the erotic field, which is needed if one is to experience the reality of the psyche. As a result, they have relational problems and have never had a genuine experience of psychic vitality and creativity. An authentic Eros experience in the analysis is healing and allows the client to overcome a lack of relatedness and "lack of soul."

2. The conditions related to the analytic vessel

The analytic vessel must fulfill certain conditions that make it into a container for soul experience, and thus for spiritual fertility. The analytic relationship is an odd mixture between a natural human relationship and an unnatural (therapeutic) technique. It awakens the need for close friendship while simultaneously forcing its participants to realize that its aim is something else: healing. It has the qualities of a unique relationship and yet both parties know that the next client is already sitting in the waiting room and, despite being fully present, the therapist has a private life in which the client takes no part.

We may feel irritated by the fact that analysis takes place somewhere between a natural and an artificial relationship, between a spontaneous and an intentional encounter, between closeness and distance. The experience of a healing relatedness remains mixed with an element of unrelatedness that also has beneficial effects. At the same time, we may choose to consider this lack of relatedness to be an expression of the *suave malum* (agreeable evil) that Jung quoted (CW16, p. 167).

The expression "agreeable evil" expresses the ambivalent reality of the analytic relationship. Yet this ambivalence should not be considered unfortunate. As shocking as this may feel, the ambivalence has a deeper meaning. It gives the therapeutic relationship the character of a ritual. As such, it goes beyond a natural relationship, to which attraction and familiarity – and sometimes possessiveness – are inherent.

3. The analysand's experience

The analysand must have experiences in order for the analysis to become a container for a relation to the psyche and for the creativity that it brings. Among these experiences are disappointments and hurt feelings.

a. The analysis may reactivate fears arising out of disturbances in the analysand's relationship to parents or to a partner: disrupted relationships, abandonment feelings, break-ups that provoked feelings of hurt.

b. Archetypal images of lack of relatedness may be constellated, without the person having had the concrete corresponding experience. For instance, the analyst may appear in a dream as a business man who has no time for spiritual things.

c. Fears are constellated that are linked to collective roles and to gender: for example, the abandonment of the child by the parents, the possessiveness of the egocentric mother, the rejection by a father who is unable to show his feelings. These stereotypes are present in society and may interfere in the analytic relationship.

d. Real wounding may occur in the analysis: for instance, the analyst does not inform the client properly about an intention to raise the fee, or reacts in a wounding manner to the transference feelings that have been expressed by the analysand. These are wounds that are suffered in the here and now of the analytic relationship.

We may wonder what the meaning of this unavoidable dimension is. It reminds me of the second part of Jung's quote from John Gower: *dulce vulnus* (sweet wound). It seems that one needs to experience the wounding aspects of Eros – in its past, archetypal, imaginary or present form – in order for its creative dimension to become active.

What conclusions does this suggest in relation to the practice of therapy? The aim is to be open to this type of wounding in such a feeling way – and not through rational thinking – that we may take in its power along with the pain involved. Surprisingly enough, this process will give us a sense of the vitality and healing contained in Eros. Eros makes it possible to relate to oneself with an attitude of quiet acceptance, and also to relate to life, to the past and to our own fate. This is a paradox: the pain suffered by the soul giving birth to the creativeness of Eros.

As analysts, we meet people who may have very different attitudes to time and to development (in their own life), that is, to a process of creative evolution. Four possible attitudes come to mind.

1. One type may be described as "hysteroid." These people tend to become completely absorbed in change. They throw themselves enthusiastically into any new experience or relationship. For them, life is an eternal promise. On the other hand, they find life difficult as soon as it involves repetition, or any limitation. The shadow side of the "puer aeternus" attitude is that nothing really changes and nothing is being genuinely created. These people remain eternally young, behaving like children or adolescents. And despite their enthusiasm for new things and for the future, they remain dependent on their family and their childhood. They are not able to be creative, in relationships or in their profession; life runs like sand through their fingers. True creativity is replaced by a pseudo-creative activism.

2. Another type may be called "compulsive." Their basic creative attitude is the exact opposite of the "hysteroid" one: not ruled by youth, by novelty, by constant change – the child archetype – but by the "senex." A "senex" attitude to life manifests itself through a tendency to impose order on everything. Creativity is thus experienced as differentiating, classifying, and structuring – a genuine dimension. But, in case of a senex attitude, a neurotic one-sidedness defends against life and the psychic reality of autonomous change and a kind of "home-made" rigid planning is constantly being used by the anxious ego to repress genuine creativity.

3. People with a "depressive" attitude experience creativity as a connection with the past and with their origins. They consider what they are familiar with to be valuable and worth keeping, and refuse to go with the spirit of time or to innovate. Innovations are considered uncreative and suspect. This is an attitude in which the true reality of creativity is reduced to a limited position of consciousness, albeit to a position connected to the "mother." Consciousness attributes absolute value to the connection with its origins in the past and to the motherly unconscious. Thus, genuine creativeness cannot be present, since it would require a connection to the time dimension and to the outer world.

4. And finally, people may have a "schizoid" attitude to creativity: trying to anticipate what is coming. They attempt to forestall the future by remembering earlier experiences and by generalizing what these have taught them. Yet one is trapped in mentally anticipating

events and changes; because "father" sun dominates consciousness nothing really new can be experienced.

These four attitudes include all authentic aspects of creativeness: the "puer" energy of change, the "senex" energy of order, a "mother" energy related to the past and a "father" energy oriented toward the future. Yet they simultaneously turn one or the other into an absolute value that is at the core of a neurotic strategy. Paradoxically, a genuinely creative existential quest and personal experience are blocked in the name of creativity. Processes staged by the ego are running idle, outside real life. Life itself is never really involved or accepted.

What provokes this type of behavior and how should we deal with it in therapy? First of all, we may assume that it has to do with a refusal to confront suffering and that the aim of therapy must be to reconnect these people with the existential dimension of pain. This will allow them to give up their fixation on pseudo-creativity and to experience genuine creativity.

People like that do not want to know about illness. This does not mean that they do not experience it in their life. When I think of some of my analysands and of the way that they represent the four neurotic types described above, I see that illness is always there, sometimes in the form of severe somatic symptoms. It is there as an autonomous entity that is experienced as repulsive instead of being accepted as part of life. Illness that is experienced in this form cannot bring transformation. The one-sided conscious attitude remains untouched, the creative strategies that have been chosen dominate consciousness.

Thinking of the "hysteroid" type, I remember a woman who lived her life in an intense manner. She could hardly keep up with all the beautiful and fascinating things that each day had to offer; but she had had a bad car accident and, unconsciously, she constantly feared that something similar would happen again. In relation to the "compulsive strategy," I think of a young man who has been quite a good student and is leading a well-ordered professional and love life, yet who keeps having unpleasant experiences: helping a stranger push his car and my client's kneecap becomes unhinged, working in his lab and hydrochloric acid sprays in his face because one of the valves is not tight. The "depressive" type is represented, for me, by a woman who, having broken a relationship to a man, suddenly became sick with polyarthritis, for which her doctor saw a bad prognosis. And the "schizoid" type by a man who, because he had

had a break-down and was considered invalid by the insurance, had lived on disability benefits ever since then. It is as if the suffering that these people excluded from their life by remaining one-sidedly fixated on the positive aspects of creativity had to be manifested through a kind of crude, oblique event.

Taking these attitudes into account, what should the therapeutic objectives be? Certainly to help these people experience authentic creativeness, without pain and illness being excluded from their life. For them, neurosis or physical illness must become a reference point and a support in achieving their creative quest for identity and for life.

This approach requires two elements. One, the therapy must include work on the physical illness, aiming to bring it closer to consciousness. Any disease that manifests in an autonomous and unrelated manner needs to be integrated and its potential for transformation experienced. Two, the therapy should promote the experience of psychic suffering, even though it seems to stand in contradiction with creativity. At the core, both are aspects of the same process.

By "integrate" I mean that physical illness, whatever its form or the time of its manifestation, should be respected and accepted. It is not enough to talk about it, to interpret and to explain it while the ego keeps a distance and does not really experience the dimensions of illness. The point is to go into the experience of illness and to accept the fact that there is nothing there that can be explained or understood. Illness leads to a dead end, to a feeling of helplessness and fear.

Illness contains great potentials for experiencing transformational potential for and, thus, consciously discovering creativeness. It scares the sufferer and because it tends to corner him, it may move him to act in an authentic manner, which he was not able to do when he was healthy.

There are several avenues for illness to make people become more authentic:

1. Illness often makes the ego genuinely perceive its own existence and take it seriously. This applies of course to the simple flu that forces me to retire to my bed, but it also applies to more serious physical diseases and to paralyzing depressions. Illness makes one turn to oneself at a very existential level and liberates one from collective expectancies.

2. The pain involved in illness brings the person to a limit of what is bearable. In the desperate hope of finding relief, one may be ready to try out things that would have seemed improper before. In this way, disease helps us open to the unusual and gives us the courage to follow unfamiliar paths.

3. Illness makes it clear to consciousness that it cannot have absolute control and make all the decisions. The ego finds itself at the mercy of a mysterious reality, of being powerless in the face of something that may send health or illness. One feels confronted with destiny, with something against which one cannot do too much. Thus, illness can help us to accept the fact that we are being shaped by an unfathomable reality.

4. The experience of illness also includes the experience of weakness, of having lost a fight. This leads us to open to something greater and stronger than we are and to accept another dimension of reality. It helps us overcome an ego-centered perception of life.

In brief, illness brings a concentration of the ego, an opening, a grounding and a "conversion." These combine in an attitude that allows a natural experience of genuine and lively creativeness.

The relationship between physical illness and creativity has been described by Jung, in an interesting report of a concrete experience. At the beginning of 1944, Jung had broken a foot; shortly after that, he suffered a heart attack that nearly killed him:

> *After the illness a fruitful period of work began for me. A good many of my principal works were written only then. The insight I had had, or the vision of the end of all things, gave me the courage to undertake new formulations. I no longer attempted to put across my own opinion, but surrendered myself to the current of my thoughts.*
> ...
> *Something else, too, came to me from my illness. I might f'ormulate it as an affirmation of things as they are: an unconditional "yes" to that which is, without subjective protests – acceptance of the conditions of existence as I see them and understand them, acceptance of my own nature. ...*
> *It was only after the illness that I understood how important it is to affirm one's own destiny. In this way we forge an ego that does not break down when incomprehensible things happen; an ego that endures, that endures the truth, and that is capable of coping with the world and with fate. ...*
> *I have also realized that one must accept the thoughts that go on within oneself of their own accord as part of one's reality. (MDR, p. 297)*

What Jung wrote about his experience is similar to what has been reported by people who have had a near-death experience. This type of experience is probably also the closest to the focus of archaic mystery cults.

The most important point in the examples I have given is that transformation does not occur as a result of a psychological interpretation. Creativity has a freeing effect, but not because we know the meaning of an illness or of a near-death experience. As psychologists, we tend to overvalue conscious knowledge, perhaps leading us to believe that it is by understanding the hidden meaning of illness that we may discover the key to its creative potential. This would be wrong since, on the contrary, it is experiencing – without understanding – the limits of the ego and the aspects that transcend it that may open the door to a creative reality situated beyond any ego ambitions.

The ego expressing its suffering and the reality of the psyche reacting to these emotions are linked by a remarkable alchemical *enantiodromia*. A woman, whose husband had committed suicide and who was fighting against similar impulses in herself, was astounded when she saw that the more she accepted her painful emotions, the more unknown energies were available to her. This is an experience with which, as therapists, we are quite familiar. Psyche seems to depend on suffering's being expressed directly, vocally and sensually before it can react by offering vital energies. Something seems to contain both poles, the pain and the healing creativeness. And creativity can be freed only if the ego is open to expressing its suffering.

These mysterious opposite processes can be expressed in pictures. I often advise analysands to use painting and to start by representing the suffering that is actually constellated: for example, melancholy, feeling of emptiness, physical sensations. Painting may help them go more deeply into the diffuse pain that they are experiencing, to amplify it and to clarify it so that, at an emotional and/or experiential level, they may come as close to it as is possible. Surprisingly, this process often leads to a paradoxical reaction from the unconscious, bringing a symbolic image as an answer to the authentic self-expression of the suffering ego. Here again, we seem to have a bipolar reality that manifests itself and, in so doing, provides a creative insight into the other side of authentic suffering.

How can we help the analysand see suffering as a way to find a new orientation, instead of expecting the therapist to aid in overcoming this unpleasant experience? An important step in this direction is made if we try not to provide support in the form of behavioral strategies or advice. We should bear with the fact that we do not know, that we don't understand and, thus, help the analysand to adopt a similar attitude. If we both succeed in being honest about the fact that we clearly do not know, the psyche may come up with a surprising hint. I have seen often that this shadowy reality cannot give birth to a genuine insight until both therapist and analysand become silent and face the pain together.

It is sometimes helpful to have to confront a crisis, which makes it easier to accept going into the suffering. For instance, an analysand may have to face an existential crisis and to make important decisions while being unable to act or to ask someone for a friendly piece of advice. In such a situation, where despair blocks any action, a freeing impulse may come from within the self and help solve the crisis. Here again, it is as if we are faced with contradictory dynamics in which, once the crisis has been "created," the enlightenment that will help solve it is provided.

Certain aspects of analytic reality are shown in Jung's quote, "A psychoneurosis must be understood, ultimately, as the suffering of a soul which has not discovered its meaning" CW11, 497). The analyst, too, is influenced by the relation between illness and creativity.

1. A therapeutic approach must find a way to experience and confront illness in all its dimensions: this is done so that people will see life in a negative light or will become masochists. On the contrary, it will enable them to achieve the existential identity and autonomy that was foreseen for them by the soul, including the necessary negative experiences. However, this adequate attitude toward "suffering," the limitations and the pain that it brings, cannot be constellated unless the therapist is aware of his or her own limits, impotence and weakness. To participate creatively in the healing process, the therapist must be a "wounded healer."

2. Therapists must be aware of their limitations: be conscious of feelings of weakness and impotence and of their own problematic, pathological sides. They must experience all of these time and time again, at a deep emotional level. Otherwise, the roles are distributed too simply, at the expense of the patient: in one chair the healthy therapist, in the other the patient who is sick – and must be sick.

3. It is also important that therapists work at remaining in a state of creative curiosity. If this stops being the case, because they are

going through a phase of "spiritual stagnation" or because they feel painfully impotent, they risk making the patient into the object of their own creativity. Then, the therapist may become too involved, or too directive, or will pretend to know it all. An unconscious process takes place; the patients become the whole contents of the therapist's life and are being psychically annexed. This over-involvement prevents the patients from being independent and from experiencing their own creativity.

Translated from the original German by Francoise O'Kane

Transsexualism or Transcendence Unattainable

Claude Bourreille
Paris, France
Société Française de Psychologie Analytique

My interest in the phenomenon of male-to-female transsexualism began after I watched a television series. I was struck by the emotional intensity of these men who were involved in this startling, dangerous and terrible adventure. I wondered about it and then looked for information. At the individual level, where it is certainly painful, it seemed to me that transsexualism is a phenomenon that exemplifies the crisis of modernity.

Wondering about this singular phenomenon, I focused on the question of meaning. What do those want who, while knowing that they are anatomically men, call themselves women and ask others to help them bring their external reality into accord with their internal one? Does it involve a destructive impulse, an intuition that is creative in its way although questionable in its form? What role does society play in the production of this phenomenon? What response does it make?

The case of a German magistrate, Daniel Paul Schreber, became famous after Freud's account (SE12) was published in 1911; it was based on Schreber's *Memoirs*, which appeared in 1903. Since then, numerous studies have been published on this case. It may seem arbitrary that I identify in the memoirs themes that seem to go along with my analysis. In fact, this selection is justified insofar as the words excerpted relate to a more general context, that of all the works about the transsexual phenomenon. In this way, one can see Schreber as the prophet of today's mass society, and also as a symptom. The second psychotic episode suffered by Schreber – in 1893 – started with the thought, early in the morning between sleep and waking, that "It must be so beautiful to be a woman giving herself in the act of love." Such a reference to beauty can be found in the desires of numerous transsexuals. His case, even without reference to castration – which was not conceivable at the time – is particularly meaningful to us. The transsexual theme unfolds in Schreber's delirious words expressing his "metamorphosis into a woman." He speaks about his constant and intimate relationship with God, leading to "the most acutely voluptuous sensation." He is waiting for "conception by divine rays of a new race of men" different from ordinary men who are "hastily built." Therefore, a divine race would be built out of his body's transformation into "the cult of femininity." His metamorphosed body has become "the wife of God plunged in a voluptuous ravishment. ... The requirement is that I have to look at myself as man and woman in one person, performing coitus with myself."

Divine fusion, similar in its content but very different because free of anguish, exists in the Hijras, the men-women of a community in India. Emasculation becomes an initiation by mystical identification with the divine Mata, goddess of fecundity, and with Shiva, god of destruction and rebirth. During the castration ceremony, the risk of death – by surrendering to her requirement of sacrifice – is essential to obtain the goddess' favor. An ideal woman's profile appears, a woman very different from the "hastily built" as Schreber would have it. According to an anthropologist Castel (1995): "Sexuality and the mode of corporal existence are transcended by a projection absolutely other" (p. 559). It is the meaning of this projection that we need to discover.

Schreber's quest, as that of the Hijras, illuminates what transsexuals in our Western societies express more or less explicitly. In spite of the perception of a body anatomically masculine, what transsexuals claim is Womanhood – which observers write with a capital W – because it projects an idea of the feminine not expressed by real women, but a feminine embodiment whose captivating power belongs to the imagination. The transsexual is situated both "outside the body" and "outside of sex." His position consists in "the will to be all woman, entirely woman, more woman than all women and being worth them all," according to Millot (1985), a Lacanian psychologist. This feminine feature, alien to a sexual identity, excludes any division. It is the essence of the "real woman": a superior being gifted with the ability of parthenogenesis.

Search for Meaning Through the Myth of Narcissus

The demand for transformation can appear at different moments in the life of a transsexual man. In broad strokes there are three main stages: young (20 to 30 years of age), middle-aged (between 40 and 50), and finally the transsexual who makes his passage at an advanced age (around 60 or even more).

What is striking in the first case is often the physical beauty of the young man, ephebe-like, whose grace erases the distinction, still uncertain, between man and woman. The middle-aged transsexual has generally led the life of a man and may be married, with a family. He tries to take on feminine being at an age when it is no longer possible for him to actualize such beauty. From the mature man he could have been, he takes on the appearance of an aging woman. It is important to note this in connection with the transsexual's idea of feminine beauty. The third type, who is older, gradually escapes the formal structure of the human body and materializes the female dimension with the help of hormone treatments.

In comparing the different forms of transsexual transformation, there appears, like a watermark, an image of Narcissus and Echo representing the symbolic model. The myth, told by the Latin poet Ovid, seems to be an archetypal model capable of clarifying the process.

Disdainful of the women whose love he attracts by his beauty, Narcissus angers the goddess Nemesis, who condemns him to love only himself. Bending over the mirroring water that reflects his image, he cannot stop looking at himself. He languishes, wastes away and finally is transformed into the flower that bears his name, while the nymph Echo, who loved him, is transformed into the rock which reverberates the spoken word. The disappearance of human form signifies involution to a state denying sexual differentiation, from the identification with the vegetable world, still relatively sexual, through to the mineral world where the distinction is totally erased. Narcissus becomes a flower and Echo a rock. Echo is none other than Narcissus, having finished the cycle of his regressions.

The story of a transsexual seems close to that of Narcissus and Echo. Like Narcissus, by not accepting sexual differentiation and giving himself the illusion of absolute power over himself, a trans-sexual risks losing himself. He does not appropriate the feminine, and he castrates himself from his masculine reality. Torn between a male with whom he cannot identify and a female whom he tries to possess, the transsexual lives in a dead-end loneliness. His insistent demand to be acknowledged expresses his feeling of loss over the identity which he could not obtain and which he is asking others – society at large – to give him. In this sense, tied to a death wish, one can perceive a desire of rebirth through a medical intervention.

In the story of Narcissus, the watery mirror becomes Narcissus' protagonist. What role does it play in a transsexual's story? Considering the mirror, *speculum* in Latin, with the meaning of both reflection in the intellectual sense and as an image in a mirror – itself sometimes called "psyché" (e.g., in French) – we can see that, between nature and culture, between the carnal and spiritual realm, it occupies a transitional position between masculine and feminine.

In a letter to Richard Hull (Let-II, p. 79) and referring to the late Prof. Wolfgang Pauli, Jung mentions the "mirror-reflection, causing the existence of two worlds [physical and psychological] which are really united in the *speculum*, the mirror, that is lying in the middle. … Thus, 'speculation,' a very typical form of consciousness, becomes the real centre of the world, the basis of the *unus mundus.*" This proposition, valid on a macrocosmic scale, is also valid at the scale of the psyche, which realizes its identity through the test of the mirror, as Lacan (1966) demonstrated. He saw the mirror as the gaze of the other.

From his connection with the mirror – the water in which he contemplates himself – Narcissus belongs to the feminine side, which constitutes a necessary component. It becomes pathological only when the relation with the mirror closes on itself, in an interrogation which does not open onto what could be heard as an answer.

Consequently, the mirror that reunites can also separate by the construction of two opposing worlds: one aiming at an abstraction more and more unilateral, the other burying itself in concrete materialism. Instead of uniting, the feminine and masculine exclude each other.

In his letter to Hull, Jung mentions the ensuing pathological stages. After a reminder about Freud's fascination for a human's dark side which he calls the "*Mysterium iniquitatis,*" and offering his own conclusions about it, Jung adds: "In modern literature, there is a whole library of *psychopathologia sexualis*, criminology, detective novels. … The only problem with all this literature is that nobody seems to realize that it is dictated by a *Mysterium*. It has been my destiny to recognize it.

We are now confronted with the pathological side of Narcissus and the trap into which he fell. In the myth, the relationship with the mirror is represented by a young man, not by a woman, in spite of the natural link of the woman with her mirror exemplified in so many works of art. The myth indicates that fascination for his feminine side leads man to a loss of virility, without reaching the female stage, which remains an illusion. The passage into action of the male transsexual ends in a castration whose high price makes him wonder what unconscious idea or what irrepressible intuition led him to give his consent.

Before wondering about meaning, some psychological subsets can be mentioned. Relationship problems with parents tend to underlie deviations in the establishment of the sexual identity, as numerous studies have shown such disturbances can be the result of a fixation at the pre-oedipal stage well before the father is to play a role in separating the mother from the child. When speaking about her son, a mother said: "I watched him too much; I chewed up his life." Mignet (1998), a Jungian psychoanalyst, mentioned the case of a young man whose mother wanted to have a girl. Before giving birth, she declared: "If it is a boy, he can die." Mignet wonders if the desire to have a girl and the "death sentence" on a boy, had, through the mother, the power to effect changes in the neuro-cellular structure, dissociating the psychological program from the physiological. She evokes the possibility of "unconscious programming at the intra-uterine stage resulting from the symbiosis between the intra-uterine environment and the mother's unconscious" (p. 68) The questioning traces the transsexual's desire back to the very origin of the child's biopsychological development during the embryonic stage. This would explain the lack, at least momentarily, of castration fear in transsexuals who don't perceive this as a loss but as a gain, a restitution of their true being which was unjustly denied. If sex for a man is on the feminine side, the penis – flesh without reality due to a lack of symbolization – is left to surgery.

The transsexual phantasm has been viewed, also, as a response to a trauma of the sadistic-incestuous type exercised by one of the parents – usually the father, as was the case for Schreber – who "submitted without a respite to so-called educational practices which offered to the father's sadism a permanent access to his son's body, on which to impose a totally perverse libido" (C. Maritan 1996, p. 173). And this without any recourse on the mother's side, who did not see or hear anything and let it all happen. The fear engendered by a divided self can worsen into a psychotic fear of the void. What place must the contemplating subject occupy in order to start a positive relationship between himself and the mirror of the other and, especially, the other's gaze?

In the first place, a child needs to gather a sense of self when reflected in the mirror offered by the other, usually the mother. The child must then detach from this external mirror and find a reflection in another mirror called the auto-erotic double, creating an interior space in which the child starts to individuate through finding autonomy.

A transsexual, like Narcissus, looks desperately outside for the mirror he lacks inside. He works himself into a frenzy over his fear of disintegration and void, a state in which fascination with the object becomes a mode of protection. He experiences a terror of the non-representation of the ego, which may occur because of his inability to distinguish himself from the object, or because of the impossibility of building an identity when forced to submit to aggression. (The situation of Schreber is seen in another form in cases of pedophilia.)

Narcissus could not reach the stage of inner being, and his reflection in the water is a substitute for an unrepresentable empty shape which maintains him in a fragile self-realization, an existence as a reflection without depth. The transsexual requires the reflection to maintain his being in the mirror of the other, the mother, or the society that will play this role later.

Narcissus and Perseus

These musings about the mirror, its function and its position within the perspective of an analysis of transsexualism's signifi- cance has brought to the surface the mythological symbol of Perseus which is opposed to that of Narcissus. Perseus was the son of Danae and of Jupiter, who came to visit her in the guise of a shower of gold in the tower where her father Acresios had locked her, so that she would have no contact with men. He had been warned by an oracle that he would be killed by his grandson.

When Acresios discovered the child, he ordered mother and son to be locked in a trunk and thrown into the sea. Washed ashore on an island, they were rescued by a fisherman's family who surrounded them with tenderness and care. Perseus became a young man. One day his still-beautiful mother was seen by the king of the island, the brother of the fisherman. He fell in love and wanted to marry her. Perseus announced that he would surpass any other guest's gift. He would cut off the head of Medusa, one of the Gorgons, who had the power to turn to stone any man looking at her – and give it to the king.

After some dangerous adventures while searching for the Gorgon, Perseus met a handsome young man, the god Hermes (in whom I see the auto-erotic double) who offered him a sword and a bag to store the head in. Then he met the goddess Athena (perhaps a mother figure who accepted her son's separating from her). She gave him the bronze shield which protected her chest and told him: "Hold this in front of you and look at it when you attack Medusa. You will see her mirror image and you will avoid her mortal gaze." In this way, Perseus succeeds in acquiring the head of the Gorgon. Some other adventures will lead him to an encounter with Andromeda (the daughter of a queen of Ethiopia. He will save her from a horrible death–being devoured by a serpent.. He will marry her and will know, as the myth tells us, "a long happy life" after accidentally killing his grandfather. These two heroes can represent the archetypal models for two attitudes. The first leads to failure; the second brings an ending to a tragedy.

The etymology is revealing. Narcissus comes from *narke*, which means sleep. Narcissus is the man who has not yet awakened to self-consciousness, a lack that condemns him to psychological death. Perseus is someone who is *per se*, for himself; he acquires an inner reality and can access the subjective point of view. We can see that everything revolves around the mirror. For Narcissus, it is the intermediary necessary for the distinction between subject and object to happen and an object of fascination. In his face to face with the vacillating watery mirror, from which Narcissus cannot separate, he is engaged in a process of involution through his identification with an idealized object. Whether it is called Mother, Sun, God or Goddess, the myth's lesson is that the object must not be sought after and contemplated in a direct manner. To look at it is to condemn oneself to a psychological, if not physical, death.

In the opposite way, the mirroring shield of Perseus allows him to take an indirect look at the Gorgon, the terrifying goddess whose direct gaze brings death. It becomes possible to make a distinction between subject and object which, in a confrontation, are linked while staying apart, thus eliminating death by the fusion of coitus.

What Intuition Leads the Transsexual;
What Error Destroys Him?

Let us go back to Jung and his letter to Hull. Pathological sexuality surfaces when the mirror, instead of playing a linking role, leads to separation into two opposing worlds. Jung wrote at the end of his letter, "It is a Mysterium; it has been my destiny to recognize it" (p. 79).

What Mysterium is this? The answer is given by the title of Jung's last work, his crowning achievement: *Mysterium Coniunctionis* (CW14). Narcissus' mistake, which matches the transsexual's error, is to believe that the union with the god or goddess – whatever the name – could have happened in a direct fashion. Out of the fear of falling to pieces, the transsexual is looking for transcendence. This makes the quest moving, but he is mistaken in the illusion of a concrete realization; the union of opposites relies on a prior differentiation, resting on a symbolic verbal stage, not on an actual one.

The transsexual uses his body as the place for an alchemy which, beyond the apparent transformation of a man into a woman, aims at the unconscious transmutation of masculine values of distinction, separation, formalizing and intellectualization into the feminine values of materialization and incarnation. Beyond the individual conditioning – important but relegated to the background if we consider this delirium in its universal aspects – the comprehension of the problem calls for an underlying religious and aesthetic dimension that is more or less visible.

The aesthetic dimension is illustrated by Schreber when he says, "It must be so beautiful to be a woman giving herself up in the act of love." It is also mentioned by numerous transsexuals when asked why they want to become women. The word comes often: "It is beautiful." It is important to understand this oft-mentioned link between femininity and beauty. It is not in the sense of women being more beautiful than men in their physical appearance. It is the beauty of femininity in the mode of approach to life according to a natural order and sentiment (as Schreber says), by opposition to the logical, institutional mode of organization of the masculine structure. What the transsexual rejects, unknowingly, are ways of thinking from a masculine model. And this in the name of a myth of femininity which takes shape, beyond individual expression, in collective hysterical explosions echoed loudly by the media. Thus, transsexualism appears as a vector of modernity's crisis, among other recent spectacular events – for example, Diana's death and the Gay Games of Amsterdam–which express collective hysteria.

A religious dimension appears when the relationship with the divine is called on for the creation of a new world. This was true for Schreber, with the forces of Christian culture which had shaped his thoughts, as demonstrated by Devreese (1996). It is equally true for the Hijras. For Westerners and others whose religious culture is not acknowledged, this dimension sometimes comes out during analysis. Mignet's (1998) patient dreams of Baby Jesus between his mother and father. He does not have a sex. This dream exemplifies sexuality's enigma. A choice must be made between the father's and mother's sex. In the sexless zone, the transsexual shows that he can identify with neither. His attempt to solve the enigma by twisting nature is a failure. When the religious dimension is completely repressed, the result is often tragic during the phase of decompensation following sex-change surgery, which is never the case in primitive populations still under the influence of myth.

With castration, a change in the body, the transsexual ultimately is looking for, paradoxically, is a supplement of the soul. At the same time, by negating the sexual dimension, he is acting out the angelic temptation well expressed by the title of a transsexual's autobiography, *The Angel's Leap* (Marin 1987). In his transcendental quest, he short-circuits the channels which, symbolically, could open the way. In his own way, the transsexual is an inverted mystic on a quest for a transcendence that is nowhere to be found. Schreber's case fully illustrates this. He was a mystic who wanted to escape the sexual dimension. Delusional about a change which would sublimate his body and take him away from dangerous fixations and aggressions, he was not graced by a word which could have reconciled him with himself by opening up the sacred dimension.

Deeply human in his dream of transcending the difference through the revelation of something beyond the ineluctable and fundamental difference between the sexes, the transsexual, along with modern Pygmalions, is a pathetic expression of the desire to be like God, in an act of creation which leads to his doom because he does not recognize that the right path leads not to the elimination of opposites but to putting them in their proper relationship.

Conclusion

The transsexual offers a fundamental challenge to us and to those who encourage him in his illusion. By twisting nature in the name of an illusory femininity, transsexualism calls into question a society with a masculine structure. But it must fail when negating the role of the other in the constitution of the subject. It is a fall into the psychotic which concerns not only the individual but also society, when it shares and even encourages the phantasm. We note the definition of psychosis: absence of separation between subject and object. Speaking of the psychotic, Lacan used to say: "He put his object in his pocket." Between the mystical I have discussed and the psychotic, there is only a small decisive step, the one which leads from creation to destruction by the substitution of a concrete act for the symbolic word.

Translated from the original French by Martine Nagy

References

Castel, P. (1995). Quelques problèmes relatifs à la définition de l'identité sexuelle dans l'anthropologie sociale contemporaine. In M. Czermak et al. (Eds.), *Sur l'Identité Sexuelle; A propos du Transexuallism*. Paris: l'Association Freudienne Internationale.

Devreese, D. (1996). Anatomie du meurte d'âme. In: Prado, L. (Ed.), *Schreber et la Paranoïa: Textes Réunis et Présentés*. Paris: L'Harmattan.

Lacan, J. (1966). *Ecrits I*. Paris: du Seuil.

Marin, M. (1987). *Le Saut de l'Ange*. Paris: Fixot

Maritan, J. (1996). *Pulsions de Mort et Tragiques Grecs*. Paris: L'Harmattan

Mignet, M. (1994). Possession et métamorphose de l'identité: Le crapaud et l'Enfant-Jésus. *Cahiers Jungiens de Psychanalyse, 81*.

Mignet, M. (1998) Transexualisme, sexuation et contre-transfert. *Cahiers Jungiens de Psychanalyse, 91*.

Millot, C. (1985). *Horsexe, Essai sur le Transexualisme*. Paris: Point Hors Ligne.

Schreber, D. (1903). *Deukwirdigkeiten eines Nerveukranken*. Leipzig: Oswald Putze.

Culture Diversity

Panel: Analytical Psychology in Various Cultural Settings

This panel is dedicated to the memory of Vera Bührmann, who did so much to further understanding across cultures and who died on the day of the Panel, August 25, 1998.

Analyst as Anthropologist

Henry Abramovitch
Jerusalem, Israel
Israel Association of Analytical Psychology

When one works with someone in and of one's own culture, one takes many things for granted such as a shared understanding of the meaning of words, images and actions. People from the same culture have something of a shared symbolic access to the archetypal world. In work with people of other cultures, many of these implicit assumptions are challenged, so that even familiar issues seem strange or unintelligible. Many cultural traditions have a strong collective orientation; thus, even the idea of individuation appears bizarre or even a betrayal of the collective. Patients from such cultures often have great difficulty with the traditional "sealed room" analysis. An analyst who is metaphorically away from home base, needs to function akin to the anthropologist, seeking to understand the cultural context of the analysand. In the process, the analyst will make mistakes and indeed, must make mistakes. I recall one such mistake during my first fieldwork in a small island off the east coast of Madagascar. It was the first time I was called upon to play the role of host, when I had invited an old, honoured storyteller to relate some of the classical tales of the region. Seeking to honour him, I started to pour some ancestral rice beer directly into his glass. I knew I had made a terrible mistake when everyone suddenly stopped and stared at me in horror. Finally, a local schoolteacher, turned to me and said, "Haven't you forgotten something?" and when I remained motionless, he pointed to the ground, "The ancestors!" I finally realized that the first drops of every bottle must be poured into the earth as their due offering. More than anything, this "necessary mistake" taught me about the pervasive omnipresence of the ancestors, that everywhere and always they must be taken into account. Failure to do so will lead to misfortune, which the Malagasy understand as the ancestors' way to discipline an unruly child. Illness is seen as the disturbed ego-self axis between the collective unconscious of the ancestors and the living. Healing involves restoring the balance.

Jung stressed the importance of seeing individuals in their specific cultural and historical context: "A psychotherapist has to acquaint himself not only with the personal biography of his patient, but also with the mental and spiritual assumptions prevalent in his milieu, both past and present, where traditional values and cultural influences play a part and often a decisive part." (CW16, p. viii). In this spirit, I offer a conceptual framework for "doing analytical psychology" in different cultural settings.

1. When analyst and analysand are members of different cultures.

a) Analyst is a member of the dominant culture, analysand a member of an "oppressed" minority. Elements of inequality may be enfolded into the analytic situation so that a submissive analysand never challenges the authority of the powerful analyst. Alternatively, analysis never gets off the ground because the analysand feels not understood by such an outsider. In Israel, individuals from certain Afro-Asian backgrounds occasionally come for treatment as if to a wonder-rabbi. They expect to be the passive recipients of archetypal blessings and wisdom and receive interpretations like holy oil and water. It is difficult for them to understand that they are supposed to take an active part in their own treatment. To do so would show disrespect to the high status healer. Unless they do become socialized to the "culture of therapy," failure is inevitable.

b) Analyst is a foreigner, analysand a member of the dominant local culture. Going for analysis is itself a symbolic act of individuation, separating from the collective. Cultures differ considerably in how tolerant or restrictive they are; some allow everyone to do one's "own thing," while others are rigid and repressive. We often have a tendency to idealize and romanticize culture but, in the name of tradition, the negative power shadow may have full force. Ultra

Orthodox Jewish (*haredi*) individuals, with whom I work, live in a world of a rigid social code of behavior. Within this community, there is no possibility of dialogue or compromise. Some have great difficulty speaking negative feelings since they feel that they are speaking *lashon hara*, literally evil tongue (malicious gossip). Likewise, "evil thoughts" are dealt with by culturally approved methods of suppression and repression. On one occasion, the analysand was able to proceed only when his rabbi granted him a special dispensation to speak *lashon hara* as necessary for his treatment. All *haredi* analysands faced difficult choices when their path of individuation clashed with collective norms; some paid a terrible price. I recall one woman whose husband lost his job because she had "immodestly" uncovered her hair at home. For this woman, the need to uncover herself was the beginning of a process of extricating herself from the ultra-orthodox world.

c) Analyst and analysand are members of the same culture, but both are living "in exile" away from their home country. I often feel an unusual sense of connectedness with other Jewish Canadians living in Israel, in a sort of countertransference nostalgia, the shared yearning for a lost home. Yet such external, persona togetherness has its shadow side. Difficult issues may be avoided in a cozy attempt to remain triangulated with an idealized or de-idealized lost home. Political exiles or refugees, whose social world no longer exists, often suffer from acute nostalgia, yearning for a world that no longer exists. Without access to this lost imagined community, it is often impossible for them to move either forward or backward: adjust to a new reality or mourn the old one. In this case, the analyst needs to encourage a symbolic holding of the lost reality through active imagination (see Papadopoulos & Hildebrand 1997).

d) Analyst and analysand are members of the same culture, but analytical psychology is perceived as foreign. In many parts of the non-Western world, analytical psychology is considered a Western intrusion on traditional values. *Aion* (CW9-II), the study of Christ imagery, is certainly the least studied of Jung's writings in Israel; *Answer To Job* (CW11) is rather more popular (see Weisstub 1993). Some individuals still feel that Judaism and Jung are incompatible. Ultra-orthodox analysands, who read Jungian books, do so only in secret, and I still encounter the question, "How can a Jew be a Jungian analyst?"

2. When the archetype of the healer has an important and distinctive local character.

Normally, the analyst should learn as much as possible about local traditions. Difficulties may arise when the image of the healer in dreams or active imagination violates cultural consensus. Two situations in Israel come to mind. Many children of holocaust survivors often display "identifications with Christ" as one who suffers for the sins of others and must provide salvation to innocent victims (see Baumann 1977). Outside Israel, such imagery might be seen as indicative of the healing power of the self-sacrificing Self. In Israel, patients tend to identify Christ with anti-semitism and find it difficult to see Jesus positively; for example, as a figure for symbolic healing. Similarly, it is difficult for secular Israelis, polarized with orthodox Judiasm, to accept that traditional Jewish religious figures might represent the Self.

3. When there is an important local tradition of dreaming and dream interpretation.

Many cultures have explicit guidelines about dreamsharing: when and with whom which types of dreams are shared. There are public dreams that must be told at large gatherings or rituals; secret dreams told only to one other person, and private dreams never told to another person. In many cultures there is a tendency to tell bad dreams to rid one of the bad karma but withhold good dreams lest the hearer "steal" the good karma contained therein. Hebrew tradition has many important dream rituals, of which even many of my Jewish colleagues are unaware: dream request ritual, ritual for undoing bad dreams, prayer to prevent nightmares, incubational dream rituals (see Abramovitch 1997) as well as an extensive tradition of dream interpretation (see Covitz 1990).

4. When collective ethnic identities carry important political meanings:

Analysis is most difficult when "indigenous people" and "new-comers" have a history of political conflict. In this case, there must be a confidence that, in the temenos, we are able to escape the harsh external political realities. In Israel, there is a need to protect the therapeutic vessel from the intrusiveness of external events. Political violence tends to trigger collectivization in which the individual ego is reabsorbed into the collective identity of the ethnic group. This is especially true of my work with Israeli Arab analysands; the collective can overwhelm the personal so that we are no longer suffering and healing together, but experience the animosity of our group identities. "You Jews!" or in countertransference recollectivization "We Jews! You Arabs!." Such collectivization undermines the individuation process. I think of a young Israeli Arab woman whose father spent her entire childhood in an Israeli prison as a suspected terrorist. She chose a Jewish therapist, she said, for reasons of confidentiality. Once a bond was formed between us, she could finally blurt out, "I hate the Jews!"

5. When there is a need to develop new ways of doing analytical psychology.

In many settings the private, individualistic context of traditional analysis is culturally inappropriate and analysis too often comes at the cost of one's collective identity. Some of my colleagues in this panel describe innovative experiments in bringing analytical psychology outside the 'sealed room' and into the community. In many cultural settings, we will need to explore and discover new forms for analytical psychology.

From Living in Two Worlds to Living in One World

Astrid Berg
Cape Town, South Africa
Southern African Association of Jungian Analysts

With this presentation I pay tribute to Dr. Vera Bührmann, whose trans-cultural work as an analytical psychologist has opened the door to viewing another culture with genuine respect. She was invited to participate on this panel, but advancing age prevented her from accepting the invitation.

In 1984 she wrote a book in which she described in deceptively simple language the rituals she participated in and her subsequent analysis of them. At that time political repression and splitting were at their height. Bührmann's focus on different cultures was misunderstood often as lending credibility to the policy of apartheid. I know that nothing was further from her mind. We are thankful that South Africa has become one country in which many cultures are alive and valued. We no longer must live in two worlds, as and the majority of South Africans had to do.

My work is different from Bührmann's. It is in post-apartheid South Africa, in an urban setting, and I concern myself with parents and their infants. I must know, however, about the customs and beliefs of my fellow citizens. The cultural roots run deep and ultimately affect infants – sometimes to the extent of a life-and-death struggle. I am indebted to Bührmann, without whose teaching and writings I would not have been able to understand and enter the traditional world of the Xhosa people. I am focusing here on what I believe to be the foundations of this particular African cosmology: the concept of ancestor reverence and the enactment of this reverence.

The Xhosa are the African people predominant in the Cape, amongst whom Bührmann had done her research in the rural area and with whom I work in the city. Central to their world-view is the notion of ancestor reverence. The ancestors are the "living dead," members of the family and clan who have died, but who continue to live as "shades." There is a human, live relationship between individuals and their ancestors, who act as guides and mentors, manifesting themselves through dreams and bodily sensations. The relationship is a symbiotic one, with the living keeping the deceased in mind and honoring them through ceremonies, in return for their protection. Bührmann (1984) wrote:

> *To me as an analytical psychologist the belief in the ancestors, the way they are experienced and the obligations towards them have many similarities to the Westerner's concept of the unconscious, his experience of the archetypes and his obligations to pay attention to these as they appear in his dreams, visions, fantasies and his spontaneous, creative activities. To remain relatively healthy, mentally and physically, and to have some light on the path of life, the ego should have a respectful attitude towards the manifestations of the unconscious and not brush these aside as nonsense or "just imagination." (p. 31)*

When the obligations to the ancestors are not being honored, the individual is left unprotected and at the mercy of evil spirits and witchcraft. This belief in evil spirits continues to be ever-present;

most of the infants I see have been taken to traditional healers to be given medicine, for better or worse, to strengthen them against evil.

In order to maintain a living link to the ancestors, to invoke their guidance or to establish the why and who of events, ceremonies are performed. These are called *intlombe*. The structure of the *intlombe* remains essentially unchanged: what Vera described in a rural, more natural setting, I have observed to be present also in an urban environment. The structure of an *intlombe* follows is in four circles. The first circle is the center of the hut or room. In the rural situation this is formed by the ashes of the fireplace; in the urban setting the center contains that which is to be taken in: the beer, the alcoholic spirits, the cool drinks and the tobacco. The ancestors like the warmth of the fire as well as the nourishment of the beverages. The second circle is formed by the people who dance, and for whom the ceremony is being performed. They move with a stamping rhythmical dance in a counter clock-wise direction. The family, friends and visitors who attend the ceremony form the third circle; they clap and sing and sit against the wall of the hut. The wall of the hut forms the outer ring; in the house I visited it was the square wall of the living room. The drummer is situated opposite the entrance of the hut or house: near the special place where the ancestors reside, called the *entla*.

This basic four-ringed structure forms the framework within which ceremonies of different types are performed: that of the universal mandala, with two non-human and two human circles as its basis. Within this structure drumming and singing, clapping and dancing alternate with the taking in of ritually brewed beer, the telling of dreams and the divination of the healer. For the very important ceremonies such as those that punctuate the training of a healer, a goat or cow is slaughtered. Bührmann (1981) summarized these rituals as follows:

> *The Xhosa, for mental health and health in general, have to live with, be in communication with, and in the proper relationship to, the ancestors. The intlombe can be seen as a confrontation with the unconscious, especially its archetypal contents, experiencing and integrating some of it. This usually leads to psychic changes in the participants, which they volunteer but which can also be objectively perceived. (p. 96)*

These ceremonies are numinous and deeply moving for the participants. Words cannot describe the atmosphere evoked through the steady drumming, the singing of melodies that are repeated time and again, the dancing that involves a strong pounding of the feet onto – even into – the earth – to the point of exhaustion. Even if one just observes, one is transported into a state of altered consciousness, into an ancient world.

Now I ask: Through which psychic processes does healing take place? There are two basic processes: those of containment and linking. When there is psychic turmoil, it is containment that is needed above all. The ceremonies offer physical structure and emotional holding in which the smaller, the more vulnerable is held by the bigger and stronger. The mandala configuration of the ritual, the authority of the healer, the collectively-accepted old age customs provide a structure in the present that is rooted in a very long past.

Within this physical and emotional containment a space is opened up in which connections can be re-established. Links can be formed, or, using more symbolic language, the process of *coniunctio* can take place. The links are formed on many levels: body and mind, ego and Self, nature and culture, individual and clan. Healing takes place because a sense of physical wholeness and emotional meaning are found. The effects are dramatic and profound because of the simultaneous involvement of the body and the mind.

I hope to have shown the profound psychological truths that lie within the customs of one particular group of people in Africa. When Jung described the collective unconscious he wrote: "It is the mind of our unknown ancestors" (CW9-I, 518). Among the people with whom I am familiar the ancestors are known in a very literal manner. Jung wrote further: "The primordial images are the most ancient and the most universal thought forms of humanity. They are as much feelings as thoughts; indeed they lead their own independent life." (CW7, 104) He went on to describe the ideas of angels as a manifestation of the autonomy of the psyche. In African culture the ancestors are the embodiment of the angels and gods of western culture – they represent the collective unconscious in a living, on-going, connected way. The ceremonies performed for them are intense, immediate experiences; the setting, the people and their actions form a whole that cannot be abstracted into one or two comprehensive images. One has to be there to know.

Amongst the depth psychologies of the West, analytical psychology has a particular contribution to make to cross-cultural understanding. The notion of an objective psyche and the concept of the archetypes form an intellectual container within which we are able to honour difference and confront self and other, while knowing that we are connected to one another by our universal humanity.

Analytical Psychology and Cultural Sensitivities

Renos K. Papadopoulos
London, England
Independent Group of Analytical Psychologists

Analytical psychologists often feel that they possess a special sensitivity to cultural differences (e.g., Henderson 1990). This perception could be the result of Jung's own intense involvement in cultural issues. He travelled to Africa and the East, he wrote about various cultures and prided himself on being a person who could be aware of other cultures beyond the confines of his own Swiss and central European roots. However, analytical psychology's position with regard to cultural matters has not been without difficulties.

The notion of culture often leads to confusion and emotionally-charged debates because it is a complex concept and encompasses a wide variety of phenomena. Therefore, it would be useful to distinguish at least two types of "cultural settings" when addressing these phenomena: 1) the external characteristics of a culture; for example, differences in dress, customs, behaviour. 2) one's own sense of cultural identity. The first type includes all the tangible aspects of culture that create a sense of the exotic, the "ethnic," the different, the other. The second is not always visible and it contains all the personal sensitivities of belonging; for example, a Middle Eastern person living in London may not act exotically, may indeed be dressed and behave in ways that are indistinguishable from the ways of English co-workers, but the sense of belonging and sense of cultural identity may be utterly different from that of English counterparts. Cultural differences are subtle and do not always follow visible formulas.

Thus, it would be erroneous to follow a causal-reductive method to trace one's sense of cultural identity. The mere fact that one was born in a certain place does not necessarily mean that one "belongs" exclusively culturally to that locality. A personal and historical approach is not always the best method of understanding a person's cultural sensitivity. Instead, a more dynamic and contextualised approach is required to grasp the complexities of cultural identities. Finally, it would be wrong to assume that each person has a single cultural identity. Modern (and indeed, post-modern) life makes us inhabit different cultural locations and assume several cultural identities. Therefore, when we consider cultural issues, we should appreciate that we are dealing with a network of interactive and dynamic relationships between individuals and their surrounding cultures.

Some of the difficulties analytical psychology faces today with reference to culture lie in Jung himself and the conflicting way he addressed cultural differences. It could be argued that there are two distinct and different positions that Jung adopted at various times, without being aware of their contradictory nature. On the one hand, he was extremely sensitive to the limitations of the psychology of his time, due to its Eurocentric nature. He noted that "the predominantly rationalistic European finds much that is human alien to him, and he prides himself on this without realising that this rationality is won at the expense of his vitality, and that the primitive part of his personality is consequently condemned to a more or less underground existence" (MDR, p. 273). This shows that Jung was aware of the limitations of the European culture and valued the enriching contribution of other cultures.

"Another Jung" can be distinguished – in a less obvious way – when he comments about the various cultures and times as if he were above them. Jung placed himself above all traditions and limitations of culture and time when he offered his "expert" assessment of various cultural phenomena without any sense of self-reflexivity. He did not comment on the fact that the stance he was assuming was itself a product of his own conditions, personal circumstances and context. This stance contradicted Jung's awareness of the limitations of the psychology of his culture and his time.

Adams (1996) distinguishes an additional pair of contradictory "Jungs" in relation to culture. He identifies the Jung who claims that all people share the same archetypal heritage and are thus the same, and the Jung who maintains that people are different due to their cultural or ethnic differences. The fact that the two pairs have been identified indicates that there has always been a tension within Jung himself with reference to culture; moreover, this tension has continued within analytical psychology as well.

Behind these contradictory positions in Jung lies another difficulty. Essentially, he felt that there is an irreconcilable opposition between the individual and the collective. Characteristically, he wrote that "the unconscious symbiosis [between an individual and the collective] is practically unavoidable, but it has the disadvantage that the more we hide behind the nation the less conscious we are of ourselves" (CW10, 910). Thus, Jung seemed to feel that the conscious individual is antithetical to the unconscious collective and that it is impossible for a person to be an individual whilst enjoying membership in a collective. Jung did not seem to have an idea of a positive and nourishing collective, such as a sense of community. These ideas were not unrelated to his conflicting views on culture and to his essential conservatism. For example, he argued that: "The essence of culture is continuity and conservation of the past; craving for novelty produces anti-culture and ends in barbarism" (CW18, 1344). Such statements show how Jung could not conceive of the possibility of development and innovation coming from what he calls "anti-culture." In a paradoxical way, his view is not very "Jungian," in that Jung is usually (and correctly) associated with the view that the alchemical union of opposites can create new qualities.

The various tensions between the contradictory positions within Jung himself cannot be resolved easily at an abstract and logical level but can be overcome in the context of practical applications. In my own work with survivors of violence and trauma I have found that culture (and the collective) may have a healing effect on individuals who struggle to deal with their own traumatic experiences. My other paper in the present volume discusses the issues involved in such situations.

In short, I have found that, under these adverse conditions, individuals need to identify with their culture (even at the expense of their own individuality) as a necessary phase of overcoming their trauma. Different facets of our cultural identities are activated at different times and with varied intensities, producing a rich kaleidoscopic approach to our being, rather than a fixed mono-dimensional perspective. In addition, a Eurocentric view of trauma as a pathological condition needs to be adjusted when working with people from other cultures who manage, under the most appalling conditions and in an admirable way, not only to display remarkable resilience but also use the adversity and their suffering in creative ways to find deeper meaning in their lives. Finding growthful meaning in suffering is also a Jungian view; indeed, as analytical psychologists we should be able to distinguish the contradictory sides of the Jungian theories.

Ultimately, over-identification with one's own culture can be either enriching and nurturing or restrictive and negative. It all depends on the timing and the context.

C. G. Jung and the East

Shirley S.Y. Ma
Toronto, Ontario, Canada
Ontario Association of Jungian Analysts

A Canadian woman wanted to talk in her session about the meaning of *cheng-ming* (Rectification of Names) – a term introduced by Confucius (551 – 479 BC). I was surprised at this request from a Western person. Working with her prompted me to reflect on the relevance of Confucian concepts to our post-modern times, and especially to notice how compatible Confucian teachings are with Analytical Psychology.

In the *Analects*, it is recorded: "Let the ruler be ruler, and the minister minster; let the father be father, and the son son" (Waley 1938). The name then defines a person's status and its corresponding duties and responsibilities.

As an ordering principle, *cheng-ming* is grounded in *jen*, generally translated as "human-heartedness." This ideogram is composed of the characters for "man" and "two." The term *jen* embraces all those moral qualities that govern one person in relation to another. It is on the basis of *jen* that a person can relate to other persons and become oneself. Confucius' focus on *jen* as the bonding principle in society was innovative, and can be seen as the first appearance of interpersonal psychology in China – some 25 centuries ago.

Jen also symbolizes the awakening of a relationship to the transcendent. *Jen* can be interpreted as an archetypal dynamism that arises from the foundation of one's being, a drive that seeks fulfillment of one's original nature. This transcendent dimension suggests that selfhood is a necessary and sufficient condition to approaching the subtle meaning of *Tien-ming* (Mandate of Heaven), a concept close to "the teleological meaning of the Self and the archetypal constellations of individuation" (Rhi 1992).

Thus, a person of *jen* is one who knows the inner Mandate of Heaven, who cultivates self-knowledge as the basis of thought and action. This person is called *chun-tzu*, a person of superior wisdom. Confucius introduced the term "*chun-tzu*" to signify the internalization of the ideal of sacral kingship on the human level. The ideals of the *chun-tzu* represent the same ideals that we Jungians see in the development of personality through the individuation process.

In contrast to Taoism and Buddhism, Confucian teaching insists that society is both necessary and intrinsically valuable for self-realization. This view echos Jung's claim that one does not individuate alone on Mt. Everest. Confucian selfhood entails the participation of the other as a mirror for self-development, for our Heaven-endowed nature unfolds, not in isolation, but in the depth and breadth of human relationships seen as part of a spiritual quest. Jung's psychology of Eros mirrors this aspect of Confucius' social philosophy.

Confucius also introduced the concept of *li* (translated as ritual and propriety) as the grammar of action to protect, contain and help develop *jen* to its fullest potential. *Li* is the application of symbolic meaning to ritual actions performed in a sacred space. *Li* interacts with and reinforces *jen* in the development of personality. The Confucian Tao requires both the cultivation of personal awareness and the practice of the symbolic life via rituals and learning. From a Jungian perspective, the awareness of *jen* alerts us to the transcendent needs of the ego; while the knowledge and practice of *li* assists us in the relationship to the Self. When practised consciously, rituals enrich the practical art of living the symbolic life. A contemporary awareness of the interrelationship of *jen* and *li* can address the current needs to live an authentic life in our post-modern times, which are deeply fragmented and much in need of rituals to assist in the transformation process inherent in personal development.

The woman I mentioned earlier is representative of most Western analysands who are generally curious and interested in Oriental philosophy and religion. Many have entered Jungian analysis to augment their spiritual quest. They are open to new ideas and are eager to incorporate mind-body practices such as yoga, tai-chi and chi-kung (breadth) meditation into their daily lives. Many are believers in alternative medicine and are familiar with acupuncture, shiatsu and the use of Chinese medicinal herbs.

In working with Chinese analysands, especially those who have migrated from Hong Kong, Taiwan and Southeast Asia, I am generally guarded in using Confucian terms. The mere mention of *cheng-ming* would trigger a negative emotional reaction. This is not surprising, given the fact that Confucius' teaching had been abused for centuries as ideological tools to maintain political power and control. The Confucian legacy has shown us that, without the grounding of *jen*, the literal renderings of the meaning of *li* turned rituals into mechanistic rules and regulations governing conduct and behaviour. Then the hierarchy of primordial ties and interpersonal relationships were turned into social resources for exchange, manipulation and exploitation. For centuries, women bore the brunt of the abuse of power in the implementation of such practices as footbinding, the chastity cult, and outright slavery.

In general, Chinese analysands are reluctant to express their feelings about relationship problems in the family. In working with them, I have come to see the less desirable influences of Confucianism on psychological development. These influences are reflected in the typical child-rearing and socialization practices that are defined by Confucian philosophy.

Confucian teaching assumes that the central unit of society is the family, not the individual. Confucius stressed five cardinal relationships: between ruler and subject, father and son, husband and wife, brother and brother, and friend and friend. He believed that with clearly defined male position and authority, respect for the status of others, and the subordination of self to the good of the family, peace and prosperity will prevail. In this light, assertiveness and emotional expressions are discouraged because it is considered selfish and an infringement on others.

Within the hierarchy of the family, children are seen as fitting into a fixed social structure based on age, sex and kin. Age has its privileges, and being male is considered superior to being female. The true mark of maturity is the ability to conform to one's role and perform one's duties. It is on this contractual basis that love is expressed; that is, love is not unconditional. The central focus is on teaching children impulse control, and proper behaviour; there is less interest in the child's expression of opinions, creativity and independence. Even less attention is paid to expressions of feelings and of individual needs. Thus, while Westerners value independence, autonomy, assertiveness and openness of expression of feelings and opinions, the Chinese value interdependence on the family, restraint in emotions and personal views, and conformity to the rules of good behaviour.

In this family orientation, with its lack of stature reserved for the individual, the actions of the individual are considered to be reflections of the family and of the ancestors. In child-rearing practices, shame, guilt and implicit threats of abandonment are brought to bear on any action that could be seen as demeaning to the family. Because of this, Chinese analysands have a great deal of resistance in approaching emotional problems associated with parents, siblings and relatives.

On the other hand, work-related issues are discussed freely in self-exploration. This practice may reflect the residue of the strenuous adaptation process encountered by first-generation immigrants. Work focus is also an acceptable way of managing anger and aggression and of gaining self-esteem. Psychological problems then are seen in terms of somatic processes. I have observed and recent research has suggested that somatic expression of psychological problems is prevalent among traditional Chinese as a way to avoid loss of face, and as a defense against shame which could be brought to bear on the family as well as the ancestors.

With analysands of Chinese descent who were born and raised in Canada, I have found a greater willingness to be open to discussing their emotional problems, even though it brings a sense of anomaly toward the culture of their immigrant parents or grandparents. In working with them, I try to focus on the distinction between primordial dictates and real life experiences. I have found dream analysis to be very useful in helping them to differentiate the relationship between the ego and the personal and family unconscious. Once they learn to access their spiritual resources from within the matrix of their own being, they can begin to shed their cultural and psychic baggage and to participate more fully in Canadian cultural life.

My analytic experience with both Westerners and Asians has taught me the importance of relating to individual life experiences and to be open to the manifestations of the unconscious. I have learned to be flexible in the use of Jungian concepts as they apply to people from different cultures. For example, the terms "persona" and "shadow" do not seem to sit well with Asians, as they seem to imply judgement. Winnicott's "true self" and "false self," however, seem to strike a sympathetic cord among Chinese. Given the age-old emphasis on ritual and learning in the pursuit of the Tao, the Confucian ego ideal for a traditionally-raised Chinese could be described more aptly as a healthy "false self" that functions well in society, with a great capacity for cultural life. The "true self" by

logical extension, would remain private and be very different from
that of a Western person.

In my work, I continue to be impressed by Western receptivity
and openness to Chinese culture. Increased exposure and growing
interests in Analytical Psychology among Asians will lead inevitably
to a re-discovery and reconnection to China's rich cultural and
spiritual resources. Jung's exploration into the unconscious has built
a bridge for understanding between the East and the West. I believe
that, through this bridge, a cross-fertilization of world cultures will
usher in a New Renaissance in the twenty-first century.

For the purpose of this panel, I have chosen the Lotus as the
symbol for self-realization. The lotus symbolizes one who realizes
Tao and thus lives an ordinary life while his mind is like the lotus
flower, so that the flower blooms from the body of mud which
represents the realization of the negative aspects of one's personality, as well as the suffering and sorrows of life. The lotus thus
signifies the consciousness of living the transcendent life that
embraces both the sacred and the profane.

A Rebirth of Tragedy

The Myth of Dionysus in a Central Australian Setting

Craig San Roque
Alice Springs, Australia
Australian and New Zealand Societyof Jungian Analysts

*[Note: This segment of the panel featured an extract from a video
documentary record of the rationale, preparation and performance
of parts of the epic myth of Dionysus in a Central Australian setting.
The video gives a glimpse of the involvement of the group of
European and Aboriginal Australians in a community project that is,
in fact, a practical application of Jungian-based work in the milieu
of social distress: specifically, alcohol-related cultural breakdown.
The entire project began as an attempt to answer a Walpiri-
Aboriginal man's query along the following lines: What is the
European's Dreaming story for alcohol and drunkenness? If there is
a creation story for alcohol, can possession of this story by Aboriginal people give power over the destructive effects of alcohol use?]*

The unravelling process and content of the Sugarman (equivalent of Dionysus) project may be understood as an example of a therapeutic amplification that is familiar to Jungians from the consulting room. This work, however, proceeded in the matrix of community relationships, in conversations, in paintings, in rehearsals and finally on the open-air performance ground, in aboriginal country – since previous experiences had shown that collective alcohol abuse was not amenable to individualistic solutions. A theatrical enactment proved to be the best way to present the string of primal metaphors, using a 100-page poetic script, retelling the Dionysus epic as a contemporary song cycle, including an adaptation of Euripides' tragedy The *Bacchae*. The myth embodies Western civilization's formulation of alcohol-making and its effects on the human being; delusion, mayhem and dismemberment are some of the elemental states present in the psychological pantheon of Dionysus.

This re-enactment of the Dionysus creation/destruction myth of origin was shown first as a trial performance in August 1996. About 200 people were sitting in the shadows, on the rim of a European mystery, watching deranged Bacchic women destroy Pentheus: their own relative, their king and their community's stability. Then they break down in a paroxysm of remorse – too late. Three of the Aboriginal women watchers said, "It made us think. It opened our minds. We didn't realize that you white fellers could cry. That you could feel sorry too." That moment of insight was a moment of fateful connection in which perhaps "Tragedy" was conceived for the first time in the Warlpiri Aboriginal mind.

My argument is that "Western culture," through the Greeks, has formulated something, code named "Tragedy," which has helped Europeans comprehend and even survive successive fateful self-destructive acts. A "tragic mentality" has become part of the Western psychological repertoire, which has helped us to survive horrors and genocide as a psychic capacity to read life-destroying events as tragedy followed by rebirth. However, "a tragic mentality" and the concept of "Tragedy" may not be part of the indigenous Australian mentality. Thus, the aboriginal Australians, when faced with catastrophic physical and psychic invasion may well be mentally unprepared for it. The European tragic sensibility with its implicit sense of death and rebirth is missing.

The indigenous people of Australia have been trained to a different beat, a different music; they read life-destroying events in a different way. Their experience of invasion and being eaten by animals is different from ours. Except for the crocodile there really are no human-eating animals there. Survival is based on strong kinship obligations, knowledge of country, endurance and perhaps on conducting ceremonies. There appears to be no implicit notion of organized resistance, of self-sacrifice, as in war, for the good of others or the culture. Sacrifice or propitiation of gods for personal benefit seem absent and there is no seasonal dying and reborn civilization god in the way we seem to construct it. There does not seem to be any implicit mythic image which prepares the aboriginal for the predations of Dionysus.

If, in Australia, we are witnessing the tentative rebirth of "Tragedy," I do not mean simply that something tragic is happening. Rather, I mean that a concept of tragedy is up for renewal, reinterpretation or even challenge. There is an implicit sense in European mentality that if you are guilty of "hubris," you offend the "gods" or you fail to honour a divine power, then there will be consequences, as Dionysus showed so brutally to Pentheus, king of Thebes. At its crudest, in the Christian fundamentalist faith, if you do not treat God the Father with respect, He demands that you will go to hell and burn – like Semele (the immolated second mother of the infant Dionysus.). At its most subtle, the offence against the gods is reconstructed as offences against the unconscious or offences against the Self, with nasty consequences and ghastly symptoms.

However, the point requiring investigation is that the structure of offences, guilt and consequences of actions as understood by European cultural tradition does not appear to have a place in the aboriginal psyche. Similarly, the structures of psychological illness and the methodology of cure are quite different.

In our project we reached for the tragic theatre form almost unconsciously because the great tragic epics have helped Europeans to mediate between the ever-present realities of creation and destruction. If the great Dreaming stories of Australia were constructed, psychologically, in the same way as the European Creation myths and mysteries then it would be easy for us to swap stories and devise mutually useful therapeutic metaphors. But if the underlying metaphysical/psychological structures are different, those implicit structural assumptions may have to be learned first, before meaningful content can be communicated effectively between us.

As a result, even though aboriginals recognized Dionysus/Sugarman as a powerful story akin to a traditional aboriginal creation story – seeing and confronting what happens when you turn your life over to drunks, when you fail to recognize the power of the god you invite into your midst, when violence breaks out, when babies are swallowed up by Dionysus' grandfather, when mothers kill their own sons – nevertheless, the revelations of Dionysus as tragedy and as an injunction to take survival action remain uncertain.

References:

Abramovitch, H. (1997). Temenos lost: Reflections on moving. *Journal of Analytical Psychology*, *42*-4, 569-84.

Adams, M.V. (1996). The Multicultural Imagination: "Race," Color, and the Unconscious. London: Routledge.

Baumann, A. (1997). The Torch bearers. In M. Mattoon (Ed.), *Open Questions in Analytical Psychology: Proceedings of the 13th International Congress for Analytical Psychology*, 211-221). Eisiedeln: Daimon.

Bührmann, V. (1984). *Living in Two Worlds.* Cape Town: Human & Rousseau.

Bührmann, V. (1981). The Xhosa healers of Southern Africa. *Journal of Analytical Psychology*, *26*-3, 187-201.

Covitz, J. (1990). *Visions of the Night: A Study of Jewish Dream Interpretation.* Boston: Shambhala.

Henderson, J.L. (1990). *Shadow and Self: Selected Papers in Analytical Psychology.* Wilmette, IL: Chiron.

Papadopoulos, R. & Hildebrand, J. (1997). Is home where the heart is? Narratives of oppositional discourse in refugee families. In R. Papadopoulos & J. Byng-Hall (Eds.), *Multiple voices: Narrative in Systemic Family Psychotherapy.* London: Duckworth.

Rhi, B. Y. (1993) Heaven's decree: Confucian contributions to individuation. In M. Mattoon, (Ed.), *The Transcendent Function: Individual and Collective Aspects. Proceedings of the Twelfth Congress of the International Association for Analytical Psychology*, Chicago, IL.

Waley, A. (1938). *The Analects of Confucius*, A Vintage Book. [City: Publisher].

Weisstub, E. (1993). Questions to Jung on "Answer To Job." *Journal of Analytical Psychology*, *38*-4, 397-418.

Cultural Transformation in China

Where the Twain Shall Meet

Laurie Layton Schapira
New York, New York, USA
New York Association for Analytical Psychology

Editor's note: This session featured a screening of "Up Against the Wall," the author's 37-minute documentary which views the feminine in China through a historical-psychological lens. A central image is "the wall" as a metaphor for patriarchal repression: from prehistoric times, through dynastic rule, to the People's Republic.

There is a legend from the Western esoteric tradition that, according to the Akashic Record, there was a meeting of the Wise Ones of the world during the first millennium AD, in which a conscious decision was made to divide up the evolution of the psyche: The East would develop spiritually and the West materially. In his commentary on *The Tibetan Book of the Great Liberation*, Jung (CW11, 770) wrote about this division along the typological lines of introversion/extroversion. East sees Western extroversion as illusion and the West sees Eastern introversion as narcissistic. I add the terms "collective" versus "individual" to describe the East/West polarity. As disciplined and developed as are the Chinese collective sensibilities, there is a primitivity when it comes to individual identity and personal ego boundaries. At the 1998 summit meetings in Beijing, the discussions were stalled repeatedly when there was an attempt to define "democracy." President Clinton spoke in terms of personal freedom and Zemin talked about the collective rights of the people. In my experience at the United Nations Conference, I often saw communication break down when a Westerner would challenge some seemingly arbitrary or personally uncomfortable rule of policy set up by the Chinese, and their friendly hospitality would change suddenly to defensive rigidity, with no room for negotiation or creative problem-solving.

Walls are ever-present in China – both concretely and metaphorically. The Great Wall was built as a magic circle designed to protect the civilized Chinese from the barbarians, more to intimidate than actually repel the enemy. Psychologically, walls have functioned as boundaries, to keep the barbarian shadow out and the feminine controlled within. Now, as the Chinese let down their walls and open up to the West, they will have to develop psychological boundaries on the level of the personal ego. Here, they can actually learn from us, the new barbarians.

On the other hand, we in the West must learn from the East to sacrifice personal gratification for the greater collective good and to comprehend the "One Mind." Certainly we have some difficult times ahead, to overcome mutual fear and distrust.

During the Piscean Age, the Aeon of the Two Fishes, the alchemical opposites have differentiated and polarized. In 1954 Jung observed that "the two contradictory worlds have met. The East is in full transformation; it is thoroughly and fatally disturbed" (CW11, 778). He was referring, of course, to the Communist revolution. A great deal more has happened on both sides in the last 50 years. One of the greatest dangers facing us today is enantiodromia. The East seems to be possessed by ruthless materialism and soulless imitation of the West. And we in the West are dissolving our egos in substance abuse and religious cults. As psychotherapists, we are in a unique position in the New Age to understand the Aquarian task of the Water-Bearer which provides a container for holding the opposites.

I conclude with a refrain from a poem of Rudyard Kipling:

Oh, East is East, and West is West,
And never the twain shall meet,
Till Earth and Sky stand presently
At God's great judgment seat;
But there is neither East nor West,
Border, nor Breed, nor Birth,
When two strong men stand face to face,
Though they come from the ends of the earth!

The Search for Cultural
and Personal Identity
of Second Generation Foreigners

Linda Briendl
Baden, Switzerland
Schweizerische Gesellschaft für Analytische Psychologie

An increasing number of patients from foreign countries have been consulting me: adults between 22 and 40 years of age who report a socially well-adjusted life history. From my work with them, I realize how the development of identity and the process of individuation in second-generation foreigners are affected by various conditions that can give rise to psychological illness.

Personal and Cultural Identity

Identity is determined by the person's distinctive characteristics, unique biography and a life-long developmental process, in which the influence of social environment plays a significant role. Reciprocally, individual characteristics influence events in the environment. Thus, identity is a crucial prerequisite for every relationship. The culture in which a person grows up – including religious, familial, historical and linguistic membership in a group of people – creates an emotional system of values which is linked closely with personal identity.

Second generation foreigners live in an area of tension between two worlds. In many cases, they are not really at home in either of the two worlds, which can lead to feelings of "bicultural inconsistency" (Hausser 1995, p. 178). The feeling of one's continuity in internally- and externally-directed contacts is no longer experienced as consistent, as the result of an orientation toward two very different frames of reference. The result is a strong impairment in feelings of self-worth, an important factor of identity. Bicultural inconsistency impairs the areas of sex roles, sexual norms, religion, and especially language.

In the development of language, personal and cultural identity are joined inseparably. The mother tongue is of high emotional significance. In the dialogue between mother and child, the sounds that are important for the acquisition of language in a culture are passed on, as are mimicry and gesture. Problematic for the second generation of foreigners is the fact that, although the mother tongue usually is imparted in the parents' home, it cannot be learned in a differentiated manner, as a result of changing care-givers and insufficient encouragement at school.

The language of the host country plays a key role in the mastery of the new environment. Because the local language (German) is, in many families, merely the language of the job or for dealing with bureaucrats, a separation between private and public spheres often is maintained. Soon the children have more mastery of the German language than do the parents. The children represent the family to the outside world, interpret and present requests – a role that belongs to the parents but which they often cannot master adequately. This role reversal leaves its tracks in the psyche.

In addition, arising from the need to belong, the child attempts to identify with both cultures. As a result, conflicts and anxiety are triggered. If, in addition, one considers the lower social status of immigrants and the limitations of their language skills, it becomes clear how much the child is dependent on a stable ego structure. But the development of this ego as an organ of self-control and integration appears to be particularly difficult, as a result of external circumstances.

Special Conditions for the Development of Psychological Disorders

According to studies by Riedesser (1982), foreign workers' children in all age groups are especially at risk for psychological disorders. Even in infants and toddlers, serious weaknesses of bonding, empathy, and self-control are observable. These manifest later as symptoms of neglect, as a result of both parents' working and the frequent change in caregivers. As early as preschool age, emotional and somatic disorders occur, out of familial and socio-cultural difficulties. Moreover, the psychosocial development of the foreign child is particularly endangered during adolescence, a time which is difficult also for indigenous teenagers. For those growing up in the tension between differing cultures, serious identity crises can occur.

Erikson (1956) showed, in his model of identity, that the successful accomplishment of each developmental phase is required for construction of a stable identity in the subsequent age level. Correspondingly, disturbed developmental progressions result in increasing impairment in psychological health, which can manifest as a developmental crisis. When such crises cannot be resolved, the result is an "identity diffusion." In the Jungian theory of complexes, this situation corresponds to a *"wenig kohärenten Ichkomplex"* (insufficiently coherent ego complex).

An identity diffusion, according to Erikson, is the inability of the ego to form an identity. It is usually manifested in adolescence, when the young person needs to integrate the largest number of differing roles. Conflicts, tensions, and anxieties can lead to delay of these decisions. The avoidance of decisions leads to a feeling of isolation and inner emptiness. The individual remains in a diffuse stage of waiting, and is incapable of committing to personal goals. Among the complications which result from this situation are:

1. Problems with intimacy. The attempt to engage in close comradeship or sexual intimacy comes to nothing. To become involved with others would mean also that one could differentiate oneself from them. Relationships are often replaced by narcissistic phantasies of greatness, which the person attempts to realize through a strong drive toward achievement. The same problem can manifest also in a hope for salvation through a leader who will take on the function of the intimate interrelationship. Due to the absoluteness of the demands, this hope usually is doomed to disappointment.

2. Dissolution of temporal perspective. Loss of ego-function interferes with time sense and future expectations. The ability to function adequately (e.g., punctuality) is disturbed. According to Erikson, this disturbance is related to the earliest life crises.

3. Interference with the ability to work. An acute disorder in feelings of capability often diminishes concentration on required tasks.

4. Flight into a negative identity. Striving toward undesirable roles (e.g., delinquency and drug abuse) during critical stages of development. This flight can express itself also as contempt for one's heritage, even to a reconstruction of one's origins.

In all the second-generation foreigners in my practice, I have found that one or another expression of identity diffusion – as

OVERVIEW

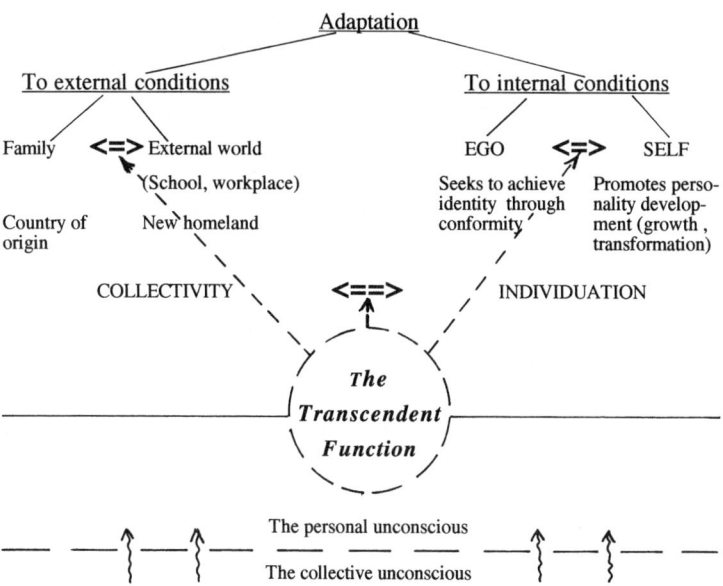

extreme cases of an unfinished adolescence – was present. A recent research result confirmed these indications. Ferron (1997) studied psychosocial adjustment in 9300 adolescents, among whom were 1200 second-generation foreigners. Marked differences between the Swiss and the foreign adolescents manifested themselves in the areas of future perspectives and risk-taking behavior (sex, drugs, and alcohol). A significantly greater percentage of immigrant adolescents showed signs of a high degree of depression and difficulties in their relationship to their parents.

Adolescence is the time of a search for identity. Herzka (1988) characterizes the increasing difficulty for adolescents in integrating the heterogeneous values of the frames of reference in which they grow up as a *"seelisches Grenzgängertum"* (psychic commuting). How difficult the search for identity must be for adolescents whose parents come from a different culture. The second-generation immigrants somehow must fill the gap between the two worlds. Psychological illness is a result of a cumulatively increasing developmental disturbance that is related to all the problems of migration. The age at entry, and the conditions under which a child has come into the host country, play fundamental roles in this situation. In the case of most of the second-generation foreigners in my practice, there had been experiences of psychological traumatization in childhood.

Often an attempt is made, through a strong achievement-orientation, to compensate for an inability to choose an identity for oneself. Thus, achievement becomes an identity aid: the meeting of advancement expectations of the parents and the socially recognized values of the host country. However, the "emergency ego" is not functional over the long term, because whole areas of personality need to be split off. The unintegrated emotions can be warded off only through repression, which results in increasing self-estrangement. The intrapsychic tensions and conflicts with the environment increase and reach unbearable intensity. A regulating counteraction from the unconscious does not fail to appear: irritable emotional states or events breaking into one's life, apparently without cause. The problems of adolescence reappear as new crises of maturation, and no longer can be overcome with one's own resources.

An adequately stable feeling of self-worth is helpful in acquiring a secure identity. Markou (1981) determined that foreign children who had feelings of self-worth enjoyed good emotional support from their parents and were not separated from the parents during early childhood. Learning the adopted language as early as possible, and a predictable perspective for the future, also influence meaningfully a stable sense of self. In my conversations with people of the second generation, outside a therapeutic setting, I found these results confirmed, when I could question them regarding the theme of feelings of identity. Thus, immigration should not be equated with uprootedness or illness, even if we therapists are primarily confronted with this manifestation. Nevertheless, one should not ignore the fact that the second-generation foreigners are more susceptible to personality developments characterized by crisis (see Leyer 1991).

Possibilities of an Analytic Psychotherapy according to Jungian Principles

When they presented to my practice, the second-generation immigrants were all in a state of psychosocial decompensation, helpless and full of anxiety. Thus, it appears to me necessary to work with the methods of crisis intervention at first; the anxiety which takes up much space in any crisis is transculturally identical. The most important goal of crisis intervention is to reduce anxiety and to communicate guidance for anxiety reduction (see Kast 1987). In the case of foreigners, however, the visit to psychotherapists triggers more anxiety and makes the process more difficult. Stigmatization experienced earlier, and the shame that one's own efforts have failed, may be the reasons for this. In addition, the conviction that it is useless to talk about problems is deeply rooted. In this regard, it is particularly difficult for second-generation foreigners to express feelings of grief, pain, guilt, or aggression. They seem not to know how to "put into words" their emotional state. Consequently, it is all the more necessary for us to listen carefully, inquire, and attempt to understand, in order to become acquainted with the nature of the crisis, its inner meaning for this person, and the relevant social situation. Only when relief from the anxiety and a certain structuring of the chaotic emotions have been achieved through the methods of crisis intervention is it possible for the work on the coherence of the ego-complex to step into the foreground.

Hildenbrand and Lanfranchi (1996) describe how children and adolescents need more transitory spaces to overcome their *seelisches Grenzgängertum*, in order to be able to establish connections between the parts of their lives. They need transitional worlds, such as undisturbed rooms for play, or neighborhood structures as a social practice field, in order to experiment with their explorations of self and world.

The therapy room can become also a transitory room, an in-between space, which I call an "approximation field of the transcendent function," because here it can be studied how the worlds of the analysand can be connected, without remaining in the either-or of polar opposites. This is a first step in bringing into conscious awareness the opposites, which the analysand has believed, – only partly consciously – that it is necessary to eliminate in order to avoid conflict.

The knowledge and the conceptions of the client and the therapist flow into the encounter between the two cultures: similarities and commonalities on the one hand, differences and contrasts on the other. This encounter can be worked out in the interpersonal dialog, without intending to regulate at the intrapsychic level. In practicing the ability to recognize contradictions between the two cultures and to tolerate the stress connected with this, however, I also see a learning process that represents a preparation for transcending the contradictions between the inner and the outer world. Meanwhile, a new viewpoint is possible, through each decision that is made about what may be valid for this second-generation immigrant regarding the travel between two influencing cultures.

In order to communicate the approximation of the transcendent function to the second-generation foreigner, a therapeutic ability for dialog is necessary: to perceive two differing and contrasting realities, with one eye toward each. One eye should be on the consciousness of how we therapists are influenced by our own culture – with respect to our thinking, feeling, and behavior. Stereotypes can often slip in without our awareness Thus, vigilance regarding our prejudices always must accompany us in our work.

The other eye must be ready to take in the perspectives of the foreign culture. A cultural versatility, acquired through travel and other sources of information, is an advantage here. Above all, the patients themselves can help us; they are superb conveyors of culture if the therapist is interested and inquires. Through the reports about life in the culture of origin, much that is emotionally authentic about the patients and their history becomes tangible. A certain joy in discovery can develop: a joy that helps a relationship to develop.

Contrasts and similarities should be verbalized by the therapist, as much as the fact that there are limits to the efforts to understand a foreign culture. One's own experiences of migration may be of help in empathizing with these clients, but hides inherent dangers through contagion of feelings, being unable also to see the other side.

In addition, the therapist should pay attention to which personality characteristics are part of the cultural identity and which portions belong to the intrapsychic conflicts of the personal identity. If one too quickly ascribes every problem to the cultural world of the analysand, one runs the danger that important elements of the personal biography will be omitted.

Ultimately, it is also important to view the child who has not continued to develop – and the adult – in terms of a dialog: the child, who is emotionally needy, and the adult, who has been able to overcome a great deal in spite of a difficult life situation. A comprehensive case history, in which the individual fragments of the life story are brought together and placed into context, can help fill the gap between the two.

This way of looking at the situation – swinging back and forth – provides us therapists with an increasingly multicultural understanding, which makes available to the analysand a viewing of a situation in terms of a dialog. The migration history should be examined particularly carefully in this respect, as it is bound up inseparably with the identity of the analysand.

Identity is shaped through relationships; the human relationship is the most important factor in the analysis, particularly when it is concerned with working on the coherence of the ego-complex. The emotional process, in this case, should actually take precedence over the consideration of cultural differences. However, in working with second-generation immigrants, this is a difficult area, because the identity diffusion is reflected in the transferences and resistances. In addition to the limited ability to engage in a relationship, there is also the danger that bad experiences with society could repeat themselves in the therapy. A further conflict of loyalty, which could result from the visit to a therapist, also feels threatening for the patient. It is helpful to address all these difficulties and to indicate that they are understandable.

Transference, however, remains mostly diffuse; although the clients show respectful behavior, they are distanced. That one is not really able to make contact with them shows how little these people are in contact with themselves. Instead, there is a noticeable need of the patient to maintain feelings of identity and self-concept. In the therapeutic work, the identity confusion is exhibited through multiple defense mechanisms, especially splitting and denial. The therapist, however, also can be confronted with displacement of the "*Ichgrenzen*" (ego boundaries) in experiencing the patient; attentiveness switches without transition to sleepiness, and anger leads into exaggerated submissiveness. Acting-out behavior is a constant danger. In cases of acute identity diffusion, defense and compensation strategies become the core problem of the therapeutic encounter.

In such a case, according to Erikson, the therapist must maintain respect and understanding for the patient. Only then is fruitful work possible. Nevertheless, the encounter can "derail." The real difficulties can lead also to anger, estrangement, and contempt in us. Such behavior also mobilizes our defense mechanisms. Analyzing the countertransference helps to share a deep experience with the patient: to feel not understood, helpless, disoriented, and enraged. Access to the experience of the client allows a feeling of commonality, within which new things become possible. When we respect the resistance of the client as self-protective, we frequently cannot make the knowledge gained from our analysis of the countertransference directly useful in the therapeutic process, because it does not correspond to the processing ability of the patient at the time.

The language competence of the second-generation immigrant, which is often low, increases the difficulties. It requires the therapist to create understanding, even with limited verbal means. A simple, pictorial language is of great advantage in this situation. As Jungian analysts many other means are available to us, such as music, dance, stories, or fairy tales, and – not least – painting or sculpting, in order to express feelings and help the client to verbalize. I have had good experience with this group of people in the use of painting and guided imagery.

The experience of being able to make oneself understood through other means of expression has a positive effect on the relationship within the therapy. Kast (1990) emphasizes, in her observations of working on the coherence of the ego-complex, the importance of modeling the relationship of an *emotionale Verlässlichkeit"* (emotional reliability) within the therapeutic relationship. She means by this that all the feelings of the analysand should be taken seriously, understood, made understandable to that person. Differences are to be expressed, and rules declared, which have validity within the therapeutic relationship. Ego strength and identity cannot be imparted through unconditional acceptance alone.

In general, the task is to make accessible the correspondence between the experiences and the emotional impressions of the person. Conscious emotional experience and the expression of emotional states is an expression of one's identity. However, the feelings must be observed by the therapist over a long period of time. The analysand who is able to absorb and formulate the therapist's observations becomes more sure of the feelings; an important aspect of identity is strengthened.

Through the work on the coherence of the ego-complex, the feeling is strengthened of the analysand's existence having been responded to. The experience of being understood within the therapeutic relationship, and the improved self-perception that results, can be the impetus for a deeper transformation. Realistically, however, these potentialities often cannot be achieved in therapy. As soon as the persona has been "patched up" and again functions to some extent, or when the panic attacks have disappeared and the depression has receded, most of my clients have ended their work with me. Terminating therapy, however, means that they have gained a small piece of autonomy. When I came to understand their possibilities, I could let these people go, without considering all that was still missing.

We live in a multicultural society that is subject to vast processes of change. As a result, we cannot restrict ourselves to working only with people with backgrounds similar to our own. We need to modify our therapeutic concept in order to develop an adequate treatment concept for people of dissimilar backgrounds.

The working methods of Jungian psychology offer, in my opinion, a good basis for a solution of this multicultural problem; in our work, we view the experiences and behavior of people in connection with unconscious processes: of meeting strange and, for the moment, incomprehensible feelings. Such encounters are familiar to us and thus less threatening; we know that our own identity also has its unconscious and, thus, strange sides. Indeed, Kristeva (1990) characterizes the ability to experience oneself as a stranger as a fundamental prerequisite to being able to relate to a stranger.

The following reflections, as well as the Overview at the end of this paper, have been stimulated by a passage from Jung's essay, "Adaptation, Individuation Collectivity" (CW18, 1084-1106). In collective consciousness are the two cultural frames of reference as well as the person's conscious attitudes. The ego wants to conform to external conditions, because it does not feel strong enough to deal with the contradictions. But conformity to the interior is neglected in the process. Because the relationship to the Self is disturbed, neither the current illness nor other messages, such as dreams, can be understood by the afflicted person as a request by the Self for individuation. The entire psychic energy is required to repress the contradictions. In analytic psychotherapy, work on bringing contradictory external conditions into conscious awareness therefore takes precedence.

Thus, for immigrants of the second generation, the connection of the ego-complex to collective consciousness is of great importance. A well-functioning persona permits a comfortable relationship of the person with the environment. To be able to incorporate the striving of the psyche toward individuation, the ego (as the center of consciousness) needs a certain coherence. Only then can an attempt be made in analysis to bring the conscious and unconscious into contact, and to differentiate the ego functions. To the extent that a person can perceive the contradictory personality parts – inner and outer – and bring them into relationship with each other, identity develops. For this work, the transcendent function – the union of pairs of opposites of the psyche in successful synthesis – is of central importance; it therefore appears as an acting center between consciousness and the unconscious, between collectivity and individuation. Increasing ego strength enhances the ability to symbolize and permits the transformation to a new view of life.

We approach the analytic process through the perception and consideration of the natural expressions of the unconscious, such as dreams, pictures and other symbols, symptoms, or moods. Kast (1990) described the development of new symbols within the transference-countertransference, a process in which can be brought to life the *"Annäherungsfeld der transzendenten Funktion"* (approximation field to the transcendent function). The therapist attempts to empathize in all aspects of the symbolic situation of the patient. To be fully understood results in deeper self-understanding. If the analysand can accept the empathy of the therapist, the confrontation and the dialog between the areas of conflict will succeed. Jung (CW8) described how the transcendent function develops and how it can lead to a new stance for the ego. Here is the turning point in the analysis: a symbol, a new decision, a good solution resulting from this transformation process. Through imagining, painting, or sculpting, the effect of the symbol is deepened. The integration of the deepened knowledge into the conscious ego frees up energies from the unconscious, which are available to the analysand for coping creatively with life.

Focus on individual symbols brings us into living contact with the controlling power of the psyche, the Self. The symbols from the personal unconscious actively participate in this exchange. But originally, symbols arose autonomously in the collective unconscious; here is the primary area of work for the transcendent function. In the archetypes of humanity, as they appear to us in myths and fairy tales, as well as in individual symbols of our dreams and phantasies, we participate in the fields of activity that are common to all people. And here we are all related to each other.

Long-term Possibilities for Development: Cultural Mediators

The development of one's own identity can be seen in the attainment of psychological health and the personality's becoming whole. Through the strengthening of the ego, an increasingly social stance also becomes possible; the contact with the contents of the collective unconscious leads to a feeling of connectedness and security.

However, collectivity and individuality are also a pair of opposites. How far the path to individuation can be followed by second-generation immigrants within the framework of analysis remains an open question. The requirements of individuation, according to Jung, include being "against all conformity with others" (CW18, 1094). The search for one's innate personal identity could, for these people, be burdened with excessive anxieties. The loneliness that is connected with the process of individuation perhaps could not be tolerated.

Nevertheless, Jung saw a way in which conformity to both opposing requirements could be successful: through the work on symbols as a value-producing function. A creative attitude develops, which makes it possible for a person to contribute new values to the society through the development and presentation of one's own ideas. Here, I believe, would be a chance for second-generation foreigners to meet the demands of the collective for conformity and participation and, at the same time, through their own individual development, have a transforming effect on the collective. Some of the individuals I questioned in parallel interviews have discovered this path from inside themselves. In the conversations regarding the question of their dealings with their bicultural identity, they asserted that the confrontation with the two worlds placed high demands on an ability to deal with contradictions and conflict. At the same time, they acquired energy for their own creative accomplishments from the combination of the two cultures. Through the creation of new values, it was possible for them to watch the individual shaping of their own identity and, through that, to experience recognition from society.

Thus, the ties to two cultures no longer need be characterized by stress, but can lead to enrichment. As cultural mediators, second-generation foreigners could experience valuable synergistic roles within the society. They are experts in both cultures, and would be superbly suited to negotiating in both directions, reducing potential conflict, and building bridges to better understanding.

During an anxiety attack, a 28-year-old Italian woman of the second generation drew a picture of a river which separated two areas of land, without any connecting crossing. A short time later, this woman dreamed: "I was on a bicycle trip with my fiancé. We found ourselves in X [place of residence of the parents] and rode downward in the direction of the Reuss [a river]. We saw some people below, in discussion in front of a bridge. It was the dedication of the new Reuss bridge. We went swimming in the river for a short time, and then walked across the bridge. I walked carefully, one step at a time, slowly over the new bridge."

For a long time, the collective unconscious has held ready the symbolic depiction of the "bridge walker" for the recognition process of the ego-consciousness. The ability to connect the opposing areas, inside and out, and to recognize the existence of a bridge which can carry a load, spanning between them, this becomes the central point of the entire regulation of identity.

Translated from the original German by Sigrid Koates

References

Erikson, E. (1956). Das Problem der Identität. *Psyche, 10,* 114-176.
Ferron, C. et al. (1997). Health behaviours and psychological adjustment of migrant adolescents in Switzerland. *Schweizerische. Medicinische Wochenschrift, 127,* 1419-1429.
Hausser, K. (1995). *Identitätspsychologie.* Berlin/Heidelberg: Springer.
Herzka, H. (1988). Pathogenese zwischen Individuation und psychosozialer Oekologie. *Praxis Kinderpsychologie, Kinderpsychiatrie, 37:* 180-184.
Hildenbrand, B. and Lanfranchi, A. (1996). Kinder im "seelischen Grenzgängertum" Das Wandern zwischen den Welten beim Verlust transitorischer Räume. In: P. Dillig and H. Schilling (Eds.), *Erziehungsberatung in der Postmoderne.* Mainz: Mathias-Grünewald.
Kast, V. (1987). *Der Schöpferische Sprung: Vom Therapeutischen Umgang mit Krisen.* Olten: Walter.
Kast, V. (1990). *Die Dynamik der Symbole: Grundlagen der Jungschen Psychotherapie.* Olten: Walter.
Kristeva, J. (1990). *Fremde Sind Wir uns Selbst.* Edition Suhrkamp, *604.* Frankfurt: Suhrkamp.
Leyer, E.M. (1991). *Migration, Kulturkonflikt und Krankheit. Zur Praxis der transkulturellen Psychotherapie.* Opladen: Westdeutscher.
Markou, G. (1981). Selbstkonzept, Schulerfolg und Integration. Eine empirische Untersuchung griechischer Schüler in der Bundesrepublik. *Zeitschrift für Pädagogik, 27,* 893-910.
Riedesser, P. (1982). Die psychischen Gefährdungen des Gastarbeiterkindes. *Caritas-Jahrbuch,* 133-137.

Beyond the Story

From Interpretation to Impact of Stories from Different Cultures

André de Koning

Perth, Australia

Australian and New Zealand Society of Jungian Analysts

To PETER REID (in memoriam)

The Parable of the Greedy Sons

> *There was once a hard-working and generous farmer who had several idle and greedy sons. On his deathbed he told them that they would find his treasure if they were to dig in a certain field. As soon as the old man was dead, the sons hurried to the fields, which they dug up from one end to another, and with increasing desperation and concentration when they did not find the gold in the place indicated. But they found no gold at all. Realizing that in his generosity their father must have given his gold away during his lifetime, they abandoned the search. Finally, it occurred to them that, since the land had been prepared, they might as well now sow a crop. They planted wheat, which produced an abundant yield. They sold this crop and prospered that year.*
>
> *After the harvest was in, the sons thought again about the bare possibility that they might have missed the buried gold, so they dug up their fields again, with the same result.*
>
> *After several years they became accustomed to labour, and to the cycle of the seasons, something which they had not understood before. Now they understood the reason for their father's method of training them, and they became honest and contented farmers. Ultimately they found themselves possessed of sufficient wealth no longer to wonder about the hidden hoard. (Shah 1974, p. 144)*

Before we turn to an interpretation of this Sufi story from the lens of analytical psychology, let us look for the context in the broader tradition of psychoanalysis. After all, the history of psychoanalysis begins with the interpretation of stories.

In an attempt to return to Freud, the psychoanalyst Lacan (1988) has provided us with some seminars that deal with the interpretation of stories. The debate between the post-modern philosopher Jacques Derrida and Lacan might well be conceived of as the most important discussion of psychoanalysis in recent times. We turn, therefore, to Lacan and the story of "The Purloined Letter." This story by Edgar Allen Poe is the third of a series of three stories, the others are "The Murders in the Rue Morgue" and "The Mystery of Marie Roget." It was interpreted psychoanalytically, first by Bonaparte (1956) and then as the centre of the famous seminar by Lacan. He argued that the structure of the story displays the ultimate triangular structure of the Oedipus complex. The characters in the story undergo a rotation of roles, which is determined by "their relation to the purloined letter or signifier just as the moves of chess pieces are subject to the rules of the game" (Gans 1989, p. 82). Derrida (1985) criticizes Lacan for his conception of a universal design of the Oedipus configuration. This is very close to Jung's critique of Freud and his emphasis on the protection of the core of psychoanalysis as a bulwark against the occult.

"The Purloined Letter" is about a letter of compromising content (although we never know the actual content), which the Queen is reading whilst the King is sitting next to her. The sharp Minister D – enters and looks at the letter, sees the situation and takes the letter with him. The prefect of the police asks the clever Dupin to be of assistance in retrieving the letter and to return it to its rightful owner, the Queen. The prefect, of course, follows his usual way of investigating and has the apartment of the Minister D – thoroughly searched inch by inch, but cannot find it. Dupin, the master detective, knows the cleverness of the Minister and quickly finds it in a most obvious place. He sees through the attempt to hide the letter by having turned it inside out and scribbled over as if it were an unimportant note stuck on the knob amidst other notes. The letter is returned and it is this trajectory that interests Lacan.

The first glance, that of the King, is of the ostrich that does not see, is blind. This position shifts to the police, who also do not see. The second glance is that of the Queen, who sees that the King does not see and, in hiding it, imagines that the letter is safe. Then the Minister thinks it is well-hidden and safe. The third glance sees that the other ones leave the letter enough unveiled and transparent for it to be seized. This third glance is first the position of the Minister and then of Dupin and can be compared with that of the analyst.

Characteristic of the third glance is that it moves in the interpersonal space, where Truth is what is heard and spoken of and perhaps shared by others. Thus, what we mean by what we say is always mediated in language or the "symbolic order," as Lacan called it. Lacan pointed out that Freud had illustrated the conception of truth as interpersonal and based on language in his telling of the Jewish joke which points up the third glance:

> *"Why are you lying to me?" one person says, adding "Saying you're going to Cracow so I should think you're going to Lemberg, when in reality you are going to Cracow?" (Freud, SE8)*

According to Johnson (1988), Lacan shows us that "The story obeys the very law it conveys; it is framed by its own content" (p. 236). The story of Poe is also about a repetition compulsion that can lead to an uncanny kind of repetition, which is contained in the story content as well as in its frame. The author of the last word is not Poe, but a citation from an author, Crébillon, who has rewritten the story or myth of Atreus. This account is remarkably complex; it tells of King Atreus who is informed, by letter, of the betrayal which his brother Thyestes has performed in relation to Atreus' wife. The fruit of this relationship is the child Plisthenes. Atreus has kept the purloined letter a secret for 20 years and acts out his revenge by trying to make Plisthenes commit patricide. This does not happen and Thyestes is made to devour the son. There is "A queen betraying a king, a letter representing that betrayal being purloined for purposes of power, an eventual return of that letter to its addressee, accompanied by an act of revenge which duplicates the original crime" (p. 236).

The story of "The Purloined Letter" as a story of repetition is also itself a repetition of a story from which it purloins its last words. The psychoanalytic truth of the repetition compulsion is demonstrated by the story as well as being a theme of the story. There is a shift from repeating the "primal scene" to a repeat of a previous story of repetition.

There are more stories with the compromising letter featured, such as Lady Macbeth's reading a letter of destiny, relating to Macbeth's killing of the King and taking his place. The crossroads of these stories might be the tragedy of King Oedipus that repeats all the letters that have been purloined from the interior of the "The Purloined Letter." Marie Bonaparte (who had kept the Freud-Fliess letters when Freud was exiled) makes an interpretation of the content of the story by saying that the return of the letter to the queen is similar to the return of the missing maternal penis to the mother. The phallus is then considered to be a real, anatomical referent.

Lacan differed from this approach and put the lack at the centre of his understanding. For Derrida this still means a frame of reference that is phallocentric, The act of psychoanalysis, then, is one of mere recognition of the expected. Or, as Johnson (1988) puts it: "The theoretical frame of reference which governs recognition is a constitutive element in the blindness of any interpretative insight" (p. 240).

For Lacan, language – the word or letter – is a symbol of a pact: of an initiation into a symbolic order of meaning and exchange. The word, the signifier, is a symbol of an absence. The reference to Freud is related to the well-known example of a child who strives to master the mother's absence by a game in which the child repeats throwing something away and making it return, saying the words "fort" and "da" ("go away" and "come here") to indicate that the child is keeping control of the actual separation from the mother. The compulsive game symbolizes a kind of control over the separation by means of language, which then functions as a medium. The infant moves from an imaginary order (where the fusion with mother is still present) to a symbolic order and, in doing so, accepts the rules or laws of language. Through language the child can imagine being human and having an ability to recognize and represent. The pain of the original separation from the mother is repressed by the child, but returns via the repetition compulsion and through language. What is left is desire, because there is a lack, a not-being unified with the object of the desire. The object of desire is symbolized by the phallus, but the phallus is present only through its absence; this is what is meant by castration. The castration complex therefore has to do with a gaining of consciousness and an awareness of loss.

The phallus, for Lacan, is the ultimate signifier. The letter in the Poe story is the signifier and phallus symbol which follows a certain and definite trajectory in returning to the owner. While the letter circulates, the characters take their different positions and become subject to the power of the signifier.

Lacan says he returns to Freud in the sense that language, the word, is the castration of natural infantile omnipotence surrendering to the laws of language. Avoiding the castration is the deferring of this law, the flight from the truth with its resulting neurotic or psychotic patterns. Lacan remains truthful to the pillars of psychoanalysis because the repetition compulsion, identity, constitutes the unconscious. "Without the repeatability no sense can be made of censorship and repression, the pillars of the analytic experience" (Gans 1989, p. 87). The letter is the lack, an absence made presence by a word, both veiling and unveiling.

Derrida's Critique

Derrida's creative contribution to philosophy and post-modernism finds its crucial element in the concept of *différance*, a word that refers to "differ" and "defer" and to the distinction between being and the being-of-being.

He hesitates in accepting the version of Truth as given by Lacan, because it still presupposes a centre and is therefore a logocentrism. His introduction of the term différance means that there is never one centre and that every presumed centre yields to another that follows as its trace. In a chain, the meanings slide and take on a different significance; there is ultimately not one meaning. There is an interweaving which he calls, in his punning way, a textile, a text which is not simply present as a given.

Please note how close this idea is to Jung's notion of the sliding meanings of symbols or the notion that archetypal meanings can be expressed by many different images, in which not one of them can exhaust its ultimate meaning. Even in a text there are references to other texts, each term marked by the trace of another term, just as images refer to other images and meanings.

Jung has said that there is only one archetype (the Self) or as many as there are symbols, but never is an archetype conceived as a definite centre or given being. The archetype itself cannot be conceived, but only approached by a similar play of difference, as Derrida uses in his thought on writing. I am not saying that these conceptions are identical, but that both Jung and Derrida are reacting against a position where there has to be a centre of fixed meaning and one ultimate carrier of all signifieds.

Lacan says he returns to Freud in giving the letter in Poe's story a fixed place or centre of meanings, around which all the others move in a definite circuit. Derrida, on the other hand, says there is no fixed place, no core or centre, just as there is no core-complex. The meanings of texts or symbols escape the psychoanalytic framing, as it cannot be enclosed within certain structures of the symbolic. The letter stages its own frame and does not submit to one law or norm and even traps those who try to do so. They fall into this trap by becoming blind themselves. Taking the position of the analyst, in the Freud-Lacanian sense, is like becoming blind, just as blind as the King in the story.

Jung seemed to see that Freud was blinded by the conviction of having arrived, through Oedipus, at the core-complex. With Derrida, Jung would agree that the letter is capable of infinite division, by dissemination, just as symbols are inexhaustible in their interpretations.

Another play on words is the word dis-semination instead of semination. Lacan's "Séminar" would assume one semen to operate from a single origin. Germination and dissemination mean that meanings are already swarming and always have been. Meanings of symbols already have been disseminating and germinating without depending on a first or primal insemination.

Does not all this sound very familiar when we look back at the major disagreement between Freud and Jung? The monotheistic paradigm of psychoanalysis is just this raising to the absolute certainty of a signifier. It is like the new religion which was to oppose "the black mud of the occult."

Jung's declaration of independence from Freud was *The Psychology of the Unconscious* (now *Symbols of Transformation* CW5), in which there is a constant sliding of meanings of symbols without referring to one centre – apart from references to the Self. The Self, however, is not the same as the phallus as a transcendental signifier; the Self presupposes a wholeness that cannot be encapsulated and remains a totality that cannot be enclosed in a structure. Just as Derrida criticizes Lacan, so Jung was critical of Freud where it concerned singularity of meaning of myths and stories.

In the story of "The Emperor's New Clothes," for instance, the Emperor is showing to the crowd his beautiful new garment, with nobody (apart from a child in the crowd) willing to admit that he is, in fact, naked. There is nothing added in meaning, according to Derrida, by interpreting the story (as did Freud) as referring to exhibitionism and castration anxiety. The fable is about veiling and unveiling, about an invisible garment and invisible nakedness; nothing is added to this theme by interpreting what is already the theme of the story. "The fable already shows what the psychonalytic reading merely repeats" (Gans 1989, p. 89).

In the story of the greedy sons, we find it hard to encapsulate one meaning of the story or to relate it to one signifier, because stories can have different functions and aims. At one level, it is just a moral story, bent on teaching the young the law of the father: that happiness is earned, never as in a mother-complex fantasy bestowed as a gift. But if we notice that it is about the search for gold and use it as an analogy of alchemy and the process of transformation, then it also says something of alchemy as a path, a road in which one has to learn to understand that which is revealed through the hidden. Campbell (1976) said that we may think of any myth as a clue to what may be permanent in our nature or as a "function of the local scene, the landscape, the history, and the sociology of the folk concerned" (p. 461). The two meanings to discovering what is true and essential might be contained in the regional or particular ethnic expression of a people or folk. Campbell speaks here of "the psychological force, or way of service, of the two aspects of a mythological image" (p. 462). A story or a myth, therefore, might actually contain an antinomy of interpretations which is fundamental to its effect. The force or impact of the mythological symbol needs to have a local and ethnic quality through which it can allow to act on the soul. Campbell even goes as far as to say that "the distinctive challenge of mythology lies in its power to effect this dual end; and not to recognize this fact is to miss the whole point and mystery of our science" (p. 462).

Systematic theorists such as Lacan and Freud arrogate the right to say what the ultimate signifier of any story is, by folding the story into their own ongoing fascinating narratives. By contrast, Derrida and Jung would agree – at least at times – that this approach does not interpret the story finally and that only a suspension of this kind of constructed knowing will allow the ambiguous and polyvalent impact of symbols to impact a listener with their difference, their capacity to shake up fixed sets of thought. A clarification of this contrast is perhaps clearer if we first look at the manner in which alchemy, for example, can be used or interpreted.

In the Sufi tradition, the seeker has to carry out the search for truth in complete faith. If it is an alchemical study, it may be impossible to reach the aim of making gold out of lead, but the framework in which the application and mental development are carried out makes up the result of the spiritual development. Shah (1977) says of this process: "It is not the framework which is altered by the effort, but the human being" (pp. 199-200). The function of the Philosopher's Stone as a universal medicine and a source of longevity is, in Sufi tradition, "a state of mind, concentrated by the doctor within himself and transmitted to the patient by means of his mind" (p. 201). Thus, it is about the mind being concentrated in a certain way that the result is the stone, a certain power, knowledge or wisdom. It is about salt, mercury and sulphur combined in a certain way, as Jung understood. But where do we read about salt, mercury and sulphur as other than elements, whether understood as analogies or not?

Shah has pointed out that many early Arabic alchemists did use these words to illustrate the process of regeneration of an essential part of humans. The stone, the hidden thing, is also called Azoth, in Arabic "el-dhat," meaning "essence" or "inner reality." Shah (1977) shows us that sulphur is kibrit, a homonym of Kibirat, meaning "greatness, nobility;" salt is milk, "goodness, learning," and mercury relates to zibaq – sharing the root for "to open a lock, to break" (p. 195). The right combination of these elements produces the Azoth. The loss of knowledge of the uses of these words, as well as their meanings, made the unlocking of alchemy problematic. In setting himself to unlock alchemy, Jung proceeded in this spirit and transformed himself in doing so, but the final interpretations of the content might not be correct. Thus, many of us "Jungians" who follow the interpretations given by Jung might accept an incorrect story that has lost its impact.

The great contribution of Lacan has been that significance lies not in the conscious sphere only, but that the signifier can be analysed in terms of its effects without even knowing the meaningful content. That is, it is the lack of meaning that should be interpreted. The significance of the letter in the story of Poe is the displacement and repetition of a situation that is not a confirmation of identity, but of difference. Each person in the chain who has the letter repeats something and yet is in a different position. The effect of symbols and stories therefore is not necessarily best analysed via its content, but should exercise the impact via that which is hidden, or that which Lacan called "lack."

In the story of the greedy sons it is also the lack that makes up its essence and subsequent effect on the reader or listener. What is hidden is what Jung had been looking for, ever since his adolescent fantasies in which he started his interest in alchemy. The hidden is related in the stories he created, such as the one on the castle and the copper tree that made golden coins in the basement (MDR). The ploughing of the field of the unconscious transformed him as well as allowed him to gain knowledge that cannot be subsumed under one signifier. Thus, his story is different from Freud's, just as Derrida's reading of Poe's story is different from Lacan's.

Story and Culture

Aesop's fables are amongst the oldest recorded stories, often known for their moral interpretations which, in the old texts, appended to the stories themselves. The interpretations are ironic in their way of disowning understanding of the stories at other levels. Shah (1977) gives an example of Aesop's story of the little mole who went to his mother and told her that he could see. His mother decided to test him. She put some frankincense in front of the little mole and asked him what it was. "A stone," said the little mole. "Not only are you blind," his mother said, "but you have lost your sense of smell as well." The story can be interpreted in terms of its content or as: "It is easy to unmask an imposter." Now, mole in Arabic also stands for eternity, paradise, mind or soul, according to the context. In Sufi tradition, "Moses made a stone as fragrant as musk" (p. 11).

The story shows that the mother of the thought (its origin, matrix) presents frankincense (impalpable experience) to the soul. The pupil mole is concentrating on "sight" and loses the power to use the one he should develop.

Just as we found above with the use of alchemical terms, there are ways of decoding the other meanings of the word "mole," which leads to a matrix of words, all conveying essentials for human development. The thirteenth century mystic Rumi pointed out that the canal may not itself drink, but it performs the function of conveying water to the thirsty.

Thus, the vehicle of the story contains an essence, which can be revealed only in this hidden way. This way of thinking about truth may be praised by philosophers, scholars and psychoanalysts alike, but the treatment of many stories from various cultures often have led to an interpretation that might fit someone's habit of relating everything in the story to a favourite theory. Therefore, you can relate a story such as the "Emperor's New Clothes" or "The Parable of the Greedy Sons" or "The Purloined Letter" to whatever the existing pattern of thought allows. Freud seemed to need the protection of such a system to a greater extent than Jung, who was more open to the space-time curvature of thought.

If Jung criticizes Freud or Lacan has a critique of Derrida, each is still framed by his own view of the other. This understanding is reminiscent of the story of the delusional jealousy of a woman who is always finding a hair on the jacket of her husband, ready to frame him. When, one day, she does not find one hair, she asks him: "All right then, who is this bald woman you are going out with?" This is also close to the paranoid kind of interpretations made by some psychoanalysts, where the frame of reference has to be such that all phenomena fit into it. The frame or the theory will not allow ambiguity.

The fact that stories of a certain kind have their effects via différance, such as in the parable of the greedy sons, does not mean that the story must refer to the phallus. The story refers to truth and, in taking literally what is referred to in the hidden part of the text, the sons learn about process and the nature of truth as not being literal. At the same time, there is no necessity to conceive this aspect of truth in terms of the psychoanalytic frame of reference.

In the play of difference between Lacan and Derrida, another aspect of truth might be conceivable without doing injustice to the nature of truth as being non-substantial or as an absence. In other cultures, the stories that are used as vehicles to convey certain truths are not in need of analysis, but need to be read and, thus, allowed to have an effect. Such teaching stories would have their impact or be useful as channels, whereas analysis or disentanglement of the knots would best be left alone. Sometimes untying the knots would leave the fabric disentangled and wear it out. The repetition of the debates between the thinkers might lead to an interesting form of one's trying to outwit the other, but it does remain a repetition. Jung, however, created his theory and insights under the hieroglyph of the mandala rather than the phallus and refers to wholeness as the signifier.

Freud and Jung, Lacan and Derrida, all masters of interpreting stories (or of repeating, at times) a traumatic interpretation), have managed to get into a kind of one-upmanship in their relation to each other. Whether the actual essences of the stories are to fit in with their theories and philosophy, or whether they would allow stories from different cultures to maintain their essential teaching value, is doubtful. To go beyond their stories and history is essential.

To close this text with an uninterpreted story seems appropriate, especially when it contains, amongst others, the reference to the work as a process and the way we could look at symbolic material in a different light.

There was a statute with pointing finger, upon which was inscribed: "Strike on this spot for treasure." Its origin was unknown, but generations of people had hammered the place marked by the sign. Because it was made of the hardest stone, little impression was made on it, and the meaning remained cryptic. Dhun-Nun, wrapped in contemplation of the statue, one day exactly at midday observed that the shadow of the pointing finger, unnoticed for centuries, followed a line in the paving beneath the statute.

Marking the place7 he obtained the necessary instruments and, by chisel blows pried up the flagstone, which proved to be the trapdoor in the roof of a subterranean cave. The cave contained strange articles of a workmanship that enabled him to deduce the science of their manufacture, long since lost, and hence acquire the treasure and those of a more formal kind which accompanied them. (Shah 1974, p. 55)

References

Campbell, J. (1968). *The Masks of God: Primitive Mythology*. New York: Souvenir Press

Bonaparte, M. (1956). *Female Sexuality*. Madison, CT: International Universities Press.

Derrida, J. (1988). The purveyor of truth. In J. Muller & W. Richardson (Eds.), *The Purloined Poe*. New York: Johns Hopkins University Press.

Gans, S. (1989). *Thresholds between Philosophy and Psychoanalysis*. London: Free Association Press.

Johnson, G. (1988). The frame of reference. In J. Muller & W. Richardson (Eds.). *The Purloined Poe*. New York: Johns Hopkins University Press.

Lacan, J. (1988). Seminar on "The Purloined Letter." In J. Muller & W. Richardson (Eds.), *The Purloined Poe*. New York: Johns Hopkins University Press.

Shah, I. (1974). *Tales of the Dervishes*. London: Octagon Press.

Shah, I. (1977). *The Sufis*. London: Octagon Press.

Psychology and Art

Breaking of the Vessels

Destruction and Creation
in the Art of Anselm Kiefer

Mary Wells Barron
St. Louis, Missouri, USA
Inter-Regional Society of Jungian Analysts

When will you learn, myself, to be a dying leaf on a living tree?

Edna St. Vincent Millay

Behind all of Anselm Kiefer's art sounds the leitmotiv of destruction and creation, both personal and collective. My first experience of his art was physical. Walking into the largest room of the St. Louis Art Museum shortly after my return from almost six years in Zurich, I was seeking familiar and beloved images to help contain my re-entry anxiety. What I found was anything but familiar. I encountered a monumental sculpture that filled the wall between the two west doorways, rose almost to the ceiling, was made of metal, and seemed to pour out shattered glass that lay strewn on the floor in front of me.

I was stopped in my tracks in much the same way one might be who suddenly came upon a beautiful and dangerous animal. Frozen to the spot, stunned by what had seized me, I had no idea what stood before me. But my body said that my soul seemed to know, for a single tear ran down my cheek. It came from my right eye, the eye that has been blind since birth. Then there was only silence. By some fate, I was alone for the next 20 minutes. No visitors, no guards walked past. As I began to emerge from my encounter with this "terrible beauty," it felt as if I might spend a good part of my life exploring its mystery. "The symbols of the Self," Jung wrote, "arise in the depths of the body and they express its materiality as much as the structure of the perceiving consciousness. The symbol is thus a living body, *corpus et anima"* (CW9-1, 291).

Some months later I came upon the words of an art critic who spoke of seeing a woman acquaintance catch her first glimpse of Kiefer's work almost fall down. He wrote:

> *What's unclear is why so many of us experience Kiefer's works –*
> *even in the first split second of a first encounter – as so much more*
> *than gratifying aesthetic presences. His big paintings instill a feeling*
> *of conviction bordering on religious faith, an intuition of knowledge*
> *which proves remarkably inarticulate when you try to debrief people*
> *about it (Schjeldahl 1988, p. 119).*

We recognize in these words a meeting with the numinous, that which is beyond all description. Silence is our response to the presence of the divine. Silence always marks those moments in our work as analysts when words are neither adequate nor necessary.

In writing about the overwhelming power of archetypal images which reflect the ultimate reality, Jung said, "They make one convinced that they actually express it and establish it as a fact. This makes discussion uncommonly difficult if not impossible" (CW11, 558). Kiefer's sculpture, the *Breaking of the Vessels*, is an archetypal image of the alchemical opus. It is the gnostic myth of creation – a visual representation of Jung's *Answer to Job*. At its core, all of Kiefer's art is concerned with consciousness and the conscious suffering that fuels the process of creation. Kiefer invites us to see what is not visible, to discover the myth behind the history, the energy in the image. He shows us that meaning and madness spring from the same deep well, a well he often depicts as containing nuclear fuel rods – a metaphor for the energy that transforms consciousness.

Others whom I have accompanied when they first saw the *Breaking of the Vessels* expressed the paradox of its power. One friend said, "It looks like a murder machine." Another stood silently for a long time and then said, "I feel the blood running through my veins as I look at it." A third voice was that of a child about five years old. She simply said, "It's so broken."

An epilogue came when I returned to the museum months later. I found that the area of broken glass on the floor was now cordoned off by a rope about two feet high. Inquiring why, I was told, "Because a few weeks ago a woman fell into the glass and cut her leg." I was reminded of the passage in *Answer to Job:* "And just as there is a secret tie between the wound and the weapon, so the affect corresponds to the violence of the deed that caused it" (CW11, 561). Had not one friend called this a murder machine? Yet the other invoked the very essence of life – the blood coursing in her veins. A mystery Dionysian and dismembering is evoked.

What I offer here is only a glimpse into the meaning and import of Kiefer's art. I feel he holds the place in our age that Michelangelo held in his. Kiefer's genius surpasses all effort to define and any pretension to facile symbolic reading, for his art is truly symbolic, as Jung defined this word. It points to the yet unknown and unknowable while simultaneously evoking mythic metaphors and archetypal images of astonishing power.

Anselm Kiefer was born into the darkness of Germany just as World War II was ending. Much of his early work was a provocation to remember the horror of Nazi Germany. He once said, "I do not identify with Nero or Hitler but I have to re-enact what they did just a little bit in order to understand their madness" (Rosenthal 1987, p. 17). These re-enactments were images of the artist giving the Nazi salute in various locations all over Europe.

As his work evolved, remembering became a re-memberment of broken psyche and shattered civilization. He painted works entitled *Osiris* and *Isis,* in that order; destruction and then creation. Another huge painting he titled *Athanor.* Here, the alchemical vessel appears as the ruin of a great imperial room – reminding us of the room designed by Albert Speer as the embodiment of the Reich that was to last a thousand years. Kiefer shows us that this room is but a scarred and burned-out shell. We are invited to remember the mythic madness, the archetype gone berserk in the horror of the Holocaust. This once "great" room is the legacy of *Lebensraum*, its blackened walls reminding us of the crematoriums, the rooms of death.

Yet, Kiefer dares to title this *Athanor*. The destroyed room of power becomes an open air cathedral, a *temenos* that may serve as the vessel for collective transformation. In *Athanor* the hollow shell, the void-like space of Gnostic myth, made when God withdrew within himself, is the place in which creation becomes possible. Creation is for the sake of redemption, we remember, not the other way around. The *deus absconditus* has left a void, but in this emptiness the world is born. Does not the unparalleled destruction of our century require a creation myth adequate to it?

At the millennium God's hand reaching out toward Adam's on the wall of the Sistine Chapel seems a wildly innocent image. We have witnessed the Holocaust and those that continue. In our work we see the inner holocausts of psyches where there is, as Winnicott called it, "a fear of annihilation that has already happened" (Little 1993, p. 135). Giegerich (1985) says that the bomb is God. Kiefer's art seems to bear a similar message. To redeem the horror of history, the archetype of creation must be imaged anew.

Does a creation myth that begins with brokenness rather than wholeness not offer us more hope of redemption? As we can see Michelangelo's hand of God reaching out to touch Adam's as an image of all that the Renaissance meant, so we might see Kiefer's *Breaking of the Vessels* as a creation image for our age.

Before we explore this great sculpture, let us turn our attention to two earlier works that are more personal in form and feeling. In the first, a watercolor by Kiefer entitled *Reclining Man with Branch*, we are reminded immediately of the image in Jung's *Psychology and Alchemy* (CW12, Figure 131), a page from the fourteenth century Ashburn manuscript (which resides in Florence). The manuscript shows a man with a flowering tree growing from his genitals. The tree Kiefer shows us here is a lifeless branch which emerges from a wound at the place of the heart chakra.

The pendant painting is of Kiefer's wife and is titled simply *Julia*. She becomes the image of the Feminine Principle. She stands in a void with only the watery outline of a downward-pointing triangle touched by golden light behind. Beneath her feet the ground resembles a sea of blood; this redness surrounds her like an aura. She is a goddess pulsing with the liquid of life. In her hands she holds a white marble heart. It is as if Kiefer shows us that this redness, this life force that surrounds her and forms the ground of her being, will infuse this stone heart with its life. The calcinated heart, the *albedo*, will be filled by this anima image from the Red Sea. She brings a *rubedo* that might flower into greenness; a *viriditas* that can bud from the branch of the reclining man, transforming it into a tree of life. This Tree of Life, alchemy's Philosophical Tree, brings us back to the *Breaking of the Vessels*. This tree of metals is imaged as a bookcase, a container of knowledge.

Jung has told us (CW13, 119) that it is difficult for modern humans to remember that spiritual growth was once symbolized by metals. Kiefer's *Breaking of the Vessels* reminds us of this deep resonance, for he is truly a master alchemist, an alchemist of the twentieth century who is acutely aware of the fact that the transformation of human consciousness is the *opus*, that the metal to be forged is in the smithy of the soul. Kiefer's art is a *coniunctio*; it joins together word and image (he often writes across the surface of his painting), reminding us that as the word becomes flesh, so the divine is made human. His work literally embodies the word as it reconnects the material and spiritual world, the visible and the invisible. He shows us these levels of reality in a way and to an extent that are unique in history. At one glance, Kiefer's art annihilates the Cartesian split. Its physical presence blurs the boundary between object and observer. We are pulled by matter into the depth of the collective unconscious. New meaning is given to Jung's image of the spectrum of the archetype, manifesting as both image and emotion.

Kiefer lives with the tension of the opposites. Tangible matter is the *materia* of his work. Lead, iron, copper, glass, straw, ash and flowers become the ineffable. These alchemical elements, the particles of this world, create the one beyond. The *prima materia* is found everywhere and destruction is an opening to transformation. Kiefer's work might be seen as imaging anew the *mysterium coniunctionis*.

This sculpture, the *Breaking of the Vessels*, is the beginning of the work. As we look at it, we feel the enormity of the *opus* in the sheer size of this piece. It stands 17 feet tall and weighs over seven tons. It is a steel bookcase holding over 40 folio-sized books of lead interleaved with glass. Shards of glass fallen from it lie strewn on the floor. Its title refers to the Kabbalah's creation story. There are many variations on this myth but we know that Kiefer has based his work on the texts of Isaac Luria – texts used by Jung (CW14).

According to Luria, the creation has three phases: In the beginning, God was Ain-Sof, i.e., without end. In order to make space for primordial creation, God contracted himself, withdrew into himself. This withdrawal into inner exile is known as the act of Tsimtsum. Divine light, the pleroma, was left behind and from it emanated the first ontological man, Adam Kadman, who was a configuration of light, God's first form. The light of the Ain-sof streamed from his eyes, ears, nose, and mouth. This was the light of the Sefirot, divine attributes which formed a matrix of the world made from the letters of the alphabet. The light emanating from Adam Kadman's eyes was too strong for the vessels which were to contain it. The vessels of the six lower Sefirot, therefore, broke and the divine light returned to its source. However, a small portion of the light was left behind and mixed with particles of evil. Prior to creation, evil was part of divine power and then, while converging in the process known as Shivrat Ha'kelim, or 'the breaking of the vessels,' it acquired its own identity and manifested itself in the world (Le Vitte Harten 1991, p. 10).

The third phase of creation is called *Tikun*, the restoration of divine unity. In some places it is imaged as the restoration of the cleavage between the Tree of Knowledge and the Tree of Life

(Scholem, p. 108). In the Kabbalah it is the reunion of God and his Shekhinah that is the redemption or return of the Divine Feminine from exile.

With the *Breaking of the Vessels*, Kiefer invites us to contemplate this story anew. Gone is the male created by Michelangelo in the image of the divine father whose touch imparts to this human biblical Adam all that the Renaissance, and then the Enlightenment man came to be: emerging from the darkness of the Middle Ages ennobled but ultimately to become inflated by the divine touch, soon forgetting the source of human power. Kiefer's sculpture calls us back to the catastrophe of creation, to a time before story and history began to divide into two separate rivers, when the great Babylonian library of Nineveh began the process of separating knowledge from the experience of the natural world: the world of the Great Mother, Sophia, Isis, Shekhinah or the one Kiefer calls *The High Priestess* in an earlier sculpture formed of two joined bookcases.

In Michelangelo's *The Creation of Adam*, we see a lovely image of Sophia: blonde, nestled protectively in the left arm of God. She has no body visible and is less than half the size of her divine partner. She has no real role in this drama of creation and there is no darkness about her.

And then we see *The Creation of Eve*. She is fear-filled, intimidated, pleading with the great figure of God the Father. Certainly these are images of diminution of the Feminine, whether divine or human.

As one stands before this great metal tree, it feels as if the glass is still falling. And I am told that from time to time museum employees do hear a piece of glass fall. Creation continues; it does so as long as we are open to the breaking in of the numinous images of the unconscious, to what in Kabbalistic terms was the process of emanation.

Kiefer imagines this continuing of creation in a painting entitled *Emanation*. It is among the most beautiful images of all his work. Over 13 feet tall, the energy of creation is imaged as molten lead pouring from a burned sky touching the tips of the sea waves below. Like Gideon's Dew in the eighth scene of the *Rosarium* (CW16, Figure 8), it refers to new consciousness. Jung wrote, "The water is the *aqua sapentiae* and the dew falling from heaven, the divine gift of illumination and wisdom" (CW16, 484). Of this stage of alchemical transformation Jung said, "The books must be 'destroyed' lest thinking impair feeling and thus hinder the return of the soul" (CW16, 488).

With this destruction of the books, we return to the *Breaking of the Vessels*. Here, the books we see look as though they have been through some great fire, charred and broken. Kiefer's metal tree is an image of terrible brokenness. It is a shattering experience, a beginning of a Night Sea Journey. The Philosophical Tree, the work of the creation of consciousness, is made of metals. And Eliade (1978) reminds us that "The image of the Earth-Mother pregnant with every kind of embryo, preceded the image of Nature as the image of the Earth-Mother had preceded that of Sofia. It is important, therefore, to return now to the exceedingly ancient symbolism in which the earth is compared to the belly of the Mother and the mines to her matrix and the ores to her embryos" (p. 52).

As we turn to the next images, we remember that the smith, like the alchemist, is a "master of fire." It is with fire that he controls the passage of matter from one state to another, from one level of consciousness to another. Here, we see Kiefer's great tree of metal. Its shelves or branches are made of iron. Its books are made of lead. And all the elements are joined by thin copper wire, the metal of the Goddess of Love. Copper, we know, is the durable conductor of heat, the fire, the passion, the eros, that makes transformation possible.

These lead books, are they not the knowledge of Saturn's realm, melancholy, depression, and Mercurius himself? The books are the *prima materia:* lead as the bringer of wisdom and the creative force of the artist. But here Kiefer joins Lilith to this image of creation. This is the cover of the catalogue for the exhibition in which *Breaking of the Vessels* was first shown. Lying amidst the shards of glass on the floor is the lead emblem inscribed *Malchut*, the last sefirot, the earthy divine Feminine. Across it, boldly printed, is the name "Lilith." It is she who is found amidst the brokenness, connected to the Tree of Life only by the wire transmitting the energy of love.

"The Spirit Mercurius has, to say the least, a great many connections with the dark side. One of his aspects is the female serpent-daemon, Lilith or Melusina, who lives in the philosophical tree" (CW13, 288). Unlike Michelangelo's portrayal of Sophia in the crook of the creator's arm or Eve abject before him, Lilith refused to lie beneath Adam. She, who perfectly represented the shadow of an increasingly monotheistic and patriarchal world, was portrayed as dark, sensual, seductive, a witch, a biblical Medea. Here, Kiefer depicts her with fighter bombers emerging from an ash-covered dress.

The background of these paintings is a photograph of the sky-scrapers of a modern city. Kiefer covers the photograph with ash and then the ashen garment of Lilith. The devastation of war is present: the clash of inner opposites and the unleashing of raw archetypal energy into the world.

"The *Nigredo* is called a 'robe of destruction' … the garment of darkness" (CW14, 43, n. 72). Surely this is a description of these images of Lilith, whose hands and feet are fighter bombers. Kiefer has given us an extraordinary new image of the Goddess of Destruc-tion and Creation, a Kali for the Western world. She is the bearer of destruction and darkness exiled at the Red Sea. Yet she is also the possibility for redemption, the source of new creation.

All of Kiefer's images of Lilith are covered with ashes associated in alchemy with the *albedo*. "The white substance of the ash," Jung wrote, "was described as 'the diadem of the heart'" (CW14, 319).

The painting of this Goddess of Destruction and Creation is titled *Adelaide: Ashes of My Heart*. Alchemy called ash the "white foliated earth" or the purified body. It is associated with conscious-ness of a previously unconscious content. Ash has a fertilizing power and was often sprinkled on fields to increase the crops. What is the meaning of this Lilith called *Adelaide*? Adelaide is the feminine form of the German name Adelheid, from the word *Adel* meaning the nobility and *Heide* meaning heathen or pagan. Is this noble pagan emerging from the ashes of the city in the background, or will she destroy these buildings in which we live high above the earth, communing only with the gods in the sky? Giegerich (1985) has spoken of the first nuclear fission as the time when the divine was split from the animal and ascended in overwhelming brightness, extracting God from nature. He likened the earthly sensuous left below, severed from the ascended divine, to what scientists call nuclear ash. But remembering that ash is used to fertilize the earth, is Lilith emerging from it a message of hope? These works speak of Kiefer's personal encounter with her but also of some new fertility that may grow out of the fallow fields of our age. The ash of the *albedo* becomes the *rubedo*, the blood of passion and suffering and of life that comes with new consciousness of personal and collective shadow.

The Red Sea is called an *aqua pontica* and signifies baptism. At the Red Sea one encounters the animal soul "but at the same time and in the same place the meeting with the anima, a feminine psychopomp who showed him the way to Mercurius and also how to find the phoenix" (CW14, 282). For Kiefer, Lilith is this soul guide, the anima and the *anima mundi*. Another work he titled *Lilith at the Red Sea*. In alchemy and in fairy tale, the Red Sea is the passage of transition from one world to another, from exile and bondage to unconscious forces to the *gnosis* of one's larger, deeper identity. In Gnostic symbolism, the sea represents the world of matter or the darkness into which the divine has sunk. And the Red Sea was identified with Saturn, with time and becoming. This sea of the unconscious and the crossing out of exile is one of danger and suffering – made possible, we remember, only *deo concedente*.

In late Kabbalistic works, melancholic people are referred to as "daughters of Lilith." Kiefer's work is titled *Lilith's Daughters*. Images of Lilith or Lilith and her daughters are the only paintings Kiefer exhibited with the *Breaking of the Vessels*. Lilith is the shadow or dark face of the Shekhinah. Like Isis or the Shulamite, she is related to the *nigredo* of alchemy, to the darkness that is the beginning of the work of transforming consciousness.

The human soul in Gnostic myth is personified as the daughter of the Great Mother. And "the garment" represents the body as container of the soul. Kiefer represents Lilith and her daughters as garments, dresses covered in ashes. In *Lilith's Daughters*, we see a photograph attached to the largest garment. It appears to be the Milky Way, the path by which souls ascend to heaven. Below we see a snake skin draped inside another ash-covered dress. Kiefer reveals that Lilith, the one associated with the heavy darkness of Saturnian time and depression, is the path of transformation, both personal and collective; this is the Milky Way.

On the Tree of Life in the Kabbalah there is a place that is unrepresentable. It separates the upper triad of the Sefiroth from the seven below. It is the opening into the world called Emanation. We might call it the Self. This place is *Daath*.

In the painting titled *Daath*, Kiefer's image is of a bridge, a Jacob's ladder horizontal and on its side. One Spanish Kabbalist (Patai 1967) gave an astonishing description of Lilith as "a ladder on which one can ascend to the rungs of prophecy" (p. 247). That she is the link to a world beyond time and space was known to a thirteenth century writer. We call this world the unconscious; he called it the world of prophecy. "In medieval times *Daath* was called the veil or abyss before the face of God, but the notion of a 'Black Hole' like those found between the universes might give a sense of its mystery and function" (Halevi, 1986, p. 11). Kiefer depicts *Daath* as a bridge extending from the left into a seemingly endless expanse toward consciousness: in Kabbalistic terms, from the World of Emanation to the World of Creation – the transcendent function.

In this image we view a detail or portion of the bridge to which Lilith is attached. The airplane here is like a bird or image of spirit. But it is made of lead. Kiefer titled this work *Karfunkel Fee* (The Carbuncle Fairy). According to myth, a new mine or an untapped vein is discovered only through the intervention of a god or a divine creature, sometimes a fairy. Lilith, as Carbuncle Fairy, shows the way to the untapped sources of riches, the embryos in the great womb of the unconscious.

As the Carbuncle Fairy, Lilith is related to the heart. "The Shulamite's heart too will shine like a carbuncle" (CW14, 608). A carbuncle is a red sore or wound filled with poison, as well as a gemstone. In alchemy the poison is transformed into medicine. The wound is also the jewel. This airplane, like those that carry us so rapidly that our souls need time to catch up, is like a fallen Icarus brought down to earth as it is caught in Lilith's energy field. As Carbuncle Fairy, Lilith is a dark Venus whose bed chamber "is lit by carbuncles" (CW9-1, 580n). She is the sacred harlot cast out of the temple to return as demon and destroyer, as all repressed energies do.

Humans have always known that images possess the power to change consciousness, that images create revolutions. The works I have cited are collective dreams that compensate the totalitarian grip of Apollonic consciousness. Hillman (1972) calls it a myth of feminine inferiority that has permeated Western consciousness; it has meant the loss of the bi-sexuality of the God-image and we must take back these projections of inferiority, that to do so "frees the feminine and her body and matter itself from its Apollonic contempt and compulsive fascination" (p. 294).

Lilith refused to be inferior. Kiefer's images bring us face to face with her essential place at the base of the Tree of Life. She is the only way that God can be rooted in the world. Without her the act of *Tikun*, the *coniunctio*, the return of the Feminine from exile is not possible. She lives in the collective unconscious, the Red Sea, to which she fled when required to assume an inferior place. She is the darkness that is a beacon. For Kiefer, Lilith – not Lucifer – is truly the light-bringer.

Seven years after exhibiting the *Breaking of the Vessels* and the *Lilith* paintings, Kiefer created a series called *The Palaces of Heaven*. Here glass is no longer broken but forms this great *Tree of Life* window. *Tikun*, a restoration of wholeness, has come to pass. In front of this great window stands a glass case like those we find in a museum of natural history. Inside are dresses, feminine ethereal garments that seem to move up and down this ladder in a kind of eternal return. These images touch me, for I have never felt comfortable with the notion that clothes in our dreams represent merely persona. No, they are soul clothes. In gnosticism we read about the "Heavenly Garment." At death, an angel comes to meet the dying with a "garment of light." This garment came to symbolize "the heavenly or eternal Self of the person, his original idea, a kind of double or *alter ego* preserved in the upper world while he labors down below. ... It grows with his deeds and its form is perfected by his toils. Its fullness marks the fulfillment of his task and therefore his release from exile in this world" (Jonas 1958, p. 122).

We are told with this image, called *The Unborn*, that there is a great work of consciousness yet to be done. In this powerful painting, we see a wasteland of garments not yet filled. Kiefer's museum of natural history is an image of the ascent and decent of the psyche in the alchemy of transformation. The window acts as the filter, the veil of eternal light into this world of history, personal and collective. We see the unmistakably feminine nature of the soul where the original image brightens with the light of consciousness and the dresses – the garments – are filled with it.

Then Kiefer suddenly gives us this image. It is a window in the world of creation through which we see a "real tree." Or is it? It is the same window that we have seen in the images of *The Palaces of Heaven*. I feel that Kiefer says all the windows are the same; it is only the light in which we see it that reveals which world we apprehend.

References

Eliade, M. (1978). *The Forge and the Crucible: The Origins and Structure of Alchemy*. Chicago: University of Chicago Press.
Giegerich, W. (1985). Lecture, C.G. Jung Institute of Chicago.
Halevi, Z. (1987). *Psychology and Kabbalah*. York Beach, ME: Samuel Weiser.
Hillman, J. (1972/1992). *The Myth of Analysis*. New York: Harper Collins.
Jonas, H. (1958/1991). *The Gnostic Religion*. Boston: Beacon.

Le Vitte Harten, D. (1991). *Anselm Kiefer – Lilith*. Catalogue of Exhibition. New York: Marian Goodman Gallery.

Little, M. (1993). Margaret Little: Psychotherapy with D.W.W. In D. Goldman (Ed.). *In One's Bones: The Clinical Genius of Winnicott*. Northvale, NJ: Aronson.

Patai, R. (1967). *The Hebrew Goddess*. Detroit: Wayne State University Press.

Rosenthal, M. (1987). *Anselm Kiefer*. Catalogue. The Art Institute of Chicago and the Philadelphia Museum of Art.

Schjeldahl, P. (1988). Our Kiefer. *Art in America*, March.

Scholem, G. 1965). *On the Kabbalah and its Symbolism*. (R. Manheim, Trans.) New York: Schocken.

The sculpture, *Breaking of the Vessels*, and all the paintings of the Lilith series appear in the catalogue of the Marian Goodman Gallery, 1991, text by Le Vitte Harten. *The Palaces of Heaven* images are from the catalogue *Anselm Kiefer* for the exhibition at the Museo Correr, Venice, 1997. All other paintings appear in the catalogue by Rosenthal, 1987.

Destruction and Creative Interplay
in Artistic and Therapeutic Processes

Ingrid Riedel
Konstanz, Germany
Schweizerische Gesellschaft für Analytische Psychologie

Despite our knowledge of the need for destruction in creative interplay, as therapists we often are at a loss when faced with clients who, after hours of careful production of their pictures, ultimately destroy them or cover them with brown sticky paint, thus erasing them at the same time. In the dream of a 58-year-old woman, the motive for the destruction of a self-produced relief picture becomes comprehensible. She dreamed:

> *My husband and I are at an art fair with many people. He talks with many people, doesn't stop at all, until we finally are the last, persistent guests. I make no contact, am not even interested in it. Then I take a picture which I have made myself, and destroy it: There aren't any paints on it, but a half-inch thick layer of grayish-white silicone rubber. In it I had modeled the picture, like a relief. It was a landscape, houses in the background. I scrape off all the stuff. Only in the background I leave a few houses standing. A big heap of this scraped-off, rubber-like scrap develops, which is truly disgusting to me.*

In the discussion about the dream her comment was: "You can throw away dead things, as well as an overhauled self-image. No fear of too much dirt. I'll manage it."

While her husband makes contact at an art fair with many people, in a manner which she feels is inappropriate (in a session, she had stated she couldn't permit herself to be excluded) now she picks up this picture, her self-made picture of a landscape, of a philosophy of life, and quite consciously destroys it. It was, after all, the picture of a landscape of life without color but with the quality of a tough, sticky, easily conforming rubber mass. As this became clear to her – and even more, that she was the one who produced this relief picture

364   *Ingrid Riedel*

– she was seized with rage – in fact, a holy wrath – toward herself: how could she have produced such a grey model of life?

This destruction is equivalent to a liberation. The dreamer knows what this dream is about, as indicated by her comment.

Because every picture we produce is essentially a self-image, the destruction of a picture is equivalent to the destruction of a self-image. This is not necessarily self-destruction, but rather the destruction of a view of oneself – perhaps even for the sake of the true self which demands, and even compels, a transformation of the self-image, in order to open a further possibility for individuation. Can the danger of self-destruction be entirely excluded from this?

When I look at the pictures of Arnulf Rainer, an Austrian artist born in 1929, and particularly his series of over-painted photos of himself, it appears that the danger of self-destruction cannot be excluded. And yet, behind these over-paintings of his photographic portraits which, to a certain extent, destroy them, one can sense an intention to capture the real person behind numerous self-images of the persona. At least, all that remains connected with it, and until now was lying – negatively and positively – in the shadows. This productive process in more and more self-images of Rainer seems to be almost a meditative exercise in the sense of Zen Buddhism, in which someone constantly and repeatedly asks: Who am I, and who is it who asks this?

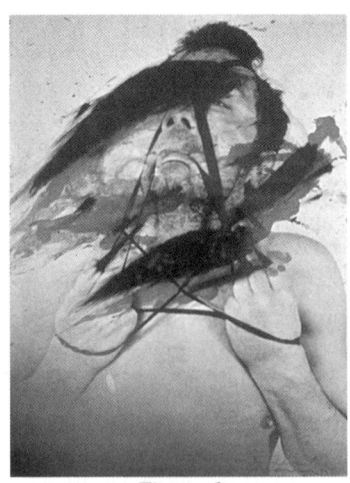

Figure 1

If we look at some of these pictures which were exhibited at the Documenta 5 (the large international art show in Kassel), a radical process of self-perception and self-production, as well as self-torture, is reflected in them. He calls one of these photos of himself, with the corresponding overpainting, *Ohne Titel* ("Without Title," Figure 1). Rainer (1967) himself wrote of it:

I want to reproduce myself in concentrated form. That which I was, am, will be, what I could be; is what I am making myself to be. Exaggerations, transformations, expansions from seeds, wishes and memories which I find in myself. I also produce and mold myself only through these acts of physical self-expression or symbolic production of the self. The result: incarnate concepts of oneself, communication systems with oneself. (p. 16)

So far, so good, but Rainer also views his self-portrayal as self-critical, namely as "auto-expressions, pretensions, manic euphemisms, catatonic self-monuments, monologues of the body exhibited in an autistic theater." [p. 16] At the same time, Rainer builds a bridge to the efforts at expression of everyone, to which paintings which arise from the unconscious also belong: "Everyone dabbles in what I pursue" (p. 16).

In his pictures, Rainer repeatedly presents himself as not free, bound, tortured; he translates this experience into merciless expression. He spans his face and his upper body with straps, photographs himself thus, and then may cross out the photograph with covering paint which often looks like whip lashes. He destroys the likeness; at the same time, he raises the photos of his own face to extreme expression through such over-painting. The face, crossed with straps – as if he wants to define and simultaneously cross it out – becomes, for him, a *Tränenbrand* (Burn by Tears, Figure 2a) and a *Wundgesicht* (Face of Wounds, Figure 2c).

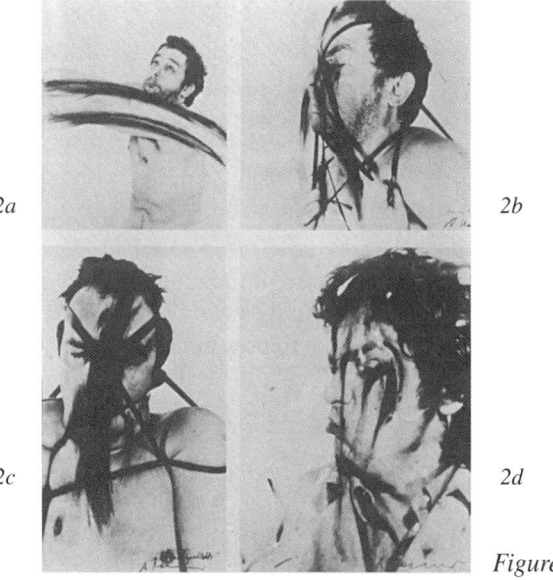

2a

2b

2c

2d

Figure 2

Through his own extreme suffering however, Rainer finally achieves the freedom for a *Sternensang* (Star Song, Figure 2d), where bright lights flash over the face, which is hung with black strands and streaks, and where the lips shape themselves to sing. He could even have named the second of this series *Sternensang* (Figure 2b): The arms stretch above an arch, of which the parallel brush strokes remind one of a rainbow, and the gaze is directed upward. In *Tränenbrand*, the face appears to be obliterated under a stroke of black paint. Black burns as tears might burn, and the face seems to be charred by fire.

The *Wundgesicht* also appears to be obliterated by a stroke of black paint, in the center of the down-turned face. In addition, the entire upper body appears to be bound by sharply cutting straps. It is human passion that Rainer creates here as his own however, on the forehead of this man. A curious figure forms: a rune of life, the symbol of birth, by the way in which the two straps running upward – with the point at the bridge of the nose – form a fork that opens upward. In the midst of suffering, new birth announces itself which, in the next picture, obviously leads to the possibility of the *Sternensang* [Star Song] through all the stigmata of pain. Multiple destruction occurs in all these pictures. First, the face – the body – is interfered with in its freedom of movement, its free expression, through the binding with straps. Then this disturbance is fixed and documented.

Finally, the photo appears crossed out, destroyed by the overpainting, as with black stripes of a whip. Through this interference, however, the passion of Rainer, but perhaps of humanity in general, is expressed.

That Rainer is not playing with suffering, at least at the time of the creation of these pictures, is shown by the fact that he consciously sets his pictures near the symbol of the Cross; that he repeatedly creates the Cross in parallel to his self-images. In *Kreuzübermalung* (Overpainting of a Cross, Figure 3), he injures himself on this symbol as he injures himself, actually, then attempts to cross out the injury, to make it invalid. *Kreuzübermalung* dates from 1956-57. Thus, he gives this symbol new meaning, whether or not intentionally.

The Cross, as a symbol of both death and resurrection, indicates here an inner process. Otherwise, Rainer rejects the conventional world of pictures, including the religious world, over-painting it with black. For Rainer himself, however, these over-painted pictures are not obliterated and empty, but instead "full of overwhelming silence." The silence obliterates the old and makes room for the new. Rainer's series of pictures relativize the individual picture and insert it into a comprehensive surveying movement, in which Rainer ascertains, through production, all that is really part of him as a person, all that is really part of humanity. His destruction particularly interferes with the fixation on particular pictures of humans. Humans are always more than a single picture. Rainer's picture series open one to this recognition, in which a

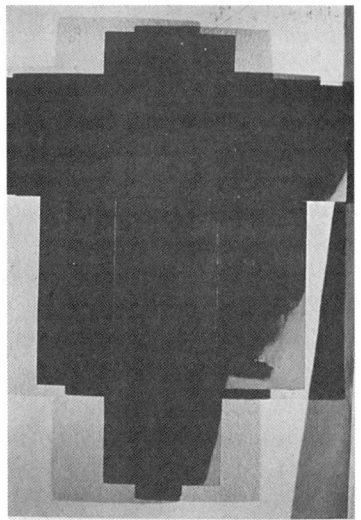

Figure 3

picture often appears to delete the one following; for example, as the "*Sternensang*" does with the "*Tränenbrand.*" And yet they all belong together, in order, as Rainer (1967) says, "to exemplify the opening and expansion of the human personality" (p. 16).

Profound and cryptic human faces, showing many signs of destruction, such as the grotesque faces of Bosch and Goya, the self-portraits of Rembrandt and Van Gogh, left deep impressions on Rainer. He even over-painted Rembrandt's 1628 *Self-Portrait in his Early Years* and titles his over-painted picture *Rembrandt als Rembrandt*) as if Rembrandt's dark face were his actual face. He is just as fascinated with the true faces of the mentally ill, as well as those of the dead. *Totenmaske* (Death Mask), accentuated by only a few characteristic strokes, puts us behind the head of the dead person; with him we look upward and to the right, along his sharply defined nose, into the zone where symbols of transcendence sometimes appear. As cited by Presler (1998) Rainer wrote, "Direct spiritual and creative principles come to fruition: erasing, turning away, breaking of taboos, curiosity about dying, mysticism surrounding death" (p. 171). Rainer's (1977) text *Als Kröte* (As a Toad), belongs to this context:

*Because, with advancing age, much becomes less clear to me, every
point, once seen, dissolves again, and the great overview does not
occur, I needed to act. ... I had a peculiar experience in this respect,
but I forgot it again each time. Each time, after finishing work – as
soon as the paintbrushes are put down, the fingers and feet scrubbed,
the paint brush soaked, the monogram and the signature applied, the
cartoons laid in the furthest corner – new standards manifest
themselves. To hell with it, or thank God, I misjudged the dimensions. It was clear that it was all only mincing around in the studio
about a little heap of paint mush. At the most, swimming amok in the
room aquarium. (p. 54)*

As soon as the work is completed, it is no longer enough for
Rainer. Already his devaluation of his creation is equivalent in that
moment to its destruction. Rainer mentally crosses it out as soon as
it is finished. But he would not be a creative person if new standards
did not open up for him at the moment of this crossing out.
Otherwise he would be afraid of "drowning in drowsiness" or
"sitting in a small niche cage, to lie in wait for my senility."
Destruction and production thus as a law of the creative process,
even of life itself in the face of death? Around 1978, a new cross
form appeared in Rainer's creations. The Cross as dress, coat, or
angel: "The scream transforms itself into a silence full of expectations" (Presler, p. 170).

A new, deeper seriousness and a devotion to a greater reality,
which transcends Rainer's person, appears after 1982, for example,
in his Hiroshima cycle, a series of drawings on top of photos of the
destroyed city. This exhibit is being shown in 17 European museums. With the print *Kosmischer Schauer* (Cosmic Shower) and a
whole series of pictures of the cosmos, Rainer again succeeds in
finding a meditative calm, and now uses his over-painting technique
for the creation of layers, in which the cosmos changes. His
surprising series of 25 pictures with the cosmos as a theme appeared
in 1994. They all have been created as oil paintings, which permits
multiple over-paintings and layers of color, and are painted on
uniform circular wooden boards, 123 centimeters in diameter.

Through the round shape alone, they acquire something closed
and calm. It has to do with the circular whole, the macrocosm –
perhaps also the microcosm – of the psyche. They are pictures of
wholeness, which appear to have overcome circulating the small
self, which for a long time was characteristic for Rainer. At the same
time, the technique of over-painting, which had been practiced for
his entire life, is now transformed in a direction in which not a

simple crossing out, but rather a multi-dimensional, multiple layering of the colors can be expressed through it. Rainer knows about the subtle color tones that arise from the overlayering of two or more colors. I point only to the subtle picture *Der verlorene Mond im Märchen des Lichts* (The Lost Moon in the Fairytale of Light). They are the most delicate compositions; previous means of destruction become sovereign means of production here. Without the previous techniques of destruction, there would not be these differentiated productive techniques. That which he lives through, suffers through himself – particularly in the artistic production – Rainer (1977) also does not spare his viewers. He attests to a "ruinous overexertion": "Now I am sitting with my worked-out spine, and muscle cramps, internally burned out from a pile of formal, banal and smeared to death, beaten and spoiled pictures, and don't know how I will ever be finished with all this, without new battles and cramps" (p. 53).

The impulse toward devaluation and therewith intellectual destruction of that which has been accomplished, generally has been, for Rainer, stimulus toward further creative development.

There is also the impulse toward material destruction of the works which one subsequently does not accept, or tears up under the influence of emotion, such as a reaction to a negative response. When an analysand destroyed a series of her pictures, I became aware of another motive for such an action. In the series she had given form to the examination of her mother complex, which controlled her, including in many transference situations. She wanted to close this phase and not fall back into it. Thus, she needed to put behind her the entire series which was evidence of her years' long struggle. She destroyed the entire series, without discussing it with me, as she regarded these pictures – rightfully – as her intellectual property, over which only she had the right to decide and to act.

I was very sad at first. That this act, with which she primarily wanted to free herself from the past, was concerned not only with destructiveness, was illustrated by the fact that, without talking about her intention to destroy the pictures, she first offered to photograph her series of pictures for my recollections and use. Even such production can lead to destruction; we are all familiar with the process in which one ultimately destroys the picture through a constant desire to improve it and paint it over. Or there is the process in which we somehow destroy the original picture through passionate production, in that we rub through it until it develops a hole, or in that we add further sheets of painting paper, or cut away sections of the picture which no longer appear to fit. We hear of such destructive tendencies, not only from Arnulf Rainer, but also from other top-class artists.

In the case of Georgia O'Keeffe, it was dissatisfaction over the lack of originality in all she had created to that point that drove her, in her twenty-eighth year of life, to destroy all of her previous work then in existence. Regarding this, she wrote (Fall 1915): "I said to myself I have things in my head which are different than the things I was taught – they express so well my nature and my thinking, that it never occurred to me to express them. I decided to start at the beginning – to throw out everything I had learned – to recognize my own thoughts as true."[*] A year later, O'Keeffe sent some of her newest works to her friend Anita Politzer in New York, though with the request not to show them to anyone. Politzer, however, was so impressed with the simple abstract drawings, that she presented them to Alfred Stieglitz, the famous photographer, publisher, and art dealer. He became Georgia O'Keeffe's gallery exhibitor and, ultimately, her husband. The completely abstract drawings and water-colors created by Georgia O'Keeffe from 1916 on are among the first and most important of this type in America.

In the case of the Russian painter Wassily Kandinsky, on the other hand, it was an overwhelming experience when he saw one of his own pictures defamiliarized to an abstraction in the twilight, in which forms are blurred. In *Rückblicke* (Retrospectives), Kandinsky described this experience, which occurred in about 1910:

> *Already in Munich, I was once entranced by an unexpected sight in my studio. It was the hour of advancing twilight. I came home with my paint box after doing a study, when I suddenly saw an indescribably beautiful picture, saturated with an inner glow. I hesitated at first, then I quickly went toward this mysterious picture, in which I saw nothing but form and color, and in which the subject was incomprehensible. I immediately found the key to the mystery: it was a picture painted by me, which was leaning against the wall on its side. The next day, in daylight, I tried to acquire the impression I had had of the picture on the previous day. But I was only halfway successful: even on its side, I continually recognized the objects, and the fine glaze of the twilight was lacking. I now knew precisely that the object harmed my pictures. (quoted in Riedl 1987, p. 31)*

---

[*] Nancy G. Heller (1989), Künstlerinnen, VGS, Köln, S. 126.

As was the case earlier with Monet, Kandinsky's vision in seeing a haystack – the visionary illumination of a new spirituality of art – appears to overtake everything that has preceded it, even if he didn't destroy the pictures he had painted up to that point. This vision was followed by the dramatic change in Kandinsky's style toward abstraction, which can be followed, above all, in his All Saints' Day paintings, which were all produced within a few months' time.

How can the spontaneous production and destruction processes, which arise from the unconscious of our analysands, now be interpreted from the perspective which we have gained from the pictures of professional artists?

A woman, in her late fifties at the time of the creation of the pictures, carries from the Nazi era a severe trauma, which slowly became clearer during the painting process. She experienced, with great shock, the abduction of her beloved Jewish grandfather and several uncles, all related on her mother's side. Her father, a lawyer, was forced out of his profession because he had married into a Jewish family. During the childhood and youth of the woman, the family experienced years burdened by anxiety, characterized by multiple displacements. Thus, her symbol for *Haus* (House, Figure 4) which in fact should express security, had become an extremely fragile cross, a symbol for swaying walls, which no longer can hold up the roof. Ultimately, this remainder of a dwelling collapses totally

Figure 4   Figure 5

for her; for months, she confronts her bottomless desolation, and is like a person dying of thirst *In der Wüste* (In the Desert, Figure 5).

Figure 6

In connection with mythical and New Testament stories of healing, with which she is occupied in her studies, she finally dares to express disunity and destruction in her pictures, such as *Zerstückelter Mensch* (Cut-up Person, Figure 6). She paints a chaotically dismembered person, which reminds one of Picasso's *Guernica.*

Ultimately, she dares to paint the *Krankheitsdämon* (Demon of Sickness, Figure 7), who appears in the New Testament story of the epileptic boy (Matthew 17:15), as his tormenter. With partial awareness, she thus paints the self-destructive impulse, which afflicts her, which has her between its teeth. She afflicts herself; the impulse, as in many victims of violence, continues to function as an internalized aggressor. By painting it, she is able to ban it, which also means that she can engage in an internal discussion with it. In the process, she experiences the devouring violence, but

Figure 7

is able slowly to differentiate herself from it. In a later picture, she depicts the "*Suchende Demeter*" (Searching Demeter, Figure 8):

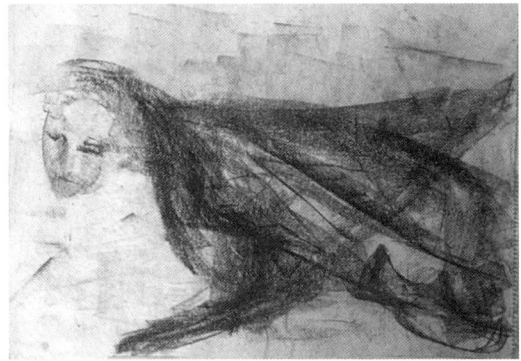

Figure 8

searching through nine nights with her torch for her daughter, who was abducted from her into the underworld. Here, too, in principle, she is depicting herself. She has found a new picture: She is no longer simply the victim, the abducted daughter, but is now herself also the mother, who passionately seeks the portion of her soul, her daughter, and simultaneously her own possibilities for development, which had been banned to the underworld, only to regain it ultimately. With this, she has, in a certain sense, become a mother, takes responsibility for the traumatized part which had ended up in the underworld.

The page has turned, even if the search at this point is far from over. The delicacy and care with which she creates *Demeter mit der Fackel* (Demeter With the Torch, Figure 9) another time, who now stands up, and, with her torch, brings a hint of red into the series of pictures which, up to that point, had been exclusively black.

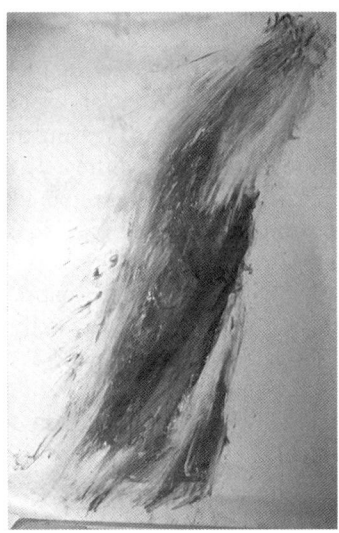

Figure 9

Figure 10

This change shows unmistakably that the painter's worst self-destruction has been overcome. Its expression through painting appeared to me to be absolutely necessary, however, to become aware even initially of her self-destructive power – which was, after all, like a demon – and then to be able to engage in a conscious internal dialogue with it. She was not only the victim; she was also the one who, for a long time, robbed herself. In the midst of darkness, peace finally enters, and after all the self-destruction, she is able to draw a person in a well, who is struck by a beam of light: *Mensch im Brunnen* (Person in a Well, Figure 10).

Production, destruction, and reorganization appear in these series as a law of life, which includes death; a law of production, which is not there to be feared, but rather to be more and more deeply understood. The occasional destructiveness of our patients derives its value from this law of life and production. In many respects, destruction can act in service to the self, as we saw:

In productively expressing the destructive impulse itself, in which it is recognized and ultimately resolved;

In shrugging off surmounted issues of a life problem that one does not wish to fall back into, an artistic attitude which one has outgrown;

In finally exploding an entire tree of life which was not one's own, but that of an oppressive family;

In personally destroying a whole landscape of life, a colorless plastic landscape, a false self image.

In all of these, destruction occurs in the service of the true self, which, after all, can be born only through this destruction.

Translated from the original German by Sigrid Koates

References

Presler, G. (1998). Schwere Ruhe, der Maler Arnulf Rainer. *Evangelische Kommentare, 3*, 169-171.

Rainer, A. (1967). *Ohne Titel*, Catalogue Documenta 5. Kassel: Dierichs.

Rainer, A. (1977). *Ohne Titel,* Catalogue Documenta 7. Kassel: Dierichs.

Rainer, A. (1994). Kosmischer Schauer. *Kosmos 25.* Stuttgart: Radius Verlag.

Rainer, A. and Härtling, P. (1992). *Engel – Gibt's Die?* 30 over-paintings. Stuttgart: Radius.

Rainer, A. (1993). *Malerei 1980-1990.* Stuttgart: Hatje.

Rainer, A. (1972). *Selbstdarstellungen: Fotoübermalungen* 1968-1972. München: Prestel.

Riedl, Peter A. (1987). *Wassily Kandinsky.* Rororo Monographie 313, Hamburg.

Art Within the Analytic Relationship

Scapegoat and Transformation

Joy Schaverien
Leicester, England
Society of Analytical Psychology

Art plays a central role within many an analytic relationship. We know that it has a healing effect but too rarely do we ask the questions of how and why that should be. Pictures may be interpreted as manifestations of unconscious material but there is more to the healing qualities of art than this. Before I became an analyst I trained as a painter, worked as an art therapist and psychotherapist and spent many years attempting to articulate the processes I observed in clinical practice. I analysed several series of pictures in order to understand the role of the pictures within the transference-countertransference (Schaverien 1991, 1995).

My concern here is with the object nature of the artwork, the imagery it reveals, as well as its aesthetic qualities. These may combine to offer means of psychological mediation in states which are otherwise inexpressible. Thus, potentially destructive impulses may be transformed into creative enactment. At times, pictures may be considered an embodiment of the "scapegoat transference," a particular means of mediating and, subsequently, integrating shadow material. This process may be understood by attention to the "aesthetic countertransference."

The Scapegoat Transference

The scapegoat is a ritual for purging a community or individual of ill-affect and disease. In the West the scapegoat is best known in its Biblical form as part of the Jewish Day of Atonement (Leviticus 16). The scapegoat was transformed, through prescribed ritual, into an embodiment of the sins of the community, and was banished into the desert. In this way the sins, in embodied form, were disposed of. It is my premise that pictures may play a similar role in analysis.

Transformed into an embodiment of ill-affect and disease the picture too may be disposed of. However, I hope to show that this is not merely a rejection of the scapegoated affect. There are numerous other forms of scapegoat in cultures throughout the world. Some involve complex rituals, including the sacrifice of an animal and, in its earliest forms, even human sacrifice (see Fraser 1913, Maccoby 1982). Others are simple rites involving the use of inanimate objects. Fraser gives examples of sticks, stones and other objects – made or found – which are used to cause harm or disease to be transferred from a sufferer.

Common to scapegoat rituals is that an inanimate object or animal is embodied, transformed, and ultimately disposed of. These conscious and curative enactments are based on the philosophical worldview that a "transference of attributes and states" is both possible and healing. Cassirer (1955) makes a connection with alchemy. Fundamental in both is the somewhat magical idea that attributes and states are both "transferable and materially detachable" (p. 66). The process is more than a symbolic substitution; it is a "real physical transference."

It is this concrete form of transference that interests me in relation to pictures created within the analytic frame. Similar processes – often unconscious – may be observed in the analysand's relation to her or his own art work. Furthermore, if we consider that, "purely 'spiritual,' purely moral attributes [sometimes may be] regarded as transferable substances" (Cassirer 1955, p. 56), we begin to see a link with the psychoanalytic concept of transference. The transference to the analyst is a form of attribution that brings affect "live" into the present and makes transformation possible. The psychological processes involved in the analysand's relationship to the art work similarly bring affect live into the present. The picture then may be regarded as an object of transference and a scapegoat in this positive sense. In a subsequent phase it may be transformed into a talisman: valued for what it holds.

Within analysis scapegoating is usually regarded negatively, as an unconscious and potentially destructive attempt to rid the self of some rejected element. Klein's (1946) concept of projective identification may be understood to be a form of unconscious scapegoating, and Perera (1986) proposes the "scapegoat complex" as a psychological attitude, derived from the role of the individual in the family. The patterns of behavior that result from these forms of scapegoating involve the attribution of disowned (shadow) personality traits to another person. Therefore the final part of the act, disposal, is unacceptable; it is neither possible, nor desirable, to dispose of a person. This fact distinguishes one specific feature of art in analysis. It is possible and at times beneficial to the analysand, to dispose of an art work, providing that its contents are ultimately integrated within the personality.

Disposal may entail the destruction of the art work but it is more often a benign act, such as its safe-keeping – perhaps by the analyst – until the analysand is ready to own it consciously. Like the earlier scapegoat rituals, this form of disposal may be considered a positive enactment. A picture offers a neutral area for mediation in the space between analyst and analysand. It reveals, captures, and holds elusive or potentially overwhelming imagery "out there" separate from the analysand – and so renders it manageable. Intense, chaotic and incomprehensible emotions may be expressed, acknowledged and contained within the art work, until such time as they can be owned or integrated. The picture may be experienced as holding aspects of the analytic relationship and so it may be valued as a talisman. This process is a feature of the concrete and temporal nature of art.

The Aesthetic Countertransference

Jung greatly respected the innate healing potential of art but he eschewed the aesthetic qualities in his own pictures, as well as those of his analysands. Nevertheless, the illustrations in his books contribute to our understanding of unconscious processes. There are numerous examples which show how integral are art and interpretation of pictures within Jungian analysis today (see Edinger 1990; Rosen 1993; Ulanov 1994). Although not always explicitly stated it is clear that, in commenting on art work made in analysis, the analyst draws on aesthetic sensibilities.

Attention to the subtlety of the analyst's aesthetic responses to art, within the context of an analytic relationship, enriches therapeutic understanding. Therefore it is important to distinguish the aesthetic effects of pictures from responses to other more transient imagery such as dreams. Different from dreams, pictures are concrete, material objects with a temporal and spatial existence as well as enduring aesthetic qualities. Engagement with the complexity of these aesthetic effects, even when the picture is not very good as "art," reveals a multi-layered set of processes which are both conscious and unconscious. For example, a picture may appeal to the analyst; the work may seem to be very skilled, beautiful or seductive. Alternatively it may repel, appearing unskilled or horrific. All these are reactions to the aesthetic impact of the work but, unlike the more neutral setting of the art gallery, the response takes place within the context of an intimate relationship. Thus it may resonate with other countertransference responses. Attention to such responses may reveal much about the analysand and the transference.

Attention to the aesthetic qualities of pictures, created within the therapeutic relationship, led me to make a distinction between two types of image. Influenced by Langer's (1967) distinction between "sign" and "symbol," I have identified the "diagrammatic" and the "embodied" image respectively. The difference reflects the depth of psychological engagement of the client in the therapeutic relationship and also in the scapegoat transference. The diagrammatic image is very often a simple line drawing, made to recount some situation or feeling state. But the image alone is insufficient; it needs words to express its meaning fully. The embodied image is rather different; this is an image for which no other mode of expression can be substituted. It is a picture or art work that articulates a state which can be conveyed in no other way.

The Diagrammatic Image

The diagrammatic image is made to tell something to the therapist. It is a sign in that it refers to something outside itself. Very often it is a conscious form of communication made with the therapist in mind: perhaps to help in recounting some feeling state, dream or memory. The picture may be of rather poor aesthetic quality, using only line or pin figures. It is an aid to telling the therapist about a dream or memory; it records the basic relationships but in itself it effects little change. Feeling may be evoked in relation to it, but the picture itself does not transform the psychological state of the analysand. This was the case with "Bel's" picture (Figure 1).

Bel's childhood experiences had continued to haunt her several years into her analysis. Her envious mother had continually played cruel tricks on Bel contributing to a sense of madness. In order to prove to herself that her mother was not malevolent Bel had had to live a lie, pretending not to notice the abuse. When her mother died Bel was in her mid-forties and suddenly and devastatingly became

Figure 1

aware of the impact this abuse had had on her life. She entered analysis under great pressure from previously-repressed fury. At first, when she recounted the tales of abuse, they moved her greatly and also touched me. As time went by, however, they became repetitive and lost their impact. Yet the memories still haunted her. Two years later she continued to puzzle over what her mother might have meant by certain repeated phrases. I admit that I became quite bored by this. Eventually I asked her if she thought that making a picture of the situation might help her. She had not previously used the art materials but she made the drawing "Bel's Picture" (Figure 1) and several similar to it, and was quite alarmed at the scenes portrayed.

As Bel told of the situation depicted, it evoked a strong reaction. This was followed by acknowledgement of her anger and sorrow at the injustice of the events related to the picture. Bel did not want to throw away the picture but neither did she want to keep it with her. Her solution was to leave it in my room. She did look at the picture a few times soon after making it but then it was forgotten. She no longer recounted this story and it seemed that this particular painful incident had been acknowledged and then integrated.

My interest here is in the aesthetic impact of the picture and in the transference. This is a simple line drawing which records the forms in the most basic manner; its aesthetic appeal is limited. One way of noting the difference between the diagrammatic and the embodied images is to pose the question to oneself: "Could this be conveyed in any other way?" With this picture I think it could; it is a story that can be told; therefore, this is a diagrammatic image.

The picture is also a simple but extremely effective scapegoat. It seems that the initial recounting of the memory had enabled some understanding of the influence of the past on the present but this had not altered the attitude to the memory. It was the picture that fixed the image and, through it, the incident was finally laid to rest. I think this was because, in the picture, Bel could view the situation outside herself rather than frozen within her and because, at last she had a witness to affirm her point of view. This presented a new perspective; the picture confirmed her experience and provided a psychological distance by which she could begin to escape the tyrany of the inner world mother.

It was as if the incident now had concrete form and, like the scapegoat, it could be disposed of – not by its rejection, but rather by my keeping it safe. This was a significant and semi-conscious enactment, within the transference, which transformed the psychological state of the artist. However this picture was never important to her for itself nor was it valued as a talisman. Thus it was different from an embodied image.

The Embodied Image

The embodied image is a picture which conveys a feeling state for which no other mode of expression can be substituted. It is what Langer (1957) calls the "art symbol." This is different from the symbols that appear in pictures, and takes account of the whole picture as a profound and irreducible entity. The embodied image engages the client in its making; it is as if the picture seems to lead, becoming rather different from the original intent. Often such a picture reveals some previously unconscious element in the psyche. The embodied image may begin with the intention of conveying a dream, for example but, in the making, the picture leads on from the original dream. Similarly it may be based in a memory but again – as it is made – the memory develops, very often revealing aspects that previously were unconscious. The point about the embodied image is that, in the process of its creation, feeling becomes "live" in the present. This may be understood to be a result of a transference – of "attributes and states." Very often the aesthetic quality of such a picture is commensurate with the engagement of the artist/

client in the transference. Five pictures selected from a series of embodied images show psychological transformation.

"Chloe" was in four-times-a-week analysis. In her late twenties, she gave the impression of someone much younger: slim and fair-haired, with a boyish appearance. The younger of two children, Chloe had yearned for her mother's approval but felt that her mother favoured her older brother. Her jealousy was fuelled by witnessing an emotionally incestuous relationship between her mother and brother. Chloe experienced him as the mother's partner. When her brother bullied Chloe – mercilessly – her mother expressed indifference. This inter-generational confusion produced oedipal fantasies of stealing her brother, to get revenge on their mother. It was he, rather than her father, who excluded Chloe from the intimacy she desired with her mother. This left her father available but, when Chloe looked to him for support and love, she was profoundly disappointed; he did not intervene on her behalf.

Thus, she had developed with the impression that it was preferable to be a boy. Her mother seemed to take no pleasure in the potential identification with her daughter; she rejected her own feminine state and favoured her son. Perry (1991) and Deickmann (1985) have written about the role of the father in helping the girl to separate from her mother and find her place in the world. Samuels (1985) has discussed the necessity for erotic playback between fathers and daughters if the girl is to develop a sense of herself as a woman. Lacking this interaction, there was no one take pleasure in Chloe. As a result, in her inner world, the relationship between the parental imagos, and male and female in general, were confused. This confusion was reflected in her first picture, which was both an embodied image and a scapegoat.

During the first Christmas break, she sent a picture in the post. She had written on the envelope, asking me to keep it for her, unopened. She said later that she could not bear to keep it with her, it was too disturbing, but she did not want to destroy it. She was admitting, thus, the power of the image and unconsciously treating it like a scapegoat. It was clearly of value within the analysis and a talisman, holding the feelings live and carrying them between us. Chloe trusted that I would understand her need for my help to take care of this aspect of her nascent self during the break. After the break she opened the envelope and showed me the picture (Figure 2).

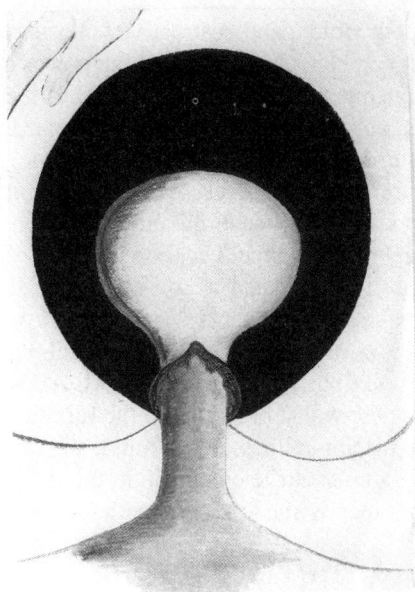

Figure 2

This work was well-executed, hence instantly compelling. Its aesthetic quality reveals embodiment of a feeling state that no words could substitute. If we pose the question: "Could this have been conveyed in any other way?" I think that the answer is "no." No words could speak the depth of experience that the picture reveals. It does not demand immediate explanation but it communicates at a profound non-verbal level. It is an irreducible entity, an embodied image, an art symbol.

When we look at pictures there is a temptation to be selective. Hence, by describing what I see I hope to notice all that is presented. But when these pictures were first made I did not know what I now begin to understand. The forms are undifferentiated. They are reminiscent of bodily parts and suggestive of sexual intercourse but the male and female elements are ill-defined. The white circular form, at the centre, is puzzling; it looks like a light bulb or a breast and appears to be penetrated by a penis. It is surrounded by black void or womb-like form and held within an outer shape seeming similar to buttocks. At the top left side of the picture is a right hand wearing a ring which, Chloe told me, is my ring. Thus it is my hand which seems to guide this intercourse. On many occasions she imagined the intercourse between us as sexual, sometimes loving and at others as rape. The theme, which commenced with this picture, developed; violent and destructive fantasies followed.

Chloe's quiet demeanour often belied the power of the emotions she was experiencing. In the way she related to the room and the objects within it, and outside, it often seemed to be animated as the inside of the maternal body. Early on, Chloe told me she thought she would need to remove her shoes. At that moment the theme of revenge was uppermost in her mind and she feared that her anger would destroy my room and me. I acknowledged the intensity of her feelings but made it clear that I would not let her destroy either; I sensed, from the beginning, that it was necessary to make explicit between us the limits of the imaginal and physical. I could accept her destructive impulses but not destructive acts. After that she often imagined kicking the walls, breaking up the furniture and smashing everything in sight. Sometimes, in her mind, she wrecked the room and destroyed all the "male" elements in it: the images of her father and brother. Only then is she left alone with me/mother.

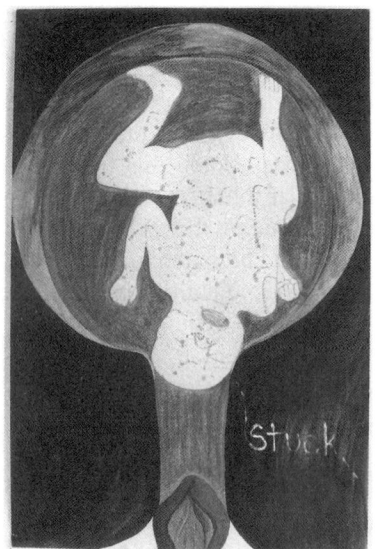

Figure 3

In the next picture (Figure 3) we see her impotent rage. Trapped within a bloody womb is a girl baby. If we compare this with the first picture we see that, where previously there was a shaft of an apparent penis, now there is a vaginal passage. It seems that the intercourse has produced a baby. This embodied image conveys the stuckness of her psychological situation in a way that no words could express. Yet the word "stuck" is written on it, seeming to confirm the image and fix its meaning. This unborn aspect of her "self" rages but cannot escape. We might understand that it shows how her growth and creativity are blocked; the girl part of Chloe is desperate to be born. This picture embodies and holds the feeling state "out there," separate from Chloe. It is a scapegoat, creating distance and offering her a perspective on her own psychological state. She kept it with her other pictures in a folder in my room and often returned to them during sessions, thus gradually becoming familiar with them and acknowledging their meaning. In this way the analyst takes care of the pictures until the analysand is ready to own them.

One of Chloe's expressed fears was that, if she used the couch, she might be pinned down and raped. This would be by an abusive and unspecific male ele- ment, or else by the phallic, spider/mother/analyst who would squash her. When she brought this picture (Figure 4) it brought out into the light the shape of this terror. It also is the beginning of separating and differentiat- ing the disparate male/ female elements which so terrified her in the first pic- ture.

At first there appears to be only one figure in this picture, but Chloe pointed

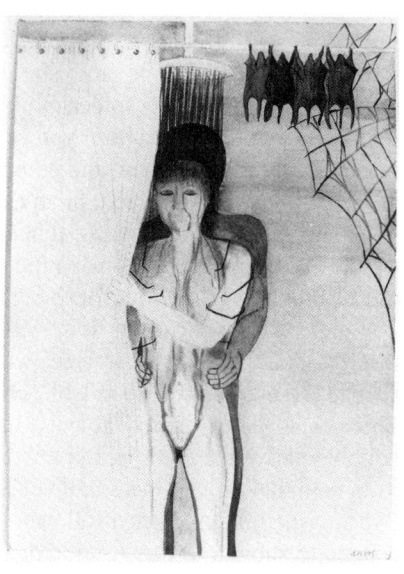

Figure 4

out that there are three. The spider mother is an image of archetypal proportions that haunted Chloe. Here a female figure stands in a shower of blood, a shower curtain in part concealing her right arm. The shadowy figure close behind, she said, is male. Between the two there is a spider, attached to the back of the woman. Chloe pointed out its legs holding onto the woman's arms. To the right is a spider's web, and bats hang from the frame of the shower.

Her associations to this picture were with her mother who is "on Chloe's back." The shadowy figure is male and penetrating her from behind – but she said that it too is the mother. The aesthetic quality of this picture reveals that it is an embodied image; it has tremen- dous impact. When Chloe showed it to me, she was terrified and the archetypal nature of this terror connected directly with me too. Chloe returned to this image many times and worked through its potential meanings, but the impact of the picture remains. I suggest that this is because it conveys the state of the artist, at the time it was made, and she holds it "live." The elements of her terror take form and so begin to become conscious.

On her return after the summer break, it became clear that the break had been nearly intolerable. In the session following it she was so frightened of her potential destructiveness that it was only at the end of the session that she would even enter the room. It was clear she was terrified of me and she later confirmed that she was experiencing me as the spider/mother of the shower room. Chloe said, "Once you've been born you can't go back in again."

Soon after this a violent, and potentially destructive, attack on the maternal body/room ensued, in an episode bordering on acting out. After sitting in silence looking at her feet, Chloe announced that she would like to make a picture. In the corner of the room was a large roll of brown paper, about four feet high. She got up, took this roll of paper and put it on the floor behind her chair. She set to work where I could hear, but not see, what was happening. There was silence except for the sound of scribbling for about 25 minutes. There was then frenzied activity in which I could see her head bobbing above the chair as she tore the paper, violently. Eventually from behind the chair, in a small voice, she said "I drew a breast. And I've smashed it." A silence followed. Then I said I wondered if she wanted to show it to me. A good deal more tearing followed before she emerged from behind the chair carrying a sheet of torn paper about four feet square; she sat in the chair and reassembled it into the shape of a breast (Figure 5). At the centre it was screwed up into the form of a nipple.

Figure 5

This enactment can be considered in terms of the scapegoat: permitting expression of the violence of feelings which could not have been expressed otherwise within the session. Chloe could not actually attack or tear me to pieces but the picture permitted the expression of this impulse. The picture was a scapegoat for her otherwise inexpressible rage, embodying the feelings and permitting them to be "live." It could be created and destroyed and yet survive. This may be understood with reference to Winnicott's (1971) distinction between object relating and object use. The transition from the undifferentiated state of object relating, in infancy, is facilitated by an attack on the breast. The breast, initially experienced as a subjective element, survives and is then perceived objectively. Then the mother is conceived of as a separate whole person – object use – and the potential for a new relationship, including love and hate, is established. Thus this potentially destructive act is transformed into a creative one.

Chloe described quietly and without eye contact how she imagined wrapping herself in the roll of paper. Her arms would be pinioned at her side and she would fight to get free. Then the paper in which she was held would come free from the main roll. There was a strongly angry feel about her communication and she curled up in the chair with her back to me. I said "I sense that you want to destroy me but also have me survive and hold you." She turned further away from me and said "I am still angry" but I heard her say "I am still crying," and acknowledged that. She corrected me ("I am still angry") and then added, almost inaudibly, "But I am crying underneath."

Thus it seemed that, in this session, she had permitted her rage with me to be live in the room. Further, in the wish to be constrained and to tear free, there is a sense of a struggle to be born, to be free of the mother and yet have her survive. Perhaps this is the birth of the raging baby we saw in her earlier picture (Figure 3). Her crying may indicate the beginning of the necessary mourning process.

This session was followed by a very intimate one in which Chloe took the torn breast object, which was lying in front of her on the floor, reassembled it and said, "I want to lie on it." She did so; her head rested on the paper with her hand beside her face. The whole sense of it, the scale of the picture to her head, the position and the atmosphere felt like a baby going to sleep at the breast. She said "I did a picture this weekend and it is of a baby in a mother's body but it is on the outside" (Figure 6, see following page).

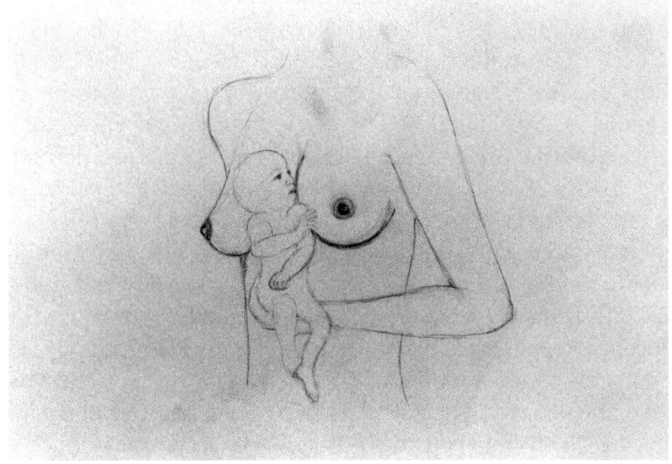

Figure 6

This very lovingly drawn image reveals the way in which the destructive fury and anger, which had been expressed in paint and torn paper, now gave way to a creative feeling. By noting the aesthetic quality we see that she used the more intimate medium of pencil and a small piece of paper. It seems that some of the violence had been a struggle for birth and both of us understood that there was the beginning of genuine psychological transformation. The girl-baby aspect of herself is now on the "outside;" it has been born into a receptive maternal environment.

Conclusion

These embodied pictures mediated as scapegoats, in a positive sense, within the analytic relationship. They brought into the light imagery which could not have been conveyed in any other way, providing a means of externalisation and containment for almost unbearable internal imagery. Their role within the transference and countertransference dynamic enabled a process of integration of potentially disowned shadow material. The form of disposal as safe-keeping contributed to this. Thus the concrete nature of the pictures played a significant part; providing a means of externalisation and transformation of potentially destructive impulses into creative, self-affirming enactments.

References

Cassirer, E. (1955). *The Philosophy of Symbolic Forms* (Vol. 2). New Haven, CT: Yale University Press.
Dieckmann, H. (1985). Some aspects of the development of authority. In A. Samuels (Ed.), *The Father: Contemporary Jungian Perspectives.* London: Free Associations.
Edinger, E. F. (1990). *The Living Psyche: A Jungian Analysis in Pictures.* Wilmette, IL: Chiron.
Fraser, J.G. (1913). *The Golden Bough.* London: Macmillan.
Klein, M. (1946). Notes on some schizoid mechanisms. In *Envy and Gratitude.* London: Hogarth.
Langer, S. (1957). *The Problems of Art.* London: Routledge & Kegan Paul.
Langer, S. (1967). *Feeling and Form.* London: Routledge & Keegan Paul.
Maccoby, H. (1982). *The Sacred Executioner.* London: Thames & Hudson.
Perera, S. (1986). *The Scapegoat Complex: Toward a Mythology of Shadow and Guilt.* Toronto: Inner City Books.
Perry, C. (1991). *Listen to the Voice Within.* London: S.P.C.K.
Rosen, D. (1993). *Transforming Depression.* London/New York: Penguin.
Samuels, A. (1985). *The Father.* London: Free Associations.
Schaverien, J. (1991). *The Revealing Image: Analytical Art Psychotherapy in Theory and Practice.* London/New York: Routledge
Schaverien, J. (1995). *Desire and the Female Therapist: Engendered Gazes in Psychotherapy and Art Therapy.* London/New York: Routledge.
Ulanov, A. B. (1994). *The Wizards' Gate: Picturing Consciousness.* Einsiedeln, Switzerland: Daimon.
Winnicott, D.W. (1971). *Playing and Reality.* London: Penguin.

Sandplay: A Place of Transformation

Livia Crozzoli

Rome, Italy

Associazione Italiana per lo Studio Della Psicologia Analitica

Analysis with children who demonstrate aggressive, violent and destructive behavior directed toward themselves, their environment and toward the therapist presents a complex relationship that is especially difficult for the analyst. In such situations, Sandplay provides a method that can facilitate the analysis significantly. The sandtray comes to represent a privileged middle space in which destructive and violent dynamics can be freely expressed, then more readily shared with the analyst.

Whether it is with the sand or the objects, the physical contact with the substance, the tactile and visual sensory nature, the corporeity of the Sandplay itself activates the playing out of those internal dynamics that disturb and yet are never translated into word or image. Rather, these dynamics are acted upon through destructive and violent actions or expressed in psychosomatic symptoms.

By attending to the emotional gestures of children, one discovers that these gestures reveal feelings that are relevant to the process and that belong to the most varied and deepest levels of the psychic apparatus. The most primitive of emotions, those that are connected to the corporeity and preverbal levels of experience, are triggered. Archaic channels of expression are activated that can reveal strong, emotionally-charged physical structures.

To work in direct contact with sand awakens a potentiality to provide visual, clear form and – later – words that favor a relationship with one's own internal reality. To give representation to one's internal world is a psychic act that is classified in the category of "thinking through images," a fundamental point of Jungian theory.

To realize the effort involved in this analysis, it is sufficient to observe the effort of the player, who chooses only that which corresponds to the emotions aroused and deliberates as to where and how to place the chosen object, in relation to the other objects. This process lends itself to a confrontation with the suppressed, unconscious image. This confrontation occurs from the emotions in relation to the object or from the imprint ingrained in the sand to the feelings awakened and provoked later in the analytic process.

The scene brings to the surface the internal dynamic that was not yet in presentable form and even less communicable with words. Whether it is destructive or constructive content that emerges, the emotional contact profoundly influences the player's thoughts and renders it possible in the clinical situation to see the beginnings of a dialogue between the conscious and the unconscious.

During Sandplay, consciousness offers spatial-temporal parameters to convey emotions, even without form and without defined relationships. The Sandplay space constitutes a sturdy and safe base, a free and protected space within the analytic relationship.

The closed and limited space of the container organizes the symbolic act. It promotes a search for order and favors the acceptance of limited space and definition to the scene. Within the sandtray, certain positions and significant distinctions are activated that are connected closely to the penetration of emotions and the manifestation of feelings.

Emotional experience has always been connected to spatial experience. Each of us is a body that occupies a space; this body colors that space with its own emotions. Joy makes us expand, enlarge, move toward others. Confusion disorients us and pushes us in all directions without a central point of reference. Fear closes us; anxiety squeezes us into a limited space. Destructiveness knocks us down and breaks us up. Depression collapses and immobilizes us.

The configuration of the scene then reveals an important field of emotions in play. The space reveals its specific archetypal meaning of experiential space that is connected closely to the corporeal experience and the alternating emotions of the player.

The dominant value of the play space is as an intermediary between the external and internal worlds: a space that allows us to stage our internal life and observe it from the exterior. At the same time, the represented scene allows us to become aware of the existence of our own internal space. Within these representations emerges the structuring, dynamic or static quality of our internal space: openings, closings, emptiness, fullness, deepness, flatness, elevations, immobility and movement.

Every patient has an individual handwriting in the construction of Sandplay scenes. In addition, the patient demonstrates a repetition of similar and recurring structures that segue each other with minimal variations. Then each one changes and turns into a different form which can even be opposite to the previous one.

It is of great importance to designate a center in the sand, either in the course of analysis or predetermined and preset. The subject is positioned in the play space and in the world in accord with internal dynamics.

Beyond the real and symbolic significance of the play space, Sandplay constitutes a possible path to the transformation of destructiveness and anxiety. When disturbing emotions take shape and become visible and shared with the therapist, they constellate a possible point of analysis and transformation of one's own psychic situation. Following a course of analysis, it is possible to recognize images and destructive, devastating and violent themes that are apparent in the psyche of every individual and are manifested in creative play.

The process is expedited also by virtue of the fact that the patients involved in Sandplay present their personal interpretation of their own internal conflicts. They use their conflicts as an initial function of distinction between themselves and their emotions. They try not to suffer passively through their anxiety, but rather confront it actively and directly.

When conducting therapeutic work that uses gesture and words, it is possible to be thoroughly present "live" at the transformative exchange between the patient and the represented scene: to hear the quiet dialogue between the conscious and the unconscious. To illustrate these theoretical elements that pertain to the configuration of the space and the confrontation between the conscience and the unconscious, the following description illustrates a few episodes in the course of analysis with an eight-year-old boy, who was in therapy for three consecutive years.

During therapy, the images of Sandplay and the dramatizations expressed by the young patient through his gestures, both within the sandtray and in the room, established "an organizer of analytic listening." My verbal interventions were toward represented events which were prompted by the patient himself, using his suggestions, his language and his metaphors.

I was able to treat his conflict as if the sandtray were a mirror, where the child could observe and see in action in his internal dynamics and then later to learn to distinguish them. The insight was discovered together with the child and an emotional experience was realized between us in the here and now.

From birth, Alessandro demonstrated urinary and fecal incontinence day and night, with alternating bouts of constipation. In addition to this macroscopically pathological aspect, other problems appeared that pertained to his relationships with his parents, other adults and especially with his peers. According to his parents, their only child was different from others: hyperactive, disturbed and aggressive, with outbursts of anger at which point he would break his own belongings and those of the household. If he was annoyed, he would yell, cry, scream, pull his hair out and assault other people. Both at home and school he showed the same behavior. Nobody wished to be around him because of his smell and his violent and dangerous behavior.

The child first manifested difficulties when he was four months old. This was the moment at which he entered day care and was first separated from his parents, particularly his mother. From the moment she re-entered the work force she began to suffer from "nervous breakdowns," which resulted in a diagnosis of schizophrenia. She subsequently underwent both psychological and pharmacological therapy.

There were severe marital tensions between the parents, which became evident in their manner of parenting. There also arose great differences and conflicts between them when pertaining to discipline. The father felt that the mother was too lenient, almost negligent. "She lets him do everything, she treats him like a small child." Contrary to her husband, the wife felt that her spouse was distant from their son, too rigid and violent: "I have to intervene when you hit him; you're not yourself when you shake him."

For his parents, Allessandro appeared to be split into two opposite parts. According to his mother he seemed a small child. The mother saw him as a part of herself, someone to take care of: an image that was connected to negative events in her relationship with her own mother. From the paternal view, Alessandro appeared large, strong, violent, "with too much power," connected to the vicissitude of his relationship with his own father, who was a gigantic man, strong and violent like his son. Alessandro's father had received blows with the belt to the point of blood and had no relationship with his father. Alessandro's symptoms and behavior seemed to correspond to each of the parents' images: a small baby to clean and take care of and a large, violent and aggressive child.

Figure 1

Episodes in Analysis with Imagery

From Alessandro's analytic sessions, I have chosen five sandtrays. The first represents an interpretation of his situation in the initial moments of analysis. The second, after six months, gives witness to the initial encounter between the conscious and the unconscious. The third frame follows the opening into the unconscious, which occurs also in the fourth frame, but where the presence of a center appears, revealing a new orientation toward the play space and his conscience. The fifth frame occurred after one year of therapy. Here, a clear transformation is evident: from the initial "catastrophe" with violent, desperate and devastating fights that blocked all energy, to an industrious, quiet village with a different configuration of the space.

The child began his first Sandplay experience (Figure 1) by deploying three adversarial parts in the sand. There was the American army close to him, the Japanese army on the opposite side and armored cars and amphibians with no definite nationality in the middle. He added dividing barriers: three flags on the ground, three airplanes and three helicopters.

There was a brief pause to observe everything. While trying to get closer to the scene he accidentally placed his hand in the middle of

Figure 2

the sand. He paused to take a bit of the sand in his hand. Then, he carefully let it fall through his fingers as if experiencing a pleasurable sensation.

This intense experience allowed him to add to the scene something more alive and natural: some trees in all the defined spaces including the middle – the only area to have trees with colored fruit. Then he exclaimed: "Here, finished."

I asked "Where would you place yourself"? The child answered "Here": at the helm of the amphibian which had been placed in the middle toward the right, on which he had poured sand earlier.

He informed me that the middle zone was was going to be attacked and he would have to defend himself and attack on both sides. "The three armies will fight each other." At the end, he looked seriously and with great concentration at the situation and said, "It's a catastrophe; everyone dies, I mean everyone."

Subsequently, he enacted a catastrophic battle with the death of all the soldiers, devastation of all military parties, air raids, the destruction of trees and the dividing borders, and sand strewn everywhere. He re-enacted these battles numerous times, adding explosions, bombings with sounds, gestures and falls to the ground. The space of the sandtray and that of the room seemed filled by devastation and deadly violence.

A double dramatization occurred: One among the figures and objects of the game, another with Alessandro himself. He would reproduce the events: throwing himself on the ground, enacting the soldiers' deaths or wounds, and destroying objects within the sandtray.

The child appeared completely stunned and confused with his own emotions and images. He was without distinction between himself and the scenes represented, between the internal or external space, and certainly without any relation to me. The battles concluded in a complete heap, together with disorder and confusion in the sandtray (Figure 2). What did Alessandro portray with these first images? There are several positions from which to approach the complexities of the play scene.

We could read the first frame, which had the tripartition of the sand space as the child's familiar *imago*: the destructive, violent and dangerous function. Both in the attack and defense, the characters were capable only of hurting and destroying each other: "It's a catastrophe; everyone dies." This unconscious persecutory identity that holds them together, stunned and confused, with a visible result of a chaotic heap that seems to represent the "shadow" part of the family.

We can read this frame also from a diagnostic point of view. It is a representation of Alessandro's individual demands and prevalent characteristics: his impulses, aggressivity, depressive and persecutory anxieties, and defenses which are visible in the rigid and hard mechanical toys. The heap seems to symbolize the problematic and conflictual knot, the child's "shadow" part that must be recognized and elaborated.

This same representation can be read also through a real and symbolic corporeal dimension that is brought in by the contact with the sand. The final pile, the fecal heap, demonstrates a lack of flow in the energetic and corporeal functions which cannot be transformed or expressed completely. Rather, it is detained or evacuated involuntarily in the urinary and fecal incontinence, comparable to the explosions of motors during clashes.

There is another reading that is connected to our interpersonal dynamic. On his path he did not represent himself as entirely alone, as indicated by the presence and the function of the two amphibians that "were opening up the street" from the changeover. It is interesting and prognostically valid that he could enjoy the sand which he discovered and poured over the amphibian.

A structural analysis of the scene helps to highlight the configuration in the play space, which represents a background to this method. The initial image seems to demonstrate an ability to spread out over the whole surface and to distinguish himself from the others. It shows an ability to take his own space in the center even if he was in danger or in battle. But in the final image, Alessandro represents himself as being coerced into a restrictive and catastrophic space where he is utterly confused and without distinction between himself and others, his emotions ending in a dramatic annihilation of his living space.

The theme of military battle and its dramatization goads the child on to repeat this with slight but progressive changes for months to come. It continues to function as a release, but also serves to confront his deep and catastrophic fears of death and annihilation.

In order to change, Alessandro had to start from this primitive, catastrophic experience. He had to enact it, confront it and then find his own living space again.

For almost a year, the child presented the same war scenes, slowly freeing up the center space and limiting the battles to two opposite factions, always ending with a final destruction. The scene slowly expanded and occupied the whole space in the sandtray.

During therapy, the possibility of not destroying the whole scene was introduced, saving six missiles and one airplane and then eventually not letting everyone die. Initially it was one soldier, then a group of soldiers from one of the groups and then soldiers from both groups. The war scenes also changed from a counter position of three battle lines facing each other to only two armies with a victory for one.

After six months of analysis, an important event occurred with the emergence of a new image. It was the "birth" of a grassy field in the middle of the war scene. In truth it was a field in the center space which separated the two fighting armies (Figure 3). While working, Alessandro commented: "The field must be full. It's becoming something strange, something that is completely full, completely alive; it doesn't look like a battleground." His voice was eager and fragile. The child's surprise and the change in his voice demonstrated the communicative and transformative power of the represented images. A feeling of life and an interior fullness seemed to be expressed which surprised both of us.

The experienced representation of the field seemed to correspond to a part of the child that is born from within. It comes forth from

Figure 3

deep inside and appears unexpectedly. This image makes us think of a more tender, vital and creative side to Alessandro's personality. It seems to melt the rigidity of the repetitive portrayal of war. The image also seems to bring out the possibility of absorbing and integrating consciousness which previously was split and partly unconscious.

The deep emotional and verbal experience that we shared seems to illustrate the form reached through the image that corresponds to an active and free energy. Ammann (1994) has defined this emergence of the field as the birth of the "interior garden," where later on Alessandro gives himself license to open himself up to a new outlook defined by a different organization of the play space.

Alessandro continued along similar military themes. But after a month, he created a scene in which a clear unifying trend toward the middle appeared (Figure 4). He placed the soldiers from three nationalities; Japanese, American and English in the middle. He added the partitions and, between these, the grassy field and said, "The leaders are giving orders to pull back. They are doing drills, each group on their own." For the first time he did not enact a battle.

This image displayed a sense of order and definition. It shows the humanizing of the soldiers, the beginning of an integration and the adding of a gentler side to the hard and militaristic side. There are many elements to highlight but, with respect to the organization of the sandtray it seems important to stress the appearance of the center. From the center the partitions disappear which framed and organized the space into four definite parts. With such a structuring of the space, the point of reference at the center testifies to a different orientation of consciousness, which starts to be more unified and integrated.

In difficult moments, Alessandro naturally returned to the portrayal of battle scenes. But it was much easier to help him regain his ability to distinguish himself from his emotions.

After a month, there was a very important session. While showing a great fear of annihilation, Alessandro created a war scene between cowboys and Indians (Figure 5). "The enemies are armed, nobody must be seen or else he'll be blown to pieces and killed." Numerous times he returned to his moods, rage and fears, but he slowly diminished his battles and stopped to look at the scene. He said with a deep, interior voice, "It looks like a massacre; a real, live massacre."

A new expression was introduced. It "looks like" a massacre, not it "is" a massacre, which is what he would say at the beginning of our therapy together. There was an "as if" present. It was no longer an identification with the presented dynamics, but rather a possibility to observe them, distinguish them and enter into relation with them with a new word and a new voice.

In this exchange between the child and the scene, it is possible to gather a penetrating and changing force of the image. Alessandro

Figure 4

Figure 5

allows the emergence of a new level of structuring. This is in relation to consciousness and the deep content. It is also a move from the impulsive enactment to a point of observation and interpretation, discovered by Alessandro himself.

This child is always in battle, and he appears not to completely blocked and overwhelmed by the conflict. He also appears able to notice the internal, emotional dynamics, showing a distinction between himself and the game, and the emotions that might over-whelm him.

Generally, when there is a new experience in the sand that surprises us, a change is about to occur. In fact, in the frames that followed, a new theme appeared. He created a small village where automobiles and people circulated in place of armored cars and soldiers. At home and at school there was also a noticeable change in his physical and relational symptomatology.

With an occasional battle scene at difficult moments, Alessandro continued to stage village scenes with livable and recognizable contents and events. I chose the last enactment created before our summer break. Behavioral descriptions and the structural analysis of the space show how the child's interior experiences began to change after one year of analysis.

On that day, while playing with the sand in his hands, Alessandro told me that he didn't have "any ideas." But after burrowing in the

Figure 6

sand, he made a cross in the middle. The two lines – one vertical and the other horizontal – gave him a new idea. In fact he said, "An idea came to me." He worked calmly in silence (Figure 6). He built roads and placed cars, trees, and a fountain in the middle. He placed different people in the sand, pointing out to me that there is a "man who is looking at the fountain." He added more trees and the grassy field. Then, with a sigh, he said, "I'm done, I wanted to put everything in. It's only a neighborhood, just one."

Alessandro no longer appeared consumed by his emotions, nor constrained in an unlivable and restrained space as he did at the beginning of therapy. But now he seemed to have arrived in first person to the center in a peaceful and everyday life. A man was near the fountain in the center position and, placed in one neighborhood, hence much more an individual, symbolizes the presence and the centrality of the function of the ego. It is here where he can watch and express himself verbally with a new and meaningful knowledge of self.

This last image of the child seems to point to the beginning of an evolutionary phase in analysis. The evolution goes from the initial session, which displayed a chaotic and catastrophic heap, to the appearance of a new order and organization – both within the space and in consciousness – which is clearly visible in his compositions and his verbal expressions.

The changes in the composition, structural elements and, especially, in the organization of the space demonstrates in concrete terms Alessandro's active integration and deep emotional change. Here Alessandro aspires to a balance aiming toward a complete psyche. The principal enactment shows us a symbolic, archetypal form of spatial organization around the center. It offers us and the child a direction and psychic orientation toward the Self. The fountain, with its vital, pulsating water, placed in the middle of the scene shows a manifestation of the Self. It is a dynamic, inexhaustible and regenerative center. Either as a center of concentration or of outward expansion, it is the source of development toward the four directions of the space.

Sandplay in analysis with children, adolescents and adults provides a preferential space where it is possible to symbolize one's own psychic world. In Jungian thought, these geometric structures refer to internal images, energy forces and the framework of the human being. When these structures become evident, they influence the development of a person and point in search of a space for one's existence.

As Aite (1989) has pointed out, we refer to that central moment in the psychic economy in which the experienced emotion, which is still unclear, acquires a mental, representational characteristic. It is brought into "imaginative visibility." Hence, it may become recognizable.

When the unconscious dynamics of suffering become evident within the sandtray, those events that are present stimulate the possibility of distinguishing and analyzing, and thus the opening of a dialogue to confront one's own internal reality.

Of course, it is not enough to express or enact these disturbing, internal subjects; one must bring about a change in the psychic, internal order. The represented images are useful tools only in the development of consciousness. Depending on the aptitude and ability to become responsible for one's own suffering and the ability to confront the surfacing unpconscious, Sandplay can activate transformative and evolutionary responses both in the creative and destructive aspects seen during these enactments.

Translated from the original Italian by Elizabeth Teefy

References:

Aite, P. (1989). Percorsi dell'immagine: Note introduttive, *Rivista di Psicologia Analitica*, *39*, 7-15.
Ammann, R. (1994). The sandtray as a garden of the soul. *Journal of Sandplay Therapy*, *4*-1, pp. 47-65.

Training and Practice

What Constitutes a Good Jungian Analyst?

Implications for Training

Eli Weisstub
Jerusalem, Israel
Israel Association of Analytical Psychology

At the previous IAAP Congress in Zurich (1995) we dealt with the subject of "Power and Eros in Training." The present panel deals with another question basic to the training of analysts: "What constitutes a good analyst?" Our aim is not to arrive at a consensus. Rather, we seek to deal with the complexity of the question in the hope of clarifying some of the goals and ideals of analytic training. A secondary intention is to shed light on difficulties encountered in evaluating candidates and determining whether they are suitable and ready to become Jungian analysts.

The question of what constitutes a good analyst underlies the admission and evaluation processes in every training institute. Yet committees involved in training usually do not address this basic issue directly. Differences of opinion on the subject of what constitutes a "good" Jungian analyst can become the basis for conflict between training analysts, sometimes to the extent of causing a split in a Society. Such a conflict reflects differing values and beliefs about what an analyst is or should be.

Some training analysts regard training as primarily the preparation of a trainee to be a competent and responsible therapist who is able to integrate theoretical and clinical knowledge contributed by Jung and others to the field of depth psychology. Others consider the role of an analyst to be closer to that of a spiritual guide. They are concerned with symbolic, spiritual and creative development, and tend to evaluate a prospective analyst on this basis.

Most analysts would consider themselves to be "good." They tend to regard favourably their own analysands and those in control analysis with them, while they may be critical of other analysts and their candidates, especially if those candidates are perceived as belonging to another theoretical or "political" group. Problems may arise when decisions are being made to determine whether someone should be accepted for training and ultimately suitable to be certified as an analyst.

Apart from the ability to learn Jungian theory and integrate it in analytic practice, there are many other issues to consider in evaluating whether a candidate is likely to become a good analyst. It is difficult to define what a "good" analyst is. Are we to emphasize a candidate's intellectual or creative capabilities or are we primarily concerned with the ability to relate to human suffering and deal with clinical issues? Is it more important to evaluate a candidate's ability to analyze, interpret and amplify or to assess ability to be an empathic, related therapist?

Jungian analysts have differing views and convictions on what constitutes a good analyst. For the purposes of today's panel discussion, the question was left open to the interpretation of each panel participant. The panel members are experienced training analysts who have been involved in leading roles in their various training institutes. They represent differing theoretical, clinical, cultural and personal orientations.

The Necessity of Talent

Adolf Guggenbühl-Craig
Zürich, Switzerland
Schweizerische Gesellschaft fur Analytische Psychologie

To be a good Jungian analyst, I have concluded, is a talent with which, if you are lucky, you are born. A Jungian analyst is like a musician; to be an excellent musician you must have a basic musical talent. Then, of course, you can refine that talent by training. But if somebody has no talent, all the training is lost.

But what is this talent to be a good Jungian analyst? Talents are mysterious phenomena. I choose to look at this question from the purely psychological side, from the archetypal side.

We always have all the archetypes in our psyches, but some are more central and stronger; others stay in the background and hardly ever appear. The archetypes that are in the center of our psyche are, perhaps, the ones that constitute our talents. For example, a musician may be under the archetype of Apollo. In the talent to be a good

Jungian analyst we are confronted with three dominating archetypes.

The first such archetype is the healer. Oddly enough, many candidates reject this. They even say: "I am not interested in healing – only in making the patient conscious." When the archetype of the healer is powerful in the analyst, the healer in the patient is constellated.

Healing is a technique that can be learned. But the medical man or woman whose inner healer is very weak, despite a good learned technique and a wide knowledge, can do harm to the patient. Conversely, someone who is a strong inner healer often has a strong healing influence. The healer archetype must be powerful in the analyst.

The second archetype is the shaman. Officially, there are hardly any real shamans left. Classical ethnography describes the shaman as a man or a woman who is, for instance, able to leave the body, to enter and make contact with demons, with gods, with other dimensions of our human existence. Shamans usually have the ability to heal, too, but that is not their main ability. Their main ability is to get themselves and their fellow human beings in touch with more dimensions than are usual in our daily lives.

We analysts show the patients these other dimensions. For instance, we put them in touch with the unconscious. Of course, everyne is more or less in touch with the unconscious but, as the word says, this part of our psyche is largely hidden. For example, our working with dreams is based on the shaman archetype.

The shamanistic archetype has its dangers. It leads us into twilight zones. Lots of bluff, cheating and fakery go on in that twilight zone. An old North American shaman, whose name I have forgotten, was asked: "How can you recognize if somebody is a genuine shaman or just a fake?" He answered; "You can recognize a genuine shaman when he, until the day of his death, is never sure if he is a genuine shaman or not." I think this applies also to us analysts. Good analysts are never sure until the day of their deaths if they are actually fakes or genuinely good Jungian analysts.

The third archetype, which is very important and which constitutes the talent to be a good Jungian analyst, is the alchemist – as Jung understood it. In alchemy the psyche, the happenings within the psyche, and the inner figures were projected on to the outer *materia*, on the chemical processes. The alchemist became conscious by using chemical processes as symbols of psychic development. Certainly some alchemists took alchemy very concretely. They really thought they could make gold, or they thought they could find the stone of wisdom. But certainly none of them went so far as to think that, in the laboratory, Rex and Regina copulated and made love. They must have understood this symbolically.

All our psychological images and ideas are, of course, symbols. For instance, the anima designates something that cannot be described purely rationally. Our psychological language, insofar as it is really psychological, is closely related to alchemy. Nevertheless there are analysts who think concretely, just as alchemists thought they were actually able to make gold.

The alchemist archetype in us is usually described or shown in the ability to symbolize, to understand symbols. So these three archetypes – the archetype of the healer, the shaman and the alchemist – help us to be good Jungian analysts.

There is a fourth dimension to our work which is usually taken for granted. A good Jungian analyst has to have a very strong moral side. As Jung said: "Die Moral versteht sich von selbst" (morals are taken as a matter of course).

The importance of morality in our work is shown in the nearly feverish activities in our profession to evaluate our work mainly from the ethical point of view: to have ethical committees, to have ethical guidelines, and to take actions when we think the ethical guidelines are transgressed. I begin increasingly to think that this activity around ethical guidelines does more harm than good.

What does it mean when I say that to be a good Jungian analyst is really a talent? I cannot go into detail here, but I find generally that training should be less rigid, to make it freer and to have fewer regulations. Anyone who has the talent to be a good Jungian analyst will be glad for any help in developing that talent, but such a person does not need innumerable rules and regulations because of the inner drive to develop the specific form of the prospective analyst's own talent.

We need less compulsion in training. We should offer the people who have a talent to be Jungian analysts more opportunities to develop this talent, but we should lower our minimal requirements. For instance, we should reduce the compulsory hours for personal analysis. Only the candidate can know how much analysis is needed; it may be 800 or it may be 200 hours.

The clinical training is given much emphasis in all our institutes. There are many rules and regulations in this field. Yet, if the inner healer is very strong, the candidate is extremely interested in sickness and in healing and does not need many precise rules and regulations.

One conclusion has to be drawn from my reflections, namely that the selection of future analysts is more important than the precise compulsory organisation of the training. We must receive with open arms the ones who have talent and refuse the ones who have no talent.

But this is not so easy. Maybe people who have a decided talent to be good Jungian analysts themselves are better at selecting people with this talent than the ones who have no talent or very little. Unfortunately we have among ourselves many who have very little talent but, by our rigorous training, have acquired the illusion that they possess talent; these people may then select other untalented candidates.

I said that three archetypes constitute a good Jungian analyst: the healer, the shaman and the alchemist. It is unfortunate that the genuine shaman is not sure all his life of being a genuine shaman or a fake. Thus, we have a difficult profession. We always have to search and can never be sure if we are doing the right thing. Our profession is a fascinating adventure.

A Reliable Jungian Analyst

Kathleen Newton
London, England
Society of Analytical Psychology

I have reservations about the word "good" in our title. I prefer the word "reliable." For me, the quality of our analytic work depends on our capacity to relate in depth to our analysands: providing a relationship with a containing space in which the analysand's intrapsychic dynamics can come into play and be expressed inter-personally. Our different ways of doing this depend both upon the nature of the conflicts that the analysand brings and who we are as persons, in relation to our own inner conflicts.

Jung's hypothesis of the self as our totality, with its own regulat-ing centre that brings about a conscious/unconscious dialectic, is central for me. Michael Fordham's amplification in terms of the

primary self and the archetypal and personal dynamics in development, has enabled us to think of this dialectic as a process continuing
throughout our lives. Given this model, one factor in the way we
relate to our analysands depends on what quality of ego integration
we have achieved. This in turn will influence which theoretical
models we can resonate to and use creatively in our work. Knowledge, whilst it can be intellectually stimulating – if emotionally
undigested – is unlikely to be fruitful in an analytic relationship.
Here I refer to Jung's statement:

> *The patient by bringing an activated unconscious content to bear*
> *upon the doctor, constellates the corresponding unconscious mate-*
> *rial in him owing to the induction which always emanates from*
> *projections in greater or lesser degree. Doctor and patient thus find*
> *themselves in a relationship founded on mutual unconsciousness.*
> *(CW16, 364).*

Jung went on to say that, in this situation, it is vital that the analyst
find a conscious position so that a process evolves in which both
change. He opened the inter-relatedness of the archetypal and
personal dimensions, and elaborated on the challenge to the analyst
to stay related to the process – which involves a considerable
emotional burden – and not withdraw behind a professional persona.
Thus, Jung enlarged on the depth of the challenge to work with the
countertransference, although he did not use that term. He linked
this discussion to the opposites and the conjunctio in alchemical
symbolism. The concept of projective identification has been valuable in increasing our understanding of, and ways of working with,
the unconscious bond that Jung describes.

There are many different ways that we as Jungians relate to and
develop Jung's ideas. Samuels (1985) has explored this in detail.
These differences can lead to creative clashes and widening perspectives, or to splitting, if certain approaches are passionately identified
with as the only way to be a "Good Jungian Analyst." I think it is
generally accepted today that the developments in ideas amongst
both Jungians and psychoanalysts make it possible to remain rooted
in Jung's metapsychology whilst also making creative use of other
approaches. Here, of course, we all need to find our own orientations, as influenced by our psychopathology.

What has all this to do with our title and our training? Given that
a central professional aim is to be involved in a healing process, we
are all vulnerable to idealising our roles; being a "Good Jungian

Analyst" could play into a persecutory ideal and inhibit our capacity to address and work with our feeling responses. These involve us in the opposites: positive and negative affects in the conscious/unconscious interplay with the analysand, including times of not knowing, times of misunderstanding, times when it is important to stay with projections and contain experience of depression and failure – which may then be weathered with the analysand – and moments of satisfaction with a deeper sense of integration.

Staying and working with these vicissitudes illustrate for me some aspects of what constitutes a reliable Jungian analyst. I am aware that there are many other factors involved. In training, the combination of a personal analysis, supervision and seminars seems vital. Clearly the seminars need to provide a good grounding in Jung's metapsychology and the many ways in which his ideas have been clinically applied and developed. It is important, also, that seminars by different seminar leaders include the ways in which psychoanalytic ideas have been found clinically fruitful. In this way, trainees will be introduced to many different channels of understanding, which will be challenging and at times confusing. The positive aspect however, is that trainees will have to work to individuate and find a personally valid position in relation to their analysands' material. Thus, they must realise that they are involved in an ongoing process which will open up avenues of understanding rather than giving final answers.

Finally, our search for meaning involves us in the challenge to an ongoing individuation process both in our lives and in our work. Here I am thinking of a spiral: the process in which we deepen our ego position both in relation to our inner world dynamics and to cultural patterns in the outer world. The remark Jung has been quoted as saying that is "I am so glad I am Jung and not a Jungian" seems relevant. He seems to be saying that, although we can be enriched by his creativity, the last thing he wants is that we should stay exclusively identified with him, rather than finding our own orientations.

The Analyst and the Client's Individuation Process

Nairo de Souza Vargas
Sao Paulo, Brazil
Sociedade Brasileira de Psicologia Analitica

A good Jungian analyst is the result of a series of variables, some constitutional and some acquired. Those with a genetic basis are sensibility, interest and attachment to the human being. Add to these technical knowledge, ethical development and a wide humanistic culture. Such are the basic ingredients, probably, for the formation of any good therapist. Our task is to distinguish what would be desirable for a good Jungian analyst specifically.

What characterizes the Jungian analyst is the concept that, through the archetypes that produce symbols, the human being is searching for individuation, trying to reach one's potential and to become oneself. The Jungian analyst should have an open mind for all possibilities of individuation without preconceived ideas about what the process of individuation should be, or in what way an individual should live.

This openness, which brings enormous richness to Analytical Psychology, is nevertheless its weak point. For this reason, more than any other, a Jungian analyst must have solid ethical and professional training and is expected to have a keen sense of differentiation. Otherwise this great openness and freedom will become an excuse for an attitude of "anything goes." Everything could be justified as being "my way of individuation" or "my moment" or "in my typology" or "following my symbols."

Sensitivity, common sense, maturity and a sound knowledge of psychotherapy can help a great deal, but the understanding of the process as a whole always will be a difficult and risky process. More than the facts, it is the careful analysis of how, for whom, and when they are being lived – the personality and symbols of the client as a whole – that will give us the answers.

A good Jungian analyst will work with one eye on the unconscious and another on the conscious mind of the client and, likewise, one will look toward oneself and the link with the client. The most difficult science and art for a good Jungian analyst may be the ability to keep "to the middle of the road": not to take a one-sided position.

Sensitivity and symbolic thinking are some of the most needed characteristics for the Jungian analyst. It is a necessary condition that one should be able to expand, respect, value and live out one's symbols, in order to be able to help clients to do the same. It is basic for a qualified professional to be prepared to perceive, to value and to deal with transference bilaterally. In order to accomplish this, the analyst must have gone through a good process of analysis as well as supervision, in addition to formal education. Therefore, it is important that a good Jungian analyst should have self-assurance, a certain degree of self-assertion and life-fulfillment, in order to cope with clients' projections which can carry rejection, aggressiveness and seduction. The analyst should have an open mind also, along with determination and courage to deal with a client's shadow – which can be revolting and destructive.

Good Jungian analysts differ in their theoretical approaches and techniques, some making more use of resources available through their natural skills, others more through technical and professional training. To characterise oneself as a Jungian analyst, however, one must recognise in the life of each human being a process of individual development. Such a process depends on potential archetypes and genetic peculiarities and on the specific environmental factors of each person's world, as well as psycho-emotional experiences and social-cultural background. This amazing complex of variables does not interact by chance. There is a sense of search that leads to the development of each person's potential. Although this search archetypally exists in every human being, not everyone realises it and very few use it to its full extent, although it is an important factor in a lesser or major degree in the structuring of one's life.

The good Jungian analyst helps the client to self-knowledge, in transcending defences and symptoms: adjusting to a larger reality, being able to recognise limits and not wishing to go beyond the client's possibilities but not falling short of these possibilities. Such an analyst will need to study a great deal: to learn about human biology and psychology as well as acquire a wide knowledge of humanistic culture, in order to see the human being as a whole that can manifest itself and be approached in a wide variety of ways.

A good Jungian analyst must be able to diagnose situations in which the psychological approach may be limited, insufficient or even blocked, and when the use of medication is necessary or other measures: counseling or teamwork with other professionals such as psychiatrists, occupational therapists, medical doctors. The analyst will use any other resource that is available through professional training and technical background.

Psychotherapy must adjust itself to the client. Thus, a good analyst must be able to diagnose and offer the best for the development of the client. It is important, also, to point out another characteristic of a good Jungian analyst: the ability to detect the client's need, wish and capability for further analysis and development. The therapist must attend to the client's wishes and possibilities and not to the therapist's own expectations. It is an essential characteristic of a good Jungian analyst to recognise and respect the limits and expectations of the client as well as to take into account his own limitations, avoiding thus to act in a therapeutic furor.

Another consideration is that there is no such thing as a good Jungian analyst for every client. The link between analyst and client is essential, each "deserving" the other. Most important is that this encounter should be true and creative: the main factor of healing and transformation.

A good Jungian analyst may experience changes during the life span; one's characteristics may be altered with losses and gains. Consequently, a good analyst must evaluate whether he or she is the adequate analyst for that specific client in that particular moment of both their lives: whether there is a significant encounter both consciously and unconsciously.

The question of a good analyst must be considered in a relative way, taking into account the link analyst-analysand and not the analyst alone. It is the link that must be good, adequate, effective and creative.

Some Thoughts from the Belly of the Beast

Lyn Cowan
St. Paul, Minnesota, USA
Inter-Regional Society of Jungian Analysts

The topic could be stated: What is a good analyst like? The first image that came to me was an alchemist in modern dress, preoccupied with modern questions and problems, willing to experiment with nature even at great risk, but not having a clue about how to change anything. This alchemist appears on the surface somewhat demented, a bit disheveled, and worries about the laboratory's blowing up. The alchemist sits up late at night plotting to overthrow the status quo that is conventional psychology and mainstream thinking, concocting new ways to practice in a world increasingly hostile to psyche, feels occasionally persecuted and ineffective, suffers from lack of recognition for the good work being done in that dim subterranean laboratory, and wonders daily why one went into this line of work.

Having been given this image, my focus is on the subversive aspect of analysis and training. To the extent that analysis works to bring about radical changes in attitude, it is a work of subversion – in the service of psyche. Ours is a psychology that poses a threat to established values and assumptions, that works toward a chronic discontent with the status quo. It is a sub-versive psychology – not only turning experience under to get at the roots but attempting to change culture through individual change.

In a 1929 essay, Jung wrote: "My aim is to bring about a psychic state in which my patient begins to experiment with his own nature – a state of fluidity, change, and growth where nothing is eternally fixed and hopelessly petrified" (CW6, 99). Thus, a good analyst practices subversion by experimenting with one's own nature and the nature of patients. This idea is no less radical now than it was in 1929, because it is truly alchemical in design and intent: to effect change by experimenting with nature, creatively, and without knowing exactly what one is doing. This approach is not acceptable to the status quo, not in conformity with the medical model, not acceptable to traditional psychotherapeutic theories and practices, and appalling to insurance companies in the United States.

An analyst who practices subversively to foster radical change in the patient knows that stasis, entropy, and inertia are synonyms for psychic death. At its best, Jungian psychology – as practiced through analysis – can become the life-giving shadow of the conventional profession of psychology.

In addition to my private analytic practice, I am a professor of psychology at a graduate school offering a doctorate in professional psychology. The best way I can describe what this is like for me, as the only depth psychologist on the faculty, is to say that I work in the belly of the beast. All my faculty colleagues are cognitive behaviorists and developmentalists who are hard-working, compassionate individuals, but who collectively are members of a profession that is, in America, paranoid about original thinking, terrified of malpractice lawsuits, and enslaved by managed care and insurance companies.

In the belly of this beast I see it as my mission to stir up as much trouble as possible, to radicalize students as best I can. I keep prodding them to know themselves as well as they know how to score assessment tests. I alarm them often by suggesting that there are ways to be psychological and to practice which may be unacceptable to their clinical supervisors, their professors, their employers, their licensing boards, but which may be life-saving to patients and to the collective psyche. I regale them with stories of all the failures and failings and misconduct of the revered giants of the field – including Jung – in the hope they will find the courage to be who they truly are as clinicians, and not just wear the conventional persona of professionalism. My purpose is to let them know that there is a large shadow cast by our profession – a shadow of power, greed, ineptitude, and distrust – and then to remind them that there are also limitless possibilities for creative change in that shadow. I keep trying to help them see that they, too, are in the belly of the beast, and we must help each other to survive, by subversion if necessary.

There are many people who disregard Jungian psychology and the practice of analysis because they think it is unscientific, or occult, or theoretically dense. But the real reason for their disregard or hostility is that a psychology of depth poses a vital threat to the status quo. Analysis is one very effective way an individual life takes all the traditional values, takes the conventional perception of the world and one's place in it, and subverts it, turns it under so that the hidden parts of life, the roots and source, may be examined in privacy, slowly and with care. Alchemy calls this process the "corruption" of the material in the vessel, and much of Jungian analysis works through corruption.

The idea of subversion, with its political overtones and associations of instability and revolution, has itself been cast into the shadow. Anyone undertaking to work in shadowy areas – certainly including Jungian analysts, their analysands and candidates – takes on some of the characteristics of the subversive: a growing discontent, if not outrage, against collective systems that are damaging to individual life; a deepening resistance to majority thinking (even when one agrees with it); new survival skills within one's profession; and the ability to live one's real life "underground," keeping the new changes of great value hidden from profane and persecuting eyes. One begins almost to lead a double life, one above ground going about in the world making a living, giving out business cards, collecting fees, making love, all that – and another life deeply subverted underground. Both lives are eminently real, each of critical importance: not a paranoid dualism, but a doubleness.

Doubleness means neither duplicity nor oppositional dualisms. A good subversive analyst has a sort of double vision which is clear sightedness of two or more visions. There is a paradox in this, of course. Though much of the work we do as analysts may be corrupting and subversive and intent upon radical change, we also live as pretty ordinary people; at least most of us aren't criminals.

Jung noted that the unconscious psyche is, paradoxically, both conservative and creative. On the one hand, he said the collective psychic heritage of our species is made up of the accretions of millennia – instincts, functions, archaic forms and reactions. As an "intricate web of achetypal conditions," said Jung, "the unconscious is seen as the collective predisposition to extreme conservatism, a guarantee, almost, that nothing new will ever happen" (CW16, 99).

He went right on to say, "If this statement were unreservedly true, there would be none of that creative fantasy which is responsible for radical changes and innovations. ... Generally speaking, [such a change or innovation] is an intrusion from the realm of the uncon-scious, a sort of lucky hunch, different in kind from the slow reasoning of the conscious mind. Thus the unconscious is seen as a creative factor, even as a bold innovator, and yet it is at the same time the stronghold of ancestral conservatism. A paradox, I admit, but it cannot be helped" (CW16, 61).

Jung saw analysis as something of a paradox, too: The doctor attempts to help the patient to a normal and reasonable life, working toward an adaptation to reduce suffering and increase a sense of well-being. But ideas of "normal" and "reasonable" are social constructs, not *a priori* categories. And so Jung advises, more than once, that we must "follow nature as a guide," and "what the doctor then does is less a question of treatment than of developing the creative possibilities latent in the patient" (CW16, 82).

Now, anytime you encourage creative possibilities in an individ-ual you are being a good analyst, and you are also encouraging subversion, because creative possibilities rarely are used to maintain the status quo, either in individual or collective life.

It is the psyche's creativity that does the subverting in the end, not the analyst or Jungian theory. I am referring here to the wild creativity of spontaneous imagination, of fresh images invading in bizarre, outrageous, amazing, sometimes shocking ways, but which bring dramatic new themes and scenarios for one's life, one's future, one's abilities, one's capacity to love – possibilities of profoundly changing one's sense of oneself.

Training should be as subversive as analysis. Individuals who have been well corrupted in their personal analysis make the best candidates because they already suspect that training is not to be taken literally, and have a beginning recognition that a training program represents the persona of the training institute, not necessarily its soul. If a candidate goes into training with this subversive attitude, then the training process may indeed be a profoundly transformative experience – for every good training program is a mess of paradox, and thus offers wonderful and terrifying opportunities for psyche to thrive.

Some of these paradoxes of training include the eternal question of how analysts can be objective in evaluating candidates in a process that is essentially subjective: how to set collective standards in a program designed to enhance individual difference, how to examine the invisible; how to know when a candidate is "ready" to finish training when there seems to be no true "end."

We here have all been through training. Those who are involved in training others know that it is practically impossible to do good training – or even to know just what training is. Fortunately, this hasn't stopped us from trying. And we need to continue trying to do the impossible precisely because this is one of the ways we continue the necessary subversion of our own ideas and methods and assumptions about training. The paradox here is that, through training, we help to subvert and overthrow the ruling consciousness of that training program, of that institute, of the profession, of the culture. No matter how valid or well-loved those conscious attitudes may be, at some point they must be subverted and perhaps even thrown away, or else nothing new can enter. We know this from myths and fairy tales, that the dying king must be replaced by a new king or queen. And the analyst with a subversive eye will recognize that sometimes the new attitude enters through deception, but is no less vital and legitimate for that.

We ought to encourage difficult candidates to be difficult We ought to teach candidates to be subversive, to cultivate a double life, to remind them that training is not what it seems and we do not always intend what we require. We ought to encourage candidates to keep looking at the underside, the shadow side of our training as well as their own personal psychology, and to see in that darkness a rare chance to instigate a small individual psychological revolution that some day might change the world.

My father was an artist who drew comic books for a living. In the 1950s in America this was considered a subversive activity. The United States was choked with fear about communist plots to overthrow America by subverting American youth. In those years there was a powerful committee in Congress called the House Un-American Activities Committee, which decided that comic books caused juvenile delinquency and made the youth of America vulnerable to communist propaganda. Reading comic books, said the old congressmen, destroyed moral fiber and the innocence of youth and turned children instantly into violent, godless revolutionaries. Well, like millions of other kids, I read comic books as part of my literary diet, and I can tell you, more than 40 years later, that Congress completely misread the source of my corruption. Comic books had nothing to do with the fact that, by the age of 11, I was already having creative fantasies about overthrowing everything that was making me crazy: dress codes at school, anti-Semitism, rules for being a girl that warped my self-image, the whole oppressing conformity by which we all had to live. The very values Congress was trying to preserve drove me psychologically underground, where some years later I found myself in Jungian analysis, far more corrupted by that process than by any comic book I ever read.

I know it may sound strange, but when I die, I hope the question of whether I was a good analyst or not will be measured by how subversively I tried to live and how many people I successfully corrupted.

The Naked Truth

Gustav Bovensiepen
Cologne, Germany
Deutsche Gesellschaft für Analytische Psychologie

In recent years, I have been preoccupied with what I would like to impart to the trainees as the most important element in analysis, and where, in my own work as an analyst, I have the most difficulty. It is not hard to see that these two questions are closely related. The reason for this is my belief that a large part of what I am trying to achieve as an analyst, the ideals I am striving to impart to the trainees, stems from exactly those problems with which I am confronted in my own work: How do we come into a close emotional contact with the inner world of the patient? This question concerns the essence of analytic method, as I currently understand it, and distinguishes analysis from non-analytic therapy.

A clinical vignette may help clarify the problem with which I am frequently confronted. With one of my former patients, I constantly had the feeling that I never really reached him. He told me numerous dreams and fantasies, had "appropriate" associations and seemed to be intensely engaged in the project of working on himself. Nevertheless, I never lost the sense that he was only "acting" analysis. He also reported on his progress and it seemed that the analysis was becoming more and more important to him, while I was plagued increasingly by dissatisfaction and boredom. He frequently countered my interpretations by adding comments such as: "Yes, but ..." or "Another aspect would be ..." We often discussed my impression that his real expectation of analysis was less the solution of his personal problems than the secret wish to have his false healer-self sanctioned by an authoritative Jungian analyst-father. Such discussions, however, had no recognisable effect. One day, he came to the session, lay down on the couch, assumed his usual, strained thinker-position, with a hand on his forehead, and remained silent. While he was lying there like that, I suddenly had the feeling that the patient smelled of faeces, that there was an unsympathetic, stinking person: an ageing little boy, who had shit in his pants! My sense of smell and the image were so powerful that I could hardly step back from it. And while I was thinking about why I had to depreciate the patient in such a way, he began to talk and the stink was suddenly gone. In the ensuing hour, the patient proceeded to talk very touchingly about his inner emptiness, and that he had felt like a piece of shit his entire life.

This little episode serves to illustrate that my primary concern in analysis is to partake in and absorb the emotional truth, the psychic reality, the inner experiences of the patient as directly as possible. This attitude may be a self-evident prerequisite of our profession. Nevertheless, I have the impression that, because of our training, we have an extraordinary number of possibilities in analytic situations to fight against, to evade, and to protect ourselves from being woven too closely into the fabric of the patient's inner world. This complex problem has to do with what Jung referred to as the necessity of the analyst's being "infected" by the patient. This is only part of the problem, however, and Jung himself explained it in symbolic rather than in clinical terms, describing the situation to which I am referring with the third picture of the *Rosarium Philosophorum*, "The Naked Truth." The couple sits facing one another, naked: "The chaste disguises have fallen away" (CW16, 450-451). Jung interpreted this phase of the *Rosarium* according to the psychology of the shadow.

If measured against the alchemical/analytic grand opus of individuation, this confrontation with the shadow may strike one as nothing but an initial difficulty. For two reasons, however, this confrontation can present a strong obstacle to becoming a "good" analyst. First, in the analytic setting, the realisation of one's own bodily reality and domination by one's instinctual urges can be irritating. Second, the "primitive or archaic psyche," as Jung called it, activates primitive fears, affects, and fantasies not only in the patient, but also in the analyst. The integration of the shadow is not easy, and it is already a big step if I, as a busy therapist, can get to know and appreciate my shadow.

I interpret Jung's term of the "naked truth" in the *Rosarium* as the immensely difficult intuition of the patient's psychic reality, without having to resort to disguises in the form of thoughts or image representations. To stay within the confines of my example, the fact that the patient stinks is not a perception of the senses, but rather an intuition of his shame. Shame does not smell or taste, is invisible and can be perceived only indirectly.

From the point of view of therapy technique, the intuitive registration of psychic reality presupposes, above all, the precise perception and observation, as personal and as detailed as possible, of what the patient communicates to me and of what I detect within myself, namely my own bodily feelings, emotions, and finally fantasies. I do not conceive of precise observation and perception as taking place under a neutral, "scientific" microscope. Rather, these elements form a relationary process, which facilitates personal access to the patient, without prematurely distancing oneself from the "true" experiences of the patient through interpretation, amplification or other interventions, as "correct" as these may be. The process of precise perception already represents a form of containment. But what is "true"? I cannot answer this question objectively, but can search for it primarily in the responses of the patient to my communications.

The analyst who succeeds in this type of precise observation and perception can develop "freedom of thought": the notion that I can form my own thoughts from my perceptions, instead of having to rely prematurely on ready-made concepts, theories, or even metaphors and images. If successful, this process can lead to joint thinking in each unique analytic situation, a thinking that can further the joy of discovery between the analytic couple. Having said all this, I do not mean to deny that theoretical equipment is necessary as well as often helpful. My own difficulty with it, however, lies in needing to leave it out, rather than in employing it. It intrudes between me and the patient all too easily, particularly since the naked psychic reality is often so difficult to bear.

If the goal of individuation has something to do with self-knowledge, then it consists in the search for the truth about oneself. This process requires, first of all, a considerable amount of curiosity and, subsequently, the ability to endure one's own psychic reality, which can unfold in the here and now of the analytic situation but which, at the same time, can hide so easily that it is often very difficult to grasp it.

One might object here that this is valid for any analytic therapy, not just for a Jungian one. It is true that Jung and many Jungians seem more interested in the search for transpersonal truth, in the sense of gnosis or of the alchemists, than in the search for personal truth. The search for transpersonal truth is one for which I harbour a deep respect. It is also one that probably does not exclude the search for personal truth. Nevertheless, I do believe that the objective psyche – like the personal one – can spin a web of tricksterlike "lies" (Bion 1984) around itself in order to hide its true, inner reality. This fact certainly does not facilitate our efforts to become "good" Jungian analysts.

A Well-Seated Clinician

Christian Gaillard

Paris, France
Société Francaise de Psychologie Analytique

Sitting in my office, reflecting on this good and difficult question: "What constitutes a good Jungian analyst?" Reflecting not without difficulty. Sitting ... seated ... And the first answer that came to me, and then pressed itself upon me, is that a (good) Jungian analyst is a well-seated clinician.

That we are clinicians seems to go without saying. Those who come to us suffer from diverse handicaps and disorders that are too costly for them, or for those around them. They hope and expect that their work with us will liberate them, allowing an opening in their lives and giving them new or renewed momentum for moving forward. If our work is one of listening, as we repeat often, it is truly also one of treatment, of accompaniment and aid to a life seeking, as best it can, to fulfill itself.

More precisely, since the words "clinical" and "clinician" come from the Greek "klinein" which means "to lie down" or "to be lying down," let us recall that many of us use the couch. I myself use it very often, although less with analysts in training. The difficulty lies in finding a way to insure that the work of an analysand seated in an armchair offers all the advantages of work done lying on a couch. And this is no small difficulty.

Thus, the Jungian analyst is a clinician in the most concrete sense of this term. This statement is no scoop, but it is useful to recall. For this means that analysis is a profession. And it is not – or not only – a philosophy, a *Weltanschauung* (world-view), or an inner experience. It is a profession that requires specific qualities and qualifications. A (good) Jungian analyst must prove to be first a (good) clinician.

But why did I hear myself say that a (good) Jungian analyst is a well-seated analyst? For I know well that Jung often received his patients by the lake of Zurich – especially when the weather was warm, or warm enough for the beetles to be flying. And that Jacques Lacan sometimes received his patients for an analytic session, in a taxi, which contributed to relaxing his conception of the length of the sessions.

In spite of such examples, which are impressive, I observe that in our French Jungian Society we rarely advise our analysts in training to practice analysis while strolling along the Seine, or riding in a car – even though in a car one normally is seated. Why so rarely? Because it is not really so easy to be well-seated, in the right place.

This is rarely the case in a taxi. And if you intervene with your body, or even your hand, in the life of your patients – even if it is seemingly for their own good – you will have a hard time remaining well-seated in your chair. Indeed, what does it mean for an analyst to be "well-seated" in an armchair?

To be well-seated is to find a position whose center of gravity is rather low, and toward the rear. One's attention is open, and sometimes even lively but in retreat; my body is then hollowed. This position allows me to resonate, to hear and feel the echoes, within myself, of what is said to me, or of that which I perceive. I am a well-seated clinician. I do not know if I am "good." But I now live the sensation function more fully and perhaps better than in my everyday life. I am speaking, of course, of introverted sensation.

This position may allow me the best use of my feeling function. Concerning feeling, I have long heard with an obscure but insistent wariness the phrase of the alchemists which is so often applied directly to analysts: "ars requirit totum hominem" (art requires the whole person). Isn't this forgetting that the alchemists often rashly burned hand or soul at their furnace? and for pure loss? and to their own ruin? and even quite wrongly? Isn't this mostly forgetting that feeling which lives in and through the introverted sensation of the well-seated clinician is interrogative feeling, feeling that asks questions, that wonders what we have here, that thus constantly assesses and judges the situation, and that is in the process of becoming?

When feeling is thus in place, I do not carry myself so much toward the other person who is there with a request and even momentary suffering. Rather, more radically, I give all my attention and all my care to that which is emerging in what the person is saying, which may or may not be desired by either of us – to that which is emerging and embodied between us, as a curious third party, which is working at its own speed, with its own means and its own point of view.

I have noticed that, through this way of practising sensation and feeling, which one learns, the (good) Jungian analyst acquires a good practice of breathing. Like the long-distance runner, the swimmer, or the mountaineer. The analyst learns to take time, to watch things come in from a distance, sometimes from far in the past, and to accompany one in a long-term evolution. The intuition, in fact, is then at work.

It is, I think, through this way of exercising intuition well-inscribed in the body that the Jungian analyst differs most radically from the Freudian. For that which concerns us and mobilizes us is less the accomplishment of desire than the accomplishment of the self. Less "WånscherfÅllung" (wish-fulfillment) than "Selbstver-wirklichung" (self-realization). Thus we find ourselves at the heart of an astonished participation in an on-going story that fulfills itself on the scale of a human life, and a transgenerational scale as well. That gives one's breath back, and makes one humble in the present.

But, you may ask, what about thinking? We have mentioned sensation, feeling and intuition, so where is thinking? I am not very concerned about the thinking function of the (good) Jungian analyst, I must confess. For three reasons. The first is that it is always a good thing to make thinking wait for a while. Thinking always has a tendency to hurry, and this is not good for the achievement we are seeking.

The second reason is that it is well known today that a (good) Jungian analyst – just as a (good) musician, painter, sculptor, or architect – can no longer be content with feeling without understanding. As for us, we are supposed to have known that since 1916, when Jung wrote about the "transcendent function."

The third and main reason is that these days, indeed, analytic practice – especially Jungian practice, like the arts – makes one intelligent. A (good) Jungian analyst who was not very intelligent at the outset would almost necessarily become so with experience. Thinking is one means of giving form to the unknown that we encounter, so as to recognize it better and communicate it to others. This is one of the advantages of turning our back squarely, as we do, on any sort of orthodoxy; the work of the thinking function of each of us must, now, make itself creative.

It remains for us to wonder if Jung himself was a (good) Jungian analyst in the diverse ways that I have described. Perhaps he wasn't always. Perhaps not at every moment of his life and of his work. It is for you to decide if this would be a shame or, on the contrary, a comfort, or even a reason to rejoice.

Translated from the original French by Leslie de Galbert

Analytic Training and the Freedom to Think
JoAnn Culbert-Koehn
Beverly Hills, California, USA
Society of Jungian Analysts of Southern California

My decision to become a Jungian analyst came from my experience of being a patient. In 1975, I had just given birth to my second child, and my marriage was in trouble. The marital difficulties had stimulated my desire for analysis three years previously. One day I went to my analyst with a specific dream after a break in the analysis. I remember him saying to me, "I'm not a dream machine. You need to be serious about this work and make up your mind if you are committed to analysis."

Initially, I was hurt that this man I respected thought I was treating him mechanically, since that was not the way I felt about him or the work. I soon realized that working with dreams the way Jung and my analyst did was very important to me. It gave me a broader view of my life and made me more aware of the depth of my feelings. To me, becoming a Jungian analyst meant being committed to a relationship with the personal and collective unconscious and mediating this relationship for others in a way that facilitates growth and development.

I began training when I was 32 and finished when I was 40. I was fortunate to have powerful and important analytic experiences during that time with a number of analysts though, at the time, having a number of analysts didn't seem fortunate. My first analyst died two years into the training, the next two moved away, and the fourth retired. As one of them put it, "You got a lot of experience working on your separation complex." Each of my analysts' personalities, as well as their analytic skills, had an impact on me and the course of my life. I think it is hard to imagine that one can become a passionate analyst unless one has had a transformative experience of the analytic process. Therefore, I see one's personal analysis as the cornerstone of training.

In my early thirties, I was affected by *Memories, Dreams, Reflections* and by Jung's essay on "Marriage as a Psychological Relationship." The curious, intense, serious way Jung approached his life and work impressed me. The memory he reports from early adolescence of the image of the turd falling on the roof of the cathedral in Basel exemplifies his courage in the face of psychic pain. So does the process of his break with Freud. I think it is essential for an effective analyst to tolerate, endure and respect intense psychic pain.

Implications for Training

1) Since I doubt that a curious and passionate relationship with the unconscious can be taught, I propose this relationship as a requirement for admission to training. Since both passion and curiosity can be dulled by an environment which does not encourage freedom of thought, we have a responsibility to provide training in which these capacities are nurtured.

2) The capacity to bear intense psychic pain can be increased through the experience of analysis and supervision in which primitive affect is engaged, contained and metabolized.

3) The capacity to bear not knowing is important. Analysis and supervision that are dominated by the analyst's need to be all-knowing, worshipped or narcissistically fed are counter-productive.

4) Jung developed his theory of typology to explain individual differences. He said explicitly that he was a Freudian analyst with one patient, an Adlerian with another. Yet I have been witness to candidates' being discouraged from reading psychoanalytic theory other than Jung. This lack of respect for differences is counter to the curiosity and freedom of thought necessary for growth and development, and dishonors the intent of Jung's typological theory.

5) Certain functions and typologies tend to be idealized in training, particularly introversion and intuition, while the development of other functions and extraversion is neglected. In my own community, analysts have skills to help develop intuitive and feeling functions, but they often try to think for their patients rather than helping them to develop this capacity.

Jones (1995) sees one of the tasks of analysis as helping the patient develop the ability to think:

culminating in the achievement of a certain type of mindfulness that leads to a deeply felt appreciation of life, including its tragic aspects. ... Helping the patient learn how to think, however, is radically different from telling him what to think. What is critical is that the analyst, in his heart, truly value the independent mind of the patient. If he does this, then the technique will probably follow; if he doesn't, then no amount of silence can possibly hide the fact and salvage the analysis. (pp. 219-220)

It is imperative that our trainees receive a training and an analysis in which their independence of mind, heart and spirit is valued, so that they can offer this to future analysands and trainees.

6) The ability to wait is a fundamental component of an analytic attitude. In the film "The Horse Whisperer," Robert Redford plays a horse trainer who works with traumatized horses. In one scene in the movie, the horse, retraumatized by the intrusive ringing of a cell phone in the corral, has bolted and run away. The trainer/analyst waits quietly at a distance. He plants himself firmly where the horse can see him and he can see the horse, but he moves no further. He is available but does not intrude. The light of the afternoon shifts; the trainer waits You sense his reverie, his deep quiet knowledge of the horse's nature, and his sense of the horse's painful trauma. As the sun goes down, the horse returns. We as analysts work with repressed, traumatized, dissociated, or perverted instinct. Even a healthy feeling or thinking function may be shy and need a slow, steady, non-intrusive waiting by the analyst to emerge.

Singer (1982) wrote about the training of Jungian analysts:

> *But growth is not always apparent, and like a seed in winter, the would-be analyst often has to endure long periods of inaction, of aimless waiting, of confusion, and of being in the dark. It is necessary at times to just 'let it be,' and analysts who cannot tolerate this in themselves cannot be expected to supply the patient husbandry that the analysand will require when the time comes. (p. 370)*

I included this quote in the write-up of my control case. Now, with fourteen additional years of experience, Singer's words, along with the image of the horse whisperer firmly planted on his own emotional earth and thoughtfully waiting, speak to me of the essence of our work.

References

Bion, W.R. (1984). *Attention and Interpretation*. London: Maresfield Reprints.
Jones, J. (1995). *Affects as Process*. Hillsdale, NJ: Analytic Press.
Samuels, A. (1985). *Jung and the Post-Jungians*. London: Routledge & Kegan Paul.
Singer, J. (1982). The education of the analyst. In M. Stein (Ed.), *Jungian Analysis*. La Salle, IL: Open Court.

Panel: Poisons and Panaceas in Analytic Training

Harry Fogarty
New York, New York, USA
New York Association for Analytical Psychology

Our approach to the formation (training) of analysts combines, to a large degree, unconscious complexes and canonical professional positions. Not quite the clone approach. Not quite the fully conscious approach we claim. As an example, consider that our training with regard to issues of professional practice and ethics has evolved less as profound reflections on various koan-like sayings from Jung, and more as reactive correctives inspired by litigation and other heightened public concerns. Thus, the process of formation morally obliges training institutes and faculty as educators in ways rarely acknowledged. Jung held that educational processes risk moral bankruptcy unless the educator's shadow and propensity to displace unresolved issues onto students has been metabolized consciously.

Training and formation are not clear endeavors to which we can aspire without major disagreements and confusions. The one-sided attitude "the faculty knows" is belied by the reality recurrently discovered that training and formation are and only can be dialogic. Such dialog occurs on at least three levels: 1) within the individual as needs and potentials become dynamically alive; 2) between the individual and the institute as well as within the institute as it engages the individual; and 3) between the institute and the individual as cultural and societal shifts are encountered.

The fundamental paradigm for a personal analysis, as suggested by Jung, is one in which the process has a life of its own and the material of the individual as well as of the analyst, each and together, manifest the objective psyche. Thus, as with St. Paul's description of "charisms" and collective life (I Corinthians 12:4-13:13), each person's process has its own distinctive charism or gift and voice. Each, in turn, must be held in a tension of multiples: intersubjective mutuality with other voices and collectives. Boal (1995), the theoretician of theater, would have us view training processes, and institute structures, only as dialogic encounters in which the essentials arise continuously within the process, from the engagement of all participants as equals possessing distinct gifts. Following Boal, only such an approach can yield non-colonizing faculty analysts and non-imperialistically missionized analysts-in-training. Jung would have it no other way.

The positioning of analytic training within an institute, however, instantly places in jeopardy what each of us values in our work. Famous theories, important texts, systems of treatment and so much else must be appropriated. To do less is to betray the analysts-in-training who, correctly, have approached the training process to integrate their own truth and deepen their gifts by means of engagement with others. These others can give what they have appropriated themselves even as, ideally, they learn freshly from the candidate. Yet archetypal tugs predispose institutes to fail in meaningful dialog. Bridging between the nerve center of an individual learning process and the needs of an institute process is analogous to constructing the transcendent function which, in this case, links the opposing yet related force fields of the institute and the individual. We affirm building the transcendent function in an individual process, yet it seems we lack confidence that the transcendent function can be built also in the engagement of the institute with the individual. Such an institute would itself be a "living stone." Scarcely what we expect from an institute. Yet exactly such a living stone is what analysts in training require if they are not to emerge from training with unnecessary and heavy shadows on their backs.

A halfway point for many has been the experience that training is a mentoring experience. Following some type of apprentice model, the analyst-in-training hooks up with a *mana*-bearing senior analyst and learns the craft. Here there seems to be more room for a dialog of voices rather than an eating at the banquet table of learning as if the candidate is only an empty stomach, not also offering something to the banquet table.

Our concern with training reflects larger issues within contemporary society: what makes for good formation and how are the trainers to avoid the stereotypic issues of power, infighting, Chronos-like devouring, and envy of the younger and perhaps more talented. That is, a training in which analysts, candidates, and the institute each function as the living stones they are called to be – yet never fully can be – would represent a true ethical encounter with the issues of contemporary society, not just a continuation of its flaws.

Instances of shadow in training include: projections onto faculty and supervisors by candidates and by other faculty and supervisors; projections onto candidates by faculty and supervisors and other candidates; contaminations of the training process of the analyst-in-training within the analytic process; materials that the analyst-in-training brings into the analysis that are concretized and not analyzed (e.g., course selection, supervisory selection, reactions to faculty and candidates as introjects, and materials that the analyst has failed to metabolize), which leak into the dynamic field of the personal analysis and contaminate it.

I suspect we can all find ourselves on this map. As an analyst I have caught myself sighing when a candidate proposes a particular supervisor. As a supervisor I have caught myself sighing when I wonder what in the world is occurring in the candidate's analysis. As a faculty member I have been astonished at what other faculty members do and don't do as teachers. As a faculty member I have wondered if I want to be a member of the club that has as its member also faculty member "X." As an Institute Board member I have sighed at the short-sightedness of faculty and Board members who confuse purity of learning with reality of learning and of the constraints of creative tension in an institute. As president of an institute I have grappled with the interface between us and them: how we are perceived in the world, what we are to do with the missing fourth. Candidates, analysts, institute AND analysands are four, as are evaluatory panels (often three in number) AND candidates. As a committee member I have valued highly the process and colleagueship of the committee and sighed at how the other committees just don't understand my committee, or how they just don't seem to do their work well. You no doubt can add to my list.

What fuels the skewing of the training process? Perhaps the ceaseless urgings of the objective psyche as we are encountered by it, pressing us further forward: as unending travelers, rounding a new turn of the individuation spiral, awash with new *prima materia* (if not in a dream, then perhaps in a new societal urging that catches us). These urgings are understood – falsely – as capable of being "integrated." We too are to become perfect as some "heavenly self" is perfect. Such perfection bleeds into static and shadowless Platonism.

Much as we know and revere Jung's work, we lose sight too often of what his work on "the missing" makes clear. The only procedure apposite to our work is one of experiencing the Self in process, as opposed to our or the candidate's or the co-faculty member's or the institute's itself being fully cooked. We want the perfectly divine meal, four star, the *creme de la creme*, the perfect. To want less is to stop short and to starve. But we confuse just what "perfect" is. Perfect is the limpid process of consciousness held in three-way tension: inner, with others (faculty and candidates), and with the societal face of the objective Self. Such tension reflects the whole. Wholeness in process is what we can have as we are urged forward by the perfect.

The confusion that arises is that the phenomenal (perfect in the moment), becomes merged with perfection itself, which is archetypal and unattainable. This confusion sets up the projection of what is missing rather than an engagement with what is known only as the shadow that comes to meet us through our projections so that our anemic "perfectness" can become more complete. Such shadow yields a tastier meal, with bits of Leviathan thrown in. A wholesome, never completed meal!

There are several vital reasons for our pursuing this material. First, what we do in training becomes not only pernicious in itself, but also embodies exactly what the analytic process is not. Thus, analysts-in-training, faculty, and future analysands are wounded by being enslaved to a faulty sense of the perfect. Second, we can work, by means of our dialog, toward some models of training and its process that would obviate this circumstance. A kind of one-sided madness arises otherwise. We force ourselves, our institutes, and our candidates into a place of disturbance; what is being carried and acted upon, insofar as it is incomplete, is afflicted and neurotic.

Perhaps it is this circumstance that has contributed to the often celebrated notion that one's analysis starts after training certification has been attained. The newly-graduated analyst most definitely is imperfect, a rank beginner as a full analyst. Legitimacy of being, however, has been conferred by certification; hence it is safer to pull back projections of perfection placed on the faculty and institute and to repulse further introjections of shadow.

What then is to be done? Many traditional solutions run afoul of the need for a secure analytic framework. For example, in addition to candidate group process meetings and retreats, and faculty meetings and retreats where we can teeter toward directly engaging one another within the safe framework of our shared endeavor, one might imagine a candidate and faculty process distinct from typical candidate/faculty meetings in which, at the end, each group splits off to arrive at its own determinations and the faculty, hypothetically, has more of a final say. But such process meetings conflict with analytic relations. Or do they? Do we perhaps use the analytic frame defensively so that we don't have to experience ordinary engagement as colleagues in the training process? It may well be that the inability of the analyst-in-training to handle what might arise in such settings is as much the projected inability of the senior analyst as not.

Last, institute training programs would do well to utilize the clinical lens as a way of giving input to analysts-in-training. This works with trainees on the level at which they have approached institute training, and it keeps feedback focused on the project at hand. Other types of feedback, more "analytic," inevitably invade the personal analysis. Most importantly, I believe that the ways in which we give feedback at all junctures in an analytic program may be done best if done dominantly through the "clinical lens." That is, exploring the issues at hand – at admissions, at ongoing evaluation meetings, in evaluating theses, at the time of concluding evaluations and graduation through a focus on the clinical work of the candidate – generates precise and appropriate feedback. Thus, competency is seen as it manifests in actual clinical work. We would give feedback in a style similar to that of the supervisory process. Thus, issues that are "analytic" are addressed but without affecting the analysis.

Praxis and ethics are the staff of life. Only through them do we digest the beast that brings forth the shadow which is necessary to make perfection whole rather than complete. This strikes me as the kind of hearty meal that we all need for the life work that being and becoming an analyst is, and that being and becoming an institute is.

Mercurius, Regression and Revelation

Sherry Salman
Rhinebeck, New York, USA
New York Association for Analytical Psychology

> *The psyche harbours contents, or is exposed to influences, the assimilation of which is attended by the greatest dangers. If the old alchemists ascribed their secret to matter, and if neither Faust nor Zarathustra is a very encouraging example of what happens when we embody this secret in ourselves, then the only course left to us is to ... admit that the psyche is a reality which we cannot grasp with our present means of understanding.*
>
> C.G. Jung

The notion of "grasping the psyche" is one of the most vexing issues in analytic training. Training analysts attempt to grasp the psyche of candidates in order to see whether candidates have grasped the psyches of their patients. Many analysts and candidates alike have suggested that this is the wrong way to go about training or evaluation, and have proposed more objective systems (see Kugler 1995). Jung himself seemed to suggest that the psyche can not be grasped anyway, unconscious factors being too great, and was happy not to be a professional Jungian.

But however much we improve the mechanics of our training systems and acknowledge the powerful, intangible influence of the unconscious, we will still find ourselves in the peculiar – some would say unholy – endeavor of grasping psyches. To maintain integrity within this potentially Faustian scheme necessitates opening up in two directions: to the outside world, in the form of objective discourse with the scientific and academic communities (see Homans 1998), and to our collective inner world, in the form of analysis of the interiority of our training institutes.

Kohut (1978) suggested that training institutes form a "group self," held together primarily by idealizing transferences; candidates idealize faculty who in turn mirror these idealizations. While this allows for a high degree of control, self-esteem, cohesiveness, and a rapid transmission of knowledge within institutes, it inhibits conflict and innovation. But, said Kohut significantly, training institutes were not ready for analysis of this collective transference.

My contribution to this analysis is to engage three related symbolic images which represent some of the archetypal dynamics constellating unconscious factors behind the scenes in training. They are: 1) The substance we are trying to grasp, the psyche as Mercurius, and its dual nature as both Poison and Panacea. 2) The issue of regression in training as it is informed, or misinformed, by the image of the Mystery Cult Initiation. 3) The archetypal daimon of revelation, which I believe lies at the heart of many of our troubles in training.

Mercurius

Jung was clear that the psyche, imaged as both the spirit Mercurius and the amphibious Melusina (a mythological figure, part woman, part sea serpent), was deceitful and shifty, comprised of both good and evil: *duplex*. Jung wrote: "Mercurius truly consists of the most extreme opposites; on the one hand he is undoubtedly akin to the godhead, on the other he is found in sewers" (CW13, 269) and that from his "snout there comes a spreading poison that has brought death to many." The *magnum opus* of the alchemist was to bring forth "everlasting life" from this "poison-dripping dragon" (CW13, 267).

Many candidates would resonate with this statement as a description not only of the mercurial substance, but of the training process as well: both a *magnum opus* and a spreading poison. Like the myth of the ambivalent *pharmakon*, a drug simultaneously poison and antidote, or the Gorgon's blood used by Asclepius which brings both plague and healing, the mercurial substance of the psyche as it lives in the training faculty spreads both disease and health. Who has not received and administered a dose of this "medicine"?

But Jung, following the alchemists, felt that Mercurius was a danger only to the ignorant. Although in the search for the panacea much poison is generated, once Mercurius became volatilized into spirit the poison was transformed, yielding a stable panacea. I question this fantasy as containing a controlling idealization, reflective of an inflation born of a paranoid identification with only the "good." The panacea/poison duality often appears split rather than contained or volatilized in training, manifesting predictably during evaluation interviews – where faculty calmly and helpfully reveal candidates' pathology, and candidates emit the appropriate dreadful, soulful responses. The training process and faculty carry the healing panacea, acting in the interests of the "good," while candidates carry the complex-ridden spreading poison in need of healing, namely a good regression.

Regression and the Mystery Cult Initiation

It is generally accepted as "just so" that there is a strong potential for malignant fragmentation during training: a risk that accompanies the creative potential inherent in the regressive aspects of the training process (see Addenbrooke 1997). This regression is presumed to take place along the lines of an analytic mystery cult initiation, wherein the unborn-initiate encounters good and evil, gods and demons, psychologically realized as the ego's fragmentation/integration by the ambivalent push/pull of the unconscious. In training, this initiation is projected into the training analysis, the personae of supervisors, faculty, peers, and the evaluatory and graduation process itself. The goal is a transformed, illuminated "volatilized" candidate, now called an analyst, who is empowered by virtue of successful initiation to administer the panacea.

But are the goals of the mystery initiation the same as those of training? The goals of analysis are intensely personal and subjective; its initiation is into the mysteries of the person's own depths while the needs of the collective are secondary. But in training the opposite is true; the candidate is initiated into a collective, professional body, and – rightly – must in some fashion conform to this collective body.

While the regression in analysis may resemble the mystery initiation, the regression in training may be more informed by collective, adolescent *rites d'entrée*, wherein the candidate becomes a member of a tribe, bound primarily by tribal directives and needs. One implication of these different archetypal dynamisms is that, while the candidate's pathology is an appropriate focus of analysis, it should not be the primary focus of supervision and evaluation during training, because pathology is that in which an institutional or tribal body is least able to engage, in an appropriate and non-invasive fashion. However, when overshadowed by the daimon of "revelation," this difference becomes obscured.

The Daimon of Revelation

To the extent that the guiding spirit behind our work is expressed in the image of alchemical transformation, we are prey to specific inflations. In the alchemical vision the one in need of redemption is not a man or woman, but the lost and sleeping deity. The alchemical work is not primarily for the alchemist's own salvation through the grace of God, but for the revelation of God from the darkness, through the work of the alchemist.

This psychological understanding is one basis for accusations that Jungians are hopelessly inflated, identified with the gods and with the revealed truth. Richard Noll (1994) has painted a picture of training institutes as economic pyramid scams and secret churches, conning unwary seekers with bogus ideas of individuation. Aspiring candidates are promised a revelation of the mysteries, along with referrals, in return for economic and religious loyalty to the tribe. Noll claimed that analysts believe themselves to gain their authority by virtue of direct knowledge of the divine revealed in initiation mysteries, thus becoming vessels themselves for creation and revelation.

For Noll, who seems to assume any engagement with the unconscious to be virtually pathological, Jungian training becomes a house of cards constructed upon nothing. Misguided as Noll's assumption is, two things do ring true: the peculiar and frightening danger of promoting initiation as the archetypal dynamic behind training, and the ever-present threat of identification with a creator-redeemer fantasy that flows from the daimon of revelation. This daimon naturally arises during most subjective experiences of personal gnosis, including analysis. But history has shown what crimes have been committed when it gets loose in collective human affairs. Crimes committed by training faculty in the name of our "intuition," arcane readings of candidates' pathology, our certainty of superior knowledge and the will to foist this upon others all may be seen to arise as a consequence of identification with the experience of revelation. Such identification veers close to religious fundamentalism and psychological terrorism, and may inflict "voodoo death" upon candidates and colleagues alike.

In the search for panacea, poison is generated. This much seems as true in training as it is in analysis. In order for our good intentions not to pave the road to hell, difficult archetypal issues need to be made conscious and contained. In the end, the duplicity of the serpent Mercurius may intend the unification of its own double nature. How may the training community creatively and humbly accept the continuing emergence of its own destructive shadow material and contain the daimon of revelation? An acceptance of the cycles of creation and destruction in training hints at the possibility of "everlasting life," rather than the slow death of "a spreading poison."

Panacea and Poison

Samuel L. Kimbles
Santa Rosa, California, USA
C.G. Jung Institute of San Francisco

My training was neither a poison nor a panacea. Rather, I think of it as an ordeal. It was part of a larger pattern of initiation that I could grasp consciously only when it was practically over. My perspective here is speaking from the archetype of initiation (see Henderson, 1967).

Each candidate brings to the training situation a basic issue that needs to be addressed during the process of becoming an analyst. The issues that grip candidates will vary but include narcissistic needs: to be valued and to have analytic elders whom they can idealize; or the problems associated with authority, autonomy, assertion, gender, power and control. The issue that was constellated for me was that of seeing and being seen; it was activated within a "complexed" field that included personal, institutional, cultural, and archetypal dimensions.

As an African-American man I am not surprised that the issue of seeing and being seen would come up within the training process. It has a long cultural, racial, and institutional legacy within the American landscape. However, it is the way this issue came up in the process of my becoming an analyst that I would like to explore. My major points are:

1. The Jungian intra-psychic bias tends to see the cultural as an exogamous factor, hence the significance of culture for individuation can be missed.

2. There is a tendency among us to confuse the collective unconscious with the cultural unconscious. Hence, cultural stereotypes often can pass for archetypes; for example, the threatening black as a "classic" shadow figure. The black is regarded as a negative or inferior aspect of the patient; symbolic blackness replaces race as a social and political reality.

3. The central emotional dynamic of my training revolved around my feeling that there were important aspects of myself which the training committee did not see. Indeed, the members could neither see me nor could I see them. This mutual blindness created an emotional field in which the tensions between cultural and archetypal reality, collective and cultural unconscious, and our different personal dynamics had to be disentangled.

Two dreams occurred during critical transitions in my training experience. The first occurred the night before my first interview with the Admissions Committee.

I am meeting in a mosque with a number of Black Muslim men. Suddenly it is time for my interview with the admissions committee. When I get up to leave the mosque, several men prevent me from leaving until I can demonstrate to them that I know and remember the secret handshake. This handshake will acknowledge my continued connection to them.

The second dream occurred just prior to my meeting with the Certifying Committee for the first time, to review my control paper.

I had surprised a senior analyst who is looking through the files of another analyst. He seems embarrassed that I know there are files on analysts. I do not see other analysts, but there is a committee meeting of some sort taking place in another room. I have a discussion with the analyst about sharing the file with me, but he is reluctant. Then suddenly a blond, all-American looking man drives up in a large red sports car. I realize that he was the analyst whose file was being reviewed.

I put these two dreams side by side to illustrate how, from the very start, what I would call a cultural and archetypal field had been constellated in my training. Together the two dreams show a pair of opposites. In the one there is a picture of the conservative, race-conscious Black Muslims; in the other there is an image of the Aryan ideal under review. This joins the issue of kinship and loyalty to racial and tribal ties, and separation from that which constellates the Aryan Other. These opposites are joined through a cultural history of power dynamics, oppression, suspicion and guilt. Could it be that this pair of opposites, which are expressions of the cultural – not the archetypal – unconscious, was contributing to my difficulty in showing myself and to the committee's having difficulty seeing me? I was clearly in the archetype of initiation, leaving my original group in order to be tested by others, and I could not leave this field without sacrificing my opportunity to be transformed.

One example of these complexed dynamics managed to appear during the certification phase of my candidacy. When I passed from being reviewed by the Reviewing Committee to evaluation, as a control-stage candidate – by the Certifying Committee for the first time – a member of the committee shared a dream which he said he had had the night before our meeting. The dream was *that he was standing in line at the airport when a black man pushed into the line ahead of him.* This is as much of the dream as he reported, but he went on to say that he had associated the black man with me and asked for my thoughts about the situation depicted in the dream.

I felt immediately confused. At a thinking level, I could follow the logic of his intervention; he evidently wanted me to check out if there was possibly an authority complex in me that wanted to pass on into becoming an analyst without having to deal with him or this committee. But at the level of feeling I was in a double bind. I had been asked to comment on his dream and his projection of my possible complex by associating myself to the black man in his dream. Where were his own associations? Was his bringing up this dream an attempt to introduce a discussion of race into our meeting? If so, were we ready to go the distance and share, both of us, the history of our relationship to racism, power, alienation, boorishness and counter-boorishness? What would be the role of the other members? Should we try to enter such a dialogue? Were they, too, willing to disclose and share their assumptions about a black man in training? If the dream suggested a shadow problem, were we ready to speak frankly to each other about the issues of power in the training situation?

I was tempted to point out that the power problem in this training situation had started already to mimic the discrepancy of power between blacks and whites in the larger culture. And I certainly wondered what the topic of the meeting had become. My individuation as an analyst? His individuation as an evaluator? The problem of the committee or even of the larger Jungian community in dealing with the threat of a black candidate who does not wait his turn? At the time, I wondered at what level we should be discussing all of this. The ensuing conversation proved unproductive, because all I could say was something to the effect that I couldn't really deal with the black man in his dream. None of the analysts present responded.

Although I did have a follow-up exchange privately with the committee member, and there was an effort at mutual assurance of good will on our parts, I continued to feel too much in a bind and overwhelmed by the power of the cultural complex field that had been constellated to deal with the issue at that time.

In preparation for this paper I asked the analyst who had shared his dream if I could discuss it with him again and use the interaction as an example in my paper of how a cultural complex can operate in the training process. He agreed to it, saying he trusted my discretion. In his note to me, however, he said that when he offered his dream he meant nothing racial by it. Nevertheless, his response deepened my sense of a continuing misunderstanding of what had been constellated and what we were trying to say to each other. I think the problem is that we have not had a psychological language that works for all of us to access such cultural complexes.

Perhaps we have never been clear enough about the nature and reality of cultural complexes and how they differ from individual complexes, on the one hand, and archetypal reality on the other. We have to ask: Can major cultural signifiers of experiences be spoken of in a neutral way that does not constellate defensiveness? Clearly, neither he nor I felt seen in our exchanges; and this lack tells me that there is much work to be done in our psychological community. For me the experience of not being seen was an indication of a cultural complex at work. On the surface, my evaluator's handling of his dream with me seems so dumb and off base that it is only when one realizes that he/we may have been in the grip of a cultural complex that the overt blindness, stupidity and inhumaness of his comments can begin to make sense. Blindness, stupidity and inhumaness are aspects of not being seen: hallmarks of being caught in a cultural complex.

My personal regret is that, whatever was constellated around race, power and training was not explored enough to make meaningful to me how this cultural complex was related to my professional individuation and my responsibility toward it. For such an exploration to occur, the members of my committee would have had to risk being vulnerable, too. Instead, at this juncture I think a split in my initiation process occurred. One part, the cultural complex, stayed separated and inappropriately intrapsychic, while the other – the personal complex – was played out on an interpersonal level to successful certification.

For me as an individual, intrapsychic resolution did occur between my first meeting with the Certifying Committee and my last. The help I got came while on a walk with a friend who was already an analyst. She compared analytic training to bull fighting. In the bull-fighting ritual, after the bull has been taunted, teased and set up for the matador, the bull and the matador meet in a sacred moment. She said, that is a moment of grace (charisma), with great power and numinosity for the bull and matador. Suddenly, I could see that this was the state of induced narcissistic vulnerability which Beebe (1996) has spoken of as the state so particular to candidates undergoing the prolonged evaluation that is the passage through analytic training. I realized that this is also the essential core vulnerability of any person conscious enough to be aware of his dependence on selfobjects. To quote Beebe (1998) in another context: "Such vulnerability is an inevitable part of the incarnated human condition; ... our vulnerability is less a function of the immaturity of our egos than an inescapable part of our integrity as incarnated creatures, whose very selfhood is throughout our lives ecologically dependent upon a matrix of self-objects" (p. 94).

Summary

I discovered early in my training that there was a level of the cultural unconscious that manifested in what I am now calling the "complex of invisibility": seeing and being seen. The cultural unconscious is a manifestation of the collective unconscious at the group level. To be conscious of this level is to see it as a field phenomenon that acts like a group complex in collective situations. It organizes in-group/out-group feelings, the sense of belonging to a specific group: loyalty and identity processes associated with such areas of concern. It organizes all the aforementioned dynamics vis à vis another group that seems to have a distinct, uncomplicated identity. That these issues are socially constructed does not diminish their archetypal significance for kinship (or belonging) and for individuation (or identity formation).

In the training, archetypal contents are sometimes activated that are nearly pure expressions of the cultural unconscious. These contents – which may include such loaded issues as race, ethnicity, and sexual orientation – are not reducible to archetypal dynamics of either an individual or intrapsychic collective nature. They are collective group forms and contents.

For me something very basic and valuable did distill out of the invisibility complex that the training experience constellated. In retrospect, I can see that from very early in my life I was not deeply in touch with my vulnerability to the evaluations of others. I did make a shift to experiencing an essential vulnerability in my training. This occurred beyond the personal, yet was very personal. It was the gold that I obtained in my candidacy. I hope, like alchemical gold, it is a homeopathic substance and that my story will touch others in a healing way.

The Group Shadow in Jungian Training

Thayer Greene
Amherst, Massachusetts, USA
New York Association for Analytical Psychology

In addressing the subject of the group shadow in the process of Jungian analytic training, I find myself confronted by the dangers and limitations of any generalized critique; it does not do justice to the variety and uniqueness of the particular. I can only ask that you reflect on my observations – drawn from my limited experience – in the light of your own training and involvement with the training process.

I began my training in 1962 when the Jungian movement was at a very different stage in its development. In 1969 I was invited onto the Training Board of the New York Institute and have been deeply involved in a broad spectrum of training issues and responsibilities until two years ago, when I resigned from my last committee and withdrew into the leisure and delight of semi-retirement where important things like golf, tennis, movies, music and especially grandchildren become primary areas of interest. Over the 34 years of my direct involvement as both trainee and then trainer, I have seen a number of phenomena which seem to repeat themselves with such regularity in the group dynamic of training that one can suspect, legitimately, an archetypal pattern is at work behind the personal and particular variety of our training experiences.

First and foremost, I maintain that the attitude of Jung himself toward group process and any form of collective institution has had an influence that is difficult to measure on both the conscious assumptions and unconscious dynamics of the Jungian community.

What we know of his childhood would seem to indicate that the interpersonal world of family relatedness and authentic communication was both limited and impoverished. Joseph Henderson of San Francisco, who knew Jung personally, shared with me some years ago that his impression of Jung's view of the family was that one should get away from it as soon as one could and stay away as long as possible. Jung certainly had the suspicion, if not conviction, that individuals could achieve a much greater consciousness than any group. In that sense, the parts were viewed as being intrinsically greater than the whole.

From my perspective as someone with an extraverted orientation and raised in a relatively positive and functional extended family system, I find Jung's introverted bias and dysfunctional family experience may well have introduced one-sided distortions into our approach to training people to be analysts and the trainers' dealing with each other. In contrast with the early ideological evangelism of Freud and his need for orthodoxy and control in the institutional formation of the psychoanalytic movement, I have always enjoyed telling the tale of Jung's famous remark following the inauguration of the Jung Institute in Zurich: "Thank God I'm Jung and not a Jungian." That story has its shadow side, however: Jung essentially absented himself from any institutional responsibility in the formation of a growing collective that bore his name.

It may be that Jungians today carry on his profound ambivalence and suspicion toward organizational life, so that we do not do a very good job at it. Most thoughtful critics of Jung describe his words and actions in the 1930s as having been extremely politically naive. Could those words apply to us as well, in the way we do training? I'm not sure what the typological distribution of Jungian analysts is today, but I do know that in the mid-seventies, roughly 82 percent were introverted and 75 percent were intuitive. Extraverted sensates, feelers and even thinkers were in very short supply. If we follow the logic of Jung's typological theory as expanded by others, we should not be surprised to find that our professional community and therefore our training process suffer from a one-sided introverted and intuitive bias with a somewhat primitive, undeveloped, and naive extraverted sensate feeling shadow. This is likely to affect our institutional empathy and our capacity to listen to feedback from candidates with discriminating realism, obscuring or distorting the objective reality and feeling quality of their individual situations.

Frequently I have sat on evaluation committees where the intuitive projections of the group became a combustible energy that obscured and distorted the real person sitting before us. Because of our naiveté about group shadow, we often put into the candidate – through a group form of projective identification – what were in fact pieces of our own unconscious and unresolved psyches. The candidate leaves such encounters feeling psychically violated rather than challenged because we had failed to allow a genuinely personal unfolding and self-revelation to take place.

Another related phenomenon which I have observed at times in our training program is the failure to distinguish between the inevitable transference-countertransference dynamics of the individual analytic container with the typical need for a regressive process, sometimes quite lengthy, and the very different dynamics and psychic container appropriate to the candidate's relation to the training community. In the former one can allow the regressed child to be recovered and infantile feeling to emerge and be examined with relative safety. When the training community itself operates on the explicit or unconscious assumption that it is carrying the parental archetypes and functioning in that role vis-à-vis the candidates, it leads almost inevitably to the infantilization of those being trained. They are the children; we are the parental figures who know what is best for them. Such an attitude, however subtle, ignores the adult and professional status of candidates and leads to an inequity and lack of respect that is deeply injurious to training. In our own consulting rooms we must carry parental projections, both highly idealized and very negative, until they are ready to dissolve, but in the institutional training process we must remind ourselves that we are adult professionals training adult professionals.

Such a perspective means that our perceptions and evaluative standards must have as objective a character as possible on these slippery slopes of evaluating the psychic potentials and limitations of fellow human beings. The group shadow of the evaluation process is to pathologize those candidates who do not fit our norms and idealized expectations, who are not the good children but the bad ones, the odd ones, sometimes even the outrageous ones who challenge our established norms and frequently bring creative change for the whole community by their willingness to be in conflict with the established order.

A further source of confusion is our understanding of the initiation process in its relation to training. Years ago one of our candidates gathered his own dreams and those of his fellow candidates around the theme of training. Within a total of about 150 dreams he found that by far the greatest number dealt with the training process as a rite of passage and initiation. In my mind the critical issue in understanding this phenomenon is our capacity to distinguish between the candidate's interpersonal experience of initiation into a professional group on the one hand and the qualitatively different experience of the personal analytic encounter of the individuating ego with the initiatory demands of the Self. The first belongs to the individual's initiation into the group with all its appropriate standards and disciplines and therefore is legitimately under the direction and authority of the training elders. The second, however, is both personal and private and uniquely individual. It belongs to the container of personal analysis and should be approached by the group with the greatest sensitivity and caution, if at all.

A related phenomenon is the frequent projection of the Self by candidates onto the training community and the training experience. Any idealization of training institutes and training elders can only lead to disappointment, as those of us who do the training know only too well. The shift from idealization to demonization can be very swift indeed and can lead to a negative group spirit which can infect the whole training process and community in very destructive ways. Those who train must block their ears from the siren song of idealization or demonization in order to keep the training process on course toward the goal of producing "good enough" analysts from a "good enough" training program.

A related phenomenon in both the admission and evaluation process is what I describe as the "raising of the bar." I have observed frequently that, when recent graduates of the institute come into positions of authority and power in the training process, they become advocates for more rigor and exactitude in the very same program which they had been complaining about for its pressure and excessive demands a few years earlier. While some of these new standards are creative and appropriate to the training and development of better analysts than we were or ever shall be, I suspect that the unconscious is often at work putting into the candidates our own desire for perfection which will relieve the burden of our imperfection. I sometimes wonder whether such brilliant theorists and remarkable therapists as Harry Stack Sullivan, Frieda Fromm Reichman or even Jung himself would have survived in some of our training programs. They all had dramatic and well-documented flaws that would make them highly questionable candidates for training in our present era.

Finally, I believe that the single most destructive element in the group shadow of training is the shadow struggle of training analysts with each other. Since we are not organizationally well trained and the majority of Jungians have not been in group therapy nor do they work with groups psychodynamically, we as a professional community are singularly unequipped to deal with our own shadow problems with each other. Jung has shown us that, when we ignore or avoid our own personal shadow issues, they gather into a collective energy that breeds destructive consequences. Training candidates are likely to pay the price for the covert conflicts between training analysts. Frequently, candidates become the pawns in a power struggle between conflicting personalities, standards of clinical practice, and very different visions of what makes a Jungian analyst. Many candidates quickly learn to read the political landscape of the training process so that they do not make a false step, but they should not be forced to carry our shadows as well as their own in order to survive six or so years in training. We as trainers need a much greater consciousness of the dynamics of groups and organizations on the one hand and some purposeful and established method through which we can confront each other with greater compassion and acceptance of genuine difference. In my view, this consciousness is the very essence of the vision of psychic reality which Jung has passed on to us. Our task now is the discovery and formation of real psychological community from which a more conscious and balanced training process can emerge. The group and its shadow can not only poison but heal.

References

Addenbrooke, M. (1997). The creative potential of play and regression in analytical training: a personal reflecton. *Journal of Analytical Psychology* *42*-3, 507-520.

Beebe, J. (1996). In Kugler, P. (Ed.), *Jungian Perspectives on Supervision.* Einsiedeln, Switzerland: Daimon.

Beebe, John (1998). Review of D. Kalsched, *The Inner World Of Trauma: Archetypal Defenses of the Personal Spirit. Quadrant, 28*-1, 92-96.

Boal, A. (1995). The *Rainbow of Desire.* (A. Jackson, Trans.). London: Routledge.

Henderson, J.L. (1967). *Thresholds of Initiation.* Middlefield, CT: Wesleyan University Press.

Homans, P. (1998). The plight and promise of contemporary psychoanalysis in the light of its social history. *Journal of Analytical Psychology 43*-1, 155-165.

Kohut, H. (1978). Creativeness, charisma, group psychology. In P. Ornstein (Ed.), *The Search for the Self: Selected Writings of Heinz Kohut: 1950-1978* (Vol. 2). New York: International Universities Press.

Kugler, P. (Ed.) (1995). *Jungian Perspectives on Clinical Supervision*. Einsiedeln, Switzerland: Daimon.

Noll, R. (1994). *The Jung Cult*. Princeton, N.J.: Princeton University Press.

Alchemy in the Image of the Analyst

Brigitte Allain-Dupré

Paris, France

Société Française de Psychologie Analytique

The incest element ... is the hiding place for all the most secret, painful, intense, delicate, shamefaced, timorous, grotesque, unmoral, and at the same time the most sacred feelings which go to make up the indescribable and inexplicable wealth of human relationships and give them their compelling power. Like the tentacles of an octopus they twine themselves invisibly round parents and children and, through the transference, round doctor and patient.

C.G. Jung

Reflection upon archetypal transference – that is, on the incestuous dimension of the relationship between patient and analyst – can be a means of uncovering intriguing hypotheses about the currents of destruction and construction at work in the transference process. Moreover, by examining the incestuous transference in clinical practice with children, it may be possible to shed new light on the operational use of a concept that is not easy to handle in work with adults.

I have often pondered the question whether, in considering transference an unconscious phenomenon, we are likely to deprive ourselves of placing its manifestations in the center of the work of gaining consciousness. Although we are often perceptive enough to understand the contents of a transference image, we are sometimes inept when it comes to giving the patient, in the experience of the session, the keys needed to take full advantage of these resources that enrich the patient's ego. Although I am ready to accept the idea commonly shared by Jungians that archetypal contents should not be interpreted, I still feel it necessary to study how their action can be stimulated, especially in the matter of archetypal manifestations of transference.

Why are we so hesitant to analyze transference? The incestuous theme of transference, as described by Jung (CW16), is presented in the form of images which evoke an intimacy so profound that it defies verbal description. Indeed, Jungian archetypal transference is much more readily identifiable as a life experience than as a theory. The intimacy of this experience opens a "sacred realm," which lends itself poorly to examination and casts heavy doubt upon us as analysts and individuals.

Jung says that this intimacy is distressing: "[The doctor] is merely drawn into the peculiar atmosphere of family incest through the projection. This necessarily leads to an unreal intimacy which is highly distressing to both doctor and patient and arouses resistance and doubt on both sides" (CW16, 368).

It is important to emphasize the juxtaposition of the adjectives: distressing and unreal. The juxtaposition makes it possible to grasp and ponder the paradox of transference: genuine feelings which only the setting and its conventions transform into projections. The setting, an arbitrary and temporary construction, gives these real feelings their unreal status and, lest we forget, applies to both partners.

Although Jung makes clear to us the importance of analyzing this kind of transference, it is only with a view to eliminating it. Jungians often are heard to say that it is only at the end of analysis, with that goal in sight, that transference should be analyzed.

I propose to make a small contribution to the enterprise of desacralizing the icon known as archetypal incestuous transference and to show that this enterprise generates contents which, when subjected to analysis, open interesting perspectives on the imago world of both the patient and the analyst. Based on the transformation processes described in alchemy, we shall see how the transference constitutes a meaning in the subject's there and now and orients an ego which integrates and utilizes it.

One image that frequently appears in patients' material is that of the analyst, in every possible variation: in dreams or in fantasies the patient formulates about wanting to become an analyst. This image, as the reactivation of the archetype of incest, is the goal of my exploration. As Jung says, "Every archetype, at its first appearance and so long as it remains unconscious, takes possession of the whole man and impels him to play a corresponding role" (CW12, 558). My exploration exploits this propensity to live the corresponding role in a way that serves the ego, when it is a question of identification with the analyst.

The image of the analyst can be considered to derive from the archetype of incest, because the crucial factor in identifying the incestuous dimension is not, for me, primarily and/or necessarily its sexual aspect. Incest is symbolized by this movement of erotic embrace, which can be described as collusion of opposites, or even as combined bodies, to borrow a metaphor from alchemy.

The crux of the analytic work will be to allow this pair of undifferentiated opposites to fulfill its destiny to unite in relation to the whole of the ego. The subject will be enriched with a new ability to feel and understand the inner world. This ability will enable the subject to integrate the introspective energy specifically associated with the image of the analyst. As a result, the image will be desacralized and stripped of its numinosity. As successive differentiations occur, the archetypal image will shed its aura of perfection, the idealizing transference; it will progress toward integration in the ego's realm of competence: integration of the analyzing function of feeling and understanding. The complex dissolves, is integrated, and reorganized in relation to other aspects of the psyche, with a corresponding expansion of the field of consciousness.

If this potential competence is analyzed on the objective level alone – the only perspective being the patient's love for the analyst – a large part of its resources will be lost to the inner self. If, on the other hand, the image of the analyst is analyzed on the subjective level – as an autonomous psychic reality that belongs entirely to the patient's psyche – the role that it can play in the internal analyzing function will become apparent. If the same image of the analyst is acted out too soon, as a real identification with the analyst (for example, if the patient becomes an analyst), it would be lost to the interiority and would need to be projected again to be recognized.

"Pierre," a seven-year-old boy who was referred to me by his homeopathic pediatrician, sat down in the armchair and began to describe in full detail nocturnal terrors haunted by terrifying witches which kept him awake until far into the night. Even his frequent visits to his parents' room did not keep them at bay. As for the rest, his life was going fairly well. The interview was lively and energetic.

When I asked him how he imagined he could get rid of this unpleasant problem, he replied, in a mischievous tone of voice, "The plant remedy didn't help, so Mrs. D. (the pediatrician) told me to come see you. She knows that you know the witches." "Is that what she told you?" I asked. "No, but I'm sure that you do. I can see that." I queried, "Really! How can you see that?" He thought for a moment, and then rejoined, "Because I think you're a witch too, but a nice one." I responded, "Oh, I see. How will it help you if I'm a nice witch?" He concluded, "You'll get rid of the witch who scares me at night."

This little vignette is a good illustration of how, in the childhood phase, the dialectical relationship of the forming ego and the unconscious creates a true *nigredo* state: an experience of darkness which stimulates the search for a solution in union with an opposite. We thus see the *nigredo* appearing simultaneously as "the initial state and as a developed state" (Conesa & Guilbaut, p. 80). In this case, the union of opposites was projected onto the analyst, via transference, as if it were an image characterizing the relationship to the analyst. Pierre's perception of me was organized immediately in the special rapport which existed between his inner world and mine. His attitude, in its search for a combination giving rise to a conjunction of opposites, is remarkable; often at his age a fantasy of heroic omnipotence would attempt to obliterate the more uncomfortable of the two terms.

The *nigredo* state can be understood as a state of dissociation between day and night: the impossible bridge between the strides towards separation and independence that Pierre is taking in his diurnal life, and the regressions from the opposite tendency tugging him backward at night, topped with a powerful and nostalgic oedipal curiosity. *Massa confusa*, one might say, between mother and son, which Pierre must painfully learn to dissolve (*solutio, separatio* from the witch/mother) to make way for the differentiation of his identity as a boy.

We can see that Pierre swiftly set up a transferential relationship with the adult I am, by means of our witches. The image of the analyst, from the outset, was identified according to its good witch element, which will combine in transference with the evil witch, the one who came to life in nightmares. The product of this combination was reorganized as a union of witches, the good witch then entering into an egalitarian dialogue with the evil one, bringing about the emergence of a third term: ego growth.

The transference to witch images is archetypal, because it is weighted with elements not yet metabolized by the ego. They belong to the realm of the self and are organized according to the inclusion-exclusion principle; that is, in other words, all or nothing. These huge images in their original state are not yet differentiated by the experience of the personal unconscious, along an ego/self axis; the images will lose their numinosity and increase in complexity as the drives acquire an oedipal quality.

Although the incestuous configuration is a powerful undercurrent, this type of transference is not oedipal; the absence of a third party, however, yields an identical, albeit inverted, image of the same. True, the transference is strongly erotic; it sets the stage for a future wedding between the good and bad witches. With flawless intuition, it draws its energy from the deepest resources of the analyst's incestuousness (see Racamier 1996).

It is interesting to note that, with children as well as with adults, narcissistic problems – which are essentially related to the avatars of the bond in infancy – can be expressed according to symptomatologies and unconscious material which usually have more to do with an original erotic state than with the later Oedipus complex.

"Juliette" was nine years old. She had been in psychotherapy for three years, and her eczema had disappeared. Although a painful feeling of worthlessness persisted, it had been attenuated. This feeling had taken shape as a paranoid type of defense, and Juliette felt less isolated from other people. She could now say that they loved her, "even if it is not perfect," to use her own words. Nevertheless, it was difficult for her to accept the idea that our relationship was coming to an end. She felt cured, but she did not want us to separate, and she said so clearly.

After we had attempted to see each other at two-week intervals, and then once a month, no change had come about; she was still unable to admit that our relationship might end. The situation troubled me; I wondered how and why, as an analyst, I was keeping her prisoner. To me, the transference bond was feeling oppressive; I tried to understand why Juliette was making me feel these things. What psychic oppression had escaped my understanding and thus our work together? To seek an answer to this difficult question, we decided to work on fairy tales. As it happened, our work on "Sleeping Beauty" was the key that unlocked the enigma, enabling Juliette to envisage and accept the end of our therapeutic relationship.

What puzzled Juliette most in "Sleeping Beauty" was trying to fathom why the king and father is so careless and inattentive as to allow an old woman with a spinning wheel, whose spindles are so fascinating and dangerous for his daughter, to live right under his own roof. When Juliette free-associated on the relationship between the king and the spinning woman, she thought that her own father might be baffled by her psychotherapy, that he was the main person who was in a hurry for the relationship to end. Her remark aroused a lively curiosity in me, a suggestion that I probe my possible unconscious collusion with this man who, in my opinion, urged and stimulated Juliette to grow, sometimes a little more quickly than is reasonable. Perhaps I am a part of this process?

Together, we understood how much the incestuous symbolism of the father/daughter relationship was activated in her difficulty in ending her therapy. She simply said, "I'm afraid my Papa asks too much of me," as if she saw therapy as an outlet for her regressive needs, although she never showed any sign of such needs in our sessions – except for the issue of ending therapy.

Juliette, however, continued her association work: "So the old woman with the spinning wheel isolated in a forgotten tower of the castle could be you, the psychologist." Sleeping Beauty's slumber is a metaphor for the patience which is necessary for a girl to mature into womanhood, into her sexual identity, and fulfill her destiny as a woman, a wife, and a mother. Juliette told me that, if she had been Sleeping Beauty, she would have tried to stay with the old woman as long as possible – taking care, of course, not to touch the spindle. Staying would have enabled her to remain in a static condition; she would have been spared from having to return to her parents who either kept her in a childhood state (incest with the mother) or asked too much of her (the father pushing her toward puberty). Nevertheless, she would avoid falling into the 100-year sleep, during which she must wait for the advent of her womanhood.

Thinking through the image of the analyst as the woman with the spinning wheel, I became aware that she remained the princess in incest with her mother, who unconsciously allowed her to escape from her father's authority, giving her access to a fantasy stand-by space, a static condition. This new awareness was a product of our work together, and it revealed the hidden bond that had been keeping Juliette prisoner. When I subjected my countertransference to analysis, I was able to see a part of me which could not accept being abandoned by Juliette.

In work with children, transference is not easy to analyze. As analysts, we are often satisfied by the projection of their pleasure in

being listened to and understood, a pleasure which does not immediately prompt us to think about the impact of the erotic on the
patient-analyst relationship. Too often, the issue of transference
begins to be examined only when a difficulty arises.

In the archaic problems presented by children, the archetypal
dimension of incest activated in the transference will often elicit in
the child an idealization of the analyst, whose negative aspects will
be projected onto someone else – usually the mother. If the analyst
is not alert to this phenomenon and the destiny of the projections, it
will be very difficult for the mother to tolerate the destructive effect
therapy may have on the child's image of her. In order for the therapy
to be effective, the elements of inclusion-exclusion of the incestuous
transference must be contained in a third arena: that of the analyst's
thoughts.

In Juliette's case, the image of the analyst (the woman with the
spinning wheel) contains evolutionary potential, but a wicked partner in the very core of the transference maintains the fantasy that
time can be stopped and change arrested. The immobility projected
onto me activated the non-differentiation of the mother/daughter
incest, which engenders sameness at the risk of stifling the daughter,
by cutting off her access to a father and a masculine principle that
fosters growth.

Jung pointed out that "the patient by bringing an activated
unconscious content to bear upon the doctor, constellates the corresponding unconscious material in him, owing to the inductive effect
which always emanates from projections in greater or lesser degree.
Doctor and patient thus find themselves in a relationship founded on
mutual unconsciousness" (CW16, 364).

For several years, I have paid particular attention to what came
out in patients' material relative to a desire to become an analyst.
Several patients expressed such a desire, whether they were children, adolescents, or adults. I consider this desire to be an expression
of an incestuous element of the archetypal transference.

"Florian" was three years old when he began a three-year psychotherapy with me. He was an extremely anxious little boy who acted
out terrible destructive and violent tendencies which expressed the
abandonments and symbioses which he had been forced to experience in early infancy.

By the end of his therapy, he had learned to read and entered first
grade. His violence had been transformed into a form of omnipotence which was more or less acceptable, personally and socially. He

often operated in the context of rivalry and competition, but could deal with failure adequately. His relationships were authentic. He was 12 years old when he expressed a desire to have a few more psychotherapy sessions with me. In the course of these few sessions, Florian had often spoken to me of his desire to become a psychologist. We had analyzed the most complex aspects of this desire to understand the unconscious elements it contained. Paradoxically, his motivation for becoming a psychologist was not related to any sort of altruism. On the contrary, it was rooted in an impeccably logical egocentrism: "If I were a psychologist, I'd know how to take care of myself when I feel bad." Initially, he insisted on the undeniable fact that, as a psychologist, one has to be very knowledgeable of one's own psychology. He insisted also on the neutral terrain represented by the psychologist. Florian made it clear to me how an imago had formed inside his personality, based on a very old and solid transference. (I had resisted his violence.)

This imago is difficult to name; for the moment, I am calling it "imago of becoming an analyst." It is pregnant with a future that finds its source in an identification with the analytic function and, as I have been able to verify, quite distinct from any aspect of parenthood identified with the analyst. It may be that introjecting into the self a dimension of the analyst imago implies a transformation of a dimension of parenthood.

This imago animates and supports an inner bond between feeling and thinking. As a result, it has the potential to bring about a new differentiation of the ego, with a capacity for introspection. It gives the subject a reference point from which to listen to the inner world in total security. The feeling of identity based on this imago seems to exist fleetingly. Therefore, I prefer to call it a "temporary imago." Winnicott might term it an "illusory experience." It is destined to dissolve (*solutio*) as an ego competence. It will be visible only as a good capacity for insight, or perhaps as heightened awareness in relationships with the self and others. In adult patients, it finds expression when they speak of having thought over a session, or voice inner dialogues which they have carried on with the analyst outside the session.

I am convinced that this imago is constituted according to the processes Winnicott described for the transitional object. Perhaps it serves the same purpose of providing support, differentiation, and bonding. It offers a new angle from which to engage in reflective thought, the self as the mirror of the self: ego-non-ego possession,

Winnicott would say. According to Winnicott, the transitional object is the source of symbolic thought in the child. Likewise, in a child, the temporary imago I have described could be seen as a fairly sophisticated form of expression of self-awareness. Jung wrote:

> *The terms he uses for the attitude of the adept – amor perfectissimus – expresses an extraordinary devotion to the work. If this "serious meditation" is not mere bragging – and we have no reason to assume any such thing – then we must imagine the old adepts carrying out their work with an unusual concentration, indeed with religious fervor. Such devotion would naturally serve to project values and meanings into the object of all this passionate research and to fill it with forms and figures that have their origin primarily in the unconscious of the investigator. (CW12, 389)*

In a letter to Freud, Jung admitted how much his transference was imbued with the above mentioned religious fervor. My next example shows how the religious fervor associated with the incestuous transference must be deconstructed before the patient enrolls in a training program to become an analyst.

"Olga" was a 33-year-old psychologist. At our first meeting, she revealed her desire to change analysts. For the past four years, she had been in analysis with a woman, twice a week on the couch. She wanted to break off this relationship, although she was determined to continue – and end – the analysis elsewhere. She appreciated the value of the work accomplished with the analyst; however, for the past six months, she had been going into sessions gripped by an anguish which was unresolved when she left. The only symbolic solution she could envisage was this desire to consult a different analyst, a desire that was making her feel guilty.

Olga's anguish was rooted in a fantasy that she and this particular analyst were trapped in an overly symbiotic, static relationship. The discomfort of the symbiosis showed itself mainly as an impression that her analyst could attach a meaning to everything. Olga had the feeling that even her infractions of the rules, missed appointments, mistakes related to paying for the sessions, and so on, were interpreted in the analysis in a way that wrapped her even more tightly in this unbreakable bond which was beginning to feel suffocating. It was as if all the analyst's suggestions, whatever they might be, inevitably led to a feeling of excess, either of love or of meaning.

I immediately responded with the standard speech on such issues: "These feelings need to be worked out in your analysis. ..." and thought of Jung's statement:

[It] is emphasized that the tincture or divine water is far from being merely curative and ennobling in its effects, but that it may also act as a deadly poison which penetrates bodies as pervasively as the pneuma penetrates its stone. (CW12, 407)

Two months later, Olga scheduled another appointment with me. More than ever, she felt trapped "in the tentacles of an octopus," and she had announced to her analyst that she was leaving her. After two more months of latency, I accepted her as a patient for face-to-face sessions, once a week.

The work on analysis of the transference in her first therapy had made it possible for her to question herself deeply about her career as a psychologist and her plan to become an analyst in the distant future. She often dreamed of her former analyst, and we made use of this material by giving special importance to it on the subjective level. That is, we explored in depth the figure of the analyst as a personification of the traits of one of her own complexes interacting with the other elements of her inner world. This technique was quite new to the patient, but she quickly perceived the liberating effect it could have. She was able to recognize what was projected onto the analyst, on one hand as a mirror image of her own story, but also as what had been introjected from the analyst as a function of the bond and access to meaning, in the very interior of her psyche.

Since a higher degree of awareness had been attributed to the image of the analyst in the idealizing transference, this degree of consciousness could be absorbed. It could work to the ego's advantage instead of being subjected to the idealizing tendency.

Looking back, she could become aware also that it was not so much the excessively good mother analyst who was persecuting her inside. Actually, the vague idea of becoming an analyst had resisted her examination, so fascinated was she by what she called her analyst's "perfection." In the same way that the totally good great mother – activated in an archetypal transference – is never endowed with a human dimension, the psychologist's identification with an analyst – experienced as infallible – had remained in the register of archetypal possession. Before it could be evaluated by the ego, the identification with the analyst had to be submitted to several deconstruction processes which made its humanization and integration in the imago world possible.

In the transference with me, the second analyst, Olga allowed herself to doubt all that she felt of the analytic omnipotence with which she had unconsciously identified. She became aware that, in

460   *Brigitte Allain-Dupré*

truth, she had no desire whatsoever to devote herself to a profession that treats psychic suffering. She refused to consider her choice in any other light than as a matter of her individual free will. Several times, she said "Of course, it could be interpreted as resistance, but there are times when it is healthy to cease interpreting."

Olga is now capable of analyzing why she turned to psychological studies. When she arrived in France, fleeing very neurotic parents, these studies enabled her to remain in contact with her inner world at a time when she felt as though her whole life had fallen apart. She told me, "When you major in psychology, you do it for yourself in the beginning, of course; then, one day, the emphasis shifts, and you begin to want to do it for other people. I have the feeling that for me, the emphasis never shifted. At first, I blamed myself for it, I thought it was my fault. Now I am fairly convinced that I was not cut out for this career, simply because my desire is absent." Olga feels quite relieved to be living and thinking her life "away from psychology," that it is "a vocabulary which is no longer necessary," now that she has found her "personal language." She dreamed of

a country scene which could be a kind of year-end show over which I reigned, with my husband and many young women. I am enthroned in a rickety old wicker armchair, which is unsteady on its four legs. The young women come up and, in an ironic way, present me with worthless gifts; they are all making an effort to act as though they have immense respect for me, but their suppressed giggles and shared winks signify the comedy of the situation. In the dream, I receive the tribute with gravity, but everyone understands that I too find it very comical. Olga is one of the irreverent young women. The dream ends with a kind of banquet where we are all dining with great gusto; the attitudes have returned to normal, and there is a great deal of shared friendship and warmth.

Olga understood this dream according to the Carnival tradition which is strong in her home country, a time when one frees oneself by mocking and ridiculing the authority figures to whom one is subservient the rest of the year. It is a sign that her work with me has ended. I also understand it in my countertransference as the possibility of feeling nourished while remaining detached from the derisory gifts presented by the young women. Jung wrote:

Time and again the alchemists reiterate that the opus proceeds from the one and leads back to the one, that it is a sort of circle like a dragon biting its own tail. ... He is the hermaphrodite that was in the beginning, that splits into the classical brother-sister duality and is reunited in the conjunctio to appear once again. (CW12, 404)

Union, duo, brother-sister, and separation, until the next union, such is the rhythm that animates our work. With the incestuous transference, our patients are ceaselessly driven to ask us about us as analysts, and about this couple they and we form. It cannot function unless its incestuous aspects are continually deconstructed, differentiated, and analyzed, even though this process is a Sisyphean task which must be set in motion again as soon as it is completed.

Translated from the original French byAnita Conrade

References

Conesa E. & Guilbaut D. (1997). Nigredo. *Cahiers Jungiens de Psychanalyse*, 88.
Racamier, P. (1996). *Inceste et Incestuel*. Paris: Editions du College.

Panel: Supervision

Hester McFarland Solomon
London, England
British Association of Psychotherapists

Working under supervision is an integral part of training to become an analyst and is often an integral component of ongoing professional development. Yet, when we approach the concept of supervision in Jungian analytic training, we evoke a variety of different designations and functions. It is an old chestnut (something hard to chew – and sometimes hard to digest) to try to discern the differences and commonalities between what is meant by such various terms as supervision, control analysis, didactic analysis, and consultation (by which is often meant post-qualification supervision, or post-qualification control analysis). Many questions arise.

There is great variation in the use of these different terms across the IAAP Societies. Does that mean there is an equivalent variation in function, or do the words merely designate similar functions with relatively minor variations in emphasis? Do the different designations have implications for theoretical understanding and clinical practice regarding, for example, concepts such as transference and countertransference? And then again, how are we to think about the supervisory relationship – those particular qualities and processes that make up that very special couple, supervisor and supervisee – and the various triangles surrounding that couple – supervisor / supervisee / patient; supervisor / supervisee / supervisee's personal analyst; supervisor / personal analyst / training patient; supervisor / trainee / training committee?

To add to this roll call of questions, we can ask also how we should understand the differences between supervision undertaken during training, and analysis undertaken during training. Do we keep a boundary between the two functions? Is the boundary permeable? Of what might consist the overlap, if any, and on what occasions?

And what does the role of post-qualification supervision play in the professional development of an analyst? Is there a difference in content or method between supervision during training and supervision after training? One distinction to be noted is that, although there may be a requirement of post-qualification supervision when an analyst applies to become a full professional member, or indeed to become a training analyst/supervisor of candidates, there is not a similar requirement of post-qualification personal analysis. And yet, personal analysis and intensive regular supervision of cases, along with theoretical and clinical seminars, are the pillars of our professional training.

Yet another question concerns whether the qualities necessary to become a supervisor are different from those needed to become a training analyst. What are the qualities that a supervisor should have; can these be learned? If so, how? And how can they be assessed and monitored by the Training Committee? What are the minimum requirements that an analyst should meet in order to be approved as a supervisor for trainees? Do the requirements differ from those to become a training analyst?

The four very different papers that follow have seemed to find rich common ground in the recognition of the unique quality of relationship that pertains between supervisor and supervisee. Each paper attends to the quality of this relationship in its own way.

Getting the Analytic Baby Back in the Bath Water

Donald Kalsched
New York, New York, U.S.A
New York Association for Analytical Psychology

My focus is the question: "What moments during the supervisory process are truly mutative and contribute to a candidate's ability to work symbolically"? To be able to think symbolically and maintain a symbolic attitude is an essential capacity that our professional Societies expect well-trained candidates to have before they graduate.

A short vignette of group-supervision process illustrates how Jungian understanding of "the symbolic" might be revisioned to apply to the supervisory process. This example serves to open the question what "symbolic capacity" really is, and whether we should continue to consider it as inherent in an individual, to be developed and evaluated. Perhaps this ability is much more context-dependent than we usually think it is: dependent on the inter-personal, inter-subjective field between or among people. Many candidates are capable of constellating a rich, playful and symbolic field with their patients, but in the supervisory process "the symbolic" often breaks down. It breaks down even more in the evaluative process, because of the candidate's anxiety. The relevant questions then become: What if symbolic capacity cannot be developed or evaluated outside a symbolic inter-subjective field? What implications would this have for our training programs and the way we supervise?

The supervision group that I conducted struggled through con-flicted feelings, moving slowly toward a symbolic field, got a brief foothold in it, fell out of it into a group complex full of anxiety and splitting, then recovered and regained symbolic space. This small group of three women psychotherapists has been working together for two years now; the participants know each other quite well. The group meets weekly in my office for an hour and a half. It is not part of a training institute, although the level of analytic awareness and skill is comparable to advanced training seminars which I have led at analytic institutes.

As the group opened on a particular occasion Sarah, one of the social workers in the group, said she had a crisis with one of her patients. She needed some of the group's time; Ellen and Liz, the other two members, readily agreed.

The crisis concerned her difficult patient Matilda, otherwise known as "Matty." Sarah wondered whether some action on her part outside the usual analytic frame might be necessary to protect Matty's newborn son from her violent affects. She had suffered an enormous amount of early trauma and, on account of her unbearable, unremembered suffering, had developed a defensive, counterdepen-dent facade that constituted a huge resistance in her psychotherapy with Sarah.

As an infant, Matilda – while in the care of her father – had fallen from a rooftop pool facility, four stories onto the ground. Her head had been split open and she had severe internal bleeding and broken bones. Many operations followed, as well as many painful hospital-izations and separations from her parents. As a handicapped child, she was picked on mercilessly by other children and retreated into an inner world shared only with her pet cats and a younger sister she loved and cared for. Nevertheless, Matilda had recovered most of her functioning and lived an increasingly normal life, thanks in large part to her mother's ceaseless devotion to her care. Despite a withered arm and epileptic-like seizures – now controlled with medication – she left home, completed college, dated a man some 15 years older than herself whom she eventually married, and just six months earlier, at the age of 29, Matilda had become a mother for the first time to a bright baby boy, Max.

Over the previous three years, Sarah had provided a warm holding environment for Matty, replicating the earlier support from her mother, while trying slowly to expand the patient's affect tolerance and autonomy. Matty had come into therapy, severely depressed, on the third anniversary of her younger sister's suicide. The sister had thrown herself out the window of a tall building. Matty had cried so hard she couldn't breathe. The sister had been her "child" when she was younger and Matty had been very protective of her.

Along with this traumatic history Matilda reported a few sparse dreams, one a repetitive childhood dream in which *a cat and a child were drowning in a pool*. In the first few weeks of therapy with Sarah, there was a similar dream – *a child drowning in the bottom of a pool and she was unable to reach the child. She saw his face underwater; he had no eyes and no mouth.* Sarah wanted to work with this autistic, schizoid inner figure but was afraid Matty was simply too wounded. Matty would come in week after week reporting the incidents of her life verbatim, without affect. If Sarah poked around for feelings, her patient would go blank and on to another subject. If Sarah used her empathy and modeled the affect implicit in Matilda's painful stories (such as, "How sad that must have felt"), Matilda would say "of course" and go on to still another subject.

Sarah felt repeatedly pushed away, insignificant and invisible. She wanted to do more uncovering work but all Matty seemed able to take in was advice on what to do. What to do with George (the then boyfriend), what to say to his parents, how to handle her boss at work.

Resigning herself to a supportive therapeutic stance, Sarah had helped Matty with many practical concerns. She had helped with communications skills with George (now Matty's husband); she met with Matty and the baby and talked about child-rearing. She had some emergency sessions with Matty and her husband over crises in their relationship and helped mediate the volatile affects that kept erupting. Lately, in addition to Matty's regular sessions, Sarah had

seen the couple more frequently because George was constantly
critical of Matty's inadequacy as a mother. She didn't change the
baby enough or feed him on schedule. She had even dropped the
baby because of her withered arm. The more George criticized his
wife, the more accident-prone Matty seemed to become.

On this day in supervision, Sarah herself had some practical
concerns and anxieties about "what to do" with Matilda. An accident
had just happened with the baby. Matilda had Max in a stroller at a
hot food cafeteria. Paying her bill, she had set the tray full of hot
food on the stroller table. By the time she was finished with the
cashier, the child had pulled the plate of hot food all over himself and
was screaming at the top of his lungs. At this moment George had
walked in and, seeing his beloved son covered in burning-hot food,
he flew into a rage at Matilda for her stupidity, grabbed the child and
ran home to their apartment.

From there George phoned Sarah and told his version of the story,
together with his great alarm about the safety of the child with
Matilda. After this phone call, Sarah had felt anxious and resentful
of the intrusion. Yet she admitted that she, too was worried for the
baby. Only the previous month, Matty had reported a fantasy from
teenage years about hurting her future baby. In the fantasy, which
she had told her mother, Matty would have a baby and then make it
suffer exactly as she had suffered as a child: the tragic fall, the
injuries, the operations, so that there would be someone in the world
who would understand completely how she felt as a child. Sarah had
heard this originally as a longing for empathy, for someone to share
Matty's unbearable childhood pain, and had hoped to work with this
in the transference, to no avail. After George's anxious phone call,
Sarah wasn't so sure.

Hence Sarah's supervisory crisis. Soon she would be meeting
with George, Matilda, and six-month-old Max. How should she
approach this session? Wasn't it possible that George was right: that
this baby was either being deliberately abused or that Matty might
be unconsciously acting out this abuse in her "accidents"? Perhaps
Sarah needed to enlist child protective services? She did not trust
Matty's judgment with the boy. What were Sarah's professional
responsibilities?

After Sarah laid out these details, the other two group members
began to ask questions for clarification. Ellen, the other social
worker in the group, identified with Sarah's concerns about the
child's welfare. Perhaps we had an untenable situation here – a

mother who was too damaged to care for him – maybe too damaged to learn anything about herself in psychotherapy. Liz, the creative-arts therapist, disagreed. Much good analytic work had been done already. Why not work symbolically with Matty's fantasies of hurting her baby and then help her to normalize them as a part of what all mothers feel? Sarah was torn. She had tried to help normalize Matilda's reported angry feelings toward the baby, somewhat helpfully. But now she was beginning to think that such work was a luxury, that maybe the child really was at risk. Liz kept pressing. Maybe Matty needed to be confronted with her fantasy again to find out whether it was essentially a cry for empathy or something to worry about. Sarah could discuss this very directly and also express her own concern about the welfare of the child. Ellen disagreed. She felt Matty was simply too wounded and concrete to be able to work with unconscious material. What if the child really was abused? Couldn't Sarah be sued?

I found myself in a revery listening to all this, letting my awareness drift back over the material of Matilda's life. I could not get the image out of my mind: of her own infant self smashed on the pavement, head split open like a melon. And her earlier dream of that half-drowned eyeless, mouthless child underwater in the pool also haunted me. A smashed innocent child, a dropped child, a destroyed childhood. Aware of my anxiety around this image, I had the vague feeling that, because of the husband's intrusive anxiety, this symbolic image had escaped the analytic vessel: just as Mercurius sometimes escapes the alchemist's retort, resulting in disaster.

My anxiety about the treatment increased. A victim/perpetrator psychology – a trauma complex – was taking hold in the group. I could feel how the symbolic space was collapsing around it. The wounded innocent child part of this complex was now projectively identified with little Max and its diabolical persecutor had now become identified with Matty herself. I could see this insidious scenario unfolding, as clearly as if it had been laid out as energy vectors on a grid. A symbolic child had escaped and the splitting of the therapeutic vessel had allowed this. My job, so it seemed at the time, was to rescue this analytic "child."

Out of my revery I came on a mission: "Wait a minute, wait a minute," I said. "It seems to me we're in danger here of throwing the bathtub out with the baby. What about the analysis? What about the child in our patient? What about Matty? Let's imagine how she might be feeling as her husband and therapist prepare to meet with her to discuss her incompetent mothering."

With this comment, Sarah seemed annoyed. "I don't think you get it," she said. "Matty's feelings aren't the issue. As a professional I'm legally obligated to report an abused child. It's part of my social work license."

"I understand that," I replied. "But why are we so sure we have an abused child all of a sudden? Let's look at what happened here. An harrassed, handicapped mother just had an accident with her baby in a busy foodline ... the child is burned slightly. ... the husband blows up in a rage. ... and suddenly drastic action is being contemplated. I'm not sure. ..."

"Listen!" Sarah said. And then, fixing me with a knowing gaze, she said emphatically and patronizingly, "Good mothers don't drop their babies" I felt my stomach tighten and my breathing stop. My ears got hot and out of the churning confusion inside, I heard myself say sarcastically, "Maybe not, but good therapists don't drop their patients either!"

At this point, a deafening silence fell over the group. Sarah seemed hurt and momentarily speechless. For that split second, I didn't care. I felt cocky and righteous about my rejoinder – pleased with myself for the analytic truth in my acerbic comment and the perfect timing of it. I had now fallen into the group trauma complex myself.

"What do you mean?" Sarah asked incredulously.

"I mean that you've lost your analytic attitude toward the patient!" I said, still caught in my side of the complex. "It feels to me that the husband's anxiety has gotten into you somehow to the point where you're in danger of colluding with him." I launched into a long explanation about the split tandem-image of the trauma complex (the innocent child and its protector/persecutor), how easy it was to get sucked into that split structure and taking up one side or the other. Then, realizing to my horror that I was slipping deeper into the same quicksand I was describing, I sweetened my explanation with some reassuring comments about the good work Sarah had done with Matty. All this was technically elegant and theoretically sound, but interpersonally as disconnected as I was from my body at the moment.

At the end of this long interpretation, Sarah looked at me like a stunned fish, overwhelmed and confused, now starting to doubt herself. She could no more hear me and take in what I said, than

Matty could hear her analytic forays into symbolic "meaning." There was simply too much splitting and anxiety in the room. The supervision had now come completely off the rails and I knew it.

Liz quickly picked up the tension. "Oh God," she said … "Look what's going on here – it's all borderline dynamics. The group is splitting two against two. All this anger and hurt. We're repeating the dynamics of the case!"

I felt immediately grateful for Liz's observation; I knew that she was right. I even knew dimly that my revery image of that smashed child might be a key to the primitive levels of anxiety now replicated in the room. Not that I could intervene yet; I was only beginning to come out of my complex and back into my body.

"And what are you feeling, Sarah?" Liz continued. "You must have a lot going on right now."

"I'm upset," Sarah replied, tears coming into her eyes. "I feel hurt and misunderstood somehow. And I'm angry at you, Don. It feels like you've just dismissed and belittled my professional concerns as if they're misplaced or beneath the higher value of analysis you stand for. You're not in my shoes. I'm down here in the trenches with this case. … It's easy for you to say there's nothing to worry about!"

I sat silently for several minutes, letting Sarah's comments seep into me as the tension receded. Now the dropped child was back in the room again in the person of Sarah, my supervisee, and I felt as though I'd just split her head open myself with my "high" analytic interpretations. I could feel the genuineness of her feelings and regretted my heavy-handedness. I, too, had felt belittled and my analytic values put down, following her comment about how "Good mothers don't drop their babies." It was these mutual injuries that prevented us from hearing each other.

"I'm sorry," I said. "I think I've been so anxious to rescue the analytic vessel that I haven't been able to listen to your concerns. You're right. I'm not in the trenches with you. Only you know the true picture of your client. So keep talking. I'll try to listen better."

With this Sarah smiled and softened. Tears came up in her eyes again. "I haven't been able to hear you either," she admitted. "I'll try to take in what you're saying better too, because I know there's something important in it for me. I just haven't been able to hear it. I've been so concerned about the baby!"

With this reconciling moment, the group complex fell away, and we were back in symbolic space. We had now metabolized a piece of the paranoid/persecutory anxiety that belonged to this case –

anxiety with which we had become infected. At this point, Liz and Ellen chimed in and we could begin to look at that "parallel process" between where we got stuck in the group and where Sarah felt stuck with Matty.

One thing was clear. Our process had deteriorated from a symbolic exploration of meanings to a concrete obsession with what to do – precisely what was frustrating Sarah with Matty's demand for concrete information. Questions about what to do are what you're left with when the search for symbolic understanding breaks down under the pressure of unbearable anxiety. Matty was riddled with this anxiety from her early traumas, but somehow Sarah had lost sight of this fact and, acting under its pressure, had retreated from the search for symbolic understanding to providing concrete answers to endless concrete questions. Meanwhile she was feeling less and less useful as Matty's depth psychotherapist. In the group we went through a similar process. Sarah had come into the group full of anxiety. Instead of letting the archaic levels of this anxiety emerge in the group as images, we also became "complexed" and retreated from the symbolic into concrete arguments about what to do.

As we explored our process together, I reported to the group my revery about the smashed child and the faceless drowning baby and suggested to the group that this image might be the source of both Sarah's and the group's unconscious anxiety and resulting complexed reactions. Sarah said this made a lot of sense to her. She said, if truth be told, that she had "fallen in love" with Matty's little boy over the last few months and had begun to see him as "innocent" and healthy and in need of protection, whereas Matty was becoming associated with "badness," damage, and persecutory neglect. Meanwhile the dropped, wounded autistic infant in Matty had been lost to the analytic process. This smashed baby image was a combination of innocence and destruction – opposites that were simply too traumatic to hold. They were split between innocence and protection versus persecution. In the group we had gone through that split and recovered the center.

In a follow-up, Sarah reported that her conjoint session with Matty and George had gone extremely well. "I couldn't believe how identified I was with George's anxiety," she said, "and I had lost my empathic connection to my patient. So, when George opened the session with a diatribe against Matty, I said we had to slow everything down and go back to the moment in the cafeteria where it all started. After we got it straight finally, I asked Matty how she would have liked George to respond at that moment. ... and Matty burst into tears. For the first time, she felt that somebody understood her feelings."

When I heard that, I felt a wonderful sense of fulfillment and gratitude for the way this supervisory process had worked and for the way the members of this group, struggling in and out of symbolic space, had found and recovered the fragmented pieces of Matty's life and process. For Sarah and her patient, the baby was back in his bath, and the process of her psychotherapy could proceed.

Anxiety and Containment in Supervision

Jane Knight
London, England
Society of Analytical Psychology

The task of the supervisor is to be available to reflect with the analyst on that person's work and the analysand's psychological states. Also to guide and stimulate the supervisee in the process of growth and discovery of skill and analytic attitude.

The role includes various responsibilities that occasionally conflict. These comprise: furthering the aptitude of the analyst for the work; taking care that the analysand has as effective an analysis as possible; and, if the analyst is in training, reporting to a training director or committee. These responsibilities give the supervisor a degree of power over the supervisee's professional life. This in itself is a factor in the supervisee's anxieties.

In supervision of a trainee-analyst, the supervisor is important in establishing a place of containment for the analytic pair. Although trainee analysts begin work with analysands only after a searching selection and a period of work with their fellow trainees before meeting their first analysand, their fear that their selection was a mistake and that they will now be found out frequently remains untouched. Only by going through the ordeal of the training can they discover themselves as analysts. Such anxieties are often denied, covered by various defensive ploys such as superiority, anger, humour or compliance.

The experience of undertaking such a rigorous training often seems – at first – to diminish skills. People who have reached the heights in previous professions seem to lose their capacities under the pressure of their expectations of themselves and assumptions about their supervisors' expectations. Here is a stimulus for shame, a painful emotion with historical and inner roots. It may be hard for supervisees to admit how much anxiety they are feeling. Perhaps they spend all the supervision time describing the analysands and giving all the details of their part in the sessions, omitting reference to the supervisees' own feelings regarding the analysands. This approach leads to the elaboration of the analysand's psychopathology, problems and history and prevents the supervisor from grasping the transference and countertransference. Similarly, repeated references to a previous professional role, for example as a psychiatrist or social worker, can deflect from this issue. These are interesting points that need attention, but is there an extraneous reason for bringing them? Do they reveal or hide the interaction between analyst and analysand?

The supervisor promotes openness in reporting and discussion, by conveying respect for the supervisee as a colleague. Given acceptance, transference and countertransference can be revealed and the supervisee's emotional response is available as a means of understanding interactions between analyst and analysand. It may be very difficult to reveal negative feelings such as envy, hatred or fear. At the same time, the relationship between supervisor and supervisee may reflect what is happening in the analysis.

Beginning work with a new analysand is a very uncertain stage. The novice analyst's insecurity may exacerbate the analysand's anxiety and lead to rejection or contempt. Alternatively, we often observe the analyst's relief at the trust which the analysand demonstrates. Analysands come with a pre-formed transference. They often see in the analyst their own projection: someone who is going to take care of them, on whom they can depend or who can be seduced; or else and even at the same time, someone who will criticise, punish or coerce them. The trainee bears the anxiety of these projections and brings them to the supervisor, we hope, in order to share the burden and to understand it. Often the projection is transmitted to the supervisor directly, together with the anxiety evoked in the analyst. The supervisor's task then is to contain the emotion and work to free the supervisee from pressure in order to prevent returning the undigested affect or retaliation. We may observe the evocation of a complex in a supervisee which corresponds with that which is in the analysand.

For example, a trainee was working with a person whose only emotion seemed to be rage. During the first year he felt constantly threatened that she would end the analysis. My comment that he was suffering her fear of abandonment did not cut much ice until they had passed the first anniversary. Gradually he relaxed, although still threatened and literally abandoned, as she often missed sessions. Then he could allow himself really to know his own frustration and anger and use them to further the analysis, by playing back the anger which she had evoked in him.

It has been my experience, fate or fortune to have inherited the supervision of some trainees whose original supervision had ended prematurely through the death of the supervisor or their moving away from London. To have to begin again in mid-stream may mean negotiating a period of testing, self-protectiveness and anxiety about exposing the work and intimate feelings. These situations confirmed for me the value of the containing function of the supervisor.

In one case there had been a gap of over two months. The analysand was a very contemptuous, narcissistically damaged young woman, a therapist in her own field. In the face of her attacks the trainee analyst had regressed to working in the way that was familiar to him, as a counselor. He picked up the outer reality, helped to resolve problems and occasionally advised on the analysand's work with her clients without addressing the symbolic meaning of this material. I felt that I had to find a way to get the train back on the rails, taking into account the analyst's anger at being abandoned. In fact he quickly understood what had happened because he really knew it all the time, but felt unsupported in the absence of his supervisor.

Another analyst had had a very good experience with her former supervisor, who had died. She was grieving when she came to me. She managed the loss and the sense of being uncontained by holding on to and continuing to apply everything the previous supervisor had said. I was aware that the work with her analysand had become stereotyped. The analyst was interpreting at the oedipal level, but I felt increasingly in touch with a desolate baby and struggled to bring this aspect into our discussions – with very little success. The analysand solved the dilemma for us by suddenly announcing that she was going to end the analysis. The analyst was bewildered and became angry. The analysis had lasted for one year and seven months and she needed it to continue for a minimum of two years to qualify as part of her training course. Would she have to begin again?

There was a pause. Then I asked her what was happening to the analysand at one year and seven months of age. The next baby was born when she was two years old. Then we could talk about the analysand's unconscious assumption that there would be no room on mother's lap for her because of the baby inside and the defense against this anxiety shared by the trainee analyst in their talk about more "grown up" oedipal matters. Then the analyst could begin to use me. The analysand stayed.

A crisis is encountered, frequently, at about two years into the analysis. It is marked enough for trainees and supervisors to question the assessing clinic director as to what was actually said to the analysand about the duration of analysis. But I wonder if this crisis is demonstrating a developmental experience which may be the mother's pregnancy, but is also an increased push towards independence, walking, talking and saying "No" (see Strauss, 1962).

The erotic transference is often a source of great anxiety in the trainee analyst. Whether reciprocal erotic feelings are experienced or not, the analysand may have a delusion that they are. This delusion can give rise to opposite emotions – feelings of hatred, fear and entrapment – in the trainee analyst who is in as much danger of colluding with and reassuring as of rejecting the analysand. It is a very difficult situation and one in which the anxiety may be transferred directly to the supervisor. There are occasions when the supervisor feels that the trainee analyst is not anxious enough.

Emotional reactions evoked in the supervisor may be very useful in understanding the process of the analysis. They may be the same, but are often different from or opposite to those experienced by the trainee analyst. Sometimes, when hearing about an analysand who is described as highly defended and denying all emotion, my eyes fill with tears. Does this indicate the underlying feeling, that there is a much more alive, unconscious interaction between analysand and trainee analyst than the latter can be aware of? Or I might feel suddenly angry and then realise that the supervisee is conveying an unconscious sense of being attacked.

Often the supervisor has to bear being in the dark. This situation may reflect the trainee analyst's state of not knowing and waiting, or analyst and analysand are together in a necessary, mutual, exclusive experience. It can be difficult to decide when to try to unpack the parcel. Does the supervisor become the strict father interrupting the mother/baby togetherness? It may be the other way round: the supervisor perceiving the trainee analyst as pushing the analysand to differentiate too quickly. Then the supervisor may become the mother. Sometimes the analysand's family situation is reproduced in the supervisory pair. We often see this happening in group supervision when everyone present plays a part in the family drama. Unless these dynamics can be understood and unraveled, the supervisee is left holding the anxiety.

Fordham (1995) stated: "Candidates are put under greater stress than is any trained analyst and so we need to find out how to diminish it. My contention is that the provision of containment is an essential element in diminishing the candidate's stress and freeing her or him to function according to his or her best capacity" (p. 50).

References

Fordham, M. (1995). Suggestions towards a theory of supervision. In P. Kugler (Ed.), *Jungian Perspectives on Clinical Supervision*. Einsiedeln, Switzerland: Daimon.

Strauss, R. (1962). The Archetype of Separation. In A. Guggenbühl-Craig (Ed.), *The Archetype*, Basel/New York: S. Karger.

Conditions of Supervision/Control Analysis

Anne Springer
Berlin, Germany
Deutsche Gesellschaft für Analytische Psychologie

The question of whether analysis can be taught has been more controversial in the Jungian world than in Freudian psychoanalysis, as has the question of a modifiable and teachable theory and technique. The process and the contents of control analysis form a complex structure of didactic and more narrowly analytic training components, including the relationship between control analyst and candidate. It is within this framework that the techniques of treatment are taught: the formulation of interventions, including interpretation; advice on relevant literature, indications for analytic work and prognosis, as well as those about the setting, the frequency and the rules of our work. The latter two items cover such issues as vacation and cancellation fees.

The essence of control analysis, however, is the attempt to understand the complex pattern of transference and countertransference that develops and surfaces during control analysis and the patient's analysis and to use it for both the patient's and the candidate's benefit. An important side effect of this is the control analyst's own continuous learning process.

The terms "supervision" and "control analysis" are used synonymously in Berlin; "control analysis" is by far the older term. It dates from the institutionalization of psychoanalysis around 1920, when analysts were debating the questions of how knowledge could be imparted to the candidates and how the quality of teaching could be safeguarded. The first standards were set by the old Berlin Psychoanalytical (Freudian) Institute, which was founded by Karl Abraham. In 1922, Max Eitington spoke of "control analysis" for the first time as one of the important educational tools, along with training analysis, first insisted upon by Jung, and clinical work with patients.

In analytical psychology, the beginnings of control analysis date back to Jung's seminars after 1920. In 1948, control analysis became an integral part of the training with the founding of the Zürich Institute. After 1960, at least 250 supervised hours were required. In the early years of the IAAP (1958 and after) the requirement was that candidates spend one and a half years in control analysis, since 1971 at least 50 sessions with the control analyst – increased in 1983 to 100 hours. Plaut and Fordham published – in 1961 – the first important Jungian works on the technique and problems of control analysis.

If I had to choose between the terms control analysis and supervision, my preference would lie with control analysis. "Supervision" originated in the realm of social work and is thus not specific to analysis. Control analysis, on the other hand, is a term that has matured over time and that, at least in German, facilitates the adequate labeling of a combination of different factors. It denotes, among other things, the analysis of the candidate's countertransference as well as the control of the patient's analysis. Other languages require at least two terms for these activities. In English, for example, they may be labeled supervisory analysis and supervised analysis respectively. At the same time the word "control" seems to evoke negative associations both in the candidate and in the control analyst, thus prompting them to use the term "supervision." In my view, it is more honest, however, to express linguistically that control analysis is part of our training and that it will also be evaluated by the training institute as such.

This view leads me to the external conditions of control analysis. Training analysts are identical to control analysts. In the whole of

Germany, at least 150 hours of control analysis are required to complete an analytic training. Of these, a maximum of 75 hours can be done in group sessions. In this context, six treatment hours correspond to one control session of 50 minutes. It is fundamentally undesirable to work on several cases with one control analyst and, in the last several years, it has become unusual to do a control analysis with one's own analyst. But this policy was decided upon formally only a few months ago by our committee of training analysts. In Berlin, we have the peculiar situation that we work in a common institute with a Freudian department and one for child and adolescent analysis. In this joint institute, our Jungian candidates have some of their cases controlled by Freudians, although these should not be the first of their training. At the end of the analysis and the control analysis, following either a formal application to assume more than six patients or to take the final exam, the candidate receives a written assessment from the control analyst regarding the quality of the candidate's work. These assessments contain qualitative judgments and form much of the basis for the decisions made by the training committee. The candidate usually receives the assessment in time to register a formal protest, in case of feeling unfairly judged.

The initial stages of control work, when the candidate chooses a control analyst, are characterized by a mixture of transference onto this one control analyst – understood as a part of the transference in the context of training analysis – and of personal acquaintance via the institute. A candidate may choose a certain control analyst for a number of reasons: because the candidate expects the control analyst to have a specific expertise, has the reputation of being influential, has published a great deal, is rumored to be "easy" or "difficult," there was no other convenient time slot, or even because the control analyst's practice is conveniently located. Control analysts, on the other hand, choose candidates because they like them personally, because they do not like them at all and are curious to find out why, because they have a slot available, because they have a professional obligation to do control analysis, because they were charmingly and/ or urgently asked for a slot, because they like doing control analyses as a welcome change from their own practice, or even because they feel flattered that they are wanted.

I have been a training analyst for about eight years and perform quite a few control analyses. During this time, I have been a member of the Berlin training committee, which I have headed for the last six years. This fact is not a negligible factor of the process of my control analyses. All of the candidates' transferences onto the institute and training – with the concomitant attitudes, affects, and feelings – form an integral part of the choice of those trainees who register with me. As has been mentioned above, these special circumstances are complemented by their transferences onto me as a person and an analyst.

From my vantage point, my actual or presumed knowledge about the candidates registering with me plays a considerable role. My inner images of the candidates are prejudiced by their appearance in seminars, conferences, personal encounters and before the training committee. I usually know, for example, with whom the candidates are doing their training analysis. The process is at its most complicated when a new control candidate has played a part in the "material" of one of my own analysands. My primary task, consequently, is to perceive my projections onto the new control analysand and possibly to understand the person in terms of my own ongoing self-analysis. If I succeed somewhat in this effort, I can then open myself to the candidate as a "new person close to me."

This is also one of the most important attitudes that I can bring to a patient who enters my practice for the first time. If I succeed at least partially in this respect, I feel that I have made a good start. From candidates, I usually experience a mixture of excitement and curiosity, fear and even anger (yet another appointment, yet another hurdle!) in varied intensities and combinations.

Over the past few years, I have cultivated a habit that marks the start of a control analysis. In the very first hour, possibly before a patient has been selected, I ask the trainee to speak as "uncollectedly" as possible about the prospective patient and our anticipated first encounters. During this time, I try to ascertain what initial questions and hypotheses I have regarding the material. I attempt, moreover, to form as clear an image as possible of the exterior framework of the treatment: the premises, the furnishings, the lighting, position of the couch? The location of easy chairs? Where the candidate is seated, and at what distance to the analysand? In this way, I develop my own interior image of the analysand – with significant gaps and distortions – and an image of the candidate as a less experienced colleague who symbolically grants the analysand access to the candidate's rooms.

Additionally, I tell the candidate at the outset of the control analysis that, for me, it makes more sense to decide before or during each control hour whether the session will be based on minutes or on a free report. In my opinion, the control analysand's occasional recourse to written notes reflects fears in most cases. The fear of "having done something wrong" represents fear of me, whereas the fear of "forgetting something important" expresses the candidate's resistance to feeling internally close to the patient. Trainees who are particularly anxious often insist on taking notes during treatment and control sessions and are loathe to let go of them, physically and symbolically. Initially or for quite a time, I have to live with this, although I sometimes find it difficult. On the other hand, this was precisely the way I "grew up" in my own training, without questioning the method at the time. I consider working without written notes to be crucial because this is the most important way to foster the candidate's trust in his or her ability to get close to the patient and to experience analysis as a living process.

In general, control analysis is made up of two essential elements. On the one hand, it comprises the teaching of treatment techniques, the theory of technique and the essential literature. On the other hand, it consists of examining the countertransference processes in the treatment actions of the candidate. It is this second aspect that I consider much more difficult, for a number of reasons.

The candidate is in training analysis. The formation of my own hypotheses on countertransference in treatment necessarily contains, among other elements, assumptions on the inner world of the candidate. This results in a partial intimacy, which is otherwise reserved for training analysis. It can be tempting – both for the candidate and for me – to institute a kind of disguised or competing "undercover" analysis, where I could act out positive and negative attitudes toward the training analyst, thereby enabling the trainee to stage or act out resistances that actually belong to the training analysis (see Fordham 1961). In my opinion, the only way out of this dilemma is via a functioning committee and group of training analysts which, in facilitating professional exchange and debate, ensure that these are not carried out at the trainee's expense.

I concede that it is idealistic and a sign of neurotic omnipotence to assume that this problem can be solved completely. For myself, I have found a sentence that helps me temper disturbingly positive or negative attitudes toward the trainee or the trainee's analyst: "I will respect that the training analyst is a very important human being for the candidate at this time and carries considerable weight in the analytic process and in the interior world of the candidate, an importance which is and should be fundamentally outside my purview."

In order to distance myself from the trainee's personal analysis, I have also devised the technique of repeatedly communicating my own thoughts on the material in a manner that seeks to relate them to those of the younger colleague and in which I sometimes explain my professional, but rarely my personal, background. Another immensely important aspect that distinguishes me from the training analyst is that – different from analysis – I encourage, console and/ or directly criticize the trainee. Although this looks like supervision, it remains a control analysis because, with the help of analytic thinking, I try to decide what I do or, more sensibly, what I refrain from saying or doing.

A large and possibly unsolvable dilemma arises if candidates unconsciously make themselves inaccessible to control analysis by chronically submitting to me, idealizing me or by fighting me – through competition or disempowerment – thus using me, but not making good use of me. Candidates may proceed in this manner because they unconsciously resent the control analysis per se, feeling that they are not being supported, but attacked, and because they resent the institution which, to them, wages the attack. Since all institutions are unjust, the Institute – and thus I as one of its representatives – repeatedly furnish material that justifies the candidate's feeling of being attacked. Until now, I have been fortunate never to have had to break off a control analysis for this reason. However, when such difficulties arise, rarely, I formulate for the candidate my assessment of the dilemma more clearly than normal. I also ask the candidate whether the problem as I experience it is well known and then point to training analysis as the proper arena in which to work on it. Occasionally, this problem concerns candidates who have not yet decided whether they want to become analysts, but who have invested a great deal of time and money in the training. In these cases, in particular, I consider it indispensable to exchange views with the candidates' other control analysts. Such an exchange is my only chance of finding out whether and how my own unanalyzed transferences onto the candidate, the candidate's patients or training analysts are possibly obstructing the candidate, or whether this is truly the candidate's problem.

If I look back on my own development as a control analyst, I come up with at least two questions that have not yet been solved satisfactorily. The first is that control analysts do not receive training for this work and thus grow up "naturally," so to speak. It depends on the environment of the respective institute whether control analysts regularly scrutinize themselves and their work through intensive discussions with colleagues. Some other analytic associations are more advanced in this regard. In the German Association for Analytical Psychology, we have only recently created a central committee of training and control analysts in our new statutes. This committee could discuss such professional and substantive questions outside the institutional context.

Second, control analysts are responsible for safeguarding their own quality within their respective local institutes, a task made more difficult – as is well-known – by all of the personal entanglements there. Because of this, I sometimes think that we should encourage each candidate to discuss one case with a control analyst from a completely different analytic organization – even one outside of our "mixed" institute – and then to include this evaluation in our own work. Such an arrangement would have to be mutual. It is equally clear that, in order for such an endeavor to work, the analysts of the different theoretical schools would have to approach one another in an atmosphere of mutual trust. The wounds of the historical division of analysts, however, are probably still too fresh for this.

In this work I am touched most deeply when I am privileged to experience how a trainee suddenly, sometimes even during a control session, has self-discovery experience – intensively, cognitively, and emotionally as an analyst – saying, in effect: "This is how analysis is, in precisely this proximity and intensity, when I create my own inner realm, guard it and make myself available as an analyst. I can accept that I am uniquely and unmistakably important for the analysand in an internal way." These moments are precious and well worth the effort. We cannot attain them without a foundation of knowledge in theory and technique, but they transcend acquired knowledge. These are the moments in which new analysts are born (not only in final examinations), and it is very satisfying to have contributed something to the process.

Translated from the German by Margaret Ries and Fabian Hilfrich

References:

Fordham, M. (1961). Suggestions towards a theory of supervision. *Journal of Analytical Psychology*, 6-2, 107-115.
Plaut, A. (1961). A dynamic outline of the training situation. *Journal of Analytical Psychology*, 6-2, 98-101.

Some Special Features of the Transference in Consultation and Supervision

John Beebe
San Francisco, California, USA
C.G. Jung Institute San Francisco

The transference relationships that develop between a Jungian psychotherapy consultant and consultees and supervisees apply to a range of consultation and supervision relationships, not only to those in which the person in training is in an analytic institute studying to be a Jungian analyst. As Jungians are called upon increasingly to share their skills with budding psychotherapists at all stages of training and development, it is important for us to think about the transferences we are likely to elicit, particularly in people at the very beginning of their training as psychotherapists – where we have the potential to be most creative or destructive in fostering the personal and cultural transformation of a psychologically-oriented individual.

I feel anxious even talking about this work, because these relationships are very precious containers. There is something quite personal about them, and I need to bite back some of what I could say, to protect the privacy of colleagues.

Talking about the transference in supervision would not seem to be pioneer work, but to a surprising extent it is. We have not tended to focus on the transferences between supervisor and supervisee. We have talked, rather, throughout the literature on supervision, mostly about the "parallel process" – that now generally accepted idea that if somewhere there's something going on with the patient, it creates a dynamic or, in Jungian terms, an archetypal field which gets into the consultation. (See Zabriskie 1997).

The invitation to be part of this panel gave me an opportunity to think systematically about some phenomena that I had found perplexing. Here I am concerned with what hides behind the parallel process, and consider the primary relationship: between supervisor and supervisee. In my supervisory work with relatively new psychotherapists, for instance, I had noticed an erotic countertransference almost each time the work starts to take off. On further reflection it seemed that these erotic countertransferences were just the tip of the iceberg of an extremely charged field.

As an experiment, I tried to recall everyone I have ever supervised, listing just those people who immediately came to mind, without going through files of my 27 years of this work. As soon as I recalled the names, I remembered not only erotic countertransference feelings toward many of them, but also extremely angry "hate-in-the-countertransference" feelings, and sometimes extreme anxiety.

I tend not to get very close to former supervisees. Nevertheless, when I've allowed a former supervisory relationship to develop into a collegial friendship, the friendship often has had an unusually difficult, stormy course. Not infrequently, angry confrontations directed toward me, or at the very least irritated feelings on my part, have created a noticeable distance that contrasts ironically with the former period of relative ease and intimacy within the supervision itself. When I looked over my list of former supervisees and consultees and considered the feelings that had come up, I was amazed at the enormity of the emotional field that seems to be created by the fact of supervision. I realized that it wasn't just eros, but also aggression, dependency, and competition that gave this field its weight. This seems to be a largely unexplored territory.

Recently I was asked to speak to a cross-disciplinary analytic meeting in San Francisco. The psychoanalyst who preceded me on the panel that day talked about an attempt within her psychoanalytic group to present a panel on relationships after termination of supervision. The cases that were chosen for discussion were those in which the analysts being trained were now fully qualified psychoanalysts. In preliminary interviews with those setting up the panel, the training analysts acknowledged that they had become friends and colleagues with their former training analysands. However, just before the event some of the training analysts who had agreed to speak were advised by their colleagues not to speak about these relationships because to do so would be professionally compromising. Although all the people contacted, both analysts and former analysands, reported a very interesting series of stages by which they developed these post-termination friendships, and expressed satisfaction in them, in the end none were willing to come forward because of the risk of exposure. The panel had to be canceled.

It seems to me that we really need to begin to let the cat out of the bag – acknowledge that there is something else going on in analytic supervision, and perhaps all supervision, than simply a very controlled professional relationship.

As soon as I heard, in Don Kalsched's presentation of the case he was supervising, in which a child had once fallen several stories, I immediately thought what a precious thing a new psychological identity is! How easy it is to lift it up too high and then to let it drop in a way that it can be smashed. We have to remind ourselves that for many people it is a new thing to think and work psychologically. That budding psychological self, which is entrusted to the supervisor, as to a parent, to foster is extremely vulnerable and precious, and can easily be hurt.

Because of the vulnerability of the supervisee, supervision can be compared to psychotherapy. All psychotherapeutic interventions proceed on the hope for some kind of change, and sometimes, as a therapist, one gets very specific notions of one's role in facilitating that change. Stein (1984) has written about what he calls the maieutic countertransference. Maieutics means midwifery, and the maieutic countertransference refers to the attitude on the part of the therapist that therapy is, or ought to be, a process of birthing. With the maieutic attitude, Stein observes, one views oneself as midwife to the new self being born out of the client. This is a common fantasy among psychotherapists. I must remind you, therefore, that few patients actually come to psychotherapy with the expectation of a whole new identity being born. Rather, they come with the expectation of relief from significant stress, some understanding of a situation. Perhaps, if they stay long enough, as a dividend of the therapy, this whole new identity may come. Usually, it does not.

In supervision, however, the client does come – in fact should come – with the expectation of a new identity being born, because he or she is supposed to be turned into a psychotherapist or made into a more competent one. The unconscious of the supervisee takes up that expectation in all the ways of an infant getting itself born and nurtured, using the supervisor as father, mother, and initiator to foster a budding self. These transference roles, as we know from one hundred years of psychoanalysis, are extremely charged, both erotically and in other ways. Michael Fordham used to say that the business of babies is being loved, making themselves loved. So we have to expect that from the infant psychotherapist selves that come to us for supervision there is going to be a pull for love. We must accept and hold that, and we should also expect it to structure the "pairing culture" that Bion (1959) talked about, where the two anticipate that their coming together will produce a new life. This means that, in supervision, often there will be a feeling of a friendship developing and the sense of the two people getting connected in some exciting way. It is a potential tragedy when that initial fantasy of pairing off to reproduce is taken literally, as it too often is in recently or prematurely terminated supervisory relationships, and sometimes in the midst of supervision itself.

And if the charged nature of the consulting relationship does not present enough difficulties, there is yet another problem. This primary relationship is in some ways disavowed by the supervisee. Making my list of former supervisees and consultees was an astonishing experience: it was as if all those countertransferences returned to haunt me. So then I decided to do an experiment and list all the supervisors I have had. I recalled hardly any great sense of transference on my part. They were nice, they were friendly. I thought a few of them were a little overly interested in me, but I was there to talk about my patients and to learn and I felt I made that clear. Occasionally there were competitive feelings toward my supervisors, feelings of which I was conscious, or was made conscious of by the supervisor. For the most part, however, I was amazed at the discrepancy between the countertransferences I had been aware of toward my supervisees and the transferences I had clearly not owned toward my own supervisors.

This makes me suspect that the supervisee is often in a kind of denial about the relationship in a way that a regular analytic patient would not be. A regular analytic patient really does gratify that part of us as analysts that is interested in relationship, because the analysand is so evidently also interested in the relationship.

As I was putting this talk together I had a dream which I think may be appropriate to share. In it, I was to have lunch with a former supervisee. This was not someone toward whom I had an erotic countertransference. This person sought me out a long time ago, before he was in the Institute; now we are colleagues. In reality, we have an extremely distant relationship, but in the dream we were meeting for lunch. I was disappointed, however, when I arrived for that lunch to find that he had invited a third person. Apparently he wanted to have lunch with one of his patients as well as with me, and he had brought that person along. I felt in the dream that I was participating in some kind of boundary violation because my former supervisee had chosen to have lunch with one of his patients. I didn't think it was a good idea, but in the dream I recognized that I felt resentful, not because I was asked to be complicit in a possible ethical compromise, but because I had expected to have lunch with my colleague alone.

Especially since it came in connection with this presentation, I have had to think very carefully about this dream. It seems to hark back to what was probably happening for me with my supervisee when we were working together: the patient got in the way. Just as at the dream lunch, when my supervisee actually wanted to talk about his patient, I often wanted to have the relationship just with him. Now I don't think that's crazy on either side; I think it's just-so. But you can see how frustrating such a state of affairs can be for the supervisor, and how tempting it is for the eros of the supervisor to develop in a compensatory way to pull for the relationship that the supervisee is disavowing. I believe this is one of the usual complications in the emotional field between supervisor and supervisee.

There's another kind of bind that I know very well, where the person coming for supervision is on the face of it very interested in the relationship with me, but the interest proves to be passive-aggressively tangential to the task at hand. Such supervisees are interested in everything about me except the part of me that knows something about psychotherapy and wants to pass that along. Such a way of connecting to me as supervisor is, I think, an instance of the defense the Kleinians call adhesive identification: only the personal surface and not the core of what I am about is being taken aboard. My response to such a fundamentally disavowing interest in my role as clinical teacher is to get increasingly angry. What is likely to emerge from me then is not a compensatory eros, but a compensatory logos that has a rageful quality. I start teaching like a maniac.

Someone who is in training to be a psychotherapist cannot be expected to take full responsibility for an unconscious relationship. We who are supervising are normally in the position of holding a relationship the supervisee is not yet ready to explore.

The unconscious aspects of the supervisory relationship not only are apt to be more intense, and more disavowed; they're often even more dangerous than the usual patient-analyst relationship. That's saying something, because we know how dangerous the usual patient-analyst relationship is. At least in therapy, however, we know that the playing field is not level. There is an obvious differential in power that requires greater responsibility on the part of the therapist. It's easy, on the other hand, to underestimate the power differential with someone we already know is en route to being a colleague and will thus be "a therapist too." One can entertain the fantasy that all you have to do is give them a tug and they'll be on your level. In that line of thinking there's a tremendous underestimation of the difference in status, and that, I think, is the reason people sometimes imagine that they can turn these relationships so quickly into friendships, or love affairs, or marriages. I'm not saying that former supervisees can't survive such role changes. Some obviously have, but for many people there is hurt in the attempt of former supervisors to make them peers, one which sometimes never gets worked out.

The supervisory relationship is dangerous in part because so much kinship fantasy gets channeled into the relationship. As supervisor, you literally are going to produce a new member of your professional community. If this work goes well, the two of you will become colleagues. But the realizability of this desirable goal can create a literalizing pull toward more destructive outcomes as well.

The supervisee is particularly aware of the potential for great benefit, and is also equally aware of the potential for great harm. Our supervisees realize they are boarding a very big ship: they know that they don't want to fall as they're going up the gangplank. The supervisee readily feels the opposites of destruction and creation, and when opposites are strongly felt and greatly polarized, a powerful energy field is generated. Both supervisor and supervisee may be tempted, given the concrete thrust of the transaction, to take that energy field as evidence of the literal strength of their relationship.

Both partners will concede that supervision can be enormously creative. But if we are to be better supervisors, we must also face the destructive potential within this very interesting work.

References

Bion, W.R. (1959). *Experiences in Groups*. London: Tavistock Publications.
Stein, M. (1984). Power, shamanism, and maieutics in the countertransference. In N. Schwartz-Salant and M. Stein (Eds.) *Transference/Countertransference*. Wilmette, IL: Chiron Publications.
Zabriskie, B. (1997). Thawing the "frozen accidents": The archetypal view in countertransference. *Journal of Analytical Psychology*, *42*-1, 25-40.

Clinical Issues

In My End Is My Beginning

Exploring the "Breakdown/Breakthrough" Cycle

Nathan Field
London, England
British Association of Psychotherapists (Jungian Section)

The incentive to write this paper arose from a phenomenon I noticed with certain cases that got badly stuck. After prolonged struggles to make the therapy work, I would be driven eventually to admit myself beaten. But when I reached this desperate point, something interesting happened. Soon afterward, sometimes even at the very next session, the patient would arrive to tell me the impasse had ended and that, at long last, things were definitely getting better. I found this very puzzling. But it happened too many times to ignore, and prompted me to think more deeply about the way change takes place. I suggest it happens in two different ways.

The first is linear. Linear growth is the way, for example, a sapling grows into a tree, upward. But there is another – cyclic – pattern of growth. Development goes forward, but not only in a straight line. Instead, it first goes backwards, then takes a large step forward.

The cyclic pattern, although not so obvious as the linear, is hardly new. We are all familiar with the notion that "things have to get worse before they can get better." In mythology, it is symbolised by the phoenix repeatedly rising from the ashes. New life emerges from death. In psychotherapy, it helps to remember the cyclic pattern because, when things seem to be going very wrong, we readily think that the therapy has failed.

I have three major concerns. The first is rather theoretical: what I call the "breakdown/breakthrough process" across a broad range of phenomena, personal and collective, human and non-human, material and abstract. The second illustrates the breakdown/breakthrough pattern in its clinical aspects, as exemplified by the case of a rather damaged young woman with whom I once worked. In the final section I round off her story and discuss the relevance of this case to the destruction/creation cycle.

The Breakdown/Breakthrough Cycle

The breakdown/breakthrough pattern can be observed across a spectrum of existence far beyond the human. It has been applied even to the evolutionary development of all living forms. The biologist Garstang (1922) termed it paedomorphosis, a process whereby evolution itself can be seen to have retraced its steps repeatedly, as it were, along the path which led to a dead end, then made a fresh start in a more promising direction. The human species, by all accounts, is an offshoot not of the fully-developed ape, but of the ape embryo; it was from this malleable half-formed stage that human stock emerged. Koestler (1967) notes further that the same pattern applies to the evolution of ideas:

> *The revolutions in the history of science are successful escapes from blind alleys. The evolution of knowledge is continuous only during those periods of consolidation and elaboration which follow a major break-through. Sooner or later, however, consolidation leads to increasing rigidity, orthodoxy, and so into the dead end of overspecialisation. ... Eventually there is a crisis and a new "breakthrough" out of the blind alley, followed by another period of consolidation, a new orthodoxy, and so the cycle starts again. (p. 163)*

Thus, Koestler links the linear and the cyclic processes. Although manifestly different, they can be seen to complement one another. The historian Toynbee (1972) traced the breakdown/breakthrough pattern in the collapse and rise of whole civilisations. Over the centuries they become top heavy, with an increasingly oppressive aristocracy, eventually provoking a revolution from below. Or they are invaded by "barbarians" from outside, who set up a new regime and, in due time, go through the same process.

At the individual level, the cyclic growth pattern was described by the late Michael Fordham in terms of the "de-integration/re-integration" cycle as typical of normal childhood development. In a more dramatic way the cycle can be traced clearly in biographical records of virtually all the major figures in religious history. St. John's "dark night of the soul" is one of the best-known examples of spiritual development. In clinical terms, he went through a prolonged depression which, with immense determination, he used to strip away all desire, even the desire for those gratifications he felt God had once given him. By doing so, he came out the other side into the radiant centeredness that characterises the ego-transcended individual.

The breakdown/breakthrough pattern fits particularly well with the Christian faith since its founder was reported to have gone through the same process: a prolonged, painful and despairing death ("My God, my God, why hast thou forsaken me?"), followed by a miraculous resurrection.

Zen Buddism grasps the same point in its use of the "koan" system of spiritual training. The aspirant is given an inherently insoluble conundrum, such as "What is the sound of one hand clapping?" and told to solve it. The master is offered one ingenious answer after another, and rejects them all. With each rejection the student becomes ever more baffled but is instructed to try still harder. Night and day the student wrestles with the problem to the point of losing all capacity to think any way through it. The answers are irrelevant; the aim of the training is to drive the student to such a degree of desperation as to undergo a radical change of consciousness.

The breakdown/breakthrough pattern can be observed in most accounts of the creative process; there is abundant documentation that scientists such as Albert Einstein, Friedrich Kekule von Stradonitz or Jules Poincaré wrestled for years with intractable problems until they virtually gave up – and were then presented with the solution in a dream or a doze! Milner (1973) described the process:

> *The inescapable condition of true expression was the plunge into the abyss, the willingness to recognise the moment of blankness and extinction was the moment of incipient fruitfulness, the moment without which the invisible forces within could not do their work. (p. 237)*

My main concern here is the application of the breakdown/ breakthrough pattern to psychotherapy. One especially serious manifestation of breakdown can be seen in clinical depression, which is generally regarded in a profoundly negative light. Rosen's (1993) approach is based on Jung's view that breakdown can be a path to self-healing. Rosen interviewed those few individuals who had survived a suicide leap from the Golden Gate Bridge in San Francisco. He summarises their experience as follows:

> *The ten survivors gave various reasons for jumping, but there was a common core feeling of aloneness, alienation, depression, rejection, worthlessness and hopelessness. Although the ten had widely divergent views of religion before attempting suicide, they all admitted to feelings of spiritual transcendence after they had leaped. (p. xxii.)*

We must keep in mind the dangers of breakdown; it does not always lead to breakthrough. Some people are permanently damaged, or succeed in committing suicide. There are many ways in which breakdown can be brought about, either voluntary or imposed: drugs, excessive fatigue, fear, solitude, torture, fasting, meditation – by excessive stimulation or deprivation of any kind. The purpose of interpretation in psychotherapy is to break down old, fixed defensive responses in order that more flexible ones can take their place. But the forceful breaking-down of a patient's defences, as sometimes happens in a mishandled treatment, can be a form of brainwashing, and result in failure.

In my own practice, I have worked with several patients who felt convinced that their previous analysts, over-zealous to liberate them from their crippling defences, only succeeded in undermining what little confidence they had. With hindsight, I can recognise that this was something that I, too, have been guilty of, as in the case I present here.

Portrait of a Victim.

My work with "Rachel" was in the earliest years of my practice. Even after all this time, I have not forgotten our initial meeting. It took place in the local mental hospital where she was a day patient. She shuffled into the office where I waited. Her head and jaw were thrust forward as if she were about to explode: a marked contrast to her large blue eyes, which had a dreadfully hurt look. Around one eye I noticed a large bruise. In the case notes she had been described as a "depressive schizoid, with paranoid features," and that was how she looked. I remember thinking: "O Lord, this girl is really sick. What am I getting into?"

I said hello, and there was a very long silence. Eventually she managed to utter that she did not want psychotherapy. I promptly felt stupid for having come, and wondered how soon I could leave. Having given up the prospect of working with her I had nothing to lose. I just asked, "Who gave you that black eye?" There was another very long silence. As I waited I felt quite frightened. I had the distinct fantasy that my question smashed like a huge boulder through the ice on a frozen lake, and now, up through the hole, some prehistoric monster would rear its awesome head. At last she said: "I get very angry." I replied: "Are you warning me?"

For the first time she looked up; she even gave the glimmer of a smile. With this, the atmosphere changed. Presently she asked where we would meet. I told her my address and she said: "Yes, I know." She was in her middle twenties, unattached, and had never had a relationship with a man. She lodged with a divorced woman friend, also an ex-mental patient. Rachel's father was a security guard. Her older brother was a graphic artist: gentle, homosexual, and virtually alchoholic.

Rachel had had a difficult start in life. Her mother once told her that she had tried to abort her; Rachel could never forgive that statement. At birth she was nearly strangled by the umbilical cord and took two days to be born. She was only a few weeks old when her brother, then aged two, drank a bottle of cleaning fluid and nearly died. For months afterward he occupied her mother's whole attention, which presumably left almost nothing for Rachel.

She was a very docile child and, on the rare occasions she showed any temper, her mother said: "That's not really you." Rachel said she could not remember a time when she was not terrified of her father. As a child she felt he couldn't stand the sight of her, because she was fat, slow and stupid. But she slimmed down in her teens and his attitude took a marked turn. She noticed he would kiss her on the lips and if she stood by his chair he would run his hand up her thighs. She said she did not know this was sexual but she was so grateful for his attention she would have done anything to please him. These attentions also meant that she "put one over" on her mother to whom she felt immensely hostile, and who became very jealous. Forgetting her husband's blatant infidelities with a succession of women – one of whom he actually brought to live in the house – she blamed Rachel that she and her husband no longer acted "like man and wife."

Rachel's memory of this period is vague, but she knows she became very depressed and was admitted to a mental hospital. She stayed for nearly two years. While there she went through a psychotic episode with, according to the notes, "terrifying visual delusions."

After discharge she lived on state benefit, did no work, and attended a psychiatric day hospital. Her prognosis was very poor. For months she came to each session as if it were that first meeting: her averted gaze, brooding antagonism, and constant lip-biting conveyed how desperate she was. Yet, when I spoke to her, she would hardly respond.

I found this period peculiarily agonizing: I felt useless, mentally paralysed, and full of an obscure dread. After some time I began to wonder if this was the mental state Rachel herself habitually lived in and that she had succeeded in inducing it in me? If so, I don't know how she endured it. It was as if she silently screamed to me for relief but forbade me to make the least move to help her. Eventually I came to the conclusion, with my supervisor's agreement, that the basis for analytic psychotherapy just did not exist. So I gave up analysing her.

In desperation I decided that since we could not work together, perhaps we could just play together? I knew, from the notes, that she had some talent for art. I bought a large drawing pad and some crayons and suggested she might wish to draw, or even just doodle? She flatly refused. Then she conceded she might co-operate if I doodled first. So I drew some pink flowers on the pad and handed it to her. With a fiendish glee she defaced my flowers with black jagged lines, and handed it back. I responded with green leaves growing from each of her jagged points. As we went on, at least it gave us something to talk about. During this phase I also had to give up my therapist's chair. By now, at her insistence, we both sat on the floor like two children at play. For a time she became so playful that it was difficult to control her. She turned the chairs around, covered the face of the clock with plasticine, refused to leave at the end of the session, and brought me black plastic spiders – sometimes as a gift, sometimes just to throw at me. I tried interpreting each of these "actings out," but it never seemed to register.

By now we were back in our chairs and had some sort of dialogue going, often about her fear of using the couch. I suspected it had to do with repressed sexual anxieties, but this was never mentioned. Her main theme was how much she hated therapy. It left me feeling always in the wrong: wrong when I saw her and wrong when I didn't – because she made it clear that she found it even worse when she couldn't come. During each holiday break she developed quite painful disorders, such as abscesses under her teeth. I felt very apprehensive that she was developing illnesses she had never had before. I gradually realised, that by making me feel so bad, she succeeded in giving me a direct sense of what it felt like to be in her place.

Since her verbal responses were still minimal, I was obliged to ask first one question, then another, then another. And to each question she responded like someone yielding up a layer of protective armor. Sometimes I would catch the tone of my own voice; it sounded hard and triumphant. I realized that I was now enjoying a certain predatory excitement in pursuing her and triumphantly pinning her down. Under further questioning, it emerged that she was indeed repressing sexual fantasies. Their disclosure was especially difficult because they involved being hunted down and anally raped. I interpreted her fantasy, although it depicted an abusive form of contact, as reminiscent of her connection with her father. It was a form of contact, something she had been deprived of by her mother in the earliest months of life.

She never made it clear if I was her imagined rapist, but then I realized that she and I were re-enacting her fantasy in the therapy itself; her evasiveness provoked my questioning, which turned me into a hunter and her into my prey. As these rape fantasies disclosed, she derived a masochistic excitement from imagining herself in subjugated states. This recognition led to an exploration of how, throughout her life, she had repeatedly contrived to become a victim, originally her father's, and now mine. It also crossed my mind that she had succeeded – through making me suffer at the sight of her suffering, yet refusing all relief – in making me her victim, and that we were entangled in a reciprocal sado-masochistic relationship.

To be labelled a "victim" made her feel even more persecuted, but gradually we both began to understand that she felt much safer in that role. Better the devil she knew than the devil she didn't. Even more puzzling: better the devil she knew than the angel she didn't. By angel I mean a good experience such as feeling safe, loved, valued, successful or happy.

I was wrong about her fear of the couch. It had nothing to do with sex. On the contrary, it offered the promise of a state of inexpressible contentment – and this terrified her even more. She kept imagining that, if she lay down and got really comfortable, her body would involuntarily perform a bizarre backward loop-the-loop and disappear into thin air.

Only by puzzling over this fantasy did I grasp the intensity of her regressive longing for fusion. She imagined it as something so blissful she simply would melt and disintegrate inside me. To avoid melting away, she did this strange loop-the-loop – only to disappear for ever. Both prospects filled her with dread. By comparison with the threat of annihilation, her chronic states of anger, anguish, suffering, grievance, complaint, frustration and failure – however painful – were like old friends. Any alternative, any breakthrough into trust, hope, gratitude, love and joy threatened the dissolution of her very self. It meant that she dared not get better.

Giving Up and Giving Over

Some time in our fourth year I began to think seriously of ending the treatment. After a period of relative co-operation, she became again so consistently negative that I came to the conclusion that we were utterly stuck. In my fantasy I compared her to Rapunzel locked up in her tower, guarded by a fearful witch but, unlike the Prince, I could find no way in. Moreover, she preferred the witch to me. I finally admitted myself beaten. But I knew that, with her minimal income, she would never find another therapist. I could not bring myself to terminate the therapy, and we carried on. But in admitting defeat, something changed in me. I gave up trying to cure her. I gave up calling her a victim and, in the process, extricated myself from the perverse collusion in which we had been entangled. There was no point in trying to analyse her, because I seemed long ago to have run out of new interpretations, and the old ones had become tired clichés.

Once I stopped trying to change her I found, to my surprise, that I could begin to accept her more or less as she was. Not only accept; I could begin to enjoy her. And not only enjoy, but to learn from her. I slowly cognised that, through her unique sufferings, she knew things I had never encountered. I found that I could learn from her about my own sadism and masochism and narcissism.

However, even though I was now beginning to accept her as she was, her persecutor/protector never allowed her to introject that acceptance as her own. If ever we had a satisfying session, the witch promptly went to work: "You know that was not real, just therapy. He's paid to make you feel better. He can't possibly value you; nobody could. How can he, when he knows you have such depraved thoughts? And even if he does accept such awfulness, what can that say about him? Perhaps he's perverted too and actually wants to seduce you? Or is he using you to prove what a good therapist he is? Don't give him that satisfaction; he's got enough as it is" and so on.

Whenever there was any hint of real closeness between us, she defended against it by virtually going into a trance. I could see it happening: A shudder went through her, her eyes drooped and almost closed. It was eerie. But there were many occasions when the same thing happened to me. No matter how hard I fought it, I found myself afflicted by an anaesthetic condition so overwhelming that I was totally incapable of thought. The experience was very unpleasant.

Drowsiness and sleep in the therapy session, whether it manifests in the patient or the analyst, is universally regarded as countertherapeutic. In my experience this turned out not to be the case. On one occasion, when Rachel was talking, the room began to disappear into a blur, but this time I let it happen, almost out of curiosity. I felt I was passing out but managed to ask her what she was thinking. She replied: "I keep thinking I want to eat your foot." My head cleared instantly: "You want to – what?" She laughed and, for the first time in four years, she briefly looked normal: just a nice young woman. I simply laughed with her.

The next time the agonising drowsiness came on me, I didn't fight it but let it take over. I consciously gave up trying to stay awake. Then something strange occurred: The room became very peaceful, filled with a dreamy, warm, energised feeling of connection. Again I dozed off. This happened on several occasions. It was after one of these intimate silences that Rachel said: "You fell asleep again." I said, a bit defensively: "Did I?" She replied, "So did I." I realised that she regarded the experience as a breakthrough. It began to happen regularly: just a few minutes of shared, almost trance-like, quietude – like a mother and baby after a good feed.

I think that if this state of *coniunctio* can be reached and acknowledged, not once but several times, the destructive voice of the witch begins to lose conviction. It then becomes increasingly possible to protect good experiences from her poison. The value of skilled transference interpretation cannot be disputed. But I think that, with a patient like Rachel, before interpretation can have any meaning there needs to be this primary undifferentiated experience. It is the basis of primary trust, and in the absence of trust, insight is merely a cerebral exercise.

Analysis tends to emphasise the need to accept pain. This is perfectly valid; we certainly need to face painful truths about ourselves. But with masochistic patients like Rachel there is not only "gain in the pain" but pleasure in it too, and pain can become a perverse addiction. We need to supplement the tolerance of pain with the acceptance of pleasure. Otherwise we starve our internalised good angel, while the bad one grows fat. I don't mean by this a programme of positive reinforcement, but holding as far as possible to what is happening between us, whether painful or pleasurable – whether a *coniunctio* or a *nigredo* – in the present moment. And not in order to interpret it, but simply to register it. The therapy was now primarily an exercise in our shared consciousness of being present with one another.

Living in the present is hardly a revelation. Every form of spiritual exercise advocates it, but it is very difficult to sustain in everyday life. It is less difficult as a shared experience in therapy. I noticed that I had stopped becoming anaesthetised. I think her mind-numbing rape fantasies had just been forgotten; likewise her fear of dissolving and disappearing. Rachel began lying down for short periods, then would sit up to talk, then lie down, and so on. Because I had long before stopped trying to make her better, most of this went unnoticed until I began to register certain positive remarks she made. Once she interrupted a discussion to say: "You don't always under-stand. But you do try." Another time she said: "I'll say this for you, you never gave up on me." I replied: "That's not quite true. I did. About a year ago." "You gave up?" She was quiet for bit. "But you carried on?" "Yes." She said: "I'm going to find it hard to leave you." "I didn't know you were thinking of it."

By way of reply she told me that the friend in whose house she still lived was apparently having another breakdown. "Actually, compared with her," Rachel said, "I'm in a different league. Deep down I'm all right. Well 90 percent all right." I asked: "How do you know that?" She said: "The way I am with you, I know I'm all right." I realised this was true, but difficult to recognise. Outwardly her life was the same as before: She still had no job, and still lodged with her now-sick friend. But I was using the wrong yardstick. Nothing had changed, but everything was different. She felt profoundly different about herself. Previously she felt that her life had not yet begun, but now she felt it was happening. Previously everything was contami-nated by a pervasive sense of unreality. But now, by registering and sharing her awareness of the present, it had begun to feel real. Previously her life had been, as it were, one long dying, and now she was living.

I suppose this is where my paper should end. Actually she didn't leave for another year, and it was a very stormy one. We went through a reciprocal "release of bad objects." Having previously given up being the persecuting therapist, I now finally managed to give up being the nice, helpful one, and we both said all kinds of angry things. But we survived them and parted with mutual regret. She left on the understanding she could come back after a year away.

She never did, except for a cup of tea from time to time. Three years after that she took her first job – in a day nursery – and much later became a practitioner in one of the alternative therapies. The last time I met her she said that she would like to find a male partner, but it didn't seem likely, and that was sad. Thus, it was not exactly a fairy tale ending, not like Rapunzel.

In my long battle with Rachel's witch, both of us endured much suffering and disappointment. I kept looking for Rachel but encountered only this awful witch. You may wonder why I kept trying to find her. Originally I thought it was because there seems to be a strange fascination about these borderline patients. Now I think I sensed unconsciously that she could heal me. Jung long ago emphasised that psychotherapy can only be a reciprocal process. Healing heals the healer, and it works for both parties. Through Rachel I became a bit less afraid of my inner rage, or of deviating from the analytic rules I had been trained to observe. I learned to recover from apparent defeat. And I am sure that if I had been resistant to letting her change me, she herself would have remained essentially unchanged.

When I began to put this paper together, it was my intention to present my decision to give up trying to change her as the turning point. It would be another demonstration of the breakdown/breakthrough process which is the theme of my paper. In fact, my professional ego broke down on repeated occasions, but each time a new solution seemed to present itself. While I think that giving up played a decisive part, it doesn't comprise the whole story. Giving up didn't work until I was driven to the despair that Rachel herself experienced. Without the years of struggle, my giving up would have been a non-event, and no breakthrough would have come out of it. This sounds a very painful process but, with a patient as damaged as Rachel, I suspect it was the only way. This seems to be the way all creative achievement comes about: long years of struggle, until you are forced to admit defeat and give up. Then something new emerges. I gave up, but carried on, without hope. Or did I rather give it over to the unconscious, or to the patient's inner healer, or to some autonomous interactive process that healed us both?

I have described a dual process: mutual transformation, and breaking down in order to break through. I see now that these are the two defining characteristics of the alchemical opus.

References

Garstang, N. (1922). The theory of recapitulation. A critical restatement of the biogenetic law. *Journal of the Linnaean Society*, *35*-81.

Koestler, A. (1967). *The Ghost in the Machine*. London: Arkana.

Milner, M. (1973). *The Madness of Sane Men*. London: Tavistock.

Rosen, D. (1993). *Transforming Depression*. New York: Putnam.

Toynbee, A. (1972). *A Study of History*. Oxford: Oxford University Press.

A Dark Talent

Silence in Analysis

Catherine Crowther
Victoria Graham Fuller
London, England
Society of Analytical Psychology

There are some patients whose silence stretches over years. Their silent attacks on analysis and their inability to use it conventionally constellate the need in us to talk, to relieve projected anxiety and test disturbing countertransference reactions. Our conversations provide containment of destructive fantasies resulting from lack of verbal interaction. Unlike patients who project onto an analyst in the unconscious hope of containment, silent patients project the need for containment, which they disavow, leaving the analyst helpless, and undermined in therapeutic identity. We have found that our collaboration about the meaning of chronic analytic silence has helped to counteract its destructive effect on the analytic relationship.

Profound silence, while not in itself archetypal, is the product of archetypal processes and is not merely resistance, as classical psychoanalytic literature proposes. We argue that there are two types of silence: one actively destructive, the other deadlocked, in death-like suspension; the nature of each depends on the patient's defensive motivation.

Our patients are two women in their mid-thirties. "Gisella" is red-haired, rather beautiful, with a calm, competent appearance. Her self-sufficiency, however, is sacrificed to relationship and is achieved by withdrawal. She makes no eye-contact with her analyst and says she would not recognise her if they met in the street.

Gisella's analysis lasted six years, scheduled at three times a week. One session was regularly not attended, conveying her resentment, and was probably unconsciously preventing some devastating criticism from being voiced. Long tracts of the first years were spent in marmoreal silence, interspersed with periods when she could speak more trustingly of her childhood and current life. There was little continuity between sessions, making it difficult to renew any hard-won contact. During a talkative phase, it was extremely difficult to discuss the silence without provoking withdrawal. Profound silence could descend like a weather front. Gisella paid acute attention to her analyst's comments about her silence, indicating neither acceptance nor agreement.

During Gisella's childhood, her mother became progressively mentally ill, requiring several hospitalisations. Hopes for her recovery were raised and dashed as her bi-polar illness fluctuated: a cycle mirrored in the analysis. Gisella was a self-reliant, undemanding child, responsible and competent, but in her teens the disappointment with her mother turned to contemptuous withdrawal. Her father evaded pain by having affairs. His eventual desertion was said to be the cause of the mother's subsequent suicide. Her parents' irredeemable actions confirmed for Gisella the hopelessness of dependent relationships. She felt guilty about her rejection of her mother. Inevitably, her adult sexual and emotional relationships foundered when her dependency needs arose, condemning her to a cycle of fear, rage, emotional hunger and being rejected.

The childhood origins of her angry mistrust in the analysis, and the cruel fluctuations of hope and despair that afflicted both Gisella and her analyst were explored in the transference-countertransference, evoking Gisella's silent trickling tears. One recurring dream image symbolised Gisella's ambivalence towards the nourishing potential of the analysis:

> *She had a sensation of something lodged in her mouth, something to be desired and paradoxically to be rejected. She felt stuck with the discomfort of being unable either to swallow or to spit it out.*

"Fiona" habitually dressed in hiking boots and nylon shell suit which failed to disguise her bulky figure. She seemed to care little about her femininity. Her analyst discovered almost nothing of her history. Like Gisella, she was referred following an analytic failure with her first therapist. Fiona was unwilling to discuss the earlier therapy and could not remember the therapist's name. She could not tolerate interpretations. Rather than bringing clarity or understanding, they made Fiona feel humiliated and used.

Fiona attended four times weekly. Gradually, she became less verbal until speech lapsed entirely. In preparation for this presentation her analyst discovered a passage from *The God of Small Things* (Roy 1997).

It had been a gradual winding down and closing shop. As though he had run out of conversation and had nothing left to say. It wasn't an accusing, protesting silence as much as a sort of aestivation, a dormancy, the psychological equivalent of what lungfish do to get themselves through the dry season. (p. 10)

This passage suggests weathering an inhospitable season which would be relieved eventually by the forces of nature. Content from a session during this period illustrates the predicament:

In Fiona's birthplace the farmers had rich soil but not enough water. They irrigated the land but the hot climate evaporated the water, leaving behind deposits of toxic metals. The analyst suggested to the patient a parallel with the way she grew up – conditions were essentially good but the nurture she needed couldn't be used and left residues that threatened growth. In a rare moment of collaboration, the patient accepted the analogy but insisted that these failures could not be remedied.

The analyst, her efforts to "weather this season" exhausted, sought consolation with a colleague. He advised reducing sessions to once weekly on the grounds that the patient was too exhausted by the burdens of the analysis to manage greater frequency. He recommended that the analyst lower her expectations of renewed speech to "ground zero."

Years later, this seems to have been a basic mistake, especially as the patient was shocked by the suggestion, but accepted it. The analyst may have overridden her instincts, leading her and her patient to participate in a form of defeat, so typical of this difficult work. Although the reduction allowed the impasse of the silence to be addressed, we now conclude that it was solved, rather than therapeutically resolved.

Countertransference

A patient's silence stimulates isolation and disorientation in the countertransference, which poses technical problems: for example, unspoken pressure for the analyst to self-disclose or to enact counter transference reactions. Our patients' speechlessness inspired in us blankness, inhibition, shame and fear. Orthodox techniques of inducing speech failed, and we suffered despair and frustration due to non-involvement in the verbal exchange of more typical analyses. We knew our patients suffered profoundly, unable to communicate to us. For months they would remain inert and stony; we would try to interpret and empathise with their paralysis but after trying – and failing – to break what we perceived as deadlock, we would feel tyrannised by helplessness and paranoia. Impulses to hate and reject our patients disturbed our professional equilibrium, and we would often dread their arrival. All this made us aware of how destructive silence can be.

Both patients demanded a pristine space exactly attuned to their immediate felt needs. Consistent with borderline pathology, they had difficulty free-associating, and were vulnerable to boundary disturbances. For example, Gisella surprised her analyst by reproaching her vehemently for presenting the monthly bill three days late. Fiona, when her analyst wore a jumper with a design of swimming dolphins, protested that no analyst should wear such a garment. In each case, we suppose the patient fantasised that flexibility meant a lack of containment by the analyst. Outrage masked a fear that a nascent, fragile not-yet-self may be annihilated by the mutuality of an open exchange. Our patients were right to fear this, as in their youth they had experienced psychic annihilation. In developmental terms, the patient's split-off infant feels safe only with closely bound "swaddling." This may be one root of her difficulty in associating freely, allowing words to flow. These sudden attacks provoked our retaliatory anger, with a concurrent loss of analytic stance. We could be lulled into forgetting our patients' vulnerability by their apparent self-sufficiency – a common misinterpretation of silence.

We hypothesise that we were used as ego functions: Kohut conceptualised that objects are not experienced by the traumatised self in terms of personal qualities, but rather as functions they perform for the psychically disabled self. Kohut's "selfobject" is experienced by the child as available exclusively to the ego, as a person may experience a limb that is taken for granted. When, inadvertently, the analyst fails as selfobject, the patient's disappointment can turn quickly to silent hostility. These times felt punishing, deliberate and merciless (see Siegel 1996). Altman 1957) pointed out that suspension of effort and reliance on time to rescue the situation are symptomatic for these patients and characteristic of an infantile transference to the ever-available parent. This symptom can arise from a wish to be cared for without necessity of one's own volition. The experience is like suspension rather than gestation.

In learning to accommodate unconscious demands for consummate availability, we were under pressure to monitor the precise quality of silence. Caught in a tension between desire to allow silence and the urge to manage it actively, we repeatedly found ourselves at a technical choicepoint: whether to attempt to meet or to challenge the patient's demand for a perfectly fitting selfobject. Protracted silence could be experienced by the patient as neglectful and withholding; attempting interaction could feel intrusive and demanding. The experience of both in the same session was not unusual.

> Gisella's analyst, after half an hour of unreadable silence, noticed the grim expression on her patient's face and, aware of how torn she was between needing help and her resentment of that need, was moved to ask empathically, "Would you like something done about this silence or are you content to stay with it?" After another silence came the reproof, "Well, you've done it now."

Gisella instilled in her analyst the desire for contact which she herself could not acknowledge, or even allow herself to feel. The analyst's countertransference indicated that both knew the analyst could not get it right. This example of what we call "deadlock" is typical in that it creates an unresolvable double bind for the pair.

We sensed vast reserves of hostility in our patients; this provoked our own, leaving us exhausted, sometimes callously indifferent. We became inhibited about disturbing the patients' silent universe. This was directly destructive of our capacity for concern. It was rare to sense the loss and hurt which were the infantile roots of hostility. Often at these lowest points our patients would surprise us with an image which symbolised the experience.

> One day Fiona broke a silence during which she had been staring at a painting above the mantelpiece of a group of quail eggs reflected in the surface of a brass jug. One egg was not reflected. "Where is that egg for the jug?" she asked. The analyst thought she was saying she felt unmirrored, but knew from experience that to voice this would risk the patient's retreat into opaque silence. Fiona stood before the painting to demonstrate her idea physically, not trusting words alone. The analyst left her chair to join her, moved literally to actualise the patient's unconscious wish to control the space between them, to bring them closer.

The egg image generates strikingly apposite associations with fragility, containment, silent incubation and potential hatching. Fiona's brief offering mobilised her analyst's awareness and brought relief from internal masochistic pressures. However, she had enacted a countertransference reaction, by leaving her chair. It was difficult to interpret this without making Fiona feel criticised and blameworthy, feelings left instead with her analyst.

Fiona would follow such moments of connection with unconscious efforts to re-establish deadlock. At the next session she blamed her analyst for not taking up "clues": "You should know what I wish to speak about and introduce it." Previous efforts to empathise with Fiona's wish to have her needs known wordlessly had been fruitless. This time, Fiona's reply was telling: "But if I start a conversation, then I am responsible for the outcome." As a child she would join family conversations but her father insisted that she support opinions with facts, something which tongue-tied her. Eventually, her spontaneity crushed, she took revenge by refusing to contribute. Fiona's unconscious restoration of this status quo ensured that no spontaneous analytic development arose from therapeutic contact. Although this destroyed the analyst's hope, Fiona's sense of internal security was preserved.

Chronically silent patients react to the asymmetric analytic environment with primary distrust. Prone to shame, they often perceive speech as dangerous entrapment. Silence serves to preserve their distorted self representations and to avoid the humiliating possibility of actively using the analyst as an auxiliary ego.

Psychological Literature

Papers by Freudian psychoanalysts helped us to think about chronic silence, but they frequently stressed ego-defences. Early authors (Sándor Ferenczi, Wilhelm Reich, Edmund Bergler) felt that non-compliance with the rule of free association was defiant and held the patient entirely responsible for lapses of analytic rigour. A 1961 psychoanalytic symposium questioned the traditional view of silence as mere resistance on the part of the patient. (See Arlow 1961, Greenson 1961, Loomie 1961, Zeligs 1961)

Loomie represented a watershed in psychoanalytic thinking about the silent patient. He noted that the rigid solution of opposing silence with silence is yielding to more patient-oriented approaches; for example, that the analyst engage in a monologue in the patient's presence. Loomie noted the prevalence of countertransference problems and the frustration of the analyst's therapeutic aspirations. Rather than interpreting silence as a reaction to childhood trauma,

Loomie observed a trend toward seeing it as a patient's generalised reaction to the analysis, as a negative therapeutic reaction.

Khan's (1963) groundbreaking work showed his use of countertransference as an instrument to register the patient's unspoken feelings about disturbed childhood relationships. Khan's judicious withholding of therapeutic intervention enabled his adolescent patient to communicate inner conflicts in words.

The technical question inspired by silence, wrote Coltart (1991), is whether the patient needs the therapist's mutual participation in silence or, alternatively, a facilitating comment upon it. This question correlates with our tension between allowing silence or attempting to foster speech. Such technical challenges encouraged Coltart to develop her therapeutic arts: negative capability, endurance, attention to information via the senses, and countertransference reactions. She advocated genuine benevolence in the face of the patient's perceived hostility and rage, since the patient is observing the analyst's silence as keenly as the analyst is studying the patient's. While we are in sympathy with Coltart's aim, we think it is an ideal that sidesteps the value of the analyst's own negativity.

Coltart stressed that the analyst's mute acceptance of silence is a technical abandonment, tantamount to neglect of the patient. Remaining silent may be a masochistic reaction on the analyst's part, or may constitute an unconscious abuse, which silent patients can provoke. Interestingly, she did not develop this point as evidence of destructiveness inherent in silence.

Wilson (1963) reiterated D. W. Winnicott's belief that silence may express the need for personal isolation in the search for identity. Wilson feels this pertains in the treatment of women who have suffered sexual abuse. The trauma re-enacted in the transference is not only a repetition of an original violation of bodily integrity, but also represents an intrusion into a woman's developing sense of self. Justifying the abused patient's right to silence, he described a woman whose core self was in a state of partial formation requiring protection and respect. The analyst's attempt to communicate with her was experienced as dangerous. Wilson concluded that the patient's chronic silence functions to control her psychic boundaries, thus preventing his untimely entry.

The theme of abuse also has absorbed Kalshed (1996). He hypothesized that patients who have suffered severe childhood trauma develop a "self-care system," ensuring self-sufficiency but cutting them off from relationships and resulting in disintegration, which Jung called "dissociation." Thus, normal continuous elements of consciousness are not allowed to integrate. "Dissociation appears to involve a good deal of aggression ... [and] an active attack by one part of the psyche on other parts" (p. 13).

Kalsched (1996) explained that children who have been emotionally abused cannot mobilise aggression to expel noxious not-me elements of experience. They take external aggression into their inner worlds: "The introjected hatred (now amplified by archetypal energy) attacks the links between body and mind in an effort to cut affective connections" (p. 17). The damage to the patient's psyche is from an archetypal rage directed against the self.

Silence in Film

The heroine in the 1996 film "The Piano," Ada, reveals with "her mind's voice" that her silence is a reaction to an undisclosed traumatic event. As the film opens, Ada arrives on a lonely beach with her young daughter and various articles of furniture, including the piano. The significance of the instrument becomes apparent when Ada removes its packing to play with an urgent concentration emphasising her deliberate muteness. Her father called this her "dark talent," from which we take the title of this paper. When Ada's mail-order husband arrives to collect her he declares the piano too heavy to carry. The silent piano, abandoned to the encroaching sea, is a poignant symbol of Ada's precarious domestic and psychic position. It is the instrument, literally as well as symbolically, through which she can protest against a coercive system supported by her father, who dispatches her to a faraway stranger as if she were a piece of furniture. Her husband, increasingly helpless and alienated by her mute protest, sells the piano to a neighbour, George, who manipulates Ada into a sexual relationship. We hypothesise that her husband's retaliation for her inevitable sexual betrayal with George – severing her index finger – is a concrete enactment of an earlier, exquisitely painful psychic wounding, which she also suffered in silence. By rejecting her power of speech, Ada believes she can subvert prevailing social norms and oppose her husband (as well as her father).

Kalsched (1996) theorized that our patients may have projected onto their analyses a powerful and oppressive regime imposed by an internal dictator who enthrals them. While Ada maintains her opposition, the potential creativity of her love for George cannot be realised. Although the piano can symbolise simultaneously Ada's hatred of a heartless system which suppressed her individuality as well as her new-found love which allows her to regain it, Ada must concede that speechlessness has become an emotional cul-de-sac. In order to resume a path toward individuation she must relinquish her symbol of power. Sailing away from the island, she asks for the piano to be thrown overboard. As the ropes speed past, Ada "out of a fatal curiosity" steps into a loop. She is immediately dragged overboard by the piano, underscoring its potential destructiveness. While it descends into the depths, Ada, fighting free, surfaces. "What a death! What a chance! What a surprise!" she thinks. "My will has chosen life!?" Ada's story supports our clinical impression that one of the unconscious purposes of silence is a desperate attempt to maintain personal integrity – a reaction to early experiences of confusion and trauma.

While silence is the patient's most powerful weapon to keep the analyst out, we find paradoxically that the boundaries between two people's unconscious minds are especially fluid during prolonged silences. In Ingmar Bergman's 1966 film "Persona" we find a further theme: the effect on other people of an individual's silence. This film yields rich descriptions of the operation of *participation mystique,* and sheds light on the violence of our countertransference anger and despair.

An actress who has become mute receives psychiatric care from a young nurse in an isolated seaside home. The patient's silence gradually induces the nurse to confide her own preoccupations, which become intimately confessional. Roles reverse as the nurse becomes dependent on the psychological space created by her patient's silence, and then outraged when she finds the patient writing amused thoughts about her confessions. This treachery leads to violence, a measure of the strength of projective identification. The film reveals the difficulty of containing or reintegrating projections in a perpetual vacuum which attracts archetypal anger, blame and guilt. The lack of normal feedback, reality testing and affirmation rapidly provoke the nurse's paranoid anxiety. The film movingly dramatises the countertransference issues with which our silent patients daily infected us.

Attachment Theory Research

A study (Patrick et al, 1994) of borderline individuals reveals a characteristic lack of coherence in their mental representations of significant early attachments. Their attitudes toward these early relationships are "preoccupied, confused, and mentally entangled" (p. 384), particularly with respect to loss, trauma or abuse.

Main (1991) links such states of mind with poorly developed metacognitive functioning: an inability to think clearly about the contents of one's mind. This theory suggests why our patients were unable to understand their speechlessness or even to speak about it.

Research by Main and co-workers (1982, 1984) correlates rejecting mothers with avoidance in their infants. It suggests that our patients' avoidance of eye contact, lateness, extending of holiday breaks, as well as silence could be avoidance of the analyst as a potential attachment figure. Main concludes that babies who show avoidant behaviour (looking away and ignoring the departure of an attachment figure in a stressful "strange situation") are responding to the repeated experience of their early attachment overtures' being rejected by a maternal figure, hence their angry withdrawal. Main and Goldwyn (1984) describe a pattern of "a disorganising and self-perpetuating conflict situation ... in which approach, withdrawal, approach, withdrawal and anger tendencies arise in rapid sequence" and propose that "a shift in attention away from the attachment figure and from feelings aroused by that figure may help the infant to maintain self-organisation ..." (p. 210).

We believe that we experienced with our patients the perpetuation of that avoidance pattern, unconsciously protecting the self's integrity. The internalisation of chronic and confusing rejection is linked with a lack of awareness of anger or resentment towards the rejecting attachment figure, often associated in adulthood with difficulty in remembering childhood and even idealisation of the rejecting figure.

This research helped us to conceptualise the origins of our patients' incoherence and their avoidance of relationship in the transference. Reluctance to give up hope of attachment is matched by reluctance to commit themselves to hope, resulting in a progressive paralysis of thinking or feeling. This concept was consonant with our intuition that a prime analytic task was to address our patients' rage and encourage its expression in the analytic relationship, where it could be lived through in a contained way. Our experience supports Kalsched's view that the unconscious repetition of trauma in the inner world must become reality with an external object if the full extent of the inner "system" is to be exposed and unlocked. Yet the inner disintegrative figure constitutes a formidable force which is antithetic to psychotherapy or indeed any form of vitality – making imperative a minute-to-minute monitoring of the transference-countertransference.

Gisella longed for her analyst to make sense of her anxiety and bewilderment, as a baby in this state of alienation needs to experience a mother who is trying to comprehend, contain and ease the baby's contradictory demands. In the transference, Gisella's mistrust of the analyst's ability to respond with calm understanding was not derived simply from mistrust of an inconsistent mother (which might have become analysable and comprehensible). There was a legacy of a fundamental double bind, in which the baby Gisella had had to adapt to the overwhelming inconsistency of her environment (the see-saw of her mother's moods from hope to despair, availability to absence) by fragmenting, dissociating, and splitting her self-representation into several autonomous complexes.

Clinical Technique

One effect of silence on our technique was our need to be unusually outspoken about our own feeling states, assuming these to be a product of unconscious projection between ourselves and our patients. For instance, we would talk about the pervasive mood of feeling abandoned or tongue-tied, fearful, helpless – states which the patient could not express. The intense silences impelled us to try to create a climate in which feelings and imagery from the inner world could be granted currency. Often our self-revelations had a "hit or miss" quality, but the patients appeared receptive as we spoke, even if they remained silent.

We dared to answer direct questions in the hope of starting a conversation. These incidents of boundary-breaking seemed temporarily to bring the patients to life, but also shifted the emphasis of the work away from the systematic analysis of psychic states. We concluded that, through projective identification, we were being used as containers for our patients' craving for contact. Paradoxically, the patients had objected to our lapses from the analytic stance, and feared any revelation of our humanity.

Because we felt more emotionally exposed than with verbal patients, we used our collegial conversations to contain despair and retaliation, discussing trial interventions which could firmly, yet compassionately, confront our patients' terrible reality. Our mutual support saved us from enacting destructive impulses by putting them into analytic context.

Imagery

Throughout silences, our trust in the self was rewarded by gradual emergence of our patients' dreams and images. Gisella felt her dreams came to her rescue because they enabled her to talk about her conflicts. In one dream:

> *Myself and a man are struggling in the sea to reach shore. We are contending with a massive undertow, and take it in turns to be the drowned, and then the saved.*

The dream portrays mutual danger and dependence in the analytic relationship and was instrumental in initiating a rapprochement. Gisella brought a crayon drawing to demonstrate her feelings about the isolation and silent suffering of her childhood. It shows her as a screaming child, in a room smeared with faeces, confronting the huge feet and legs of an enormous mother, whose face and upper body are out of view, beyond reach. A small window reveals a child's swing, on which Gisella could rock herself for comfort.

Through this drawing Gisella shared her story in a way that words had never achieved. More importantly, like her dream images, it enabled her to speak about herself symbolically, and elicited sadness and warm concern in the analyst.

Clinical outcomes

Although both patients left analysis suddenly, we are not convinced the terminations were premature. Gisella has returned on three occasions, somewhat happier and able at last to talk. Her analyst felt encouraged by her contemplative, friendly mood. Something had been gestating. As further evidence Fiona, halfway through her analysis, produced a live baby, having kept her pregnancy a secret. Fiona's analyst often felt the analysis was stillborn, yet it apparently helped Fiona to sustain a marriage and motherhood. We are left with events we do not understand, but hesitantly conclude that the destructive forces unleashed during the analyses have been balanced by a measure of creativity and growth.

Conclusion

We have highlighted features such as intolerance and avoidance of positive emotional involvement: marked countertransference reactions including destructive fantasies. Although not in itself archetypal, we have hypothesised that profound and prolonged silence is a product of archetypal processes. Avoidance of attachment to the analyst is protective of the integrity of the self, but also paradoxically threatens the existence of the self.

Our respect for silence as protection for the patients' integrity meant that orthodox methods of maintaining therapeutic alliance were challenged. Our patients made pre-symbolic use of us which speech would have disturbed. We believe now that we should not seek at first to foster whole-object relating with silent patients. Rather, there may be a benefit in allowing oneself to be used, or even abused, as a self-object in the transference, possibly for years, with careful monitoring of the countertransference for signs of masochistic surrender. Weathering the silence is what we offer such patients and, with interpretation, may transform its destructiveness.

References

Altman, L. (1957). The waiting syndrome. *Psychoanalytic Quarterly, 26,* 508-518.

Arlow, J. (1961). Silence and the theory of technique. *Journal of the American Psychoanalytic Association,* 9-1, 44-55.

Coltart, N. (1992). *Slouching towards Bethlehem: And Further Psychoanalytic Explorations.* London: Guilford Press.

Greenson, R. (1961). On the silence and sounds of the analytic hour. *Journal of American Psychoanalytic Association,* 9-1, 79-90.

Kalsched, D. (1996). *The Inner World of Trauma.* London: Routledge.

Khan, M. (1963). Silence as communication. In *The Privacy of the Self.* London: International Psychological Library.

Loomie, L.S. (1961). Some remarks on the role of speech in the psycho-analytic technique. *International Journal of Psycho-analysis. 37:* 460-467.

Main, M. (1991). Metacognitive knowledge, metacognitive monitoring, and singular (coherent) vs. multiple (incoherent) models of attachment. In P. Marris, J. Stevenson-Hinde, and C. Parks (Eds.), *Attachment across the Life Cycle.* New York: Routledge.

Main, M. & Goldwyn, R. (1984). Predicting rejection of her infant from mother's representation of her own experience: Implications for the abused-abusing intergenerational cycle. *Child Abuse and Neglect, 8,* 203-217.

Main, M. & Weston, D. (1982). Avoidance of the attachment figure in infancy: Descriptions and interpretations. In: C.M. Parkes & J. Stevenson-Hinde (Eds), *The Place of Attachment in Human Behaviour.* New York: Basic Books.

Patrick, M.; Hobson, R.P.; Castle, D.; Howard, R.; Maughan, B. (1994). Personality disorder and the mental representation of early social experience. *Development and Psychopathology, 6,* 375-388.

Roy, A. (1997). *The God of Small Things.* London: Harper Collins.

Siegel, A.M. (1996). *Heinz Kohut and the Psychology of the Self.* London: Routledge.

Wilson, P. (1963). *A time to think.* Paper presented at the meeting of the University of Hertfordshire Counselling Service.

Zeligs, M.A. (1961). The psychology of silence: Its role in transference, countertransference and the psychoanalytic process. *Journal of the American Psychoanalytic Association, 9-1,* 7-43.

Creating and Destroying

Dionysiac Images of Dismemberment, Death and Renewal

Gary D. Astrachan
Portland, Maine, USA.
New England Society of Jungian Analysts

In this offering to the Greek god Dionyso, we trace the themes of looking, mirroring, reflecting and their connections to images of dismemberment, death and renewal. We explore these motifs in the analytic situation, as well as take them up within a discourse concerned with establishing a ground for doing depth psychological work in a post-holocaust context. The analytic container must provide a holding vessel for the overwhelming and opposing urges we all bear, both to create and to destroy.

There are basically two traditions regarding the birth of Dionysos. In the classical version, he is the offspring of Semele, the mortal daughter of King Cadmus of Thebes; and Zeus, her nocturnal lover. Instigated by Hera's insinuating envy, Semele prevails upon Zeus to appear to her in his true form, so that she can actually see him. Unhappily obliging, Zeus comes to the ill-fated young woman as a lightning bolt and incinerates her on the spot. At that same horrific moment, however, he snatches Dionysos from her womb and clasps him up in his own male thigh, there to complete the intra-uterine maturation.

Thus, from his very beginnings Dionysos is the god of the double birth, who enters the world through a double door, *dithyrambos*: born out of the womb of fiery death. He is the god of dividedness and duality. His immolated mother's longing to see – and thereby know – her mysterious paramour proves disastrous, literally setting the stage in Euripides' tragic drama, *The Bacchae*, with the ruins of a palace and Semele's still-smoking, vine-covered tomb as the god's originating *topos* (place).

In a later, underground Orphic story of this god's early life and times, Dionysos is once again begotten by Zeus, but by Zeus

Katacthonios: Zeus in his underworldly form and identical with Hades, lord of the dead. His mother in this variation is Persephone, *Kore,* the abducted maiden daughter of Demeter who now presides as mistress in the deep realm of shades. In this tale, as the infant god sits amusing himself amidst his toys; The Titans, a banished race of primordial, brutal beings, persuaded by Hera's murderous wrath, sneak up on the innocently playing infant. Their faces daubed and smeared with white chalk, they seize the unwary god as he looks at this own reflection in a mirror and tear him apart limb from limb. Adding horror to infamy, they boil, roast and eat the body of the slain child, except for one body part which they overlook in their cannibalistic frenzy.

Some unnoticed god or goddess lingering at the obscene feast picks up the scattered organ, the phallus, or – in some versions – the heart, and brings it to Rhea, the venerable mother of all the gods. She places it in a casket on her head and carries it there for nine months. Dionysos is then re-birthed, actually re-membered, from his own mangled body part. Again, this constellation of looking, seeing the other, whether directly or in the mirror, is fatal for the protagonist and leads inexorably to tragedy. Dismemberment, death and destruction are integral, then, not only to the Dionysiac mythologem, but appear necessary for ordinary psychological development, as well as for possibilities of renewal.

Zeus, learning of the slaughter of his beloved son, blasts the god-gorged Titans with his lightning bolts, reducing them to heaps of burning ash. As the remarkable culmination of this tale, he creates out of this still smoldering stuff nothing less than the human race. So we human beings, ever since that distant time, are comprised of an ineradicably dual nature. We all bear a double-fold destiny: a flesh-eating, lawless, Titanic part – the body – as well as a divine Dionysiac spark, the soul.

Psychotherapy – the care and cultivation of our immortal, god-like aspect – is, in a real sense, grounded upon this grisly infanticide. We, not unlike the ancient Orphics, devote our entire lives to honoring this deep split between body and soul at the very base of our being, while at the same time attempting through our analytic art and dedication, to heal it. It is here at the intersection of soma and psyche where we must build our temples to Dionysos. Here, at this critical disjuncture between our all-too-human worldly condition and our divine birthright, we must acknowledge that we all partake deeply of the body and blood of a murdered and eaten god. We pay homage to a god whom we kill and devour and is then reborn, a god who comes and goes and who asks only that we respect and remember him.

Perhaps, if only we too could be reborn, like Dionysos, from our own madness, fragmentations and deaths, he would not appear to have such a bipolar countenance, or such a split nature, as ours. As the lord of both worlds, whatever pair of opposites one might choose, Dionysos reigns at the edges of our lives, in the twilight zone, at the fluid border between sanity and madness, wholeness and division, body and soul and, ultimately, life and death. He is the purplish wine, resinous sap and glutinous semen that hold together body and soul, life and death; who gives staining, gluey and redolent body and life to both soul and death.

"Be in advance of all parting, as though it were behind you like the winter that is just going. For among winters, one is so endlessly winter that, overwintering, your heart once for all will hold out. Be ever dead in Eurydice. ... Here, among the waning, be, in the realm of decline, a ringing glass that shivers even as it rings. Be – and at the same time know the condition of not-being, the infinite ground of your deep vibration, that you may fully fulfil it this single time."

As he feverishly wrote these *Sonnets to Orpheus* in the Château de Muzot in Switzerland's Valais in February 1922, Rilke evoked for us today the dark terrain of the god who looms large in the *mythos* behind the figure of his frail and beloved poet Orpheus. He calls up in his poems the scorched, earthy *topos*, which is the provenance of Dionysos, the place of strangeness and alienation belonging to this god born from death, who dwells in the borderline between creating and destroying.

The epiphanous and cacophonous arrival of Dionysos, *Bromios*, the roarer, is always preceded by a deafening silence, a loss, a wandering in the underworld, abandonment, a falling into depression, a death. This is his psychological ground. His absence creates sorrow and a yearning for his return. Time and again, Orpheus dies, Dionysos leaves, and we are left alone.

Yet again Rilke reminds us: "A god can do it. But how, tell me, shall a man follow him through the narrow lyre [entrance]? His mind is cleavage." How then do we, men and women, follow this god, with his beckoning promises of vitality, enthusiasm and ecstasy, surrounded as he is by dissolution, terror and annihilation?

Pursuing the problematics of the gaze, looking and seeing, within the Dionysiac mythologem with its frequently consequent reprisals of dismemberment and death, we now turn to justly famous Orpheus himself. This lyre player's magical song is the most renowned of all the figures who fall under the wrenching sway of Dionysos *Mainomenos* (the mad god). When "dark" Orpheus violates the sole injunction laid upon him by the powers of the underworld to refrain from looking back at his beloved wife Eurydice; he loses her to death for the second time and forever. Later in his myth and in his misogyny – for he abjures all women after losing Eurydice; by some accounts he introduces homosexual love into Greece and institutes initiatory rites exclusively for men. He is ripped apart by the raving women followers of Dionysos.

Another alter-ego and sacrificial victim of Dionysos is his first cousin Pentheus, "man of sorrows," the young king in Euripides' *Bacchae*. Throughout the tragic drama, Pentheus refuses to recognize the triumphantly returning Dionysos. In the penultimate scene, Pentheus – dressed as a woman – is led through the streets of his own kingdom of Thebes by Dionysos whom, by then, he sees delusionally as a bull. Consequently, he is dismembered by his own mother, aunts and other women of the city when he goes to spy, lasciviously, upon their orgiastic rites in the wilderness. They, in their own hallucinatorily transfigured vision, see him as a mountain lion perched in a tall fir tree, which they tear to the ground, tumbling him out before swarming upon his helplessly protesting body. The literal vision of all these Thebans swept up in this devastating tragedy reverts back to its atavistic paleo-hominian ancestry and origins in hunting and cannibalism, the Dionysiac bodily ground of our animal instinct.

Finally, in this fatal confluence of looking and the reprisal of dismemberment, we find the young princely hunter Actaeon, another first cousin of Dionysos from the royal house of Thebes, who unwittingly views the virgin goddess of wild nature and the hunt, Diana/Artemis, in her bath. Outraged, she transforms him into a stag and in his full human awareness, he is ripped apart by his own pack of hunting dogs.

With this bloody legacy as our background, we note that the forbidden gaze, looking and seeing, even when guileless, is paired for all these protagonists with terrifying destruction and death. The young mother Semele, the infant Dionysos, Orpheus, Pentheus and Actaeon, are all torn apart and obliterated in connection with the act of seeing. The desired object of their glance, the other, becomes eventually the perpetrator of their death. These tragic voyeurs all become the hunted prey of their own desiring vision. Their fates exemplify the processes of disintegration, dissociation and the splitting of the psychic functions which led Eugen Bleuler to coin the term "schizo-phrenia," the splitting apart of the vital, bodily self. The gaze always risks eliciting responses of hate, jealousy and retributive rending which lurk within its perceptual field. And the punishment for looking and seeing is enacted upon and within the body.

As the patron god of theater and tragedy in particular, Dionysos is the only Greek god who has a *dromenon* (dramatic enactment) as part of his ritual. He is also alone among the Olympians in offering his devotees both the spectacle and experience of corporally becoming one with him, *entheos* (enthusiastic or possessed by the god), and the recipient of his blessings. Whether in rending retaliation or intoxicating bliss, Dionysos reflects our own visions back to us, toward their source in us, in sublime identification with his uncanny powers. For better or worse, Dionysos forces us to own our projections.

Arriving now at the *temenos* of the analytic drama, we can appreciate that our patients' needs to look backward, to recollect, reflect and be reflected – mirrored and held within the therapeutic gaze – constitute the basic conditions for doing depth psychological work. Depth analysis is thus fraught with the same dire possibilities of psychic destruction and death as we have seen in the Dionysiac mythologem. In encouraging the capacities to regress, to free associate, and to renounce seeing, analysis can follow only upon the establishment of a safe and secure container which promises to hold the tearing conflictual tensions that may be unleashed.

In the myths of his infancy and early years, Dionysos represents the embattled, regressed and schizoid aspects of the divine child – aspects that form the central piece of some of our deepest work with analysands. The pairing of the gaze with the terror of dismemberment points in a developmental context to the possible insufficiency of positive mirroring experiences within the early maternal environment. Such pairing would seem also to indicate the tremendous risks intrinsic to the analytic context of experiencing intimacy or vulnerability, allowing oneself to be truly seen, or even sometimes of gaining insight.

Persecuted throughout his entire mythologem by the "schizophrenogenic mother," Hera, Dionysos must flee into the deepest recesses of nature in order to protect and preserve his bodily integrity. Escaping his aggressors on one occasion, he dives into the sea to stay for nine months with the nymph Thetis, who becomes his foster mother. Another time, he plunges into lakes to avoid destruction. Fleeing brutal attack, he runs to distant mountain tops, secluded wooded valleys, or deep forests, often with his attendant nurses, nymphs and mother/lover figures surrounding him.

This image is of a withdrawn and isolated core bodily self, the hidden and fearful Dionysiac divine child, run away to the wild, to the preserve of inner wilderness which is his domain. The archetypal child corresponds on the unconscious level to what we see consciously manifest in the consulting room: the false self, intense lack of trust and impaired capacity for reflection and symbolic thinking that we meet in the borderline patient. Dionysos the child god, image of the self though not dead, has fled and is revealed only by his absence. The *deus absconditus* (hidden god), the concealed self appears only in the traces it leaves: symptoms, defenses, resistances, emptiness, depression, despair and paranoia.

The development of a sense of bodily self – a true self – and its innate value stem from the cumulative, good-enough experiences of mirroring and mirrored dismembering occurring in infancy and throughout childhood. When there is inadequate or distorted mirroring due to loss, narcissistic injury, deprivation, neglect, abuse, or trauma; pathological splitting constellates, as well as other defenses of a paranoid-schizoid type. Such rigid defenses continued into adult life through an "archetypal self-care system" (Kalsched 1996, p. 4) may preclude securing the minimal interpersonal trust necessary for developing genuine relatedness or for interiority, the capacity for enriching and nurturing aloneness. The soul, inherently reflective by nature, becomes dulled, tarnished and dimmed by conflicts and concerns over concretely physical, bodily safety. There is no room for a safeguarded soul space, allowing for reflection when issues of survival are dominant.

Psychotherapeutically, this situation necessitates the entire reconstruction of a nourishing environment and transitional space, an analytic/alchemical container secure enough for the immersion of both participants in this work upon soul. The bodily self, the divine Dionysiac child, needs to engage in a re-creation. The child in the patient needs to learn how to play.

With these thoughts in mind, I now turn to some clinical material from two female analysands. The first piece is a dream from a 52-year-old woman:

> *After showering, I dress and go over to the mirror, an oval mirror over a counter. I notice the door to the bathroom is ajar. I go to close it and meet with resistance. There is a man on the other side attempting to force his way into the bathroom. He overpowers me and pushes the door open. I am terrified because I know he wants to harm me. I manage to escape, but know he will pursue me. I run outdoors to get help and find neighbors, an elderly couple. Just as I begin to tell them what happened, I wake feeling the terror I was trying to escape.*

This dream, stunning in its simplicity, ordinariness and economy of symbolic expression, holds within its infinitely mirroring depths all the complex and tangled motifs of Greek mythology that we are touching upon here.

The main symbolic connection to be made now is that, as in the myth of the infant Dionysos dismembered, the dreamer's looking into the mirror becomes linked with the terror of being attacked. The conjunction of narcissistic reflection with the threat of rape or other bodily harm, points to the negative valuation of looking and being seen which has characterized this woman's life. Her excruciating physical vulnerability, intense loathing of her body and severe inhibitions against being seen in any sense, are associated further for her with fears of being overwhelmed and attacked literally, splitting apart and going mad, or being abandoned. She has always had a sleep disorder and finds it extremely difficult to stay in her own house overnight when her family members are not present.

She grew up fatherless and was raised by a non-nurturing, narcissistic mother who also exhibited some paranoid traits. Doting on the first-born boy, her mother relegated the patient to the status of a Cinderella who had to do the housework and cooking from an early age, while the mother worked in an office in the nearby city. Controlling and intrusive, the mother fostered a symbiotic relationship by insisting that her daughter sleep in the same bed with her until age 14. The mother always had to have the window curtains drawn so that people could not look in – although they lived in the country. And despite spending nearly two hours every morning making herself up before work, she forbade her daughter to look in mirrors, spend any time shopping or on her own appearance, or consort with boys or men. There was only one thing, she warned, that they wanted.

When the patient was about seven – on the rare occasion of sleeping at an aunt's house because her mother was in the hospital – the patient was sexually abused by an older female cousin who put sharp, pointed objects into her vagina. She reports that she has felt almost no sensations of sexual arousal or erotic pleasure throughout her life, and instead, often experiences anxiety, abhorrence and revulsion in sexual situations.

At the very end of the session when the above dream was recounted, she mentioned that, earlier in the evening of the dream, her husband wanted to have sex with her, just as the dream's man forcefully pushed his way through the door. She ambivalently complied. Associations to the mirror included a recent shopping excursion for a bathing suit and her inability to try one on in the store. Later, when she went upstairs to try on the bathing suit in the privacy of her own bedroom and bathroom, she stood looking into the mirror, crying with shame and disgust when her daughter walked in. She apologized to her daughter for having such negative feelings about her own body.

The second patient is a woman who, over the course of a long analysis, recounted some of her experiences. During the first four years of her life, her mother was away a great deal: literally due to various sicknesses, including some hospitalizations; and more often emotionally unavailable. When the mother was resting at home, the patient used to go into her room and watch her sleep, sometimes trying to pry her eyelids open, getting her to look.

When still a little girl, the patient would play, unobserved under the dining room table, gazing out at others in the house while wishing herself to be seen and found. She knows that she tore and twisted all the eyes off her stuffed dolls, including her favorite ones, though she does not remember actually doing it. One doll had decals for eyes, which she peeled off again and again. Each time, her mother replaced them.

Attending a workshop I was presenting, after beginning analysis with me, she recalls the great luxury of being able to sit there and watch me, feeding contentedly on me with her eyes without worry about being seen herself.

During an eight-months' period of working analytically on the couch, she would become extremely distressed nearly every session because she could not see or hear me and did not know if I was sleeping, looking at her, bored, uninterested, or even there at all. She felt as if she was disappearing or falling, did not know what to say, and between bouts of shame and failure, desperately pleaded for help. The silence, the ticking of the clock and the lack of visual and emotional contact created such a continuously unbearable tension and panic that we had to stop using the couch.

The associations are important between looking and feeding and this patient's need for face-to-face mirroring in order to maintain even a semblance of a sense of self. In the absence of benevolent mirroring and holding interpretations, the patient felt hopelessly abandoned, rejected and worthless. Unable to see the analyst, the inner capacity for reflection became completely shattered, making the verbalization of internal experience nearly impossible.

Though not overtly abusive, this patient's mother was hypochondriacal and foisted unnecessary medical interventions upon the patient, including minor surgery when she was five years old. Her mother became frankly paranoid for periods of time throughout her later adult life and into old age; she thought her mail was being read and her phone tapped.

The patient's father was a seductive charmer who made promises he never kept, was away for up to a year at a time in the armed forces and never dealt with or discussed any of his comings and lengthy goings. He also had a marked sociopathic side, was twice convicted of fraud and theft, and even served a brief sentence in prison. After 48 years, he mentioned in passing that he was not the patient's father, concocting a bizarre story involving the patient's recently-deceased mother in a number of sexual affairs.

As a result of these intensely negative and apparently envious and rivalrous mother-daughter relationships, each patient developed a harshly self-critical, devalued sense of herself and her body: a punitive, persecutory inner mother. Their absent fathers provided shadowy, unreliable, tantalizing and frightening inner male figures who continue to haunt them. As partial compensation for their low self-esteem, they expanded their gifted intellectual capacities and are both empathic, knowledgeable and talented psychotherapists. They are also, remarkably, loving and devoted mothers.

With the breakdown of the maternal environment and the absence of positive bodily mirroring experiences, the relationship to the world of matter becomes extremely conflicted. In addition to being emotionally absent, the madness of these women's mothers, themselves abandoned by husbands, took a particularly virulent attacking and dismembering form. The combination failed to provide the silvery material backing necessary to the psyche's capacity to reflect. It is as if the inner mirror is shattered, splintered into many glinting sharp fragments and whole objects cannot be held within its reflections with any degree of permanency.

The lack of physical security and bodily well-being also made it difficult for the women, as children and as adults, to feel free enough to play or to imagine. Transfixed by the dreadful stare of serpent-haired Medusa, the intolerably negative mother, the child's gaze becomes petrified, frozen and horror-struck in awe-filled emotional trauma. Their relationships with men easily become characterized by sado-masochistic tendencies, deep dependency longings and a reactive resentment and rage at not being perfectly mirrored or fulfilled in their expectations of an idealized father.

The capacities for regression and free association in the analytic process hinge upon a groundwork of trust provided by an adequate facilitating environment. The tendency toward concreteness and literalness, in both inner and outer looking, results in a Narcissus-like fixation on words, reflection itself, or on physical appearances, which fixation acts defensively to split or dismember the self, in order to protect the deeply regressed, infantile portion. Lacking a healthy capacity for self-reflection, the ego fluctuates wildly between poles of inflated grandiosity and self-abasing depression.

With both these women, a general hyper-vigilance, high anxiety, strong intellectual defenses and tendency toward splitting all militate against any kind of direct, heroic, or forceful approaches to emotional issues. Confrontation is often met by fierce resistance and a hatred barely disguised by an animus-possessed rationality.

There is no reason to assume, however, that the general psychological picture of these two women is by any means extraordinary in analysis. Normal development includes suffering major frustrations, disappointments, losses, rejections and abandonments. It is, however, just at the junctures of characterological "stuckness" and rigidity that we may invoke the god who can take us gently, albeit via oblique routes, even more deeply into these gaping splits and rending tears within ourselves. Through the transferentially-gained therapeutic alliance, our patients may gain the possibility of becoming free. A second dream of the first patient illustrates this slow, but perhaps hopeful, process:

*I am in a relatively large, bright, but empty room in my house. I find
a broken, injured man. He is in his early thirties, has very light skin
and is wearing a true red, short sleeve shirt. I want to help him, but
I am so overwhelmed and sickened by the sight that I am incapaci-
tated. I realize that I have neither the skill nor the experience to help
repair or heal this man. The man is dismembered. His left arm and
leg with bloody shredded edges are lying next to him. He seems quite
comfortable there on the floor, unaffected by his serious, gaping
wounds.*

*My brother arrives and offers his help. At this point my brother turns
into [my analyst]. He gathers the man and his body parts, carries
him into the adjacent room and fixes him. I am relieved, grateful,
surprised and in awe. I feel safe.*

The dismembered man is the dreamer's father who left the family
when the patient's mother was six months pregnant with her and also
had a four-year-old son. The father was in his early thirties when he
finally, totally abandoned the family. His favorite color for clothing
and other gift items was always red.

The dismembered man also points to the *rubedo* phase of
alchemy: the reddening, the red man who unites with the white
woman. He is Mars, the red planet and the aggressive, bellicose god
of macho masculinity. He is the color of blood, wine, rage and
passion.

He is also the analyst, regularly dismembered in fits of fury
usually precipitated by patient-perceived countertransferential reactions of abandoning through distancing, rendering judgments, tearing criticism and lacerating insensitivity. He is the patient's father
imago, repeatedly ripped in revenge.

Though still within a relatively passive, magical and idealized
transference fantasy, the dream points to a possibility of renewing
and reconstructing a potentially healthier masculine attitude within
this woman's life and of healing a tragically split father archetype.

Dionysiac mirroring strives to hold within its gaze the fractured
shards of a soul in tortured struggle. The Dionysiac gaze reflects
from its own crazily shattered pieces of a mirrored self, repeatedly
broken and painstakingly recreated. The dissolving cauldron of
analysis takes place in the mutual dismemberment and death of the
ego's defensive moves against completely exposing itself in the
presence of the other. Risking dismemberment, one may find acceptance.

Dionysos *Lysios* – the loosener, liberator, releaser, untier of knots and bonds – whose epithet lysios is cognate with lysis – as in the name of our art, ana-lysis – allows us to dissolve and break down into our many complexes and fragments, to arrive at our essences, the essentials, what really matters. Separating and sorting through the dis-membered pieces of ourselves, we re-member the forgotten and disjointed body. We re-collect the disowned parts. We slowly put back together the torn and scattered limbs of the divine child we all bear within.

In all the stories of Dionysos, his life is fraught with the terrors of persecution, attack and destruction. His bodily presence and sheer being – as neonate, infant, youth and young man – are attended by violence, hate and death. He constellates the deepest and darkest impulses that threaten his own life. The very image of Dionysos, especially as divine child – whole, helpless, ineffable, needy and vulnerable – calls up and elicits an archaic urge to attack and destroy that which is most sacred. The Dionysiac body of the child – as pure untrammeled nature, unbearably numinous and miraculously other – entails the looming danger of its own abuse and even murder.

Dionysos represents the bodily self that resides wild, in the divine wildness of our own natures. And both our inner and outer wilderness is under furious attack and is rapidly disappearing. Objectively, the natural wilderness environment of the world, unprotected and unpreserved, is daily despoiled, ravaged and becoming rapidly extinguished by a greedily rapacious consumerism that denies the intrinsic value of matter, the indwelling of soul in nature, self-evident to the divine child. This lack of human and ecological safety and security creates our postmodern condition of dis-ease, a cultural atmosphere of profound paranoia, cynicism and fragmentation concerning both our own personal and social bodies and the besieged body of the world. We live in times of catastrophe and dismemberment. Body and soul are both endangered.

Dionysos is indissolubly connected to the sustaining body of the matriarchal earth goddesses. Raised entirely by women, he is the avatar of the ancient and repressed orgiastic powers of the mothers. Arriving as a male – nourished, feted and surrounded by the mad nymphs and nurses of his native Nysa – he is always and everywhere perceived as a threat by the hard-won heroic ego of patriarchal Western consciousness. In the many myths of resistance to him, he comes and goes from the depths of oceans, seas and lakes. He roves with his maenads over rocky hills and through lush fields and deserted plains. His home is with the deep feminine sources of nature. Forced into severe repression through centuries of harsh instinctual renunciation, the god now manifests himself through the darker sides of human nature, threatening to tear apart our psychosocial fabric of values, beliefs, goals and ideals. This essentially enlivening and invigorating god has become sickened and corrupted for our time. Unable to create sufficient vessels for containing his basically liberating and gladdening gifts, we fall prey to the regressive and primitive trends which are his retaliations for being dishonored. Dionysos is a force of nature, scorned and vengeful, calling to us from the diminished, exploited and scarred body of the world for redemption and healing. His rent and strewn body inseminates the earth with a deep resonance and instills a divine frenzy into matter.

Radiant in his occlusion, he speaks cryptically in the veiled utterances of nature's disfigured text. We search for him in climates of conflagration and holocaust. In the dispersed and fragmented signs of his absence which litter our contemporary landscape with ruin, Dionysos *Zagreus* (great hunter) hunts us down for his own restoration, recollection and interpretation. He reveals himself through incompleteness. Despite his ambiguity, formlessness and non-representability, he nevertheless establishes the reality of the bodily self, its precious historicity; while simultaneously naming its nothingness, its emptiness in the groundless ground of our being, in our non-being, in death and in soul.

Dionysos invites us to relinquish our fixed and concrete visions of solidity and substance and follow instead in his violently churning wake. In the ebb and tide and flux and flow of his rhythmical comings and goings, he may find us creating a clearing for his homecoming upon the ever-shifting shore: awaiting his return, like Ariadne on Naxos; like his lovers and devotees throughout the Greek world who always invoked his coming from the watery depths; like the women of Elis who would dance and sing:

> *Come, Hero (of the underworld) Dionysos to the temple by the sea*
> *with the Graces to the pure temple*
> *raving with the bull's foot (Kerenyi 1976, p. 182)*

References

Kalsched, D. (1996). *The Inner World of Trauma*. London: Routledge.
Kerenyi, K. (1976). *Dionysos. Archetypal Image of Indestructible Life*. Princeton, NJ: Princeton University Press.

Panel: Letting Go of
the "Unified Theory" Concept

Brigitte Allain-Dupré
Paris, France
Société Française de Psychologie Analytique

The International Workshop of Analytical Psychology in Child-hood and Adolescence was founded at the Jerusalem Congress in 1983, when the IAAP recognized officially Jungian therapy with children and adolescents.

Mara Sidoli and Gustaav Bovensiepen organized the workshop as a three-day meeting of 40 attendees, each year in a different European country. The aim remains to work together on our practice and to discuss theoretical issues, taking into account the fact that there are many ways to be Jungian; each country has its own style and its own Jungian culture. When working on case material, one shares one's own Jungian culture with colleagues, to enrich the reflection about child therapy, not to teach to convince each other. Meeting differences obliges us to be clearer about our own theoretical and clinical positions.

Since 1991, a committee of eight child therapists, from seven European countries and the United States, organizes the Workshop. The papers here are designed to make known our work and to give ideas to one who would like to create such a creative, vivid and friendly way to work. Seven years ago we started a journal (with the financial support of the IAAP and of our national societies) called *Materia Prima*, as a link between the workshop and Jungian child therapists all over the world.

The Workshop Background

Gianni Nagliero

Rome, Italy

Associazione Italiana di Psicologia Analitica

Our Workshop history can be traced, from its founders' initial determination to seek a unifying idea for child therapists, to the establishment of the different ideas and theories. The difficulty and indeed the impossibility of adopting a common theory caused a crisis within the Workshop and the resignation of its leaders, Mara Sidoli and Gustav Bovensiepen. Since many members were motivated enough to continue an experience that had been most productive, the group survived and was transformed. The sharing of a solid leadership and an efficient organizing committee made it possible, despite initial difficulties, to compare and confront our different ideas. My present reflection stems from the decision to abandon the search for a common theory for all Jungian child analysts, opting instead for recognition of different opinions and theories as an enriching element for all: an exchange of views that we have experienced during the years of our group's existence.

Once again there is a desire for change; some of us want to leave the organizing committee to make room for people with new ideas and fresh enthusiasm. There are many reasons for this but, for me at least, it is the result of a desire to deepen "my" theory, the theory to which I feel closest, which I consider most useful for my work – which is closer, perhaps, to my typology. Obviously it is an incomplete theory that I want to explore further with someone who "speaks my language," the "language" of the importance of transferential relation, of setting and of interpretation.

Perhaps our German colleagues' decision to re-introduce moments of theoretical discussion – as well as clinical cases – into the last Workshop meeting, is connected to this desire for moments of confrontation on the very theoretical aspects that have been avoided during these years by concentrating exclusively on clinical cases, preventing potentially dangerous conflicts and schisms within the group. The will for a return to confrontation on these theories has been expressed by many Workshop participants. This is a sign of the strength acquired by the group over these years, where fears have diminished of a break-up because of different theories. I think this is a sign that our work has been important over these years precisely because it has reinforced everyone's ideas, making confrontation possible today without so many worries of a consequent disintegration of the group. On the other hand, confrontation can and must take place between different and powerful ideas because only through the strong defense of one's personal convictions, while respecting those of others, can something new be created.

My last thoughts are for the Jungian environment which we know to be represented by many theories. In no other school is it possible to meet colleagues who work so differently from one another. It is said that this derives from the fact that Jung was imprecise on one side and open on the other. Thus, when Jungian minds meet, there is a tendency for some reconciliation on everything; the belief prevails that basically we all think the same thing, that Father-Jung unites us all. This has caused a weakening in Jungian thinking, but it has regained its strength over the last few years by recognition of the diversity of the various opinions. I like to think that this is partly due to the merits of our Workshop.

Significance of the Workshop

Lois Ione Hunt Khan
Barrington, Ilinois, USA
Chicago Society of Jungian Analysts

When the invitation came in 1984 to attend a workshop for Jungians interested in working with children and adolescents, I was thrilled. At the time I was in progressive training programs in the Inter-regional Society of Jungian Analysts and the Chicago Jung Institute but, despite the range of interests and experiences they represented, my colleagues were not interested in work with these age groups.

My early training and work experience led me to work with children and youth: as a social worker in a child guidance clinic; as a nursery school teacher; as a child welfare worker and probation officer; as a rehabilitation counselor and psychologist in a state institution for the retarded, epileptic, and psychotic; as a vocational counselor and director of a training facility to work and train disadvantaged youth; and, finally, as a clinical psychologist in private practice working with children, youth, and adults.

Educationally, my university training in developmental theory included Eric Erickson, Anna Freud, Arnold Gesell, Frances Ilg and Louise Ames, T. Joseph Stone and Joseph Church, and Daniel Stern. Also Virginia Axline in play therapy and – in later years – Robert Coles, who addressed the spiritual, moral, and ethical crises faced by children in every level of society. Coles was especially significant as he echoed Jung's sensitivity regarding how individuals seeking their own meaningful story must and do confront their own soulful-spiritual issues. My experience is that, for children more than for adults, issues are carried more keenly in the archetypal form and recognized in their play, and in the stories with which they identify and in which they find significance.

I have attended nearly all the workshops over the years. What has been so significant for me was the sharing of ideas. It amazes me that we all call ourselves Jungian analysts and candidates, and yet have different approaches, from Melanie Klein and Michael Fordham to body work. Even more than the theoretical learning has been the value of our working in a case colloquium model, wherein we are able to discuss cases and to share our experiences and resources. It has increased my respect for each school of thought and has increased the repertoire that I bring to the analytic session. I have learned much over these past 14 years, and I have come to respect even more Jung's edict: to know the theory but be with your patient where that individual's life story takes you. While I may disagree with some interpretations, it matters little; in their working relation-ship, the patient and analyst seem to sail or muddle along toward greater consciousness.

Because of my training and style, I have been frustrated that more of the illustrative children's stories with their wonderful problem-solving techniques are not brought into relatship to the issues the patient brings. Initially I was also somewhat frustrated by the "politics," until I realized the importance of bringing pressure on the Jungian community at large to recognize the value of child and adolescent training and work. I only wish that it would percolate to the United States. The only training facility that insists on all candidates' having some work experience with young people is Los Angeles. It was always such a relief and joy when Edith Sullwold, the director of that program, would come to Chicago and we would have seminars – on the inner child, of course – but it gave me someone to talk to.

Now I have a whole community to talk to, albeit mostly in Europe. Americans are still very slow to embrace this work. Even those who are working with children and adolescents are neither visible nor sharing, as the European community is. I am so grateful to have not only a supportive community, but to represent that community back here in the States to those who have begun to indicate an interest in the field.

Factors in the Healing Process

Hildegard Thomas
Leonberg, Germany
Deutsche Gesellschaft für Analytische Psychologie

Participation in the International Workshop has been an important event in my work with children and adolescents. The variety of ways of working in different countries surprised me initially. How could it be that there were such huge differences when we all had a Jungian training? It made me feel insecure, and I had to fight for my own approach. My idea that there was a certain framework, which provided the best way of working with patients, broke apart when I saw how many different kinds of frameworks there are.

In the Workshop we work in small groups on clinical cases. The first thing I have learned among so many colleagues was to listen – really listen – to find out what the other person means. I have learned that the different approaches were based on working in different symbolic areas:

1. the image of the therapeutic relationship in which the patient's personal attitudes and difficulties are to be interpreted.

2. the image of the therapy space as a womb, in which the patient's infantile needs and difficulties are to be interpreted.

3. archetypal images, in response to which the therapist offers archetypal material so that they can be embodied and interpreted.

All my colleagues, using these different frameworks, were working seriously and had successes or failures, as I did. From this experience I concluded that it is the personality of the analyst that is the deciding factor, that provides the "interactive field." This is the space within which patient and analyst meet to understand and deepen the analytic process. For me, this means that I must look very carefully at my own values: Am I authentic?

During my training, work with the symbol and its healing, transformative quality was of crucial importance. Over the years in the Workshop, I have realised that we have a variety of fields within which to experience the symbol that can open a new path and new possibilities for the patient. For me, this opens a large area; in addition to drawings, and dreams and sand, feelings can be expressed through the body, in music or through writing stories. The choice of field can be talked about. For example, some patients come asking for therapy that includes body work. It enriches the work with our patients if analysts can work in several fields of symbolic expression.

I was encouraged to look into the field of body work. An example is a vignette from work on the theme of shame and humiliation. I asked an adolescent patient how he would express his feelings with his body. He lay on the floor, face downward: a secure position where he could let go without losing face. In later sessions we worked with an apt body image: Make yourself small, keeping eye contact, and straighten up. At first he was unable to raise himself and turned away but, little by little, by raising his body he had the experience of being a person who can be looked at and liked.

In this way, the International Workshop has broadened my view as I got to know different concepts and approaches within the Jungian world. And at the same time I have been stimulated to look at the fundamentals of my work, my own position and my authenticity.

Michael Fordham and the London Child Training

Jane Bunster
London, England
Society of Analytical Psychology

I am a child analyst, trained at the Society of Analytical Psychology in London. The child training was pioneered in the early 1970s by Michael Fordham. The program continues to this day, although consisting of smaller numbers and feeling depleted by Fordham's death in 1995.

Differing from Jung, Fordham pioneered the idea that individuation starts at the outset of life. With this in mind he put forward the idea of the Primary Self: a unique potential-containing integrate from which the baby unfolds – "deintegrates" – in the course of development. This deintegrative experience is described most easily in a feeding sequence; the baby instinctively moves towards the breast, has a good feed and reintegrates the experience as good. The baby's development occurs gradually on the basis of these deintegrative/reintegrative experiences.

Fordham emphasized the individuality of the infant and that the innate, archetypal expectations of the infant bring influence to bear on the environment. These expectations are based on the instincts, which include the innate releasing mechanism. The ideas challenged Jung's idea that the infant at first is part of the mother's unconscious, and has no life of its own, as it were.

Fordham also differed markedly from Jung's ideas with regard to treatment of disturbed children. Jung seemed to believe that, if children were troubled, the parents' disturbance was causing it and, therefore, the parents needed the treatment.

In founding the child analytic training in London, Fordham was influenced greatly by the ideas of Melanie Klein: making links between archetypes and unconscious phantasies. Here is a table of links that he made:

Jung	*Klein*
Archetypes	Unconscious phantasies
Concept of an inner world	Concept of inner world
Concept of psychic reality	Concepts of psychic reality
Importance of the symbol for development of personal and cultural life	Symbols as the basis for the development of the mind
The urge for knowledge and the spiritual life	The epistemophilic instinct
The ruthlessness of the unconscious	Paranoid-schizoid position
The two mothers, nurturing and terrible	Good and bad breast mothers
Battle with and triumph over the mother	Manic defence
The uniting symbol	The breast-penis
Conjunction	Primal scene

When I first met my international colleagues, I was struck at how differently from me they approached their work with children. There seemed to be an inhibition about confronting their instinctual impulses through regression and interpretation. The Sandplay technique, for example, seemed to keep a distance between the therapist and the child, relying more on the child's being able to work symbolically and produce images in the sand. I must confess to some envy here; the few occasions when I had used sand, the child usually threw sand around the room or at me. Also, in our child guidance system, we are working mainly with severely deprived and disturbed children, some of whom are rigidified in an acting-out, pre-symbolic stage of being.

The approaches to child analytic work seemed to be poles apart, each at one end of the archetypal spectrum: the negative mother approach and the positive. Those of us who work with instinctual impulses have been thought to be far too negative and invasive: a kind of deadly, suffocating mother. And I thought my colleagues were far too keen to be received as the good, all-embracing, all-nurturing mother archetype figure.

How to get these two views closer together? Over the years, an international group of therapists has met to discuss clinical material from these differing standpoints. We must acknowledge that the group is now self-selected, so that there is much more a spirit of co-operation, rather than confrontation. For my part, I am inclined to have less of a proselytising spirit – in that my way is "the way, the truth, the life" – and I am interested in hearing about other people's ways of working.

The influence this experience has on me is to lose some of my rigidity – but not my rigour. I still feel sincerely that what the SAP child analytical training has to offer is of supreme importance. This statement particularly applies to analytic boundaries, analytic attitude, transference/countertransference issues and providing a container for very primitive affects to come to light, so that a rich deintegrative/reintegrative process can ensue.

"Unified Theory" vs. Conflictual Thinking

Verena Rossetti-Gsell
Rancate, Switzerland
Schweizerische Gesellschaft für Analytische Psychologie

Our Workshop makes me feel part of a network of colleagues and friends, which stretches over long distances and where the openness for different ways of being and working gives me the sensation of independence while still being connected.

My analysis and training in Zurich had enriched me greatly, opening a new dimension both on a personal and professional level: the symbolic dimension. I had learned to consider every communication from my patients within the therapeutic space as having a symbolic sense, which could be shared and understood by putting it into relation with the personal and collective context of the patient's history.

My first contact with the Workshop (1984) surprised me for its diversity in approach; I felt opposition toward certain positions, because they seemed reductive or incomprehensible. I queried the foundations of my approach, deep-rooted in my experience participating in the evolution of symbolic play with many children.

The Workshop became then a place of translation for me. Translating my colleagues' contributions from one analytic language to another, I progressively opened up to the different "analytic languages" and translated them into my own.

The wish, activated in the Workshop, to communicate my experience at the Paris Congress (1989) caused me to delve further into questions regarding archetypal aspects. I realized the fundamental importance in my therapeutic work – with children suffering from early psychic disturbances – of the positive and negative maternal archetypal constellations, visible in images of the maternal-matter, the maternal-container and the maternal-nourisher.

Asking myself where these symbols were born I hypothesized a transference space, where the unconscious contents were activated and put into images (in the form of play, drawing or handwork) that were influenced from three unconscious levels: actual, personal and collective. Later I became aware of my particular "symbolic attitude," which leads me to speak of a "sensorimotor symbolism," considering every gesture within the therapeutic framework as symbolic expression.

Analytical Relationship

body
instincts

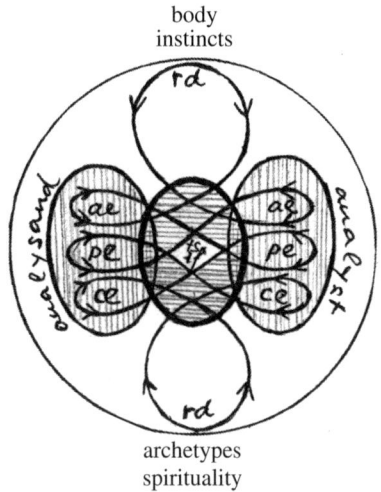

rd = relational dynamics
ae = transference / countertransference of the actual emotional experience
pe = transference / countertransference of the personal emotional experience
ce = transference / countertransference of the collective emotional experience
ts/if = transference space / interactive field: here is activated
the symbolic experience
through images and play

archetypes
spirituality

Moved by the conflicts within the Workshop, I learned to pay more attention to the actual emotional transference and counter-transference experience, especially concerning primitive needs for attachment and containment relative to the anxiety of annihilation and abandonment – as well as the archaic feelings of greed, envy, jealousy and revenge. Dominated by the negative mother archetype they need to be shared, understood and contained by a precise "fatherly" setting.

Preparing a seminar with a Workshop colleague for the Chicago Congress (1992) made me discover the richness of the "transcendent function" concept for infant analysis, which emphasizes the importance of two aspects in the confrontation with unconscious contents: that of representation and that of comprehension. Through following exchanges within the Workshop on negative transference and coun-tertransference, I was prompted to question myself regarding the basis of my countertransference.

Since then, the awareness of the relational dynamic is growing in me: a continual dynamic that runs across the psyche of the analysand and the analyst through the unconscious: different levels, from the instinctive and actual sphere into the archetypal one. It is through this dynamic and inside the transference space (or interactive field) where the symbolic experience is activated and thus generates meaning.

My focus on this dynamic will always be bound to my personality. Clashing with other insights, my own can be deflected or multiplied. This process may reduce the pieces that remain hidden in the shadow.

Differentiation as a Pre-condition for Integration

Giuseppe Maffei
Lucca, Italy
Associazione Italiana per lo
Studio della Psicologia Analitica

The reporting of clinical cases – the main subject matter of the Workshop – has highlighted the differences in theoretical methods, schools and backgrounds. The description of clinical work has opened the way and allowed us to come into contact with that hidden psychic region where personal tendencies and anxieties determine theoretical options and merge with them. By learning the procedures of clinical work we are allowed to see the origin and therefore the individual human aspect of theoretical diversities. Every therapeutic relationship is one where two people interact at a deep level and where the very bases of their beings are questioned. The reporting of clinical cases makes it possible to perceive this deep level of meeting and mutual transformation, as well as the emotional roots of theoretical options.

It is interesting, also, to notice how within the field of the Workshop – made up of people with such remarkable theoretical differences – each of the members perceived the theoretical options of the others as forms of resistance. We were all strongly tempted to ask ourselves: "What am I doing here with people whose ideas are so different from mine? Hadn't I better be with colleagues more similar to me?"

The consequent question is why these thoughts, marking individual resistances, did not lead to a breaking point. There seem to be two reasons. The first is that the contact with other people's styles allowed understanding of our own styles. In confrontation with such different approaches, each one experienced loneliness in perceiving the limits of one's point of view. But in this process individual ideas acquired more definite contours.

The second reason is more interesting to discuss with those who did not share our experience. The general problem concerns the existence of various analytical psychologies and their future developments. It seems clear that each such psychology has its own coherence and its own development. The wish not to break contacts with totally different views might be interpreted as dictated by fear of differentiation within oneself. This problem asks for serious reflection. On the one hand, diversity is necessary to our mental health; it provides the essential corrective to the natural tendency of the human soul to transform its own convictions into truths and to issue them as such. On the other, in order to make the confrontation useful, it must provide an occasion to question the limits necessarily present in every theorization. In my view, in order to be useful, such a confrontation must be radical.

Panikkar (1988), a theorist of pluralism, says that, as long as we think of something in a non-exhaustive way, this something will still be outside our thoughts; it will exist and therefore it can be thought about. Consequently, we can say that the experience of diversity allows us to keep our opinions non-exhaustive and therefore open to what we do not know yet. Panikkar also says that, when something contrasts with our thoughts, it shows its reality by this very fact. The experience of differences continually shows their reality, which reality must be unyielding so that our own difference may develop in a creative way.

On Workshop Identity

Wanda Grosso
Rome, Italy
Associazione Italiana di Psicologia Analitica

My stance on "reading" the workshop history relates to the concept of identity. The Workshop's image has changed through time, necessitating an assessment of the group's current needs and sense of identity.

Looking back to the 1984 beginning of the Workshop, there was a strong drive for Jungian child analysts to assert their existence and function, and to gain national and international recognition. Speaking of identity raises the question about the Self and how to conceive it: a self-representation or a psychic entity?

According to Mitchell (1992), all the theories of the Self fall into two categories. One states that the self is a relational product of a discontinuous and multiple nature. Self representation is not always the same; it changes according to subjective experiences and, with time, there are many selves. The other considers the Self as a separate entity not directly dependent on the outside; a psychic structure integral and continuous, it will stay the same with time and experience. Mitchell tried to integrate these two categories, suggesting that both help to define identity so long as there is no exclusion. "Being oneself" depends on both multiple and discontinuous self-representations and on an inner feeling of unity and cohesion based on a psychic structure.

Is it possible to think that to be defined as Self-feeling, one aspect or the other predominates at different times? At the time of the Workshop's formation, because of the fragile group identity, it seemed that we were searching and fighting for a unifying factor that would bond the group's sense of Self. Since there were various theoretical differences, it was impossible to get a unified position. But we struggled eagerly for it. Over time, the Workshop developed as a resource for members and observers, structuring our identity both as a group and as individuals.

Then in 1990, the search for a unifying thought was given up. The pleasure of being together overrode the theoretical differences. Pursuing a common idea was no longer the goal. Rather, the group's multiple theoretical outlook became the basis of our sense of identity. This second phase of the Workshop seemed defined by a multiple relational self. In fact, we presented ourselves as a group of individuals representing different cultural and procedural attitudes, all the while bonded by respect and affection.

Acknowledging that there is richness in diversity has been a milestone in the Workshop's history. Complacency can dull the challenges of exploration. Creative tension leads to clarification. For this to be possible, I believe it necessary for the various positions to continue questioning their identities, based on what Giuseppe Maffei calls "the ideas that cannot be relinquished" in one's clinical and theoretical approach. The common elements among the different positions could be thought of as the structural Self of the group. While the elements of differentiation would remain as the expression of the multiplicity of numerous Jungian spirits, there are many representations of the relational Self.

Now another phase seems to be emerging. It may not be incidental that the theme chosen for this year's workshop is to reflect upon what and how to determine the change in therapeutic processes. Could it really be a reflection on what and how to change the Workshop itself, or at least to reflect upon the reflection?

Analysing the Transference To Theory

Brigitte Allain-Dupré
Paris, France
Société Française de Psychologie Analytique

In his correspondence Jung (Let-I) showed insistently how Freud's ideas are close to his own, as if he had previously thought them. The strong identification thus set up creates jubilation of "being-together-thinking." Thus, thanks to a massive and reciprocal transference, Freud and Jung were stimulated in their intellectual creativity. Building a theory was the container and the ferment of their relationship.

When they parted in 1912, their identifications untied themselves and Jung worked hard to make precise his own thinking, focusing on fundamental differences with Freud's. Needs of individuation pushed each one to take new positions, producing more differentiated ideas. In their break, as in concluding an analysis, Jung tried to take his idealising projections off Freud. Free of the pressures of obedience to Freud's ideas, a new creativity started for Jung.

In a psychoanalytic Society, training analysts and supervisors represent theoretical positions that are perceived acutely by every candidate. The candidate's unconscious is projected onto the theory, as it is projected onto each object of the external world. The aspects of the theory that a training analyst uses are experienced as one of the many aspects of the transference. Thus, training analysis deeply influences theoretical positions. How would one analyse the transference to the theoretical expectations of the society one is entering?

Analysing the transference in training analysis is not easy to manage. By entering the Society of one's analysts, one never leaves them. This endogamy is inherent to the constituting of societies; the core of the transition is related to the timelessness and wholeness fantasies about family.

Great Congresses help to make clear that the transition is dynamic and viable in broadening and diversifying relationships in the family, including distant cousins. As a result, the links we have with theory are diversified. But it is not enough, because so many members are not really active during a Congress.

Thus, we need intermediary places to be active, to confront our truths and uncertainties. The Workshop is a good melting pot to individuate our thinking about theory in our Jungian practice. This confrontation is neither easy nor fast. But it allows a deeper analysis of our transference to the theory transmitted by those who are or were our mentors in our training. Specifically, in the work of presenting our own cases to our colleagues of different cultures and styles, we are obliged to realise that there is not one truth and that our approval of a theory is the result of many subjective factors.

For me, the awareness of this subjectivity helps me to feel not so torn among different tendencies of Jungian assumptions, to make better choices and to develop a space for uncertainty, where I meet my patients and my colleagues from other countries than my own French group.

The extra-territoriality of the Workshop – horizontally organised, using varied languages – creates this *lieu tiers* (third place), which allows me to analyse my transference to theory and many other things that I received from my own group.

References

Mitchell, S.A. (1992). Contemporary perspectives on Self: Toward an integration. *Psychoanalytic Dialogues*, 1-2.
Panikkar, R. (1988). Personal communication.

Research

Panel: Current Developments in Infant Observation Research

Brian Feldman
Palo Alto, California, USA
C.G. Jung Institute San Francisco

Some creative and destructive elements are inherent in the infantile psyche. I am interested in understanding the capacity for symbolization in children and adults, as well as difficulties in symbolization processes in the context of analysis. I believe that the precursor of the capacity for symbolization – the capacity to utilize thought, image and emotion in an integrative manner for the purpose of psychological growth and development – has as its foundation the sensorial development of the infant during the first year of life: differentiations through touch, smell, sight and sound, and the infant's experience of the skin as a defining boundary between what is experienced as internal as opposed to what is experienced as external to the self. These differentiations are fundamental to psychological development.

My focus is on the psychological experience of the skin in infancy and its relation to the development of a concept of an internal space where symbolization processes take place. My interest in the psychological function of the skin began when, several years ago, I was doing research into Jung's infancy and childhood, and the impact that this had upon the evolution of his psychology. In *Memories, Dreams, Reflections* – written when he was 83 years old – Jung described his infancy and childhood with candor and insight. When he was three years old his mother was hospitalized for several months, for what appears to have been a severe depression. Jung wrote that her hospitalization was related to difficulties in the marriage relationship. During his mother's absence he was taken care of by a maid. He developed severe eczema, which he connected with the estrangement of his parents and his mother's hospitalization.

It seems probable that Jung's eczema was linked to the sense of psychic catastrophe that he experienced on his separation from his mother. It was as if he was unable to contain torturous and painful emotions within himself and they burst out in somatic form. These skin difficulties were a precursor of other emotional difficulties, which I relate to problems in maternal containment. The child Jung suffered from what appears to have been a childhood depression resulting in self-destructive fantasies and behavior. He reported having a serious accident while crossing a bridge over the Rhine Falls at the time of his mother's hospitalization. He noted that "the maid caught me just in time – I already had one leg under the railing and was about to slip through" (MDR, p. 24). This experience points to an unconscious suicidal urge or, it may be, to a fatal resistance to life in this world. His accident-proneness could be related to a feeling of being uncontained in the mother-child relationship and to a sense of rage directed against the self and not at the emotionally unavailable and abandoning mother.

As I began to untangle some of the autobiographical origins of Jungian thought, I began to realize that his psychology was in part a structure to help Jung contain primitive infantile anxieties. While I think he made an important contribution in elucidating the nature and significance of symbolic thought as a kind of primitive and universal language, he failed to emphasize its infantile origins and hence failed to see the importance of analyzing the developmental origins of the capacity for symbolization. Because of this lacuna in Jungian thought I was drawn to explore the origins of the capacities for symbolic thought and emotional containment within a Jungian framework. This led me to a deeper exploration of the object relations and attachment literatures, as well as to exploration of the possibilities of infant observation and the analysis of autistic and psychotic children, in helping to understand primitive infantile states of mind. In pursuing this work I found that the concept of the "psychic skin" was fundamental in understanding these primitive infantile states.

In my own observations of babies, I have been struck by their need to give shape to the bodily self by pushing the body up against hard and soft surfaces, and by the mouthing of and grasping of animate and inanimate objects. The experience of the infant's being held securely in the arms of the mother or another significant caregivers, and the exploration of the body of the other – especially the touching of the skin of the breast during feeding as well as the touching of the other's face by the infant, and the way in which the infant's body is handled during bathing – all are important and fundamental experiences that give rise to a stable and secure sense of self as well as a stable and secure sense of attachment to a significant other.

An infant observation that I conducted illustrates the creative, forward-moving elements within the infant, which facilitate development. The observation, which took place when baby Emily was four weeks old, demonstrates the importance of the skin contact during feeding.

I was sitting across from mother; Emily was in a carrying basket. I noticed that she was whimpering gently in her basket. Mother said that she put her in the basket in anticipation of my coming to observe, as she wanted to make sure that I could see the baby even if she were sleeping. She also said that it would be easier to carry Emily around during the observation. Emily's whimpering continued, not in an overly fussy manner, but I had the feeling that she wanted to be held, that she wanted bodily contact. Mother picked Emily up out of her basket. As she did so, Emily started to whimper more and made several motions with her mouth pursing her lips and opening them into an oval shape. Mother then held Emily against her shirt and offered her the right breast. Emily slowly opened her mouth, leaned her cheek against the mother's breast, and then opened her mouth in an oval shape to accommodate the nipple. There appeared to be a playful interaction between mother and infant, and mother spoke of Emily as having a big appetite. Emily stretched out her legs and arms, holding onto the breast with her hand and sucking forcefully. Her toes were extended and her legs appeared taught. She started to stroke and then knead the skin of the breast while sucking. Slowly her legs became more relaxed and dropped down over mother's legs. She nursed for about five minutes and then stopped. She appeared to fall into a reverie while mother held her on her lap. Emily had a half-smile, Mona Lisa-like. Her half-smile conveyed to me a feeling of contentment, happiness, and fulfillment. Then Emily made some motions with her arm toward mother's left breast. She gently brushed her wrist against her mouth in a delicate way, and then again opened her mouth into an oval to feed. Mother gave her the breast. Emily went through a similar sequence, feeding and stroking mother's skin. Then she fell quickly into a deep sleep.

My emotional response and countertransference to this episode was strong. As I was observing the feed I noticed that I myself was experiencing some of the reverie that was occurring between the mother-infant couple. As I left the observation I sensed that I was disoriented and I became lost driving home in my car. I felt that I, like Emily, was attempting to hold onto the good feeling generated by the nursing couple.

In retrospect I think that this was a good experience for Emily of feeling well held and sensitively responded to. Her desire for contact with mother's skin appeared equally as strong as her desire for feeding. I sensed that her whole body was involved in the feeding experience, as she also desired tactile contact with mother's warm and soft breast, while being held by mother's strong arms, and while reclining on mother's firm lap. My imaginative experience during this episode was that Emily's sensorial capacities for touch, taste, smell, sight and hearing were all activated, and that she experienced being held securely by mother, who in turn felt some auxiliary holding by me as an attentive and interested empathic observer. Infant observations such as these have helped me to become attuned to the profound impact which sensory/bodily experience has for the infant's emotional development.

The first in-depth study of the psychological function of the skin was made by the Kleinian analyst Esther Bick. In an important article, Bick (1968) postulated that the psychological function of the skin is akin to holding, and that the skin is experienced by the infant as holding together the parts of the personality, which are not yet differentiated from parts of the body. Initially, the containing or mothering function is introjected by the infant through the experience of an adequate holding relationship such as I depicted in the episode with Emily. Until the containing maternal functions have been introjected the space within the self where thought and symbolization take place cannot exist. For Bick the need for a containing object leads the infant to search instinctually for an object to hold the personality together. Optimally this is the breast, which together with the secure and firm holding of mother, gives the infant an experience of being a coherent whole. My own observations indicate that there is a desire for a containing experience which involves the nipple securely held in the mouth, the sucking motions which provide a good feed, the tactile feel of mother's skin, and the experience of being securely and firmly held in mother's arms. I think that Emily's Mona Lisa-like smile indicates the depth of satisfaction, mystery and pleasure which this experience can induce. Bick felt that the primary containing object for the baby is the skin. Faulty developments in the skin or containing function can occur as a result of deficits in the mother-infant relationship as well as from the infant's fantasized attacks upon mother, which can impair a good introjection. When a faulty skin function develops, a defensive process can emerge which Bick terms a "second skin" formation. When a second or faulty skin function develops, the infant can develop a precocious independence from the mothering figure. A second-skin defensive pattern can lead to the excessive use of thinking or muscularity to help create a feeling of containment. The precocious development of speech, when the infant provides the sound of its own voice for self-soothing, or a muscular development that leads to holding the body rigidly together during periods of stress, are examples of this type of defensive pattern.

I observed this type of second-skin phenomenon in Emily at five months, in a sequence that depicts the use of muscularity as an attempt to contain unbearable, painful emotions. It points to the possibility of defensive elements emerging within the infant, as psychic development is impeded.

When I arrived for the observation Emily was in her baby seat in the family room; mother was about to leave for work, bustling around the room, and the *au pair* was sitting in the kitchen. Mother went in and out of the room several times. Emily's mouth was slightly open; her lower lip was out a bit and covered over by her upper lip. I wondered if she was pouting and perhaps protesting. After a few minutes mother emerged down the stairs, dressed for work. She said hello to me, but did not go over to Emily, who was looking at her. After a few minutes mother, who appeared quite rushed, left – still not interacting or saying good-bye to Emily. As mother left the room I was careful to look at Emily to see her response to the separation. I saw that she was staring intently at the door. Her body was taught and frozen; she was holding it rigidly together. I experienced a slight chill running down my spine. I wondered if this was in response to the "chilly" separation. After a few minutes Emily started to rock her body back and forth in the chair and to make back and forth head movements. After a few more minutes the caregiver went over to her and took her out of her chair. Emily became more and more fussy; the caregiver placed her on the floor. The au pair went to the kitchen and brought back a bottle and gave it to Emily. As she held Emily, I saw that Emily was holding on tightly to the plastic nipple with her mouth and gulping down the formula. She continued to do this in a frantic way until the formula was finished.

Emily's response to separation from mother, which included a lack of transitioning, seemed to lead her to bodily defenses of a second-skin nature. Her body became rigid and frozen as a way of coping with the unbearably painful feeling surrounding the abrupt separation. When the *au pair* came over to her, she was inconsolable. Then Emily focused on the rubber nipple and ate voraciously as a way of coping with what at the time were unbearable anxieties and emotions. She seemed uncontained by mother and dropped from mother's mental and emotional preoccupation. Being separated from mother in this way meant, for Emily, being torn away from mother and her containing presence. Emily tried to gain control over these dreadful feelings by having her musculature become frozen and stiff. In this way she could attempt to control and stop feeling flooded by unbearable primitive affects. When she latched onto the rubber nipple and gulped down the formula, she appeared to be in frantic search of an object that she could hold onto and control. By voraciously drinking the formula she could fill her stomach with a warm substance which could give her the illusion of a nourishing mother, and at the same time fill up the dark internal spaces with something good and warm that momentarily could take away the cold, empty and rageful feelings. The frantic aspect of this sequence reminded me of my work with women with eating disorders who, often in a dissociated state, binge in order to control emotional states that are filled with anxiety and dread. Often these women talk about their binges as being triggered by feelings of disconnection, and a nameless dread to which it is difficult to give shape. In the histories of these women, often their mothers were viewed as rejecting of their deeper emotions, and this lack of containment led to a feeling of nameless dread.

Some of these thoughts and observations may help in understanding the importance of infant observation and its role in both helping to elucidate the foundations of psychic life, and the capacity for symbolization which is at the heart of Jungian analysis.

Is Infant Observation Relevant?

Jane Bunster
London, England
Society of Analytical Psychology

Many studies of infancy have sprung up in recent years. Infant mental health has been described as one of the most exciting and rapidly developing areas in the entire field of mental health. The Association for Infant Mental Health has been established, with a United Kingdom branch. Research projects are developing all round the world, evidence of the serious consideration that is being given to the psychological needs of infants and their parents. Research has shown that babies who are attached securely to their parents are likely to develop more confidently and completely: something we have known for a long time, but now is well validated by laboratory research. Similarly, post-natal depression in the mother has been known to have a potentially adverse effect on the baby's development; research shows that such difficulty needs to be spotted and alleviated as quickly as possible, to the advantage of both mother and baby.

Systematic infant observation, over a period of two years, is conducted in weekly visits to the infant's home, each lasting 50 minutes to an hour. It is sometimes difficult to find a family that is willing to make this commitment. The first inquiries often are made via health visitors and general practitioners. Both parents are involved, and we look for a family that is likely to stay in the geographical area and has a stable network of support from family and friends. The aim of this type of observation is to have an opportunity, quite privileged and prolonged, of being absorbed in the baby and then reflecting on the experience. The former process is done by the observer, writing up each observation, in as descriptive a way as possible (no thoughts or comments), without taking notes during the visit. The reflection process takes place in a weekly seminar group where five or six observers (in my situation, all female) meet regularly and study one child at a time. Each observer presents her baby twice each term, and has a permanent scribe taking notes about the discussions. At the beginning of each seminar (after the first), notes are read out by the scribe of the previous discussions to bring that particular baby back into mind. Then the observer reads aloud her new observation in detail, and perhaps one or two earlier ones more superficially. Each group member has a copy of the observations. Seminars last 60 to 90 minutes and are nearly always too short to absorb fully the material provided.

An observation requires strict discipline and regular commitment. We reckon on about five hours' work each week, including travel and seminar; I am always humbled by the dedication of the students. It is not an easy task being an observer. Thus, we take great care in selecting a family. Students are in my group two to three months before making any move to find a family so that they have a really good idea what they want and can present this request to the health visitor or physician. When a contact has been made, two assessment visits are recommended, one of which includes the father. This process is two-way; it is important that the parents make an assessment whether they feel comfortable with the observer. An observation succeeds or fails on this mutually facilitating environment in which a space can be created for intensive observation. Based on mutually satisfactory assessments, the observation proceeds.

A "successful" observation provides a containing, rewarding experience for both parent and observer, and can be creative for both. Many parents express their appreciation of this special relationship, even though the observer seems to do nothing. And critics feel that it can be an imposition.

Primarily the observer focuses intensely on the baby. Often the parents, too, develop an attentiveness about which, previously, they may have lacked confidence. Infant observation is an affirmation of the value of the baby's individuality, with attendant feelings and emotions. Close attention to the child's movement and responses can be of infinite importance in facilitating this affirmation. It is not based on "doing." As one mother put it, "I really enjoy the observer's visit as it is one time in the week when I can sit and watch my baby, without feeling I should be doing the chores." Thus, the emphasis is on observing the baby within the mother-baby couple.

I am influenced in this approach by the work of Michael Fordham, who pioneered many innovative ideas throughout his long life. Fordham, who was steeped in the ideas of Jung, was a founding member of the Society of Analytical Psychology. As early as 1947 he put forward the hypothesis that individuation starts at the beginning of life, whereas Jung thought of the individuation process as belonging to the second half of life, when such ego-developing functions as job-seeking, work successes, and bringing up families become less pressing.

It is the pioneering work of Fordham that has developed the idea of the individuality of the child, encapsulated in the theory of the Primary Self. This Primary Self includes all the child's potential and is complete in itself but as yet unformed and undeveloped; Fordham calls it an integrate. From this Primary Self, the baby needs to move out to another person, rather like an amoeba with pseudopods. For this process Fordham coined the term "deintegrate." The baby unfolds from the self, putting out feelers – towards the breast, for example – has a satisfactory feed and then digests and reintegrates the experience. Development gradually builds, involving – one hopes – a consistent enough deintegrative-reintegrative process to form the basis for ego development and its attendant functions such as movements, perceptions and learning.

The observer pays very close attention to the infant, remaining a "participant observer": closely involved but not passing judgments, not interfering such as picking up baby (except in extremes), not giving advice, remaining at a distance but wholly involved. Both baby and mother respond to this interest. Finally, the situation becomes therapeutic when the observer provides a container – especially for anxiety – but without any interpretive work taking place. Quite remarkable.

There are some broad patterns of development that we observe, in a very general way. First, that the experience of the birth has quite an impact on how baby relates to the outside world and particularly to the feeding situation. We have noticed that, for a baby whose birth has been over-quick or over-long, what looks like intra-uterine movements seem to continue for several weeks. Long separation of baby and mother at the beginning is quite traumatic for both parties. The most confident fit at the breast seems to develop if baby and mother are able to be in close contact from the beginning. Even here, the enormous range of behaviors amongst babies is interesting: some who latch on immediately, others needing coaxing. Especially traumatic births, although we have not much experience of these, take their toll.

One example comes to mind of a birth experience, long and frightening, wherein the mother was virtually unconscious after the birth for several hours. Baby was taken away for various interventions to do with breathing. Attempted breast feeding for three weeks was painful in the extreme with sore nipples and colic, both mother and baby being quite desperate. Change to the bottle brought some relief, but there was an inhibition of contact between mother and baby. Feeds were inclined to be matter-of-fact or edgy. Real trouble came at weaning time, when baby steadfastly refused all changes. The months went by with hardly any adaptation; all baby would eat spontaneously was yogurt. We came to think that new food for this child evoked a kind of terror. At the sight of any mashed up solids whatsoever she would scream. Help from the clinic was of no avail and the situation was extremely distressing. Alongside this, however, baby made great strides with her motor development, walked well and was highly verbal with well-developed use of language. She seemed to present a kind of false self, confident and in control. In discussions about this, the group would nearly always hark back to the fear and terror of the birth situation, about some fear of intrusion into the mouth and throat. (There was always a lot of choking on new food and then it would be spat out). Even though mother's anxiety may have exacerbated the situation, we also felt that there was an internal terror, possibly to do with the fear of suffocation and difficulties due to nasty tubes being thrust down the throat at birth: terror which had affected deeply the baby's first deintegrative experience.

This traumatic weaning situation leads naturally to our less dramatic findings in infant observation at this very important developmental stage. However, we find that weaning is always a traumatic experience. "Teething troubles" are very real, perhaps physically but certainly psychically. Nearly every baby suffers, and mother too. After birth, teething is the first separation experience and has enormous implications for development. It seems to hinge round the ability to bite or chew. The arrival of teeth heralds the ability to manage without milk. Until now, baby's nourishment is entirely dependent on sucking milk and, although baby may be bottle-fed by this time, nourishment relates to the dependency between baby, mother and breast. With teeth, baby can manage without mother, as it were. Baby can also bite her and push her away. There is no longer the same dependency. Baby has the power to take control of its own intake: still dependent on mother for providing food, but there is a subtle shift of power. "Weaned" animals and birds can find their own food. For human babies, too, there is this possibility, when they begin to move around. But in so many observations babies become ill with sore throats, runny noses and coughs – mothers too, sometimes, so that there is loss involved for her, too. There is also vomiting. We wonder whether these "illnesses" provide an opportunity for baby to regress and be a real baby again; then another move forward can take place. Backwards and forwards they go, neatly described in the lovely French phrase, *reculer pour mieux sauter* (regress for better health). An example of a written observation of a six-month-old baby, during the weaning stage:

> *On arrival the mother announces that S. is grumpy. In the living-room, baby is in the walker with feet on the floor. She bounces the walker towards the observer, takes her lip off the dummy [pacifier], smiles, then sucks it again. She keeps her eyes on the observer, then the dummy falls on the floor. She pushes her tongue with her lip and then puts thumb and forefinger into her mouth feeling the sides of her tongue. She puts a third finger into her mouth and chews at all three. She then throws two soft toys onto the floor and pushes herself backwards and gazes out the window into the garden. Then she moves a plant pot, feels the side of the pot and puts her hands in the soil. She looks at her fingers and puts them back in the soil. She looks at her grubby hand and puts her fingers in her mouth. She makes a grimace as though responding to the taste of the soil. She pushes her tongue around her mouth and begins to hit the table looking miserable and starting to grizzle. "Time for breakfast," Mother says and she ties bib round baby's neck. Baby becomes excited, banging on the table, and looking up expectantly.*
>
> *Mother spoons cereal into baby's mouth. The lip and spoon collide, as if the timing and fit are not quite right, and baby pushes cereal out, on the top of her tongue. The food dribbles out. Mother scoops it back, baby grumbling mildly throughout. Mother wipes baby's mouth with tissue and leaves it on the table. Baby picks it up and strokes it. She holds it to open lips, feeling it but not putting it in her mouth. She smoothes it on the tray, then gently crumbles it and takes it back to open lips. She smiles and murmurs. The tissue drops on the floor and she looks down for it. Mother picks it up and baby continues to feel it, gently scrunch it and put it to her lips. This "playing" with the tissue goes on between spoonfuls of cereal.*
>
> *Cereal eventually finished, Mother fetches bottle, and gives it to her at first in chair and then on her lap, where baby lies against her – but feeling her own clothes. She sucks steadily and there is also steady eye contact between the two from time to time.*

In this example, I think we see a combination of enactments. One minute baby tries something new, then returns to the familiar: the soft tissue. Some mothers combine solids with a breast-feed afterwards. The process, usually, is negotiated sensitively and gradually.

But one situation has to be confronted: fury and rage against the breast that has gone away, perhaps often compounded by a new baby coming or, at any rate, parents having it in mind with the resumption of intercourse. Where has the breast gone? Has Daddy got it or the new real or fantasized baby? Has it been stolen or has the baby been so greedy that she has robbed mother of all her milk and goodness? Sometimes mothers may say that they feel emptied out and gutted by baby's demands and so want to start the weaning process.

As I mentioned earlier, baby – and mother sometimes – become ill. It is as though the conflicts of the complex emotions cannot be contained safely within the baby. By becoming ill, baby can regress to early infancy and not experience the trauma of separation with its attendant pains. But maturational development presses on of its own accord, for a baby who is not able to wean will be in danger of dying, a literal or a psychic death. Hence an unsuccessful weaning time may be a precursor of anorexia.

This is an example is a baby girl who had a good breast-feeding experience. When weaning time came she did not like the spoon and seemed to become rather dissociated from the feeding process. Baby seemed to look everywhere during the feed except at the spoon and mother, whereas with the breast there had been an intimate tactile contact. She became ill and listless, slept badly at night and some-how seemed more interested in her two dummies than anything else. During the feeds, she would suck at a piece of toast or fill her mouth with her fingers, while mother slipped in the solid food. She swallowed it but there was no affect or sensual enjoyment of it, just a routine that had to be got through. Then one day, at the observer's visit, baby was holding some hard bread during the feed. She put the bread into her mouth and pulled her lips back so that four fully-emerged front teeth were visible. She bit, and tore the bread with her teeth. She ate the piece in her mouth, and looked at the remaining piece in her hand. She stuffed the entire amount in her mouth. It was too big so she took it out and looked at it carefully. She tore it into two pieces. She tossed one away over the side of the chair and looked over to see where it had fallen. Then she returned her attention to the remaining piece and ate it.

I hope I have given you enough thoughts about the feeding-weaning process, which involves both creation and destruction. In order to be weaned, baby must have the confidence to attack or bite the breast, without the fear that nothing will be left. In the last example, the baby could bite the toast, explore it, throw away what she did not want and enjoy what was left. This is a good example of weaning.

Reference

Bick, E. (1968). The experience of the skin in early object relations. *International Journal of Psychoanalysis, 49*, 184-86.

Panel: Empirical Research
in Psychoanalysis and Analytic Psychotherapy

Wolfram Keller
Tilman Grande
Berlin, Germany
Deutsche Gesellschaft für Analytische Psychologie

Psychoanalysts are convinced, generally, of the effectiveness and benefit of their treatment. In recent years this persuasion has been shocked by increasing criticism of long-term psychoanalysis. Thus, psychoanalytic psychotherapy has come under pressure to offer convincing evidence of its effectiveness. This development was forced by increasing competition among different schools of psychotherapy and limited financial resources. In Germany, disqualification of psychoanalysis is being proposed by health care authorities. Nevertheless, this threatening situation includes the chance of developing and investigating our own varying theoretical positions by means of a systematic and empirical approach.

Since the beginning of the 1990s, controversial discussions within the Jungian community led to some systematic studies as a first approach to empirical research: in Berlin, Zürich, San Francisco and other places. Empirical research in psychotherapy is no longer a marginal issue for some incorrigibly enthusiastic researchers living in an ivory tower and producing results that are not useful to practitioners. Rather, many differentiated methods have been developed to demonstrate effects of the psychoanalytic process.

Many empirical studies exist already on the effectiveness of short-term psychotherapy, but there has been a lack of studies on the effectiveness of long-term psychoanalysis, especially in a naturalistic (non-laboratory) design that includes analysts in private practice. A proved effectiveness of shorter and less expensive psychotherapeutic procedures could result in restricted insurance coverage for long-term analysis.

Research in this field is geared to legitimacy in the eyes of the public, such as health insurance companies and political institutions.

But, aside from the question of effectiveness, there is an interest on the part of psychoanalytic organizations in evaluating their own work and gaining a deeper understanding of the psychoanalytic process and theory with the aid of systematic research. Usually, in short-term psychotherapy research, conventional instruments are used which intend to show changes in symptomatic impairment and behaviour. "Dose-effect" models (Howard & Orlinski 1986), however, demonstrate convincingly significant effects in the first 50 sessions of treatment but in the further course only small effects could be detected. As a consequence, long-term psychotherapy is criticized as ineffective and costly.

These results led us to conclude that the specific effects of psychoanalysis, which, experience shows, follow long and intensive treatment, cannot be revealed with the aid of conventional research instruments. Analysts suppose that essential changes in psychoanalysis develop at the level of personality structure. Therefore, a method is necessary to assess such changes.

Some efforts have been made to close this gap. In 1992 a working group was formed: 40 scientists and clinicians, each with a psychoanalytic background, from 12 universities. Four years of work led to a classification system (Arbeitsgruppe OPD 1996) for research, teaching, and practice: the Operationalized Psychodynamic Diagnosis (OPD), a standardized system based on psychoanalytic constructs and thus going beyond the descriptive approach of existing systems. Since then, the OPD system is on its way to become a well-known and important assessment tool in the entire psychoanalytic community in Germany and Switzerland, independent of schools of psychoanalysis. It is applied not only in research but in teaching and private practice.

In 1993 the Confederation of German Psychoanalysts (DGPT) decided to support research on long-term psychoanalysis, and a project proposal (Grande et al.1997) was developed. The plan was evaluated by several independent experts and deemed suitable. A review committee agreed in 1995 to support our concept with a grant. The IAAP and another German society (Stiftung für Bildungs- und Behindertenförderung Robert Bosch) followed with additional financial support.

Based on their experience in psychotherapy research, the study centers of Heidelberg, Berlin and Zürich started toward the end of 1996 with data collection. This study was created as a consequence of a discussion among psychotherapists and health care providers on the state of research with respect to long-term psychotherapy. We decided on a naturalistic research design with patients treated in private practice. The "Praxisstudie analytische Langzeittherapie" (Practitioners' Study in Analytic Long-term Psychotherapy; PAL) investigates patients being treated by Jungian and other practitioners of psychoanalytic schools. The aim of this multicenter study (Heidelberg, Berlin, Zürich) is to examine the process and effectiveness of long-term psychotherapy and psychoanalysis. This study includes 36 cases in psychoanalysis (three or more sessions per week) and 36 psychodynamic psychotherapies (one session per week) examined on several perspectives – psychoanalyst, patient, examiner and social perspective – regarding the treatment process and outcome, using a combination of quantitative and qualitative approaches.

A major characteristic of the study is the concentration on psychoanalysis-specific assessments, via the OPD system. It records those relationship patterns, conflicts, and structural characteristics that, in the view of psychoanalysis, make up the background of a patient's symptoms, assigns the patient to an OPD diagnosis, and are the object of treatment.

The clinical material required to assess an OPD finding can be obtained using a video-documented interview – initially in a free form and later focused on interpersonal relationship episodes, central life-long conflicts, and structural capacities.

The OPD conceptualizes a set of psychodynamic findings as a combination of five axes: 1) experience of illness and treatment preconditions, 2) habitual relationship patterns, 3) basic conflicts, 4) structural capacities, and 5) ICD-10 (International Classification of Disease, Revision 10). Only the relationship axis, conflict and structure axes are used for a psychodynamic diagnosis.

The structure axis describes six structural capacities and assigns them, in terms of their level of integration, to a four-stage scale. The following capacities are defined: self-perception, self-regulation, defenses, object-perception, communication, and attachment. For research purposes, each of the six structural capacities is subdivided and therefore much more differentiated.

The conflict axis assesses the patient's enduring and life-defining conflicts. The eight conflict types defined here are rated on a four-stage scale in terms of their presence, significance and passive or active modes of coping. The types are: dependency versus autonomy conflicts, submission versus control conflicts, need for care versus autonomy conflicts, self-esteem conflicts, super-ego conflicts, oedipal-sexual conflicts, identity conflicts, and deficient awareness of conflicts and feelings.

To conceptualize the relationship axis, we note the patient's central habitual, dysfunctional relationship pattern. The elements of this pattern include the interpersonal positions habitually assumed by the patient, and objects in the dominant relationship constellation. The quality of these positions is assessed on the basis of a list of 30 items derived from the model of the Structural Analysis of Social Behaviour (Benjamin 1974). The experience of relationship from two perspectives, the patient and the examiner, are assessed and integrated to form a concise relationship figure.

In a second step, we select those five problem areas of central significance in the areas relationship, conflicts, and structure axis that can be used to observe changes in the course of therapy. This choice is based on a spectrum of findings encompassing a total of 30 areas. These areas result from the core dysfunctional relationship pattern, 8 conflicts and 21 points from the structure axis. The problem areas rated here as central are those that are presumed to sustain the patient's psychic and psychosomatic symptoms as well as interpersonal problems.

The Structural Axis
in Operationalized Psychodynamic Diagnosis

Sabine Stehle
Berlin, Germany
Deutsche Gesellschaft für Analytische Psychologie

The OPD does not rely on a specific psychoanalytic theory, but follows an integrative psychodynamic approach. Concepts of object relations theory, self psychology and ego psychology meet here. On the structural axis of the OPD, capacities and deficits of mental structures are assessed, four disorder stages differentiated.

The psychic structure of personality is defined by OPD authors (Arbeitsgruppe OPD 1996) as the functional mechanisms and shaping of the self in relation to the other. Capacities and deficits of the self are described on the self axis, based on six dimensions:

Figure 1. Structural Dimensions of the OPD

Operationalized Psychodynamic Diagnosis OPD		Heidelberg Set of Problems based on OPD
I. Relationship	Identification of patient's core dysfunctional relationship pattern	1. core dysfunctional relationship pattern
II. Conflicts	Rating the significance of conflict types for patient; see list opposite =>	2. dependency versus autonomy 3. submission versus control 4. need for care versus autarky 5. self-esteem conflicts (narcissistic conflicts) 6. super-ego and guilt conflicts 7. oedipal-sexual conflicts 8. identity conflicts 9. deficient awareness of conflicts and feelings
III. Structure	Rating the patient's level on the following structural abilities (well integrated, moderately integrated, poorly integrated, disintegrated):	
	a. Capacity for perception and experience of the self	10. self-reflection 11. image of self 12. identity 13. differentiation of affect
	b. Capacity for self-regulation	14. tolerance of affects 15. regulation of self-esteem 16. regulation of impulses 17. anticipation
	c. Capacity for defense	18. intrapsychic defenses 19. flexibility of defenses
	d. Capacity for object perception and object experience	20. self-object differentiation 21. empathy 22. awareness of total objects 23. object-related affects
	e. Capacity for communication	24. contact 25. decoding others' affects 26. encoding one's own affects 27. reciprocity
	f. Capacity for attachment	28. internalizations 29. detaching 30. variability of relationships

1) Self-perception. The capacity for self-reflection and gaining a self-image, keeping this self-image coherent and constant over time (identity), and the capacity for differentiating intrapsychic processes, especially affects.

2) Self-regulation. Requires the capacity for tolerating and integrating ambivalences and (even unpleasant and strong) affects, establishing a feeling of self-esteem on a realistic level and regulating vacillations, being able to deal intentionally with drives and aggressive impulses as well as anticipating reactions from one's enviroment.

3) Defenses. Using specific mechanisms to maintain a mental balance in conflict and stress situations. (One differentiates here between the object and the success of defenses as well as the flexibility and maturity of defense mechanisms.)

4) Object-perception. Capacity for self-object differentiation, that is, assigning feelings, impulses, thoughts to the self or to the object as well as the capacity for experiencing object-related affects; also the capacity for empathy, for perceiving the object wholistically, with her/his interests and positive and negative sides.

5) Communication. Capacity for making contacts, understanding the affects of others, communicating one's own affects, and the capacity for reciprocity.

6) Attachment. Capacity for internalization, forming stable inner representations of important persons in order to become independent of their external presence. Also, the capacity for detachment; that is, tolerating separations, mourning losses, dealing with the variability of relationships and being capable of building up and maintaining different and triadic relationship patterns.

These structural dimensions are further differentiated into 21 concretely described aspects (see Rudolf et al.1998).

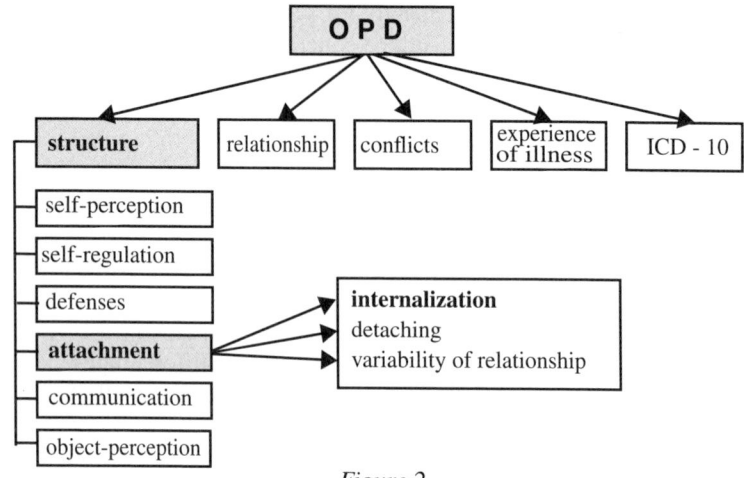

Figure 2

In each patient examined in the PAL study, all dimensions and subpoints are assessed on a four-step scale in terms of their integration level: good integration, moderate integration, poor integration and disintegration. For this purpose a number of criteria are formulated for each integration level. As an example, Figure 2 shows the criteria for the integration levels of the capacity for internalization as one subpoint of the structural dimension attachment.

At the top of Figure 2 are represented the five axes of the OPD. On the left is pictured the structural axis with the capacity of attachment as one of the six dimensions used in the case example in Dilg's paper. The related aspects are given in the right box. At the bottom are the integration levels for internaliza

Thus, it is possible, using the structure axis of the OPD, to differentiate and crystallize structural deficits, that are often recorded only globally as personality disorders. Since all structural characteristics on this axis are assessed independently of each other, it is possible to obtain a differentiated picture of the structural capacities and deficits of the subjects.

CAPACITY FOR INTERNALIZATION the four levels of integration			
good integration	**moderate integration**	**poor integration**	**disintegration**
Capacity for long-term constant emotional relationships; relationships are characterized by constant basic affects	Reduced capacity for developing stable inner pictures of significant individuals in order to be more independent from their external presence; internal images can get lost in conflict situations (out of sight, out of mind)	Seriously disturbed capacity for developing stable inner pictures of significant individuals in order to be more independent from their external presence.	An almost complete lack of the capacity for developing stable inner pictures of individuals in order to be more independent from their external presence.
Other people are of emotional importance. Rules of interaction are developed to protect existing relationships; no object dependency	Emotional importance of the significant other may be exaggerated: strong object dependency.	Emotional importance and sense of belonging only when the object ist physically present, and thus changing, short-term, dependent relationships.	Highly symbiotic relationships or anxiously preserved autonomy avoiding object relationship
Central fear is to lose the love of the object.	Central fear is to lose the significant, supporting, controlling object.	Central fear is that the self being at the mercy of other people can be destroyed by the loss of the good object or by the bad object.	Central fear is merging of self- and object representation with loss of own identity.

Selection of a (Structural) Therapy Focus Based On OPD

Reiner Dilg
Berlin, Germany
Deutsche Gesellschaft für Analytische Psychologie

An example of assessing a structural therapy focus is a patient – from the PAL study – with a poor integration level. Every six months we conduct a 60- to 90-minute interview with each patient as a basis for the OPD assessment. My impressions are based mainly on the interview.

The patient is 32 years old. She is obese, wears glasses, is friendly but slightly nervous. She starts the interview by saying; "I didn't really want to come here. This is all too much for me: the therapy, my job." She appears naive. She is asking herself what she is doing here, talking about herself in the third person. "Not wanting to think about oneself." Then she adds abruptly: "I just thought: I stay right here in the clinic, I already have my bag with me." Behind the insecurity about what is expected of her stands the tension between the unpleasantness of coming here and the desire to stay in the clinic right away. These feelings come up again in the course of the interview. "If you gave me a bed now, I would hide in it. At the moment I feel like hiding, I don't exist."

She reports that she works as a family helper and is there 24 hours a day. "My current problem is that I do not know when I am being referred to; I relate everything to myself. I quickly start feeling panicky" Her self-perception in this family becomes even clearer elsewhere: "I used to take things along for drawing and pottery. I don't do this anymore. I once sat down to draw something. I have difficulties when somebody says something negative, even if it is not meant to be unfriendly. I don't do it anymore. The father of the family made a remark, what kind of doodling is that, so I packed everything away."

She said about her relationship with a man: "I always get myself to a point where I take care of the other one." After three months, her relationship was almost completely reduced to shopping and eating. She spends weekends with him, does his shopping, and often goes home again without having had any other kind of contact. "Sometimes I like my partner very much; five minutes later everything is different. Sometimes, on the weekend, when I go there on Friday, I am ready to break off the relationship. I don't know anymore what I feel. It is hard to keep up a relationship over a distance." To the question if she remembers having gotten angry, she replies: "I don't do it very often. I know that I am under an incredible amount of pressure. Anger, mourning, many feelings are all mixed up. When my former partner left me alone or had drunk some alcohol, I really flipped out. One time, I trashed the kitchen, throwing food and eggs on the floor. Today I don't know why I did it, whether it had something to do with being alone. Afterward, this turned into complete hatred; I would have been capable of killing him. It was the situation: me or him. There was a situation when I choked him a little bit longer. I don't know anymore. With my arm, I just choked him; I would have had to do it only a little bit longer. Fortunately, something clicked in my head, so that I didn't go on with it. Thank God, the relationship ended soon after. I should have ended the whole thing much earlier so that I don't develop such a hatred."

When asked to describe another person, her answer clearly shows how blurred are the borders between self and object, and that the threatening object is also part of the self-image. "When I think of work, the father of the family, there are situations where he just sits and gets on other people's nerves. I once described my father like that – me too – like a king on a garbage dump; that's how I see him, reigning there. I arrive and say please, please." I will close the impressions from this interview with the image of the patient as the "princess on the garbage dump."

The impressions and description of the patient are now followed by an assessment based on the OPD. We have selected five foci for this patient: a relationship focus, need for care vs. autonomy conflict, affect differentiation, regulation of self-esteem, and internalization.

You see in Figure 1 of Stehle's paper above that internalization is a dimension of "attachment" on the structural axis. We have described the internalization focus as follows: The patient does not seem to have any stable object images and does not appear able to establish a continuous relationship to an important other. Feelings of belonging and emotional importance are already vacillating and insecure in the presence of the object. The inner attachment gets totally lost when the object is absent. The patient lives with the family for which she is working and does not see her partner during the week. On Fridays, she is often ready "to break up, because it is difficult to keep up a relationship over a distance." The reverse of the instability of the object images is the fear of being left alone, which led to the described devastation of the kitchen and is probably an important reason for her having almost strangled her former partner.

This patient has a poor integration level for the internalization focus. (See Figure 2 in Stehle's paper.) The patient meets the first criterion of the poor integration level of internalization in that she can barely tolerate a one-week separation from her partner; a relationship can be maintained only by being there in person. Otherwise "the emotional importance and feeling of belonging disappears quickly."

She therefore fulfills the second criterion also: emotional importance and sense of belonging only when the object is physically present. Therefore she has changing, short-term, dependent relationships. Here dependency is demonstrated also by her work situation: in a family, present 24 hours a day. But she reports that she wants to quit her job in three months. Otherwise she'll lose herself and exist less and less, as she formulates it. It becomes clear that she fulfills the third criterion for an integration level: the central fear that the self might be destroyed by the loss of the good object or the bad object.

Her feeling at the mercy of the family feeds the central fear that, unless she quits her job, she will lose more and more of herself. The bad object embodied by her employer, the father of the family in which she works, threatens to destroy her when he makes critical or perhaps just inquisitive remarks about her drawing and pottery. Considering drawing and pottery as a special form of self-expression from a Jungian point of view, this patient's withdrawal from these activities is a valid symbol of her fear of destroying herself.

This brings me to the relation between OPD and Jungian concepts. It is not possible to discuss here the question of compatibility of OPD and the Jungian self-concept, but the example of internalization shows that it may be worthwhile to carry out a theoretical in-depth analysis in light of Michael Fordham's concept, disintegration/reintegration. I find that Jungian concepts are very much in agreement with the OPD.

Measuring Structural Change
in Psychoanalytic Psychotherapies

Tilman Grande
Gerd Rudolf
Claudia Oberbracht
Heidelberg, Germany
Deutsche Psychoanalytische Gesellschaft

We have developed a research strategy to conduct the PAL. A preliminary study using this strategy deals with inpatient treatments. Our considerations centered on the fundamental question whether the specific effects of psychoanalysis can be detected by applying conventional research instruments. These instruments measure surface characteristics: symptoms or behaviors. From the psychoanalytic point of view, however, essential changes proceed at the level of personality structure. These considerations lead us to conclude that a project dealing with the effectiveness of long-term analytic therapies could be successful only if a standardized method were available to assess personality from a psychoanalytic point of view.

Steps in the Method

1) Assessment of the criteria according to OPD.

2) Selection of five main problems of the patient from the relationship, conflicts, and structure.

3) Recording of what restructuring processes have taken place in the patient with regard to the problem areas. For this purpose, we use a modified form of the Assimilation of Problematic Experiences Scale (APES) of Stiles et al. (1992). This scale permits us to describe even subtle changes in a patient's handling of given structural problems. We refer to this instrument as the Heidelberg Structural Change Scale. (HSCS).

Each stage of the scale marks a therapeutically significant step, beginning with an increasing awareness of a problem area not perceived until then, extending through the therapeutic working-through of the aspects and experiences associated with this area, down to the restructuring resulting from it in the patient's experience as well as in external behavior. Using the scale, the degree of structural change the patient has achieved is assessed.

Heidelberg Structural Change Scale (HSCS)

Stages	Examples from the Manual
1. Problem warded off	No awareness of conflicts; problematic behaviors ego-syntonic; for the patient there is "no problem" at all
2. Unwanted occupations with the problem	Unwanted thoughts and feelings regarding the problem area; collisions with outer reality; patient behaves defensively and tries to avoid problematic experiences
3. Vague awareness of the problem	The patient is aware of a problem which cannot be warded off; has an idea that this problem could be related to him/herself; nevertheless the attitude is mainly defensive
4. Acceptance and exploration of the problem area	The difficulty is acknowledged as a problem which can be formulated; the patient seeks to explore the problem area actively; now a working alliance related to the problem is possible
5. Deconstructions in the problem area	Destabilization in concepts of self and other persons; the patient is aware of his/her limitations and injuries; efforts alternate with resignation
6. Reorganizations in the problem area	The patient owns up to his/her new situation and has dismissed the old; he/she tries to find new solutions in respect to the problem; there is a change in concepts of self and other persons
7. New integration of the problem, solution	Problem solved; in the problem area the patient behaves in a self-confident way; problem is remembered as something past.

Results and Discussion

Forty patients were measured twice, once at admission and again before discharge. At the beginning of therapy, patients displayed average restructuring levels for two of the five problem areas selected for them. This indicates that the patients have unwanted confrontations with their structural problems at the beginning of therapy (see Figure 1). This situation may be due to unconscious enactments, unpleasant thoughts and feelings, or confrontation with difficulties in their social environment. This finding corresponds to the clinical experience that, for most hospitalized patients, the initial concern is to build a motivation for psychotherapy. By the end of therapy, the HSCS averaged 3.5. Thus, the patients have on average reached the threshold of "acceptance and exploration of the problem area," a good precondition for the start of outpatient therapy after inpatient treatment.

Another method of evaluation also indicates the validity of the HSCS. The patients were divided into two groups, depending on whether they reached level 4 or not. We found high correlations between this dichotomizing measure and the global assessment of success made by various raters: therapeutic rounds ($r = .44$); therapist ($r = .41$); both statistically significant. Staff ($r = .62$) highly significant. The high correlation is surprising, since the assessments made by the external researchers were completely independent of the ratings made by the therapeutic team; that is, the researchers knew nothing of the assessments of the clinicians, nor were they informed on the patient's therapeutic course.

In a further step we examined the extent to which the restructuring processes we registered are associated with symptomatic change. We found that there is no connection. In the period of inpatient treatment, structural changes do not lead regularly to symptom alleviation, and an improvement of symptoms can take place without any structural change occurring. (An exception was a depression scale). These results indicate that with the HSCS we have been able to register a significant level of therapeutic success different from that observed by conventional surface measures.

In a follow-up study we found that patients who reached level 4 of the HSCS are able to initiate changes in very problematic areas of their real lives. This fact leads us to infer that level 4 of the HSCS is a precondition for the ability to cope successfully with the significant psychological difficulties formulated in the five selected problems. The higher levels of the HSCS represent further steps toward a genuine structural change of personality, in the sense of new conflict solutions and integration. We assume that such progress is most likely to be reached in long-term psychotherapy. This hypothesis will be tested in the ongoing PAL.

Qualitative Strategies in the Zürich PAL

Guido Mattanza
Zürich, Switzerland
Schweizerische Gesellschaft für Analytische Psychologie

Quality control for the health service profession in Switzerland was established in 1996. It requires that treatment methods that are covered by basic health insurance periodically verify their usefulness and show proof of ongoing quality control, using scientific methods. Accordingly the Zürich analysts under the auspices of the SGfAP, IAAP and the Zürich Jung Institute have joined an ongoing empirical research project (PAL Study) with two other centers, one in Heidelberg (psychoanalysts) and one in Berlin (Jungians). The results, based on 50 individual therapies, will enable us to substantiate the usefulness of analytic psychotherapy following Swiss legislative guidelines and make comparisons with two other significant therapist collectives.

Our study has been in process for about a year now, with 22 cases represented. Present efforts focus on the collection and logging of data. In the year 2002, after a total of five test-years, we hope to present results that will:

1) Verify the usefulness of our methods and the quality within the framework of a meaningful PAL Space Study;

2) Make a contribution to a better understanding of the process of psychotherapy;

3) Demonstrate how characteristic Jungian concepts and interests are accommodated in the otherwise psychoanalytic framework of the study.

The study design provides for analysts to describe in their own words the analytic process in general, as well as important individual sessions during the given time period. (Because of the personal quality of a the free text, the result is a collection of material that is characteristic of the specific test group; in this case, the Zürich

Jungians.) Then the texts will be evaluated in Zürich as well as in Heidelberg and Berlin. The same methods will be used at each center to facilitate a comparison of the three sets of results.

Qualitative Evaluation of Test Results

At the beginning of the therapy the analyst fills out an initial diagnostic questionnaire. For this discussion two items have been selected from it that deal with the description of the psychodynamic formulation of the problem and of the diagnosis. The evaluation of the responses to these two questions involves identifying specific categories in the texts, using a catalog designed for this purpose. The catalog lists categories of responses that would be expected. It serves to reduce a large amount of information into individual elements, and has inherently a structuring or ordering function that is a constant for the method. Thus it will be possible to document the course of a therapy over two-and-one-half years, using the changes apparent in the session descriptions over the given time.

For the study, main categories were identified: relationship, structure, conflict, experience of the illness (disturbance), syndrome diagnosis, Jungian concepts, and compensatory functions of the disturbance. The texts were then examined to determine how frequently the different categories were represented, and their relationship to one another. Example: An analyst contributed the psychodynamic formulation of the patient's central problem:

In spite of this the fragility of his personality structure is clearly evident. With his wife's continuous attempts to win more room for herself, and independence within the relationship, the patient feels threatened and insecure. The feelings of worthlessness and loss of identity that are normally suppressed by a strong, albeit fragile persona, resurface. The resulting threat of collapse of the patient's dependent-narcissistic personality pattern results in a panic state and depressive mood.

All the main categories can be found in this paragraph, which brings structural elements together with the patient's partner relationship, experience of the situation and conflict. Thus, this analyst has formulated a comprehensive psychodynamic description of the problem: using the everyday Jungian term, "persona," and assigning it a compensatory function on the conflict level as well as on the structural level. The analyst also has identified a personality disturbance as the syndrome diagnosis. This disturbance is entered again later in the questionnaire with the numerical identification according to the ICD-10 *Manual for Diagnosis*, which is the main reference used in Switzerland. This analyst seems to have a relationship- and conflict-oriented dynamic understanding of the psychotherapy.

Summary of Results

Following the procedure used in the example, the text for each case was evaluated. In 16 of the 19 texts an easily recognizable psychodynamic problem formulation, that contains fully or even partly the expected categories, is not apparent. Consideration must be given to the fact that the category pattern is dependent upon the patient's disturbance.

It is evident that the categories are connected with one another. In three cases, either the question was not understood or there was not a clear understanding of the psychodynamics. Information from the anamnesis was reported, and comments were made about the results. In order to derive a psychodynamic problem formulation from such information, one would have to take the risk of a false interpretation.

Psychodynamic diagnosis formulations that meet the expectations of the study were found in nine cases. However, in twelve cases was found the use of a kind of syndrome diagnosis containing Jungian concepts such as "father complex" through which a psychodynamic understanding is "implied." In three cases a syndrome diagnosis according to the ICD-10 is given, either alone or with other information, as the psychodynamic diagnosis.

Jungian terms appeared rather frequently. The terms persona, self, mother or father complex (with or without positive/negative descriptive), animus, and the term "complex" – in various combinations such as authority complex – are found in nine of nineteen texts.

The 19 evaluated texts varied from one another at first glance but, at closer examination, a commonality became apparent. In 85 percent of the texts analyzed, a comparable pattern of description is used. In addition, 50 percent of the texts contain Jungian concepts that apply well, either in the psychodynamic descriptions or in the diagnosis, and therefore can be considered to belong to the analysts' everyday professional jargon.

Concepts from the categories "relationship" and "conflict" were used frequently, in reference to the patient's experience. Concepts from the category "structure" were used less frequently.

Conclusion:

A compensatory line of thought on the part of the analyst is predominant in the texts. It appears that the analysts understand psychotherapy, above all, in terms of relationship and conflict, and have the tendency to attribute a compensatory function to the disturbance. A comparison of these descriptions with those of the psychoanalysts from Heidelberg would indicate whether we are dealing with a specifically "Jungian" characteristic.

The example is not mature enough to make useable hypotheses. Interesting aspects have appeared, however, that give hints for new working hypotheses. The evaluation of the description of the individual sessions and the descriptions of the analytic process, that will follow, provide even more insight to the psychotherapy process.

The qualitative evaluation of our research results is an intriguing chapter in our own developmental processes. In addition to providing data to show the quality and usefulness of our methods, it provides us with the possibility of looking at ourselves from a new perspective (we all know the value of doing that), and to compare ourselves with other therapist collectives in similar positions.

A Jungian Approach to Psychic Structure of the Psyche Using OPD

Marianne Junghan
Bern, Switzerland
Schweizerische Gesellschaft für Analytische Psychologie

The structure of the psyche is one of the axes evaluated by the OPD (see Rudolf et al. 1995). As psychic structure is conceptualized variously within the psychoanalytic community, we must comprehend structure in the OPD framework and then apply this understanding of psychic structure to analytical psychology. This application is important in allowing use of the OPD without sacrificing important Jungian concepts.

Jung outlined a structure of the psyche consisting of consciousness and the unconscious, personal and collective. Jacobi (1940) went into more detail, describing the structural characteristics of the psyche as consciousness, ego, persona, the unconscious, the complexes and the archetypes. For Jacobi, the complexes were located at the very core of the structure of the psyche.

Jung and Jacobi considered the quality of consciousness to be of vital importance when it comes to ascertain the severity of a psychic disturbance. They, however, took the quality of a person´s consciousness more or less as a given. It was the research done by Neumann (1963) and Fordham (1958) that provided more detail on the developmental process that leads to ego-consciousness.

To understand evaluation of OPD structure and to explain this evaluation in Jungian terminology, a comparison of the terms "ego" and "Self" in the OPD and in analytical psychology is crucial. In the OPD, structure is defined as the "emerging shape and the functioning of the Self in its relation to others." The Self in the OPD is regarded as the highest level of integration of the psyche. Self emerges as the result of a self-reflective process that is initiated when the ego becomes an object of reflection. Ego at the center of this process of self-reflection is assumed to be present from birth and is the "central organizer of the psyche." Thus, ego that is present from the beginning and governs the course of development is later on subsumed under the structure that emerges along with the process of self-reflection, the Self. In contrast the Self within the theoretical framework of analytical psychology is assumed to be present from the beginning and to be the structure that gives birth to the rising ego and ego-complex.

It becomes obvious that the Self in the OPD contains all elements of the ego-complex which, in analytical psychology, can be seen to include the persona. The ego of the OPD, as an inborn structure which is the central organizer of all psychic processes, relates to what analytical psychologists would term the Self. We must keep in mind, however, that both in the OPD and in analytical psychology the Self is considered to represent the totality of the psyche even though the Self is defined differently in analytical psychology and OPD. The contradictions arising from conceptualizing the Self as the totality of the personality, as well as the central archetype, in analytical psychology have been elaborated extensively (see Samuels 1985, Fordham 1963).

For our purposes, it seems legitimate to state that the Self of the OPD closely resembles the ego-complex of analytical psychology. Hence, OPD structure within the framework of analytical psychology is characterized by the relation of the ego-complex to the other complexes. In this context, the term complex refers to the work of

Knox (1997) who defines complexes as mental representations of objects, combining an innate archetypal predisposition with real external personal and interpersonal experience which has been internalized. As a consequence, complexes and the relationship of these complexes to the ego-complex can be experienced by observation of interpersonal relations.

Describing the structure of the psyche as is done in the OPD procedure would require, therefore, a detailed description of the ego-complex and its relationships to other complexes in a given person. Such a description employs the six dimensions of OPD assessment. These dimensions illustrate four different levels of structure, based on the description of observable behavior. To give a more practical impression of this evaluation process, those six structural dimensions are summarized.

1. Self-perception. The capacity for self-reflection and for drawing a clear picture of one's own Self (as defined by the OPD). This picture should be detailed and consistent over a lifetime, giving the impression that the person has an adequate feeling of Self and is able to experience and describe one's own feelings in a rich and varied way. In terms of analytical psychology such a stable self-image and clear-cut sense of one's own identity would point to a stable and coherent ego-complex.

2. Self-regulation. The capacity of a person to tolerate emotions including strong and unpleasant ones, as well as to maintain self-esteem. Such a capacity includes the ability to control feelings and impulses and to foresee the impact of one's behavior. Dieckman (1991) describes this ability as a function of the ego-complex. As evaluation is made to determine whether the energy freed by the activation of a complex can be controlled by the ego-complex or whether the activated complex gains control over the psychic functioning.

3. Defenses. Defense mechanisms as defined by psychoanalysis are evaluated. The theoretical concept of defense mechanisms has its roots in classical psychoanalysis, but was introduced to analytical psychology by Neumann (1963). Defense mechanisms, according to Neumann, protect the ego-consciousness from being overwhelmed by inner experiences or by threats from outside. Neumann and Fordham (1960) see the defense mechanisms as a function of the ego to maintain the stability of the ego-complex. The defense mechanisms addressed here are the so-called "mature ones." Somewhat different are the defense mechanisms that Fordham describes as the

defense of the Jungian-defined Self: "primitive" defense mechanisms that predominate on a poorly integrated level of the structure. Examples are the processes of splitting, idealizing and projective identification.

4. Object-perception. The capacity to differentiate between inner and outer reality, between self and the object. In Jungian language, this capacity is measured by the relationship of the ego-complex to other complexes: whether other complexes govern the ego-complex. This relationship can be evaluated by testing a person's aability to describe significant others in a differentiated way or to show empathy with others. A person lacking this capacity would project the inner world onto others without being able to reflect on this process or to recognize the border between the inner world and the outside reality.

5. Communication. The capacity to communicate that could be lost whenever a fragmentation of the ego-complex occurs and some of its basic functions get lost. Alternatively, the activation of a complex that is not connected to the ego-complex could lead to a restricted ability to communicate. For example, a strong negative parent complex activated during the course of an interview could lead to strong and uncontrolled projections on the interviewer and so affect the communication negatively.

6. Attachment. Describes whether there is a reliable internalization of objects, enabling a person to build a stable inner representation of others and the outer world, and to achieve and keep an adequate affective connection with these object representations. Assuming that predominantly negative object representations hinder the development of attachment or prevent a person from adequately dissolving existing relationships, OPD evaluates to what extent positive object representations had been internalized.

In terms of analytical psychology, the evaluation would raise the question of the relationship between positive and negative father/mother complexes and how these complexes are related to the ego-complex, especially because these relationships strongly influence the capacity for attachment.

Pictorial-Hermeneutic, Qualitative Methods

Manfred Krapp

Berlin, Germany
Deutsche Gesellschaft für Analytische Psychologie

Jung saw the image as a concentrated expression of the psychic situation in its totality. For investigating this hypothesis, the data consist of eight paintings of a borderline patient and her comments on them. They represent inner images and process fantasies which emerged some months before the start of therapy. She painted the paintings after her first therapeutic sessions. Under the supervision of an expert in qualitative research, an art historian and I are are performing a comparative analysis of the verbal and pictorial modes of expressing inner images. Thus, three methods are connected: Jungian images from the unconscious, qualitative research and the pictorial-hermeneutic method of the history of art. The aim is to create a systematic, empirically verifiable basis for this Jungian therapeutic approach.

The pictorial-hermeneutic analysis of the paintings follows Panofsky's (1957) iconological-iconographical method, which refers to Cassirer's (1973-1975) symbolic forms and shows remarkable similarities to the Jungian theory of symbols. Semiotic and structuralistic approaches also are employed, and, especially for "non-figurative" paintings: French semiotics as applied by Thürlemann (1990).

In the 1980s, new scientific methods became established in psychology and the social sciences, methods that are in contrast to quantitative-empirical methods. This so-called "qualitative" research "has led to an alternative understanding of social inquiry and to the systematic study of meaning based on the experience of subjects – phenomenology. It is to this trend of twentieth century thought that Jung properly belongs; the contemporary research methods that have evolved within this strand of thinking include a specifically Jungian contribution of psychotherapy research" (Lepper 1997, p. 638).

Qualitative strategies are now used increasingly in process research, especially to investigate the therapeutic relationship. They make transparent the bases of interpretations at all stages, from theory-driven data collection to the development and application of categories and the evaluation and interpretation of results. They are

Figure 1

directed at the complexity and totality of the subject under investigation, including both its inner perspective and the subjectivity of the investigator. Here we have an analogy to the alchemical attitude of investigating nature, "with true and not with fantastic imagination;" CW12, 218).

In our project we are applying the "Grounded Theory" (Corbin & Strauss 1990), a "method ... of discovery ... which grounds a theory in reality." It is based on a code paradigm. "A more abstract concept must be developed in terms of its properties and dimensions of the phenomenon it represents" (p. 4). The computer program ATLAS/ti is based on the procedure of Grounded Theory. This "Interpretation Support System" was developed at the Technical University of Berlin for the requirements of qualitative, hermeneutic research. Codes, categories and comments are compiled on specific units of meaning in text and paintings to form semantic networks and theories: "In contrast to linear, sequential representations (e.g., text), network representations of knowledge resemble more closely the way human memory and thought is structured. Some cognitive 'load' in handling complex relationships is reduced with the aid of spatial representation techniques. ATLAS/ti uses networks to help explore conceptual structures and to make them transparent. The networks add a heuristic 'right brain' approach to qualitative analysis" (Muhr 1997, p.61).

Picture 1

Far-reaching into the horizon there is an all enclosing black-grey background –; before that a brown, mouldy bottom with only a few clumps of grass –; at this bottom or directly out of the mould arises slowly a shapeless tiny black-brown mass –; probably my "Ego"

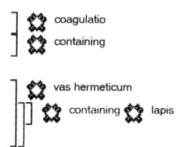

Developing this image I felt: the bottom is very soft and deep, smells like a <u>swamp</u> and "I" want to grow.

Picture 2

Far-reaching into the horizon there is an all enclosing black-grey background –; before that again a brown, mouldy bottom with a few more clumps of grass -; the shapeless mass is consolidating a little bit –; now a lilac covering is arising –; "Ego"

Developing this image I felt: The covering is transparent, probably consisting of bullet-proof glass, the covering is slowly arising around my "Ego".

Figure 2

Jungian research requires this "right brain" methodological approach to do justice to the subtlety of inner images. Using semantic networks it is easy to relate the patient's paintings and comments to the theories in the analyst's mind. For example: In Figure 1 you can see the first painting which the patient has divided into picture 1 and picture 2. In Figure 2, to which I applied ATLAS/ti, are the comments of the patient on this painting and my codes, which almost all consist of alchemical images. The quotations relating to the codes are underlined.

Inspired by Edinger (1985), I created a semantic network (Fig. 3) of the alchemical operation of the "solutio." Each term is linked to the corresponding literature. This hypertext representation of the theoretical background makes the computer an "auxiliary ego to imagination" (see Krapp 1997). Comparing this network with the patient's alchemical images it is striking that the water symbols of the *solutio* are represented only in the swamp. The *solutio* has not the purification capacity of water, and therefore the process of transformation, the *solve et coagula* (dissolving and coagulating), is fragmented. Indeed, the patient later experienced the *sublimatio* in a dissociated way, as other paintings demonstrate. The threat of sinking into the swamp, which is visible in the pictorial mode, was articulated verbally only much later.

Within the therapeutic process the patient's images become linked with the therapist's symbolic attitude, empathy and identifi-

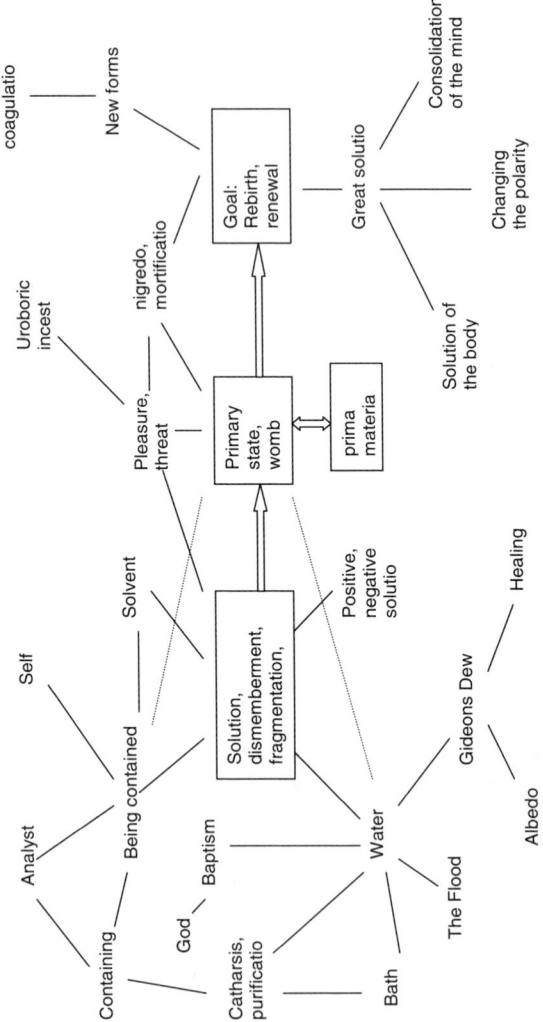

Figure 3

cation with the patient. Interaction and communication about painted images from the unconscious create a *coniunctio* that amplifies the therapeutic process. This could be a factor of therapeutic efficacy, which may be specific for analytical psychology. The comments of my patient demonstrate that she has introjected my therapeutic attitude of becoming emotionally involved with her inner images and of creating a container for her with the help of the archetypal image of "Die and Become."

"Inwards I have to die a 'little bit' in order		*Stirb* (die)
to create some space for the new.		*Werde* (become)
That's the way within the nature and		imagnatio vera (see CW XII. par. 218)
that's happening probably in my soul too.		introjection of the therapist' attitude
I had difficulties to accept this kind of dying.		therapeutic progress
Since more than half a year, I defended it."		

Figure 4

This is just the beginning of the study and my first step with ATLAS/ti. There is much more to do to refine this method for analytical psychology.

References

Arbeitskreis OPD (1996). Operationalisierte Psychodynamische Diagnostik (OPD): *Grundlagen und Manual.* Huber: Bern/Göttingen/Toronto/Seattle.

Benjamin, L. (1974). Structural analysis of social behaviour. *Psychological Review, 81,* 392-425.

Cassirer, E. (1973-1975). *The Philosophy of Symbolic Forms.* Darmstadt: Wissenschaftliche Buchgesellschaft.

Corbin, J.; Strauss, A. (1990). Grounded theory research: Procedures, canons and evaluative criteria. *Qualitative Sociology, 13,* pp. 3-21.

Edinger, E. (1985). *Anatomy of the Psyche.* Chicago: Open Court.

Fordham, M. (1958). Individuation and ego development. *Journal of Analytical Psychology, 3,* 2, 115-130.

Fordham, M. (1960). Ego, self, and mental health. *British Journal of Medical Psychology; 33:*249-253.

Fordham, M. (1963). The empirical foundation and theories of the self in Jung's Works. *Journal of Analytical Psychology, 8-1,* 1-23.

Grande, T., Rudolf, G. & Oberbracht, C. (1997). Die Praxisstudie Analytische Langzeittherapie. Ein Projekt zur prospektiven Untersuchung Struktureller Veränderungen in Psychoanalysen. In: M. Leuzinger-Bohleber, & U. Stuhr (Eds.). *Psychoanalysen im Rückblick.* Giessen, Germany: Psychosozial Verlag.

Howard K. & Orlinsky, P. (1986). Process and outcome. In S.L. Garfield & A.E. Bergin (Eds.), *Handbook of Psychotherapy and Behaviour Change* (3rd ed.). New York: Wiley.

Jacobi, J., (1940). *Die Psychologie von C.G. Jung*. Frankfurt a/M.: Fischer, 1992.

Knox, J. (1997). Internal objects: A theoretical analysis of Jungian and Kleinian models. *Journal of Analytical Psychology, 42*, 653-666.

Krapp, M. (1997). Alchemy in the computer? In M. Mattoon (Ed.), *Open Questions in Analytical Psychology*. Einsiedeln, Switzerland: Daimon.

Lepper, G. (1997). Research and Jungian psychotherapy: Outcome studies. In Mattoon, M. (Ed.), *Open Questions in Analytical Psychology*. Einsiedeln, Switzerland: Daimon.

Muhr, T. (1997). ATLAS/ti. *The Knowledge Workbench*. Berlin: Scientific Software Development.

Neumann, E. (1963). *Das Kind*. Fellbach-Oeffingen: Bonz.

Panofsky, E. (1957). *Meaning in the Visual Arts*. New York: Doubleday.

Rudolf, G.; Buchheim, P.; Ehlers, W.; Küchenhoff, J.; Muhs, A.; Pouget, D.; Rüger, U.; Seidler, G.; Schwarz, F.; Struktur und strukturelle Störung. *Zeitschrift Psychomatische Medizin, 41*, 197-212.

Rudolf, G.; Grande, T.; Oberbracht, C. (1998). Die Struktür-Chekliste: Eine anwender-freundliches Hilfsmittel für die Strukdiagnostik nach OPD. In H. Schauenburg, H.J. Freyberger, M.Cierpka, P. Büchheim (Hrsg.). *OPD in der Praxis*. Bern/Göttingen/Toronto/Seattle: Verlag Hans Hüber.

Samuels, A. (1985). *Jung und seine Nachfolger*. Stuttgart: Klett-Cotta.

Stiles, W.B., Meshiot, C.M., Anderson, T.M. & Sloan, W.W. (1992). Assimilation of problematic experiences: The case of John Jones. *Psychotherapy Research, 2*, 81-101.

Thürlemann, F. (1990). *From Picture to Space*. Cologne: Dumont.

Closing

Reflections from the Presidency

Verena Kast
IAAP President, 1995-98

In my tenure as president of IAAP I did not belong to the uroboric phase of the organization, as did Hans Dieckmann, nor was I bound to Jungian Psychology from the beginning by birth, as was Tom Kirsch: In contrast to them, I have been a completely "ordinary" President of a worldwide professional organization that is growing, that is thriving, but that also has come of age. It is no longer a "family affair." Thus, "Mother" and "Father" have needed to be replaced by brothers and sisters. This is one of the reasons why I have strived to make structural changes in the Executive Committee and to render it more democratic. An organization like ours needs to be carried by a large number of our member societies – but this means that a large number of our societies also need to have a realistic possibility of being represented in the Executive Committee.

I was struck again and again during my presidency at how much more important it seems to be for small groups to be members of the IAAP than for larger ones. That makes sense. It feels good to be not alone in the practice of this kind of psychotherapy, and to be a part of a greater whole – that may be better able to provide ideas for solutions to certain problems. Thus, I am extremely happy that statute amendments – providing for single terms – were approved at the Delegates' Meeting. I am convinced that these changes will give our society new stimulation and enhanced life.

And now, to speak about some experiences that I have had over the past 12 years as vice-president and president of IAAP, and then to reflect about the future of our Association.

We can say that Jungians are very creative, when we look at the great number of publications appearing each year. This remains true when we look at the content, which includes a wealth of theoretical and therapeutic ideas. There is a great abundance in our midst but, sadly, very little is done with it. We pay too little attention to publications and research; we do not adequately make use of these rich resources: discussing and exchanging them. My wish is that, at some Congress, a young colleague would bring together at one table authors who represent diametrically opposed views and challenge them with hard and relevant questions, so that they would really have to become involved, and to define their positions. And then I would wish for some thinkers among us to reflect further on the implications of these points of view. This could be the beginning of a Streitkultur, a "culture of debate": an atmosphere of fair confrontation and debate, not an anti-culture of devaluing what often has not even been read, of ignoring interesting contributions, of secretly mining little treasures from the contributions of colleagues and never giving them credit. We hear the complaint again and again that not enough attention is paid to Jungian literature. This is certainly not fundamentally true. But at the same time, we naturally can ask the question, "Why should others pay any attention to us if we pay so little attention to each other?" My present hopes are with the Internet: perhaps this new medium will provide a means for a discussion, particularly among younger colleagues.

I have always been very impressed by the admirable efforts of colleagues to provide good and reliable training opportunities. It isn't only a question of how psychotherapy based on Jungian psychology might look in general, but also often that adaptations need to be made for the particular needs of each country. This may be a reason why there is ever more concern with structure and ever less with content – about which we need to be ever vigilant. Ever more training analysis and ever more supervision are no guarantees of better preparation of analysts. I have asked often if there might not be a requirement that could be eliminated from the regulations. This question has usually been met with bewilderment although, in the best case, with reflection.

In spite of ever more hours of training analysis, every training program has its shadow sides, which usually are projected onto the institutes that have programs with different emphases. These projections occur most of all in situations where colleagues living in the same area have been trained by different institutes, and then wish to found a society together. Even the fascinating process of starting something new cannot hide the respective prejudices – or even downright condemnations. A lengthy development is usually necessary before the differences can be seen as an enrichment and not a threat, so that a climate of mutual respect can grow.

Frequently, it appears to me, this last stage is not really accomplished at all. Then, a few years later, the differences erupt and are seen as unbridgeable.

It also appears to me that many societies have difficulties with the integration of the younger generation. The new analysts are kept in daughter- and son-roles, and told that they need more experience. Some then rebel, while others remain in states of dependency. If we take the theory of individuation at all seriously, we cannot possibly wish for such a state of affairs! Is it a matter of defending our own stature, which we have worked so hard to achieve? What will happen when the need for still more psychotherapists has been fulfilled? Will we simply cease training, so that we can continue to live comfortably, or will we have faith that a transformation can occur? Is the principle of generativity – the caring for the next generation and thus the future of our own profession and our society – intact?

What else is ahead of us? In my opinion, we need to address the question of how better to train supervisors. Since not all societies have the same understanding of this term, I will say that, with the word "supervision," I refer both to colleagues who focus primarily on transference/countertransference in connection with the training of candidates, and to those who help the analyst-in-training in very practical ways to see, understand and solve the problems that arise in the course of an analysis. In many institutes and societies, these functions are united and I am including them under the single word, "supervision."

We all practice supervision in some form and the number of required hours of supervision is on the increase. It is my strong opinion that we should be far more reflective of what we are doing: not in the sense that future supervisors should undergo still more training, but rather that creative niches be created in our institutes where we can investigate how we practice supervision and how it might be improved. Out of this exercise there might emerge new hypotheses for research: What does supervision really consist of, what improves it, what weakens it? Reflection on an activity helps us to gain a certain distance from it and, out of this, new questions and insights can emerge. ... Sometimes new possibilities are not considered seriously because it could become apparent that the training of the trainers is not as good as that of those being trained! Continuing to learn throughout life, which is very necessary in today's world, is naturally true for analysts and concerns not only the professional aspects, which anyway are more obvious. If training is to be worthwhile, then it always needs to be in transformation. If we do not address this phenomenon, we will not be able to describe, teach and learn a specifically Jungian supervision.

Although the empirical aspect was a part of Jungian therapy in the beginning, it fell into a region of shadow; only in recent times has it been brought back into the light, along with considerable mistrust. To our good fortune, this mistrust is a valuable function for us: it forces us to seek the investigative means appropriate to psychotherapy as an independent science, including the unique characteristic of the encounter in the analytic relationship. In some countries – Switzerland, for example – payments are dependent upon whether hard evidence can be found that Jungian therapy is effective, appropriate and economical. If Jungian therapy were to be excluded from medical insurance coverage, that would lead to a drastic reduction of trainees, which would be a terrible blow to Jungian psychology.

Research into Jungian psychotherapy was at first viewed with skepticism and even considered by many to be a betrayal of the soul. Subsequently, various research projects have been launched; the colleagues who have been involved feel enriched and say they have received new impulses. These new impulses will accelerate the reflection about our profession and our therapy. This does not mean that traditional Jungian research work, such as on archetypal images, is no longer of value. It also does not mean that we should not always think seriously about whether we are selecting the appropriate people into our training programs, and whether our training is "good enough."

In the German-speaking world, there is a magical phrase: "quality control." We need to reflect about what we in our profession understand by quality control, and how we might exercise it. It would be of the utmost importance for this discussion to take place among Jungians from many different countries. Of course, we never would come to complete agreement, but perhaps the discussion could lead, for example, to the publication of a paper formulating the main emphases of the different societies in this regard.

It would be important for us to be clear among ourselves about how we would like to deal with this issue and then to formulate a point of view, before some outside authority defines for us how quality control is to be understood. This provides us with a perfect opportunity to discuss and to formulate not only in terms of structure, but also in terms of content.

There are many tasks ahead that we will have to take on together. It would be wonderful if it weren't always the same people doing the work, and also not always the same people tending more to criticize than to contribute in terms of the work needing to be done. We need input from everyone.

Jungian psychotherapy is, and will be ever more, just one psychotherapy among many. We need to determine what the strengths of our approach are, and of course, what the weaknesses are. If we do not do this ourselves, it will be done for us from outside, often in an unqualified manner. But we also need to determine and to formulate what our particular identity is, what our contribution is, and how this may change. We are not privileged, as a result of our heritage, to be something exceptional, and we should not try to argue in terms of any such privilege when we are attacked; rather, we should demonstrate what our form of therapy really is. We have a therapy that is based upon a very interesting theory; it is an effective and valuable form of psychotherapy. It comes as no surprise that, in present times, an integrative model of psychotherapy is now in fashion. This is completely normal, after the many years of battle among the various schools, and the widespread bickering within the schools. Openness toward the other schools, along with reflection about our own foundations, is something that I experience as very enlivening. At the same time, our form of psychotherapy is not so narrow and specialized that we have to borrow from others.

After a tradition of 40 years of male IAAP presidents, I have been the first woman president of this organization, and I hope that it won't be another 40 years before the next woman is elected president, from a membership consisting of more than two-thirds women. What we need are women who will run for office, and colleagues who are ready to entrust these women with responsibility. We also need delegates who accept a feminine style of leadership, and who might even be able to enjoy it! From the beginning, it was my intention to be president for three years, and three years only. This is because I am deeply convinced that an international association such as ours is most dynamic when as many different societies as possible are actively participating. For this to occur, it is necessary for the officers not to remain in office for long periods, to stay glued to their seats.

The presidency is also a responsibility that requires tremendous amounts of time and energy. To invest the required time and energy into all of the fascinating – but also the less-fascinating – tasks is much easier if there is an approaching end in sight.

I thank you all for having elected me, and for the trust you placed in me. I thank also the executive committee and my vice-presidents, and especially my honorary secretary, Robert Hinshaw, who has been a great support to me.

It was always my goal to establish what I call a "flat hierarchy" in the executive committee; in other words, to have a very democratic style. This demanded both creativity and hard work from everyone involved.

To my successor, Luigi Zoja, with whom I have had a very pleasant collaboration, I extend my best wishes for his presidency, including many pleasant moments – and unpleasant ones only in homeopathic doses!

Author Index

Subject Index

423, 471-474, 478-479, 494, 496-
497, 500, 504-506, 523, 531, 541,
556, 558, 570
female 36, 54, 87, 95, 97, 105, 107,
127, 189, 208, 210, 212, 218, 261,
293, 295, 316, 347, 357, 382-383,
385, 389, 523-524, 553
feminine 48, 67, 97, 190, 209, 211-
215, 217-218, 255-257, 261, 264,
292-295, 298, 322-323, 354, 356-
361, 382, 529, 593
femininity 292, 298, 300, 504
fetus 85-86, 202
film 46-47, 226, 430, 510-511
fire 113, 188, 201, 226, 309, 357, 366
fixation 106, 285, 295, 299, 367, 526
flow 24, 33, 37, 99, 101, 103-104, 121-
122, 153, 178, 227, 271, 329, 396,
439, 506, 529
flower 118, 206, 211, 241, 270-272,
293, 318, 354-355, 496
fluid 154, 168, 495, 511, 519
forest 43-44, 91, 201, 203, 522
formation of symbols 103
freedom 25, 30, 37, 162-163, 186, 322,
366, 414, 424, 428-429
French 80, 150, 174, 176, 235, 250-
251, 294, 300, 426-427, 461, 544,
557, 581
French Revolution 176
Freudian 18, 147-148, 150-151, 155-
158, 427, 475-477
Freudian analyst 429
Freudian psychoanalyst 508
Freudians 152, 477
friendship 19, 212, 218, 281-282, 460,
483, 485, 487
fullness 184, 190, 192, 361, 391, 397
gender 97, 261, 264, 283, 440
Genesis 117, 157, 159, 204
genius 119, 210, 353, 362
genocide 173, 176, 184, 319
gesture 14, 72-73, 78, 124, 154, 218,
325, 390, 392, 395, 538
ghost 502
God 23, 25, 41, 57-58, 109, 130, 133-
134, 137-142, 149, 151, 158-159,
162-166, 168-172, 177, 206, 213,
269-270, 277-278, 292, 297, 299,

320, 323, 347, 353-356, 358-360,
368, 439, 446, 469, 492-493, 504,
516, 569
goddess 126, 177, 210, 212-213, 215,
241, 292-293, 297-298, 354, 357-
358, 362, 518, 520
god-image 149, 166, 176, 360
Goethe, J.W. von 170
Gogh, Vincent van 367
gold 104, 126, 217, 269, 271, 296, 337,
343, 410, 445
good mother 459, 468-469
Gorgon 297, 437
Goya, F.J. de 367
grandfather 156, 297, 321, 371
grandmother 56-57
grandparents 317
grape 117, 277
gratification 95, 102-104, 323, 492
great mother 356, 359, 459
Greek 119, 121, 203, 205, 212, 224,
242, 319, 425, 517, 521, 523, 529
grief 95, 98, 108, 329
group therapy 449
guilt 37, 56, 74-76, 101, 140, 142, 170,
173-175, 181, 185, 317, 320, 329,
389, 441, 511
Hades 518
hammer 16
harmony 16, 19, 45, 129, 190-191,
275, 280
hate 84, 93, 113, 116-117, 159, 307,
387, 506, 521, 528
healing 32-33, 65, 82, 86, 90, 92-93,
104, 106, 112, 124, 127, 195, 209-
210, 214-217, 220, 231, 233, 268,
270, 272, 274-276, 282-283, 288-
289, 304, 306-307, 310, 313, 372,
376-378, 409, 411-412, 416, 437-
438, 445, 501, 527, 529, 534-535
health 58, 204, 221, 223, 252, 287,
309, 326, 334, 336, 437, 541, 553-
554, 557, 560, 562, 574, 585
hearing 118, 469, 474, 537, 550
heart 62, 97, 102, 122, 124, 178, 195,
204, 215-216, 218, 287, 321, 354,
358, 360, 427, 429-430, 437, 518-
519, 552
heartbeat 78

NEW TITLES FROM DAIMON

Ann and Barry Ulanov

The Healing Imagination – The Meeting of Psyche and Soul

This eloquent work speaks of the centrality of imagination in the life of the spirit. Ann and Barry Ulanov describe the imagination as a bridge between the psyche and the spirit.

Using rich imagery drawn from literature, film, and their own experience as therapists, they unlock for us the healing power of our imagination.

"Imagination heals by building a bridge sturdy enough to link us up, each of us, to the river of being already present in us, to the currents flowing through us and among us in our unconscious life."

After describing this healing power of imagination, the authors go on to show how it is vital in the spiritual life: in preaching, prayer, teaching, counseling, and politics. (200 pages, ISBN 3-85630-591-2)

Yehezkel Kluger & Nomi Kluger-Nash

A Psychological Interpretation of Ruth

The biblical Book of Ruth is a love story, apparently personal and simple – of love between women and between man and woman – told in poetic imagery and style. Barely hiding within this immediate beauty are the archetypal depths which reveal nothing less than the eternal mystery of a love which brings about redemption and individuation both personal and transcendent, human and divine.

Dr. Kluger wrote the original interpretation as part of the requirements of the first graduating class of the Jung Institute in Zürich. He later updated his work, but the thesis remains the same: the return of the feminine principle in the Bible. To this end, he examines the fate and role of the feminine as "she" travels from ancient times through various goddesses to the person of Ruth, and her destiny as restoring the original totality of masculine and feminine in equal, interacting, balance.

In counterpoint to the scholarly style of her father – while in unison with his interpretations – Nomi Kluger-Nash has written a woman's subjective reactions to the story of Ruth, Naomi and Orpah. To this associative style she brings further amplifications from Kabbalah into the meaning of these women who carry aspects, both light and dark, of the Shekhinah, the feminine presence of God.

(232 pages, ISBN 3-85630-587-4)

Aniela Jaffé

Death Dreams and Ghosts

A collection of death dreams and ghost stories were gathered and presented to C.G. Jung and the author, who approaches this fascinating material from the depths of her analytic experience.

"... among the Swiss, who are commonly regarded as stolid, unimaginative, rationalistic and materialistic, there are just as many ghost stories as, for instance, among the English or Irish. Indeed, as I know from my own experience ..., the kind of magic practiced in the Middle Ages ... has by no means died out, but still flourishes today ... I recommend this book to all who know how to value things that break through the monotony of daily life with salutary effects, that (sometimes!) shake our certitudes and lend wings to the imagination."

– from the Foreword by C.G.Jung

(200 pages, ISBN 3-85630-580-7)

Regina Abt, Irmgard Bosch & Vivienne MacKrell

Dream Child – Creation and New Life in Dreams of Pregnant Women

Foreword by Marie-Louise von Franz

The broad scope of the dream material analyzed in this book allows the authors to touch upon many subjects associated with the nature of the psyche, not only those relevant to pregnant women. The careful interpretation of the amplificatory material drawn from a wide range of cultures also makes this an inspiring aid for the understanding of dreams, valuable to psychologists, doctors, midwives or anyone else interested in this human subject.

(ca. 520 pages, richly illustrated, ISBN 3-85630-592-0)

Eva Langley-Dános

Prison on Wheels – From Ravensbrück to Burgau

Prison on Wheels is a remarkable diary kept by a young Hungarian woman, Eva Dános, during sixteen horror-filled days and nights of deportation by the Nazis in 1945. It is an eyewitness report of a 700-kilometer rail journey from Ravensbrück, north of Berlin, to Burgau, near Munich, one of the countless such operations that took place within Nazi Germany's vast network of labor- and concentration-camps.

(112 pages, ISBN 3-85630-585-8)

Images, Meanings and Connections

Essays in Memory of Susan R. Bach

Edited by Ralph Goldstein, 192 pages, ISBN 3-85630-586-6, richly illustrated

The title of this book reflects the main themes from 50 years of Susan Bach's analytical work with spontaneous pictures and in her 'blue room'. In working with spontaneous pictures and drawings, she perceived the expression of deep connections between psyche and soma and learned that 'it knows within us' when either healing or death is imminent.

Talking with Susan Bach about her work was inspiring and humbling and one felt deeply privileged to be studying with someone who brought so much intuition and intellectual understanding to the contemplation of the human psyche.

The humbling part of the conversation came from wondering how to move one's own work towards the paths she was opening up. The purpose of this collection of essays is to show how the work of connecting and finding meaning continues and advances, whether through pictures, objects, dreams or other images and myths.

The contributors have in common both a Jungian orientation and their having made distinguished contributions in their own specialities.

Available from your bookstore or from our distributors:

In the United States:

Continuum
P.O. Box 7017
La Vergne, TN 37086
Phone: 800-937 5557
Fax: 615-793 3915

Chiron Publications
400 Linden Avenue
Wilmette, IL 60091
Phone: 800-397 8109
Fax: 847-256 2202

In Great Britain:

Airlift Book Company
8 The Arena
Enfield, Middlesex EN3 7NJ
Phone: (0181) 804 0400
Fax: (0181) 804 0044

Worldwide:
Daimon Verlag   Hauptstrasse 85   CH-8840 Einsiedeln   Switzerland
Phone: (41)(55) 412 2266   Fax: (41)(55) 412 2231
e-mail: daimon@compuserve.com   Write for our complete catalog!
http://daimon.webjump.com